Education and the Law

Cases and Materials on Public Schools

WILLIAM R. HAZARD

Education
and the Law

---

*Cases and materials on
public schools*

Fp *The Free Press, New York*

Collier-Macmillan Limited, London

Copyright © 1971 by William R. Hazard

Printed in the United States of America

All rights reserved. No part of this book may be
reproduced or transmitted in any form or by any means,
electronic or mechanical, including photocopying, recording,
or by any information storage and retrieval system,
without permission in writing from the Publisher.

The Free Press
A DIVISION OF THE MACMILLAN COMPANY
866 Third Avenue, New York, New York 10022

Collier-Macmillan Canada Ltd., Toronto, Ontario

Library of Congress Catalog Card Number: 79-143512

printing number
1   2   3   4   5   6   7   8   9   10

To Lynne and Andy

Contents

5 TEACHER-BOARD RELATIONS

Table of Cases

Preface

This book is an introduction to school law. It deals primarily with laws relating to public schools (both elementary and secondary) in the United States, and concerns non-public schools only inasmuch as they are affected by general statutes. The book is designed not only for students of educational administration, but also for others concerned with the implications of school law, and the approach is such that an interested layman can readily grasp the content.

We live in a time of rapid social change, and many of today's most significant legal decisions stem from civil and political unrest. This is evident in our schools as well as on our campuses; increased civil rights involvement has been coupled with growing dissent, general civil unrest, and a sharper delineation of individual rights in a more and more complex society. Teacher militancy and student militancy are here and now; the time for talk grows short as demands for action grow louder.

School law should not be viewed as a separate branch of law. Although most states have codes of law relating to certain school problems, many legal principles in this area operate in a broader framework. Some laws apply specifically to schools and school personnel, but most apply equally in non-school settings.

My focus is on urban schools, since most pupils attend schools in urban (rather than rural) settings, and most legal problems in schools arise in urban districts. I was fortunate to be able to spend a year conducting a research project to investigate which areas of school law are of most relevance to practicing administrators in urban school systems. I have also benefited from the opportunity of teaching school law and from the practice of law.

Each of the seven chapters contains (1) a brief narrative outline of the broad legal issues involved in that chapter's area of consideration, (2) readings from law reviews and general periodicals, (3) cases selected from state and federal courts, (4) problems and questions for discussion, and (5) a selected annotated bibliography.

Certain resource materials, particularly legislative and constitutional provisions, have not been readily available to many students in the past. Limited access to such materials has frustrated efforts by students to understand school law. Hopefully the cases included here will provide students with these basic resource tools.

The cases were selected to show: (1) the development of this area of law; (2) the present state of school law; and (3) what basis there is for anticipating legal developments in such volatile areas as teacher-board relations, student dissent and militancy, and civil rights.

The glossary lists legal terms and phrases frequently encountered in the cases, with definitions written in non-technical language. The narrative outlines are also in a non-technical style and should provide a grasp of the basics involved in school law. The selected readings extend the narratives and offer the best available analysis and comments on selected issues.

All these materials, especially if used in conjunction with state school codes, constitutions, and education legislation at the state and federal levels, provide the individual with ample background for case study, discussion, and analysis of the salient legal issues in schools.

WILLIAM R. HAZARD

Evanston, Illinois

Credits and Acknowledgements

This volume reflects the efforts of many people. The articles, commentaries, and cases included herein constitute a major portion of the book and the authors' contributions are gratefully acknowledged. Miss Elaine Teigler, Assistant Librarian, and Mr. John Campbell, Reference Assistant, were particularly helpful in placing the resources of the Northwestern University Law School Library at my disposal. Their personal interest and assistance in the research was most helpful.

The countless chores in manuscript preparation were ably handled by Mrs. Sally Goodman, Mrs. Nancy Dornbos, Mrs. Dorothy Salene, and Mrs. Joan Dolan. They are invaluable colleagues and too often bear the burdens of the task and too rarely share in any benefits. The manuscript was reviewed by my brother, Dr. Forrest E. Hazard. Even discounting fraternal criticism, his comments and suggestions were helpful and I am indebted to him.

The able assistance of James Fletcher must be acknowledged. Jim devoted the better part of a year to the research and analysis of the legal problems in the urban schools. As a senior law school student, he is an able researcher and a perceptive critic of the laws concerning schools. Without his capable assistance this book would never have seen the light of day.

Finally, I wish to thank my wife, Jean, for encouraging me to complete this manuscript. After I completed this project, she rediscovered the kitchen table, the den floor, and my patience.

The contributions of these able people do not cloud the fact that the errors, omissions, and bad judgments in the book are mine. Thoughtful readers perhaps will bring shortcomings and critical comments to my attention and facilitate improved versions of this book at a later time.

Education and the Law

Cases and Materials on Public Schools

1

Public Schooling and the Law

INTRODUCTION

The management and control of public education are an ultimate responsibility of the state. Subject to restrictions imposed by the state and the federal constitution, state legislatures create, fund, and regulate public schools through various state, intermediate, and local agencies. The state legislatures provide for the schools' financial support, curriculum, qualifications of teachers, policies concerning pupils, and a vast range of school management policies and procedures. Most operational decisions are made by the local school boards, generally elected by and responsible to the voters in local school districts.

The constitutions of most states specifically mention the legislative responsibility for public education. Article 11, section 1, of the New York State Constitution, for example, states that:

The legislature shall provide for the maintenance and support of a system of free common schools, wherein all the children of this state may be educated.

The Illinois state constitution, article 8, section 1, expresses a similar intent.

The General Assembly shall provide a thorough and efficient system of free schools, whereby all children of this State may receive a good common school education.

Subject to constitutional restrictions, the state legislative body possesses plenary (complete) power over the public schools. If it chose to do so, the state legislature could redistrict the state (change local district boundaries) and prescribe curriculum, textbooks, school calendar, hours of school operation, and practically every other detail of school operation. This control by the state legislature is subject, however, to review by the state courts, to the rights of citizens under the federal constitution, and to review by the federal courts for violation of constitutional rights.

"Control of public education" means little in the abstract; there are many levels of control and many contextual meanings. One may speak of state control or local control of education. State control may refer to legislative authority, executive authority, or judicial authority in school matters. Local control may

1

refer to the powers and duties of local school boards, the right of citizens to elect board members and vote on local tax issues, or the power of local opinion to affect policies, regulations, and decisions in the schools. Control of the schools includes the exercise of political, social, and economic power. As used here, control of schools means the power to enact, implement, and review the laws under which schools operate and to which they may be called to account. Thus, the primary meaning is a legal control, but there is a secondary meaning too: the executive control exercised through state and local agencies (the state superintendent of public education or its state-level counterpart and the local board of education).

LEGAL STRUCTURE OF EDUCATION

The Constitution of the United States does not expressly mention schools or education. The Tenth Amendment, however, does state that "the powers not delegated to the United States by the Constitution, nor prohibited by it to the States, are reserved to the States respectively, or to the people." Since the federal constitution does not mention schools, the power and responsibility for public schools devolves on the states or the people. As noted above, article 8, section 1, of the state constitution of Illinois mandates the General Assembly to provide a thorough and efficient system of free schools to all the children of the state. Under this authority, the Illinois General Assembly (legislature) enacts laws creating school districts, raising revenue for the schools, providing for local school boards, and regulating many specific aspects of the public schools. The Illinois constitution also provides for an elected superintendent of public instruction to "perform such duties as may be prescribed by law," specifically prohibits use of public funds for aid to church-controlled schools, permits an elected county superintendent of schools in each county, and exempts school property from taxation.

Under this constitutional mandate, the General Assembly shares its school powers through laws empowering the state superintendent, county superintendent, and local school boards to exercise complete control of school matters, subject to the rights of the citizens under state and federal constitutions and the judicial review by the state and federal courts.

State laws concerning schools comprise what is frequently known as the state's school code. School laws, though varying widely among the states in scope, degree of specificity, and complexity, generally provide for school elections, taxing and bonding power for the local district, school board membership and duties, certification and employment guidelines for teachers, and curriculum matters deemed important to the public interest.

Historically, the "common school" meant elementary schools. By state law and judicial interpretation, the term "common school" now includes public preschool, kindergarten, high school, and junior college levels. Current legislation in many states provides for public preschool education, programs for exceptional children, and extensive post-high school technical, vocational, and junior college programs. Adult education and noncredit community-service activities are included in some state-supported educational systems. Provisions for scholarships, loans, transportation, and other direct aid to pupils and parents are not uncommon among the states. Permissive legislation in some states encourages local school districts to enter various types of consortia to provide specialized services which, because of limited need and high per-pupil cost, might be prohibitive to a single district. Personnel and facilities for such specialized areas as medical and dental services, special education, and distributive and career training are examples of the purposes behind such consortia. These foregoing provisions concerning "common schools" are representative of the scope of school laws designed to create, support, and control public education. (It should be noted that state laws also usually define a system of college and university education. But since these laws are outside the scope of this book, they will be included only casually in the selected cases and readings.)

Local school districts, created by law and managed by elected or appointed board members, implement the state laws. Through tax levies and school bonds, local districts raise revenue to build, maintain, and operate the district schools. Consistent with curriculum mandates in the law, local boards of education determine the courses taught, the facilities, the equipment, and the supplies used in the system. With advice from the district teachers and administrators, they also determine the day-to-day instructional program for the pupils. Citizens of the district exercise political influence on the school operation by electing board members, serving on lay advisory committees, and by individually and collectively monitoring the school board meetings. Legally, school boards act as agents of the state legislature; politically, they represent the district electors, the pupils, parents, and community interests.

EDUCATION AS A STATE FUNCTION

Subject to the limitations imposed by the civil protections in the federal constitution and the case-law developed from it, the states are free to shape their systems of public education. The varying legislative opinions about public school systems explain the differences in scope, emphasis, support mechanisms, and structures of the fifty state school systems.

State laws concerning schools generally provide broad guidelines in either mandatory or permissive language. The structural details come either from central administrative agencies (state education departments or state supervisory offices) or from the local district implementation. Mandatory legislation (in such areas as teacher certification, specific curriculum components, and procedural steps in school elections) seeks to define state goals for education; permissive legislation encourages local initiative in education programs, services, and facilities. The local school districts, through delegated powers from the state legislature, carry the major responsibility for day-to-day operations. Unless challenged by a lawsuit instituted by an unhappy citizen or by a supervisory state agency, boards' decisions control the local schools. The state control in most school matters is so remote to the public view as to constitute little impact. Unless some conflict erupts, the local school board's plans and decisions are the prime forces in the nature, extent, and quality of local education. The state's valid concern for the substance and form of education is manifested in curriculum components required or encouraged in the schools. Illinois, for example, requires the public schools to provide courses in health, physical education, history of the United States, the content of the Uniform Traffic Act, periodic training in "honesty, kindness, justice, and moral courage," and specified instruction in American patriotism and the principles of representative government, and the nature and effect of alcoholic drinks and beverages.

In addition to required or permitted courses of study, states frequently provide for the selection, sale, loan, or free distribution of textbooks, transportation of pupils, scholarships and loans, and machinery to facilitate consortia of local districts for specialized instruction such as training for adults and school dropouts.

RIGHTS AND DUTIES OF LOCAL SCHOOL BOARDS

School boards are quasi-corporate bodies, created by state law to exercise certain delegated powers over local schools. The board's power extends over the school district for which it is constituted. The board, however, may not have the complete control of all public education in the district. Some states provide for separate school districts to handle the education of exceptional children, vocational and career training, and junior colleges. But in the main, the local school board acts as the state's agent for public education. Most school boards consist of members elected by the district voters. This means that board members may be regarded as dual representatives—agents of the state and of the voters. Although the duality may present political and personal tension, the board's ultimate legal responsibility is to the state government and the state laws concerning education.

School boards hold three kinds of power: (1) express power granted by law, (2) implied power arising from the express, and (3) those powers reasonably necessary to achieve the purposes of the granted powers. The express powers are frequently broad in scope and general in language. For example, most states charge local boards with the duty to operate and manage the local schools. Implied in this express grant is the power to select, employ, and dismiss teachers. The power to supervise, evaluate, and rate teachers may be neither expressed nor implied, but it would be reasonably necessary to achieve the purposes (that is, "operate and manage the schools") for which the board exists.

School boards can act only in their official capacity. Individual members have no power to perform official acts and must act as a duly constituted board to conduct school business. Statutes generally define the procedural requirements for board elections, meetings, records, and official acts.

Boards may only enter contracts which fall within the three broad areas of authority noted above. Unauthorized board action is *ultra vires* (outside the scope of authority). The uncertainty of the law concerning *ultra vires* contracts by the school boards stems from the conflict between the protection of the district (by preserving district assets from unauthorized use) and the protection of innocent people who rely on the board's apparent lawful contracting transactions. In dealing with school boards, one should prudently ascertain the scope of board authority and enter into only those transactions clearly within it.

Board meetings (except for executive sessions), records, and official business are public. Statutes usually exempt certain school business from public view where the need for privacy (deliberations about land acquisition and personnel matters) outweighs the public's right to know. Even for such delicate matters, the law usually requires that boards conduct some kind of open hearing to permit expression of public opinion, and that the vote be conducted in an open meeting. To require public hearings of all matters within the purview of the board would inhibit free deliberations and might well create more mischief than benefit. Although the law recognizes and honors the public interest in school management, it likewise attempts to balance the public interest and the realities of school board operations. Such a delicate balance exemplifies the dual responsibilities (to the state and to the district voters) vested in school boards.

THE FEDERAL ROLE IN EDUCATION

The federal role in education, though indirect, has become real in matters of curriculum and finance. Through comprehensive legislation, substantial federal support has been channeled into research and curriculum development in mathematics, science, foreign languages, vocational education, and, to a lesser extent, the humanities. The Elementary and Secondary Education Act of 1965 provides federal funds to improve the education for poor children and to strengthen library, supplementary educational services, and state departments of education. Although most federal support has gone to colleges and universities for research and teacher training, the benefits of the federal effort are for pupils in the public schools. The federal legislation for improved teachers, curriculum, teaching materials, and specialized training facilities has pumped vital resources into the state public education systems. With the exception of aid to impacted areas (schools affected by nearby government installations such as military bases and substantial government employment), federal aid is categorical rather than general and is administered to the states and the public schools through several executive agencies, such as the U.S. Office of Education (Department of Health, Education and Welfare) and the National Science Foundation (a quasi-governmental agency).

Although public education is primarily a function of the state, the federal government has taken an increasing responsibility for some aspects. As the historical church control of higher education gave way to secularism, state and federal ties to education developed to the point of domination. The waning influence of church-controlled common schools is evident from the rash of parochial-school closings in the past decade. Some states face the prospect of deciding whether constitutional means can be found to divert public funds to private-school support, a question laden with legal and social consequences. Public interest in education was manifested in the Northwest Ordinance (1787), which set aside certain land for educational purposes. Federal support for public education gained impetus from the Morrill Act (1862) which created "land grant" colleges in the states. The second Morrill Act (1890) authorized federal appropriations to each land-grant institution, and subsequent legislation (Smith-Lever Act of 1914, Smith-Hughes Act of 1917, and George-Deen Act of 1937) stimulated vocational training in several areas in the public schools.

Federal involvement in education is based on (a) the "general welfare" clause (Article 1, section 8 of the United States Constitution), which authorizes congressional action on behalf of the people, and (b) the protection of citizens under the federal constitution, particularly the First, Fifth, and Fourteenth Amendments. The First Amendment protects freedom of religion, speech, and press, and the right of petition. The first clause concerns schools most directly:

Congress shall make no law respecting an establishment of religion or prohibiting the free exercise thereof. . . .

This prohibition originally affected only the federal congress. Subsequent decisions of the United States Supreme Court, however, have extended this prohibition to the states. The result of such extension and judicial interpretation is a prohibition of both federal laws and state laws purporting to "establish" or "prohibit the free exercise of" religion. This principle will be explored in several contexts in subsequent chapters.

One of the most important consequences of the First Amendment concerns the use of federal funds to support private education. The orthodox interpretations of the federal constitution prohibit public support of parochial schools except by subterfuge. The "child-benefit doctrine" (the idea that the funds benefit the child, not the church) has developed to enable church schools to share, to a limited extent, in federal support for books, equipment, and other educational materials. This matter is dealt with in Chapter 2.

The Fifth Amendment appears frequently in cases concerning self-incrimination by teachers and pupils in school settings. The implications of this amendment appear in cases involving loyalty oaths concerning teachers and school administrators. The Fourteenth Amendment defines United States citizenship and bars state laws which abridge the privileges and immunities of such citizens and includes the right to "due process" and "equal protection of the laws." The latter two rights have spawned considerable litigation in school matters concerning segregation, flag-salute, rights of parents to provide private (vis-à-vis public) education for their children, and a variety of others. The Fourteenth Amendment has supported a sizable body of federal legislation aimed at achieving and protecting equal educational opportunity for racial, cultural, and economic minority groups.

EDUCATION AND THE COURTS

A brief description of the legal procedures will clarify the judicial role in the state system of education. Most laws seem completely clear and unambiguous. They direct public officials or citizens to do certain clearly defined acts (call elections, submit budgets to public hearings, provide schools for certain children, and so on) and are never the subject of a lawsuit. In the instances where disputes arise on school laws, however, it is clear that laws mean very little in the abstract. Whatever meaning the law has comes through litigation and court decisions. Most state court systems consist of three levels: (a) trial courts (where cases begin), (b) appellate courts (where most appeals from trial courts are heard), and (c) the state supreme court of last resort (where the final decisions in cases not dealing with a substantial federal question are made).

Civil cases begin when the aggrieved party (plaintiff) files a complaint against the alleged wrongdoer (defendant). The defendant usually responds to the complaint by filing an answer which either denies all or part of the complaint or admits the allegations in the complaint but sets out some legal justification for his behavior. With these two documents (the complaint and the answer), the issues are typically joined for trial. Various procedural maneuvers may be used to delay the trial, but the court ultimately sets the matter for hearing. Evidence is introduced on the dispute, the court (in nonjury cases) or the jury reaches a verdict, and the court renders an opinion. If the parties to the suit are not satisfied with the decision, one or both may appeal.

The appellate court's jurisdiction (the power to hear and determine) is appellate only; it has no power to hear the case until the trial court has reached a final decision. The appellate court does not hear testimony. It reviews the recorded trial proceedings and may either affirm or reverse the trial court's decision or, in a few instances, will remand (send back) the case to the trial court for further hearing. For most disputes, the appellate court decision is final. Although the state supreme (or final) court may have the power to hear almost any case, the court actually hears a small percent of the cases instituted at the trial court level. Most cases, obviously, are not of such public importance as to justify the time and expense of appeal to the highest state court.

The state supreme court generally takes appeals from the appellate court decisions. In some states, however, certain types of cases may be appealed directly from the trial court to the highest state court. The supreme court sets the rules by which it hears appeals from lower courts. Some cases may be started in the state supreme court, bypassing the trial court. The Illinois constitution, for example, provides that the state supreme court shall have original jurisdiction in "cases relating to the revenue, mandamus, prohibition and habeas corpus, . . . and only appellate jurisdiction in all other cases."

Most cases involving schools are civil, rather than criminal, matters. Civil cases involve alleged wrongs against the individual; criminal cases arise from alleged wrongs against the state. Cases concerning school matters frequently go through the federal court system to the United States Supreme Court. The Supreme Court picks and chooses the cases it hears. Unless the Court believes the case involves an important federal (or national) issue, it will not hear the matter. The issues in such cases touch upon rights guaranteed by the federal constitution or affected by federal legislation. During the past two decades, cases concerning segregation, flag-salute, church-state relations, and other civil-rights issues have been decided by the Supreme Court.

Once a case is before the Court, its task is to fairly interpret the law applicable to the facts. The Court carefully refrains from legislating school policies and recasting school legislation. If the matter has come before the Court in an earlier case, the doctrine of *stare decises* (abide by or follow decided cases) guides its decision. This doctrine, also known as the *rule of precedent*, removes some of the guesswork from lawsuits and serves as a guide to both litigants and the Court.

Many cases involve the school board's discretion in making rules, policies, and procedures for the schools, the teachers, and the pupils. As the cases demonstrate, the Court looks to the reasonableness of the school board's actions and rarely substitutes its wisdom for the board's. Because of the peculiar and awesome responsibility placed on the school boards, courts are most reluctant to overturn the boards' decisions unless they clearly breach either the manifest intent of the law or the bounds of reason. The test of "reason," however, has no application where the case clearly involves the denial or interference with a constitutional right.

In many ways, public schools are creatures of law. Their creation, control, management, and the countless day-to-day decisions are directly or indirectly products of the law. The matters of school finance, teacher-board employment relations, curriculum, policymaking and its effect on teachers, pupils, and parents, and a variety of relationships among schools, the churches, and community agencies all derive from constitutional and legislative mandates. Although most school problems arise from human interaction, the framework in which they develop and through which they are resolved comes from the state and federal laws. The overlapping control of schools by the state legislature, state department of education, the local school board, and the Congress creates problems of management and organization. The bureaucratic regulations at the various governmental levels, coupled with the normal red tape at the local school level, constitute serious barriers to either sensible or efficient education. The schools have survived this layer-cake management in the past; the future may be something else.

Readings

Do School Districts Need an Ombudsman?

Howard J. Grossman

American School Board Journal (December 1967), **155**, 6–7.

The ombudsman has arrived at the shores of America.

Born in Sweden in 1809, the ombudsman concept is a way of life in other governments. He acts as the people's representative in handling complaints and redressing grievances against the individual. He can investigate and order corrections and can alleviate much work of the legislative branch, allowing them to concentrate on their prime responsibilities of establishing legislation and creating policy.

The basic purpose of the ombudsman is to bring government back to the people in an era of larger and larger public actions, bodies, and systems which threaten individual liberty. Some call the post a commissioner of investigation, a people's representative, the tribune of the people, an agent of redress, and other similar names. The word actually means "one who represents someone" and is used quite frequently in many aspects of Swedish life.

The ombudsman concept also represents the one, fresh, new idea to reach the mainstream of governmental reform in many years. What this really means in the context of federal, state, county, municipal, and school district governmental actions remains to be seen, since few communities or governmental units in America have as yet accepted it as a way of life. But the ombudsman offers a potential for providing redress for the average citizen in a way he possibly could never attain elsewhere, as well as bringing to large school districts a creative concept for making school boards more responsive to community needs. . . .

POWER OF SCHOOL DISTRICT OMBUDSMAN

What exactly are the powers of the ombudsman if he were to be created as a United States school district institution? He would be appointed by the school board for a term of office, usually to coincide with that of the board. He would be eligible for reappointment and generally would have discretion in deciding which matters to investigate. He would receive citizen complaints and make announced and unannounced inspection tours. He could take matters up by his own volition and could compel testimony and the production of evidence. He could make available to the press the results of his investigations when he deems it advisable.

With a small staff, the size depending upon the type of school district, the ombudsman is alerted by squeaking wheels as one expert has put it—citizens' grievances and newspaper reports. He relies on the departments under investigation to supply the facts he needs to judge the merits of the complaints he receives, at least in the first instance. The experience in other lands has been that this cooperation does exist and is forthcoming. The majority of the complaints which the ombudsman receives are without merit, and the bureaucrat welcomes the opportunity to sustain his actions. In fact, government employees themselves may initiate complaints about working conditions and other matters.

The ombudsman would have to work closely with the school administrative staff, particularly the superintendent. Every effort would have to be made to prevent the problems resulting from change which erupt in most public agencies when new concepts are placed into longstanding administrative situations. The ombudsman should not remain apart from the school administration although he should be independent to investigate and report findings without interference by the administration. On the other hand, the ombudsman should be completely conversant with the operation and administration of the school district, so he probably should be structured within the office of the superintendent and, in many respects, made a part of the staff of that office. The fine line of independence versus close cooperation must be formed and implemented to the specific situation of the school district. The school board must resolve how this can best be accomplished. While the ombudsman is "not a God," as Nassau County Public Protector Greason has said, he offers the chance to create representative government at a new level in the United States. This is as true for school districts as it is for other forms of American government.

NATIONAL EXPERIMENTS

On the national level, Congressman Henry S. Reuss has appointed James P. Buckley to act as ombudsman for Reuss' 5th District in Milwaukee on a trial basis. Congressman Reuss points out that "a member of Congress is today a harried man. The days are hardly long enough for him to think and act soundly on all the great issues. So why don't we hire a professional grievance man to serve all of us, to take as much of the load off our backs . . . and at the same time give our constituents better help by putting their problems in the hands of a truly expert staff?"

Additionally, Congressman Reuss has continually submitted bills before Congress to establish the ombudsman concept, but thus far none has been enacted. His proposal has run under fire by other Congressmen who claim, as does Representative William A. Carey of Massachusetts, that "if they (congressmen) can't represent the people, then they should get out and let someone else do the job. We were elected to represent the people, not to pass the buck to an Ombudsman." This argument, of course, could apply to school boards as well, but neglects the facts of American trends toward larger and more complex agencies, including school districts. As districts become bigger, the need for the ombudsman as a safety valve to protect the citizen from possible school district bureaucracy, intentional or otherwise, will be even greater—particularly in large urban districts.

Over sixteen states have introduced bills to establish a state ombudsman, and Michigan has established one under the Secretary of State. Utah, New York, Pennsylvania, California, Rhode Island, Connecticut, Illinois, Colorado, Indiana, Maryland, and others have expressed serious interest.

To cite one example, Representative Robert J. Butera, Majority Whip in the Pennsylvania House of Representatives, co-sponsored a bill to establish an ombudsman post in Pennsylvania. Butera states that "what we need is a champion of the Little Guy—to attack the red tape and rescue the people from the sometimes insolent attitude of government bureaus and bureacracy. The office of Ombudsman must be above partisan politics. . . . The elimination of groundless fear and distrust is essential if we are to expect state government to meet the growing challenges of the 20th century."

The ombudsman concept deserves to be experimented with by those school districts confronted with the problems facing many urban communities, that is, being responsive to citizen needs. The ombudsman's psychological effect on school district officials who are conscious of his existence may be its chief benefit. The ombudsman is an innovation which could create the kind of school government needed to cope with the changing demands of society.

Summary of the Elementary and Secondary Education Act of 1965

This summary originally appeared as part of the article, "The First Work of These Times," *American Education* (published by the U.S. Office of Education, April, 1965) pp. 1–8.

AN ACT

To strengthen and improve educational quality and educational opportunities in the Nation's elementary and secondary schools.

Title 1. Financial Assistance to Local Educational Agencies for Special Educational Programs in Areas Having High Concentrations of Children of Low-Income Families

BACKGROUND. It has long been apparent that there is a close relationship between poverty and the lack of educational development and poor academic performance. The 10 States with lowest per capita personal incomes have Selective Service rejection rates for mental tests well above the average for the 50 States. Dropout rates are high where income rates are low. Economic deprivation often precludes children from taking full advantage of such educational facilities as are provided.

There is no lack of techniques, equipment, or materials which can be used or developed to meet the problem of educating the economically and culturally deprived child. But those school districts which need these materials most are least able to pay for them.

PROVISIONS. This title authorizes approximately $1,060,000,000 to help local school districts broaden and strengthen public school programs where there are concentrations of educationally disadvantaged children. The money could be used to hire additional staff, construct facilities, acquire equipment, etc.

The amount each local school district would get would depend on two factors:
1. The average annual current expenditure per school child in the entire State.
2. The number of school-age children in the district from families with annual incomes of less than $2,000 and those in families receiving more than $2,000 annually from the program of Aid to Families with Dependent Children.

One-half the first, multiplied by the second, would be the amount for which a local district would be eligible.

The local educational agency could use these funds as it saw fit for the benefit of deprived students of both public and nonpublic schools, through such arrangements as dual enrollment, educational radio and television, educational media centers, and mobile educational services and equipment. Administrative supervision and control of the programs—and title to any property constructed or purchased—would rest with a public agency.

The President is required under the Act to appoint a National Advisory Council on the Education of Disadvantaged Children. This Council would review the administration and operation of Title I each year, particularly the title's effectiveness in improving the educational attainment of deprived children.

Title 2. School Library Resources, Textbooks, and Other Instructional Materials

BACKGROUND. Educational specialists from the fields of both instruction and library science—have pointed up the growing importance of well-stocked libraries, audio-visual materials, and up-to-date textbooks and materials in an effective program of instruction.

Quality in school library programs is related to students' academic achievement, to remaining in high school, and to continuing on to college or a job. Where there are central libraries in elementary schools, research has found that children not only read more but show significant educational gains between the fourth and sixth grades. Despite this and other evidence of the value of elementary school libraries, nearly 47 percent of public and more than 50 percent of nonpublic elementary school students have no library. Secondary school students are somewhat better off, but the number of libraries is still inadequate. Approximately 12,000,000 of 41,000,000 public and nonpublic elementary and secondary school students in the United States—nearly a third of them—attend schools without libraries.

The need is not confined to small school systems or to particular geographic regions. In 1963, public schools in the 21 largest U.S. cities provided fewer books per pupil and spent less per pupil than did many smaller systems which themselves had inadequate libraries.

As far as textbooks are concerned, school systems in 33 cities of over 90,000 population do not provide free high school text-books. Nonpublic schools rarely provide free textbooks. A family with children in high school may have to spend $15 to $20 per student for up-to-date texts. In 1961, parents spent more than $90,000,000 for textbooks—40 percent of that year's total textbook expenditures.

PROVISIONS. This title authorizes the allotment of $100,000,000 to States for school library resources, textbooks, and other instructional materials. Materials could include books, periodicals, documents, magnetic tapes, phonograph records, and other printed and published materials. Allotments would be made on the basis of the number of children enrolled in public and nonpublic elementary and secondary schools within each State.

For the first fiscal year in which the program is in operation, up to 5 per cent of each State's grant would be available to defray administrative costs; after the first year, up to 3 percent.

Title 3. Supplementary Educational Centres and Services

BACKGROUND. Among the variety of supplementary services that make the difference between a poor school and a good school are special instruction in science, languages, music, and the arts; counseling and guidance; health and social work; access to such resources as technical institutes, museums, art galleries, and theaters; and the availability of informal model innovative programs to serve as stimuli to local planning and operation.

Seventy percent of the Nation's public secondary schools have no language laboratories. Seventy-five percent of our elementary schools do not have the services of a guidance counselor as often as once a week. In 40 States, there are still secondary schools without science laboratories. Model programs have traditionally been developed only in local communities with extraordinary financial capacity and a strong commitment to education.

Many other examples of uneven distribution and inconsistent quality of educational, scientific, and cultural resources could be cited. Enrichment of the curriculum of elementary and secondary schools through supplementary services is essential.

PROVISIONS. Title III authorizes $100,000,000 for supplementary educational centers and services. The program would serve three basic functions: (1) To improve education by enabling a community to provide services not now available to the children who live there, (2) to raise the quality of educational services already offered, and (3) to stimulate and assist in the development and establishment of exemplary elementary and secondary school educational programs to serve as models for regular school programs.

A State's allocation would be based on a formula taking into account both the school-age population and the total population of the entire State. Grants, however, would be made to local public educational agencies by the Commissioner after review and recommendation by the State.

The Commissioner would have to ascertain that grants are equitably distributed according to size and population of the States, the geographic distribution of population within each State, the relative need of people in different geographic areas within the State for the kinds of services to be offered, and the relative ability of particular local educational agencies to provide these services.

The Act provides that an Advisory Committee on Supplementary Educational Centers and Services be established, consisting of the Commissioner, as chairman, and eight appointed members. This Committee would advise the Commissioner on action to be taken regarding applications for grants, on policy questions arising in the administration of the program, and on the development of evaluative criteria.

Title 4. Educational Research and Training

BACKGROUND. During this fiscal year, $34,000,000,000 is being devoted to education—which, with 26,000 operating school districts and 2,100 institutions of higher education, is America's largest industry. But only $72,000,000—less than one-fifth of 1 percent—is being spent on education research and development. Many private industries devote as much as 10 percent of their annual expenditures to research and development activities.

Since 1954, the Cooperative Research Act has supported education research by colleges, universities, and State educational agencies. Such research has made significant contributions to improve students' learning. In some schools 2- and 3-year olds are learning to read and write. First-graders are dealing with the concepts of economics. Fourth-graders are using the set theory in mathematics. Junior high school students are studying concepts of anthropology. High school students are studying advanced science and literature courses formerly taught only in a college.

For fiscal year 1965, some $16,000,000 was allocated under the Cooperative

Research program. This is far from adequate. Moreover, even if more money was available, few colleges or State agencies have the equipment or plant to carry on extensive research and training programs.

PROVISIONS. Title IV amends the Cooperative Research Act to authorize $100,000,000 over the next five years for the construction of national and regional research facilities. In addition to the construction funds, there is authorization for an expansion of the current programs of research and development. There would also be established a new program of training for education researchers.

Title 5. Strengthening State Departments of Education

BACKGROUND. If American elementary and secondary education is to be both free and effective, State departments of education must be strong. The alternative to strong State departments is an educational lag and a default of leadership.

In one medium-sized department in a middle-income State, there are 75 professional staff members. These 75 must assist 1,300 schools and 20,000 local school people in the administration of State and Federal funds and programs, in the improvement of instruction, and in the solution of technical problems relating to building, equipment, etc. Some estimate they visit each school in their State on the average of one-half day every seven years. Under such circumstances —believed to be widespread—effective State educational leadership for the challenges of today and the awesome responsibilities of tomorrow is impossible.

PROVISIONS. Title V authorizes $25,000,000 for the development, improvement, or expansion of a variety of programs and projects designed to improve the effectiveness of operations of State departments of educations.

For the first two years the Federal Government would bear the entire cost. Thereafter, grants would be on a matching basis, with the Federal share ranging from 50 percent to 66 percent.

Two types of grants are authorized: basic grants and special project grants. Eighty-five percent of authorized funds would be basic grants. The remainder would be for the support of experimental projects or the establishment of special services which hold promise of contributing to the solution of problems common to all or several of the States.

Provision is made for an interchange of personnel between the Office of Education and State educational agencies. The Commissioner of Education might arrange for assignments of Office of Education personnel to State departments, or State personnel to the Office of Education, for a period not exceeding two years.

An Advisory Council on State Departments of Education is to be appointed by the Secretary of Health, Education, and Welfare. This council would review the administration of programs for which Federal funds are appropriated, not only under this title, but under all other acts which provide funds to assist State education agencies in administering Federal programs in education.

Equal Education
and the Law

Hershel Shanks

Hershel Shanks, a graduate of the Harvard Law School and a partner
in a Washington, D. C., law firm, combines his practice with writing
on law, sociology and biblical criticism. His articles have appeared
in *Commentary*, the *Jewish Quarterly Review*, and numerous legal
publications. His first book, *The Art and Craft of Judging*, was a
selection of the Lawyer's Literary Club. Mr. Shanks has participated
in much of the litigation described in this article.

From *The American Scholar* (Spring, 1970) **39**, no. 2, 225–269

Well over one hundred years ago Alexis de Tocqueville observed that Americans
tend to transform their political, or social, problems into legal problems. The
observation was as much a prophecy as a then present fact; the tendency persists,
to say the least.

To some who observe the outcome only when it hits the morning paper, a
decision of the Supreme Court often seems fore-ordained. The result either so
conforms to one's own predilections that the Court's conclusion appears to be
obvious, or is so at variance with those predilections that the Court's conclusion
can be attributable only to a perverse, result-oriented liberalism, or worse. In
truth, however, the outcome—as it appears before the event—is often far from
clear and is worked out with a prodigious amount of legal effort and creativity.

Still very much in doubt is the outcome of one of these struggles in which
educators and lawyers are attempting to transform—at least partially—a social
problem into a legal problem. This account is in the nature of a progress report.

The social problem, in its broadest context, is the dismal state of many of the
nation's public schools, especially in urban slums and poor rural areas. On the
other hand, many of the nation's schools—especially in the affluent suburbs—
are very fine indeed. Is there somewhere in this situation a legal wrong that a
court might redress?

The obvious differences in quality between one public school and another
immediately suggest to the constitutional lawyer the possibility of relief under
what he refers to as the equal protection clause. This clause is contained in one
of the post-Civil War Amendments to the Constitution—the Fourteenth—and
provides simply that "No State shall . . . deny to any person within its jurisdiction the equal protection of the laws."

One of the astonishing facets of our political democracy is that a simple
phrase like Equal Protection should have been so monumentally extrapolated
that it is now a major grant of legally enforceable rights. As interpreted by the
courts, equal protection of the laws really means the protection of equal laws.
The emphasis is not on "protection" (a more clinical work like "application"

would serve as well), but on "equal." The laws must be "equal." Because black schools and white schools are not "equal," the Supreme Court struck down state laws requiring their separation. Because a city vote was not "equal" to a rural vote in most areas of the country, the Court struck down laws that malapportioned legislatures. As Mr. Justice Harlan has recently put it, "The equal protection clause prevents states from arbitrarily treating people differently under their laws."

Like that one, all definitions of equal protection reflect the fact that the law often treats its citizens unequally (or differently) for very sound reasons. Convicted criminals, unlike other citizens, are denied the right to vote. Men, unlike women, are required to serve in the armed forces, and even among men the law treats those between the ages of eighteen and thirty-five differently from men of other ages. Clearly the equal protection clause does not condemn the laws that make these distinctions, even though they apply or "protect" unequally. The equal protection clause forbids only distinctions that are inadequately justified, unreasonable or arbitrary. Thus the government may treat young men differently from old men, with respect to the draft. But it may not treat Negro children differently from white children, with respect to public schools.

This background may help the reader to appreciate why a constitutional lawyer might focus on the equal protection clause as a means of translating the social problem of inadequate schools into a legal problem. The vague perception, however, that the equal protection clause may offer some hope of relief is only the beginning of analysis, not the end.

This analysis has been undertaken by a dozen organizations, in a hundred seminars and meetings, and, by now, in a handful of scholarly articles and books, and it has been carried forward by the Urban Coalition, the Lawyers' Committee for Civil Rights, the National Education Association, the University of Chicago's Center for Policy Study, the newly established Law and Education Center at Harvard University, and local groups throughout the country that have been formed to develop and prosecute cases designed to bring some judicial relief to the problem of inadequate schools. The result has been a number of law suits—in Illinois, Michigan, California, Texas, Virginia, Florida and elsewhere—seeking a judicial solution to the quest for equal education.

The initial question for the groups behind these lawsuits was a policy question, rather than a legal one: Would a judicial victory based on the equal protection clause actually improve the schools? The social problem at the outset was inadequate schools, not unequal schools. But the legal consideration focused on the contrast that existed between inadequate schools and certain other better schools. In this contrast lay the possibility that a legal wrong might be found for which the courts would give redress. Even if the legal effort based on the equal protection clause were completely successful, this would result only in a judicial order that the states equalize schools, not that they improve them. In short, victory might mean a reduction in the quality of schools to the lowest common denominator, not an improvement so that all the schools within a state would be equal to the best. And this could destroy the public school system. A system of private schools for all who could afford them might well grow up in the more affluent areas, leaving the public school system as a whole in worse condition than ever. In addition, some have argued, too much emphasis on equality might eliminate the diversity, the freedom to experiment, that is the greater hope for improvement.

But those who decided to go forward obviously concluded that these risks were worth running, that as a practical or political matter a judicial command to equalize schools would improve, not destroy, them. They guessed that those who control both the public schools and the legislatures, supported by the broad middle class who are entirely dependent on those schools, would force state legislatures to improve the schools in response to a judicial victory based on the equal protection clause.

The next question was to decide on the particular inequality that was to be the target of the legal attack. This involved conceptual problems concerning the meaning of equality in this particular context, as well as practical factual questions about the possible justification for a particular kind of unequal treatment.

There is so much that is unequal about schools within a state, it is hard to know where to begin a consideration of the inequality—textbooks, course offerings, school buildings, special programs, teaching staffs, more subtle environmental factors such as the abilities of a student's classmates, their socio-economic status, their values and outlooks. And the justification—or lack thereof—varies with each inequality. Or one may take a different tack and ask whether providing an equal education requires a state to provide more and better facilities—that is, more education—in the slums to overcome the disadvantages with which slum children start the race; to provide an equal education, it can be argued, the state must take account of the differing educational needs of each child. Still another approach would be to attack the variations in per pupil expenditure within a state. In the end, the demonstrably unequal expenditures per pupil were the focus of most of the cases. Although more money would not automatically solve the problem, it would, most people believed, at least provide the poorer schools with an additional means of attacking the problem.

An attack on the inequality in per pupil expenditures within a state requires an examination of financing systems for the support of public education to determine the causes of the inequality and whether there are justifications that the state might use to support the inequality. Sometimes the inequality stems from an unfair state formula that distributes more money per pupil in the suburbs than in the central city. More often the inequality results from the fact that a major burden of school financing is placed on local governments. In poverty areas, the school district simply cannot afford to finance adequate schools by local taxation; in the affluent suburbs, the local school district has no difficulty in providing adequate funding for its own schools. Is a state financing system adequately justified that places unequal burdens on different local communities, depending on their wealth?

The first case to be decided presented this question. Since it is now the leading case in the area, we shall look at it more closely. It is entitled *McInnis* v. *Ogilvie*, or simply the *McInnis* case.

The *McInnis* case was brought by a group of parents from Chicago's West Side who had banded together under the sobriquet Concerned Parents and Teachers of the West Side. The central thrust of the complaint they filed in the Federal District Court in Chicago was that the state scheme for financing public education necessarily results in a larger per pupil expenditure in some school districts than others, because it requires local communities to raise about two thirds of their school funds from local real estate taxes, and that this financing scheme violates the equal protection clause of the Fourteenth Amendment to the Constitution.

In elementary schools, where the variation in per pupil expenditure is the greatest, some Illinois schools spend three times as much per pupil as others. On a school district basis—which includes not just elementary schools, but all levels of education—per pupil expenditures in Illinois vary from $480 per pupil in some school districts to $1,000 per pupil in others. While this disparity is extreme, the general pattern is clear, not only in Illinois but throughout the nation: the poorer school districts spend far less per pupil than do wealthy school districts. Nationally, spending levels in suburban schools average almost thirty percent in excess of the average for city schools ($573 to $449). And the extreme variation in expenditures per pupil in Illinois is not atypical. In California, expenditures per pupil vary between $265 and $1,353. In New York, they vary between $470 and $1,600.

The defendants in the Illinois suit (state officials from the Governor on down) promptly filed a motion to dismiss the suit on the ground that the plaintiffs had not stated a valid constitutional claim, that the state had no obligation to finance public education by a scheme that would equalize per pupil expenditures. The federal district court agreed with the defendants. The court conceded that "the inequities of the existing arrangement are readily apparent," but it could find no constitutional wrong. "The allocation of public revenues is a basic policy decision more appropriately handled by a legislature than a court." The court found in the Illinois scheme sufficient justification to satisfy constitutional requirements.

The Illinois scheme allowed responsibility for local schools to remain with local residents, and thus accrued the attendant benefits of decentralization and community participation. Local school districts were free to experiment in educational financing, which was a reasonable legislative choice, especially since Illinois assured a minimum school fund of $400 per pupil, regardless of the poverty of the district. And individual localities were free to determine their own tax burden according to the importance that they placed upon public schools. The Illinois legislative scheme for financing schools may be unwise, but it is not wholly without a basis in reason. And thus, said the court, despite the obvious inequality, the inequality is justified by an adequate rational basis to sustain its constitutionality.

The *McInnis* decision was indeed a setback, especially as it was the unanimous decision of a three-judge court. (A constitutional attack on a state statute brought in federal court must be heard by a district court of three judges.) Fortunately, however, the Supreme Court still sat in Washington, and it was there that the plaintiffs promptly repaired.

The Supreme Court's decision in the *McInnis* case was handed down on March 25, 1969. It is short enough to quote in its entirety. The Supreme Court said simply, "The motion to affirm is granted and the judgment [of the lower court] is affirmed."

There was no place else to go. The highest court in the land had spoken.

As might have been expected, the *McInnis* case was soon cited as precedent in a number of other similar suits in which the plaintiffs were thrown out of court. The question remains whether the issue is now dead.

The answer is no—for at least three reasons. The first requires us to delve more deeply into very recent and far-reaching developments in the meaning of equal protection. The second requires us to ask why the Supreme Court ruled as it did in the *McInnis* case. And the third reason involves a look at another case that is already making its way through the courts.

Earlier in the discussion of equal protection, we said that it was not inequality that was unconstitutional, but unjustified inequality, unreasonable inequality. As stated in a 1935 Supreme Court case, which was quoted by the lower court in the *McInnis* case, "A statutory discrimination will not be set aside as the denial of equal protection of the laws if any state of facts reasonably may be conceived to justify it." It was by this standard that the lower court in *McInnis* made its determination that the Illinois statutes were sufficiently justified that they did not violate the equal protection clause.

In recent years, however, a stricter standard appears to have been applied in some cases. The emergence of this stricter standard began in cases where the Supreme Court declined to accept "any reasonable" justification for distinctions based on race. As early as 1944, the Court said that classifications based on race were "suspect" and therefore had to bear a greater burden of justification.

More recently, the Supreme Court appears to have required a greater burden of justification in certain cases in addition to those involving racial discrimination, although it was not very explicit about the matter.

Then on April 21, 1969, in what may well have been the most significant opinion of the 1968-69 term, the Court articulated more explicitly and in greater detail than it had ever done before a new—and far broader—standard for judging the constitutionality of legislation subjected to attack under the equal protection clause. And in a second case handed down on April 28, 1969, the Court enumerated the classes of cases to which the new standard was applicable. Taken together, these cases give the courts far broader power to strike down legislation on the basis of the equal protection clause than they have ever had before.

The first case, handed down on April 21, involved the constitutionality of a one-year state residence requirement as a pre-requisite to eligibility for welfare assistance. The plaintiffs claimed that the statue violated the equal protection clause because it treated residents of less than one year and residents of more than one year differently, without adequate justification. The importance of the case lies not so much in the fact that it struck down one-year residence requirements for welfare assistance, but in how the Court did it. The Court did not simply say that the one-year residence requirement was unreasonable because it has *no* legitimate legislative justification. The Court went on to say that even if there were reasonable grounds for a legislature's imposing a one-year residence re quirement, this was not enough. In some cases, of which this was one, reasonable grounds for the law were not sufficient to sustain it against constitutional attack; in cases like this, an adequate justification required the state to demonstrate that the legislation in question served a *compelling* state interest. Said the Court:

... [T]he traditional criteria [Does the legislation have some basis in reason or is it completely arbitrary?] do not apply in these cases ... [The] constitutionality [of the inequality under attack here] must be judged by a stricter standard of whether it promotes a *compelling* state interest. [Italics in original]

This new interpretation of the equal protection clause vastly increases the scope of judicial review that the Court exercises over legislation, both state and federal. For a litigant to demonstrate that a statute is completely without reason is difficult indeed. But the test under the new standard is, "Does the legislative classification under attack promote a compelling state interest?" The shoe—or the burden—is on the other foot. Now the *state* must justify the statute, and do it by showing a compelling state interest.

In what cases does the new standard apply? First of all, as the welfare case makes clear, the new standard applies to legislation that impinges on the exercise of a constitutionally protected right. (In the welfare case, the constitutional right involved was the right to travel.)

Other kinds of cases are more specifically identified in an opinion handed down a week after the welfare case, on April 28, 1969. The Court there made clear that the new and stricter standard it had articulated in the welfare case was also applicable where "fundamental rights," such as voting, are impinged upon by the legislation and also where the legislation under attack draws lines on the basis of race *or wealth*.

The significance for the equal education cases of this post-*McInnis* constitutional development of the equal protection clause may be easily seen. In the first place, education, like voting, may involve "a fundamental right." As the Supreme Court said in *Brown* v. *Board of Education*:

Today, education is perhaps the most important function of state and local governments ... [Education] is required in the performance of our most basic responsibilities, even service in the armed forces. It is the very foundation of good citizenship. Today it is a principal instrument in awakening the child to cultural values, in preparing him for later professional training, and in helping him to adjust normally to his environment. In these days, it is doubtful that any child may reasonably be expected to succeed in life if he is denied the opportunity of an education.

Secondly, state financing statutes also appear to classify students according to wealth. The wealthier suburbs can afford an education far beyond that of the urban ghetto. What kind of education a child gets depends in large part on how valuable the real estate is in the school district in which he happens to live. Thus it would seem that the plaintiffs have an excellent argument that the "compelling state interest" test is applicable to the equal education cases, both because a fundamental right is involved (the right to an education) and because the state statutes discriminate on the basis of wealth. It would be extremely difficult to find a compelling state interest that justifies the complex of state statutes that provide a $1200 education to the suburban child and a $400 education to the ghetto child.

Why then did the Supreme Court affirm the decision of the lower court in *McInnis*? There is no way to know for certain, because the Supreme Court did not give any reasons for its ruling. But it seems safe to assume that, by its affirmance, the Supreme Court did not intend to put its imprimatur on the broad rulings of the lower court. To have done so would have been inconsistent with its own rulings of less than one month later in the welfare case. Much more likely, the Supreme Court's decision in *McInnis* can be accounted for on very narrow grounds, grounds that may not be present in a subsequent case. For example, the plaintiffs sought to obtain a decree that would apportion public funds according to educational need (a highly unmanageable concept from a court's point of view), rather than to obtain only the elimination of discrimination based on the wealth of the local district. The Supreme Court's affirmance may represent only a rejection of the plaintiffs' unnecessarily broad position. There are a number of similar, if technical, bases on which the *McInnis* case will likely be distinguished from cases that will be presented in the future.

Moreover, it can be argued that the Supreme Court's decision in *McInnis* is nothing more than a refusal to review the lower court's decision. Although the *McInnis* case is not one in which the Supreme Court technically had the option to decline to review (as it can in most cases where its review is sought), the Court nevertheless treated the case in much the same way as it does those cases where it is free to announce simply that it will exercise its discretion *not* to hear the case. This is evidenced by the fact that the Court made its decision only on the basis of a jurisdictional statement and without full briefs addressed to the merits of the case; the Court did not permit oral argument on the case; and the Court gave no reason for its decision. If this is indeed tantamount to a refusal to review, then the Supreme Court may have based its decision on nothing more than the conclusion that the issue was not ripe for review at that time or that the record was defective.

That the *McInnis* case does not foreclose success in other similar cases is suggested by the final case that we will examine, *Hargrave* v. *McKinney*, which may well turn out to be the first victory in the equal education cases.

The *Hargrave* case, which is being underwritten by the National Education Association, grew out of the school crisis that gripped the state of Florida in

February and March, 1968, a crisis that included the first statewide teacher walk-out in history. As part of the package passed by a special session of the legislature to increase state appropriations for education and end the walkout, Florida also passed a statute limiting to a maximum of ten mills the tax rate that a county could impose on local real estate for purposes of public education. If a county exceeded the ten-mill limit, its state school funds would be cut off. Twenty-four Florida counties had imposed tax rates on themselves exceeding this ten-mill ceiling. In one county the rate was eighteen mills. The new legislation required each of these twenty four counties to reduce its tax rate (since they could not possibly do without state funds), and for this reason the legislation was known popularly as the millage rollback act.

After the teacher walkout ended, discontent at the inadequacy of the financial support that the legislature had given to public education continued to smolder. Especially rankling was the millage rollback act, which effectively prevented counties from raising funds previously approved by their own voters. Was there any way to invalidate the millage rollback act? the teachers asked their lawyers.

On the surface, it would appear that the millage rollback act was well within the power of a state legislature. After all, the counties are the creatures of the state and they cannot collect taxes not authorized by the legislature. But a state legislature is also bound by the Constitution's equal protection clause.

What is unequal, however, about a ten-mill limit on a county's taxing authority for educational purposes? The answer proceeds along the following lines and explains how this case, the only purpose of which was to invalidate a piece of legislation that Florida teachers believed unwise, came to affect—perhaps crucially—the equal education cases: The legislature, by its ten-mill ceiling, authorizes Charlotte County, Florida, for example, to collect $725 per pupil, while Bradford County is authorized to collect only $52 per pupil. This is inequality with a vengeance, and arises from the fact that Charlotte County's tax base per pupil is approximately fourteen times that of Bradford County. In other words, Charlotte County is far richer (in relation to its school population) and as a result of that fact the Florida legislature allows it to tax itself far more per pupil than other counties may.

Whether this is constitutionally permissible depends, first of all, on what standard of justification is applicable—do we ask whether the inequality is based on a compelling state interest or do we ask whether there is any rational basis to a statute that creates this inequality? Secondly, we must ask whether the justification for the statute meets the applicable standard. As we have already indicated, the stricter standard—the compelling state interest test—would seem to be applicable here because of the fundamental rights involved and the fact that lines are drawn on the basis of wealth.

The only justification for the millage rollback act that has thus far been advanced is that it prevents local governments from taxing themselves or the county into a depression. Given the state of the economy and the extent of federal and other governmental controls over the economy, the millage rollback act hardly seems to be supported by a compelling state interest. It may well lack adequate justification even under the "any rational basis" test.

The first judge to rule on the *Hargrave* case, however, threw it out on technical grounds, without even convening a three-judge court. While a ruling of a three-judge court is appealed directly to the Supreme Court, a ruling by a single district judge is appealed to the Court of Appeals. Accordingly, the plaintiffs in the *Hargrave* case took an appeal to the United States Court of Appeals for the Fifth Circuit, which hears appeals in desegregation cases from most of the federal district courts in the Deep South. It is a court that is accustomed to difficult cases.

In the *Hargrave* case, the Fifth Circuit split two to one. The dissenter, Judge Griffin B. Bell of Georgia, argued that the case was controlled by the Supreme Court's decision in *McInnis*, which had been handed down after the single district judge had dismissed the *Hargrave* complaint. Therefore, according to Judge Bell, the lower court was correct in dismissing the case even if the lower court was wrong on the technical ground on which it based its ruling. The majority, however, disagreed. "We readily observe," wrote Judge Richard T. Rives of Alabama for the majority, "that prior decisions of the federal judiciary do not foreclose consideration of plaintiffs' equal protection argument. See [the] *McInnis* [case]." Thus, Judge Rives indicated that the *McInnis* case was not the end of the line, that it really settled very little. The majority continued:

The allegations of the complaint posit a fact situation which, under recently elasticized theories of equal protection, gives rise to a constitutional claim. . . . Noting that lines drawn on wealth are suspect and that we are here dealing with interests which may well be deemed fundamental, we cannot say there is no reasonably arguable theory of equal protection which would support a decision in favor of the plaintiffs.

The court did not say that the plaintiffs were right, but it could not say they had no case either. So the court returned the suit to the single district court judge with directions to convene a three-judge court to decide it.

The Fifth Circuit handed down its decision on June 9, 1969, and that is where the case now stands. The case may ultimately be decided by the Supreme Court.

What would a victory in the *Hargrave* case mean?

A reasonable expectation is that a victory for the plaintiffs in the *Hargrave* case would establish the principle that a state may not use the wealth of the local community—which is unrelated to the educational needs of the community—as the measure of the financial support that the community may give to public education. This holding could, of course, provide the springboard for a broader attack on existing educational inequalities that result from the variations within a state of the wealth of different school districts. How far the principle would be expanded in subsequent cases is difficult to predict. It might well carry to victory the next set of plaintiffs who challenge a *McInnis*-like situation, for in both *Hargrave* and the *McInnis*-like situation the state effectually draws lines on the basis of wealth.

While a victory in a *McInnis*-like case will clearly require a revamping of state laws providing for the funding of public education, it will not, as is sometimes claimed, eliminate local taxes as a prime source of funds for public education. What success in a *McInnis*-like case will do is to break the now necessary relation between a local community's wealth and the kind of schools it gets. Once this divorce is made, there is a myriad of acceptable state financing laws. The state could, of course, fund public education solely through state taxes, distributing all necessary funds to the local communities based on some reasonable formula related to the educational needs of the local community (rather than to the wealth of the local community). But it could also break the link between community wealth and the financial level of support for public schools without eliminating local taxes as a major source of public school funding. The key to accomplishing this within the structures of a victory in a case like *McInnis* is to provide that the production of local funds depend on effort (that is, the tax rate) rather than on the wealth of the community (that is, the tax base).

To illustrate, let us say that the state will provide fifty percent of the necessary financial support for public education by appropriation to the local community. The dollar amount of this appropriation would depend on the number of pupils in the system. Additional funds would be provided by the local community depending on the tax rate imposed on itself by the local community (but *not* depending on its wealth as reflected in the tax base). Let us say ten mills will produce the additional fifty percent needed for an adequate system. Any local community that imposes this ten-mill rate will get the additional fifty percent. If the community is a poor one in which a ten-mill tax will produce only twenty-five percent, rather than fifty percent, of what is needed, the difference will be paid by the state. If it is a wealthy community in which a ten-mill tax will produce seventy-five percent, rather than fifty percent, of what is needed, the excess will be paid to the state. Thus the result in a local community will depend on effort (the tax rate) rather than wealth (the tax base). And the local community will still be free to set its own level of effort, depending on the importance it places on education.

The very fact that there is this simple alternative to remedy the *McInnis*-like inequality is a strong argument that this inequity is inadequately justified by the state, and is therefore unconstitutional.

And what is beyond a victory in the *McInnis* kind of situation? The next question is whether the state has an affirmative obligation to provide an equal education to its children, even though the inequality does not result from lines drawn on the basis of wealth—as it does in the *McInnis*-like situation. What if, for example, it costs more to educate properly a ghetto child than a suburban child? Is the ghetto child entitled to demand as a constitutional right that he be given the same education as the suburban child, even though it may cost more to educate him than the suburban child? And what of the blind child? Or the deaf child? Can they make the same demand? And what of the case where the inequality results not from differences in the tax base—as in a *McInnis* case—but from the fact that there are greater demands on local taxes in the city with its need for greater welfare expenditures and police protection? Can a city plead poverty because it must spend its money on other things besides schools? Perhaps the safest course is to note only that these are the kinds of legal questions that are opened by the thrust of current litigation. What will be the ultimate course of this constitutional development cannot be foretold.

POSTSCRIPT

The *Hargrave* case (now entitled *Hargrave v. Kirk*) was decided on May 8, 1970, by a three-judge federal court in Florida in favor of the parents and students who comprised the plaintiffs. The court thus struck down the Florida statute limiting the right of Florida counties to impose no more than 10 mills of tax for educational purposes. The opinion of Judge David W. Dyer stated:

What apparently is arcane to the defendants is lucid to us—that the [Millage Rollback] Act prevents the poor counties from providing from their own taxes the same support for public education which the wealthy counties are able to provide. . . .

What rational basis can be found for the distinctions that are inherent in the Act? . . . What interest has the State of Florida in preventing its poorer counties from providing as good an education for their children as its richer counties? We have searched in vain for some legitimate state end for the discriminatory treatment imposed by the Act.

While the state undoubtedly has a valid interest in preserving the fiscal integrity of its programs, and may legitimately attempt to limit its expenditures for public education, or any other purpose, it "may not accomplish such a purpose by invidious discrimination between classes of its citizens." . . .

. . . [T]he plaintiff's argument [which the Court accepted] simply stated is that the Equal Protection Clause forbids a state from allocating authority to tax by reference to a formula based on wealth. . . . For the reasons we have outlined we hold that the provisions of the Millage Rollback Act . . . are unconstitutional.

Florida has indicated it will appeal the decision to the Supreme Court. The door has now been opened—at least a crack—toward assuring that poor people will not be deprived of an equal share of the educational dollar.

Cases

A. Legislative Authority to Create Schools

Charles E. Stuart and Others v. School District No. 1 of the Village of Kalamazoo and Others
30 Mich. 69 (1874)

COOLEY, J.

The bill in this case is filed to restrain the collection of such portion of the school taxes assessed against complainants for the year 1872, as have been voted for the support of the high school in that village, and for the payment of the salary of the superintendent. While, nominally, this is the end sought to be attained by the bill, the real purpose of the suit is wider and vastly more comprehensive than this brief statement would indicate, inasmuch as it seeks a judicial determination of the right of school authorities, in what are called union school districts of the state, to levy taxes upon the general public for the support of what in this state are known as high schools, and to make free by such taxation the instruction of children in other languages than the English. . . .

The complainants rely upon two objections to the taxes in question, one of which is general, and the other applies only to the authority or action of this particular district. The general objection has already been indicated; the particular objection is that, even conceding that other districts in the state may have authority under special charters or laws, or by the adoption of general statutes, to levy taxes for the support of high schools in which foreign and dead languages shall be taught, yet this district has no such power; because the special legislation for its benefit, which was had in 1859, was invalid for want of compliance with the constitution in the forms of enactment, and it has never adopted the general law (*Comp. L., § 3742*), by taking a vote of the district to establish a union school in accordance with its provisions, though ever since that law was enacted the district has sustained such a school, and proceeded in its action apparently on the assumption that the statutes in all respects were constitutional enactments, and had been complied with. . . .

It was remarked by Mr. Justice Campbell in *People v. Maynard*, 15 Mich., 470, that "in public affairs where the people have organized themselves under color of law into the ordinary municipal bodies, and have gone on year after year raising taxes, making improvements, and exercising their usual franchises, their rights are properly regarded as depending quite as much on the acquiescence as on the regularity of their origin, and no *ex post facto* inquiry can be permitted to undo their corporate existence. Whatever may be the rights of individuals before such general acquiescence, the corporate standing of the community can no longer be open to question." To this doctrine were cited *Rumsey v. People,* 19 N. Y., 41, and *Lanning v. Carpenter,* 20 N. Y., 447. The cases of *State v. Bunker,* 59 Me., 366; *People v. Salomon,* 54 Ill., 41, and *People v. Lothrop,* 24 Mich., 235, are in the same direction. The legislature has recognized this principle with special reference to school districts, and has not only deemed it important that their power should not be questioned after any considerable lapse of time, but has even established what is in effect a very short act of limitation for the purpose in declaring that "Every school district shall, in all cases, be presumed to have been legally organized, when it shall have exercised the franchises and privileges of a district for the term of two years:" *Comp. L. 1871,* § *3591.* This is wise legislation, and short as the period is, we have held that even a less period is sufficient to justify us in refusing to interfere except on the application of the state itself: *School District v. Joint Board, etc.,* 27 Mich., 3. . . .

The more general question . . . is, as we understand it, that there is no authority in this state to make the high schools free by taxation levied on the people at large. The argument is that while there may be no constitutional provision expressly prohibiting such taxation, the general course of legislation in the state and the general understanding of the people have been such as to require us to regard the instruction in the classics and in living modern languages in these schools as in the nature not of practical and therefore necessary instruction for the benefit of the people at large, but rather as accomplishments for the few, to be sought after in the main by those best able to pay for them, and to be paid for by those who seek them, and not by general tax. And not only has this been the general state policy, but this higher learning of itself, when supplied by the state, is so far a matter of private concern to those who receive it that the courts ought to declare it incompetent to supply it wholly at the public expense. This is in substance, as we understand it, the position of the complainants in this suit.

When this doctrine was broached to us, we must confess to no little surprise that the legislation and policy of our state were appealed to against the right of the state to furnish a liberal education to the youth of the state in schools brought within the reach of all classes. We supposed it had always been understood in this state that education, not merely in the rudiments, but in an enlarged sense, was regarded as an important practical advantage to be supplied at their option to rich and poor alike, and not as something pertaining merely to culture and accomplishment to be brought as such within the reach of those whose accumulated wealth enabled them to pay for it. . . .

It is not disputed that the dissemination of knowledge by means of schools has been a prominent object from the first, and we allude to the provision of the ordinance of 1787 on that subject, and to the donation of lands by congress for the purpose, only as preliminary to what we may have to say regarding the action of the territorial authorities in the premises. . . .

The system adopted by the legislature, and which embraced a university and branches, and a common or primary school in every school district of the state, was put into successful operation, and so continued, with one important exception, until the adoption of the constitution of 1850. The exception relates to the branches of the university, which the funds of the university did not warrant keeping up, and which were consequently abandoned. Private schools to some extent took their place, but when the convention met to frame a constitution in 1850, there were already in existence, in a number of the leading towns, schools belonging to the general public system, which were furnishing instruction which fitted young men for the university. These schools for the most part had been organized under special laws, which, while leaving the primary school laws in general applicable, gave the districts a larger board of officers and larger powers of taxation for buildings and the payment of teachers. As the establishment and support of such schools were optional with the people, they encountered in some localities considerable opposition, which, however, is believed to have been always overcome, and the authority of the districts to provide instruction in the languages in these union schools was not, so far as we are aware, seriously contested. . . . We content ourselves with the statement that neither in our state policy, in our constitution, or in our laws, do we find the primary school districts restricted in the branches of knowledge which their officers may cause to be taught, or the grade of instruction that may be given, if their voters consent in regular form to bear the expense and raise the taxes for the purpose.

Having reached this conclusion, we shall spend no time upon the objection that the district in question had no authority to appoint a superintendent of schools, and that the duties of superintendency should be performed by the district board. We think the power to make the appointment was incident to the full control which by law the board had over the schools of the district, and that the board and the people of the district have been wisely left by the legislature to follow their own judgment in the premises.

It follows that the decree dismissing the bill was right, and should be affirmed.

The other justices concurred.

People v. Francis
40 Ill. 2d 204, 239 N.E. 2d 129 (1968)

HOUSE, JUSTICE

This is a *quo warranto* action by the State's Attorney of Kankakee County against the members of the Board of Junior College District No. 520 praying for their ouster on the ground that the Public Junior College Act (Ill.Rev.Stat.1967, chap. 122, pars. 101–1 to 108–2), under which the District was organized and the

Board elected, is unconstitutional. The circuit court of Kankakee County held the Act constitutional in all respects and dismissed the complaint. Plaintiff elected to stand on the complaint and this appeal followed.

The parties use different sequences in discussing the 13 points of unconstitutionality alleged by plaintiff. We approach them somewhat arbitrarily, therefore, and will commence with plaintiff's basic thesis that the legislature lacked authority to create junior colleges, and the powers granted to the State Junior College Board were without sufficient standards and constituted discriminatory special legislation. . . .

Plaintiff argues that four different portions of the Act, other than those previously asserted, constitute arbitrary and discriminatory special legislation and that they deny equal protection of the law. They are said to involve substantially similar questions and issues and are argued by plaintiff as a unit.

Some background may be helpful to an understanding of these issues. The Public Junior College Act was adopted in 1965. All districts were originally classified as Class II. Provision was made for upgrading districts to Class I under section 4–10 after they met minimum requirements, including a finding by the State Board that the district meets the standards fixed by the statute and after approval by the Board of Higher Education.

Section 2–17 is criticized because it provides for apportionment of $9.50 for each semester hour in a course carried by an Illinois student to mid-term in a Class II district while section 2–16 provides for payment of $11.50 in a Class I district. There is a rational difference in these classifications for payment. A Class I district must provide a comprehensive junior college program, with emphasis upon vocational education, while no such requirement is made as to Class II districts. Obviously, it costs more to operate a school with a comprehensive curriculum than one offering the minimum to qualify as a Class II district.

Sections 5–1 to 5–10 inclusive, which provide for State funds for junior college building purposes to Class I districts, but not to Class II districts, are similarly criticized. Again, there are adequate grounds for the classification. The legislature could reasonably determine that it was not to the best interests of the general public in the area of education to foster and perpetuate Class II districts by providing State funds for building programs. Since the public welfare requires a sound system for higher education, a differential can be made to encourage the upgrading of a district to Class I status. It has been long recognized that State funds need not be distributed equally. In Martens v. Brady, 264 Ill. 178, 106 N.E. 266, it was held that differential in aid for highways connecting principal cities and trading points in each county with each other was not an invalid classification.

Section 5–3 provides that no petition for funds for building purposes will be accepted unless the district contains three counties or that portion of three counties not included in a junior college district, or the projected enrollment shows 1,000 full-time students within five years in districts outside the Chicago metropolitan area and 2,000 full-time students in the Chicago metropolitan area.

Plaintiff argues that this will result in a distribution of a disproportionate share of such funds among Class I districts. It is said that there is no rational basis for so classifying eligibility since it in no way reflects the relative necessity of building needs. The Master Plan for Higher Education in Illinois, July, 1964, emphasizes the need for development of facilities to serve commuter students. The legislature recognized the differences between the Chicago metropolitan area and the balance of the State. A single standard would make it impractical for downstate areas to conduct a commuter program except on a submarginal basis. Of course, if downstate urban areas project 1,000 full time students, the three-county provision is not in force. On the other hand, in those more sparsely inhabited areas which cannot provide 1,000 students, the three-county or parts-of-three-counties provision prevails. The number of students and areas which are within commuting distance is a matter for legislative policy and the courts should not interfere save only if there is no reasonable basis for the standards fixed.

Section 3-17 requires a preference to be given students residing in the district if space is not available to all student applicants. This does not affect the validity of the organization of the district or the selection of the Board and comes into effect only after the organization. In any event this has always been recognized as proper and does not constitute discrimination.

Two points raised by plaintiff involve the one man, one vote principle of Reynolds v. Sims, 377 U.S. 533, 84 S.Ct. 1362, 12 L. Ed.2d 506, as applied in Avery v. Midland County, Texas, 390 U.S. 474, 88 S.Ct. 1114, 20 L.Ed.2d 45, to a local governmental unit having general governmental powers over the entire geographic area served by the unit. Section 3-6 of the Act provides that a Class I junior college district shall be governed by a seven-member board elected in the manner provided in article 9 of the School Code and also provides, "If more than 15% but less than 30% of the taxable property in any Class I junior college district is located in unincorporated territory, at least one member of the board must be a resident of such unincorporated territory; if 30% or more of the taxable property in such school district is located in unincorporated territory, at least 2 members of the board must be residents of such unincorporated territory." Plaintiffs argue that the quoted portion of section 3-6 requires the election of members of the Board on other than a one man, one vote population basis and is a denial of equal protection of the law. . . .

We find no invidious discrimination in the legislative scheme giving the rural area and the urban area an equal voice in the creation of a local governmental unit which will thereafter exercise authority equally over both areas without regard to their rural or urban nature. Anything in Grenan v. Sheldon, 401 Ill. 351, 82 N.E.2d 162, and People v. Spaid, 401 Ill. 534, 82 N.E.2d 435, to the contrary notwithstanding, we hold that section 3-5 does not violate the equal-protection clause of the Federal constitution, section 18 of article II of our constitution or section 22 of article IV of our constitution.

The unannounced fear of requiring separate urban and rural majorities in order to create a governmental unit with authority over both areas seems to be that the rural area will defeat the proposition. This fear would appear to be unfounded because in a great number of the some 1,000 districts created under statutes where this requirement must have been operative, the rural area had to have consented for the districts to have been created.

We also note that while plaintiffs and *amici curiae* urge us to declare the junior college district here in question unlawfully organized because the organizational election was not conducted at large throughout the district, the effect of the election was as if it had been conducted at large. The statutory requirement for separate rural and urban majorities had no effect in this case because favorable majorities were given in the rural and urban areas.

For the foregoing reasons the judgment of the circuit court of Kankakee County is affirmed.

Judgment affirmed.

B. Authority to Provide for School Governance

Vito F. Lanza, et al., Appellants v. Robert F. Wagner, as Mayor of the City of New York, et al., Respondents
11 N.Y. 2d 317 (1962)

FULD, J.

Prior to the summer of 1961, the Education Law of this State provided that the Board of Education of the City of New York was to consist of nine members appointed by the Mayor (§ 2553, subd. 2). During the early part of August, the Mayor asked those then serving on the board to resign, and all except three tendered their resignations. On August 21, the Legislature, convened by the Governor, met in an Extraordinary Session for the purpose of dealing with conditions in the school system of New York City. Finding and declaring that "The conditions existing in [such] school system . . . have shaken public confidence, cause . . . grave concern and call for prompt corrective action" (§ 1)—in short, finding that "this is a time of crisis for the New York city schools" (§ 1)—the Legislature passed the statute, now before us, under which the city's Board of Education was to be reorganized and reconstituted, the method of effecting appointments to the board materially altered (L. 1961, ch. 971).

Pursuant to the legislation, the terms of those then comprising the Board of Education were to come to an end on September 20, 1961 (§ 2) and appointments of new members of the board, as well as of their successors, were to be made by the Mayor from a list of nominees to be submitted to him by "a selection board" consisting of the heads of three universities located in New York City and the presidents of eight other organizations representing educational, civic, business, labor and professional groups interested in city affairs including education (§§ 3, 5).[1] In making its nominations, the selection board was directed to receive and consider "recommendations from representative associations [and] . . . groups active or interested in the field of education" and to select nominees who in its judgment are "persons of outstanding experience, competence and qualification for service on the board of education" (§ 3). For the purposes of the initial appointment of nine new board members, the selection panel was required to submit a list of at least 18 names by September 15, 1961 (§ 3). If the Mayor should fail to make the appointments by September 20, the State Commissioner of Education was to make them from among the nominees submitted to the Mayor (§ 3). If the selection board submitted less than 18 names to him, the Mayor was "to fill from the names submitted that number of vacancies equal to one-half the number of names submitted disregarding resulting fractions and the mayor [was authorized to] fill any remaining vacancies . . . without regard to the provisions of this section" (§ 3).[2]

Following enactment of the statute, the selection panel met, nominated 26 persons, eight more than the specified minimum, and submitted a list of such nominees to the Mayor. Several days later, the Mayor made his appointments to the board from that list. The plaintiffs, former members of the board who had not resigned and whose terms of office still had some time to run, brought this action for a judgment (1) declaring the new statute unconstitutional and (2) enjoining the Mayor from making appointments to the board—to cull from their complaint— "in [their] place and stead".[3] The court at Special Term dismissed the complaint, the Appellate Division affirmed unanimously and the appeal is here as of right on constitutional grounds.

The plaintiffs' basic contention is that, insofar as chapter 971 of the Laws of 1961 terminates their terms of office and provides for a new method of appointing board members, it violates the home rule provisions of the State Constitution

1. The selection board consists of "the president of Columbia University; the chancellor of the City University of New York; the president of New York University; the president of the Association of the Bar of the City of New York; the president of the New York City Central Trades and Labor Council; the president of Commerce and Industry Association of New York, Inc.; the president of the Public Education Association; the president of the United Parents Associations of New York City, Inc.; the president of the League of Women Voters of the City of New York; the president of Citizens Union; and the president of the Citizens Budget Commission, Inc."

2. In addition, the statute contains provisions designed to strengthen the powers of the Board of Education and to assure closer supervision of the educational affairs of New York City's school system by the Regents and the Commissioner of Education during an "emergency period", which was to continue until July 1, 1962 (§ 7).

3. The Attorney-General was joined as a party defendant because of the attack on the constitutionality of a State statute (Executive Law, § 71).

(art. IX, § 9) and, insofar as it vests the power of nomination in private persons and organizations, it not only interferes with home rule but also constitutes some sort of impermissible delegation of legislative authority. They further urge that the statute is a bill of attainder, in violation of section 10 of article I of the United States Constitution.

We may quickly dispose of the attack upon the statute on the score of its having shortened the plaintiffs' terms of office. The office held by each of the plaintiffs was concededly created by the Legislature, not by the Constitution, and there is no constitutional inhibition against the mere shortening of the term of an existing statutory office by legislation aimed at the office rather than at its incumbent. . . . Public offices are created for the benefit of the public, and not granted for the benefit of the incumbent, and the office holder has no contractual, vested or property right in the office. . . . Absent any express constitutional limitation, the Legislature has full and unquestionable power to abolish an office of its creation or to modify its term, or other incidents attending it, in the public interest, even though the effect may be to curtail an incumbent's un-expired term. . . . There is not the slightest warrant in the present case for the charge that either the purpose or the effect of the statute was to punish or im-peach the plaintiffs or any other incumbent member of the former board or to render them ineligible for consideration as potential appointees to the new board. It is clear that general legislation such as this, designed solely to provide a more effective and efficient body and aimed at the office of board members rather than at the incumbent office holders, has none of the objectionable attri-butes of a bill of attainder. . . .

[It] has long been settled that the administration of public education is a State function to be kept separate and apart from all other local or municipal functions (N. Y. Const., art. XI, § 1; art. IX, § 13, subd. B). Although members of a Board of Education in a city perform tasks generally regarded as connected with local government, they are officers of an independent corporation separate and distinct from the city, created by the State for the purpose of carrying out a purely State function and are not city officers within the compass of the Constitu-tion's home rule provisions. . . .

Since, then, education is a State, not a local, function and members of New York City's Board of Education are State, not local, officers, the home rule restrictions of section 9 are inapplicable and, under the explicit language of that section, such officers may be "elected by the people or *appointed, as the legisla-ture may direct.*" (Emphasis supplied.)

Despite this apparently unrestricted grant of power to the Legislature to direct the mode of selection of nonlocal officers, whose election or appointment is not provided for by the Constitution, it is insisted that the method of appointment provided for by chapter 971 must be condemned as an unlawful delegation of legislative authority in violation of section 1 of article III of the State Constitu-tion. As we understand the argument, it is that the Legislature may not confer on private individuals or organizations a voice of any kind in the appointment of

public officers, and that such a delegation constitutes an unconstitutional relin-
quishment of legislative authority.

We shall shortly consider the ample authority, both in this State and elsewhere, supporting the validity of legislation providing for an appointive procedure such as that prescribed by the present statute. But, before doing so, it is
worth noting that this very technique—of designating a representative panel of
responsible and knowledgeable persons to assist the appointing power by submitting a list of eminently qualified nominees from among whom the appointments are to be made is by no means a novel one in New York. Since before
the turn of the century, a similar procedure has been followed in the appointment
of State boards of examiners and committees on grievances. The Education
Law contains a number of sections providing for the appointment of members of
such bodies by the State Board of Regents from among nominees designated by
private professional societies. ... In short, though, whether we regard the
selection board as "private" or "public", we perceive no constitutional bar to the
legislative designation of a nominating panel, made up of people representing a
knowledgeable cross section of city interests, either active or vitally interested in
the educational life of the city, who could reasonably be expected to present to the
Mayor, on an objective and nonpartisan basis, the names of individuals excep-
tionally qualified for service on the Board of Education.

DYE, J. (DISSENTING)

In this action for judgment declaring chapter 971 of the Laws of 1961 (Extraordinary Session of August 12, 1961) unconstitutional and permanently enjoining the defendant Mayor of the City of New York from proceeding to
reorganize the New York City Board of Education under the challenged legislation and replacing plaintiffs with new appointees, the plaintiffs, two former
members of the board, appeal on constitutional grounds from a judgment,
entered upon an order of the Appellate Division, Second Department, unanimously affirming, without opinion, a judgment of the Supreme Court, Kings
County (Brenner, J.) which dismissed the complaint for insufficiency and also
from an incidental order which denied plaintiffs' motion for a temporary injunction restraining the Mayor from acting in the premises and granted defendants'
cross motion to dismiss the complaint for insufficiency. (The joinder of the
Attorney-General apparently is for the reason that the constitutionality of a
statute is challenged [Executive Law, § 71].)

During the hotly contested New York City mayoralty campaign in the
Summer of 1961, certain actions in the school construction and maintenance
program were disclosed, leading to sensational charges of corruption and malfeasance. Early in August, Mayor Wagner requested the resignation of all nine
members of the New York City Board of Education, all of whom were then
serving unexpired terms with varying dates of termination (Education Law,
§ 2553, former subd. 2). Six of these members submitted their resignations but

three, including plaintiffs Lanza and Rank whose terms were to expire in May of 1962 and 1964 respectively, refused to resign. Thereafter the Legislature, at an Extraordinary Session held August 21, 1961, passed, on a message of necessity, the challenged legislation (L. 1961, ch. 971). That statute (amdg. Education Law, §§ 2553, 2554), after reciting that conditions existing in the school system in New York City had shaken public confidence, caused the Legislature grave concern and called for prompt corrective action, proceeded to list four categories of irregularity, concluding that "this is a time of crisis for the New York city schools . . . the terms of office of the persons then comprising the membership of the board of education of the city school district of the city of New York shall terminate" (L. 1961, ch. 971, § 2).

The statute then made provision for a new and novel method of appointment of school board members. The Mayor's power of appointment was continued, but sharply curtailed as to whom he should appoint and forfeiture of the power of appointment if he failed to act within a specified time. The eligible list from which the Mayor was to make appointments was to be furnished by a selection board consisting of 11 members, who were to convene with the Chancellor of the Board of Regents, from the heads of certain named private business, educational, civic and philanthropic organizations, to wit:

the president of Columbia University;
the chancellor of the City University of New York;
the president of New York University;
the president of the Association of the Bar of the City of New York;
the president of the New York City Central Trades and Labor Council;
the president of Commerce and Industry Association of New York, Inc.;
the president of the Public Education Association;
the president of the United Parents Associations of New York City, Inc.;
the president of the League of Women Voters of the City of New York;
the president of Citizens Union; and
the president of the Citizens Budget Commission, Inc.

The members of the selection board thus designated but not named, no later than September 15, 1961, were to submit a list of 18 nominees to the Mayor for service on the Board of Education. No later than September 20, 1961, the Mayor was to appoint, from such list of 18 nominees only, nine persons to be members of the Board of Education. If he failed to do so within the time limit, then the appointments were to be made by the State Commissioner of Education. The statute also provides that the terms of the incumbents should expire and those of the new members begin on September 20 for staggered terms of 8 months to 7 years. Such a list of nominees was promulgated, none of whom were present or former members of the Board of Education. The Mayor made his selection within the allotted time and the nine so selected were duly sworn in as members of the Board of Education on September 19, 1961. . . .

The statute under attack provides, in pertinent part: "At least five days before the effective date of section two of this act, the selection board shall submit a list to the mayor of at least eighteen names of nominees who, *in the judgment of the selection board*, are persons of outstanding experience, competence and qualification for service on the board of education. On the effective date of section two of this act, *the mayor shall appoint nine persons from among the nominees* to be the members of the board of education of the city school district of the city of New York." (Emphasis supplied.)

Thus we find that the 11 private individuals who comprise the so-called "selection board" may, in their untrammeled discretion, decide who shall, and who shall not, be considered by the local governmental authorities for appointment to the Board of Education. Under this arrangement the Mayor, instead of being able to choose for appointment to the school board any qualified citizen from among the more than eight million inhabitants comprising the school district, including these plaintiffs, is limited to the 18 eligibles nominated by the selection board. The board, under the circumstances, is thus not merely a civic advisory committee, but a quasi-executive committee with mandatory power to limit the appointive prerogative of a duly elected public official. However well intended the statutory scheme may be, its practical effect is to delegate a sensitive legislative function to a number of private persons whose identity may not be known for certain until the moment they convene for the purpose of making a selection of eligibles and, even then, their status is a nebulous one, since they are not sworn as public officers nor are they removable as such. The tendency to run government by committee is becoming a favorite device to circumvent the democratic process which our Constitution reposes in the Legislature. Such power may not be delegated to others. The promptings of expediency to deal with momentary political problems, however well directed, furnish a poor excuse for tampering with fundamental principles of government and "can never serve in lieu of constitutional power" (*Carter* v. *Carter Coal Co.*, 298 U. S. 238, 291). . . .

Chief Judge Desmond and Judges Burke and Foster concur with Judge Fuld; Judge Dye dissents in part in a separate opinion in which Judge Van Voorhis concurs; Judge Froessel dissents in part in a separate opinion.

Judgment modified, without costs, in accordance with the opinion herein.

[The plaintiffs challenged the constitutionality of the statute and sought to enjoin the appointment of their successors. Both the trial court and the appellate court dismissed the complaint. The instant opinion sustained the constitutionality of the statute but, for technical reasons, did not agree that plaintiff's petition for the injunction should be dismissed. Hence, this court modified the opinion of the two lower courts.]

C. Authority to Restrict Curriculum

Meyer v. State of Nebraska
262 U.S. 390 (1922)

MR. JUSTICE MCREYNOLDS DELIVERED THE OPINION OF THE COURT

Plaintiff in error was tried and convicted in the District Court for Hamilton County, Nebraska, under an information which charged that on May 25, 1920, while an instructor in Zion Parochial School, he unlawfully taught the subject of reading in the German language to Raymond Parpart, a child of ten years, who had not attained and successfully passed the eighth grade. The information is based upon "An act relating to the teaching of foreign languages in the State of Nebraska," approved April 9, 1919, which follows [Laws 1919, c. 249.]:

Section 1. No person, individually or as a teacher, shall, in any private, denominational, parochial or public school, teach any subject to any person in any language other than the English language.

Sec. 2. Languages, other than the English language, may be taught as languages only after a pupil shall have attained and successfully passed the eighth grade as evidenced by a certificate of graduation issued by the county superintendent of the county in which the child resides.

Sec. 3. Any person who violates any of the provisions of this act shall be deemed guilty of a misdemeanor and upon conviction, shall be subject to a fine of not less than twenty-five dollars ($25), nor more than one hundred dollars ($100) or be confined in the county jail for any period not exceeding thirty days for each offense.

Sec. 4. Whereas, an emergency exists, this act shall be in force from and after its passage and approval.

The Supreme Court of the State affirmed the judgment of conviction. (107 Neb. 657.) It declared the offense charged and established was "the direct and intentional teaching of the German language as a distinct subject to a child who had not passed the eighth grade," in the parochial school maintained by Zion Evangelical Lutheran Congregation, a collection of Biblical stories being used therefor. And it held that the state forbidding this did not conflict with the Fourteenth Amendment, but was a valid exercise of the police power. The following excerpts from the opinion sufficiently indicate the reasons advanced to support the conclusion.

The salutary purpose of the statue is clear. The legislature had seen the baneful effects of permitting foreigners, who had taken residence in this country, to rear and educate their children in the language of their native land. The result of that condition was found to be inimical to our own safety. To allow the children of foreigners, who

38

had emigrated here, to be taught from early childhood the language of the country of their parents was to rear them with that language as their mother tongue. It was to educate them so that they must always think in that language, and, as a consequence, naturally inculcate in them the ideas and sentiments foreign to the best interests of this country. The statute, therefore, was intended not only to require that the education of all children be conducted in the English language, but that, until they had grown into that language and until it had become a part of them, they should not in the schools be taught any other language. The obvious purpose of this statute was that the English language should be and become the mother tongue of all children reared in this state. The enactment of such a statute comes reasonably within the police power of the state. *Pohl* v. *State*, 132 N. E. (Ohio) 20; *State* v. *Bartels*, 181 N. W. (Ia.) 508.

It is suggested that the law is an unwarranted restriction, in that it applies to all citizens of the state and arbitrarily interferes with the rights of citizens who are not of foreign ancestry, and prevents them, without reason, from having their children taught foreign languages in school. That argument is not well taken, for it assumes that every citizen finds himself restrained by the statute. The hours which a child is able to devote to study in the confinement of school are limited. It must have ample time for exercise or play. Its daily capacity for learning is comparatively small. A selection of subjects for its education, therefore, from among the many that might be taught, is obviously necessary. The legislature no doubt had in mind the practical operation of the law. The law affects few citizens, except those of foreign lineage. Other citizens, in their selection of studies, except perhaps in rare instances, have never deemed it of importance to teach their children foreign languages before such children have reached the eighth grade. In the legislative mind, the salutary effect of the statute no doubt outweighed the restriction upon the citizens generally, which, it appears, was a restriction of no real consequence.

The problem for our determination is whether the statute as construed and applied unreasonably infringes the liberty guaranteed to the plaintiff in error by the Fourteenth Amendment. "No State shall . . . deprive any person of life, liberty, or property, without due process of law."

While this Court has not attempted to define with exactness the liberty thus guaranteed, the term has received much consideration and some of the included things have been definitely stated. Without doubt, it denotes not merely freedom from bodily restraint but also the right of the individual to contract, to engage in any of the common occupations of life, to acquire useful knowledge, to marry, establish a home and bring up children, to worship God according to the dictates of his own conscience, and generally to enjoy those privileges long recognized at common law as essential to the orderly pursuit of happiness by free men. . . . The established doctrine is that this liberty may not be interfered with, under the guise of protecting the public interest, by legislative action which is arbitrary or without reasonable relation to some purpose within the competency of the State to effect. Determination by the legislature of what constitutes proper exercise of police power is not final or conclusive but is subject to supervision by the courts. . . .

The American people have always regarded education and acquisition of knowledge as matters of supreme importance which should be diligently promoted. The Ordinance of 1787 declares, "Religion, morality, and knowledge being necessary to good government and the happiness of mankind, schools and the means of education shall forever be encouraged." Corresponding to the right of control, it is the natural duty of the parent to give his children education suitable to their station in life; and nearly all the States, including Nebraska, enforce this obligation by compulsory laws.

Practically, education of the young is only possible in schools conducted by especially qualified persons who devote themselves thereto. The calling always has been regarded as useful and honorable, essential, indeed, to the public welfare. Mere knowledge of the German language cannot reasonably be regarded as harmful. Heretofore it has been commonly looked upon as helpful and desirable. . . .

It is said the purpose of the legislation was to promote civic development by inhibiting training and education of the immature in foreign tongues and ideals before they could learn English and acquire American ideals; and "that the English language should be and become the mother tongue of all children reared in this State." It is also affirmed that the foreign born population is very large, that certain communities commonly use foreign words, follow foreign leaders, move in a foreign atmosphere, and that the children are thereby hindered from becoming citizens of the most useful type and the public safety is imperiled.

That the State may do much, go very far, indeed, in order to improve the quality of its citizens, physically, mentally and morally, is clear; but the individual has certain fundamental rights which must be respected. The protection of the Constitution extends to all, to those who speak other languages as well as to those born with English on the tongue. Perhaps it would be highly advantageous if all had ready understanding of our ordinary speech, but this cannot be coerced by methods which conflict with the Constitution—a desirable end cannot be promoted by prohibited means.

For the welfare of his Ideal Commonwealth, Plato suggested a law which should provide: "That the wives of our guardians are to be common, and their children are to be common, and no parent is to know his own child, nor any child his parent. . . . The proper officers will take the offspring of the good parents to the pen or fold, and there they will deposit them with certain nurses who dwell in a separate quarter; but the offspring of the inferior, or of the better when they chance to be deformed, will be put away in some mysterious, unknown place, as they should be." In order to submerge the individual and develop ideal citizens, Sparta assembled the males at seven into barracks and intrusted their subsequent education and training to official guardians. Although such measures have been deliberately approved by men of great genius, their ideas touching the relation between individual and State were wholly different from those upon which our institutions rest; and it hardly will be affirmed that any legislature could impose such restrictions upon the people of a State without doing violence to both letter and spirit of the Constitution. . . .

The power of the State to compel attendance at some school and to make reasonable regulations for all schools including a requirement that they shall give instructions in English, is not questioned. Nor has challenge been made of the

State's power to prescribe a curriculum for institutions which it supports. Those matters are not within the present controversy. . . .

No emergency has arisen which renders knowledge by a child of some language other than English so clearly harmful as to justify its inhibition with the consequent infringement of rights long freely enjoyed. We are constrained to conclude that the statute as applied is arbitrary and without reasonable relation to any end within the competency of the State.

As the statute undertakes to interfere only with teaching which involves a modern language, leaving complete freedom as to other matters, there seems no adequate foundation for the suggestion that the purpose was to protect the child's health by limiting his mental activities. It is well known that proficiency in a foreign language seldom comes to one not instructed at an early age, and experience shows that this is not injurious to the health, morals or understanding of the ordinary child.

The judgment of the court below must be reversed and the cause remanded for further proceedings not inconsistent with this opinion.

REVERSED.

MR. JUSTICE HOLMES DISSENTING

We all agree, I take it, that it is desirable that all the citizens of the United States should speak a common tongue, and therefore that the end aimed at by the statute is a lawful and proper one. The only question is whether the means adopted deprive teachers of the liberty secured to them by the Fourteenth Amendment. It is with hesitation and unwillingness that I differ from my brethren with regard to a law like this but I cannot bring my mind to believe that in some circumstances, and circumstances existing it is said in Nebraska, the statute might not be regarded as a reasonable or even necessary method of reaching the desired result. The part of the act with which we are concerned deals with the teaching of young children. Youth is the time when familiarity with a language is established and if there are sections in the State where a child would hear only Polish or French or German spoken at home I am not prepared to say that it is unreasonable to provide that in his early years he shall hear and speak only English at school. But if it is reasonable it is not an undue restriction of the liberty either of teacher or scholar. No one would doubt that a teacher might be forbidden to teach many things, and the only criterion of his liberty under the Constitution that I can think of is "whether, considering the end in view, the statute passes the bounds of reason and assumes the character of a merely arbitrary fiat." *Purity Extract & Tonic Co.* v. *Lynch*, 226 U. S. 192, 204. *Hebe Co.* v. *Shaw,* 248 U. S. 297, 303. *Jacob Ruppert* v. *Caffey*, 251 U. S. 264. I think I appreciate the objection to the law but it appears to me to present a question upon which men reasonably might differ and therefore I am unable to say that the Constitution of the United States prevents the experiment being tried.

I agree with the Court as to the special proviso against the German language contained in the statute dealt with in *Bohning* v. *Ohio*.

Mr. Justice Sutherland concurs in this opinion.

Problems and Discussion Questions

1. Some critics of public education suggest a two-board system of control: one board to deal with finances and resources allocation; another board to decide on such "professional" matters as educational objectives, curriculum content, teaching strategies, and school policies. Do you consider such dual control to be feasible or desirable? Why?

2. What is the proper state interest in education? Apart from litigation, which forces the court to choose between the interests of the state and the individual, what procedures or processes might balance these interests?

3. Design a model school code to express the contemporary public interest in equitable financial support, balanced curriculum, development of the individual, and pluralistic notions of the best possible social order. Consider the relation of the federal, state, and local governments in the code.

4. Federal support for education aims at specific, categorical objectives rather than general objectives. How might the schools use federal funds for maximum benefit to children in elementary schools? In secondary schools? Would you support legislation by Congress to grant general, unrestricted support to local schools? Why?

5. The increasing demands for "community control" of the public schools expresses various dissatisfactions with the schools as they are. How can school boards be more representative of the people? What selection procedures would ensure equitable representation, as you define the notion?

Annotated Bibliography

BECKMAN, Norman, "Metropolitan Education in Relation to State and Federal Government," R. J. Havighurst (ed.), *Metropolitanism: Its Challenge to Education*. National Society for the Study of Education Yearbook, vol. LXVII, part 1, pp. 173–198, University of Chicago Press, 1968.

Beckman points out that issues and decisions of the past were accurate indicators of the "new mix" that exists today; i.e., the intergovernmental relationships that have significant impact on education. As director of the Office of Intergovernmental Relations and Urban Program Coordination (Washington, D.C.) the author is able to comment on both federal and state actions dealing with segregation and the role of education in the fight against poverty. Beckman suggests steps that might be taken to implement federal financial aid to education.

BOARDMAN, William P. "Federal Impact Fund Deduction in State School Appropriation Formulae," *Washington and Lee Law Review*, 25:237, Fall, 1968.

Under Public Law 874, Congress has authorized aid to local school districts in federally impacted areas. Boardman points out that some fifteen states offset this aid by, in effect, reducing the amount of state aid given to the impacted districts. In a 1968 Virginia case, the plaintiffs claimed such offset financing to be unconstitutional, based on their contention that the U.S. Constitution was supreme on the point. The Court upheld this view. This article reviews the case, its arguments, and the intent of P.L. 847. Boardman's suggestion is that, had more careful investigation of resource distribution been made in the Shepherd v. Godwin case (280 F. Supp. 869), a different verdict might have been reached.

CAMPBELL, Ronald F., "Federal-State Educational Relations." *Phi Delta Kappan*, vol. XLIX, no. 1, September, 1967.

Noting that the announcement of the 1967 conference of the Education Commission of the States carried the theme "power-play for control of education," Campbell discussed and analyzed some of the relationships between and among federal and state agencies. He noted two specific problems at the federal level: the rather tenuous position of the U.S. Office of Education, and the often ineffective and inefficient administration of federal programs. Other issues presented, both factually and editorially, are: federal involvement in education; categorical or general federal aid; the federal government's creation of new institutions or organizations (e.g., Head Start and Job Corps); church-state relations; and the role of federal aid in restructuring educational government. The author closed with a suggestion that these various phenomena be viewed as "an interdependent social system."

MURNAGHAN, Francis D. Jr., and Richard Mandel, "Trends and Musts in Federal Education Legislation," *Kappan*, vol. L, no. 10, June, 1969.

Murnaghan and Mandel, both graduates of Harvard Law School, initially discuss the purpose of federal legislation as the sole guarantee of equal educational opportunities—especially as regards the "environmentally deprived." Their evaluation of current legislation and appropriations implies that the goal is not being reached. Three programs are explored as suggestions for improvement of federal investment: (1) the National Education Association General Aid Bill; (2) the Federal Foundation for Equal Educational Opportunity—fostered by the Research Council of the Great Cities for School Improvement; and (3) the American Federation of Teachers' Ten-Year Plan. The article suggests the type and means of political action that must be taken in order to implement any of the programs.

WEST, E. G. "The Political Economy of American Public School Legislation," *Journal of Law and Economics*, 10;101, October, 1967.

West does not follow a conventional pattern of discussing optimal allocations or maximal gain. He does, instead, attempt to show—historically—what the basis for public school legislation has been. The intent is to study sequential economic circumstances, the political process in educational legislation, the nationalization principle in schooling, and the "genesis of the three particular features described in the terms universal, free, and compulsory." The study itself is concerned only with New York State (beginning with an act in 1795), but implications for present and future public schooling are drawn on a more national basis.

2

Church, State, and Schools

Few school problems carry so much emotional baggage as the relation of schools to religion. Since public education is secular education, the two principal school-religion issues can be framed as follows: (1) In what manner and to what extent can religious practices be permitted in public schools, and (2) can public funds go to church-sponsored schools? Responses to these issues raise still other questions about prayer, Bible reading, government support to parochial schools, parental rights in children's education, curriculum, and matters of human conscience. The extent of sectarian interest in public education is revealed by the scope and depth of public expression triggered by Supreme Court decisions on prayer, Bible reading, released time, and other schoolhouse religion cases.

Because statutes dealing with schools and religion must look to the federal constitution for their validity, questions raised about religion and public education must be considered in light of the state and federal constitutions. Section 3, article XI, New York State constitution, commonly known as the Blaine Amendment, illustrates the state ban on aid to church-controlled schools:

Neither the state nor any subdivision thereof shall use its property or credit or any public money, or authorize or permit either to be used, directly or indirectly, in aid or maintenance, other than for examination or inspection, of any school or institution of learning wholly or in part under the control or direction of any religious denomination, or in which any denominational tenet or doctrine is taught, but the legislature may provide for the transportation of children to and from any school or institution of learning.

Federal law concerning religion and schools stems from the first clause of the First Amendment to the United States Constitution, which reads "Congress shall make no law respecting an establishment of religion, or prohibiting the free exercise thereof. . . ." This clause consists of two fundamental concepts: (1) Congress shall not establish religion (the establishment clause), and (2) Congress shall not prohibit the free exercise of religion (free-exercise clause).

The establishment clause supports the doctrine of church-state separation, a doctrine reviewed extensively in such Supreme Court decisions as *Everson v. Board of Education*, 330 U.S. 1 (1947), *McCollum v. Board of Education*, 333 U.S. 203 (1948), *Engel v. Vitale*, 370 U.S. 421 (1962), and *School District v. Schempp*, 374 U.S. 203 (1963). The establishment-clause cases raise the question of how far the state (or federal government) can go with direct or indirect support of sectarian education. The crux of the church-state separation issue is whether the First Amendment requires governmental antagonism, neutrality, noninvolvement, or restricted benefit to religion. Literal neutrality would seem to mandate a total secularization of government activity. Church-state separatists range in literalism from urging the removal of mottoes from our coins to laissez-faire accommodation to the status quo.

The free-exercise clause relates to school policies and pupil behavior. School activities and curriculum requirements frequently conflict with parents' religious beliefs. Some parents, for example, object to their children studying biology and theories of evolution on the ground that such courses constitute state-sponsored interference with the free exercise of their religion. Mandatory school attendance laws may interfere with parental desires for the child's participation in religious exercises. Public expression of patriotism through classroom activities (pledge of allegiance, singing the national anthem, flag-salute, etc.) prompts some parents to object on the basis that such activities interfere with the free exercise of their religion. Mandatory school prayer, until its recent ban by the Supreme Court, irritated nearly as many parents as did the decision banning it.

In these cases, the courts attempt to achieve some balance between the interests of the state and the religious preferences of the pupils and their parents. The court decisions reflect the agony over these conflicting rights. Unless the school activities interfere with the free exercise of religion, courts are reluctant to turn the free-exercise shield into a minority-view sword. For example, the Supreme Court has sustained pupil refusal to salute the flag but has not barred the flag-salute in schools. The dissenter cannot be forced to participate, but the advocates need not halt the activity. The school-prayer cases raise even more troublesome dilemmas. The establishment and free-exercise clauses of the First Amendment are not disjunctive but complementary. To ban the establishment of religion (as seen by one) is to interfere with another's free exercise of religion. The prayer ban sustains the parent who fears governmental establishment of religion, but it frustrates the free exercise of religion by pro-prayer parents.

Sectarian practices in schools are legally suspect. Even when tied to moral guidance or abstract principles of character building, religiously based school activities have come under fire. Religious holiday observances through songs, school assemblies, decorations, or similar school practices are viewed with suspicion by the United States Supreme Court. The Court decisions are piecemeal fragments in the mosaic of the law. As noted in Chapter 1, the Court considers specific issues in cases brought before it. Some, but not all, of the specific church-state separation issues have been raised. The guidelines for prayer or Bible reading, for example, are much clearer than those for school activities of a religious nature. This lack of clarity on familiar school practices results in a dilemma for local boards of education. In many communities school boards are under pressure both to preserve sectarian "values" in the schools and to eliminate all activities even remotely tainted with religious overtones. The tension between state control of schools and religious preferences of parents, children, and community achieves a delicate balance in schools across the country.

STATE CONTROL AND RELIGIOUS CHOICE

The state's legitimate interest in the education of its citizens is well established in the law. The extent and nature of this interest are less clear. Religious freedom is an explicit human right recognized by the federal constitution and most state constitutions. The United States Supreme Court has clearly supported the parents' right to choose between sending their children to public schools or private schools of a sectarian or secular nature. Parental choice of private rather than public schooling for their children creates no legal problems; the problems arise when the state interests confront the parents' religious views in public schools.

Numerous arguments support state interests in the education system. Aside from state constitutional mandates to maintain and operate schools, the state's power to promote the welfare of its citizens (an aspect of the police power of a government) supports the concept of state-regulated schools. The desirability of an educated electorate is another, and more politically phrased, version of this ideology.

It seems inevitable that some of the public schools' goals conflict with some individuals' religious beliefs. The secular welfare of citizens does not always square with the religious tenets of pupils or parents. For example, the teaching of honesty, kindness, and moral courage raises the question, "Whose brand?" Reasonable men may agree on the fundamental concepts of honesty or moral courage but disagree sharply on the means to those ends. Many states recognize the pluralistic religious views by permitting pupil exemption from certain study. Some states, for example, excuse pupils from the study of disease if such instruction violates the parents' religious beliefs. Such exemption not only illustrates legislative accommodation but also indicates a legislative discrimination between barring certain instruction and providing alternatives for those clients who object on constitutional grounds.

Within the framework of general legislative requirements and guidelines, school boards design and implement comprehensive programs of instruction. The day-to-day operations must somehow comply with state directives in curriculum, instructional procedures, and policies while at the same time recognizing the general and specific religious views of pupils and parents. The courts have defined some of the broad conflict areas; many others remain latent. Until specific issues in the matter of *state control* versus *religious choice* arise and are litigated, the local schools can do no more than combine restraint and sensitive judgment with hope in framing policies. School boards must expect litigation from the religious conflicts in schools. There is no practical way to evade the reality that public education and religious choices will clash.

FREEDOM OF CONSCIENCE

The extent of school board power to make and enforce rules on pupils, parents, and teachers raises other civil rights questions. The flag-salute cases are examples of such questions. Most states provide for public schools to teach some kind of moral, patriotic, and democratic principles. The practice of saluting the American flag, reciting the pledge of allegiance, and singing the national anthem are common school exercises aimed at that end. The flag-salute cases arose when the school board excluded from school children who refused to participate in the exercises on the ground that participation was contrary to their religious beliefs. The issue was whether required participation, on pain of exclusion, deprived the children of religious freedom guaranteed under the First Amendment to the United States Constitution. Lower courts were divided on the question, and the first opinion on the matter by the United States Supreme Court in *Minersville School District v. Gobitis*, 310 U.S. 568 (1940), upheld the constitutionality of a Pennsylvania statute requiring flag-salute. A later opinion, *West Virginia State Board of Education v. Barnette*, 319 U.S. 624 (1943), reversed the *Gobitis* decision, enjoined the enforcement of the state law, and stated in part:

If there is any fixed star in our constitutional constellation, it is that no official, high or petty, can prescribe what shall be orthodox in politics, nationalism, religion, or other matters of opinion or force citizens to confess by word or act their faith therein. If there are any circumstances which permit an exception, they do not now occur to us.

The flag-salute cases demonstrate that individual rights under the federal constitution can be protected without restricting the rights of the majority. The *Barnette* decision is set forth in Chapter 3.

The flag-salute cases illustrate the two central points in civil rights in the schools: (1) whatever school boards do must be done in a fair manner, and (2) if the board's discretionary acts are fair and reasonable, the courts will not interfere. Boards must realize the constitutional implications of their policies and rules governing pupils and employees. The board decisions affect not only educational programs and school management but also the civil rights of the personnel concerned. The delicate balance between board judgment and civil rights is recognized by the courts. In most decisions concerning school matters the courts refrain from preempting board functions and responsibilities. Unless the board decision is patently unreasonable, arbitrary, or capricious, the courts are most reluctant to intervene. Under our fifty-one systems of law (fifty state systems and our federal system), conflicting decisions are not uncommon. There are few questions of school law on which unanimity of decisions is found. Under such conditions, boards of education walk a somewhat narrow line separating authority to govern the schools and the responsibility for miscalculation.

SHARED TIME AND RELEASED TIME

Judicial attention to schoolhouse religion awakened the public to the realities of church-school relations. For the first time since the national debates during the free school movement of the mid-nineteenth century, citizens were forced to consider the proper relationship between their schools and their religion. The recognition of parochial education as a legal alternative to public school attendance (*Pierce v. Society of the Sisters of the Holy Names of Jesus and Mary*, 268 U.S. 510 [1925]) caused no particular national concern. The two principal flag-salute cases (*Minersville School District v. Gobitis*, 310 U.S. 568 [1940], and *West Virginia State Board of Education v. Barnette*, 319 U.S. 624 [1943]) received national publicity but no widespread concern about religion in the schools. The flag-salute decisions spoke of patriotism versus the individual conscience of adherents to minor religious sects. The nation was engaged in World War II and national attention was preempted by priorities higher than classroom prayers or Christmas crèche scenes. The released-time and shared-time cases arise at a period when the American conscience was ripe for pricking.

Shortly after World War II, released-time plans for religious instruction developed in a number of school districts. The release of schoolchildren to churches for religious instruction during the school day, conceptualized in 1905, was first inaugurated in 1914 in Gary, Indiana. The school superintendent, convinced that education embraced more than classroom instruction, encouraged the wider use of community facilities for education. The school was only one agency for education. The library, the home, the playground, and the church had roles in educating children, and the Gary plan encouraged local religious groups to sponsor religious classes. Under the released-time plans, schools released pupils during school hours for religious instruction. The plans varied somewhat as to location, time, instructors for the sectarian lessons, and mechanical details of parental consent and administration, but the basic notion of releasing pupils *from* school *to* religious instruction was common to the several plans. The plans provided for alternative activities for those pupils who chose not to participate. Under the released-time schemes, religious instruction was conducted during a part of the school day, and teachers were involved only to the extent of dismissing the children for instruction and conducting or supervising activities for the children who elected to stay in school. In some plans, the religious instruction was conducted on the school premises; in others, the classes were held in churches or other locations.

Released time for religious instruction grew from 619 pupils in one program in the 1914–1915 school year to almost 2 million pupils in 2,200 programs during 1947. The growth of released-time plans demonstrates the grassroots concern for organized religious instruction for children. It also indicates the extent to which the schools were charged with societal chores. In many communities, the public schools undertook diverse responsibilities far beyond the intellectual development of children. Responsibilities once accepted by the home, the church, and the community moved into the schools. At this juncture, the released-time plan for religious instruction met with constitutional objection.

The gist of the objection centered on the establishment clause of the First Amendment. Whether the released-time plans violated the establishment clause was raised directly in the *McCollum* case. The United States Supreme Court found that the plan used the state's compulsory-attendance machinery to provide pupils for sectarian religious classes and that the "wall of separation" erected between the church and state by the First Amendment had been breached.

Shortly after the *McCollum* decision, the Supreme Court reconsidered the released-time concept through the case of *Zorach et al. v. Clausen et al.*, 343 U.S. 306 (1952), and, under facts only slightly different from those in *McCollum*, sustained the New York City plan. The *Zorach* opinion, set out later in this chapter, distinguished the *McCollum* decision on factual bases. The opposite conclusions in the two cases illustrate Justice Frankfurter's statement in *McCollum* that "released time as a generalized conception, undefined by differentiating particularities, is not an issue for Constitutional adjudication." This means that the Court does not pass judgment on released time per se but looks at the details each plan presented in litigation to determine its compatability or conflict with the state or federal constitution.

Plans to share the school day between public schools and nonpublic schools developed during the early 1960s. Under these plans pupils enrolled in nonpublic schools for a part of the school day. The pupils came to public schools for certain classes and activities. The rationale behind these shared-time plans was simple: if pupils are entitled to full-time enrollment in public schools, they are equally entitled to part-time enrollment so long as state mandatory-attendance laws are observed. Nonpublic schools, particularly parochial schools, face urgent financial problems. The cost of certain kinds of instruction, such as laboratory sciences, physical education, and specialized programs for exceptional children, strains school budgets. Through dual enrollment, the parents can both achieve their religious education objective and make use of the public school system which they support as citizens.

The arguments against shared-time, or dual-enrollment, plans are more political than legal. There is no legal principle to support the notion that enrollment in public or nonpublic schools is an either-or proposition. Nonpublic schooling has long been recognized as a valid option for parents in full compliance with the state laws mandating school attendance. Some school people have objected to the shared-time concept for its alleged complexity in scheduling classes and the additional burden on already overtaxed public schools. In light of available computerized assistance, the scheduling argument is not persuasive. Though dual enrollment doubtless can add further burden to public schools, one must remember that the pupils in nonpublic schools are entitled to attend the public schools whenever their parents choose to enroll them.

The legal status of shared-time plans is uncertain; few state courts have rendered decisions and the issue has not been presented to the United States

Supreme Court to date. The plan may offer short-term accommodation to the church-state conflict in the schools. The state's interest in a child's education is not superior per se to the parents' interest. Released-time plans, however, apparently assume some superior state rights over education by releasing children *to* parental control (religious instruction); shared-time plans suggest parity. The shared-time or dual-enrollment plan recognizes the parents' authority to choose alternatives to public schools and thus guide the child's destiny. The legal problems inherent in church-school relations are logical consequences of the two institutions confronting each other in an open society.

PUBLIC FUNDS AND PAROCHIAL SCHOOLS

The question of public support for church-controlled schools is both old and new and probably has not been settled by the several major decisions of the United States Supreme Court. From our earliest national beginnings, there are numerous examples of state and federal fund appropriations to support church-sponsored education. Sam Duker, in his book *The Public Schools and Religion* (New York: Harper & Row, 1966), cited instances as early as 1787 when Congress authorized the sale of federal lands to a private buyer with a stipulation that one lot in each township be perpetually devoted to religious use. From the First Amendment's ban, "Congress shall make no law respecting an establishment of religion . . ." and similar state constitutional provisions, one might expect the courts to reject flatly any diversion of public funds to parochial schools. Ironically, the first major test of the aid to parochial school question did not mention the First Amendment. In the case of *Cochran et al. v. Louisiana State Board of Education*, 281 U.S. 370 (1930), plaintiff argued that a state statute providing tax money for "supplying school books to the school children of the State" violated the Fourteenth Amendment. The Court, in supporting the state law, denied that public funds had benefited the church or, for that matter, any school, public or private. The Court found that "The schools . . . are not the beneficiaries of these appropriations. They obtain nothing from them, nor are they relieved of a single obligation because of them. The school children and the state alone are the beneficiaries. . . ." Thus, the child-benefit doctrine emerged to avoid the confrontation of church and state in the matter of school aid.

Seventeen years later, the question of church-school aid was raised directly in the case of *Everson v. Board of Education of the Township of Ewing et al.*, 330 U.S. 1, 1947. Unlike *Cochran*, *Everson* raised the aid question on the First Amendment. The township school board, to reimburse parents for expenses incurred in transporting their children to schools outside the township (the town of Ewing had no high school), adopted the following resolution: "The transportation committee recommended the transportation of pupils to the Trenton and Pennington High Schools and Catholic schools by way of public carrier . . ." The plaintiff claimed that the resolution was invalid for violating the First Amendment. The Supreme Court of New Jersey found the payments unconstitutional; the Court of Errors and Appeals (high court) reversed and sustained the resolution's validity. On appeal, the U.S. Supreme Court held by a five-to-four decision that the New Jersey reimbursement plan did not breach the "high and impregnable" wall of separation between church and state. The Court reaffirmed the notion that the benefit, if any, was to the child, not the church. Through this near-fiction, the constitutionality of the reimbursement scheme was upheld.

In the recent (1968) case of *Board of Education v. Allen*, 392 U.S. 236, the Supreme Court reaffirmed the reasoning of the *Cochran* and *Everson* decisions and upheld a New York State statute authorizing the loan of textbooks (purchased with public funds) to students attending parochial schools. The severe financial crises in parochial education no doubt will encourage new efforts to engineer support from public funds. It seems clear that the courts will neither flatly bar aid nor remove all restrictions. Somewhere between these extremes, the case-law will continue to grope for accommodation of the church-law interests.

Readings

Do Court Decisions Give Minority Rule?

Dale Doak

Phi Delta Kappan (October, 1963), **45**, 20–4.

On June 17, 1963, the United States Supreme Court issued an opinion which renders unconstitutional the prescription, by law, of reading from the Bible and/or reciting the Lord's Prayer in public school classrooms. These actions were held to violate the First Amendment as made applicable to the states by the Fourteenth.

The citizens who originally initiated the suit were Edward L. Schempp *et al.* and William J. Murray III *et al.* Schempp as a Unitarian and Murray as an atheist represent religious or non-religious groups which constitute only a small percentage of the U. S. population; yet they have forced action which, to judge by letters in the popular press, is disagreeable to a large majority. Superficially, this appears to be a clear-cut case of minority rule, but let us examine this concept more closely.

Mrs. Murray filed suit to compel cancellation of a rule of the Baltimore school board which required daily reading from the Holy Bible and/or use of the Lord's Prayer in opening exercises. She holds these views toward the Bible and God:

We find the Bible to be nauseating, historically inaccurate, replete with the ravings of madmen. We find God to be sadistic, brutal, and a representation of hatred, vengeance. We find the Lord's Prayer to be that muttered by worms groveling for meager existence in a traumatic, paranoid world.[1]

Edward Schempp, the Unitarian from Pennsylvania, objected to Bible reading in public school classrooms on the ground that specific religious doctrines are perverted by a literal reading of the Bible.

FACTS OF THE CASE

The Schempp family objected to this 1913 Pennsylvania law:

At least ten verses of the Holy Bible shall be read, without comment, at the opening of each public school on each school day. Any child shall be excused from such Bible

1. Letter from Madalyn Murray to *Life*, Vol. 54, April 12, 1963, p. 63.

reading, or attending such Bible reading, upon the written request of his parent or guardian.[1]

At Abington Senior High, attended by the Schempp children, opening exercises each morning included the reading of ten verses from the Bible and recitation of the Lord's Prayer in unison. Although students remained in their home rooms, the intercom system made the all-school ceremony possible. The King James, Douay, Revised Standard, and Jewish Holy Scriptures versions of the Bible were used. No prefatory statements, questions, comments, explanations or interpretations were given during the exercises. Recitation of the Lord's Prayer was followed by the flag salute and general announcements to the students. Attendance at these exercises was voluntary.

Schempp chose not to have his children excused from such exercises on the grounds that such a request would: 1) cause the children to be labeled "oddballs" before their teachers and classmates each school day, 2) connote atheism and communism instead of a difference in religious belief, 3) cause the children to miss the daily school announcements, and 4) force the children to stand in the hall while the exercises were conducted, an action which "carried with it the imputation of punishment for bad conduct."

Mrs. Murray and her son William objected to a 1905 rule of the Board of School Commissioners of Baltimore. The rule required ". . . reading, without comment, of a chapter in the Holy Bible and/or the use of the Lord's Prayer." At their insistence the rule was amended to allow children who objected to such practices to be excused upon written request of the parents. William Murray was subsequently excused from the opening exercises.[2]

This, then, set the stage for the court action. In both cases, the Supreme Court declared that the law and rule in question violated the First Amendment as applied to the states by the due process clause of the Fourteenth Amendment.

OPINION OF THE COURT

Mr. Justice Clark delivered the court's majority opinion, which reviewed many of the previous cases concerning religion in public education. The First Amendment is, in the delivered opinion of the court, divided into the establishment clause and the free exercise clause. The establishment clause acts as a barrier to all legislative power respecting religious belief or the expression thereof. The free exercise clause withdraws from federal or state legislative power the exertion of any restraint on the free exercise of religion.[3]

The court concluded as follows:

In both cases the laws require religious exercises and such exercises are being conducted in direct violation of the rights of the appellees and petitioners. . . . The breach of

1. 24 Pa. Stat., Sec. 15-1516, as amended Pub. Law 1928 (Supp. 1960) December 17, 1959.
2. Rule of Board of Commissioners adopted pursuant to Art. 77, Sec. 202 of Annotated Code of Maryland.
3. Advance Sheet, *Abington School District* v. *Schempp* (1962). No. 119. Justice Clark's opinion, pp. 18-20.

neutrality that is today a trickling stream may all too soon become a raging torrent and, in the words of Madison, "it is proper to take alarm at the first experiment on our liberties. . . ." Finally, we cannot accept that the concept of neutrality, which does not permit a state to require a religious exercise even with the consent of those affected, collides with the majority's right to free exercise of religion. While the free exercise clause clearly prohibits the use of state action to deny the rights of free exercise to *anyone*, it has never meant that a majority could use the machinery of the state to practice its beliefs.[1]

Mr. Justice Stewart dissented on the basis that the records in the two cases before the court were fundamentally deficient and that the cases should be remanded for the taking of additional evidence. He also said:

permission of such exercises [religious] for those who want them is necessary if the schools are truly to be neutral in the matter of religion. And a refusal to permit religious exercises thus is seen, not as the realization of state neutrality, but rather as the establishment of a religion of secularism, or at the least, as government support of the beliefs of those who think that religious exercises should be conducted only in private.[2]

SHOULD THE MAJORITY RULE?

Throughout the nation one hears cries of "minority rule," "atheists and deists are forcing their views upon us." But is majority rule what these persons really want? Suppose you lived in a community where, if the majority ruled, instead of the Lord's Prayer the required prayer began "Hail Mary, full of grace, the Lord is with Thee," or suppose it began "Sheme Israel. . . ." Or it might be a Mormon prayer, a Buddhist prayer, or any other prayer of the religious sect which happens to be in the majority. Then what would you think of majority rule? Should the majority rule in such a religious issue, the ultimate result would be establishment of a state church, the very concept that James Madison was fighting against in his "Memorial and Remonstrance" and that Thomas Jefferson was seeking to prevent in his "Bill for the Establishment of Religious Freedom" back in the 1780's.

In 1943 Mr. Justice Jackson said:

The very purpose of a Bill of Rights was to withdraw certain subjects from the vicissitudes of political controversy, to place them beyond the reach of majorities and officials and to establish them as legal principle to be applied by the courts. One's right to . . . freedom of worship . . . and other fundamental rights may not be submitted to vote; they depend on the outcome of no elections.[3]

Jefferson held that a "Bill of Rights is what the people are entitled to against every government on earth, general or particular, and what no just government should refuse, or rest on inference."[4]

This is what the court has reaffirmed—that majority rule is not in effect in

1. *Ibid.*, pp. 21-22.
2. Advance Sheet, *Abington School District* v. *Schempp* (1962). Justice Stewart's dissenting opinion, p. 6.
3. *West Virginia Board of Education* v. *Barnette*, 319 U. S. 624, 638 (1943).
4. Paul L. Ford (ed.), *The Works of Thomas Jefferson*. New York: G. P. Putman's Sons, 1892, p. 371.

matters of religion—that government may not prescribe religious exercises—
that the individual is entitled to worship or to refrain from worship—to believe
or disbelieve in a supreme being—in any way he chooses. This is what the First
Amendment says, that "Congress shall make *no law* respecting an *establishment*
of religion or *prohibiting* the *free exercise* thereof. . . . "

Powell Davies states it in still another way. He holds that "the right to
disbelieve is inherent in the right to believe."[1]

VIEWS OF CHURCH LEADERS

As we all know, this court decision brought varied comment from church
groups and leaders throughout the nation. It would appear that most but not all
are favorable toward the decision.

The president of the Central Conference of American Rabbis, Rabbi Albert
G. Minda of Minneapolis, said:

We are gratified to learn of the two decisions. . . . We believe that these decisions will
strengthen the voluntary religious life in America and trust that they will be accepted
by all groups in the spirit of good will.[2]

The view of the National Council of Churches is that the decision

serves as a reminder to all our citizens that teaching religious commitment is the
responsibility of the home and the community of faith [church or synagogue] rather
than the public schools. Neither the church nor the state should use the public school
to compel acceptance of any creed or conformity to any specific religious practice.[3]

However, the World Methodist Council president, Bishop Fred Pierce
Corson of Philadelphia, said: ". . . the decision penalizes religious people who
are definitely in the majority in the United States."[4]

OPINIONS OF EDUCATORS

Finis E. Engleman, former executive secretary of the American Association of
School Administrators, stated recently:

The Supreme Court decision on Bible reading and prayer in the public schools has
strengthened religious freedom in the United States. Rather than prohibiting the Bible
from the public schools it authorizes its reading as a part of the curriculum.[5]

Mr. Engleman is obviously referring to Mr. Justice Brennan's concurring opinion
which gave clearance for non-devotional use of the Bible in the public schools.[6]

The decision effects only the proscription of Bible reading and recitation of

---

1. *Newsweek*, V. 49, March 18, 1957, p. 89.
2. United Press dispatch, *The Denver Post*, June 17, 1963, p. 6.
3. *Ibid.*
4. *Ibid.*
5. Letter from Finis Engleman to the author, Aug. 23, 1963.
6. Advance Sheet, *Abington School District* v. *Schempp* (1962). Justice Brennan's concurring
opinion, p. 72.

the Lord's Prayer. It does not prohibit voluntary prayers, religious observance of various holidays, baccalaureate exercises, or non-devotional use of the Bible in the curriculum.

Max Rafferty, California State Superintendent of Public Instruction, views the recent decision with alarm. He said:

The June decision should not, in my opinion, be looked at as an isolated case, but rather as merely the latest in a long series of high court dicta. . . . Little by little, a trend has been established which—unless interrupted by factors at present unforeseeable—will lead inevitably to complete secularization of America's schools. Already in my state suit has been filed to eliminate the phrase "under God" from the Pledge of Allegiance, and school superintendents are banning the singing of Christmas carols on the school grounds. . . .

To sum up in one sentence: It is not the last Supreme Court decision which disturbs me; it is the next one, and the one after that.[1]

A professor of law at the University of Chicago, Phillip B. Kurland, has interpreted the Supreme Court's opinions in the school prayer case (*Engel* v. *Vitale*) as follows:

The states may not prescribe the conduct of religious ceremonies in their public schools. To read more into the opinions, as the court's detractors attempt to do, to see the opinions as destructive of religious life in the United States, is so patently absurd as to deserve to be ignored.[2]

PRESENT LEGAL STATUS OF BIBLE READING

Prior to this decision the U. S. Supreme Court had never ruled upon the issues of Bible reading or recitation of the Lord's Prayer in public school classrooms. On at least two previous occasions cases concerning these issues were presented to the court but were not ruled upon because of legal technicalities.[3] The writer proposes that the chaotic pattern of laws and practices concerning these matters is at least partially the result of the court's failure to face this issue squarely.

At present eleven states require by statute the reading of the Bible in public school classrooms.[4] Most of these laws provide for reading without comment, and also for voluntary attendance at such exercises. A representative statute states:

The teacher in charge shall read or cause to be read a portion of the Bible daily in every classroom or session room of the common schools of the state in the presence of the pupils therein assembled, but no child shall be required to read the Bible against the wish of his parents or guardians.[5]

Mississippi is the only state whose constitution mentions Bible reading in the public schools. It forbids its exclusion.[6]

1. Letter from Max Rafferty to the author, Aug. 29, 1963.
2. *Chicago Tribune*, Sept. 8, 1963. Section 1A p. 3.
3. *Doremus* v. *Board of Education*, 5 N. J. 435 (1950); and *Schempp* v. *School District of Abington Township*, 177 F. Supp. 398 (1960).
4. Alabama, Arkansas, Delaware, Florida, Georgia, Idaho, Kentucky, Maine, Massachusetts, New Jersey, and Tennessee.
5. Kentucky Statutes, Chap. 158, Sec. 170.
6. Mississippi Constitution, Art. III, Sec. 18.

Statutes in five states authorize, but do not require, reading from the Bible in the public classroom.[1]

Various legal bodies in twenty-three states have upheld practices of and laws requiring or authorizing Bible reading in the public schools.[2]

In eleven states legal bodies have declared Bible reading a sectarian practice forbidden by state and/or federal constitution.[3]

The total legal picture then finds twenty-six states which require or authorize Bible reading in the public school classrooms and eleven states which forbid such practices.

The legal status of recitation of the Lord's Prayer or of other prayers is somewhat less complete than is that of Bible reading. Three states authorize the repeating of the Lord's Prayer in the public schools,[4] while legal bodies in twelve states have approved such recitations[5] and have disapproved it in five others.[6]

In summary, thirteen states authorize recitation of the Lord's Prayer in the public school classroom while some five states forbid such a practice.

THE OPENING DAY OF SCHOOL, 1963

The Associated Press reported that despite the Supreme Court's ban against required religious devotions, thousands of children in public school classes began the first days of school with Bible reading and/or prayer. The AP concluded that most schools merely continued practices followed before the decision.

The one case of open defiance of the decision appeared in Alabama. Governor George C. Wallace said, "We don't care what the Supreme Court says."

Other states have handled the issue in various ways. Arkansas and Delaware are still requiring Bible reading or prayer. In Texas, South Carolina, and Florida local school officials are permitted to use their own discretion but generally with the understanding that neither Bible reading nor prayer be required; Vermont, Massachusetts and Pennsylvania have substituted "moments of meditation," while children in Washington, D. C., public school classrooms will have inspirational readings; in California regular courses of study dealing with the Bible and religious literature, as specifically sanctioned in the Supreme Court decision, have been adopted.

A United Press International survey showed that in the West most schools are abiding by the Supreme Court decision. But in New Jersey school devotions were "blatant and arrogant defiance," according to an attorney for the American

1. Indiana, Iowa, Kansas, Oklahoma, and North Dakota.
2. Alabama, Arkansas, Colorado, Florida, Georgia, Iowa, Kansas, Kentucky, Maine, Maryland, Massachusetts, Michigan, Minnesota, New Jersey, New Mexico, New York, North Dakota, Rhode Island, South Carolina, Tennessee, Texas, Vermont, and Virginia.
3. Arizona, California, Illinois, Louisiana, Nebraska, Nevada, Ohio, Pennsylvania, South Dakota, Washington, and Wisconsin.
4. Arkansas, Delaware, and New Jersey.
5. Arkansas, Georgia, Kansas, Kentucky, Massachusetts, Minnesota, New Jersey, New Mexico, Rhode Island, Tennessee, Vermont, and Virginia.
6. California, Illinois, Nebraska, Pennsylvania, and South Dakota.

Civil Liberties Union. And the UPI reported that at least nine Pennsylvania school districts have voted to continue Bible reading, despite warnings by the state attorney general that the high court left no loopholes in its decision. The Pennsylvania Department of Public Instruction said "the trend" is to abide with the court's and attorney general's opinions.

City schools in Newport, Kentucky sported signs saying, "Bring back the Bible." When the signs were taken down, students showed up with cards on shirts and dresses saying the same thing.

Tennessee has a state law requiring home room teachers to begin each school day with the reading of a Bible verse. Local school superintendents have interpreted silence from state officials as the green light to continue reading.

School officials in Kansas and Missouri said they did not issue special instructions on prayer or Bible reading. They said it was left on a voluntary basis and left it up to the individual teacher.

EFFECT OF THE DECISION

One can only hypothesize about the ultimate effect this court decision will have upon laws and practices in the states. As the preceding paragraphs show, there is a real question whether the court's voice will be heeded. The legislature in at least one state, Alabama, has moved to defy this decision. Whereas Alabama did not require, by law, reading from the Bible in the public school classrooms, its public officials have now moved to do so. I suspect, however, that most states will eventually comply, realizing that the court's decision was the only one possible if religious freedom of the individual is to be protected. Should the slightest weakening of Jefferson's envisioned "wall of separation" be allowed, the torrent of abuse to follow will destroy the wall so firmly established. And with the destruction of the wall of separation between church and state would come, in my opinion, the ruin of the public school system of America.

Religion and the Public Schools

Comment, Vanderbilt Law Review (1966–67), **20**, 1083–1113

C. Prayer and Bible Reading

1. THE HISTORICAL DEVELOPMENT. The practice of opening the school day with prayers and Bible readings has a long history. In 1684 the Rules of the New

Haven Hopkins Grammar School required that the teacher "every morning begin his work with a short prayer for a blessing on his Laboures and their learning. . . ."[1] A 1682 contract with a Dutch schoolmaster in New York required four prayers during each school day.[2] Although public schools gradually supplanted the private academies between 1800 and 1850, morning devotional exercises were generally retained. Yet Eastern educators, whose schools were exposed to religious diversities as a result of swelling immigration, soon began to question the soundness of opening the school day with compulsory prayer or Bible reading. In 1843 the Philadelphia School Board declared that no pupils would be required to listen to the reading of the Bible if their parents were "conscientiously opposed thereto."[3] A decade later, the New York Superintendent of Schools issued a decree against prayers in the public schools and declared that Catholic students could not be compelled to listen to readings from the King James Bible.[4] An even bolder position was taken by the Cincinnati Board of Education; in 1869 it resolved that "religious instruction and the reading of religious books, including the Holy Bible, are prohibited in the common schools of Cincinnati. . . ."[5]

Although the overwhelming majority of state courts sustained devotional exercises in the public schools,[6] it is significant that six state supreme courts held such exercises to violate their respective state constitutions.[7] *Doremus v. Board of Education*[8] was the first Bible reading case to reach the United States Supreme Court. Apparently not yet ready to rule on the merits,[9] the Court dismissed for lack of standing.[10]

2. STATE-COMPOSED PRAYERS. A full decade passed before the Court said anything further concerning "Religion and the Public Schools." Finally, in 1962 the Court heard arguments in the case of *Engel v. Vitale*.[11] The New York State Board of Regents had composed a "non-sectarian" prayer and had recommended that it be recited daily in the New York public schools. The prayer read:

1. Abington School Dist. v. Schempp, 374 U.S. 203, 267-68 (1963) (Brennan, J., concurring).
2. *Id. See also* W. DUNN, WHAT HAPPENED TO RELIGIOUS EDUCATION? 21-22 (1958).
3. Abington School Dist. v. Schempp, 374 U.S. at 272.
4. *Id.*   5. *Id.*
6. *See, e.g.*, Carden v. Bland, 199 Tenn. 665, 288 S.W.2d 718 (1956); Kaplan v. Independent School Dist., 171 Minn. 142, 214 N.W. 18 (1927); Wilkerson v. Rome, 152 Ga. 762, 110 S.E. 895 (1922); Church v. Bullock, 104 Tex. 1, 109 S.W. 115 (1908); Hackett v. Brooksville Graded School Dist., 120 Ky. 608, 87 S.W. 792 (1905); Billard v. Board of Educ., 69 Kan. 53, 76 P. 422 (1904); Pfeiffer v. Board of Educ., 118 Mich. 560, 77 N.W. 250 (1898); Moore v. Monroe, 64 Iowa 367, 20 N.W. 475 (1884).
7. State *ex rel.* Finger v. Weedman, 55 S.D. 343, 226 N.W. 348 (1929); State *ex rel.* Dearle v. Frazier, 102 Wash. 369, 173 P. 35 (1918); Herold v. Parish Bd. of School Directors, 136 La. 1034, 68 So. 116 (1915); People *ex rel.* Ring v. Board of Educ., 245 Ill. 334, 92 N.E. 251 (1910); State *ex rel.* Freeman v. Scheve, 65 Neb. 853, 91 N.W. 846 (1902); State *ex rel.* Weiss v. District Bd., 76 Wis. 177, 44 N.W. 967 (1890). For a discussion of these cases, see D. BOLES, THE BIBLE, RELIGION, AND THE PUBLIC SCHOOLS 108-32 (1965); Harrison, *The Bible, the Constitution and Public Education*, 29 TENN. L. REV. 363, 386-89 (1962); Note, *Bible Reading in Public Schools*, 9 VAND. L. REV. 849 (1956).
8. 342 U.S. 429 (1952).
9. *See* R. DRINAN, RELIGION, THE COURTS, AND PUBLIC POLICY 93 (1963).
10. For a discussion of the standing question, see notes 210-16 of the original article (in volume 20, *Comment, Vanderbilt Law Review*) from which this selection is excerpted.
11. 370 U.S. 421 (1962), *noted in* 16 VAND. L. REV. 205 (1962).

"Almighty God, we acknowledge our dependence upon Thee, and we beg Thy blessings upon us, our parents, our teachers and our country."[1] The Court held, by a six-to-one vote, that the use of the prayer violated the "no establishment" clause even though the prayer was denominationally neutral and its observance on the part of the students was voluntary.[2] Once again speaking for the majority, Mr. Justice Black said:

> There can, of course, be no doubt that New York's program of daily classroom invocation of God's blessings as prescribed in the Regents' prayer is a religious activity. It is a solemn avowal of divine faith and supplication for the blessings of the Almighty. . . . [S]tate laws requiring or permitting use of the Regents' prayer must be struck down as a violation of the Establishment Clause because that prayer was composed by government officials as a part of a governmental program to further religious beliefs.[3]

In answer to respondent's contention that the practice should be upheld because of its voluntary nature, Mr. Justice Black declared that government mental coercion is not a prerequisite to a violation of the "no establishment" clause. Rather, the clause is violated whenever "the power, prestige and financial support of government is placed behind a particular religious belief."[4]

3. THE RESPONSE TO ENGEL. The *Engel* decision was greeted with a storm of protest. Bishop James A. Pike of the Episcopal Church declared that the Supreme Court had "deconsecrated" the nation, and he called for a constitutional amendment to reverse this "lockout of God."[5] Cardinal Spellman, after announcing that he was "shocked and frightened" by the decision, exclaimed that it "strikes at the very heart of the Godly tradition in which America's children have for so long been raised."[6] And evangelist Billy Graham referred to the decision as "another step toward the secularization of the United States" and observed that "the framers of our Constitution meant we were to have freedom *of* religion, not freedom *from* religion."

Dean Erwin Griswold of the Harvard Law School attacked the decision for its use of a "fundamentalist theological" and "mechanically absolutist" approach. He would prefer to use a "comprehensive" or "integral" approach whereby all the provisions in the Constitution would be examined in a "living setting."[7]

1. Dean Drinan observed that although the prayer is not trinitarian or Christian, it is "clearly theistic." He explained that the Regents justified this preference of one religion over another by making reference to the "spiritual heritage of the nation and the undeniable reality of a theistic commitment underlying the legal and moral institutions of the country." R. DRINAN, (note 9, p. 60), at 100. Although the prayer received strong support from most Protestant and Catholic church leaders, some charged that it was bound to deteriorate into empty formality and would be of little spiritual significance.
2. The petitioners, who were challenging the constitutionality of the Regents' prayer, included Jews, Unitarians, Ethical Culturalists and one nonbeliever. W. DOUGLAS, THE BIBLE AND THE SCHOOLS 17 (1966).
3. Engel v. Vitale, 370 U.S. 421, 424-25 (1962).
4. *Id.* at 431.
5. W. KATZ, RELIGION AND AMERICAN CONSTITUTIONS 35-36 (1964).
6. *Id.*
7. Griswold, *Absolute is in the Dark—A Discussion of the Approach of the Supreme Court to Constitutional Questions*, S UTAH L. REV. 167, 172–73 (1963).

Under this approach he would sustain the use of the state-composed prayer as a means of teaching members of minority groups a lesson in tolerance.[1]

4. BIBLE READING AND THE LORD'S PRAYER. In the midst of this outburst of public dissent, the Supreme Court handed down another major church-state decision in the companion cases of *Abington School District v. Schempp* and *Murray v. Curlett*.[2] At issue in the *Schempp* case was the validity of a Pennsylvania law requiring the reading without comment of ten verses from the Holy Bible at the beginning of each school day.[3] The *Murray* case involved no statute; rather the petitioners were challenging the practice of daily Bible reading and recitation of the Lord's Prayer which the Baltimore school authorities had approved for the Baltimore public schools. After reaffirming the *Everson-McCollum* principle that government may not "aid one religion, aid all religions, or prefer one religion over another," the Court laid down a test for determining whether governmental activity violates the first amendment: governmental activity is unconstitutional if either its purpose or primary effect is the advancement or inhibition of religion.[4] By an eight-to-one vote, the Court held that the morning exercises in question were intended to advance the Christian religion; hence, there was a violation of the first amendment's command that "Government maintain strict neutrality, neither aiding nor opposing religion."[5] As in *Engel*, the Court held that the voluntary nature of the exercises was no defense to a challenge under the "no establishment" clause.[6] Neither was the Court im-

1. *Id.* at 176–77. Dean Griswold reasoned as follows: "The child of a non-conforming or minority group is, to be sure, different in his beliefs. That is what it means to be a member of a minority. Is it not desirable, and educational, for him to learn and observe this, in the atmosphere of the school—not so much that he is different, as that other children are different from him? And is it not desirable that, at the same time, he experiences and learns the fact that his difference is tolerated and accepted? No compulsion is put upon him. He need not participate. But he, too, has the opportunity to be tolerant. He allows the majority of the group to follow their own tradition, perhaps coming to understand and to respect what they feel is significant to them." *Id.* at 177.
2. 374 U.S. 203 (1963). The Court decided *Schempp* and *Murray* in a single opinion.
3. *Id.* The Pennsylvania statute was amended in 1959 to permit any child to be excused from the Bible reading exercises upon the written request of his parent or guardian. PA. STAT. ANN. tit. 24, § 15–1516 (1962).
4. 374 U.S. at 222. Professor Choper has proposed a slightly different test. He suggests that the "no establishment" clause is violated "when the state engages in what may be fairly characterized as *solely religious activity* that is likely to result in (1) *compromising* the student's religious or conscientious beliefs or (2) *influencing* the student's freedom of religion or conscientious choice." Choper, *Religion in the Public Schools: A Proposed Constitutional Standard*, 47 MINN. L. REV. 329, 330 (1963).
5. 374 U.S. at 225.
6. At the trial Edward Schempp explained why he had decided not to request that his children be excused from the morning exercises. The trial court summarized his testimony as follows: "He said that he thought his children would be 'labeled as "odd balls" ' before their teachers and classmates every school day; that children, like Roger's and Donna's classmates, were liable 'to lump all particular religious difference[s] or religious objections [together] as "atheism" ' and that today the word 'atheism' is often connected with 'atheistic communism,' and has 'very bad' connotations, such as 'un-American' . . . with overtones of possible immorality. Mr. Schempp pointed out that due to the events of the morning exercises following in rapid succession, the Bible reading, the Lord's Prayer, the Flag Salute, and the announcements, excusing his children from the Bible reading would mean that probably they would miss hearing the announcements so important to children. He testified also that if Roger and Donna were excused from Bible reading they would have to stand in the hall outside their 'homeroom' and that this carried with it the imputation of punishment for bad conduct." Schempp v. School Dist., 201 F. Supp. 815, 818 (E.D. Pa. 1962).

pressed with the defense that the religious practices in question were only minor encroachments on the first amendment. Speaking for the majority, Mr. Justice Clark cautioned:

The breach of neutrality that is today a trickling stream may all too soon become a raging torrent and, in the words of Madison, 'it is proper to take alarm at the first experiment on our liberties.'[1]

Finally, the Court rejected the contention that the command of strict neutrality which does not permit a state to require a religious exercise even with the consent of the majority of those affected, collides with the majority's right to free exercise of religion. Mr. Justice Clark declared:

While the Free Exercise Clause clearly prohibits the use of state action to deny the rights of free exercise to *anyone*, it has never meant that a majority could use the machinery of the State to practice its beliefs.[2]

5. COMPLIANCE WITH SCHEMPP. Once again the Supreme Court was inundated with a flood of criticism. An editorial in the *Wall Street Journal* declared that the Court had established atheism as "the one belief to which the State's power will extend its protection."[3] Bishop Pike commented that "[t]he result of the decision is not neutrality but an imposition upon the public school system of a particular perspective on reality, namely, secularism by default, which is as much an 'ism' as any other."[4] Cardinal McIntyre of Los Angeles stated that the decision "can only mean that our American heritage of philosophy, of religion and of freedom are being abandoned in imitation of Soviet philosophy, of Soviet materialism and of Soviet regimented liberty." Cardinal Cushing of Boston expressed the view that the Communists were no doubt taking great pleasure in the decision, and Cardinal Spellman of New York asserted that no one who believes in God could approve of such a holding.[5]

Other religious leaders hailed the *Schempp* ruling as a great bulwark to the preservation of religious liberty. The Right Reverend Arthur Lichtenberger, Presiding Bishop of the Episcopal Church, declared that the decision was in keeping with "the Court's sense of responsibility to assure freedom and equality to all groups of believers and non-believers as expressed in the First Amendment of the Constitution."[6] Dr. Eugene Carson Blake and Dr. Silas G. Kessler, executive officers of the United Presbyterian Church, issued a statement declaring that the decision had "underscored our firm belief that religious instruction is the sacred responsibility of the family and the Churches."[7] Similar

1. 374 U.S. at 225.
2. *Id.* at 226.
3. W. KATZ (note 5, p. 61), at 97.
4. *Id.*
5. Legal scholars have also dissented from the *Engel* and *Schempp* decisions. *See, e.g.,* C. RICE, THE SUPREME COURT AND PUBLIC PRAYER (1964); Hanft, *The Prayer Decisions*, 42 N.C.L. REV. 567 (1964).
6. *See* D. BOLES (note 7, p. 60), at 266.
7. Id.

thoughts were expressed by Rabbi Uri Miller, president of the Synagogue Council of America (which represents Orthodox, Conservative, and Reformed Judaism) and by the National Council of Churches.[1]

In the midst of this dialogue among theologians, many politicians were expressing their disapproval of the *Schempp* decision. State officials in at least four states announced that they would ignore the decision,[2] and rumblings of a constitutional amendment echoed through the halls of Congress.[3] This critical attitude even found expression in state courts in which church-state issues were pending. When requested to strike down the Florida Bible reading statute, the Florida Supreme Court boldy declared in *Chamberlin v. Dade County Board of Public Instruction*[4] that the *Schempp* neutrality command had not been breached. Inasmuch as the preamble to the statute made reference to "good moral training," "a life of honorable thought," and "good citizenship," the court concluded that the Bible reading practice was founded upon secular rather than sectarian considerations.[5] The United States Supreme Court was unimpressed with this attempt to distinguish the Florida practice from those presented in the *Schempp* case, and it reversed per curiam.[6]

Although several states sought to justify the continuance of Bible reading in the public schools on the theory that the *Schempp* decision applied only to legislative enactments and not to "local custom,"[7] other states made a dedicated effort to comply without any "chicanery."[8] In New Jersey and Pennsylvania, for example, the governors threatened local school districts with the loss of state aid if they did not comply. And in at least two instances state officials obtained injunctions to force compliance by defiant school districts.[9]

---

1. *Id.* at 265–67. The National Council of Churches also issued the following statement: "The full treatment of some regular school subjects requires the use of the Bible as a source book. In such studies—including those related to character development—the use of the Bible has a valid educational purpose. But neither true religion nor good education is dependent upon the devotional use of the Bible in the public school program." Quoted in L. Pfeffer, Church, State and Freedom 474 (rev. ed. 1967).

2. *See* C. Rice (note 5, p. 63) at 7. Gov. George Wallace of Alabama boldly declared: "I want the Supreme Court to know we are not going to conform to any such decision." He further stated that, if the courts rule that the Bible cannot be read in an Alabama school, "I'm going to that school and read it myself." Beaney & Beiser, *Prayer and Politics: The Impact of Engel and Schempp on the Political Process*, 13 J. Pub. L. 475, 486 (1964).

3. Over ninety congressmen introduced constitutional amendments designed to overturn the *Schempp* decision.

4. 160 So. 2d 97 (Fla. 1964).

5. *Id.* The Florida court relied on McGowan v. Maryland, 366 U.S. 420 (1961), wherein the Supreme Court upheld a Sunday closing statute on the ground that its purpose and effect were not to aid religion, but to set aside a day of rest and recreation.

6. Chamberlin v. Dade County Bd. of Pub. Instruction, 377 U.S. 402 (1964). Other Bible reading statutes have been summarily invalidated by lower federal and state courts. *See* Johns v. Allen, 231 F. Supp. 852 (D. Del. 1964); Adams v. Engelking, 232 F. Supp. 666 (D. Idaho 1964); Attorney Gen. v. School Comm., 347 Mass. 775, 199 N.E.2d 553 (1964); Sills v. Board of Educ., 42 N.J. 351, 200 A.2d 615 (1965).

7. *See* Beaney & Beiser (*supra* note 2) at 488–89.

8. *Id.*

9. *Id.* Of the twenty-nine states which reported Bible reading in their public schools before the *Schempp* decision, only five have completely abolished the practice, according to a 1965 survey. In fourteen, Bible reading exists in scattered areas; and in six, it continues as it did before the decision. Katz, *Patterns of Compliance with the Schempp Decision*, 14 J. Pub. L. 396, 403 (1965).

IV. VALIDITY OF OTHER PRACTICES CONTAINING REFERENCES TO RELIGION

A. Observance of Holy Days

1. PAGEANTS AND PROGRAMS. Public school observance of holy days is clearly an unconstitutional activity if conducted in a devotional setting.[1] That allowance is made for joint religious observances, such as Christmas-Hanukah and Easter-Passover, does not cure the infirmity, for the Constitution prohibits the states from aiding one religion, aiding all religions, or preferring some religions over others.[2] The suggestion that Christmas and Easter have lost their religious significance[3] and have become national holidays in the same category as Thanksgiving Day and Washington's Birthday would surely be disputed by the nation's religious leaders.

It is submitted, therefore, that the schools should refrain from any "celebration" of religious holidays. There should be no worship services of any type, no religious pageants, and no exhibition of films which are primarily religious in nature.[4]

On the other hand, it would appear to be entirely appropriate for public school teachers to "acknowledge and explain" the various holy days.[5] In fact, the American Association of School Administrators has recently recommended that the public schools recognize religious holidays "in the spirit of exposition of the differing rites and customs of families, cultures, and creeds—each with deep meaning for its adherents, and in sum revealing the many different religious, philosophical, and cultural practices and beliefs held by Americans."[6]

2. SACRED MUSIC. The constitutional command of neutrality clearly prohibits the use of religious hymns in a devotional setting. They may, however, be sung as a part of a course in music appreciation since this is a secular activity.[7] School choirs and orchestras may properly make use of religious music, including Christmas carols, as long as their performances do not take place in a devotional setting. Although the duty of neutrality would not appear to forbid public school

---

1. Chamberlin v. Dade County Bd. of Pub. Instruction, 143 So. 2d 21 (Fla. 1962); Rosenfield, *Separation of Church and State in the Public Schools*, 22 U. PITT. L. REV. 561, 572 (1961).
2. Choper, (note 4, p. 62), at 411–13; Rosenfield, *supra* note 1 at 572. For a discussion of various instances where public school observance of holy days has given rise to community turmoil see PFEFFER (note 1, p. 64) at 479–96.
3. *See* Harrison (note 7, p. 60), at 416.
4. *See* Chamberlin v. Dade County Bd. of Pub. Instruction, 143 So. 2d 21 (Fla. 1962). Professor Choper has noted that the occasional showing of motion pictures depicting religious happenings may be of considerable educational value. Choper, (note 4, p. 62), at 413. It seems doubtful, however, that he would sanction the use of religious films for devotional purposes; he would very likely restrict their use to history classes or to objective religion courses.
5. In 1963 the General Assembly of the United Presbyterian Church adopted a lengthy report on church-state relations. Among other things, the report recommended that "Religious holidays be acknowledged and explained, but never celebrated religiously, by public schools or their administrators. . . ." Quoted in PFEFFER (note 1, p. 64), at 492. *See also Church-State Report*, Presbyterian Life, June 15, 1963, at 10; Rosenfield, *supra* note 1, at 573.
6. Quoted in L. PFEFFER (note 1, p. 64), at 492. For a more detailed discussion of the recommendations of the association see BOLES, (note 7, p. 60), at 292–95.
7. *See* Choper (note 4, p. 62), at 413.

officials from setting aside a period of silence at the beginning of the school day, the period could well be turned into a devotional setting if sacred music were played over the public address system. It is submitted, therefore, that it would be improper to use sacred music in connection with the period of silence. On the other hand, religious music would appear to be unobjectionable as a part of a musical assembly if the primary purpose is to entertain—not to indoctrinate.[1]

3. RELIGIOUS SYMBOLS. Although it has been suggested that it is proper for public school teachers to acknowledge and explain religious holidays,[2] such explanations should not be accompanied by a display of religious symbols or pictures. It is indisputable that the presence of a Crucifix or a Star of David would tend to create a religious atmosphere. The display of such symbols, even on a temporary basis, would appear, therefore, to violate the school's duty of neutrality. Pictures of distinctively religious events and placards contraining the Ten Commandments[3] or other sectarian mottoes would also tend to create a religious atmosphere; hence, their presence in public school classrooms would appear to be just as unconstitutional as the presence of religious symbols.[4] On the other hand, there would probably be no objection to such seasonal decorations as pine trees, wreaths, bells, candles, poinsettias, lilies, colored eggs or rabbits, as these items merely reflect the joy and good will of the season and have only incidental religious connotations.[5]

References to religious painting, sculpture and architecture in an art class would appear to be beyond question. Many of the world's great artistic accomplishments are centered on religious themes, yet the religious element is definitely incidental to the artistic qualities.[6]

Whether an art teacher may assist his students in creating religious symbols which would violate the aid to religion test if placed on display by the school officials is a more difficult question. It is likely that the answer will turn on the purpose and primary effect of such activity. If the purpose is to teach students to paint or draw or sculpture, then the fact that the creation is a religious symbol should be of no consequence. On the other hand, if the purpose is to construct a religious display for use in the school lobby, then the art room activity takes on aid-to-religion characteristics.[7]

4. NATIVITY SCENES. The erection of nativity scenes on public school premises generally has been held constitutional on the ground that it constitutes a mere

1. *See* Harrison (note 7, p. 60), at 415.
2. *See* note 5, p. 65, and accompanying text.
3. A North Dakota statute requires "a placard containing the ten commandments of the Christian religion to be displayed in a conspicuous place in every schoolroom, classroom, or other place where classes convene for instruction." N.D. CENT. CODE § 15-47-10 (1960).
4. *See* Choper (note 4, p. 62), at 408–09.
5. *Id.* at 412.
6. *Id.* at 386.
7. But *see* Chamberlin v. Dade County Bd. of Pub. Instruction, 143 So. 2d 21, 35 (Fla. 1962), where the court refused to enjoin a display of religious symbols because it was a work of art created by the students and was set up only on a temporary basis.

"passive accommodation of religion."[1] The courts have emphasized that the scenes were displayed only during the school's Christmas recess and at no expense to the school district.[2] It also has been suggested that permission for religious displays on public property should be granted on a non-discriminatory basis.[3] The conclusion is inescapable, however, that the mere presence of a nativity scene constitutes a dedication of the premises to the Christian faith. The scene probably would be offensive to Jews and other non-Christians, and undoubtedly some Christians would look upon it as a place of worship.[4] That the school district granted permission for the erection of religious displays on a non-discrimatory basis, that they were erected only during the holiday recess, and that the costs were borne by the sponsoring church are not determinative of the constitutional question. The question is whether the action of the school district has the purpose or primary effect of aiding one religion, aiding all religions, or preferring one religion over another. The answer is obvious. By sanctioning the use of its property for the display of a nativity scene, the school district aids the Christian religion in general;[5] if the sponsoring church attaches its name to the scene, it aids one sect in particular; finally, it prefers the Christian religion over non-Christian beliefs. Patently, then, the presence of a nativity scene on public school property constitutes an establishment of religion. . . .

D. Wearing of Religious Garb by Public School Teachers

The wearing of religious garb by public school teachers has been challenged on numerous occasions, usually on the ground that it violates state constitutional prohibitions against sectarian influence in the public schools. In the absence of evidence that the nuns have injected religious dogma into their teaching, most of the courts have declined to enjoin the wearing of religious garb in the public schools.[6] It scarcely could be denied, however, that such distinctive garb tends to create a religious atmosphere in the classroom.[7] Furthermore, in view of the

1. Lawrence v. Buchmueller, 40 Misc. 2d 300, 243 N.Y.S.2d 87, 91 (Sup. Ct. 1963).
2. *Id.*; Baer v. Kolmorgen, 181 N.Y.S.2d 230 (Sup. Ct. 1958).
3. *See Church-State Report* (note 5, p. 65), at 10.
4. In State *ex rel.* Singelmann v. Morrison, 57 So. 2d 238 (La. App. 1952), the court decided that a statue or monument erected on public property violated the "no establishment" clause if it was designed and used as a public shrine or place of worship, if it was used for the propagation of a religious belief, if it was intended to hold some other religious group in public contempt and ridicule, or if it was designed to cause religious strife and antagonisms.
5. The plaintiff's brief in Lawrence v. Buchmueller, *supra* note 1, at 90, stated that "objection is made . . . not on the basis of any religious antagonism with the creche as a symbol—but, rather, precisely because it *is* symbolic of a basic tenet of the Church and, as such, has no place in a secular atmosphere. . . ."
6. *See, e.g.,* Rawlings v. Butler, 290 S.W.2d 801 (Ky. 1956); New Haven v. Torrington, 132 Conn. 194, 43 A.2d 455 (1945); State *ex rel.* Johnson v. Boyd, 217 Ind. 348, 28 N.E.2d 256 (1940); Gerhardt v. Heid, 66 N.D. 444, 267 N.W. 127 (1936); Hyscng v. Gallitzin Borough School Dist., 164 Pa. 629, 30 A. 482 (1894). After the Pennsylvania decision was rendered, the legislature quickly passed a law prohibiting public school teachers from wearing religious garb. This law was held constitutional in Commonwealth v. Herr, 229 Pa. 132, 78 A. 68 (1910). Administrative regulations banning the wearing of religious garb and religious insignia also have been upheld. *See* Zellers v. Huff, 55 N.M. 501, 236 P.2d 949 (1951); O'Connor v. Hendrick, 184 N.Y. 421, 77 N.E. 612 (1906).
7. In his dissenting opinion in the *Rawlings* case, Judge Hogg emphasized the fact that religious garb generates a religious atmosphere. He stated: "The distinctive garbs, so exclusively peculiar to the Roman Catholic Church, create a religious atmosphere in the schoolroom. They have a subtle

fact that the garb serves as a constant reminder of the teacher's religious affiliation, and that children develop impressions just as much from what they see as
from what they hear,[1] it would not be difficult to conclude that the wearing of
religious garb constitutes sectarian influence. Although such influence may fall
short of sectarian "teaching" it would appear to have a "propagandizing effect,"[2]
especially where the garb includes rosaries or other religious insignia.[3] Practices
which tend to create a reverent atmosphere and which contain suggestions of a
proselytizing purpose probably would constitute sufficient sectarian influence to
violate the constitutional command of neutrality. Hence, the practice of wearing
religious garb in the public schools would appear to be an unconstitutional
advancement of religion.

The argument that the wearing of religious garb is protected by the "free
exercise" clause can be answered in two ways. First, the religious liberty of one
person may not be exercised so as to limit the freedom of others.[4] Second, a
prohibition against religious garb in the public schools does not in any way
interfere with a teacher's freedom of belief; it merely means that during the
period in which she is employed as an agent of the state she cannot practice
those beliefs which constitute sectarian influence.[5]

One court has disqualified all nuns from teaching in the public schools,
apparently on the ground that their lives are dedicated to the teaching of religion.[6] It is unlikely, however, that the employment of nuns or ministers as
teachers would violate the neutrality concept if they wear no religious garb or
insignia and if they take care that their classroom comments contain no sectarian
implications.[7] The fact that these nuns or ministers contribute their salaries

influence upon the tender minds being taught and trained by the nuns. In and of themselves they
proclaim the Catholic Church and the representative character of the teachers in the schoolroom.
They silently promulgate sectarianism." Rawlings v. Butler, *supra* note 60, at 809.

1. See Note, *Religious Garb in the Public Schools—A Study in Conflicting Liberties*, 22 U. Chi.
L. Rev. 888, 892-93 (1955).
2. In Zellers v. Huff (note 6, p. 67), the court said: "Not only does the wearing of religious garb
and insignia have a propagandizing effect for the church, but by its very nature it introduced sectarian
religion into the school." 55 N.M. at 525, 236 P.2d at 964.
3. Speaking of teachers wearing religious garb, Justice Williams of the Pennsylvania Supreme
Court stated: "Wherever they go, this garb proclaims their church, their order, and their separation
from the secular world, as plainly as a herald could do if they were constantly attended by such a
person." Hysong v. Gallitzin Borough School Dist., 164 Pa. 629, 659, 30 A. 482, 485 (1894) (dissenting
opinion).
4. See Note, *supra* note 1, at 892. See also Commonwealth v. Herr (note 6, p. 67), where the
court stated: "The right of the individual to clothe himself in whatever garb his taste, his inclination,
the tenets of his sect, or even his religious sentiments may dictate is no more absolute than his right to
give utterance to his sentiments, religious or otherwise." 229 Pa. at 143–44, 78 A. at 72.
5. Cf. Reynolds v. United States, 98 U.S. 145 (1878), where the Court refused to allow a religious
belief as a defense against a polygamy prosecution. Speaking for the Court, Mr. Chief Justice Waite
stated: "Laws are made for the government of actions, and while they cannot interfere with mere
religious beliefs and opinions, they may with practices." *Id.* at 166. The North Dakota decision
allowing the wearing of religious garb in the public schools (note 6, p. 67), was abrogated by a public
referendum in 1948. Thereafter, the Catholic bishops of the state announced that the nuns would be
permitted to wear "modest dress" while teaching; hence, they have continued in their employment.
See L. Pfeffer (note 1, p. 64), at 497–98. It would appear, therefore, that the wearing of religious
garb is not nearly so vital to a nun's freedom of religion as the "free exercise argument" suggests.
6. Harfst v. Hoegen, 349 Mo. 808, 163 S.W.2d 609 (1942).
7. See Harrison (note 7, p. 60), at 416.

to religious purposes should have no bearing on the validity of their employ-ment.[1] No inquiry is made concerning the manner in which other public school teachers dispose of their salaries, and there is no reason why a different approach should be taken in regard to nun-teachers or minister-teachers. Indeed, it is possible that any inquiry concerning a teacher's disposition of his salary would violate the "free exercise" clause.[2]

Public Aid to Parochial Schools

Paul A. Freund

Carl M. Loeb University Professor, Harvard University. A.B., Washington University, 1928; LLB., Harvard, 1931, S.J.D., 1932. This article is based on a paper read before the Section on Individual Rights and Responsibilities, American Bar Association, August 4, 1968. *Harvard Law Review* (June, 1969) **82,** 1680–92.

Since June 10, 1968, a discussion of state aid to parochial schools can profit-ably start with the Supreme Court decision of that date in *Board of Education v. Allen.*[3] The case was brought by members of a local school board to enjoin the Commissioner from enforcing a law of New York, enacted in 1965 and amended in 1966, that requires them to lend textbooks, under stated conditions, to stud-ents enrolled in grades seven to twelve of parochial and private, as well as public schools.[4] The statutory conditions are that the book be required for use as a text for a semester or more in the particular school and that it be approved by a board of education or similar body, whether or not designated for use in any public school. By judicial interpretation in New York, this duty embraces the loan of "secular," not "religious" textbooks. On cross-motions for summary judgment on the pleadings the trial court held the statute unconstitutional under the first and fourteenth amendments; the appellate division reversed on the ground that the complainants had no standing to raise the question.[5]

1. *See* Choper (note 4, p. 62), at 404.
2. In Gerhardt v. Heid (note 6, p. 67), the court said: "The fact that the teachers contributed a material portion of their earnings to the religious order of which they are members is not violative of the Constitution. A person in the employ of the state or any of its subdivisions is not inhibited from contributing money, which he or she has earned by service so performed, for the support of some religious body of which he or she is a member. To deny the right to make such contribution would in itself constitute a denial of that right of religious liberty which the Constitution guarantees." 66 N.D. at 460, 267 N.W. at 135.
3. 392 U.S. 236.
4. N.Y. EDUC. LAW § 701 (McKinney Supp. 1968).
5. 51 Misc. 2d 297, 273 N.Y.S.2d 239 (Sup. Ct.), *rev'd*, 27 App. Div. 2d 69, 276 N.Y.S.2d 234 (1966).

The New York Court of Appeals, differing from both courts below, held, in a four-to-three decision, Judges Van Voorhis, Fuld and Breitel dissenting, that the law does not contravene either the state or federal constitution, "merely making available secular textbooks at the request of the individual student and asking no question about what school he attends."[1] It is hard to accept this bland description literally since under the law a loan is limited to books prescribed as texts in the school attended by the borrowing student. Moreover, pursuant to its statutory authority, the state Department of Education has provided forms for textbook requisition, to be filled out on behalf of students and sent to the local school board by an official of a parochial or private school.

On appeal to the Supreme Court, the decision was affirmed, Justice White writing for the majority, with a concurring opinion by Justice Harlan and dissenting opinions by Justices Black, Douglas, and Fortas.[2] The majority opinion is in terms a guarded one. There is repeated reference to the lack of a factual record. As there was no evidence concerning the nature of the books requested or concerning the character and practices of the parochial schools involved, these matters were taken most favorably to the defense. The opinion is a narrow one, too, in its stress on the formal aspects of the arrangements, namely, that the books were loaned, with title remaining in the state, and that the requests were made by and on behalf of the students, not the school. "So construing the statute," said Justice White, "we find it in conformity with the Constitution, for the books are furnished for the use of individual students and at their request."[3]

How crucial were these limiting factors? The case is obviously the beginning, not the end, of constitutional litigation—now fostered in the case of federal programs by the decision in *Flast v. Cohen*,[4] recognizing federal taxpayers' suits—to determine the bounds of public aid to parochial schools. Suppose, for example, that the Court is ready to pursue its negative pregnant and to inquire into the nature of textbooks and the character of teaching in parochial schools. That prospect might understandably offend parochial school authorities, and pressures would mount for unconditional grants of funds, free from the textbook strings, for certain curricular fields. This is precisely what has occurred in Pennsylvania, where a statute was recently enacted appropriating a fixed annual amount, to be derived so far as possible from the public proceeds of horseracing, for the support of the teaching in parochial schools of mathematics, modern foreign languages (Latin is evidently too obsolete or too explosive), and physical training.[5] The funds could presumably be used for books, equipment, buildings, or teachers' salaries, in the discretion of the schools. Gone is the elaborate minuet of the individual student's request for specific books and its approval by the public school board; all is now modern ballet, bold and muscular.

1. 20 N.Y.2d 109, 117, 228 N.E.2d 791, 794, 281 N.Y.S.2d 799, 805 (1967).
2. Board of Educ. v. Allen, 392 U.S. 236 (1968).
3. *Id.* at 244 n.6. The unsatisfactory abstractness of the record for purposes of a definitive decision is reminiscent of Times Film Corp. v. Chicago, 363 U.S. 43 (1961) which has become a derelict in the field of motion picture censorship.
4. 392 U.S. 83 (1968).
5. Pa Stat. Ann. tit. 24, §§ 5601–09 (Supp. 1969).

Will the Court re-score its composition to accommodate the new movement? Indeed, the movement may develop even more vigorously. Arguing that the aid in the New York case was sustained because it was available neutrally to pupils in all accredited schools, the proponents are likely to insist that such aid is not merely permissible, but is mandatory, since the first amendment enforces just this standard of neutrality among religions and between a religious and a secular promotion of a common public purpose. Later I will turn to this question of mandatory aid as an issue of principle. Meanwhile it can be said that whatever the force of this logic, to make public aid mandatory would seem as a matter of prediction to call for more than a re-scoring of the Court's composition; it would, more probably, require a re-composition of the Court itself.

The decision in the New York case purported to rest on the principle of *Everson v. Board of Education*,[1] a 1947 decision upholding state reimbursement of bus fares for school children regardless of the school they attend. *Everson* was a five-to-four decision, which Justice Black, writing the majority opinion, was at pains to say went to "the verge."[2] It in turn rested on the analogy of police and fire protection for church buildings: a general safety measure could be applied for the benefit of the community—indeed might have to be so applied —irrespective of the religious or non-religious character of the beneficiaries. Thus it could be said that an ordinance permitting schoolchildren to ride for half fare might (or must) encompass all, whatever school they attend. The same principle would, in my view, support free medical examinations or hot lunches for all schoolchildren, wherever they might be found. It is true that buses and nurses and lunches may well benefit the parochial school by making it more attractive to parents or less expensive for the church; the sharp dichotomy between pupil benefit and benefit to the school seems to me a chimerical constitutional criterion. It is akin to the ineffectual effort in the mid-nineteenth century to classify such local measures as pilotage laws as either regulations of safety or regulations of commerce, and to make their validity turn on the classification. It was the beginning of wisdom when the Court candidly recognized that such measures were regulations of both safety and commerce, and that before a sensible judgment could be made, a closer look had to be taken at their consequences for both, as well as their exigency, in light of the policies underlying the commerce clause.

Now buses and nurses and lunches are not ideological; they are atmospherically indifferent on the score of religion. Can the same be said of textbooks chosen by a parochial school for compulsory use, interpreted with the authority of teachers selected by that school, and employed in an atmosphere deliberately designed through sacred symbol to maintain a religiously reverent attitude? Perhaps if the atmosphere had been so delineated in the record, the result would have been different. If so, as I have suggested, either the actual significance of the decision for parochial schools is very limited or on a case-by-case basis

1. 330 U.S. 1 (1947).
2. *Id.* at 16.

such schools will confront what they would regard as a highly unwelcome and impertinent secular intrusion into their internal affairs.

In the realm of books, the apt analogy to bus fares would be the public library, accessible to every schoolchild, aiding the pupils and no doubt the schools themselves, but managed by public authorities not delegating responsibility for selection of books or personnel or symbolic decor to any religious group, and certainly not engaged in the business of supplying instructional materials, the staple requirements of denominational schools. It is hardly surprising that Justice Black, the author of the bus decision, was a fierce dissenter in the textbook case. Of course a bridge that carries you to the verge is apt to be burned behind when you discover that the verge is farther ahead after all. The judicial process resembles the episode that began when the King of England visited the White House during World War II. Both the Chief Justice and the senior member of the foreign diplomatic corps, then the British Ambassador, were invited to a state dinner for His Majesty. There had long been an unresolved issue of precedence as between those two offices, and the matter was put before President Roosevelt. Displaying more of his Columbia Law School training than was his wont, the President reasoned that the Ambassador's claim rested on his representing his sovereign; and since the sovereign himself was to be present, the Ambassador should be subordinated to the Chief Justice. Thereafter, when the same issue of precedence again arose (no sovereign being present) the protocol officer was able to announce happily that President Roosevelt had determined that the Chief Justice outranks the head of the diplomatic corps, and so the rule of law was settled—by precedent.

It is not enough, to be sure, to maintain that precedent was reinterpreted in the New York case. After all, the newer majority may have read the Constitution more recently, or they may have read further in Robert Frost than "Good fences make good neighbors"—may in fact have reached the lines:

> *Why* do they make good neighbors? Isn't it
> Where there are cows? But here there are no cows.
> Before I built a wall I'd ask to know
> What I was walling in or walling out,
> And to whom I was like to give offense.
> Something there is that doesn't love a wall,
> That wants it down.

To translate Frost into legal prose, why does observance of the ancient religious guarantees of the first amendment continue to be important? Beyond ancestral voices, are there now any grounds of policy or polity that are threatened? Three such grounds need to be considered: voluntarism in matters of religion, mutual abstention of the political and the religious caretakers, and governmental neutrality toward religions and between religion and non-religion. In a large sense, both of the guarantees of the first amendment—the free-exercise and the non-establishment clauses—are directed harmoniously toward these purposes, though in the context of specific governmental measures the two guarantees may point in different directions and the purposes themselves may be discordant.

The policy of voluntarism generates least tension between the free-exercise and non-establishment clauses. Religion must not be coerced or dominated by the state, and individuals must not be coerced into or away from the exercise or support of religion. The school-prayer decisions[1] reflected the principle of voluntarism on both counts: taxpaying families could not be required to support a concededly religious activity; nor could pupils, by the psychological coercion of the schoolroom, be compelled to participate in devotional exercises. When the state provides textbooks, taxpayers are forced to finance books selected by sectarian authorities for instruction in denominational schools maintained at considerable expense to preserve and strengthen the faith. Of course those schools serve a public purpose; that is why the loan of textbooks was held valid in the early *Cochran* case,[2] before the religious guarantees were thought to be embodied in the fourteenth amendment.

It will be argued that the general taxpayer is coerced for an improper purpose where public funds buy parochial school books, the parochial school familes are similarly coerced into paying taxes to support public schools, which, to be sure, their children are legally free to attend but which they regard either as an enemy of all religion, or, if "secularism" itself be deemed a form of religion, then as a friend of a repellent kind of religion. Note that this argument does not deny that the principle of voluntarism is violated by aid to parochial schools; the argument pleads rather by confession and avoidance, relying on an argument of reciprocity or fairness or neutrality. Note too that if it is indeed the case that public schools are an enemy of religion, or a fountainhead of an obnoxious kind of religion, then the argument, it seems, should call for the abolition of the public schools as being themselves in violation of the first amendment. I will return presently to these arguments of avoidance on the score of governmental reciprocity.

If textbooks were selected by the public school authorities to be used in public and parochial schools alike, the problem of voluntariness for the taxpayer might be mitigated somewhat, but by no means removed. It was this aspect of the New York case—the selection of books by the parochial schools—that particularly

1. Abington School Dist. v. Schempp, 374 U.S. 203 (1963); Engel v. Vitale, 370 U.S. 421 (1962).
2. Cochran v. Louisiana State Bd. of Educ., 281 U.S. 370 (1930). The decision in Pierce v. Society of Sisters, 268 U.S. 510 (1925), though it involved a parochial school, was placed on the ground of liberty to direct the upbringing of children and to pursue a lawful occupation; the opinion also encompassed a companion case involving a private military academy not church-related. Illinois *ex rel.* McCollum v. Board of Educ., 333 U.S. 203 (1948), was the first application of the non-establishment clause to the states, although a dictum in Cantwell v. Connecticut, 310 U.S. 296, 303 (1940), had stated the proposition. It has been argued with much cogency that the first amendment guarantee against a federal law "respecting an establishment of religion" was essentially a shield of federalism, and that neither historically nor textually does it lend itself (as contrasted with "free exercise of religion") to absorption into the guarantees of liberty and property in the fourteenth amendment. *See* Corwin, *The Supreme Court as a National School Board*, 14 LAW & CONTEMP. PROB. 3 (1949). Since, however, the Court has continued to treat the non-establishment guarantee as embracing both federal and state laws, the present discussion does not differentiate the sources of public aid.

troubled Justice Fortas, who, like Justices Black and Douglas, dissented. But consider the position if the selections were in fact to be made by the public authorities. The parochial schools might well consider their own autonomy—their voluntarism—compromised. In certain school districts the reverse might obtain: for the sake of uniformity the school authorities would be pressured into selecting books for the public schools that were particularly desired by the parochial schools. In that event there would be a double loss of voluntariness by the general taxpayer.

This risk of intrusion from one side or the other points up a second policy embodied in the religious guarantees—mutual abstention—keeping politics out of religion and religion out of politics. The choice of textbooks in any school is apt to be a thorny subject; witness the current agitation over the recognition of the Negro, his contributions and his interests, in the books assigned in public schools. For the identity and integrity of religion, separateness stands as an ultimate safeguard. And on the secular side, to link responsibility for parochial and public school texts is greatly to intensify sectarian influences in local politics at one of its most sensitive points.

The third policy—in addition to voluntarism and mutual abstention—is governmental neutrality, among religions and between religion and non-religion. It is this policy that is chiefly relied on by proponents of public aid. The concept of neutrality is an extremely elusive one, generally raising as many questions as it answers, because it depends on sub-concepts like comparability and on definitions (whose?) of religious and non-religious activities, on a determination whether it overrides the policies of voluntarism and mutual abstention, and on a decision whether in any event it requires or only permits public aid. Let me illustrate one difficulty of definition. One might suppose that "neutrality" requires the law to deal even-handedly with Jehovah's Witnesses and Unitarians. Yet in the school prayer cases Unitarians (speaking generally) succeeded in eliminating all ceremonial prayers from the public schools, while in the flag-salute case Jehovah's Witnesses succeeded only in getting themselves excused from a ceremony that to them was at least as unacceptable and religious in nature as the prayers were to the Unitarians.[1] In fact, the Witnesses regard the flag-salute as the profanation of a religious gesture, a bowing before idols, a Black Mass in the schoolroom. And yet their claim was recognized only to the extent of excusal, exposing them to the repugnant ceremony. Why? Because the prevailing, dominant view of religion classifies the flag-salute as secular, in contravention of the heterodox definition devoutly held by the Witnesses. Neutrality, that is, does not assure equal weight to differing denominational views as to what constitutes a religious practice.[2]

1. *Compare* West Virginia State Bd. of Educ. v. Barnette, 319 U.S. 624 (1943) *with* Abington School Dist. v. Schempp, 374 U.S. 203 (1963).

2. It may be suggested that a conventional definition of religion or religious practice is controlling in applying the non-establishment clause, while a heterodox version is entitled to protection under the free-exercise clause, which safeguards the nonconformist conscience. This analysis is indeed useful, and indicates that the apparent discrepancy in definition is not unprincipled; but from the point of view of an idiosyncratic sect the sense of non-neutrality cannot but remain.

Nor is there any general principle that requires the state to compensate those who out of religious conviction incur a handicap under law. Pupils in public schools may (perhaps must) be excused on their religious holidays; but it scarcely follows that those pupils are not responsible for the work they miss, even if they must resort to the expense of private tutoring. Businesses that close on Saturday as a religious observance and must close on Sunday under the law are disadvantaged materially because of religious faith; but exemption from the Sunday laws is not required.[1] The state requires a certain formal ceremony to render a marriage valid in law, and provides magistrates at public expense who are available to satisfy this requirement. For those couples, however, whose religious faith compels them to hold an ecclesiastical ceremony, additional expense is involved, either to the couple or to their church or both. Must the state therefore compensate the minister or the bridegroom and bride? Would it help their case to insist that no true marriage can be celebrated without churchly blessing and that a ceremony before a judge is anti-religious, a profanation subsidized with public money? Would not the answer be: If your religion prevents you from availing yourself of the public facility and impels you to make a financial sacrifice for the sake of your faith, surely the spirit of religion is the better served by your act.[2]

At this point account must be taken of *Sherbert v. Verner*,[3] which held that eligibility for unemployment benefits cannot be denied to a man who is not willing to accept a job calling for Saturday work, where his refusal is based on religious conviction. Proponents of public aid would generalize this holding to establish the principle that a public benefit (unemployment compensation or subsidized secular education) cannot be withheld where the claimant's ineligibility derives from his pursuit of a religious calling (refraining from work on Saturday or attending parochial school). Several points should be made in response to such a proposition. First, it is entirely too broad, as the *Sherbert* opinion indicates. Suppose the claimant's religious belief required him to abstain from all work, or to work only one day a week, or only in a church. The opinion points out that in the case before them, to recognize the claim would not materially affect the working of the secular program; only two of the more than 150 Seventh Day Adventists in the area had been unable to obtain suitable employment. On this ground the case was distinguished from the question of exemption

1. *See, e.g.*, Gallagher v. Crown Kosher Super Market, 366 U.S. 617 (1961).
2. A realistic appraisal of financial burdens from the standpoint of neutrality would have to take into account tax exemptions for the property of church-related and other private schools, including an inquiry into the correlation between the extent of property holdings by the respective churches and their maintenance of separate schools.
The traditional tax exemption of church-related property is sometimes advanced as a legal argument for subsidies, which are viewed as an economic equivalent. The argument, however, proves too much, since church buildings themselves are exempted, and it would hardly be argued that therefore subsidies for the building of churches would be valid. Moreover, the symbolism of tax exemption is significant as a manifestation that organized religion is not expected to support the state; by the same token the state is not expected to support the church. Psychologically, too, the exemption differs from subsidy; the former is viewed as an entrenched status, the latter as a recurring political issue.
3. 374 U.S. 398 (1963).

from Sunday closing laws.[1] Moreover, the case did not involve subsidy to a religious institution, but dispensation from a general regulatory law or condition. Dispensation granted under the free-exercise clause is quite distinct from disbursement challenged under the non-establishment clause, the very kind of measure that precipitated the historic struggle for religious liberty and disestablishment in Virginia. Finally, the *Sherbert* case at most would relate to a shared time arrangement, that is, to a plan making the public educational program available to those whose religious convictions inhibit them from full-time attendance at a public school. Whether such an arrangement can be maintained without detriment to the concept of a unified school day, like that of a unitary day of rest, would seem to lie in the judgment of those administering the secular program. I do not argue at all that shared time is unconstitutional, but only suggest that it is the limit, under precedent and principle, to which the policy of neutrality carries us; and at present the parochial school authorities do not seem, on their part, to regard it as an acceptable solution.

Their reluctance may stem from a rejection of the premise of separability of education into a religious and a non-religious component. That premise clearly underlies the Court's thinking in *Allen*, and it has been presupposed thus far in this discussion. Ironically, the premise is incompatible with the philosophy that largely fosters the maintenance of parochial schools.[2] They do, to be sure, perform a public function and satisfy state-imposed standards for compulsory education; but, their proponents insist, they do so with a difference that is of central importance for religion. Suppose a state were to require bus transportation of school pupils over long distances and made buses available to all. If a church-related school chose to maintain its own bus in order to conduct religious services during the journey, the secular interest in safety would be satisfied perfectly, and yet a serious question would surely remain whether the transportation could be publicly subsidized.

We turn, then, to this alternative thesis of public aid: that there is a religious element in education that is pervasive, inescapable, and inseparable. This position, in turn, may take either of two forms—that public school education is empty of religious content and therefore not genuine education at all, or that it inculcates a religion of its own, secularism, and hence the parochial schools are entitled to equal support for their brand of religious education.

Consider now each of these positions and its consequences—first, that public school education is not true education. If it is deficient because under the Con-

---

1. *Id.* at 399 n. 2, 408–09.
2. *See, e.g.*, Drinan, *Does State Aid to Church Related Colleges Constitute an Establishment of Religion?—Reflections on the Maryland College Cases*, 1967 UTAH L. REV. 491, 510:

The exclusion of nonsecular ideas and forces from education, even if it were possible, is absurd. Neither the secular nor the sacred is comprehensible if one is isolated from the other; for the state to try to isolate them in its schools is to attempt a task which educators, believers, and nonbelievers must all agree is impossible. . . . The crucial question, therefore, is this: what is the state to do with those individuals and groups whose basic religious convictions forbid them to separate "secular" and "sacred" in education?

A valuable compendium of views on the issue of public aid is THE WALL BETWEEN CHURCH AND STATE 55–116 (D. Oaks ed. 1963).

stitution public schools cannot impart religion (as they cannot provide devotional prayers), then the argument is simply that since by reason of the first amendment the state cannot subsidize religion in common schools, it must by reason of the first amendment subsidize religion in church schools—surely an incongruous result. Or the meaning may be that the public schools are wanting in a religious atmosphere that they could constitutionally create but that they fail to provide. Here the concept of "religious" is being employed in a different and non-constitutional sense, to mean what I have described on another occasion as concern for moral reasoning and a quality of teaching that conveys a sense of reverence for knowledge, humility in the face of the unknown, and awe in the face of the unknowable.[1] To these attributes of an educational process the Constitution sets no barriers, and I earnestly trust that they are embodied in public school teaching, as I am sure they are in the classrooms of the best teachers. But if parents find these attributes lacking, their first recourse is to seek to improve the quality of education offered in their school, or seek a transfer to another school, or move to another district. Failing that, they may be so dissatisfied that they will send their children to a school of better quality outside the public school system, whether it be a private non-church school or a parochial school. But in seeking this superior quality of inspiration they surely lay no basis for a constitutional claim to be reimbursed by the state, any more than in the case of an ecclesiastical wedding. And so I conclude, taking the ambiguous premise that education without religion (whether in the constitutional or non-constitutional sense) is not true education, it by no means follows that education in parochial schools must or may be subsidized by the state.

Now we are ready to consider the alternative view of inseparability—that public school education is itself necessarily religious, but in a perverse sense, as so-called secularism is itself a form of religion, however degraded a form. If a state school worships the Anti-Christ, equal support is due to a school that worships Christ. But we must be careful not to construct a syllogism out of a metaphor of this kind, any more than out of the countervailing metaphor, "wall of separation." To say that Americans worship what William James called the bitch-goddess, Success, is not to assert anything relevant to the usage of "religion" in the first amendment. To say that the absence of Crucifixes or Torahs in a public school is itself a religious statement is either a play on words or an idiosyncratic characterization, like the Jehovah's Witnesses' view of the flag-salute, which is not controlling as a definition of religion. To say that moral training cannot be separated from religious training in a constitutional sense is to contradict the judgment underlying the one reference to religion in the constitutional text prior to the Bill of Rights—that no religious test "shall ever be required" for "any Office or public Trust under the United States."[2] For if good moral character is relevant to holding a position of public trust, and if religious training is essential to sound morality, it would have been reasonable

1. P. Freund & R. Ulich, Religion and the Public Schools 19–22 (1965).
2. U.S. Const. art. VI.

to allow a religious test as at least a presumptive assurance of moral qualification.

Actually the confrontation between so-called secularism and the religion of
parochial schools is not as stark as I have here assumed in order to meet the
proponents of public aid on their own ground. In point of fact most parents who
avail themselves of the public schools are anxious that their children shall
receive religious training, but outside the community of the school, in the home
and the church or in an after-hours church school or a Sunday school. Taking
this into account, the idea of reciprocity or neutrality becomes more complex.
Public aid to parochial schools maintained by Catholics or Lutherans or Orthodox Jews would in some measure benefit the religious mission of these faiths,
because religion, on our present hypothesis, permeates all their instruction. As a
counterpart, the Baptists and other separationists could fairly insist that equalization would require some contribution by the state to their own churches or
Sunday schools which perform the same mission that would be subsidized in
the parochial schools of other denominations. It would be ironic if the Baptist
separationists, who triumphed over the Anglican theocrats in the historic
struggle against establishment in Virginia, should find themselves disadvantaged
in the name of a Constitution that repudiated establishment.

Are there, then, any forms of public aid to parochial schools that should be
sustained? I would enumerate the following, which are general non-religious
state activities that operate in effect to mitigate certain costs borne by parochial
schools or their patrons:

1. General welfare services for children, wherever they may be located,
   including medical examinations and hot lunches.
2. Prizes and awards in general academic competition, usable by the re-
   cipients as they please, like veterans' benefits that constitute deferred
   compensation.
3. Shared time instruction in the public schools, treating participating
   parochial school children as part-time public school children.

Institutions of higher learning present quite a different question, mainly
because church support is less likely to involve indoctrination and conformity at
that level of instruction.

One final observation. In facing the issues that will soon be raised—provision
of textbooks not on loan or not in form requested by pupils, or books of a
character or for use in schools different from the circumstantial presumptions in
the New York case; unconditional grants for specified areas of learning; lump-
sum grants—three courses are open constitutionally: to hold the aid mandatory,
to hold it permissible, and to hold it impermissible. The mandatory result seems
least pre-figured, notwithstanding the local course of the argument from "neutrality." A choice between the permissible and the forbidden is in essence a choice
whether to leave the issue to the political process in each state or locality, or to
defuse the political issue. Ordinarily I am disposed, in grey-area cases of constitutional law, to let the political process function. Even in dealing with basic

guarantees I would eschew a single form of compliance and leave room for different methods of implementation, whether in pre-trial interrogation under the privilege against self-incrimination, or libel of public figures under freedom of the press, or exclusion of evidence under the search and seizure guarantee. The religious guarantees, however, are of a different order. While political debate and division is normally a wholesome process for reaching viable accommodations, political division on religious lines is one of the principal evils that the first amendment sought to forestall. It was healthy when President Kennedy, as a candidate, was able to turn off some of the questions addressed to him on church-state relations by pointing to binding Supreme Court decisions. Although great issues of constitutional law are never settled until they are settled right, still as between open-ended, ongoing political warfare and such binding quality as judicial decisions possess, I would choose the latter in the field of God and Caesar and the public treasury. This basic preference may help to account for what otherwise may seem a too rigid, and not sufficiently permissive, view of constitutional commands.

Cases

A. Freedom of Conscience

**West Virginia State Board of Education et al. v.
Barnette et al.**
Appeal from the District Court of the United States for the
Southern District of West Virginia 319 U.S. 624 (1943)

*MR. JUSTICE JACKSON DELIVERED THE OPINION OF
THE COURT*

Following the decision by this Court on June 3, 1940, in *Minersville School
District* v. *Gobitis*, 310 U. S. 586, the West Virginia legislature amended its
statutes to require all schools therein to conduct courses of instruction in history,
civics, and in the Constitutions of the United States and of the State "for the
purpose of teaching, fostering and perpetuating the ideals, principles and spirit
of Americanism, and increasing the knowledge of the organization and machinery
of the government." Appellant Board of Education was directed, with advice of
the State Superintendent of Schools, to "prescribe the courses of study covering
these subjects" for public schools. The Act made it the duty of private, parochial
and denominational schools to prescribe courses of study "similar to those
required for the public schools."

The Board of Education on January 9, 1942, adopted a resolution containing
recitals taken largely from the Court's *Gobitis* opinion and ordering that the
salute to the flag become "a regular part of the program of activities in the
public schools," that all teachers and pupils "shall be required to participate in
the salute honoring the Nation represented by the Flag; provided, however, that
refusal to salute the Flag be regarded as an act of insubordination, and shall be
dealt with accordingly."

The resolution originally required the "commonly accepted salute to the
Flag" which it defined. Objections to the salute as "being too much like Hitler's"
were raised by the Parent and Teachers Association, the Boy and Girl Scouts, the
Red Cross, and the Federation of Women's Clubs. Some modification appears
to have been made in deference to these objections, but no concession was made
to Jehovah's Witnesses. What is now required is the "stiff-arm" salute, the
saluter to keep the right hand raised with palm turned up while the following is
repeated: "I pledge allegiance to the Flag of the United States of America and to

the Republic for which it stands; one Nation, indivisible, with liberty and justice for all."

Failure to conform is "insubordination" dealt with by expulsion. Readmission is denied by statute until compliance. Meanwhile the expelled child is "unlawfully absent" and may be proceeded against as a delinquent. His parents or guardians are liable to prosecution, and if convicted are subject to fine not exceeding $50 and jail term not exceeding thirty days.

Appellees, citizens of the United States and of West Virginia, brought suit in the United States District Court for themselves and others similarly situated asking its injunction to restrain enforcement of these laws and regulations against Jehovah's Witnesses. The Witnesses are an unincorporated body teaching that the obligation imposed by law of God is superior to that of laws enacted by temporal government. Their religious beliefs include a literal version of Exodus, Chapter 20, verses 4 and 5, which says: "Thou shalt not make unto thee any graven image, or any likeness of anything that is in heaven above, or that is in the earth beneath, or that is in the water under the earth; thou shalt not bow down thyself to them nor serve them." They consider that the flag is an "image" within this command. For this reason they refuse to salute it.

Children of this faith have been expelled from school and are threatened with exclusion for no other cause. Officials threaten to send them to reformatories maintained for criminally inclined juveniles. Parents of such children have been prosecuted and are threatened with prosecutions for causing delinquency.

The Board of Education moved to dismiss the complaint setting forth these facts and alleging that the law and regulations are an unconstitutional denial of religious freedom, and of freedom of speech, and are invalid under the "due process" and "equal protection" clauses of the Fourteenth Amendment to the Federal Constitution. The cause was submitted on the pleadings to a District Court of three judges. It restrained enforcement as to the plaintiffs and those of that class. The Board of Education brought the case here by direct appeal.

This case calls upon us to reconsider a precedent decision, as the Court throughout its history often has been required to do. Before turning to the *Gobitis* case, however, it is desirable to notice certain characteristics by which this controversy is distinguished.

The freedom asserted by these appellees does not bring them into collision with rights asserted by any other individual. It is such conflicts which most frequently require intervention of the State to determine where the rights of one end and those of another begin. But the refusal of these persons to participate in the ceremony does not interfere with or deny rights of others to do so. Nor is there any question in this case that their behavior is peaceable and orderly. The sole conflict is between authority and rights of the individual. The State asserts power to condition access to public education on making a prescribed sign and profession and at the same time to coerce attendance by punishing both parent and child. The latter stand on a right of self-determination in matters that touch individual opinion and personal attitude.

As the present CHIEF JUSTICE said in dissent in the *Gobitis* case, the State may "require teaching by instruction and study of all in our history and in the structure and organization of our government, including the guaranties of civil liberty, which tend to inspire patriotism and love of country." 310 U. S. at 604. Here, however, we are dealing with a compulsion of students to declare a belief. They are not merely made acquainted with the flag salute so that they may be informed as to what it is or even what it means. The issue here is whether this slow and easily neglected route to aroused loyalties constitutionally may be short-cut by substituting a compulsory salute and slogan. This issue is not prejudiced by the Court's previous holding that where a State, without compelling attendance, extends college facilities to pupils who voluntarily enroll, it may prescribe military training as part of the course without offense to the Constitution. It was held that those who take advantage of its opportunities may not on ground of conscience refuse compliance with such conditions. *Hamilton* v. *Regents*, 293 U. S. 245. In the present case attendance is not optional. That case is also to be distinguished from the present one because, independently of college privileges or requirements, the State has power to raise militia and impose the duties of service therein upon its citizens.

There is no doubt that, in connection with the pledges, the flag salute is a form of utterance. Symbolism is a primitive but effective way of communicating ideas. The use of an emblem or flag to symbolize some system, idea, institution, or personality, is a short cut from mind to mind. Causes and nations, political parties, lodges and ecclesiastical groups seek to knit the loyalty of their followings to a flag or banner, a color or design. The State announces rank, function, and authority through crowns and maces, uniforms and black robes; the church speaks through the Cross, the Crucifix, the altar and shrine, and clerical raiment. Symbols of State often convey political ideas just as religious symbols come to convey theological ones. Associated with many of these symbols are appropriate gestures of acceptance or respect: a salute, a bowed or bared head, a bended knee. A person gets from a symbol the meaning he puts into it, and what is one man's comfort and inspiration is another's jest and scorn. . . .

Objection to this form of communication when coerced is an old one, well known to the framers of the Bill of Rights.

It is also to be noted that the compulsory flag salute and pledge requires affirmation of a belief and an attitude of mind. It is not clear whether the regulation contemplates that pupils forego any contrary convictions of their own and become unwilling converts to the prescribed ceremony or whether it will be acceptable if they simulate assent by words without belief and by a gesture barren of meaning. It is now a commonplace that censorship or suppression of expression of opinion is tolerated by our Constitution only when the expression presents a clear and present danger of action of a kind the State is empowered to prevent and punish. It would seem that involuntary affirmation could be commanded only on even more immediate and urgent grounds than silence. But here the power of compulsion is invoked without any allegation that remaining passive during a flag salute ritual creates a clear and present danger that would justify an effort even to muffle expression. To sustain the compulsory flag salute we are required to say that a Bill of Rights which guards the individual's right to speak his own mind, left it open to public authorities to compel him to utter what is not in his mind.

Whether the First Amendment to the Constitution will permit officials to order observance of ritual of this nature does not depend upon whether as a voluntary exercise we would think it to be good, bad or merely innocuous. Any credo of nationalism is likely to include what some disapprove or to omit what others think essential, and to give off different overtones as it takes on different accents or interpretations. If official power exists to coerce acceptance of any patriotic creed, what it shall contain cannot be decided by courts, but must be largely discretionary with the ordaining authority, whose power to prescribe would no doubt include power to amend. Hence validity of the asserted power to force an American citizen publicly to profess any statement of belief or to engage in any ceremony of assent to one, presents questions of power that must be considered independently of any idea we may have as to the utility of the ceremony in question.

Nor does the issue as we see it turn on one's possession of particular religious views or the sincerity with which they are held. While religion supplies appellees' motive for enduring the discomforts of making the issue in this case, many citizens who do not share these religious views hold such a compulsory rite to infringe constitutional liberty of the individual. It is not necessary to inquire whether non-conformist beliefs will exempt from the duty to salute unless we first find power to make the salute a legal duty.

The *Gobitis* decision, however, *assumed*, as did the argument in that case and in this, that power exists in the State to impose the flag salute discipline upon school children in general. The Court only examined and rejected a claim based on religious beliefs of immunity from an unquestioned general rule. The question which underlies the flag salute controversy is whether such a ceremony so touching matters of opinion and political attitude may be imposed upon the individual by official authority under powers committed to any political organization under our Constitution. We examine rather than assume existence of this power and, against this broader definition of issues in this case, reexamine specific grounds assigned for the *Gobitis* decision. . . .

Government of limited power need not be anemic government. Assurance that rights are secure tends to diminish fear and jealousy of strong government, and by making us feel safe to live under it makes for its better support. Without promise of a limiting Bill of Rights it is doubtful if our Constitution could have mustered enough strength to enable its ratification. To enforce those rights today is not to choose weak government over strong government. It is only to adhere as a means of strength to individual freedom of mind in preference to officially disciplined uniformity for which history indicates a disappointing and disastrous end.

The subject now before us exemplifies this principle. Free public education, if faithful to the ideal of secular instruction and political neutrality, will not be partisan or enemy of any class, creed, party, or faction. If it is to impose any ideological discipline, however, each party or denomination must seek to control, or failing that, to weaken the influence of the educational system. Observance of the limitations of the Constitution will not weaken government in the field appropriate for its exercise. . . .

The Fourteenth Amendment, as now applied to the States, protects the citizen against the State itself and all of its creatures—Boards of Education not excepted. These have, of course, important, delicate, and highly discretionary functions, but none that they may not perform within the limits of the Bill of Rights. That they are educating the young for citizenship is reason for scrupulous protection of Constitutional freedoms of the individual, if we are not to strangle the free mind at its source and teach youth to discount important principles of our government as mere platitudes.

Such Boards are numerous and their territorial jurisdiction often small. But small and local authority may feel less sense of responsibility to the Constitution, and agencies of publicity may be less vigilant in calling it to account. The action of Congress in making flag observance voluntary and respecting the conscience of the objector in a matter so vital as raising the Army contrasts sharply with these local regulations in matters relatively trivial to the welfare of the nation. There are village tyrants as well as village Hampdens, but none who acts under color of law is beyond reach of the Constitution. . . .

The *Gobitis* opinion reasoned that this is a field "where courts possess no marked and certainly no controlling competence," that it is committed to the legislatures as well as the courts to guard cherished liberties and that it is constitutionally appropriate to "fight out the wise use of legislative authority in the forum of public opinion and before legislative assemblies rather than to transfer such a contest to the judicial arena," since all the "effective means of inducing political changes are left free." *Id*. at 597–598, 600.

The very purpose of a Bill of Rights was to withdraw certain subjects from the vicissitudes of political controversy, to place them beyond the reach of majorities and officials and to establish them as legal principles to be applied by the courts. One's right to life, liberty, and property, to free speech, a free press, freedom of worship and assembly, and other fundamental rights may not be submitted to vote; they depend on the outcome of no elections.

In weighing arguments of the parties it is important to distinguish between the due process clause of the Fourteenth Amendment as an instrument for transmitting the principles of the First Amendment and those cases in which it is applied for its own sake. The test of legislation which collides with the Fourteenth Amendment, because it also collides with the principles of the First, is much more definite than the test when only the Fourteenth is involved. Much of the vagueness of the due process clause disappears when the specific prohibitions of the First become its standard. The right of a State to regulate, for example, a public utility may well include, so far as the due process test is concerned, power to impose all of the restrictions which a legislature may have a "rational basis" for adopting. But freedoms of speech and of press, of assembly, and of worship may not be infringed on such slender grounds. They are susceptible of restriction only to prevent grave and immediate danger to interests which the State may lawfully protect. It is important to note that while it is the Fourteenth Amendment which bears directly upon the State it is the more specific limiting principles of the First Amendment that finally govern this case. . . .

Lastly, and this is the very heart of the *Gobitis* opinion, it reasons that "National unity is the basis of national security," that the authorities have "the right to select appropriate means for its attainment," and hence reaches the conclusion that such compulsory measures toward "national unity" are constitutional.

Upon the verity of this assumption depends our answer in this case.

National unity as an end which officials may foster by persuasion and example is not in question. The problem is whether under our Constitution compulsion as here employed is a permissible means for its achievement.

Struggles to coerce uniformity of sentiment in support of some end thought essential to their time and country have been waged by many good as well as by evil men. Nationalism is a relative recent phenomenon but at other times and places the ends have been racial or territorial security, support of a dynasty or regime, and particular plans for saving souls. As first and moderate methods to attain unity have failed, those bent on its accomplishment must resort to an ever-increasing severity. As governmental pressure toward unity becomes greater, so strife becomes more bitter as to whose unity it shall be. Probably no deeper division of our people could proceed from any provocation than from finding it necessary to choose what doctrine and whose program public educational officials shall compel youth to unite in embracing. Ultimate futility of such attempts to compel coherence is the lesson of every such effort from the Roman drive to stamp out Christianity as a disturber of its pagan unity, the Inquisition, as a means to religious and dynastic unity, the Siberian exiles as a means to Russian unity, down to the fast failing efforts of our present totalitarian enemies. Those who begin coercive elimination of dissent soon find themselves exterminating dissenters. Compulsory unification of opinion achieves only the unanimity of the graveyard.

It seems trite but necessary to say that the First Amendment to our Constitution was designed to avoid these ends by avoiding these beginnings. There is no mysticism in the American concept of the State or of the nature or origin of its authority. We set up government by consent of the governed, and the Bill of Rights denies those in power any legal opportunity to coerce that consent. Authority here is to be controlled by public opinion, not public opinion by authority.

The case is made difficult not because the principles of its decision are obscure but because the flag involved is our own. Nevertheless, we apply the limitations of the Constitution with no fear that freedom to be intellectually and spiritually diverse or even contrary will disintegrate the social organization. To believe that patriotism will not flourish if patriotic ceremonies are voluntary and spontaneous instead of a compulsory routine is to make an unflattering estimate of the appeal of our institutions to free minds. We can have intellectual individualism and the rich cultural diversities that we owe to exceptional minds only at the price of occasional eccentricity and abnormal attitudes. When they are so harmless to others or to the State as those we deal with here, the price is not too great. But freedom to differ is not limited to things that do not matter much. That would be a mere shadow of freedom. The test of its substance is the right to differ as to things that touch the heart of the existing order.

If there is any fixed star in our constitutional constellation, it is that no official, high or petty, can prescribe what shall be orthodox in politics, nationalism, religion, or other matters of opinion or force citizens to confess by word or act their faith therein. If there are any circumstances which permit an exception, they do not now occur to us.

We think the action of the local authorities in compelling the flag salute and pledge transcends constitutional limitations on their power and invades the sphere of intellect and spirit which it is the purpose of the First Amendment to our Constitution to reserve from all official control.

The decision of this Court in *Minersville School District* v. *Gobitis* and the holdings of those few *per curiam* decisions which preceded and foreshadowed it are over-ruled, and the judgment enjoining enforcement of the West Virginia Regulation is affirmed.

B. Released Time

Illinois ex rel. McCollum v. Board of Education of School District No. 71, Champaign County, Illinois, et al.
33 U.S. 203 (1948)
Appeal from the Supreme Court of Illinois

MR. JUSTICE BLACK DELIVERED THE OPINION OF THE COURT

This case relates to the power of a state to utilize its tax-supported public school system in aid of religious instruction insofar as that power may be restricted by the First and Fourteenth Amendments to the Federal Constitution.

The appellant, Vashti McCollum, began this action for mandamus against the Champaign Board of Education in the Circuit Court of Champaign County, Illinois. Her asserted interest was that of a resident and taxpayer of Champaign and of a parent whose child was then enrolled in the Champaign public schools. Illinois has a compulsory education law, which, with exceptions, requires parents to send their children, aged seven to sixteen, to its tax-supported public schools where the children are to remain in attendance during the hours when the schools are regularly in session. Parents who violate this law commit a misdemeanor punishable by fine unless the children attend private or parochial schools which meet educational standards fixed by the State. District boards of education are given general supervisory powers over the use of the public school buildings within the school districts. Ill. Rev. Stat. ch. 122, §§ 123, 301 (1943).

Appellant's petition for mandamus alleged that religious teachers, employed by private religious groups, were permitted to come weekly into the school buildings during the regular hours set apart for secular teaching, and then and there for a period of thirty minutes substitute their religious teaching for the secular education provided under the compulsory education law. The petitioner charged that this joint public-school religious-group program violated the First and Fourteenth Amendments to the United States Constitution. The prayer of her petition was that the Board of Education be ordered to "adopt and enforce rules and regulations prohibiting all instruction in and teaching of religious education in all public schools in Champaign School District Number 71, . . . and in all public school houses and buildings in said district when occupied by public schools."

The board first moved to dismiss the petition on the ground that under Illinois law appellant had no standing to maintain the action. This motion was denied. An answer was then filed, which admitted that regular weekly religious instruction was given during school hours to those pupils whose parents consented and that those pupils were released temporarily from their regular secular classes for the limited purpose of attending the religious classes. The answer denied that this coordinated program of religious instruction violated the State or Federal Constitution. Much evidence was heard, findings of fact were made, after which the petition for mandamus was denied on the ground that the school's religious instruction program violated neither the federal nor state constitutional provisions invoked by the appellant. On appeal the State Supreme Court affirmed. 396 Ill. 14. 71 N. E. 2d 161. Appellant appealed to this Court under 28 U. S. C. § 344 (a), and we noted probable jurisdiction on June 2, 1947.

The appellees press a motion to dismiss the appeal on several grounds, the first of which is that the judgment of the State Supreme Court does not draw in question the "validity of a statute of any State" as required by 28 U. S. C. § 344 (a). This contention rests on the admitted fact that the challenged program of religious instruction was not expressly authorized by statute. But the State Supreme Court has sustained the validity of the program on the ground that the Illinois statutes granted the board authority to establish such a program. This holding is sufficient to show that the validity of an Illinois statute was drawn in question within the meaning of 28 U. S. C. § 344 (a). *Hamilton* v. *Regents of U. of Cal.*, 293 U. S. 245, 258. A second ground for the motion to dismiss is that the appellant lacks standing to maintain the action, a ground which is also without merit. *Coleman* v. *Miller*, 307 U. S. 433, 443, 445, 466. A third ground for the motion is that the appellant failed properly to present in the State Supreme Court her challenge that the state program violated the Federal Constitution. But in view of the express rulings of both state courts on this question, the argument cannot be successfully maintained. The motion to dismiss the appeal is denied.

Although there are disputes between the parties as to various inferences that may or may not properly be drawn from the evidence concerning the religious program, the following facts are shown by the record without dispute. In 1940 interested members of the Jewish, Roman Catholic, and a few of the Protestant faiths formed a voluntary association called the Champaign Council on Religious Education. They obtained permission from the Board of Education to offer classes in religious instruction to public school pupils in grades four to nine inclusive. Classes were made up of pupils whose parents signed printed cards requesting that their children be permitted to attend; they were held weekly, thirty minutes for the lower grades, forty-five minutes for the higher. The council employed the religious teachers at no expense to the school authorities, but the instructors were subject to the approval and supervision of the superintendent of schools. The classes were taught in three separate religious groups by Protestant teachers, Catholic priests, and a Jewish rabbi, although for the past several years there have apparently been no classes instructed in the Jewish religion. Classes were conducted in the regular classrooms of the school building. Students who did not choose to take the religious instruction were not released from public school duties; they were required to leave their classrooms and go to some other place in the school building for pursuit of their secular studies. On the other hand, students who were released from secular study for the religious instructions were required to be present at the religious classes. Reports of their presence or absence were to be made to their secular teachers.

The foregoing facts without reference to others that appear in the record, show the use of tax-supported property for religious instruction and the close cooperation between the school authorities and the religious council in promoting religious education. The operation of the State's compulsory education system thus assists and is integrated with the program of religious instruction carried on by separate religious sects. Pupils compelled by law to go to school for secular education are released in part from their legal duty upon the condition that they attend the religious classes. This is beyond all question a utilization of the tax-established and tax-supported public school system to aid religious groups to spread their faith. And it falls squarely under the ban of the First Amendment (made applicable to the States by the Fourteenth) as we interpreted it in *Everson* v. *Board of Education*, 330 U. S. 1. There we said: "Neither a state nor the Federal Government can set up a church. Neither can pass laws which aid one religion, aid all religions, or prefer one religion over another. Neither can force or influence a person to go to or to remain away from church against his will or force him to profess a belief or disbelief in any religion. No person can be punished for entertaining or professing religious beliefs or disbeliefs, for church attendance or non-attendance. No tax in any amount, large or small, can be levied to support any religious activities or institutions whatever they may be called, or whatever form they may adopt to teach or practice religion. Neither a state nor the Federal Government can, openly or secretly, participate in the affairs of any religious organizations or groups and *vice versa*. In the words of Jefferson, the clause against establishment of religion by law was intended to erect 'a wall of separation between church and State.' " *Id.* at 15–16. The majority in the *Everson* case, and the minority as shown by quotations from the dissenting views in our notes 6 and 7, agreed that the First Amendment's language, properly interpreted, had erected a wall of separation between Church and State. They disagreed as to the facts shown by the record and as to the proper application of the First Amendment's language to those facts. . . .

To hold that a state cannot consistently with the First and Fourteenth Amendments utilize its public school system to aid any or all religious faiths or sects in the dissemination of their doctrines and ideals does not, as counsel urge, manifest a governmental hostility to religion or religious teachings. A manifestation of such hostility would be at war with our national tradition as embodied in the First Amendment's guaranty of the free exercise of religion. For the First Amendment rests upon the premise that both religion and government can best work to achieve their lofty aims if each is left free from the other within its respective sphere. Or, as we said in the *Everson* case, the First Amendment has erected a wall between Church and State which must be kept high and impregnable.

Here not only are the State's tax-supported public school buildings used for the dissemination of religious doctrines. The State also affords sectarian groups an invaluable aid in that it helps to provide pupils for their religious classes through use of the State's compulsory public school machinery. This is not separation of Church and State.

The cause is reversed and remanded to the State Supreme Court for proceedings not inconsistent with this opinion.

Reversed and remanded.

Mr. Justice Frankfurter concurred in a separate opinion in which Mr. Justice Jackson, Mr. Justice Rutledge, and Mr. Justice Burton joined.

Mr. Justice Reed dissented.

**Tessim Zorach and Esta Gluck, Appellants, v.
Andrew G. Clauson, Jr., Maximilian Moss, Anthony
Campagna, Harold C. Dean, George A. Timone and
James Marshall, Constituting the Board of Education
of the City of New York, et al.**
(343 US 306, 96 L ed 954, 72 S Ct 679) (1952)

*MR. JUSTICE DOUGLAS DELIVERED THE OPINION OF
THE COURT*

New York City has a program which permits its public schools to release
students during the school day so that they may leave the school buildings and
school grounds and go to religious centers for religious instruction or devotional
exercises. A student is released on written request of his parents. Those not
released stay in the classrooms. The churches make weekly reports to the schools,
sending a list of children who have been released from public school but who have
not reported for religious instruction.

This "released time" program involves neither religious instruction in public
school classrooms nor the expenditure of public funds. All costs, including the
application blanks, are paid by the religious organizations. The case is therefore
unlike Illinois ex rel. McCollum v. Board of Education, 333 US 203, 92 L ed
648, 68 S Ct 461, 2 ALR2d 1338, which involved a "released time" program from
Illinois. In that case the classrooms were turned over to religious instructors.
We accordingly held that the program violated the First Amendment which (by
reason of the Fourteenth Amendment) prohibits the states from establishing
religion or prohibiting its free exercise.

Appellants, who are taxpayers and residents of New York City and whose
children attend its public schools, challenge the present law, contending it is in
essence not different from the one involved in the McCollum Case. Their
argument, stated elaborately in various ways, reduces itself to this: the weight and
influence of the school is put behind a program for religious instruction; public
school teachers police it, keeping tab on students who are released; the classroom activities come to a halt while the students who are released for religious
instruction are on leave; the school is a crutch on which the churches are leaning
for support in their religious training; without the cooperation of the schools this
"released time" program, like the one in the McCollum Case, would be futile and
ineffective. The New York Court of Appeals sustained the law against this claim
of unconstitutionality. 303 NY 161, 100 NE2d 463. The case is here on appeal.
28 USC § 1257 (2).

The briefs and arguments are replete with data bearing on the merits of this
type of "released time" program. Views pro and con are expressed, based on
practical experience with these programs and with their implications. We do not
stop to summarize these materials nor to burden the opinion with an analysis of

them. For they involve considerations not germane to the narrow constitutional issue presented. They largely concern the wisdom of the system, its efficiency from an educational point of view, and the political considerations which have motivated its adoption or rejection in some communities. Those matters are of no concern here, since our problem reduces itself to whether New York by this system has either prohibited the "free exercise" of religion or has made a law "respecting an establishment of religion" within the meaning of the First Amendment.

It takes obtuse reasoning to inject any issue of the "free exercise" of religion into the present case. No one is forced to go to the religious classroom and no religious exercise or instruction is brought to the classrooms of the public schools. A student need not take religious instruction. He is left to his own desires as to the manner or time of his religious devotions, if any.

There is a suggestion that the system involves the use of coercion to get public school students into religious classrooms. There is no evidence in the record before us that supports that conclusion. The present record indeed tells us that the school authorities are neutral in this regard and do no more than release students whose parents so request. If in fact coercion were used, if it were established that any one or more teachers were using their office to persuade or force students to take the religious instruction, a wholly different case would be presented. Hence we put aside that claim of coercion both as respects the "free exercise" of religion and "an establishment of religion" within the meaning of the First Amendment.

Moreover, apart from that claim of coercion, we do not see how New York by this type of "released time" program has made a law respecting an establishment of religion within the meaning of the First Amendment. There is much talk of the separation of Church and State in the history of the Bill of Rights and in the decisions clustering around the First Amendment. See Everson v. Board of Education, 330 US 1, 91 L ed 711, 67 S Ct 504, 168 ALR 1392; Illinois ex rel. McCollum v. Board of Education (US) supra. There cannot be the slightest doubt that the First Amendment reflects the philosophy that Church and State should be separated. And so far as interference with the "free exercise" of religion and an "establishment" of religion are concerned, the separation must be complete and unequivocal. The First Amendment within the scope of its coverage permits no exception; the prohibition is absolute. The First Amendment, however, does not say that in every and all respects there shall be a separation of Church and State. Rather, it studiously defines the manner, the specific ways, in which there shall be no concert or union or dependency one on the other. That is the common sense of the matter. Otherwise, the state and religion would be aliens to each other—hostile, suspicious, and even unfriendly. Churches could not be required to pay even property taxes. Municipalities would not be permitted to render police or fire protection to religious groups. Policemen who helped parishioners into their places of worship would violate the Constitution. Prayers in our legislative halls; the appeals to the Almighty in the messages of the

Chief Executive; the proclamations making Thanksgiving Day a holiday; "so help me God" in our courtroom oaths—these and all other references to the Almighty that run through our laws, our public rituals, our ceremonies would be flouting the First Amendment. A fastidious atheist or agnostic could even object to the supplication with which the Court opens each session: "God save the United States and this Honorable Court."

We would have to press the concept of separation of Church and State to these extremes to condemn the present law on constitutional grounds. The nullification of this law would have wide and profound effects. A Catholic student applies to his teacher for permission to leave the school during hours on a Holy Day of Obligation to attend a mass. A Jewish student asks his teacher for permission to be excused for Yom Kippur. A Protestant wants the afternoon off for a family baptismal ceremony. In each case the teacher requires parental consent in writing. In each case the teacher, in order to make sure the student is not a truant, goes further and requires a report from the priest, the rabbi, or the minister. The teacher in other words cooperates in a religious program to the extent of making it possible for her students to participate in it. Whether she does it occasionally for a few students, regularly for one, or pursuant to a systematized program designed to further the religious needs of all the students does not alter the character of the act.

We are a religious people whose institutions presuppose a Supreme Being. We guarantee the freedom to worship as one chooses. We make room for as wide a variety of beliefs and creeds as the spiritual needs of man deem necessary. We sponsor an attitude on the part of government that shows no partiality to any one group and that lets each flourish according to the zeal of its adherents and the appeal of its dogma. When the state encourages religious instruction or co-operates with religious authorities by adjusting the schedule of public events to sectarian needs, it follows the best of our traditions. For it then respects the religious nature of our people and accommodates the public service to their spiritual needs. To hold that it may not would be to find in the Constitution a requirement that the government show a callous indifference to religious groups. That would be preferring those who believe in no religion over those who do believe. Government may not finance religious groups nor undertake religious instruction nor blend secular and sectarian education nor use secular institutions to force one or some religion on any person. But we find no constitutional re-quirement which makes it necessary for government to be hostile to religion and to throw its weight against efforts to widen the effective scope of religious influence. The government must be neutral when it comes to competition between sects. It may not thrust any sect on any person. It may not make a religious observance compulsory. It may not coerce anyone to attend church, to observe a religious holiday, or to take religious instruction. But it can close its doors or suspend its operations as to those who want to repair to their religious sanctuary for worship or instruction. No more than that is undertaken here.

This program may be unwise and improvident from an educational or a community viewpoint. That appeal is made to us on a theory, previously advanced, that each case must be decided on the basis of "our own prepossessions." See Illinois ex rel. McCollum v. Board of Education, supra (333 US p. 238, 92 L ed 672, 68 S Ct 461, 2 ALR2d 1338). Our individual preferences, however, are not the constitutional standard. The constitutional standard is the separation of Church and State. The problem, like many problems in constitutional law, is one of degree. See Illinois ex rel. McCollum v. Board of Education, supra (333 US p 231, 92 L ed 669, 68 S Ct 461, 2 ALR2d 1338).

In the McCollum Case the classrooms were used for religious instruction and the force of the public school was used to promote that instruction. Here, as we have said, the public schools do no more than accommodate their schedules to a program of outside religious instruction. We follow the McCollum Case. But we cannot expand it to cover the present released time program unless separation of Church and State means that public institutions can make no adjustments of their schedules to accommodate the religious needs of the people. We cannot read into the Bill of Rights such a philosophy of hostility to religion.

Affirmed.

MR. JUSTICE BLACK, DISSENTING

Illinois ex rel. McCollum v. Board of Education, 333 US 203, 92 L ed 648, 68 S Ct 461, 2 ALR2d 1338, held invalid as an "establishment of religion" an Illinois system under which school children, compelled by law to go to public schools, were freed from some hours of required school work on condition that they attend special religious classes held in the school buildings. Although the classes were taught by sectarian teachers neither employed nor paid by the state, the state did use its power to further the program by releasing some of the children from regular class work, insisting that those released attend the religious classes, and requiring that those who remained behind do some kind of academic work while the others received their religious training. We said this about the Illinois system:

Pupils compelled by law to go to school for secular education are released in part from their legal duty upon the condition that they attend the religious classes. This is beyond all question a utilization of the tax-established and tax-supported public school system to aid religious groups to spread their faith. And it falls squarely under the ban of the First Amendment. . . . Illinois ex rel. McCollum v. Board of Education, supra (333 US at pp 209, 210, 92 L ed 657, 658, 68 S Ct 461, 2 ALR2d 1338).

I see no significant difference between the invalid Illinois system and that of New York here sustained. Except for the use of the school buildings in Illinois, there is no difference between the systems which I consider even worthy of mention. In the New York program, as in that of Illinois, the school authorities release some of the children on the condition that they attend the religious classes, get reports on whether they attend, and hold the other children in the school building until the religious hour is over. As we attempted to make categorically clear, the McCollum decision would have been the same if the religious classes had not been held in the school buildings. We said:

Here *not only* are the State's tax-supported public school buildings used for the dissemination of religious doctrines. The State *also* affords sectarian groups an invaluable aid in that it helps to provide pupils for their religious classes through the use of the State's compulsory public school machinery. *This* is not separation of Church and State. (Emphasis supplied.) Illinois ex rel. McCollum v. Board of Education, supra (333 US at p 212, 92 L ed 659, 68 S Ct 461, 2 ALR2d 1338).

McCollum thus held that Illinois could not constitutionally manipulate the compelled classroom hours of its compulsory school machinery so as to channel children into sectarian classes. Yet that is exactly what the Court holds New York can do.

I am aware that our McCollum decision on separation of Church and State has been subjected to a most searching examination throughout the country. Probably few opinions from this Court in recent years have attracted more attention or stirred wider debate. Our insistence on "a wall between Church and State which must be kept high and impregnable" has seemed to some a correct exposition of the philosophy and a true interpretation of the language of the First Amendment to which we should strictly adhere. With equal conviction and sincerity, others have thought the McCollum decision fundamentally wrong and have pledged continuous warfare against it. The opinions in the court these diverse viewpoints. In dissenting today, I mean to do more than give routine approval to our McCollum decision. I mean also to reaffirm my faith in the fundamental philosophy expressed in McCollum and Everson v. Board of Education, 330 US 1, 91 L ed 711, 67 S Ct 504, 168 ALR 1392. That reaffirmance can be brief because of the exhaustive opinions in those recent cases.

Difficulty of decision in the hypothetical situations mentioned by the Court, but not now before us, should not confuse the issues in this case. Here the sole question is whether New York can use its compulsory education laws to help religious sects get attendants presumably too unenthusiastic to go unless moved to do so by the pressure of this state machinery. That this is the plan, purpose, design and consequence of the New York program cannot be denied. The state thus makes religious sects beneficiaries of its power to compel children to attend secular schools. Any use of such coercive power by the state to help or hinder some religious sects or to prefer all religious sects over nonbelievers or vice versa is just what I think the First Amendment forbids. In considering whether a state has entered this forbidden field the question is not whether it has entered too far but whether it has entered at all. New York is manipulating its compulsory education laws to help religious sects get pupils. This is not separation but combination of Church and State.

The Court's validation of the New York system rests in part on its statement that Americans are "a religious people whose institutions presuppose a Supreme Being." This was at least as true when the First Amendment was adopted; and it was just as true when eight justices of this Court invalidated the released time system in McCollum on the premise that a state can no more "aid all religions" than it can aid one. It was precisely because Eighteenth Century Americans were a religious people divided into many fighting sects that we were given the constitutional mandate to keep Church and State completely separate. Colonial history had already shown that, here as elsewhere, zealous sectarians entrusted with governmental power to further their causes would sometimes torture, maim and kill those they branded "heretics," "atheists" or "agnostics." The First Amendment was therefore to insure that no one powerful sect or combination of sects could use political or governmental power to punish dissenters whom they could not convert to their faith. Now as then, it is only by wholly isolating the state from the religious sphere and compelling it to be completely neutral, that the freedom of each and every denomination and of all nonbelievers can be maintained. It is this neutrality the Court abandons today when it treats New York's coercive system as a program which *merely* "encourages religious instruction or cooperates with religious authorities." The abandonment is all the more dangerous to liberty because of the Court's legal exaltation of the orthodox and its derogation of unbelievers.

Under our system of religious freedom, people have gone to their religious sanctuaries not because they feared the law but because they loved their God. The choice of all has been as free as the choice of those who answered the call to worship moved only by the music of the old Sunday morning church bells. The spiritual mind of man has thus been free to believe, disbelieve, or doubt, without repression, great or small, by the heavy hand of government. Statutes authorizing such repression have been stricken. Before today, our judicial opinions have refrained from drawing invidious distinctions between those who believe in no religion and those who do believe. The First Amendment has lost much if the religious follower and the atheist are no longer to be judicially regarded as entitled to equal justice under law.

State help to religion injects political and party prejudices into a holy field. It too often substitutes force for prayer, hate for love, and persecution for persuasion. Government should not be allowed, under cover of the soft euphemism of "co-operation," to steal into the sacred area of religious choice.

Mr. Justice Frankfurter, dissenting. . . .

C. Shared Time

Marie Morton, et al., Plaintiffs-Appellants, v. Board
of Education of the City of Chicago, et al.,
Defendants-Appellees
69 Ill App. 2d 38
First District, Second Division February 18, 1966

*MR. JUSTICE BURKE DELIVERED THE OPINION OF THE
COURT*

This appeal is taken from a decree dismissing with prejudice plaintiffs' complaint
for an injunction to restrain the defendants from maintaining an experimental
dual enrollment program (commonly known as the shared-time plan) created by
a resolution of the Board of Education of the City of Chicago on April 23, 1964,
and implemented by a report of the General Superintendent of Chicago Public
Schools on April 29, 1965.

The 1964 resolution provides that students residing within the Kinzie High
School attendance area who are otherwise eligible for full-time enrollment at that
High School may attend the Kinzie High School on a part-time basis during the
period of the experiment, beginning in September of 1965 and ending in June of
1969. The resolution provides that participation in the program may be effected
only upon application in writing by the students' parents or legal guardians and
that the participating students at all times during the duration of the experiment
must fully comply with the compulsory attendance laws of Illinois. The resolution
further provides that the General Superintendent of Public Schools shall request
various private schools within the City of Chicago having students residing in the
Kinzie High School attendance area to cooperate in the experiment, for the
purpose of determining whether the dual enrollment plan is in the best interests
of the Chicago public school children and the public school system. In August
of 1964, the name of the Kinzie High School was changed to the "John F.
Kennedy High School," and shall hereinafter be referred to by the latter name.

The General Superintendent's 1965 report described the progress of the
implementation in connection with the Kennedy High School and set out the
standards to be met by the students enrolled in the program as a condition to
continued participation. The report also set out preliminary steps taken in connection with the initiation of a similar plan at the Taft High School. The 1965
progress report was approved and adopted by the Board of Education in May of
1965.

The Kennedy dual enrollment plan went into effect in September of 1965.
The students enrolled in the program took all courses at the Kennedy High

School except English, Social Studies, Music and Art, which courses were taken at the nearby St. Paul High School. Credit towards a Chicago Public High School diploma is given for the courses which are taken at the St. Paul High School.

Plaintiffs' complaint, filed in May of 1964, sought to enjoin the Board of Education from maintaining the dual enrollment program on the grounds that the program violated statutory and constitutional provisions. The complaint also sought to enjoin the Board of Education from permitting the construction of the Kennedy High School building which was then in the process of construction, but this matter had become moot by the time the hearing was had on the complaint in June of 1965, for the reason that the building had been erected and was then in use.

The legality of the dual enrollment program was challenged on the ground that it permits the parents or legal guardians of the participating students to violate the compulsory attendance laws of Illinois, set out in sections 26–1 and 26–2 of the 1961 School Code. Ill Rev Stats 1963, chap 122, pars 26–1 and 26–2. The complaint also challenged the constitutionality of the program on the ground that it violates article VIII, sections 1 and 3 of the Illinois Constitution, as well as the First Amendment to the United States Constitution, with respect to the establishment and/or maintenance of religion. Ill Const, art VIII, secs 1 and 3; US Const, 1st Amend. After considerable oral argument by counsel for the respective parties concerning both of the alleged violations, the trial court found that the dual enrollment plan does not violate either the statutory or the constitutional provisions, and ordered that the complaint be dismissed with prejudice.

Undoubtedly, the Chicago School Board has the power to create and maintain experimental education programs for the Chicago public school children. Section 34–18 of the 1961 School Code specifies the powers of the school boards and states that the "specifications of the powers herein granted are not to be construed as exclusive, but the board shall also exercise all other powers that may be requisite or proper for the maintenance and the development of a public school system, not inconsistent with the provisions" of the School Code. Ill Rev Stats 1963, chap 122, par 34–18. We cannot find any intention on the part of the legislature to limit the power of a school board to adopt and develop better methods of educating the children of this State, so long as the methods so adopted are otherwise consistent with the provisions of the School Code.

Section 26–1 of the School Code compels school attendance of all children in this State between the ages of 7 and 16 years. It provides:

Whoever has custody or control of any child between the ages of 7 and 16 years shall cause such child to attend some public school in the district wherein the child resides the entire time it is in session during the regular school term; Provided, that the following children shall not be required to attend the public schools:

1. Any child attending a private or a parochial school where children are taught the branches of education taught to children of corresponding age and grade in the public schools, and where the instruction of the child in the branches of education is in the English language;

2. Any child who is physically or mentally unable to attend school, such disability being certified to the county or district truant officer by a competent physician; or who is excused for temporary absence for cause by the principal or teacher of the school which the child attends;

3. Any child necessarily and lawfully employed according to the provisions of the law regulating child labor may be excused from attendance at a school by the county superintendent of schools or the superintendent of the public school which the child should be attending, on certification of the facts by and the recommendation of the school board of the public school district in which the child resides. In districts having part-time continuation schools, children so excused shall attend such schools at least 8 hours each week;

4. Any child over 12 and under 14 years of age while in attendance at confirmation classes. Ill Rev Stats 1963, chap 122, par 26–1.

Section 26–2 relates to children under the age of 7 and over the age of 16, but only if they are enrolled in a public school. It provides:

Any person having custody or control of a child who is below the age of 7 years or above the age of 16 years and who is enrolled in any of grades 1 through 12, in the public school shall cause him to attend the public school in the district wherein he resides when it is in session during the regular school term unless he is excused under paragraphs 2, 3, or 4 of Section 26–1. Ill Rev Stats 1963, chap 122, par 26–2.

Section 26–1 requires the education of all children of this State, without regard to the place of education. Section 26–2, on the other hand, appears to be an administrative measure designed to prevent problems from arising in the maintenance of attendance and credit records of those children under 7 years and over 16 years who, by reason of their ages, are not compelled to attend school under section 26–1, but who are nevertheless enrolled in a public school. Significantly, section 26–2 does not apply to children enrolled in nonpublic schools, indicating the legislature intended such children to be governed by the regulations of the particular nonpublic school administrations wherein such children are enrolled.

The dual enrollment program does not violate section 26–1 of the School Code. Any child within the ages of 7 and 16 years is required "to attend some public school in the district wherein the child resides the entire time it is in session during the regular school term" unless the child falls within one of the four exceptions. In the event that the child does come within one of the exceptions it is not necessary that he "attend some public school in the district wherein [he] resides *the entire time* it is in session." (Emphasis supplied.) Since the object of the compulsory attendance law is that all children be educated and not that they be educated in any particular manner or place, part-time enrollment in a public school and part-time enrollment in a nonpublic school is permitted by section 26–1, so long as the child receives a complete education. See People v. Levisen, 404 Ill 574, 90 NE2d 213.

Plaintiffs contend that paragraph 1 of section 26–1, requiring private and parochial schools to offer a full curriculum of studies comparable to those offered in the public schools to children of corresponding age and grade, requires that the children attending nonpublic schools must be in full-time attendance at the nonpublic schools. While it is necessary that the nonpublic schools offer comparable courses of study, as set out, it does not necessarily follow that the children must be in full-time attendance at any particular school. Furthermore, the dual enrollment program in question does not require all students enrolled in the participating nonpublic school to be enrolled in the dual enrollment program, nor does it contemplate that the only courses taught in the participating nonpublic schools are to be solely those taken by the participating students.

Plaintiffs further argue that the legislative history of the School Code shows a "tightening of the public school requirement and a narrowing of the 'or private school' alternative to the specific exception in paragraph 1" of Section 26–1, thereby prohibiting dual enrollment programs. What has been said above disposes of this contention. Furthermore, compulsory attendance was required before the statutory change in 1945 to which plaintiffs refer. Section 274 of the School Code of 1909 required children between the ages of 7 and 16 "to attend some public or private school for the entire time during which the public school in the district wherein the pupil resides is in session." The four exceptions to public school attendance provided for in the present Code were provided for in the Code of 1909. Ill Rev Stats 1909, chap 122, par 301. As indicated by the Public School Commission which drafted the 1945 School Code, the purpose of the 1945 codification was not to incorporate substantive changes into the law but to attempt the codification of existing laws. One of its main objectives was to eliminate superfluous verbiage. SHA, 1946 Ed, chap 122, pp IX–XVII. The wording of the 1909 Code, that the children shall attend some public *or private school* was superfluous to the extent that a specific exception relating to private and parochial schools was thereafter provided. The words "or private school" were therefor unnecessary, and were eliminated in the School Code of 1945. Ill Rev Stats 1945, chap 122, par 26–1. The words "or private school" are likewise omitted from the 1961 School Code for the same obvious reason. Ill Rev Stats 1961, chap 122, par 26–1. Plaintiffs' argument, that the legislature in 1945 by omission of the words "or private school" intended to "tighten the public school requirement" is therefore unfounded. Furthermore, it is difficult to understand how the omission of these words has any bearing on the question of part-time enrollment so long as the child receives a full and complete education. See People v. Levisen, 404 Ill 574, 90 NE2d 213; Commonwealth ex rel. Wehrle v. School Dist. of Altoona, 241 Pa 224, 88 Atl 481.

Section 26–2 likewise permits part-time enrollment in a public school and part-time enrollment in a nonpublic school. As admitted by plaintiffs, section 26–2 was designed to eliminate administrative problems relating to attendance and credit records of those students enrolled in public schools who are not subject to the compulsory attendance provisions of section 26–1 by reason of their ages. Section 26–2 does not employ the words "the entire time" which are contained in section 26–1. It is of interest to note that these specific words were contained in section 274 of the 1909 School Code relating to the "under 7 and over 16" age group (Ill Rev Stats 1909, c 122, par 301), but were deleted from the comparable provisions in the 1945 and 1961 School Codes. Ill Rev Stats 1945, 1961, chaps 122, pars 26–1. The 1964 resolution and the Superintendent's 1965 progress report both specifically provide that the participating students shall comply with the compulsory attendance laws of this State, as well as provide that they shall meet the Chicago public high school graduation requirements. The students in the "over 16" age group who are enrolled in the dual enrollment program are required to be in attendance at all classes in which enrolled in order to receive the proper graduation credits. The participating students are also required to conform to all rules and regulations established by the Board of Education.

Plaintiffs' argument, that the lack of a "nonpublic school attendance" exception in section 26–2 indicates that the legislature intended to prohibit dual enrollment programs, is unavailing. As stated above, section 26–2 was enacted as an administrative necessity to eliminate attendance and credit record problems involving the public school students who are not covered by section 26–1. Since children under 7 and over 16 are not required to attend school under section 26–1, an exception for attendance at a nonpublic school under section 26–2 would have been superfluous. The legislature intended that problems of attendance and credit relating to students in the "under 7 and over 16" age group enrolled solely in nonpublic schools be left for the particular nonpublic school administration. The lack of such an exception in section 26–2 has no bearing on whether the legislature intended to permit or to prohibit dual enrollment programs. In passing it should be noted that no such exception was contained in the comparable provisions in the 1909 and the 1945 School Codes. Ill Rev Stats 1909, chap 122, par 301; Ill Rev Stats 1945, chap 122, par 26–2.

Plaintiffs' argument that there is no attendance control for participating students while in attendance at the participating nonpublic school is likewise unavailing. The participating students are required "to conform to all rules and regulations established by the Board of Education" and to "meet the High School graduation requirements of the Chicago Public Schools, including those in relation to required subjects and sequences," and shall "receive a diploma issued by the Chicago Board of Education." The program contemplates that the participating students will receive a full and complete education so as to be entitled to a public high school diploma. People v. Levisen, 404 Ill 574, 90 NE2d 213. We do not here create an additional exception to the compulsory attendance required by section 26–2, as contended by plaintiffs, since the scope of section 26–2 permits dual enrollment in public and nonpublic schools and since the dual enrollment program does provide for control of attendance.

Section 18–8.1 of the School Code provides for State aid to part-time students from the common school fund, further indicating the legislature did not intend to prohibit dual enrollment. Students who are regularly enrolled in a public school for only a part of the school day may be counted on a basis of one-sixth of a day for every class hour attended pursuant to such enrollment. Ill Rev Stats 1963, chap 122, par 18–8.1.

The program applies to all nonpublic educational institutions and not to any religious group or groups, and offers its benefits to individual students on a purely voluntary basis upon application by the parents or legal guardians of those children. As stated in Pierce v. Society of Sisters, 268 US 510, at page 535: "The child is not a mere creature of the State; those who nurture him and direct his destiny have the right, coupled with the high duty, to recognize and prepare him for additional obligations." The experimental dual enrollment plan adopted by the Chicago School Board is merely an attempt to find a better method for the education of the Chicago public school children at the option of the parents or legal guardians of those children.

The decree of dismissal with prejudice is affirmed.

Decree affirmed.

Bryant, P. J. and Lyons, J., concur.

D. Bible Reading

School district of Abington Township, Pennsylvania, et al., Appellants, v Edward Lewis Schempp et al. (No. 142)

William J. Murray III, etc., et al., Petitioners, v John N. Curlett, President, et al., Individually, and Constituting the Board of School Commissioners of Baltimore City (No. 119)

374 U. S. 203, 10 L. ed. 2d 844, 83 S. Ct. 1560.
Argued February 27 and 28, 1963 (No. 142); February 27, 1963 (No. 119), Decided June 17, 1963

MR. JUSTICE CLARK DELIVERED THE OPINION OF THE COURT

Once again we are called upon to consider the scope of the provision of the First Amendment to the United States Constitution which declares that "Congress shall make no law respecting an establishment of religion, or prohibiting the free exercise thereof. . . ." These companion cases present the issues in the context of state action requiring that schools begin each day with readings from the Bible. While raising the basic questions under slightly different factual situations, the cases permit of joint treatment. In light of the history of the First

Amendment and of our cases interpreting and applying its requirements, we hold that the practices at issue and the laws requiring them are unconstitutional under the Establishment Clause, as applied to the States through the Fourteenth Amendment.

I.

THE FACTS IN EACH CASE. No. 142. The Commonwealth of Pennsylvania by law, 24 Pa Stat § 15–1516, as amended, Pub Law 1928 (Supp 1960) Dec. 17, 1959, requires that "At least ten verses from the Holy Bible shall be read, without comment, at the opening of each public school on each school day. Any child shall be excused from such Bible reading, or attending such Bible reading, upon the written request of his parent or guardian." The Schempp family, husband and wife and two of their three children, brought suit to enjoin enforcement of the statute, contending that their rights under the Fourteenth Amendment of the Constitution of the United States are, have been, and will continue to be violated unless this statute be declared unconstitutional as violative of these provisions of the First Amendment. They sought to enjoin the appellant school district, wherein the Schempp children attend school, and its officers and the Superintendent of Public Instruction of the Commonwealth from continuing to conduct such readings and recitation of the Lord's Prayer in the public schools of the district pursuant to the statute. A three-judge statutory District Court for the Eastern District of Pennsylvania held that the statute is violative of the Establishment Clause of the First Amendment as applied to the States by the Due Process Clause of the Fourteenth Amendment and directed that appropriate injunctive relief issue. 201 F Supp 815. On appeal by the District, its officials and the Superintendent, under 28 USC § 1253, we noted probable jurisdiction. 371 US 807, 9 L ed 2d 52, 83 S ct 25.

The appellees Edward Lewis Schempp, his wife Sidney, and their children, Roger and Donna, are of the Unitarian faith and are members of the Unitarian Church in Germantown, Philadelphia, Pennsylvania, where they, as well as another son, Ellory, regularly attend religious services. The latter was originally a party but having graduated from the school system pendente lite was voluntarily dismissed from the action. The other children attend the Abington Senior High School, which is a public school operated by appellant district.

On each school day at the Abington Senior High School between 8:15 and 8:30 a. m., while the pupils are attending their home rooms or advisory sections, opening exercises are conducted pursuant to the statute. The exercises are broadcast into each room in the school building through an intercommunications system and are conducted under the supervision of a teacher by students attending the school's radio and television workshop. Selected students from this course gather each morning in the school's workshop studio for the exercises, which include readings by one of the students of 10 verses of the Holy Bible, broadcast to each room in the building. This is followed by the recitation of the

Lord's Prayer, likewise over the intercommunications system, but also by the students in the various classrooms, who are asked to stand and join in repeating the prayer in unison. The exercises are closed with the flag salute and such pertinent announcements as are of interest to the students. Participation in the opening exercises, as directed by the statute, is voluntary. The student reading the verses from the Bible may select the passages and read from any version he chooses, although the only copies furnished by the school are the King James version, copies of which were circulated to each teacher by the school district. During the period in which the exercises have been conducted the King James, the Douay and the Revised Standard versions of the Bible have been used, as well as the Jewish Holy Scriptures. There are no prefatory statements, no questions asked or solicited, no comments or explanations made and no interpretations given at or during the exercises. The students and parents are advised that the student may absent himself from the classroom or, should he elect to remain, not participate in the exercises.

It appears from the record that in schools not having an intercommunications system the Bible reading and the recitation of the Lord's Prayer were conducted by the home-room teacher, who chose the text of the verses and read them herself or had students read them in rotation or by volunteers. This was followed by a standing recitation of the Lord's Prayer, together with the Pledge of Allegiance to the flag by the class in unison and a closing announcement of routine school items of interest.

At the first trial Edward Schempp and the children testified as to specific religious doctrines purveyed by a literal reading of the Bible "which were contrary to the religious beliefs which they held and to their familial teaching." 177 F Supp 398, 400. The children testified that all of the doctrines to which they referred were read to them at various times as part of the exercises. Edward Schempp testified at the second trial that he had considered having Roger and Donna excused from attendance at the exercises but decided against it for several reasons, including his belief that the children's relationships with their teachers and classmates would be adversely affected.

Expert testimony was introduced by both appellants and appellees at the first trial, which testimony was summarized by the trial court as follows:

Dr. Solomon Grayzel testified that there were marked differences between the Jewish Holy Scriptures and the Christian Holy Bible, the most obvious of which was the absence of the New Testament in the Jewish Holy Scriptures. Dr. Grayzel testified that portions of the New Testament were offensive to Jewish tradition and that, from the standpoint of Jewish faith, the concept of Jesus Christ as the Son of God was 'practically blasphemous.' He cited instances in the New Testament which, assertedly, were not only sectarian in nature but tended to bring the Jews into ridicule or scorn. Dr. Grayzel gave as his expert opinion that such material from the New Testament could be explained to Jewish children in such a way as to do no harm to them. But if portions of the New Testament were read without explanation, they could be, and in his specific experience with children Dr. Grayzel observed, had been, psychologically harmful to the child and had caused a divisive force within the social media of the school.

Dr. Grayzel also testified that there was significant difference in attitude with regard to the respective Books of the Jewish and Christian religions in that Judaism attaches no special significance to the reading of the Bible per se and that the Jewish Holy Scriptures are source materials to be studied. But Dr. Grayzel did state that many portions of the New, as well as of the Old, Testament contained passages of great literary and moral value.

Dr. Luther A. Weigle, an expert witness for the defense, testified in some detail as to the reasons for and the methods employed in developing the King James and the Revised Standard Versions of the Bible. On direct examination Dr. Weigle stated that the Bible was non-sectarian. He later stated that the phrase 'non-sectarian' meant to him non-sectarian within the Christian faiths. Dr. Weigle stated that his definition of the Holy Bible would include the Jewish Holy Scriptures, but also stated that the 'Holy Bible' would not be complete without the New Testament. He stated that the New Testament 'conveyed the message of Christians.' In his opinion, reading of the Holy Scriptures to the exclusion of the New Testament would be a sectarian practice. Dr. Weigle stated that the Bible was of great moral, historical and literary value. This is conceded by all the parties and is also the view of the court. 177 F Supp 398, 401, 402.

The trial court, in striking down the practices and the statute requiring them, made specific findings of fact that the children's attendance at Abington Senior High School is compulsory and that the practice of reading 10 verses from the Bible is also compelled by law. It also found that:

The reading of the verses, even without comment, possesses a devotional and religious character and constitutes in effect a religious observance. The devotional and religious nature of the morning exercises is made all the more apparent by the fact that the Bible reading is followed immediately by a recital in unison by the pupils of the Lord's Prayer. The fact that some pupils, or theoretically all pupils, might be excused from attendance at the exercises does not mitigate the obligatory nature of the ceremony for . . . Section 1516 . . . unequivocally requires the exercises to be held every school day in every school in the Commonwealth. The exercises are held in the school buildings and perforce are conducted by and under the authority of the local school authorities and during school sessions. Since the statute requires the reading of the 'Holy Bible,' a Christian document, the practice . . . prefers the Christian religion. The record demonstrates that it was the intention of . . . the Commonwealth . . . to introduce a religious ceremony into the public schools of the Commonwealth. 201 F Supp, at 819.

No. 119. In 1905 the Board of School Commissioners of Baltimore City adopted a rule pursuant to Art 77, § 202 of the Annotated Code of Maryland. The rule provided for the holding of opening exercises in the schools of the city, consisting primarily of the "reading, without comment of a chapter in the Holy Bible and/or the use of the Lord's Prayer." The petitioners, Mrs Madalyn Murray and her son, William J. Murray III, are both professed atheists. Following unsuccessful attempts to have the respondent school board rescind the rule, this suit was filed for mandamus to compel its rescission and cancellation. It was alleged that William was a student in a public school of the city and Mrs. Murray, his mother, was a taxpayer therein; that it was the practice under the rule to have a reading on each school morning from the King James version of the Bible; that at petitioners' insistence the rule was amended to permit children to be excused from the exercise on request of the parent and that William had been excused pursuant thereto; that nevertheless the rule as amended was in violation of the petitioners' rights "to freedom of religion under the First and Fourteenth Amendments" and in violation of "the principle of separation between church and state, contained therein. . . ." The petition particularized the petitioners' atheistic beliefs and stated that the rule, as practiced, violated their rights "in that it threatens their religious liberty by placing a premium on belief as against non-belief and subjects their freedom of conscience to the rule of the majority; it pronounces belief in God as the source of all moral and spiritual values, equating these values with religious values, and thereby renders sinister, alien and suspect the beliefs and ideals of your Petitioners, promoting doubt and question of their morality, good citizenship and good faith."

The respondents demurred and the trial court, recognizing that the demurrer admitted all facts well pleaded, sustained it without leave to amend. The Maryland Court of Appeals affirmed, the majority of four justices holding the exercise not in violation of the First and Fourteenth Amendments, with three justices dissenting. 228 Md 239, 179 A2d 698. We granted certiorari. 371 US 809, 9 L ed 2d 52, 83 S Ct 21.

II.

It is true that religion has been closely identified with our history and government. As we said in Engel v Vitale, 370 US 421, 434, 8 L ed 2d 601, 609, 82 S Ct 1261, 86 ALR2d 1285 (1962), "The history of man is inseparable from the history of religion. And . . . since the beginning of that history many people have devoutly believed that 'More things are wrought by prayer than this world dreams of.' " In Zorach v Clauson, 343 US 306, 313, 96 L ed 954, 962, 72 S Ct 679 (1952), we gave specific recognition to the proposition that "[w]e are a religious people whose institutions presuppose a Supreme Being." The fact that the Founding Fathers believed devotedly that there was a God and that the unalienable rights of man were rooted in Him is clearly evidenced in their writings, from the Mayflower Compact to the Constitution itself. This background is evidenced today in our public life through the continuance in our oaths of office from the Presidency to the Alderman of the final supplication, "So help me God." Likewise each House of the Congress provides through its Chaplain an opening prayer, and the sessions of this Court are declared open by the crier in a short ceremony, the final phrase of which invokes the grace of God. Again, there are such manifestations in our military forces, where those of our citizens who are under the restrictions of military service wish to engage in voluntary worship. Indeed, only last year an official survey of the country indicated that 64% of our people have church membership, Bureau of the Census, U. S. Department of Commerce, Statistical Abstract of the United States (83d ed 1962), 48, while less than 3% profess no religion whatever. Id., at p. 46. It can be truly said, therefore, that today, as in the beginning, our national life reflects a religious people who, in the words of Madison, are "earnestly praying, as . . . in duty bound, that the Supreme Lawgiver of the

Universe . . . guide them into every measure which may be worthy of his [blessing . . . .]" Memorial and Remonstrance Against Religious Assessments, quoted in Everson v Board of Education, 330 US 1, 71, 72, 91 L ed 711, 752, 67 S Ct 504, 168 ALR 1392 (1947) (Appendix to dissenting opinion of Rutledge, J.).

This is not to say, however, that religion has been so identified with our history and government that religious freedom is not likewise as strongly imbedded in our public and private life. Nothing but the most telling of personal experiences in religious persecution suffered by our forebears, see Everson v Board of Education, supra (330 US at 8–11), could have planted our belief in liberty of religious opinion any more deeply in our heritage. It is true that this liberty frequently was not realized by the colonists, but this is readily accountable by their close ties to the Mother Country. However, the views of Madison and Jefferson, preceded by Roger Williams, came to be incorporated not only in the Federal Constitution but likewise in those of most of our States. This freedom to worship was indispensable in a country whose people came from the four quarters of the earth and brought with them a diversity of religious opinion. Today authorities list 83 separate religious bodies, each with membership exceeding 50,000, existing among our people, as well as innumerable smaller groups. Bureau of the Census, op cit, supra, at 46–47.

III.

Almost a hundred years ago in Minor v Board of Education of Cincinnati, Judge Alphonso Taft, father of the revered Chief Justice, in an unpublished opinion stated the ideal of our people as to religious freedom as one of "absolute equality before the law, of all religious opinions and sects. . . . The government is neutral, and, while protecting all, it prefers none and it *disbarges* none."

Before examining this "neutral" position in which the Establishment and Free Exercise Clauses of the First Amendment place our Government it is well that we discuss the reach of the Amendment under the cases of this Court.

First, this Court has decisively settled that the First Amendment's mandate that "Congress shall make no law respecting an establishment of religion, or prohibiting the free exercise thereof" has been made wholly applicable to the States by the Fourteenth Amendment. Twenty-three years ago in Cantwell v Connecticut, 310 US 296, 303, 84 L ed 1213, 1218, 60 S Ct 900, 128 ALR 1352 (1940), this Court, through Mr. Justice Roberts, said:

The fundamental concept of liberty embodied in that [Fourteenth] Amendment embraces the liberties guaranteed by the First Amendment. The First Amendment declares that Congress shall make no law respecting an establishment of religion or prohibiting the free exercise thereof. The Fourteenth Amendment has rendered the legislatures of the states as incompetent as Congress to enact such laws. . . .

In a series of cases since Cantwell the Court has repeatedly reaffirmed that doctrine, and we do so now. Murdock v Pennsylvania, 319 US 105, 108, 87 L ed 1292, 1295, 63 S Ct 870, 146 ALR 81 (1943); Everson v Board of Education,

330 US 1, 91 L ed 711, 67 S Ct 504, 168 ALR 1392, supra; Illinois ex rel.
McCollum v Board of Education, 333 US 203, 210, 211, 92 L ed 649, 658, 659,
68 S Ct 461, 2 ALR2d 1338 (1948); Zorach v Clauson, 343 US 306, 96 L ed
954, 72 S Ct 679, supra; McGowan v Maryland, 366 US 420, 6 L ed 2d 393, 81
S Ct 1101 (1961); Torcaso v Watkins, 367 US 488, 6 L ed 2d 982, 81 S Ct 1680
(1961); and Engel v Vitale, 370 US 421, 8 L ed 2d 601, 82 S Ct 1261, 86 ALR2d
1285, supra.

Second, this Court has rejected unequivocally the contention that the
Establishment Clause forbids only governmental preference of one religion over
another. Almost 20 years ago in Everson, supra (330 US at 15), the Court said
that "[n]either a state nor the Federal Government can set up a church. Neither
can pass laws which aid one religion, aid all religions, or prefer one religion over
another." . . .

The same conclusion has been firmly maintained ever since that time, see
Illinois ex rel. McCollum, supra (333 US at pp. 210, 211); McGowan v Maryland,
supra (366 US at 442, 443); Torcaso v Watkins, supra (367 US at 492, 493, 495),
and we reaffirm it now.

While none of the parties to either of these cases has questioned these basic
conclusions of the Court, both of which have been long established, recognized
and consistently reaffirmed, others continue to question their history, logic and
efficacy. Such contentions, in the light of the consistent interpretation in cases of
this Court, seem entirely untenable and of value only as academic exercises.

IV.

The interrelationship of the Establishment and the Free Exercise Clauses was
first touched upon by Mr. Justice Roberts for the Court in Cantwell v Connecticut, supra (310 US at 303, 304), where it was said that their "inhibition of
legislation" had "a double aspect. On the one hand, it forestalls compulsion by
law of the acceptance of any creed or the practice of any form of worship.
Freedom of conscience and freedom to adhere to such religious organization
or form of worship as the individual may choose cannot be restricted by law.
On the other hand, it safeguards the free exercise of the chosen form of religion.
Thus the Amendment embraces two concepts,—freedom to believe and freedom
to act. The first is absolute but, in the nature of things, the second cannot be."

A half dozen years later in Everson v Board of Education, supra (330 US
at 14, 15), this Court, through Mr. Justice Black, stated that the "scope of the
First Amendment . . . was designed forever to suppress" the establishment of
religion or the prohibition of the free exercise thereof. In short, the Court held
that the Amendment "requires the state to be a neutral in its relations with
groups of religious believers and non-believers; it does not require the state to
be their adversary. State power is no more to be used so as to handicap religions
than it is to favor them." Id. 330 US at 18.

And Mr. Justice Jackson, in dissent, declared that public schools are organized "on the premise that secular education can be isolated from all religious teaching so that the school can inculcate all needed temporal knowledge and also maintain a strict and lofty neutrality as to religion. The assumption is that after the individual has been instructed in worldly wisdom he will be better fitted to choose his religion." Id. 330 US at 23–24.

Moreover, all of the four dissenters, speaking through Mr. Justice Rutledge, agreed that "Our constitutional policy . . . does not deny the value or the necessity for religious training, teaching or observance. Rather it secures their free exercise. But to that end it does deny that the state can undertake or sustain them in any form or degree. For this reason the sphere of religious activity, as distinguished from the secular intellectual liberties, has been given the two fold protection and, as the state cannot forbid, neither can it perform or aid in performing the religious function. The dual prohibition makes that function altogether private." Id. 330 US at 52.

Only one year later the Court was asked to reconsider and repudiate the doctrine of these cases in McCollum v Board of Education. It was argued that "historically the First Amendment was intended to forbid only government preference of one religion over another . . . . In addition they ask that we distinguish or overrule our holding in the Everson Case that the Fourteenth Amendment made the 'establishment of religion' clause of the First Amendment applicable as a prohibition against the States." 333 US, at 211. The Court, with Mr. Justice Reed alone dissenting, was unable to "accept either of these contentions." Ibid. Mr. Justice Frankfurter, joined by Justices Jackson, Rutledge and Burton, wrote a very comprehensive and scholarly concurrence in which he said that "[s]eparation is a requirement to abstain from fusing functions of Government and of religious sects, not merely to treat them all equally." Id. 333 US at 227. Continuing, he stated that: "the Constitution . . . prohibited the Government common to all from becoming embroiled, however innocently, in the destructive religious conflicts of which the history of even this country records some dark pages." Id. 333 US at 228. . . .

And then in 1961 in McGowan v Maryland and in Torcaso v Watkins each of these cases was discussed and approved. Chief Justice Warren in McGowan, for a unanimous Court on this point, said:

But, the First Amendment, in its final form, did not simply bar a congressional enactment *establishing a church; it forbade all laws respecting an establishment of religion.* Thus, this Court has given the Amendment a 'broad interpretation . . . in the light of its history and the evils it was designed forever to suppress. . . .' *366 US, at 441, 442.*

And Mr. Justice Black for the Court in Torcaso, without dissent but with Justices Frankfurter and Harlan concurring in the result, used this language:

We repeat and again reaffirm that neither a State nor the Federal Government can constitutionally force a person 'to profess a belief or disbelief in any religion.' Neither can constitutionally pass laws or impose requirements which aid all religions as against non-believers, and neither can aid those religions based on a belief in the existence of God as against those religions founded on different beliefs. *367 US, at 495.*

Finally, in Engel v Vitale, only last year, these principles were so universally recognized that the Court without the citation of a single case and over the sole dissent of Mr. Justice Stewart, reaffirmed them. The Court found the 22-word prayer used in "New York's program of daily classroom invocation of God's blessings as prescribed in the Regents' prayer . . . [to be] a religious activity." 370 US, at 424. It held that "it is no part of the business of government to compose official prayers for any group of the American people to recite as a part of a religious program carried on by government." Id. 370 US at 425. In discussing the reach of the Establishment and Free Exercise Clauses of the First Amendment the Court said:

Although these two clauses may in certain instances overlap, they forbid two quite different kinds of governmental encroachment upon religious freedom. The Establishment Clause, unlike the Free Exercise Clause, does not depend upon any showing of direct governmental compulsion and is violated by the enactment of laws which establish an official religion whether those laws operate directly to coerce non-observing individuals or not. This is not to say, of course, that laws officially prescribing a particular form of religious worship do not involve coercion of such individuals. When the power, prestige and financial support of government is placed behind a particular religious belief, the indirect coercive pressure upon religious minorities to conform to the prevailing officially approved religion is plain. *Id. 370 US at 430, 431.*

And in further elaboration the Court found that the "first and most immediate purpose [of the Establishment Clause] rested on the belief that a union of government and religion tends to destroy government and to degrade religion." Id. 370 US at 431. When government, the Court said, allies itself with one particular form of religion, the inevitable result is that it incurs "the hatred, disrespect and even contempt of those who held contrary beliefs." Ibid.

V.

The wholesome "neutrality" of which this Court's cases speak thus stems from a recognition of the teachings of history that powerful sects or groups might bring about a fusion of governmental and religious functions or a concert or dependency of one upon the other to the end that official support of the State or Federal Government would be placed behind the tenets of one or of all orthodoxies. This the Establishment Clause prohibits. And a further reason for neutrality is found in the Free Exercise Clause, which recognizes the value of religious training, teaching and observance and, more particularly, the right of every person to freely choose his own course with reference thereto, free of any compulsion from the state. This the Free Exercise Clause guarantees. Thus, as we have seen, the two clauses may overlap. As we have indicated, the Establishment Clause has been directly considered by this Court eight times in the past score of years and, with only one Justice dissenting on the point, it has consistently held that the clause withdrew all legislative power respecting religious belief or the expression thereof. The test may be stated as follows: what are the purpose and the primary effect of the enactment? If either is the advancement or inhibition of religion then the enactment exceeds the scope of legislative power as circumscribed by the Constitution. That is to say that to withstand the strictures of the Establishment Clause there must be a secular legislative purpose and a primary effect that neither advances nor inhibits religion. Everson v Board of Education, 330 US 1, 91 L ed 711, 67 S Ct 504, 168 ALR 1392, supra; McGowan v Maryland, supra (366 US at 442). The Free Exercise Clause, likewise considered many times here, withdraws from legislative power, state and federal, the exertion of any restraint on the free exercise of religion. Its purpose is to secure religious liberty in the individual by prohibiting any invasions thereof by civil authority. Hence it is necessary in a free exercise case for one to show the coercive effect of the enactment as it operates against him in the practice of his religion. The distinction between the two clauses is apparent—a violation of the Free Exercise Clause is predicated on coercion while the Establishment Clause violation need not be so attended.

Applying the Establishment Clause principles to the cases at bar we find that the States are requiring the selection and reading at the opening of the school day of verses from the Holy Bible and the recitation of the Lord's Prayer by the students in unison. These exercises are prescribed as part of the curricular activities of students who are required by law to attend school. They are held in the school buildings under the supervision and with the participation of teachers employed in those schools. None of these factors, other than compulsory school attendance, was present in the program upheld in Zorach v Clauson. The trial court in No. 142 has found that such an opening exercise is a religious ceremony and was intended by the State to be so. We agree with the trial court's finding as to the religious character of the exercises. Given that finding, the exercises and the law requiring them are in violation of the Establishment Clause.

There is no such specific finding as to the religious character of the exercises in No. 119, and the State contends (as does the State in No. 142) that the program is an effort to extend its benefits to all public school children without regard to their religious belief. Included within its secular purposes, it says, are the promotion of moral values, the contradiction to the materialistic trends of our times, the perpetuation of our institutions and the teaching of literature. The case came up on demurrer, of course, to a petition which alleged that the uniform practice under the rule had been to read from the King James version of the Bible and that the exercise was sectarian. The short answer, therefore, is that the religious character of the exercise was admitted by the State. But even if its purpose is not strictly religious, it is sought to be accomplished through readings, without comment, from the Bible. Surely the place of the Bible as an instrument of religion cannot be gainsaid, and the State's recognition of the pervading religious character of the ceremony is evident from the rule's specific permission of the alternative use of the Catholic Douay version as well as the recent amendment permitting nonattendance at the exercises. None of these factors is consistent with the contention that the Bible is here used either as an instrument for non-religious moral inspiration or as a reference for the teaching of secular subjects.

The conclusion follows that in both cases the laws require religious exercises and such exercises are being conducted in direct violation of the rights of the appellees and petitioners. Nor are these required exercises mitigated by the fact that individual students may absent themselves upon parental request, for that fact furnishes no defense to a claim of unconstitutionality under the Establishment Clause. See Engel v Vitale, supra (370 US at 430). Further, it is no defense to urge that the religious practices here may be relatively minor encroachments on the First Amendment. The breach of neutrality that is today a trickling stream may all too soon became a raging torrent and, in the words of Madison, "it is proper to take alarm at the first experiment on our liberties." Memorial and Remonstrance Against Religious Assessments, quoted in Everson, supra (330 US at 65).

It is insisted that unless these religious exercises are permitted a "religion of secularism" is established in the schools. We agree of course that the State may not establish a "religion of secularism" in the sense of affirmatively opposing or showing hostility to religion, thus "preferring those who believe in no religion over those who do believe." Zorach v Clauson, supra (343 US at 314). We do not agree, however, that this decision in any sense has that effect. In addition, it might well be said that one's education is not complete without a study of comparative religion or the history of religion and its relationship to the advancement of civilization. It certainly may be said that the Bible is worthy of study for its literary and historic qualities. Nothing we have said here indicates that such study of the Bible or of religion, when presented objectively as part of a secular program of education, may not be effected consistently with the First Amendment. But the exercises here do not fall into those categories. They are religious exercises, required by the States in violation of the command of the First Amendment that the Government maintain strict neutrality, neither aiding nor opposing religion.

Finally, we cannot accept that the concept of neutrality, which does not permit a State to require a religious exercise even with the consent of the majority of those affected, collides with the majority's right to free exercise of religion. While the Free Exercise Clause clearly prohibits the use of state action to deny the rights of free exercise to *anyone*, it has never meant that a majority could use the machinery of the State to practice its beliefs. Such a contention was effectively answered by Mr. Justice Jackson for the Court in West Virginia State Board of Education v Barnette, 319 US 624, 638, 87 L ed 1628, 1638, 63 S Ct 1178, 147 ALR 674 (1943):

The very purpose of a Bill of Rights was to withdraw certain subjects from the vicissitudes of political controversy, to place them beyond the reach of majorities and officials and to establish them as legal principles to be applied by the courts. One's right to . . . freedom of worship . . . and other fundamental rights may not be submitted to vote; they depend on the outcome of no elections.

The place of religion in our society is an exalted one, achieved through a long tradition of reliance on the home, the church and the inviolable citadel of the individual heart and mind. We have come to recognize through bitter experience that it is not within the power of government to invade that citadel, whether its purpose or effect be to aid or oppose, to advance or retard. In the relationship between man and religion the State is firmly committed to a position of neutrality. Though the application of that rule requires interpretation of a delicate sort, the rule itself is clearly and concisely stated in the words of the First Amendment. Applying that rule to the facts of these cases, we affirm the judgment in No. 142. In No. 119, the judgment is reversed and the cause remanded to the Maryland Court of Appeals for further proceedings consistent with this opinion.

It is so ordered.

E. Public Funds and Parochial Schools

Board of Education of Central School District No. 1 et al. v. Allen, Commissioner of Education of New York, et al.
392 U.S. 236 (1968)
Appeal from the Court of Appeals of New York

MR. JUSTICE WHITE DELIVERED THE OPINION OF THE COURT

A law of the State of New York requires local public school authorities to lend textbooks free of charge to all students in grades seven through 12; students attending private schools are included. This case presents the question whether this statute is a "law respecting an establishment of religion, or prohibiting the free exercise thereof," and so in conflict with the First and Fourteenth Amendments to the Constitution, because it authorizes the loan of textbooks to students attending parochial schools. We hold that the law is not in violation of the Constitution.

Until 1965, § 701 of the Education Law of the State of New York authorized public school boards to designate textbooks for use in the public schools, to purchase such books with public funds, and to rent or sell the books to public school students. In 1965 the Legislature amended § 701, basing the amendments on findings that the "public welfare and safety require that the state and local communities give assistance to educational programs which are important to our national defense and the general welfare of the state." Beginning with the 1966–1967 school year, local school boards were required to purchase textbooks and lend them without charge "to all children residing in such district who are enrolled in grades seven to twelve of a public or private school which complies with the compulsory education law." The books now loaned are "text-books which are designated for use in any public, elementary or secondary schools of the state or are approved by any boards of education," and which according to a 1966 amendment—"a pupil is required to use as a text for a semester or more in a particular class in the school he legally attends."

Appellant Board of Education of Central School District No. 1 in Rensselaer and Columbia Counties, brought suit in the New York courts against appellee James Allen. The complaint alleged that § 701 violated both the State and Federal Constitutions; that if appellants, in reliance on their interpretation of the Constitution, failed to lend books to parochial school students within their counties appellee Allen would remove appellants from office; and that to prevent this, appellants were complying with the law and submitting to their constituents a school budget including funds for books to be lent to parochial school pupils. Appellants therefore sought a declaration that § 701 was invalid, an order barring appellee Allen from removing appellants from office for failing to comply with it, and another order restraining him from apportioning state funds to school districts for the purchase of textbooks to be lent to parochial students. After answer, and upon cross-motions for summary judgment, the trial court held the law unconstitutional under the First and Fourteenth Amendments and entered judgment for appellants. 51 Misc. 2d 297, 273 N.Y.S. 2d 239 (1966). The Appellate Division reversed, ordering the complaint dismissed on the ground that appellant school boards had no standing to attack the validity of a state statute. 27 App. Div. 2d 69, 276 N.Y.S. 2d 234 (1966). On appeal, the New York Court of Appeals concluded by a 4–3 vote that appellants did have standing but by a different 4–3 vote held that § 701 was not in violation of either the State or the Federal Constitution. 20 N. Y. 2d 109, 228 N. E. 2d 791, 281 N.Y.S. 2d 799 (1967). The Court of Appeals said that the law's purpose was to benefit all school children regardless of the type of school they attended, and that only textbooks approved by public school authorities could be loaned. It therefore considered § 701 "completely neutral with respect to religion, merely making available secular textbooks at the request of the individual student and asking no question about what school he attends." Section 701, the Court of Appeals concluded, is not a law which "establishes a religion or constitutes the use of public funds to aid religious schools." 20 N. Y. 2d, at 117; 228 N. E. 2d, at 794, 795; 281 N.Y.S. 2d, at 805. We noted probable jurisdiction. 389 U. S. 1031 (1968).

Everson v. *Board of Education*, 330 U. S. 1 (1947), is the case decided by this Court that is most nearly in point for today's problem. New Jersey reimbursed parents for expenses incurred in busing their children to parochial schools. The Court stated that the Establishment Clause bars a State from passing "laws which aid one religion, aid all religions, or prefer one religion over another," and bars too any "tax in any amount, large or small . . . levied to support any religious activities or institutions, whatever they may be called, or whatever form they may adopt to teach or practice religion." 330 U. S., at 15–16. Nevertheless, said the Court, the Establishment Clause does not prevent a State from extending the benefits of state laws to all citizens without regard for their religious affiliation and does not prohibit "New Jersey from spending tax-raised funds to pay the bus fares of parochial school pupils as a part of a general program under which it pays the fares of pupils attending public and other schools." The statute was held to be valid even though one of its results was that "children are helped to get to church schools" and "some of the children might not be sent to the church schools if the parents were compelled to pay their children's bus fares out of their own pockets." 330 U. S., at 17. As with public provision of police and fire protection, sewage facilities, and streets and sidewalks, payment of bus fares was of some value to the religious school, but was nevertheless not such support of a religious institution as to be a prohibited establishment of religion within the meaning of the First Amendment.

Everson and later cases have shown that the line between state neutrality to religion and state support of religion is not easy to locate. "The constitutional standard is the separation of Church and State. The problem, like many problems in constitutional law, is one of degree." *Zorach* v. *Clauson*, 343 U. S. 306, 314 (1952). . . .

Based on *Everson, Zorach, McGowan,* and other cases, *Abington School District* v. *Schempp,* 374 U. S. 203 (1963), fashioned a test subscribed to by eight Justices for distinguishing between forbidden involvements of the State with religion and those contacts which the Establishment Clause permits:

The test may be stated as follows: what are the purpose and the primary effect of the enactment? If either is the advancement or inhibition of religion then the enactment exceeds the scope of legislative power as circumscribed by the Constitution. That is to say that to withstand the strictures of the Establishment Clause there must be a secular legislative purpose and a primary effect that neither advances nor inhibits religion. *Everson* v. *Board of Education.* . . . 374 U. S., at 222.

This test is not easy to apply, but the citation of *Everson* by the *Schempp* Court to support its general standard made clear how the *Schempp* rule would be applied to the facts of *Everson.* The statute upheld in *Everson* would be considered a law having "a secular legislative purpose and a primary effect that neither advances nor inhibits religion." We reach the same result with respect to the New York law requiring school books to be loaned free of charge to all students in specified grades. The express purpose of § 701 was stated by the New York Legislature to be furtherance of the educational opportunities available to the young. Appellants have shown us nothing about the necessary effects of the statute that is contrary to its stated purpose. The law merely makes available to all children the benefits of a general program to lend school books free of charge. Books are furnished at the request of the pupil and ownership remains, at least technically, in the State. Thus no funds or books are furnished to parochial schools, and the financial benefit is to parents and children, not to schools. Perhaps free books make it more likely that some children choose to attend a sectarian school, but that was true of the state-paid bus fares in *Everson* and does not alone demonstrate an unconstitutional degree of support for a religious institution.

Of course books are different from buses. Most bus rides have no inherent religious significance, while religious books are common. However, the language of § 701 does not authorize the loan of religious books, and the State claims no right to distribute religious literature. Although the books loaned are those required by the parochial school for use in specific courses, each book loaned must be approved by the public school authorities; only secular books may receive approval. The law was construed by the Court of Appeals of New York as "merely making available secular textbooks at the request of the individual student," *supra*, and the record contains no suggestion that religious books have been loaned. Absent evidence, we cannot assume that school authorities, who constantly face the same problem in selecting textbooks for use in the public schools, are unable to distinguish between secular and religious books or that they will not honestly discharge their duties under the law. In judging the validity of the statute on this record we must proceed on the assumption that books loaned to students are books that are not unsuitable for use in the public schools because of religious content.

The major reason offered by appellants for distinguishing free textbooks from free bus fares is that books, but not buses, are critical to the teaching process, and in a sectarian school that process is employed to teach religion. However this Court has long recognized that religious schools pursue two goals, religious instruction and secular education. In the leading case of *Pierce* v. *Society of Sisters*, 268 U. S. 510 (1925), the Court held that although it would not question Oregon's power to compel school attendance or require that the attendance be at an institution meeting State-imposed requirements as to quality and nature of curriculum, Oregon had not shown that its interest in secular education required that all children attend publicly operated schools. A premise of this holding was the view that the State's interest in education would be served sufficiently by reliance on the secular teaching that accompanied religious training in the schools maintained by the Society of Sisters. Since *Pierce*, a substantial body of case law has confirmed the power of the States to insist that attendance at private schools, if it is to satisfy state compulsory-attendance laws, be at institutions which provide minimum hours of instruction, employ teachers of specified training, and cover prescribed subjects of instruction. Indeed, the State's interest in assuring that these standards are being met has been considered a sufficient reason for refusing to accept instruction at home as compliance with compulsory education statutes. These cases were a sensible corollary of *Pierce* v. *Society of Sisters:* if the State must satisfy its interest in secular education through the instrument of private schools, it has a proper interest in the manner in which those schools perform their secular educational function. Another corollary was *Cochran* v. *Louisiana State Board of Education,* 281 U. S. 370 (1930), where appellants said that a statute requiring school books to be furnished without charge to all students, whether they attended public or private schools, did not serve a "public purpose," and so offended the Fourteenth Amendment. Speaking through Chief Justice Hughes, the Court summarized as follows its conclusion that Louisiana's interest in the secular education being provided by private schools made provision of textbooks to students in these schools a properly public concern: "[The State's] interest is education, broadly; its method, comprehensive. Individual interests are aided only as the common interest is safeguarded." 281 U. S., at 375.

Underlying these cases, and underlying also the legislative judgments that have preceded the court decisions, has been a recognition that private education has played and is playing a significant and valuable role in raising national levels of knowledge, competence, and experience. Americans care about the quality of the secular education available to their children. They have considered high quality education to be an indispensable ingredient for achieving the kind of nation, and the kind of citizenry, that they have desired to create. Considering this attitude, the continued willingness to rely on private school systems, including parochial systems, strongly suggests that a wide segment of informed opinion, legislative and otherwise, has found that those schools do an acceptable job of providing secular education to their students. This judgment is further evidence that parochial schools are performing, in addition to their sectarian function, the task of secular education.

Against this background of judgment and experience, unchallenged in the meager record before us in this case, we cannot agree with appellants either that all teaching in a sectarian school is religious or that the processes of secular and religious training are so intertwined that secular textbooks furnished to students by the public are in fact instrumental in the teaching of religion. This case comes to us after summary judgment entered on the pleadings. Nothing in this record supports the proposition that all textbooks, whether they deal with mathematics, physics, foreign languages, history, or literature, are used by the parochial schools to teach religion. No evidence has been offered about particular schools, particular courses, particular teachers, or particular books. We are unable to hold, based solely on judicial notice, that this statute results in unconstitutional involvement of the State with religious instruction or that § 701, for this or the other reasons urged, is a law respecting the establishment of religion within the meaning of the First Amendment.

Appellants also contend that § 701 offends the Free Exercise Clause of the First Amendment. However, "it is necessary in a free exercise case for one to show the coercive effect of the enactment as it operates against him in the practice of his religion," *Abington School District* v. *Schempp,* 374 U. S. 203, 223

(1963), and appellants have not contended that the New York law in any way coerces them as individuals in the practice of their religion.

The judgment is affirmed.

Mr. Justice Harlan, concurring. . . .

Mr. Justice Black, dissenting. . . .

Mr. Justice Douglas, dissenting. . . .

Problems and Discussion Questions

1. If all church-related or church-supported nonpublic elementary and secondary schools in your state closed at the end of the current school year, what impact would this have on the public school system? Based on current state average spending per pupil, compute the added costs to the public school system for the next school year.

2. Can public schooling ever be "nonsectarian"? How can children be taught concepts of morality or ethics apart from some brand of theology?

3. The "child-benefit" doctrine has sustained the use of public funds for pupils enrolled in parochial schools [for transportation, see *Cochran et al. v. Louisiana State Board of Education et al.*, 281 U.S. 370 (1930); textbooks on "loan", see *Board of Education v. Allen*, 392 U.S. 236 (1968)]. Is this doctrine any more than a convenient rationalization of an otherwise unpopular legal dilemma? Under the "child-benefit" doctrine, what guidelines can a local board of education rely on?

4. Discuss the implications (to teachers, administrators, and school operations) of shared-time and released-time plans for church-school cooperation.

Annotated Bibliography

"Aid to Parochial Education—A New Era," *Notre Dame Lawyer*, 41:711, June, 1966.

This represents but one segment of *Church-State—Religious Institutions and Values: A Legal Survey—1964-66*, conducted by Frank P. Cihlar, Michael K. Cook, Joseph P. Martori, Jr., and Paul J. Meyer. Under the well-documented premise that there is a recent "shift in public opinion toward favoring equal treatment of all children, regardless of the schools they attend," this segment presents state and federal legislation, shared time, and tax credits relevant to the point. The author's brief conclusion argues in favor of governmental aid to nonpublic school children.

"Constitutional Law—Church and State—Shared Time: Indirect Aid to Parochial Schools," *Michigan Law Review*, 65:1224, April, 1967.

A concise summation of the many arguments for and against shared time sets the background for the remainder of the article. Brief discussions on the constitutionality (re: the First Amendment) of shared time, through (1) the "Child Benefit" theory, (2) the released time analogy, and (3) accommodated neutrality, are included. Further, some attention is given to the complexities of overcoming state-level obstacles to shared time.

"Constitutional Problems in Church-State Relations: A Symposium," *Northwestern University Law Review*, 61:759, November–December, 1966.

This piece consists of four papers—each extensively documented—dealing with the history of separation, federal aid to sectarian institutions, impact on school curricula, and conflicts between an individual's freedom and the government's duty.

I. "First Amendment Religion Clause: Historical Metamorphosis." The title indicates exactly the content of this paper. A possible exception is the discussion of the effect of the Fourteenth Amendment on the interpretation of the First. The paper concludes that there is no definitive, all-encompassing statement of where secularism ends and sectarianism begins.

II. "The First Amendment and Financial Aid to Religion: Limits on the Government's Conduct." This piece examines the complexities of direct and indirect federal aid, the conflict between the establishment and free-exercise clauses of the First Amendment, and the distinction between religious and secular objectives. It is pointed out, rather clearly, that both direct and indirect aid may or may not be constitutionally sound, depending on (1) whether one examines the objectives of the aid (as put to use by the recipient institution), (2) or in light of the establishment clause, (3) or if the lack of such aid would prevent free exercise.

III. "Humanistic Values in the Public School Curriculum: Problems in Defining an Appropriate 'Wall of Separation.' " "The area of concern in this paper will be that part of the educational process which departs from the mere teaching of objective facts, and leads to the exploration of ultimate values, both moral and spiritual." In fulfillment of this statement the paper considers, through considerable use of selected cases, the neutrality and duality of court opinions and school practices, the semantic problems of the word "religion," and school neutrality in context.

IV. "Legislative Free Exercise and Conflict Between the Clauses." The theory of legislative free exercise reasons that it is the most viable means by which individual religious practices may be protected from governmental "hostility;" i.e., the government may involve itself in benign adjustments when to assume a strict neutrality would precipitate undue hardships. This paper presents a study and discussion of the application of legislative free exercise in various cases which deal with schools and religion.

COSTANZO, Joseph F., S.J., "Wholesome Neutrality: Law and Education," *North Dakota Law Review*, 43:605, Summer, 1967.

Costanzo demonstrates that the "wall of separation" between church and state is a qualified "wall;" i.e., "there is to be no jurisdictional, institutional, or functional fusion of the two authorities, civil and religious." He shows, rather clearly, however, that the two are in fact interdependent and cooperating institutions. As regards governmental aid to parochial institutions, Costanzo cites numerous cases and comments at some length on the implications and interpretations of each. In a final prospectus the author notes that "the American community and its political and legal institutions . . . have a right as well as the awesome responsibility of fashioning their own church-state relations without evoking ancient fears and animosities."

DIERENFIELD, R. B., "The Impact of the Supreme Court Decisions on Religion in Public Schools," *Religious Education*, 62:445–51, September–October, 1967.

Dierenfield's study is a comparison of the results of two questionnaire surveys—one in 1960 and the other in 1966. The title of the article refers to the Supreme Court decisions of 1962 and 1963 prohibiting the recitation of prayers and the devotional reading of the Bible in public schools. Due to the sampling and feedback percentages, the author does not attempt to draw valid nationwide inferences. Although the prefatory notes, questions, and responses are interesting, the reader's curiosity may be aroused regarding the real relationship between the survey and the decisions in question.

DUKER, Sam, *The Public Schools and Religion: The Legal Context*, New York, Harper & Row, 1966.

A review of issues relating to religion and the schools, this book presents excerpts from twelve opinions of the United States Supreme Court. The cases cited range from *Meyer v.*

State of Nebraska (1923) to *Chamberlin v. Dade County Board of Public Instruction* (1964) and deal with the issues of the flag-salute, the "child-benefit" theory, religious instruction during school hours, and prayers in the class room. Introductory materials and commentary set the cases in perspective. The excerpts include majority opinions and, in several instances, the salient thrust of dissenting opinions. Brief explanatory comments supplement the excerpted opinions.

LOWELL, Stanley C., "Church Wealth and Tax Exemptions," *Kappan*, vol. L, no. 9, May, 1969.

The article is a summary of a study made by the author and Martin A. Larson. The author's intent in this article is to show that the tax-exempt status of churches is being exploited to the church's advantage—largely in the area of property taxes. Since public education is largely supported by property taxes, there are dollars missing that could be well used. Lowell's chief argument is that the exemptions are being claimed by the churches for businesses and enterprises—church-owned—whose functions do not relate to normal church activity. This practice, according to Lowell, is especially abusive in light of the growing requests by sectarian schools for public support.

3

Civil Rights and Education

INTRODUCTION

The American tradition of compulsory, universal education through a system of free, public schools carries with it the implicit notion that education is available to all. Few societies have attempted to create and implement a relevant education for such diverse clients as our own. Given the cultural, racial, religious, and ethnic pluralism in the United States, the problems inherent in undertaking universal education are monumental. Apologists for the public school, however, may be less helpful than capable critics, and the current debate about public education stems from broadly based criticism of the system's shortcomings.

Slogans and catch-phrases abound in literature about schooling. "Equality of educational opportunity," "education for democratic living," "relevant education," and "meeting the needs of all youth" are but a few of the high-sounding but hollow slogans cluttering the public school systems. The latent ambiguity of such slogans impedes the painful but necessary public examination of schools, pupils, teachers, and their educational attainments. The schools operate within the social, political, economic, and legal context of the larger society. Though they may reflect some of the social ideals, more likely they will mirror the social realities. The disparity between the real and imagined expectations and accomplishments of the public schools feeds the fire of public dialogue but does not necessarily produce appropriate action. The crises in urban schools across the nation illustrate the malfunctions plaguing our social institutions.

Schools bear the brunt of current social unrest. Public education touches the lives of the vast majority of American families, rich and poor alike. Schools are visible; pupils and parents see in them an extension of the "establishment" and a ready focus for their discontent. By accident or design, we seem to have developed the expectation that our public schools should solve the unsolved social problems and do so quickly. This expectation, however unwarranted, stems from the almost childlike faith of Western man in the magic of education; if only we knew more, all social problems could be solved. Such faith may par-

121

tially explain the evolution of public schools from a fundamental intellectual mission to multipurpose goals.

The public schools are charged with the responsibility for the socialization and the emotional, physical, spiritual, and intellectual development of all who enter. In so many areas where parents, community, church, and social agencies have failed, the schools are expected to succeed. Some of the problems hounding schools have been solicited by teachers and administrators. One characteristic of a professional is a candid awareness of his capabilities and his limitations. There is little excuse for schools, staffed by alleged professionals, to undertake tasks far beyond the capabilities of the teachers, the facilities, and the resources available to them. To do so invites unreal expectations and perpetrates fraud and deceit on innocent children and sincere parents.

American public schools are ostensibly democratic institutions. The fundamental reasons for public schools undergird the national claim to participatory democracy by informed participants. Justice demands, therefore, that approximately equal opportunities for education would be available to all who qualify to enter. To conduct a system of public education in conflict with the civil rights of pupils, parents, and teachers is a contradiction of terms. The fact that so many cases involving civil rights under the state and federal constitutions should arise in the schools does little to inspire confidence in the slogans and catch-phrases so familiar in the jargon of public education.

The civil rights issues raised in the schools flow primarily from the First, Fifth, and Fourteenth Amendments to the United States Constitution. The applicable sections read as follows:

FIRST AMENDMENT
Congress shall make no law respecting an establishment of religion, or prohibiting the free exercise thereof; or abridging the freedom of speech . . .

FIFTH AMENDMENT
(No person) . . . shall be compelled in any criminal case to be a witness against himself, nor be deprived of life, liberty, or property, without due process of law: . . .

FOURTEENTH AMENDMENT
. . . No state shall make or enforce any law which shall abridge the privileges or immunities of citizens of the United States; nor shall any state deprive any person of life, liberty, or property, without due process of law; nor deny to any person within its jurisdiction the equal protection of the laws . . .

Under rights claimed through these three amendments (and parallel state constitution provisions), citizens have raised legal issues about racial segregation, mandatory flag-salute and related exercises, and loyalty oaths for school employees. Recently students in high schools and universities have turned to strikes, walkouts, boycotts, and similar protest techniques to dramatize alleged wrongs in school curricula, rules, and governance. The legal implications of student activism are not at all clear. The resultant problems thrust upon school boards, administrators, and teachers, however, are both real and frightening.

SCHOOL SEGREGATION

School segregation cases are probably the most widely known examples of civil rights issues in school law. *Plessy* v. *Ferguson*, 163 U.S. 537 (1896), and *Brown v. Board of Education*, 347 U.S. 483 (1954), are perhaps the two most familiar school segregation cases. *Plessy* did not involve the schools; the issue arose under a Louisiana statute requiring segregated railway accommodations for travel within the state. The United States Supreme Court, in a decision widely cited, held that the state law did not violate either the Thirteenth Amendment (prohibiting involuntary servitude) or the Fourteenth Amendment to the United States Constitution. Despite the fact that the case was confined to intrastate railway accommodations, the decision was used to support the notion that "separate but equal" school facilities for black pupils were consistent with constitutional principles. *Brown* specifically overturned the *Plessy* decision and held, in brief, that racially segregated schools are *inherently* unequal. In addition to striking down state laws requiring, permitting, or fostering segregation in schools, the *Brown* opinion ordered states (and, by inference, school boards) to eliminate segregated schools with all deliberate speed. Compliance has been less than spectacular in many school districts.

Racial segregation is a fact in public education. Prior to the United States Supreme Court 1954 decision in *Brown v. Board of Education*, 347 U.S. 483 (1954), and the subsequent decision, *Brown v. Board of Education*, 349 U.S. 294 (1955), racial segregation in the schools was of two types: (a) de jure segregation supported by governmental action or inaction and (b) de facto segregation not supported by governmental action but existing in fact. After the *Brown* decision, which invalidated state school segregation laws, only de facto segregation persisted. Through various legal maneuvers and delaying action, some states continued segregated schools under color of state law. The *Brown* decision announced the law of the land. Whether each state complied is another matter. The response to the *Brown* decision was immediate and intense. States' reactions ranged from enthusiastic support and immediate legislative compliance to open rejection and complex legislative obstacles. The public schools in an entire state were closed; state support was channeled into "private" schools; and a variety of massive resistance schemes to thwart the court decision emerged in several states. Disregarding the niceties of definition, segregation in public education has not declined substantially since 1954. With the movement of whites from the "inner city" and their replacement by blacks, many urban school systems are, in fact, more racially segregated than ever before. It is not mere flippancy to observe that racially integrated schools are impossible without white pupils. The task of undoing a century or more of segregated public schools is complicated. Segregated housing, untouched by the *Brown* decision, obstructs desegregated neighborhood schools, prompts the need for busing schemes, and adds to the schools' problems. Many school districts discovered, after *Brown*, a deep and abiding need to examine pupils for the purpose of placement in schools. Many such examination and placement plans resulted in substantial segregation of pupils by race. Other complications arose from "freedom of choice" attendance plans through which pupils could transfer out of schools threatened with integration. Private schools, some with state support, have developed to resegregate pupils. The point of all this is simple: desegregation of the public schools requires more than a court decree; some measure of coercive power apparently is needed to overcome the network of resistance.

With the rejection of de jure segregation in 1954, the responsibility for eliminating segregation in the schools fell on local boards of education. The policies enunciated and implemented by local boards came under closer examination in many school districts. The result is the familiar dilemma: school boards are pressured to promote school desegregation by some community groups and to delay it by others. The dilemma is a phenomenon of the local control structure in American schools. Colloquially stated, the local school board frequently finds itself damned (by local voters) if it "does" and damned (by state or federal authorities) if it "doesn't."

Local boards have responded to desegregation pressures in a variety of ways. Busing children to schools outside regular attendance areas in an effort to achieve a viable racial balance is one of the more popular compliance schemes. Redrawing attendance boundaries to reduce racial imbalance is another. Plans to circumvent the *Brown* holding are imaginative. Various such plans result in the separation of pupils on the basis of race. So far as such plans classify pupils on racial bases, the courts generally strike them down. Intelligence tests have been known to be culturally discriminative and their use can result in plausible separation of pupils. Some boards have embraced the "neighborhood school" ideology with warmth and zeal. Neighborhood schools tend to reflect the racial segregation of neighborhoods and, in many districts, constitute de facto segregation in public schools.

STUDENT MILITANCY

The legal implications of student protests, boycotts, sit-ins, strikes, and general militancy in colleges and public schools are not yet clear. The campus and school disturbances often disrupt school operations, cause schools to close or restrict their activities, and result in extensive property damage, personal injury, and even death. Appropriate provisions exist in the law to deal with criminal acts, but the civil law regarding interference with the schools is less clear. The notion that each person is responsible for the consequences of his wrongful conduct is a fundamental principle of tort law. Assuming legal competency, students who cause injury to person and damage to property can be held accountable in damage under civil law or face prosecution and penalties under the criminal law. School authorities are empowered to take appropriate disciplinary action; the manner of its exercise in particular cases likely will raise the pertinent legal issues and ultimately establish the dimensions of the law. The law regarding suspension, expulsion, and discipline of pupils will be discussed in Chapter 5; this section will attempt only to place the student militancy phenomenon in the framework of civil rights.

The First Amendment clearly protects freedom of speech and freedom of the press. These rights, however, are not unlimited. To recall Justice Oliver Holmes' famous comment—freedom of speech does not condone one's yelling "fire" in a crowded theater. The right to free speech may be limited by a conflicting, overriding public interest. Another example is the limitation of free speech in the military. The question is, how far may school governing bodies go in restricting students' speech and conduct without infringing on their civil rights? There is no question that school boards can make reasonable rules of conduct for pupils. Likewise, boards can impose reasonable disciplinary measures on those students who violate the rules. School authorities are under no obligation to support student newspapers or other student publications. The problem seldom arises from the official board-supported student publications but rather from the "underground" publications, privately printed and distributed by and to the students. Undoubtedly, the board can ban in-school distribution of this literature and punish violators, but the board has no clear right to punish students for the writing or printing. The test required by the First Amendment is whether the board's interest in restricting free speech (to prevent disruption of the school, for example) justifies the infringement.

Serious questions arise from student picketing. Under the legal principles applied in labour disputes, peaceful picketing is permitted. Students marching, chanting slogans, and other reasonable visual and vocal protest are entitled to the same protection as are other types of peaceful picketing. The school might invoke trespass laws against unauthorized entry onto school property and might even use reasonable and appropriate means to eject trespassers from school premises. Whether boards can lawfully punish or discipline students, however, for exercising their civil rights as citizens, apart from the school day or off the school premises, is not at all clear. There are cases to support the school authorities disciplining pupils for misbehavior away from the school. The usual rationale for this disciplinary power is not *where* or *when* the offense occurs, but whether it is detrimental to the good order of the school and the welfare of the pupils. Discipline imposed for misconduct in the school may rest comfortably on the rationale; serious restriction of students' rights of speech, as citizens, may be quite another matter.

As student demonstrations and protests spread and school authorities impose discipline on participants, civil rights questions will be presented to the courts. The courts may be asked to decide where discipline ends and infringement of civil rights begins. The applicability of the freedom of speech and press to student protest and student militancy may be tested. Already there is ample evidence that the courts will give closer scrutiny to due process in pupil discipline matters. School boards should carefully review state and federal laws bearing on civil rights prior to their framing and enforcing personnel policies.

Readings

The History of Racial Segregation in American Education

Virgil A. Clift
School and Society (May 7, 1960), **88,** 220–229

If one is to understand the history of racial segregation in American education, attention must be given to economic and social forces which operated at various times and in different places in the nation. The development of schools for Negroes has represented largely the influences of social forces outside the Negro community.

Much to the surprise of many, the Negro has been a part of the American scene from the time the nation was discovered to the present. It has been claimed that Pedro Alonso Nino of the crew of Columbus was a Negro. Negroes were with Spanish and Portuguese explorers who came to the New World. Thirty Negroes were with Balboa when he discovered the Pacific Ocean, and Cortez took them with him into Mexico. Estevanico, a Negro, was one of the outstanding explorers who opened up New Mexico and Arizona for the Spanish. As early as 1501, Spain relinquished her ban and permitted Negroes to go to the Spanish lands of the New World.[1]

The development and exploitation of vast resources found in the New World made cheap labor a necessity. The economic background of American Indians, their inability to adjust to the discipline of the plantation system, and their susceptibility to disease made Indian slavery unprofitable. Landless, penniless whites from Europe voluntarily indentured themselves and were brought to the New World, but it soon was realized that this was an inadequate source of cheap labor. Once in the New World, they created problems. Many ran away, were difficult to identify when they did, and even sued ship captains and their masters to gain freedom. Therefore, Negro slavery was introduced because the supply of slaves was inexhaustible, slave traffic itself was important economically, Negro slaves were cheaper in the long run, and they presented fewer problems than indentured whites.

Slave trade to America was opened formally in 1517, when Bishop Las Casas advocated the encouragement of immigration to the New World by permitting Spaniards to import 12 Negroes each. From the discovery of America until the

1. J. H. Franklin, "From Slavery to Freedom" (New York: Knopf, 1947), p. 46.

[Reprinted with permission of the author and the publisher, Society for the Advancement of Education, Inc.]

Civil War, slavery either flourished or diminished in cycles, depending primarily upon economic conditions in various parts of America.

As we consider the history of education for the Negro in America, it is important to remember that segregation was influenced at various times and places by different causal factors. Prior to the Civil War, if and when Negroes received any of the rudiments of education, it was almost always on a segregated basis depending on the will and desire of white slave owners or white leadership in the area. In the South after the Civil War, segregated education had the sanction of state and local laws. In some of the border states, permissive segregation was written into statutes. Before the 1954 Supreme Court decision on segregated education, some states of the North had segregated schools which state laws permitted but did not make mandatory. In the 1920's and the depression years of the 1930's, some segregated schools came into existence in the North and border states at the request of some Negro leaders. Usually these requests were based on three justifications. First, separate education for Negro children was sought in order that trained Negro teachers would have employment opportunities; seldom, if ever, could they secure employment in mixed schools. Second, some thought that separate schools contributed to the development of Negro leadership, since in mixed schools Negro children rarely were given an opportunity in leadership roles. Finally, others thought that the separate school protected Negro youth from the prejudices of white teachers and youth and thereby reduced the probability of developing in them feelings of inferiority, rejection, and hostility—all of which have a lasting effect on the personality and achievement of the individual. In most areas of the North, restrictive covenants and economic factors helped to create neighborhoods inhabited primarily or entirely by Negroes. Consequently, the schools in such neighborhoods became Negro schools. . . .

DEVELOPMENTS DURING THE TWENTIETH CENTURY

In the early years of the 20th century, public education for Negroes in the South received significant impetus from the outside through the contributions of such philanthropists as Rockefeller and Peabody. The Anna T. Jeanes Fund, in 1908, inaugurated the "Jeanes Teacher" program to improve the quality of instruction in rural Negro schools. Beginning in 1913, the Julius Rosenwald Fund provided grants for Negro school construction, and by 1932 more than 5,000 Negro school buildings in 883 counties of 15 southern and border states had been built with Rosenwald aid. Rosenwald grants provided an invaluable incentive and accounted for about 15% of the money spent on school construction for Negroes. In addition, 17% came from direct contributions made by Negroes themselves. At the end of the Rosenwald building program, the per-pupil value of Negro school property was less than one-fifth as great as that of white schools. An even more telling index to the relative growth of the dual school systems is provided by a comparison of teachers' salaries. Between 1900 and 1930, the average white salary rose from slightly less than $200 to $900, while the average Negro salary rose from $100 to $400. And these figures reflect the peak of a national boom, both in national income and in school population.

The effects of this disparate policy were evident in the concentration of Negro children in the lower grades during the first half of the 20th century. As late as 1920, 85% of all Negro pupils in the South were enrolled in the first four grades. In 1916, there were only 67 Negro public high schools with fewer than 20,000 students.[1]

Between 1896, when the Plessy decision was handed down, and 1930, only three cases involving Negro education came before the Supreme Court. In none of these was school segregation directly challenged, nor did the Court find occasion to order relief of any kind for Negro Plaintiffs. In 1899, the Supreme Court heard an appeal by a group of Negroes from Augusta, Ga., who demanded an end to public support for two white high schools after the sole Negro high school had been discontinued. The majority opinion in *Cumming v. Richmond County* held that the relief requested was improper. In 1908, the Court heard the case of *Berea College v. Kentucky*, which involved the right of a privately chartered college to teach both races in defiance of the Kentucky law making segregation mandatory. The Court ruled against Berea on technical grounds. The case was generally accepted as a reflection of the Court's feeling that segregation was a matter better left to the states. *Gong Lum v. Rice* came before the Court from Mississippi in 1927. The issue was whether Mississippi could properly classify a Chinese child as "colored" and therefore require her to attend a Negro school. The Court upheld the Mississippi law and Chief Justice Taft took the occasion to offer a reminder that the "separate but equal" doctrine was still in effect: "had the petition alleged specifically that there was no colored school in Martha Lum's neighborhood to which she could conveniently go, a different question would have been presented. . . ." None of these cases directly challenged the constitutionality of segregation in education.

In 1935, almost 40 years after the Supreme Court handed down its historic Plessy doctrine permitting "separate but equal" public educational facilities, Donald Murray, a Negro, applied for admission to the law school of the University of Maryland at Baltimore and was duly refused in accordance with Maryland's segregation statutes. His complaint was based on the fact that Maryland provided no law school for Negroes within its boundaries but attempted to meet the Plessy doctrine by offering a limited number of scholarships for Negroes in institutions outside the state. The Maryland Court of Appeals upheld Murray's contention and accepted the argument that out-of-state scholarships, which covered only the cost of tuition, placed Negro students who had to live away from home at an economic disadvantage.

1. For further information on the inequality of the segregated school system in the South, see Fourteenth U.S. Census, vol. II, p. 1043; "The Negro Year Book, 1925-26"; Bulletin No. 39, Department of Interior, Bureau of Education ("Negro Education"); N. C. Newbold, *Annals of the American Academy of Political and Social Sciences*, November, 1928, p. 209; and V. A. Clift, *School and Society*, 72, Oct. 7, 1952.

The Gaines case in 1938 was the real forerunner of the decisions of the '40's which opened graduate schools in the South to Negroes. Lloyd Gaines sued for admission to the law school of the University of Missouri on the grounds that no separate law school for Negroes was provided in the state and that the out-of-state scholarships available to him did not satisfy the requirement of equal treatment. The Supreme Court reversed the courts of Missouri in an opinion which announced a new point of law. The Court removed the legal basis for providing out-of-state scholarships for Negro applicants and also laid new emphasis upon the personal rights of the applicants. Nevertheless, it still honored the Plessy doctrine by not directly ordering Gaines admitted to the university.

This set into motion in the South a feverish expansion of state-supported Negro graduate and professional schools designed especially to deny Negroes admission to white state-supported colleges and universities.[1] The decade following the Murray and Gaines Cases witnessed the most revolutionary change to take place in the entire history of education in the South. Either because of a strange fondness for the Negro and his educational welfare or because of an abhorrence for the idea of further litigation challenging the "separate but equal" doctrine, the entire South began to spend an unprecedented proportion of its income for the education of Negro children in public schools.

It came as a surprise to the South that Negroes were not impressed with the makeshift graduate schools, the increased expenditure on capital improvements, the attempts to equalize salaries, and the general pronounced increase in expenditures for Negro education. Educational opportunities for Negroes were greatly improved, to be sure, but they viewed this as irrelevant because they did not judge their conditions in comparison with those of slaves in Russia or the impoverished millions in Asia. Instead, Negroes viewed their conditions by the standards of their fellow citizens and by the guarantees the American system made for them. They were and are keenly aware that they are at the very crux of the great American Experiment and that their drive to secure full educational rights as human beings and citizens is the acid test of the American Way of Life. They are proud to be American citizens and have a burning desire to help make American democracy work.

Therefore, Negroes prepared to make an onslaught and frontal attack on the validity of segregation in higher education. From 1946 to 1948, the Sipuel, McLaurin, and Sweatt cases came before the U. S. Supreme Court. Ada Lois Sipuel initiated a case against the University of Oklahoma in 1946, which was hinged upon the Gaines case and which brought forth another significant point of law. She demonstrated that Oklahoma maintained no law school for Negroes, and the United States Supreme Court held that the state must provide her with opportunity for a legal education—and added that it must do so as it did for any other qualified applicant.

In the meantime, G. H. McLaurin, another Negro applicant, led a separate

1. For details on this new pattern of discrimination, see V. A. Clift, *op. cit.*, p. 226.

legal attack in 1948 all the way to the point of admission to the University of Oklahoma Graduate School at Norman. The Oklahoma Legislature amended the state law to permit the admission of Negroes to the university for enrollment in those courses not offered by Langston University, the Negro college. But at the same time the legislature stipulated that segregation should be maintained on the campus, and McLaurin was required to sit apart from white students in the classroom, the library, and the dining hall. In 1949, McLaurin went back to the Federal court, and in the appeal the Supreme Court moved another significant step away from its old interpretation of Plessy. The restrictions placed upon McLaurin, it held, "impair and inhibit his ability to study, to learn his profession." The Court concluded, "The Appellant, having been admitted to a state-supported school, must receive the same treatment at the hands of the state as students of other races."

Herman Sweatt had applied for admission to the University of Texas law school in 1946. The Sweatt case differed from all others in that his attorneys argued, in sum, that no segregated Negro school actually could provide equal educational opportunity. His attorneys not only argued that the new Negro law school which had been established by Texas was materially inferior, but offered the testimony of anthropologists, psychologists, and educators to show that Negroes were as capable of learning as whites, that classification of students by race was arbitrary and unjust, and that segregation was harmful to personality adjustment. The Court obviously gave weight to these contentions by ruling out segregation in specific instances and largely invalidating it in the field of graduate and professional training. Few if any state Negro colleges in the South could meet the requirements posed by the Court in its decision.

Meanwhile, the southern states had pooled their resources to set up a regional program for higher education which would serve the students of both races from all participating states. This plan was denounced by Negro leaders as another device for preserving segregation at the university level. The Southern Regional Educational Board and the regional compact were immediately challenged in 1949 when a Negro applicant was denied admission to the University of Maryland School of Nursing on the grounds that she was entitled to out-of-state training at Meharry Medical School (Negro) under the regional plan. The Maryland Court of Appeals ordered her admitted to the state university. Beginning with this decision, more public institutions have admitted Negroes, and now state universities in only five states have not admitted them—those being in Alabama, Florida, Georgia, Mississippi, and South Carolina. Enrollment of Negroes has been restricted, however, primarily to graduate and professional schools.

The relentless legal assault upon the upper ramparts of the segregated educational structure had been planned and executed with great care. Negro leaders now reasoned that the anachronistic system of segregation in public elementary and secondary schools perpetuated segregation and discrimination in all other phases of public life of the nation. They maintained that segregation in the lower schools was a divisive and anti-democratic device perpetuating an obsolete caste system which flatly controverted the basic ethical concepts of the American Judeo-Christian tradition.

By this time the Negro masses were demanding the National Association for the Advancement of Colored People to press harder and with greater speed for equal rights in all fields. The masses, in the North and South, were making such great demands on Negro leaders that the leaders actually were being pressured into action in many instances where otherwise they would have been reluctant.[1]

Therefore, in 1952, the long course of litigation over separate education in America brought before the U. S. Supreme Court five separate cases which challenged head-on the Plessy doctrine of "separate but equal."[2]

Each of these cases raised the basic issues of segregation in education in a somewhat different way. The implications reached the whole of the nation's segregated pattern as well as the basic division of authority between the Federal government and the sovereign states. The moral overtones had practical repercussions on America's effort in international politics to keep black, brown, and yellow peoples of the world from swinging into the communist orbit.

On May 17, 1954, the U. S. Supreme Court ruled unanimously that segregation of the races in public education was unconstitutional. The Court made its position abundantly clear in the following unequivocal statement:

In approaching this problem, we cannot turn the clock back to 1868 when the Amendment was adopted, or even to 1896 when *Plessy v. Ferguson* was written. We must consider public education in the light of its full development and its present place in American life throughout the Nation. Only in this way can it be determined if segregation in public schools deprives these plaintiffs of the equal protection of the laws. . . .

We come then to the question presented: Does segregation of children in public schools solely on the basis of race, even though the physical facilities and other "tangible" factors may be equal, deprive the children of the minority group of equal education opportunities? We believe that it does.

. . . Segregation of white and colored children in public schools has a detrimental effect upon the colored children. The impact is greater when it has the sanction of the law; for the policy of separating the races is usually interpreted as denoting the inferiority of the Negro group.

Desegregation was progressing slowly, even in the South, before this historic and far-reaching decision. In compliance with the decision, school desegregation began in the fall of 1954 in a few large cities, notably Wilmington, Baltimore, and Washington, and in some scattered counties in Missouri, Arkansas, and West Virginia. By the fourth anniversary of the Supreme Court's original decision, the desegregation process was at work in 10 out of the 17 states that previously had compulsory school segregation. In keeping with the Court-ordained "deliberate speed" clause, desegregation moved faster in Kentucky, Oklahoma, and

1. S. Robinson and T. Marshall, *Journal of Negro Education*, 21: 332-336, Summer, 1952.
2. These cases were from: Clarendon, S. C. (Briggs-Elliot); Prince Edward County, Va. (Davis v. County School Board); Topeka, Kan. (Brown v. Board of Education); Wilmington, Del. (Belton v. Gebhart, Bulah v. Gebhart); and Washington, District of Columbia (Bolling v. Sharpe).

Texas than in Tennessee and North Carolina. But it did spread. Out of 2,889 southern school districts with both white and colored pupils, desegregation had begun in 764 by the end of four years. Of these, fewer than 40 were compelled to desegregate by specific court order.

Then, in the fall of 1958, desegregation appeared to have been brought almost to a standstill by deep southern hostility. New desegregation moves were limited to 13 school districts in the entire South; and in contrast to this modicum of progress toward compliance, schools were closed in Little Rock, Ark., and in sections of Virginia to avoid integration. Desegregation seemed to have been stopped short by seven states willing to dispense with public schools rather than to yield to racial mixing.

By the middle of the 1958–59 school year, the situation had taken a different turn. Negro pupils had entered white schools in Alexandria, Va., without incident, bringing a third new community into the desegregation column—and not in a border state but in Virginia, the former center of massive resistance. Desegregation was thus on the move again, having met the ultimate test of school closing and having proved, at least in Virginia, that parents placed sufficiently high value on public education for their children to endure a limited amount of integration. Georgia, Alabama, and Mississippi seemed not to be ready to back away from massive resistance. But the solid front had been broken, and desegregation was making some marked advances in its sixth year; once again it began slowly to approach inevitability.[1]

The problem of providing for all American youth an adequate and equal educational opportunity which is truly democratic in all its aspects is a difficult one. This problem sometimes is made more difficult because of emotionalism, the lack of understanding of issues, and hot-headedness. In spite of mitigating factors, the story of the education of the Negro has contributed a fascinating chapter to the continuing history of education and democracy in the United States.

1. Editorial, *Baltimore Sun*, March 8, 1959.

Public School Desegregation: Legal Remedies for De Facto Segregation

J. Skelly Wright

J. Skelly Wright is a Judge of the United States Court of Appeals
for the District of Columbia Circuit.
This Article was delivered as the sixth annual James Madison Lecture,
on February 17, 1965, at the New York University School of Law.
Requests to reprint all or part of this Article should be addressed
to the Dean, New York University School of Law.
New York University Law Review (April, 1965), **40,** 297

One hundred years ago this country abolished slavery and decreed by solemn
constitutional amendment that "all persons born or naturalized in the United
States, and subject to the jurisdiction thereof, are citizens of the United States
and of the State wherein they reside."[1] Thus, at last, our Negro citizens were
included in the truths we hold self-evident, "that all men are created equal, that
they are endowed by their Creator with certain unalienable Rights, that among
these are Life, Liberty and the pursuit of Happiness."[2]

One hundred years have passed and the promise of equality remains, in large
part, unfulfilled. It seems that in these 100 years we have succeeded in changing a
system of slavery into a caste system based on race which may, in some respects,
be more difficult to uproot than slavery itself.

Before considering the problem of racial discrimination as it confronts this
country today, it may be useful briefly to recall how the great hopes and aspirations of 100 years ago were curdled in the aftermath of the Civil War. And it will
be particularly interesting to note that the instrument of destruction then—
the United States Supreme Court—is now the architect of the new dream of
equality and freedom. . . .

Whether a state can be, and should be, compelled by law to correct purely
adventitious de facto segregation in its public schools admittedly present serious
problems—both legal and practical. This question also involves the emotional
area of state's rights. How far should the courts go in requiring the states
affirmatively to afford equal opportunity to equal education? Is the enforcement
of this right sufficiently important to risk further assaults on the federal courts in
general and the Supreme Court in particular? If the Supreme Court does not
undertake this burden, at least initially, by recognizing the constitutional right to
equal educational opportunity, can we confidently assume that the Congress or

---

1. U.S. Const., amend. XIV, § 1.
2. U.S. Declaration of Independence.

the states will protect the Negro in the realization of this right? Perhaps some background on the importance of public education in this country may be helpful in answering these questions.

The importance of generalized education, at least at the elementary and high school level, is no new dogma. It is as old as the theory of popular government. On these shores, it has always been one of the principal articles of the democratic faith. In 1787, in the Northwest Ordinance, the Continental Congress declared: "[S]chools and the means of education shall forever be encouraged."[1] Jefferson termed general education the only "sure foundation . . . for the preservation of freedom,"[2] "without which no republic can maintain itself in strength."[3] Today, all the more, it remains "the very foundation of good citizenship."[4] But, because our society has grown increasingly complex, education is now also an economic necessity. "In these days, it is doubtful that any child may reasonably be expected to succeed in life if he is denied the opportunity of an education."[5] Thus, adequate schooling is no longer a privilege that can be made available to the few; it is the indispensable equipment of all men.

The critical role of education in our contemporary society gives meaning to the associated constitutional rights. But the full importance of the state's obligation to provide equal education cannot be appreciated without noticing the long and consistent history of general education as a governmental function.

Washington,[6] Jefferson,[7] Madison,[8] and John Adams[9] all advocated governmental responsibility in the diffusion of knowledge through common schools. With such leadership, the public school movement soon took root, so that, by 1850, almost every state in the Union had at least made a start toward a comprehensive system of education.[10] There was then no retreat from the view that education is a state function. On the contrary, except for the temporary disruption resulting from the Civil War, the next century is a chronology of progress, studded with important reaffirmations of the doctrine. Very soon most of the states solemnly proclaimed a right to public education in their constitutions. Significantly, the 39th Congress, which drafted the fourteenth amendment, put down public education as one of the fundamental tenets of republicanism,[11]

1. Ordinance of 1787, § 14, art. 3.
2. Letter from Thomas Jefferson to Whyte, Aug. 13, 1786, in 5 Writings of Thomas Jefferson 396 (Berg ed. 1907).
3. Letter from Thomas Jefferson to John Tyler, May 26, 1810, in 12 Writings of Thomas Jefferson 393 (Berg ed. 1907).
4. Brown v. Board of Educ. 347 U.S. 483, 493 (1954).
5. Ibid.
6. See, e.g., Letter from George Washington to Samuel Chase, Jan. 5, 1785, in 28 Writings of George Washington 27 (Bicentennial ed. 1938).
7. For Jefferson's own summary of his proposed "Bill for the More General Diffusion of Knowledge," see his Notes on the State of Virginia 146-49 (Peden ed. 1955).
8. Letter from James Madison to Thomas W. Gilmer, Sept. 6, 1830, in The Complete Madison 314-15 (Padover ed. 1953).
9. See Adams, Dissertation on the Canon and the Feudal Law (1765), in 3 Works of John Adams 455-56 (Charles Francis Adams ed. 1851).
10. See Brown v. Board of Educ., 347 U.S. 483, 489 n.4 (1954) and authorities cited therein.
11. See, e.g., Act of July 16, 1866, ch. 200, 14 Stat. 173, 176 (1866); Act of March 2, 1867, ch. 157, 14 Stat. 434 (1867).

and their immediate successors imposed it as a pre-condition to readmission of the states still considered in rebellion and to the admission of new states.[1] The full development came with the adoption of compulsory school attendance laws which necessarily imply free public education.

The courts, also, have long characterized education as a function of the state. As early as 1874, Judge Cooley, whose *Constitutional Limitations* had appeared in the year of the ratification of the fourteenth amendment, expressed "no little surprise" that anyone should question the propriety of the state's furnishing "a liberal education to the youth of the state in schools brought within the reach of all classes."[2] He "supposed it had always been understood . . that education, not merely in the rudiments, but in an enlarged sense, was regarded as an important practical advantage to be supplied at their option to rich and poor alike, and not as something pertaining merely to the culture and accomplishment . . . of those whose accumulated wealth enabled them to pay for it."[3] In 1907, the Supreme Court, speaking through Mr. Justice Holmes, recognized that education is properly considered "one of the first objects of public care."[4] And in 1947, Mr. Justice Black, also for the Supreme Court, wrote: "It is much too late to argue that legislation intended to facilitate the opportunity of children to get a secular education serves no public purpose."[5] Now even college training has become a public concern. As Mr. Justice Frankfurter put it, "The need for higher education and the duty of the state to provide it as part of a public educational system, are part of the democratic faith of most of our states."[6] The full impact of this development was summed up in *Brown v. Board of Education*: "Today, education is perhaps the most important function of state and local governments."[7]

From the fact that public education is the states' most important function, it does not necessarily follow that segregated public education, whatever the cause, is illegal. But the importance of public education in a democratic society imperatively requires affirmative action on the part of the state to assure each child his fair share, and a child in a segregated Negro school does not receive his fair share. Public education, once offered by the state, "must be made available to all on equal terms."[8] And segregated education, being "inherently unequal," is therefore unconstitutional.[9]

A racially segregated Negro school is an inferior school. It is "inherently unequal."[10] No honest person would even suggest, for example, that the segregated slum school provides educational opportunity equal to that provided by the white suburban public school. Thus children compelled by state compulsory

1. McCollum v. Board of Educ., 333 U.S. 203, 220-21 & n.9 (1948) (opinion of Mr. Justice Frankfurter).
2. Stuart v. School Dist. No. 1, 30 Mich. 69, 75 (1874).
3. Ibid.
4. Interstate Consol. St. Ry. v. Massachusetts, 207 U.S. 79, 87 (1907).
5. Everson v. Board of Educ., 330 U.S. 1, 7 (1947).
6. Board of Educ. v. Barnette, 319 U.S. 624, 656 (1943) (dissenting opinion).
7. 347 U.S. 483, 493 (1954).
8. Ibid.
9. Id. at 495.
10. Brown v. Board of Educ., 347 U.S. 483 (1954).

attendance laws to attend the segregated Negro school are deprived of equal protection of the law. The fact that the classification to attend the school is based on geography,[1] and not on race, does not necessarily make the school less segregated or less inferior. Nor does it make the classification less illegal unless it can be shown that no reasonable classification will alleviate the inequality.[2]

The touchstone in determining equal protection of the law in public education is equal educational opportunity, not race. If classification by race is used to achieve the invidious discrimination, the constitutional insult is exacerbated. But the focus must remain on the result achieved. If the untoward result derives from racial classification, such classification is per se unconstitutional. Where the result is segregation, and therefore unequal educational opportunity, the classification used, whatever it is, is constitutionally suspect and a heavy burden is placed on the school board and the state to show, not only innocent intent, but also lack of a suitable alternative.[3] In short, since segregation in public schools and unequal educational opportunity are two sides of the same coin, the state, in order to provide equal educational opportunity, has the affirmative constitutional obligation to eliminate segregation, however it arises.

Our experience with the cases involving racial segregation in Southern schools has blurred the issue presented by de facto segregation. In the Southern school cases the classification was on the basis of race. It was this classification that achieved the segregated, and therefore unequal, schools. What made the classification invidious, and therefore unconstitutional, was the inequality it produced. When the same invidious result is achieved by another classification, that classification likewise must be tested by the Constitution.

Perhaps the clearest statement of the principle involved in adventitious de facto segregation has been made by Chief Judge Sweeney of the United States District Court for the District of Massachusetts in the only case to date, state or federal, squarely holding that a state may be required to relieve racial imbalance in the public schools. In ordering the city of Springfield to file a desegregation plan for its schools by April 3, 1965, Judge Sweeney wrote:

The defendants argue, nevertheless, that there is no constitutional mandate to remedy racial imbalance. . . . But that is not the question. The question is whether there is a constitutional duty to provide equal educational opportunities for all children within the system. While *Brown* answered that question affirmatively in the context of coerced segregation, the constitutional fact—the inadequacy of segregated education—is the same in this case, and I so find. It is neither just nor sensible to proscribe segregation having its basis in affirmative state action while at the same time failing to provide a remedy for segregation which grows out of discrimination in housing, or other economic or social factors. Education is tax supported and compulsory, and public school

1. Compare the reapportionment cases: Reynolds v. Sims, 377 U.S. 533 (1964); Wesberry v. Sanders, 376 U.S. 1 (1964); Gray v. Sanders, 372 U.S. 368 (1963). See also Barksdale v. Springfield School Comm., 237 F. Supp. 543 (D. Mass. 1965).
2. McLaughlin v. Florida, 379 U.S. 184 (1964). Compare Sherbert v. Verner, 374 U.S. 398, 406–09 (1963).
3. McLaughlin v. Florida.

educators, therefore, must deal with inadequacies within the educational system as they arise, and it matters not that the inadequacies are not of their making. This is not to imply that the neighborhood school policy per se is unconstitutional, but that it must be abandoned or modified when it results in segregation in fact.[1]

There can, of course, be no mathematical formula[2] to determine at what point the unequal educational opportunity inherent in racial imbalance and de facto school segregation rises to constitutional dimension. A judgment must be made in each case based on the substantiality of the imbalance under the particular circumstances. Once substantial racial imbalance is shown, however, no further proof of unequal educational opportunity is required. What may be substantial imbalance in Boston, where the Negro school population is relatively small, may not be in Washington, where the Negro school population is approaching 90 per cent. Numbers alone do not provide the answer. The relevant population area is an important consideration. Is the relevant area the city alone or the suburbs as well? A variety of other circumstances may also be important in answering this sometimes difficult question.

The judicial process is equipped to develop the necessary evidence and to make the judgment as to substantial racial imbalance. The word "substantial" does provide a certain or mechanical guide to decision, but judicial judgments based on similar guides are made routinely. The test for negligence in every case is whether the party charged acted "reasonably" or as "the reasonably prudent person would have" under the circumstances. In every jury case, civil and criminal, the judge decides whether the evidence against the defendant is "substantial" before he allows the case to go to the jury. The examples can be multiplied, but the point is already made. The determination as to substantial racial imbalance, and therefore unequal educational opportunity, is clearly within the competence of the judiciary. As in other areas involving due process and equal protection of the law, the guidelines will have to be staked out on a case-by-case basis.[3] Once substantial racial imbalance is shown, however, the case for relief is complete and the burden of going forward with the evidence falls on the state.[4]

Assuming the constitutional question is answered affirmatively in favor of the Negro, the question of appropriate remedy arises. What can a state do—what can a court require a state to do—to relieve racial imbalance? In short, what, if any, remedies are available?

Initially, public school authorities must be cured of the neighborhood school syndrome. The neighborhood school, like the little red school house, has many emotional ties and practical advantages. The neighborhood school serves as the neighborhood center, easily accessible, where children can gather to play on holidays and parents' clubs can meet at any time. But twentieth-century education

1. Barksdale v. Springfield School Comm., 237 F. Supp. 543, 546 (D. Mass. 1965).
2. For example, a school, though mathematically racially imbalanced as compared with other schools in the area, ordinarily would not be racially segregated in the constitutional sense unless the Negro population of the school outnumbered the white.
3. Davidson v. New Orleans, 96 U.S. 97, 104 (1877).
4. See note 2, p. 136.

is not necessarily geared to the neighborhood school. In fact, the trend is definitely in the opposite direction. Educational parks, each consisting of a complex of schools, science buildings, libraries, gymnasiums, auditoriums and playing fields, are beginning to replace the neighborhood school. Although the development of the educational park idea in education is unrelated to the question of racial segregation, its use in relieving racial imbalance in public schools is obvious. Instead of having neighborhood schools scattered through racially homogeneous residential areas, children of all races may be brought together in the educational parks.

In many areas where the educational park is not feasible, simple changes in the existing school district lines may relieve racial imbalance. For example, the homogeneous character of a school in a segregated neighborhood may be changed by redrawing its district lines along with the district lines of the nearest white school so as to include Negro and white pupils in both schools. Also, under the well-known Princeton Plan, where the district lines of two racially diverse schools are contiguous, the racial imbalance can be relieved by limiting the grades in one school from kindergarten to third and in the other from fourth to sixth. And where new schools are to be built to accommodate the expanding school population, the sites for those schools should be, not in Negro or white residential areas, but near the dividing line so that the children living in both areas may be included in each school district. These plans, alone or in combination, when properly used, may well suffice to eliminate the inequality arising from the segregated school in most areas. But in some sections of our large cities, because of the density of the residential segregation, Negro schools are back to back. Princeton Plans and the like are not geared to this problem, but educational parks do provide the answer to Harlem-type residential situations. And pending the construction of the educational parks, open enrollment may be used as a temporary expedient.

An even more difficult problem is presented by the flight of the white population to the suburbs. The pattern is the same all over the country. The Negro child remains within the political boundaries of the city and attends the segregated slum school in his neighborhood, while the white children attend the vastly superior white public schools in the suburbs. The situation is accurately described in the 1964 Advisory Panel Report to the Board of Education of the City of Chicago:

Finally, it cannot be too strongly stressed that programs to effect school integration must reckon with the fact that the white elementary school child is already in the minority in the public schools of Chicago and the time is not far off when the same will be true of the white high school student. Unless the exodus of white population from the public schools and from the City is brought to a halt or reversed, the question of school integration may become simply a theoretical matter, as it is already in the nation's capital. For integration, in fact, cannot be achieved without white students.[1]

1. Advisory Panel on Integration in the Public Schools, Report to the Board of Education of the City of Chicago 12 (1964).

While a court, in proposing or approving a plan of desegregation, may find no great difficulty in ordering the local school authorities to use the Princeton Plan, or one of its variants, or under the authority of *Griffin v. School Board*[1] in ordering the local taxing authority or the state to levy taxes to raise funds to build an educational park, relieving the inequality between the suburban public school and the segregated city slum public school presents a greater challenge. Obviously, court orders running to local officials will not reach the suburbs. Nevertheless, when political lines, rather than school district lines, shield the inequality, as shown in the reapportionment cases,[2] courts are not helpless to act. The political thicket, having been pierced to protect the vote,[3] can likewise be pierced to protect the education of children.

Education, as stated in *Brown*, is "the most important function of the state." And, as shown in *Hall v. St. Helena Parish School Board*,[4] and *Griffin v. School Board*,[5] that important function must be administered in all parts of the state with an even hand. The state operates local public schools through its agents, the local school boards, it directly supplies part of the money for that operation, it certificates the teachers, it accredits the schools, and, through its department of education, it maintains constant supervision over the entire operation. The involvement of the state in the operation of its public schools is complete. Indeed, the state is the conduit through which federal money, in increasing amounts, is being funnelled into the public schools. Certainly federal money may not be used to indurate an inequality.[6] Thus no state-created political lines can protect the state against the constitutional command of equal protection for its citizens or relieve the state from the obligation of providing educational opportunities for its Negro slum children equal to those provided for its white children in the affluent suburbs.[7]

When the Supreme Court decided the first reapportionment case, *Baker v. Carr*,[8] just as when it decided *Brown*, it left to the district courts the task of fashioning the remedy. Undoubtedly, if and when the Supreme Court tackles the suburban vis-à-vis the city slum school problem, in the event of a decision in, favor of the complainants, it will again remit the remedy to the district courts, with instructions to ignore the state-created political lines separating the school boards and to run its orders directly against state, as well as local, officials.

I am aware, of course, that what has been said here this evening will not find favor with the advocates of judicial restraint—many of whom have already expressed the view that de facto segregation is a political and social matter which requires a political, not a judicial, solution, that the Congress and the states are

1. 377 U.S. 218 (1964).
2. See note 1, p. 136.
3. Baker v. Carr, 369 U.S. 186 (1962).
4. 197 F. Supp. 649 (E.D. La. 1961) (per curiam), aff'd, 287 F.2d 376 (5th Cir.), aff'd, 368 U.S. 515 (1962) (per curiam).
5. 377 U.S. 218 (1964).
6. Simkins v. Moses H. Cone Memorial Hosp., 323 F.2d 959 (4th Cir. 1963), cert. denied, 376 U.S. 938 (1964); see Bolling v. Sharpe, 347 U.S. 497 (1954).
7. See note 1, p. 136.
8. 369 U.S. 186 (1962).

equipped to remedy any inequality which may exist in the public schools, and that any attempted judicial resolution of the problem would adversely affect the balance of our federalism by trenching on states' rights.

These objections to judicial intervention into de facto segregation all have a slightly familiar ring. The Supreme Court's opinion in *Brown* was subjected to just such criticism. Yet because of that decision definite progress has been made toward the recognition of Negro rights. The Court's action unquestionably moved other branches of government to act. Is there anyone who seriously thinks that the Civil Rights Act of 1964 would be a reality today without *Brown* and other Supreme Court decisions exposing racial injustice? Is it conceivable that the Southern states would have abolished segregation compelled by law without prodding from the federal courts?

The reapportionment cases are also in point. Does anyone really believe that the state legislatures would have reformed themselves? Legislators elected via the rotten borough system ordinarily would not be expected to vote for its abolition. Perhaps the reapportionment cases do trench on states' rights, but the people who now have a full vote are not complaining.

The advocates of judicial restraint have also been critical of the Supreme Court's work in the field of criminal justice. It is true that the Court has insisted on civilized procedures in state as well as federal criminal courts. An accused in a serious criminal case must now have a lawyer available to represent him, coerced confessions must be excluded from state and federal criminal trials, and state as well as federal police must now respect the fourth amendment. How long should the Supreme Court have waited for the states to civilize their own criminal procedures before it undertook to protect the constitutional rights of persons accused of crime?

The Supreme Court's intervention into these field of primary state responsibility was not precipitous. The states were given ample opportunity to correct the evils themselves. Before *Brown*, the Supreme Court handed down a series of decisions in the field of education indicating quite clearly that, if the states did not act to eliminate racial segregation compelled by law, it would. The persistence with which reapportionment cases continued to reach the Supreme Court after it had refused to exercise jurisdiction in *Colegrove v. Green*,[1] should have been warning enough to the states that, one way or the other, vote dilution was on the way out. And civilizing of state criminal procedures, under gentle urging from the Supreme Court, has been going on since *Brown v. Mississippi*,[2] in which the Court set aside a death sentence based solely on a confession obtained by hanging the accused from a tree.

There is no indication that the Supreme Court will rush into the de facto segregation arena. Two circuit courts of appeals[3] have already denied relief from de facto segregation and the Supreme Court has stayed its hand. But this is no

1. 328 U.S. 549 (1946).
2. 297 U.S. 278 (1936).
3. Downs v. Board of Educ., 336 F.2d 988 (10th Cir. 1964), cert. denied, 33 U.S.L. Week 3284 (U.S. Mar. 2, 1965); Bell v. School City, 324 F.2d 209 (7th Cir. 1963).

guarantee that the Court will not act if the problem persists and the states fail to correct the evil. Proper judicial restraint does not include a failure to act where a state has abdicated its responsibility to protect the constitutional rights of its citizens.

Equal educational opportunity is not the only demand of the Negro Revolution of the 1960's, but it is the most important one. Education is the key to social mobility. Without it the Negro will continue to be tied to the segregated slum where the social, intellectual and educational damage suffered by his children begins the day they are born. Repeated studies have confirmed that the ability of Negro children to learn, given equal conditions, is equal to the white.[1] But, by school age, the segregated slum culture in which they are born and reared has opened an educational gap, as compared with the white child, which not only is never closed, but which actually increases as time goes on.[2]

It is not enough, therefore, simply to provide equal educational opportunity beginning at the age of six. Until society eliminates these segregated slums, cultural and educational enrichment for slum children must begin at birth. To their great credit, some enlightened states, including New York and California, are already planning just such programs. And the President of the United States, in his recent message on education,[3] has asked the Congress for legislation providing financial aid to states undertaking pre-school educational programs for slum children.

The American Negro is a totally American responsibility. Three hundred years ago he was brought to this country by our forefathers and sold into slavery. One hundred years ago we fought a war that would set him free. For these last one hundred years we have lived and professed the hypocrisy that he was free. The time has now come when we must face up to that responsibility. Let us erase this blemish—let us remove this injustice—from the face of America. Let us *make* the Negro free. . . .

1. See The Effects of Segregation and the Consequences of Desegregation: A Social Science Statement, 37 Minn. L. Rev. 427 (1953) (Appendix to Appellants' Briefs in the School Segregation Cases).
2. Ibid.
3. 111 Cong. Rec. 499-500 (daily ed. Jan. 12, 1965).

Cases

A. Racial Segregation in the Schools

Plessy v. Ferguson
Error to the Supreme Court of the State of Louisiana
163 U.S. 537, 16 S. Ct. 1138 (1896)

BROWN, J.

This case turns upon the constitutionality of an act of the General Assembly of the State of Louisiana, passed in 1890, providing for separate railway carriages for the white and colored races. Acts 1890, No. 111, p. 152.

The first section of the statute enacts "that all railway companies carrying passengers in their coaches in this State, shall provide equal but separate accommodations for the white, and colored races, by providing two or more passenger coaches for each passenger train, or by dividing the passenger coaches by a partition so as to secure separate accommodations: *Provided,* That this section shall not be construed to apply to street railroads. No person or persons, shall be admitted to occupy seats in coaches, other than, the ones, assigned, to them on account of the race they belong to."

By the second section it was enacted "that the officers of such passenger trains shall have power and are hereby required to assign each passenger to the coach or compartment used for the race to which such passenger belongs; any passenger insisting on going into a coach or compartment to which by race he does not belong, shall be liable to a fine of twenty-five dollars, or in lieu thereof to imprisonment for a period of not more than twenty days in the parish prison, and any officer of any railroad insisting on assigning a passenger to a coach or compartment other than the one set aside for the race to which said passenger belongs, shall be liable to a fine of twenty-five dollars, or in lieu thereof to imprisonment for a period of not more than twenty days in the parish prison; and should any passenger refuse to occupy the coach or compartment to which he or she is assigned by the officer of such railway, said officer shall have power to refuse to carry such passenger on his train, and for such refusal neither he nor the railway company which he represents shall be liable for damages in any of the courts of this State."

The third section provides penalties for the refusal or neglect of the officers, directors, conductors and employés of railway companies to comply with the act, with a proviso that "nothing in this act shall be construed as applying to nurses attending children of the other race." The fourth section is immaterial.

The information filed in the criminal District Court charged in substance that Plessy, being a passenger between two stations within the State of Louisiana, was assigned by officers of the company to the coach used for the race to which he belonged, but he insisted upon going into a coach used by the race to which he did not belong. Neither in the information nor plea was his particular race or color averred.

The petition for the writ of prohibition averred that petitioner was seven eighths Caucasian and one eighth African blood; that the mixture of colored blood was not discernible in him, and that he was entitled to every right, privilege and immunity secured to citizens of the United States of the white race; and that, upon such theory, he took possession of a vacant seat in a coach where passengers of the white race were accommodated, and was ordered by the conductor to vacate said coach and take a seat in another assigned to persons of the colored race, and having refused to comply with such demand he was forcibly ejected with the aid of a police officer, and imprisoned in the parish jail to answer a charge of having violated the above act.

The constitutionality of this act is attacked upon the ground that it conflicts both with the Thirteenth Amendment of the Constitution, abolishing slavery, and the Fourteenth Amendment, which prohibits certain restrictive legislation on the part of the States.

1. That it does not conflict with the Thirteenth Amendment, which abolished slavery and involuntary servitude, except as a punishment for crime, is too clear for argument. Slavery implies involuntary servitude—a state of bondage; the ownership of mankind as a chattel, or at least the control of the labor and services of one man for the benefit of another, and the absence of a legal right to the disposal of his own person, property and services. This amendment was said in the *Slaughter-house cases*, 16 Wall. 36, to have been intended primarily to abolish slavery, as it had been previously known in this country, and that it equally forbade Mexican peonage or the Chinese coolie trade, when they amounted to slavery or involuntary servitude, and that the use of the word "servitude" was intended to prohibit the use of all forms of involuntary slavery, of whatever class or name. It was intimated, however, in that case that this amendment was regarded by the statesmen of that day as insufficient to protect the colored race from certain laws which had been enacted in the Southern States, imposing upon the colored race onerous disabilities and burdens, and curtailing their rights in the pursuit of life, liberty and property to such an extent that their freedom was of little value; and that the Fourteenth Amendment was devised to meet this exigency.

So, too, in the *Civil Rights cases*, 109 U. S. 3, 24, it was said that the act of a mere individual, the owner of an inn, a public conveyance or place of amusement, refusing accommodations to colored people, cannot be justly regarded as imposing any badge of slavery or servitude upon the applicant, but only as involving an ordinary civil injury, properly cognizable by the laws of the State, and presumably subject to redress by those laws until the contrary appears. "It would be running the slavery argument into the ground," said Mr. Justice Bradley, "to make it apply to every act of discrimination which a person may see fit to make as to the guests he will entertain, or as to the people he will take into his coach or cab or car, or admit to his concert or theatre, or deal with in other matters of intercourse or business."

A statute which implies merely a legal distinction between the white and colored races—a distinction which is founded in the color of the two races, and which must always exist so long as white men are distinguished from the other race by color—has no tendency to destroy the legal equality of the two races, or reëstablish a state of involuntary servitude. Indeed, we do not understand that the Thirteenth Amendment is strenuously relied upon by the plaintiff in error in this connection.

2. By the Fourteenth Amendment, all persons born or naturalized in the United States, and subject to the jurisdiction thereof, are made citizens of the United States and of the State wherein they reside; and the States are forbidden from making or enforcing any law which shall abridge the privileges or immunities of citizens of the United States, or shall deprive any person of life, liberty or property without due process of law, or deny to any person within their jurisdiction the equal protection of the laws.

The proper construction of this amendment was first called to the attention of this court in the *Slaughter-house cases*, 16 Wall. 36, which involved, however, not a question of race, but one of exclusive privileges. The case did not call for any expression of opinion as to the exact rights it was intended to secure to the colored race, but it was said generally that its main purpose was to establish the citizenship of the negro; to give definitions of citizenship of the United States and of the States, and to protect from the hostile legislation of the States the privileges and immunities of citizens of the United States, as distinguished from those of citizens of the States.

The object of the amendment was undoubtedly to enforce the absolute equality of the two races before the law, but in the nature of things it could not have been intended to abolish distinctions based upon color, or to enforce social, as distinguished from political equality, or a commingling of the two races upon terms unsatisfactory to either. Laws permitting, and even requiring, their separation in places where they are liable to be brought into contact do not necessarily imply the inferiority of either race to the other, and have been generally if not universally, recognized as within the competency of the state legislatures in the exercise of their police power. The most common instance of this is connected with the establishment of separate schools for white and colored children, which has been held to be a valid exercise of the legislative power even by courts of States where the political rights of the colored race have been longest and most earnestly enforced. . . .

So far, then, as a conflict with the Fourteenth Amendment is concerned, the case reduces itself to the question whether the statute of Louisiana is a reasonable regulation, and with respect to this there must necessarily be a large discretion on the part of the legislature. In determining the question of reasonableness it is at liberty to act with reference to the established usages, customs and traditions of the people, and with a view to the promotion of their comfort, and the preservation of the public peace and good order. Gauged by this standard, we cannot say that a law which authorizes or even requires the separation of the two races in public conveyances is unreasonable, or more obnoxious to the Fourteenth Amendment than the acts of Congress requiring separate schools for colored children in the District of Columbia, the constitutionality of which does not seem to have been questioned, or the corresponding acts of state legislatures.

We consider the underlying fallacy of the plaintiff's argument to consist in the assumption that the enforced separation of the two races stamps the colored race with a badge of inferiority. If this be so, it is not by reason of anything found in the act, but solely because the colored race chooses to put that construction upon it. The argument necessarily assumes that if, as has been more than once the case, and is not unlikely to be so again, the colored race should become the dominant power in the state legislature, and should enact a law in precisely similar terms, it would thereby relegate the white race to an inferior position. We imagine that the white race, at least, would not acquiesce in this assumption. The argument also assumes that social prejudices may be overcome by legislation, and that equal rights cannot be secured to the negro except by an enforced commingling of the two races. We cannot accept this proposition. If the two races are to meet upon terms of social equality, it must be the result of natural affinities, a mutual appreciation of each other's merits and a voluntary consent of individuals. As was said by the Court of Appeals of New York in *People v. Gallagher*, 93 N. Y. 438, 448, "this end can neither be accomplished nor promoted by laws which conflict with the general sentiment of the community upon whom they are designed to operate. When the government, therefore, has secured to each of its citizens equal rights before the law and equal opportunities for improvement and progress, it has accomplished the end for which it was organized and performed all of the functions respecting social advantages with which it is endowed." Legislation is powerless to eradicate racial instincts or to abolish distinctions based upon physical differences, and the attempt to do so can only result in accentuating the difficulties of the present situation. If the civil and political rights of both races be equal one cannot be inferior to the other civilly or politically. If one race be inferior to the other socially, the Constitution of the United States cannot put them upon the same plane.

It is true that the question of the proportion of colored blood necessary to constitute a colored person, as distinguished from a white person, is one upon which there is a difference of opinion in the different States, some holding that any visible admixture of the black blood stamps the person as belonging to the colored race, (*State v. Chavers*, 5 Jones, [N. C.] 1, p. 11); others that it depends upon the preponderance of blood, (*Gray v. State*, 4 Ohio, 354; *Monroe v. Collins*, 17 Ohio St. 665); and still others that the predominance of white blood must only be in the proportion of three fourths. (*People* v. *Dean*, 14 Michigan, 406; *Jones* v. *Commonwealth*, 80 Virginia, 538.) But these are questions to be determined under the laws of each State and are not properly put in issue in this case. Under the allegations of his petition it may undoubtedly become a question of importance whether, under the laws of Louisiana, the petitioner belongs to the white or colored race.

The judgment of the court below is, therefore, affirmed.

MR. JUSTICE HARLAN DISSENTING

By the Louisiana statute, the validity of which is here involved, all railway companies (other than street railroad companies) carrying passengers in that State are required to have separate but equal accommodations for white and colored persons, "by providing two or more passenger coaches for each passenger train, *or* by dividing the passenger coaches by a *partition* so as to secure separate accommodations." Under this statute, no colored person is permitted to occupy a seat in a coach assigned to white persons; nor any white person, to occupy a seat in a coach assigned to colored persons. The managers of the railroad are not allowed to exercise any discretion in the premises, but are required to assign each passenger to some coach or compartment set apart for the exclusive use of his race. If a passenger insists upon going into a coach or compartment not set apart for persons of his race, he is subject to be fined, or to be imprisoned in the parish jail. Penalties are prescribed for the refusal or neglect of the officers, directors, conductors and employés of railroad companies to comply with the provisions of the act.

Only "nurses attending children of the other race" are excepted from the operation of the statute. No exception is made of colored attendants travelling with adults. A white man is not permitted to have his colored servant with him in the same coach, even if his condition of health requires the constant, personal assistance of such servant. If a colored maid insists upon riding in the same coach with a white woman whom she has been employed to serve, and who may need her personal attention while travelling, she is subject to be fined or imprisoned for such an exhibition of zeal in the discharge of duty.

While there may be in Louisiana persons of different races who are not citizens of the United States, the words in the act, "white and colored races," necessarily include all citizens of the United States of both races residing in that State. So that we have before us a state enactment that compels, under penalties, the separation of the two races in railroad passenger coaches, and makes it a crime for a citizen of either race to enter a coach that has been assigned to citizens of the other race.

Thus the State regulates the use of a public highway by citizens of the United States solely upon the basis of race.

However apparent the injustice of such legislation may be, we have only to consider whether it is consistent with the Constitution of the United States. . . .

In respect of civil rights, common to all citizens, the Constitution of the United States does not, I think, permit any public authority to know the race of those entitled to be protected in the enjoyment of such rights. Every true man has pride of race, and under appropriate circumstances when the rights of others, his equals before the law, are not to be affected, it is his privilege to express such pride and to take such action based upon it as to him seems proper. But I deny that any legislative body or judicial tribunal may have regard to the race of citizens when the civil rights of those citizens are involved. Indeed, such legislation, as that here in question, is inconsistent not only with that equality of rights which pertains to citizenship, National and State, but with the personal liberty enjoyed by every one within the United States.

The Thirteenth Amendment does not permit the withholding or the deprivation of any right necessarily inhering in freedom. It not only struck down the institution of slavery as previously existing in the United States, but it prevents the imposition of any burdens or disabilities that constitute badges of slavery or servitude. It decreed universal civil freedom in this country. This court has so adjudged. But that amendment having been found inadequate to the protection of the rights of those who had been in slavery, it was followed by the Fourteenth Amendment, which added greatly to the dignity and glory of American citizenship, and to the security of personal liberty, by declaring that "all persons born or naturalized in the United States, and subject to the jurisdiction thereof, are citizens of the United States and of the State wherein they reside," and that "no State shall make or enforce any law which shall abridge the privileges or immunities of citizens of the United States; nor shall any State deprive any person of life, liberty or property without due process of law, nor deny to any person within its jurisdiction the equal protection of the laws." These two amendments, if enforced according to their true intent and meaning, will protect all the civil rights that pertain to freedom and citizenship. Finally, and to the end that no citizen should be denied, on account of his race, the privilege of participating in the political control of his country, it was declared by the Fifteenth Amendment that "the right of citizens of the United States to vote shall not be denied or abridged by the United States or by any State on account of race, color or previous condition of servitude."

These notable additions to the fundamental law were welcomed by the friends of liberty throughout the world. They removed the race line from our governmental systems. They had, as this court has said, a common purpose, namely, to secure "to a race recently emancipated, a race that through many generations have been held in slavery, all the civil rights that the superior race enjoy." They declared, in legal effect, this court has further said, "that the law in the States shall be the same for the black as for the white; that all persons, whether colored or white, shall stand equal before the laws of the States, and, in regard to the colored race, for whose protection the amendment was primarily designed, that no discrimination shall be made against them by law because of their color." We also said: "The words of the amendment, it is true, are prohibitory, but they contain a necessary implication of a positive immunity, or right, most valuable to the colored race—the right to exemption from unfriendly legislation against them distinctively as colored—exemption from legal discriminations, implying inferiority in civil society, lessening the security of their enjoyment of the rights which others enjoy, and discriminations which are steps towards reducing them to the condition of a subject race." It was, consequently, adjudged that a state law that excluded citizens of the colored race from juries, because of their race and however well qualified in other respects to discharge the duties of jurymen, was repugnant to the Fourteenth Amendment. *Strauder* v. *West Virginia*, 100 U. S. 303, 305, 307; *Virginia* v. *Rives*, 100 U. S. 313; *Ex parte Virginia*, 100 U. S. 339; *Neal* v. *Delaware*, 103 U. S. 370, 386; *Bush* v. *Kentucky*, 107 U. S. 110, 116. At the present term, referring to the previous adjudications, this court declared that "underlying all of those decisions is the principle that the Constitution of the United States, in its present form, forbids, so far as civil and political rights are concerned, discrimination by the General Government or the States against any citizen because of his race. All citizens are equal before the law." *Gibson* v. *Mississippi*, 162 U. S. 565.

The decisions referred to show the scope of the recent amendments of the Constitution. They also show that it is not within the power of a State to prohibit colored citizens, because of their race, from participating as jurors in the administration of justice.

It was said in argument that the statute of Louisiana does not discriminate against either race, but prescribes a rule applicable alike to white and colored citizens. But this argument does not meet the difficulty. Every one knows that the statute in question had its origin in the purpose, not so much to exclude white persons from railroad cars occupied by blacks, as to exclude colored people from coaches occupied by or assigned to white persons. Railroad corporations of Louisiana did not make discrimination among whites in the matter of accommodation for travellers. The thing to accomplish was, under the guise of giving equal accommodation for whites and blacks, to compel the latter to keep to themselves while travelling in railroad passenger coaches. No one would be so wanting in candor as to assert the contrary. The fundamental objection, therefore, to the statute is that it interferes with the personal freedom of citizens. "Personal liberty," it has been well said, "consists in the power of locomotion, of changing situation, or removing one's person to whatsoever places one's own inclination may direct, without imprisonment or restraint, unless by due course of law." 1 Bl. Com. *134. If a white man and a black man choose to occupy the same public conveyance on a public highway, it is their right to do so, and no government, proceeding alone on grounds of race, can prevent it without infringing the personal liberty of each.

It is one thing for railroad carriers to furnish, or to be required by law to furnish, equal accommodations for all whom they are under a legal duty to carry. It is quite another thing for government to forbid citizens of the white and black races from travelling in the same public conveyance, and to punish officers of railroad companies for permitting persons of the two races to occupy the same passenger coach. If a State can prescribe, as a rule of civil conduct, that whites and blacks shall not travel as passengers in the same railroad coach, why may it not so regulate the use of the streets of its cities and towns as to compel white citizens to keep on one side of a street and black citizens to keep on the other? Why may it not, upon like grounds, punish whites and blacks who ride together in street cars or in open vehicles on a public road or street? Why may it not require sheriffs to assign whites to one side of a court-room and blacks to the other? And why may it not also prohibit the commingling of the two races in the galleries of legislative halls or in public assemblages convened for the consideration of the political questions of the day? Further, if this statute of Louisiana is consistent with the personal liberty of citizens, why may not the State require the separation in railroad coaches of native and naturalized citizens of the United States, or of Protestants and Roman Catholics?

The answer given at the argument to these questions was that regulations of the kind they suggest would be unreasonable, and could not, therefore, stand before the law. Is it meant that the determination of questions of legislative power depends upon the inquiry whether the statute whose validity is questioned is, in the judgment of the courts, a reasonable one, taking all the circumstances into consideration? A statute may be unreasonable merely because a sound public policy forbade its enactment. But I do not understand that the courts have anything to do with the policy or expediency of legislation. A statute may be valid, and yet, upon grounds of public policy, may well be characterized as unreasonable. Mr. Sedgwick correctly states the rule when he says that the legislative intention being clearly ascertained, "the courts have no other duty to perform than to execute the legislative will, without any regard to their views as to the wisdom or justice of the particular enactment." Stat. & Const. Constr. 324. There is a dangerous tendency in these latter days to enlarge the functions of the courts, by means of judicial interference with the will of the people as expressed by the legislature. Our institutions have the distinguishing characteristic that the three departments of government are coördinate and separate. Each must keep within the limits defined by the Constitution. And the courts best discharge their duty by executing the will of the law-making power, constitutionally expressed, leaving the results of legislation to be dealt with by the people through their representatives. Statutes must always have a reasonable construction. Sometimes they are to be construed strictly; sometimes, liberally, in order to carry out the legislative will. But however construed, the intent of the legislature is to be respected, if the particular statute in question is valid, although the courts, looking at the public interests, may conceive the statute to be both unreasonable and impolitic. If the power exists to enact a statute, that ends the matter so far as the courts are concerned. The adjudged cases in which statutes have been held to be void, because unreasonable, are those in which the means employed by the legislature were not at all germane to the end to which the legislature was competent.

The white race deems itself to be the dominant race in this country. And so it is, in prestige, in achievements, in education, in wealth and in power. So, I doubt not, it will continue to be for all time, if it remains true to its great heritage and holds fast to the principles of constitutional liberty. But in view of the Constitution, in the eye of the law, there is in this country no superior, dominant, ruling class of citizens. There is no caste here. Our Constitution is color-blind, and neither knows nor tolerates classes among citizens. In respect of civil rights, all citizens are equal before the law. The humblest is the peer of the most powerful. The law regards man as man, and takes no account of his surroundings or of his color when his civil rights as guaranteed by the supreme law of the land are involved. It is, therefore, to be regretted that this high tribunal, the final expositor of the fundamental law of the land, has reached the conclusion that it is competent for a State to regulate the enjoyment by citizens of their civil rights solely upon the basis of race. . . .

The sure guarantee of the peace and security of each race is the clear, distinct, unconditional recognition by our governments, National and State, of every right that inheres in civil freedom, and of the equality before the law of all citizens of the United States without regard to race. State enactments, regulating the enjoyment of civil rights, upon the basis of race, and cunningly devised to defeat legitimate results of the war, under the pretence of recognizing equality of rights, can have no other result than to render permanent peace impossible, and to keep alive a conflict of races, the continuance of which must do harm to all concerned. This question is not met by the suggestion that social equality cannot exist between the white and black races in this country. That argument, if it can be properly regarded as one, is scarcely worthy of consideration; for social equality no more exists between two races when travelling in a passenger coach or a public highway than when members of the same races sit by each other in a street car or in the jury box, or stand or sit with each other in a political assembly, or when they use in common the streets of a city or town, or when they are in the same room for the purpose of having their names placed on the registry of voters, or when they approach the ballot-box in order to exercise the high privilege of voting.

There is a race so different from our own that we do not permit those belonging to it to become citizens of the United States. Persons belonging to it are, with few exceptions, absolutely excluded from our country. I allude to the Chinese race. But by the statute in question, a Chinaman can ride in the same passenger coach with white citizens of the United States, while citizens of the black race in Louisiana, many of whom, perhaps, risked their lives for the preservation of the Union, who are entitled, by law, to participate in the political control of the State and nation, who are not excluded, by law or by reason of their race, from public stations of any kind, and who have all the legal rights that belong to white citizens, are yet declared to be criminals, liable to imprisonment, if they ride in a public coach occupied by citizens of the white race. It is scarcely just to say that a colored citizen should not object to occupying a public coach assigned to his own race. He does not object, nor, perhaps would he object to separate coaches for his race, if his rights under the law were recognized. But he objects, and ought never to cease objecting to the proposition, that citizens of the white and black races can be adjudged criminals because they sit, or claim the right to sit, in the same public coach on a public highway.

The arbitrary separation of citizens, on the basis of race, while they are on a public highway, is a badge of servitude wholly inconsistent with the civil freedom and the equality before the law established by the Constitution. It cannot be justified upon any legal grounds.

If evils will result from the commingling of the two races upon public highways established for the benefit of all, they will be infinitely less than those that will surely come from state legislation regulating the enjoyment of civil rights upon the basis of race. We boast of the freedom enjoyed by our people above all other peoples. But it is difficult to reconcile that boast with a state of the law which, practically, puts the brand of servitude and degradation upon a large class of our fellow-citizens, our equals before the law. The thin disguise of "equal" accommodations for passengers in railroad coaches will not mislead any one, nor atone for the wrong this day done.

The result of the whole matter is, that while this court has frequently adjudged, and at the present term has recognized the doctrine, that a State cannot, consistently with the Constitution of the United States, prevent white and black citizens, having the required qualifications for jury service, from sitting in the same jury box, it is now solemnly held that a State may prohibit white and black citizens from sitting in the same passenger coach on a public highway, or may require that they be separated by a "partitition," when in the same passenger coach. May it not now be reasonably expected that astute men of the dominant race, who affect to be disturbed at the possibility that the integrity of the white race may be corrupted, or that its supremacy will be imperilled, by contact on public highways with black people, will endeavor to procure statutes requiring white and black jurors to be separated in the jury box by a "partition," and that, upon retiring from the court room to consult as to their verdict, such partition, if it be a moveable one, shall be taken to their consultation room, and set up in such way as to prevent black jurors from coming too close to their brother jurors of the white race. If the "partition" used in the court room happens to be stationary, provision could be made for screens with openings through which jurors of the two races could confer as to their verdict without coming into personal contact with each other. I cannot see but that, according to the principles this day announced, such state legislation, although conceived in hostility to, and enacted for the purpose of humiliating citizens of the United States of a particular race, would be held to be consistent with the Constitution.

I do not deem it necessary to review the decisions of state courts to which reference was made in argument. Some, and the most important, of them are wholly inapplicable, because rendered prior to the adoption of the last amendments of the Constitution, when colored people had very few rights which the dominant race felt obliged to respect. Others were made at a time when public opinion, in many localities, was dominated by the institution of slavery; when it would not have been safe to do justice to the black man; and when, so far as the rights of blacks were concerned, race prejudice was, practically, the supreme law of the land. Those decisions cannot be guides in the era introduced by the recent amendments of the supreme law, which established universal civil freedom, gave citizenship to all born or naturalized in the United States and residing here, obliterated the race line from our systems of governments, National and State, and placed our free institutions upon the broad and sure foundation of the equality of all men before the law.

I am of opinion that the statute of Louisiana is inconsistent with the personal liberty of citizens, white and black, in that State, and hostile to both the spirit and letter of the Constitution of the United States. If laws of like character should be enacted in the several States of the Union, the effect would be in the highest degree mischievous. Slavery, as an institution tolerated by law would, it is true, have disappeared from our country, but there would remain a power in the States, by sinister legislation, to interfere with the full enjoyment of the blessings of freedom; to regulate civil rights, common to all citizens, upon the basis of race; and to place in a condition of legal inferiority a large body of American citizens, now constituting a part of the political community called the People of the United States, for whom, and by whom through representatives, our government is administered. Such a system is inconsistent with the guarantee given by the Constitution to each State of a republican form of government, and may be stricken down by Congressional action, or by the courts in the discharge of their solemn duty to maintain the supreme law of the land, anything in the constitution or laws of any State to the contrary notwithstanding.

For the reasons stated, I am constrained to withhold my assent from the opinion and judgment of the majority.

Mr. Justice Brewer did not hear the argument or participate in the decision of this case.

Brown et al. v. Board of Education of Topeka et al.
347 U.S. 483 (1954)

Together with No. 2, *Briggs et al.* v. *Elliott et al.*, on appeal from the United States District Court for the Eastern District of South Carolina, argued December 9–10, 1952, reargued December 7–8, 1953; No. 4, *Davis et al.* v. *County School Board of Prince Edward County, Virginia, et al.*, on appeal from the United States District Court for the Eastern District of Virginia, argued December 10, 1952, reargued December 7–8, 1953; and No. 10, *Gebhart et al.* v. *Belton et al.*, on certiorari to the Supreme Court of Delaware, argued December 11, 1952, reargued December 9, 1953.

MR. CHIEF JUSTICE WARREN DELIVERED THE OPINION OF THE COURT

These cases come to us from the States of Kansas, South Carolina, Virginia, and Delaware. They are premised on different facts and different local conditions, but a common legal question justifies their consideration together in this consolidated opinion.

In each of the cases, minors of the Negro race, through their legal representatives, seek the aid of the courts in obtaining admission to the public schools of their community on a nonsegregated basis. In each instance, they had been denied admission to schools attended by white children under laws requiring or permitting segregation according to race. This segregation was alleged to deprive the plaintiffs of the equal protection of the laws under the Fourteenth Amendment. In each of the cases other than the Delaware case, a three-judge federal district court denied relief to the plaintiffs on the so-called "separate but equal" doctrine announced by this Court in *Plessy* v. *Ferguson*, 163 U. S. 537. Under that doctrine, equality of treatment is accorded when the races are provided substantially equal facilities, even though these facilities be separate. In the Delaware case, the Supreme Court of Delaware adhered to that doctrine, but ordered that the plaintiffs be admitted to the white schools because of their superiority to the Negro schools.

The plaintiffs contend that segregated public schools are not "equal" and cannot be made "equal," and that hence they are deprived of the equal protection of the laws. Because of the obvious importance of the question presented, the Court took jurisdiction. Argument was heard in the 1952 Term, and re-argument was heard this Term on certain questions propounded by the Court.

Reargument was largely devoted to the circumstances surrounding the adoption of the Fourteenth Amendment in 1868. It covered exhaustively consideration of the Amendment in Congress, ratification by the states, then existing practices in racial segregation, and the views of proponents and opponents of the Amendment. This discussion and our own investigation convince us that, although these sources cast some light, it is not enough to resolve the problem with which we are faced. At best, they are inconclusive. The most avid proponents of the post-War Amendments undoubtedly intended them to remove all legal distinctions among "all persons born or naturalized in the United States." Their opponents, just as certainly, were antagonistic to both the letter and the spirit of the Amendments and wished them to have the most limited effect. What others in Congress and the state legislatures had in mind cannot be determined with any degree of certainty.

An additional reason for the inconclusive nature of the Amendment's history, with respect to segregated schools, is the status of public education at that time. In the South, the movement toward free common schools, supported by general taxation, had not yet taken hold. Education of white children was largely in the hands of private groups. Education of Negroes was almost nonexistent, and practically all of the race were illiterate. In fact, any education of Negroes was forbidden by law in some states. Today, in contrast, many Negroes have achieved outstanding success in the arts and sciences as well as in the business and professional world. It is true that public school education at the time of the Amendment had advanced further in the North, but the effect of the Amendment on Northern States was generally ignored in the congressional debates. Even in the North, the conditions of public education did not approximate those existing today. The curriculum was usually rudimentary; ungraded schools were common in rural areas; the school term was but three months a year in many states; and compulsory school attendance was virtually unknown. As a consequence, it is not surprising that there should be so little in the history of the Fourteenth Amendment relating to its intended effect on public education.

In the first cases in this Court construing the Fourteenth Amendment, decided shortly after its adoption, the Court interpreted it as proscribing all state-imposed discriminations against the Negro race. The doctrine of "separate but equal" did not make its appearance in this Court until 1896 in the case of *Plessy* v. *Ferguson, supra*, involving not education but transportation. American courts have since labored with the doctrine for over half a century. In this Court, there have been six cases involving the "separate but equal" doctrine in the field of public education. In *Cumming* v. *County Board of Education*, 175 U. S. 528, and *Gong Lum* v. *Rice*, 275 U. S. 78, the validity of the doctrine itself was not challenged. In more recent cases, all on the graduate school level, inequality was found in that specific benefits enjoyed by white students were denied to Negro students of the same educational qualifications. *Missouri ex rel. Gaines* v. *Canada*, 305 U. S. 337; *Sipuel* v. *Oklahoma*, 332 U. S. 631; *Sweatt* v. *Painter*, 339 U. S. 629; *McLaurin* v. *Oklahoma State Regents*, 339 U. S. 637. In none of these cases was it necessary to re-examine the doctrine to grant relief to the Negro plaintiff. And in *Sweatt* v. *Painter, supra*, the Court expressly reserved decision on the question whether *Plessy* v. *Ferguson* should be held inapplicable to public education.

In the instant cases, that question is directly presented. Here, unlike *Sweatt* v. *Painter*, there are findings below that the Negro and white schools involved have been equalized, or are being equalized, with respect to buildings, curricula, qualifications and salaries of teachers, and other "tangible" factors. Our decision, therefore, cannot turn on merely a comparison of these tangible factors in the Negro and white schools involved in each of the cases. We must look instead to the effect of segregation itself on public education.

In approaching this problem, we cannot turn the clock back to 1868 when the Amendment was adopted, or even to 1896 when *Plessy* v. *Ferguson* was written. We must consider public education in the light of its full development and its present place in American life throughout the Nation. Only in this way can it be determined if segregation in public schools deprives these plaintiffs of the equal protection of the laws.

Today, education is perhaps the most important function of state and local governments. Compulsory school attendance laws and the great expenditures for education both demonstrate our recognition of the importance of education to our democratic society. It is required in the performance of our most basic public responsibilities, even service in the armed forces. It is the very foundation of good citizenship. Today it is a principal instrument in awakening the child to cultural values, in preparing him for later professional training, and in helping him to adjust normally to his environment. In these days, it is doubtful that any child may reasonably be expected to succeed in life if he is denied the opportunity of an education. Such an opportunity, where the state has undertaken to provide it, is a right which must be made available to all on equal terms.

We come then to the question presented: Does segregation of children in public schools solely on the basis of race, even though the physical facilities and other "tangible" factors may be equal, deprive the children of the minority group of equal educational opportunities? We believe that it does.

In *Sweatt* v. *Painter, supra*, in finding that a segregated law school for Negroes could not provide them equal educational opportunities, this Court relied in large part on "those qualities which are incapable of objective measurement but which make for greatness in a law school." In *McLaurin* v. *Oklahoma State Regents, supra*, the Court, in requiring that a Negro admitted to a white graduate school be treated like all other students, again resorted to intangible considerations: ". . . his ability to study, to engage in discussions and exchange views with other students, and, in general, to learn his profession." Such considerations apply with added force to children in grade and high schools. To separate them from others of similar age and qualifications solely because of their race generates a feeling of inferiority as to their status in the community that may affect their hearts and minds in a way unlikely ever to be undone. The effect of this separation on their educational opportunities was well stated by a finding in the Kansas case by a court which nevertheless felt compelled to rule against the Negro plaintiffs:

Segregation of white and colored children in public schools has a detrimental effect upon the colored children. The impact is greater when it has the sanction of the law; for the policy of separating the races is usually interpreted as denoting the inferiority of the negro group. A sense of inferiority affects the motivation of a child to learn. Segregation with the sanction of law, therefore, has a tendency to [retard] the educational and mental development of negro children and to deprive them of some of the benefits they would receive in a racial[ly] integrated school system.

Whatever may have been the extent of psychological knowledge at the time of *Plessy* v. *Ferguson*, this finding is amply supported by modern authority. Any language in *Plessy* v. *Ferguson* contrary to this finding is rejected.

We conclude that in the field of public education the doctrine of "separate but equal" has no place. Separate educational facilities are inherently unequal. Therefore, we hold that the plaintiffs and others similarly situated for whom the actions have been brought are, by reason of the segregation complained of, deprived of the equal protection of the laws guaranteed by the Fourteenth Amendment. This disposition makes unnecessary any discussion whether such segregation also violates the Due Process Clause of the Fourteenth Amendment.

Because these are class actions, because of the wide applicability of this decision, and because of the great variety of local conditions, the formulation of decrees in these cases presents problems of considerable complexity. On reargument, the consideration of appropriate relief was necessarily subordinated to the primary question—the constitutionality of segregation in public education. We have now announced that such segregation is a denial of the equal protection of the laws. In order that we may have the full assistance of the parties in formulating decrees, the cases will be restored to the docket, and the parties are requested to present further argument on Questions 4 and 5 previously propounded by the Court for the reargument this Term. The Attorney General of the United States is again invited to participate. The Attorneys General of the states requiring or permitting segregation in public education will also be permitted to appear as *amici curiae* upon request to do so by September 15, 1954, and submission of briefs by October 1, 1954.

It is so ordered.

B. Resistance to Desegregation

Ruth Pendleton James, a minor, etc., et al., Plaintiffs, v. J. Lindsay Almond, Jr., Governor of Virginia, et al., Defendants
170 Federal Supplement 331 (1959)

PER CURIAM

In this action for a preliminary and permanent injunction certain children of the white race, together with their parents, seek to restrain the enforcement, operation and execution of Sections 22–188.3, 22–188.4, 22–188.5, 22–188.6, 22–188.7, 22–188.8, 22–188.9, 22–188.10, 22–188.11, 22–188.12, 22–188.13, 22–188.14, and 22–188.15 of the Code of Virginia, 1950, as amended by the Acts of Assembly, Extra Session, 1956, and the Acts of Assembly, 1958. The statutes in question have been referred to by counsel as the "massive resistance" laws. As stated by defendants in their brief, the statutes are all a part of an overall effort or plan of the General Assembly to deal with the problems created by the decision of the United States Supreme Court in Brown v. Board of Education of Topeka, Shawnee County, Kan., 347 U.S. 483, 74 S.Ct. 686, 98 L.Ed. 873, and its impact upon the social, economic, and political conditions existing in Virginia as related to the children of this state.

The defendants are the Chief Executive and the Attorney General of the Commonwealth of Virginia, as well as the individual members of the School Board of the City of Norfolk, the Division Superintendent of Schools, and the School Board of the City of Norfolk, Virginia, a body corporate.

As injunctive relief is sought against certain officers of the state, a three-judge district court was convened pursuant to 28 U.S.C. §§ 2281, 2284.

The background of this litigation may be obtained by a casual reference to certain documents introduced in evidence and a study of the proceedings in the case of Beckett v. School Board of City of Norfolk, Virginia, Civil Action No. 2214, which has been pending in this court since May, 1956, and in which numerous orders have been entered and appeals taken. Subsequent to the decision of the United States Supreme Court in Brown v. Board of Education, supra, the Report of the Commission on Public Education was submitted to the Governor of Virginia on November 11, 1955. This Report, as well as Senate Joint Resolution No. 3 known as the "Interposition Resolution" and the Governor's address to the General Assembly of Virginia at its Extra Session of 1956, have been fully discussed in Beckett v. School Board of City of Norfolk, Virginia, D.C., 148 F.Supp. 430, and need not be repeated. It is sufficient to state that the Report of the Commission on Public Education, referred to as the "Gray Report", was not adopted by the General Assembly. Thereafter, in the Inaugural Address of the present Governor of Virginia delivered on January 11, 1958, it was stated that no integration would be permitted in Virginia. While these documents are of no great moment in the final determination of the issues now before the court, they were admitted in evidence as a part of the legislative history for the purpose of ascertaining the legislative purpose and intent. National Association for Advancement of Colored People v. Patty, D.C., 159 F.Supp. 503; Beckett v. School Board of City of Norfolk, Virginia, supra, and authorities cited therein.

At the conclusion of the numerous proceedings and appeals in Beckett, the matter was again before the district court on the individual applications of 151 Negro children for admission into public schools previously attended solely by white children. The School Board initially denied all applications for admissions as filed by Negro children, assigning as reasons for such action that (1) the presence of one or two Negro children among a large number of white pupils would create among the Negroes an injurious "sense of isolation," (2) the peculiar circumstances would involve "racial conflicts and grave administrative problems," (3) many of the applicants were scholastically not eligible for considerations of transfer, and (4) as to a limited few Negro pupils, while otherwise qualified, they would be subjected to another transfer in September, 1959, because of a new school to be constructed in the area and "too frequent" transfers are not conducive to proper education. The district judge upheld the Board's reasoning in denying requests for transfer as to pupils classified in the latter two groups, but held that a "feeling of isolation" and "possible racial tension" did not constitute sufficient legal grounds to deny admission to the children otherwise qualified. The Board was then requested to reconsider all of the applications and report to the court; the district judge at all times refraining from making any specific assignments. The members of the School Board, acting in compliance with the law of the land as construed by the United States

Supreme Court, and as fully explained to them by the district judge, finally reported that seventeen Negro children *would be* assigned to certain public secondary schools of the City of Norfolk which had previously been attended only by children of the white race. On September 27, 1958, following an affirmance of the order of the district court by the United States Court of Appeals for the Fourth Circuit (260 F.2d 18), at a special session of the latter court that day held at the request of the School Board, the Board assigned the seventeen Negro children to the schools in controversy, and thereupon the Governor of Virginia, purporting to act under § 22–188.5 of the Code of Virginia, issued a proclamation declaring the affected schools closed; divesting the School Board of all authority, power and control over said schools; and assuming as Governor complete authority, power, and control over the schools, its principals, teachers, employees, and pupils enrolled or ordered to be enrolled therein, including the infant plaintiffs, each of whom is a white child enrolled or ordered to be enrolled in one of said schools.

As the opening of all public schools in the City of Norfolk had been postponed by action of the School Board until September 29, 1958, in order to obtain a final ruling from the United States Court of Appeals for the Fourth Circuit, the six schools referred to have never opened for the 1958–59 school year. Since September 27, 1958, the only activity permitted has been such as was specifically authorized by the Governor. Approximately 42,000 pupils were enrolled in all public schools in Norfolk prior to the enforcement of the school-closing laws which are the subject of this litigation. Of this number, an estimated 9,900 would have been enrolled in the six schools. No high schools heretofore attended solely by white children are in operation. Three of the four junior high schools formerly attended solely by white children are closed, and the only junior high school in this class remaining open is operating on a segregated basis in excess of its normal capacity. The schools previously and now attended only by Negro children are in full operation, also on a segregated basis, but the seventeen Negro children are not in attendance at any school.

What has happened to the 9,900 white children in the interim? Between 4,200 and 4,500 children are enrolled in various tutoring groups being held in private homes and churches, where they are receiving stopgap instruction in certain basic courses under the guidance of teachers; ninety percent of whom are public school teachers under contract to teach in the six closed schools and whose contractual obligations have purportedly been assumed by the State pursuant to § 22–188.14 of the Code of Virginia, 1950, as amended. There have been 1,621 children officially transferred to other recognized schools, public or private; but the number leaving the state is presently unknown. Approximately 948 children have been transferred to the public schools of South Norfolk, a city contiguous to Norfolk, where the vast majority attend a session beginning at 4 P.M. each day. It is estimated that between 2,500 and 3,000 children are receiving no education or tutoring of any nature.

The plight of the school children and the teaching personnel who would have been in attendance at the six schools has been adequately described as "tragic." Children who would be in their last year of high school are at a loss as to what to do, and those who had planned to attend college are completely frustrated. The value of a high school diploma is freely recognized, even as to such children who may be admitted to college on examination and without a diploma. Children not having reached the twelfth grade are equally uncertain as to their future. While the record does not reflect the reaction of the children attending other public schools in Norfolk now in operation, it is a proper assumption that at least some of these students and their parents must realize that their schools could be closed at any moment.

In this state of confusion the teachers under contract in the closed schools have endeavored to assist as a temporary measure. But they likewise must look to the future. The morale is at a low ebb; they do not know when, if ever, they will resume the noble profession of educating the youth of Virginia, to which they have dedicated their lives. While their contracts are apparently protected until June 30, 1959, they have no assurance that their services will be renewed for the next succeeding school year. Aside from the financial remuneration they receive, the teachers express the desire to teach in public schools—not merely to assist in some private tutoring group. The testimony points to a feeling of unrest and insecurity among all of the teachers; they are here today, but they will undoubtedly be gone tomorrow unless they are assured with respect to the future. If the teachers leave for a more certain field of endeavor, the public of Norfolk will lose and, even if we were to assume that private tutoring groups would and could continue, the teaching source of supply would be so limited that only a scattered number of children could receive this type of education.

In this setting we approach the statutes under consideration. The adult plaintiffs are all taxpayers and citizens of the Commonwealth of Virginia. With the exception of four adult female plaintiffs, all adult plaintiffs are taxpayers of the City of Norfolk. A portion of the public funds of the state derived from taxation of the adult plaintiffs and other citizens of Virginia is used and applied in the maintenance and operation of the free public school system of Virginia. It is unnecessary for us to discuss the rather complicated formula used by the state in determining the amount allocated for the purpose of public school education in each county and city throughout the state. In some countries the percentage of the total budget for public education received from the state will be as high as seventy percent. In the City of Norfolk the percentage of state contribution is slightly in excess of twenty-three percent. By reason of the large number of federally-connected children in Norfolk, the federal government contributes approximately twelve percent of the total budget of $10,354,406.

We are not unmindful of the difficulties confronting Virginia and other Southern States following the Brown decision of May 17, 1954. It is not for us to pass upon the wisdom of state legislation, but it is our duty to apply constitutional principles in accordance with the decisions of the United States Supreme Court, and when state legislation conflicts with those constitutional principles, state legislation must yield. Irrespective of what may be said by those in public life, we are gratified to note that counsel for the defendants, including the Attorney General of Virginia, concede that the decisions of the United States Supreme Court are not only binding upon this court, but also constitute the law of the land. If there ever existed any room for doubt as to the controlling force of the principles of law enunciated in Brown v. Board of Education, 347 U.S. 483, 74 S.Ct. 686, 98 L.Ed. 873; Id., 349 U.S. 294, 75 S.Ct. 753, 99 L.Ed. 1083, these doubts were effectively removed when, on September 29, 1958, the Supreme Court handed down its opinion in Cooper v. Aaron, 358 U.S. 1, 78 S.Ct. 1401, 1410, 3 L.Ed.2d 5, wherein Brown was expressly and unanimously reaffirmed.

In Cooper v. Aaron, supra, we find the following apt statement:

It is, of course, quite true that the responsibility for public education is primarily the concern of the States, but it is equally true that such responsibilities, like all other state activity, must be exercised consistently with federal constitutional requirements as they apply to state action. The Constitution created a government dedicated to equal justice under law. The Fourteenth Amendment embodied and emphasized that ideal. *State support of segregated schools through any arrangement, management, funds, or property cannot be squared with the Amendment's command that no State shall deny to any person within its jurisdiction the equal protection of the laws. The right of a student not to be segregated on racial grounds in schools so maintained is indeed so fundamental and pervasive that it is embraced in the concept of due process of law.* (Emphasis supplied)

Tested by these principles we arrive at the inescapable conclusion that the Commonwealth of Virginia, having accepted and assumed the responsibility of maintaining and operating public schools, cannot act through one of its officers to close one or more public schools in the state solely by reason of the assignment to, or enrollment or presence in, that public school of children of different races or colors, and, at the same time, keep other public schools throughout the state open on a segregated basis. The "equal protection" afforded to all citizens and taxpayers is lacking in such a situation. While the State of Virginia, directly or indirectly, maintains and operates a school system with the use of public funds, or participates by arrangement or otherwise in the management of such a school system, no one public school or grade in Virginia may be closed to avoid the effect of the law of the land as interpreted by the Supreme Court, while the state permits other public schools or grades to remain open at the expense of the taxpayers. In so holding we have considered only the Constitution of the United States as it is unnecessary, in our opinion, to pass upon the specific provisions of the Constitution of Virginia which deal directly with the free public school system of the state. We do not suggest that, aside from the Constitution of Virginia, the state must maintain a public school system. That is a matter for state determination. We merely point out that the closing of a public school, or grade therein, for the reasons heretofore assigned violates the right of a citizen to equal protection of the laws and, as to any child willing to attend a school with a member or members of the opposite race, such a school-closing is a deprivation of due process of law. It follows, therefore, that the defendants must be permanently enjoined from enforcing or attempting to enforce the statutes in question as the same may apply to the public schools of the City of Norfolk. . . . In the instant proceeding the six schools are closed solely because of resistance to the law of the land as interpreted by the United States Supreme Court. The underlying reason is, of course, the mixing of races in these schools by the School Board's assignment of seventeen Negro children into schools previously attended only by white pupils. The plaintiffs thereupon became a class created by reason of the operation of the massive resistance statutes. They, together with the seventeen Negro children, are the subjects of discrimination and are unable to obtain the benefits of public taxation on the same basis as the parents of other children similarly situated. The statutes and the action of the defendants thereunder manifestly constitute a clear and unmistakable disregard of rights secured by the Fourteenth Amendment to the Constitution.

In the event the State of Virginia withdraws from the business of educating its children, and the local governing bodies assume this responsibility, the same principles with respect to equal protection of laws would be controlling as to that particular county or city. While the county or city, directly or indirectly, maintains and operates a school system with the use of public funds, or participates by arrangement or otherwise in the management of such a school system, no one public school or grade in the country or city may be closed to avoid the effect of the law of the land while other public schools or grades remain open at the expense of the taxpayers. Such schemes or devices looking to the cutoff of funds for schools or grades affected by the mixing of races, or the closing or elimination of specific grades in such schools, are evasive tactics which have no standing under the law.

We cannot agree with defendants' argument that the closing of these schools constitutes a "temporary" delay in operation. Defendants presented no evidence and did not suggest when, if ever, the schools would be reopened, or as to what steps, if any, were being taken by the Governor to accomplish this purpose. Indeed, Chapter 68 of the Acts of Assembly, Extra Session, 1956, as amended by the Acts of Assembly, 1958, provides that any school in which children of both races are enrolled shall be closed and shall not be reopened as a public school until, in the opinion of the Governor and after investigation by him, he finds and issues an executive order that (1) "the peace and tranquility of the community in which the school is located will not be disturbed by such school being reopened and operated," *and* (2) "the assignment of pupils to such school could be accomplished without enforced or compulsory integration of the races therein contrary to the wishes of any child enrolled therein, or of his or her parent or parents, lawful guardian or other custodian." Code of Virginia, 1950, as amended, § 22–188.6. If we were to assume the validity of this statute, it would certainly be chimerical to conclude that the Governor could ever order a reopening of any of the six schools where an effective objection may be registered by any one parent of a child scheduled to attend the school in question. There are a large number of Virginians who are determined that there shall be no mixing of races in public schools under any circumstances, and who cannot be expected willingly to comply with the anti-discrimination rule established by the 1954 decision of the United States Supreme Court. To anticipate that there would be no objection on the part of any parent to the operation of an integrated school would require us to completely disregard what everyone knows to be the fact. To postpone the reopening of a school until the end of all opposition to racial mixing cannot possibly be regarded as a temporary measure. . . .

Where a state or local government undertakes to provide public schools, it has the obligation to furnish such education to all in the class eligible therefor on an equal basis. State of Missouri ex rel. Gaines v. Canada, 305 U.S. 337, 59 S.Ct. 232, 83 L.Ed. 208. As the United States Supreme Court has ruled out any classification by race as a condition of eligibility, it follows that all eligible children must be accorded equal treatment with respect to admission or attendance in public schools, subject to reasonable rules and regulations disassociated with racial questions. The plaintiffs herein, and the class they represent, are not being accorded education on an equal basis. . . .

It would perhaps be sufficient to answer defendants' argument by referring to the second Brown decision, 349 U.S. 294, 75 S.Ct. 753, 99 L.Ed. 1083, where it is said that all provisions of federal, state or local law requiring or permitting such racial discrimination in public education are unconstitutional and any such laws must yield to this principle. As the statutes in question effectively require a continuance of racial discrimination, they are patently unconstitutional. Aside from the foregoing, however, the short answer is that this court, while holding the statutes unconstitutional, is not directing the reopening of the schools. We merely hold that the Governor's proclamation of September 27, 1958, closing the schools was predicated upon an unconstitutional statute and hence is void. The injunction to be issued will simply prohibit the defendants, and all other persons in active concert or participation with defendants who receive or have notice or knowledge of the injunctive order, from in any manner, directly or indirectly, taking any steps in pursuance of the unconstitutional statutes here involved. The effect of this injunction will be tantamount to restoring to the School Board its rights, duties and obligations which existed prior to the enactment of the unconstitutional statutes, including, of course, its obligation to comply with the order of this court heretofore entered on February 26, 1957, in the Beckett case. The decree to be entered will not restrain the Commonwealth of Virginia in any sense of the word—it will only prevent the defendant state officials and others from endeavoring to enforce the package of unconstitutional laws designed for the purpose of defeating the "law of the land" as expressed in Cooper v. Aaron, supra [358 U.S. 1, 78 S.Ct. 1410]. . . .

An order has this day been signed by the resident judge directing a further hearing for the purpose of considering the form of decree to be entered in this cause.

C. Due Process and Equality of Educational Opportunity

Julius W. Hobson, individually and on behalf of Jean Marie Hobson and Julius W. Hobson, Jr., et al., Plaintiffs, v. Carl F. Hansen, Superintendent of Schools of the District of Columbia, the Board of Education of the District of Columbia et al., Defendants
United States District Court District of Columbia
269 F. Supp. 401 (1967)

J. SKELLY WRIGHT, CIRCUIT JUDGE

OPINION OF LAW

I. Preview

A preliminary matter concerns identification of the governing constitutional principles. In Bolling v. Sharpe, 347 U.S. 497, 74 S.Ct. 693, 98 L.Ed. 884 (1954), the companion to Brown v. Board of Education, 347 U.S. 483, 74 S.Ct. 686, 98 L.Ed. 873 (1954), the Supreme Court held that the equal protection clause's proscription against *de jure* school segregation—segregation directly intended or mandated by law or otherwise issuing from an official racial classification—was an element of due process of law under the Fifth Amendment, thereby applicable in the District of Columbia. In so doing the Court postponed consideration of which additional doctrines of equal protection due process includes, at least insofar as the District of Columbia is concerned.

In the intervening years the Court has found the due process clause of the Fourteenth Amendment elastic enough to embrace not only the First and Fourth Amendments, but the self-incrimination clause of the Fifth, the speedy trial, confrontation and assistance of counsel clauses of the Sixth, and the cruel and unusual punishment clause of the Eighth. In so doing the Court has responded with implicit and understandable revulsion to invitations to distinguish between the core and substance of a constitutional right and its supposed mere incidents or excrescences.

In the meantime the equal protection clause has consolidated its position as the cutting edge of our expanding constitutional liberty; and a constitutional amendment, the Twenty-third, has struck at the idea that denizens of the District are second-class citizens. Apart from these post-*Bolling* transitions is the consideration which *Bolling* itself adumbrated, at once eminently commonsensible and yet rooted deep in the theory of federalism: it is "unthinkable," 347 U. S. at 500, 74 S.Ct. at 695, that school practices which the Constitution forbids in New York, Birmingham and Los Angeles it should forgive in Washington, D. C. "[T]he District of Columbia is not a provincial community but the cosmopolitan capital of a nation that professes democracy." Carr v. Corning, 86 U.S. App. D.C. 173, 192, 182 F.2d 14, 33 (1950) (Edgerton, J., dissenting).

From these considerations the court draws the conclusion that the doctrine of equal educational opportunity—the equal protection clause in its application to public school education—is in its full sweep a component of due process binding on the District under the due process clause of the Fifth Amendment.

To fathom and apply the content of the principle of equal educational opportunity is the court's next project. As every student of the Constitution knows, the intense debate over racial segregation in the schools has clustered around two seminal concepts: *de jure* and *de facto* segregation. The first of these, as already indicated, adverts to segregation specifically mandated by law or by public policy pursued under color of law; this is the segregation unequivocally denounced by *Bolling* and *Brown*. School segregation is *de facto* when it results from the action of pupil assignment policies not based on race but upon social or other conditions for which government cannot be held responsible; whether segregation so occasioned does fall within *Brown*'s proscription the Supreme Court has not yet considered or decided. A third equal protection approach to the problems presented by this case questions whether the principle of equal educational opportunity does not require that schools must be materially equal whenever, for whatever reasons, these schools are substantially segregated racially or economically.

After briefly treating and rejecting plaintiff's unseasonable argument invoking the requirement that formerly (before 1954) *de jure* school systems affirmatively "disestablish" segregation, the court holds that a separate-but-equal rule, a variation perhaps of Plessy v. Ferguson, 163 U.S. 537, 16 S.Ct. 1138, 41 L.Ed. 256 (1896), does apply, and that violations of this rule have been recorded here in the District. The court then turns to the optional zones and teacher segregation concluding that these practices are condemned by *de jure* reasoning. Next, the court assesses the *de facto* segregation question and holds that the District's neighborhood school policy, as presently administered at least, results in harm to Negro children and to society which cannot constitutionally be fully justified. Finally, the court finds that the effect of the track system is to deny a majority of District students their right to equal educational opportunities.

II. Disestablishing De Jure Segregation

Until 1954 the District of Columbia's public schools were segregated by law. The question arises of what relevance this fact has to a segregation suit launched in 1966.

Plaintiffs press the argument that effectively to "disestablish" *de jure* segregation—no matter what the law on *de facto* segregation—a school board must adopt an assignment system which will achieve substantial *actual* integration. Indeed, considerable apparent support in precedent can be marshalled in defense of this position, including the Office of Education desegregation guide-lines, which in some cases require minimum percentages of actual integration, 45 C.F.R. § 181.54 (Supp.1967); the accent in all the recent cases on a desegregation plan that "works" and gets "objective" results, *e. g.*, United States v. Jefferson County, 5 Cir., 372 F.2d 836, 847 (1967); Bradley v. School Board, 4 Cir., 345 F.2d 310, 322–323 (1965) (Sobeloff and Bell, J.J., concurring in part); Dove v. Parham, 8 Cir., 282 F.2d 256 (1960); and the Fifth and Eighth Circuits' recent rejection in its application to desegregation suits of the Briggs v. Elliot, E.D.S.C., 132 F.Supp. 776, 777 (1955), "the Constitution. . . does not require integration" dictum. *Jefferson County, supra,* 372 F.2d at 861–872; Kemp v. Beasley, 8 Cir., 352 F.2d 14 (1965).

All this learning, however, has been applied primarily in situations where not only the condition of segregation persists, but the same students attend the very schools they were attending before "desegregation." The courts have shown less inclination to apply it to situations in which a complete revamping of the school system into neighborhood schools proves to have segregatory effects. *See, e. g.*, Davis v. Board of School Comm'rs, 5 Cir., 364 F.2d 896, 900 n. la (1966). The Office of Education percentage guidelines themselves do not apply to desegregation plans entailing establishment of neighborhood schools. *See* 45 C.F.R. §§ 181.31–181.35 (Supp. 1967).

The argument can be made, however, that even in these situations the court has the power, though not necessarily the duty, to insist on a degree of actual integration. Twin considerations could be thought to underlie such a remedy. One, the court, is entitled to real assurance that the school board has abandoned its earlier unconstitutional policy of segregation, assurance which only the objective fact of actual integration can adequately provide, inasmuch as only that is "clearly inconsistent with a continuing policy of compulsory racial segregation," Gibson v. Board of Public Instruction, 5 Cir., 272 F.2d 763, 766 (1959). Two, the entire community, white and black, whose own attitude toward Negro schools is what stigmatizes those schools as inferior, must be disabused of any assumption that the schools are still officially segregated, an assumption it might cling to if after supposed "desegregation" the schools remained segregated in fact.

But whatever the merits of the argument in the large, the court is not disposed to grant relief on its basis in this case, for two reasons. First, there is a failure of proof. Plaintiffs have not supplied the court with the necessary data as to the degree of actual integration in the years immediately following *Bolling*, which obviously under this theory form the crucial period. Although substantial segregation was an inevitable result of adoption of the neighborhood plan in 1954, without hard figures the court cannot be assured that actual integration was then so minor as to justify relief.

Second, the argument is untimely. This suit was begun 12 years after the institution of the neighborhood school policy, making the policy older than most of the students today attending the local schools. Many concurrent causes have combined with the Board's 1954 decisions in the evolution of present reality. If the segregation in the District's schools is not currently objectionable under either an independent *de facto* or *de jure* rationale, it would be very difficult to strike it down merely because the neighborhood school policy failed to produce sufficient integration when it replaced an overt *de jure* system 13 years ago.

III. Separate but Unequal

Section III of the findings above transcribes the court's conclusions respecting the comparative inferiority which vexes the typical predominantly Negro school in the District. The major findings can be briefly restated here. First, the school system's most ancient and dilapidated buildings can be found in the low income areas—which in Washington means in the Negro ghettos. There the typical school building is nearly 60 years old; the median building age elsewhere in the city is approximately 40 years.

The predominantly (*i. e.* 85–100%) Negro schools suffer from drastic student overcrowding (the median in 1965–66 for the 107 predominantly Negro elementary schools: 115% of capacity, which qualifies as an emergency situation), even while the 85–100% white schools flourish with empty seats and classrooms (their median: 77%). The distinction is almost systematic, in the sense that virtually every predominantly Negro school is more crowded than the majority of predominantly white schools.

By virtue of the compound of several individual ingredients of imbalance, the teachers at the predominantly white schools are a clear class above predominantly Negro school faculties in quality. Teachers at these latter schools have had much less teaching experience than their colleagues in the predominantly white schools, and more than twice as many of them have only temporary licenses, signifying their failure to compile the qualifications demanded by the school system for tenured positions; indeed, almost all the schools except those predominantly white must deal with a surfeit of temporary teachers. The large number of teachers with graduate degrees in the predominantly white schools is a feature the predominantly Negro schools do not equal. The fact that median per pupil expenditure in the predominantly Negro elementary schools has been a clear $100 below the figure for predominantly white schools, and $132 below the schools west of the Park, summarizes all the inequalities above, and perhaps significant others.

Every student within the boundaries of predominantly white schools gets a chance to attend kindergarten in his neighborhood school; the comparable opportunity is available in the predominantly Negro neighborhoods only if classroom space is available—and often it is not. In view of society's growing awareness that the children of the slums absolutely must be brought into the culturally rich atmosphere of the school at the earliest age—three or four if possible—this failure in many Negro neighborhoods to provide even kindergarten training, freely available in the white districts, cannot but be disquieting.

The predominantly Negro schools, thus, are at comparative disadvantage in major respects. True, large dosages of federal financial assistance are infused into the slum schools and those alone under the Economic Opportunity Act, the Elementary and Secondary Education Act, and the impact aid legislation. None of these, however, requires more than nominal local contributions, and so they have all but nil effect on how the Board disburses its own assets. Furthermore, these statutes are manifestly intended to provide extraordinary services at the slum schools, not merely to compensate for inequalities produced by local school boards in favor of their middle-income schools. Thus, they cannot be regarded as curing any inequalities for which the Board is otherwise responsible.

Taking what has been called "a 'new' approach to litigation over racial imbalance," the court considers whether these documented inequalities in the predominantly Negro schools deny the children who are assigned by defendants to attend them equal educational opportunity and equal protection of the law. However the Supreme Court ultimately decides the question of a school board's duty to avoid pupil-assignment policies which lead to *de facto* segregation by race and class, it should be clear that if whites and Negroes, or rich and poor, are to be consigned to separate schools, pursuant to whatever policy, the minimum the Constitution will require and guarantee is that for their objectively measurable aspects these schools be run on the basis of real equality, at least unless any inequalities are adequately justified.

To invoke a separate-but-equal principle is bound to stir memories of the bygone days of Plessy v. Ferguson, 163 U.S. 537, 16 S.Ct. 1138 (1896). To the extent that *Plessy's* separate-but-equal doctrine was merely a condition the Supreme Court attached to the states' power deliberately to segregate school children by race, its relevance of course does not survive *Brown*. Nevertheless, to the extent the *Plessy* rule, as strictly construed in cases like Sweatt v. Painter, 339 U.S. 629, 70 S.Ct. 848, 94 L.Ed. 1114 (1950), is a reminder of the responsibility entrusted to the courts for insuring that disadvantaged minorities receive equal treatment when the crucial right to public education is concerned, it can validly claim ancestry for the modern rule the court here recognizes. It was in the latter days of *Plessy* that the rule of actual equality began regularly to be applied. At that time *de jure* segregation was of very shaky status, morally, socially and constitutionally; so it is with *de facto* segregation today. If in either circumstance school boards choose not to integrate, it is just and right that courts hold these segregated schools to standards of material equality. Of course, however, there are important differences between the doctrines old and new. Under *Plessy's* provisions once a court discovered a substantial inequality between white and Negro schools its inquiry apparently came to an end: even strong justification underlying the inequality could not deprive the Negro student of his right to judicial relief. No court would advance so absolutist an approach outside the *de jure* framework.

The constitutional principle from which this modern separate-but-equal rule draws its sustenance is, of course, equal protection. Orthodox equal protection doctrine can be encapsulated in a single rule: government action which without justification imposes unequal burdens or awards unequal benefits is unconstitutional. The complaint that analytically no violation of equal protection vests unless the inequalities stem from a deliberately discriminatory plan is simply false. Whatever the law was once, it is a testament to our maturing concept of equality that, with the help of Supreme Court decisions in the last decade, we now firmly recognize that the arbitrary quality of thoughtlessness can be as disastrous and unfair to private rights and the public interest as the perversity of a willful scheme.

Theoretically, therefore, purely irrational inequalities even between two schools in a culturally homogeneous, uniformly white suburb would raise a real constitutional question. But in cases not involving Negroes or the poor, courts will hesitate to enforce the separate-but-equal rule rigorously. Through use of a generous *de minimis* rule or of a relaxed justification doctrine, or simply in the name of institutional comity, courts will tolerate a high degree of inequality-producing play, and delay, in the joints of the educational system. But the law is too deeply committed to the real, not merely theoretical (and present, not deferred) equality of the Negro's educational experience to compromise its diligence for any of these reasons when cases raise the rights of the Negro poor. Further, the inequality of a predominantly Negro school is most often no mere random fortuity unlikely to persist or recur, as these proposed rules impliedly regard it. It is instead just one more exemplification of a disheartening and seemingly inexorable principle: segregated Negro schools, however the segregation is caused, are demonstrably inferior in fact. This principle is unanimously attested to by reports from every quarter. *E. g.*, U. S. COMM'N ON CIVIL RIGHTS, PUBLIC SCHOOLS NORTH AND WEST 216–226 (1962); SILBERMAN, CRISIS IN BLACK AND WHITE 262–263 (1965); NATIONAL ASS'N OF INTERGROUP RELATIONS OFFICIALS (NAIRO), PUBLIC SCHOOL SEGREGATION IN THE NORTH 34–35 (1963); Dentler, *Barriers to Northern School Desegregation,* in THE NEGRO AMERICAN 472, 473 (K. Clark & T. Parsons ed. 1966); Peck & Cohen, *The Social Context of De Facto School Segregation,* 16, W.RES.L.REV. 572, 590, 593–594 (1965).

In any event the particular inequalities which have been uncovered in the course of this very long trial easily suffice to lay the predicate for an equal protection violation; as the Task Force commented, they may well spell the margin between "superior and inferior education." If any countervailing advantages favor the predominantly Negro schools, defendants have failed to highlight them.

And here, too, there is an absence of convincing justification for the discriminations. The school system's failure to keep up with burgeoning population in the Negro neighborhoods explains several of the inequalities, thereby showing that the Board cannot be charged with having schemed their eventuation. But the element of deliberate discrimination is, as indicated above, not one of the requisites of an equal protection violation; and, given the high standards which pertain when racial minorities and the poor are denied equal educational opportunity, justification must be in terms not of excusing reasons of this stripe but of positive social interests protected or advanced. A related line of defense is that the school administration, through its six-year building plan, is moving to close at least the most glaring inequalities. But that a party is in process of curing illegality, although that circumstance may affect the relief which equity finally grants, does not oust the court from its jurisdiction to declare the constitutional wrong. *See* United States v. W. T. Grant Co., 345 U.S. 629, 632, 73 S.Ct. 894, 97 L.Ed. 1303 (1953).

The failure to justify the teacher inequalities can also be confirmed. The attributes of individual schools' faculties are natural outgrowths of the methods by which teachers are assigned to the schools. And the court has already found that teacher assignment has been characterized by unconstitutional racial considerations. Absent strong evidence, the court will not assume that the superiorities in the qualifications of the predominantly white schools' faculties are unrelated to the infirmities in the appointment process.

The final question concerns the remedy to be administered for relief of the inequalities here identified. Once the showing of inequality is completed, it may be that until it is eliminated the Negro student has the right to transfer to one of the advantaged white schools, as he did during *Plessy*'s reign under similar circumstances. *See* Missouri ex rel. Gaines v. Canada, 305 U.S. 337, 59 S.Ct. 232, 83 L.Ed. 208 (1938). He certainly is entitled to appropriate injunctive relief directed at phasing out the inequality. These two considerations coalesce in the remedy the court is ordering for overcrowding: that the Board transport volunteering Negro students from the city's overcrowded elementary schools into the partly vacant white schools west of the Park. On this score the court is impressed that Dr. George Brain, whom defendants qualified as an expert on public school administration, as Superintendent of Baltimore's schools ordered the busing of center city Negro students into white schools along the city's periphery for this precise reason: to even out overcrowding. At the time of trial this busing project in Baltimore was in its third year. Similar projects are under way in other cities. Implicit in the court's choice of remedy is the judgment that the Board's open transfer policy, *see* Findings I–E–3–a, as relief from the disparate overcrowding is unacceptably meagre. The transfer right which places the burden of arranging and financing transportation on the elementary schoolchildren is, particularly for the poor, a sterile right, one of form only.

The court should add that the integration implications of this remedy are obvious; as such, it gets cumulative support from the court's *de facto* segregation holding spelled out in Section V, where its equities are more thoroughly explored.

The teacher inequalities need no direct rectification at this time. Pursuant to one section of this court's order entered for reasons apart from separate-but-equal, the school system will soon be integrating its faculties. Compliance with this provision will necessarily encompass the reassignment of a number of white teachers currently serving at predominantly white schools. Since in general these are the best educated, longest-experienced and highest salaried teachers in the system, integration will also serve as a vehicle for equalizing faculty. The court will therefore defer formulation of specific provisions for faculty equalization at least until the dust surrounding this fall's "substantial" teacher integration settles.

IV. De Jure Segregation

A. OPTIONAL ZONES. Optional zones, deviants from the core principles of a neighborhood school policy, allow students living within their borders to choose which of two or more schools they will attend. In Washington, zones couched between the Park and 16th Street let the whites and Negroes in that integrated neighborhood attend either nearby predominantly (85–100%) Negro schools or integrated or white schools far on the other side of the Park. In the Southwest urban renewal whites and public housing Negroes may attend either the distant, integrated Western High School or Dunbar, predominantly Negro. The theme which the court finds runs through these and other optional zones recently abolished is the school system's reluctance to make white students attend primarily Negro schools.

To place this case in the larger perspective, it can be pointed out that an unwillingness to pursue a neighborhood school policy through to its logical consequences when that entails relegating whites to Negro schools is not a habit peculiar to local school officials. The Fifth Circuit of Appeals, schooled and toughened by a decade of experience with Southern desegregation, was recently moved to comment wearily on the steadfastness with which those Southern communities that have adopted neighborhood school plans carve exceptions therefrom:

As every member of this court knows, there are neighborhoods in the South and in every city in the South which contain both Negro and white people. So far as has come to the attention of the court, no Board of Education has yet suggested that *every* child be required to attend his 'neighborhood school' if the neighborhood school is a Negro school. Every board of education has claimed the right to assign every white child to a school other than the neighborhood school under such circumstances.

Nor is this even an exclusively Southern phenomenon; across the North similarly derived optional zones besmirch the supposed racial evenhandedness of many school boards' neighborhood school policies.

Nationally common or not, these zones in the District produce *de jure* constitutional violations. Given their unmistakably segregatory aspects and the Supreme Court's broad expression in Goss v. Board of Education, 373 U.S. 683, 686, 688, 83 S.Ct. 1405 (1963), that any device which "promote[s]" or inevitably "lends itself" to segregation is unconstitutional, the optional zones might be thought to pose an easy equal protection question. Unlike the minority-to-majority transfer struck in *Goss*, however, these zones do allow the Negro as well as the white students who live within them to choose a white (or integrated) rather than a predominantly Negro school; and at first glance these zones may be thought to bear a slight resemblance to student freedom of choice plans now being approved in the South, if only on a provisional basis. These are plans which let all the students within a school system elect which of two or more schools they will attend. On closer analysis the similarity vanishes.

For, whatever the value of a free choice plan adopted city-wide, anomalies flower when islands of free choice are planted selectively in the midst of a neighborhood school system. These zones in the District admittedly were created to accommodate white families anxious not to send their children to Negro schools; they were created in Crestwood, Kalorama Triangle, and in the Southwest because of the residence thereof of a significant number of whites, probably a higher density of white families, the court can note, than anywhere else in the Roosevelt, Cardozo and Dunbar High School districts. They were not established in any of the nearly exclusively Negro neighborhoods which typify the Roosevelt-Cardozo-Dunbar swath of the central city.

Thus the racial basis for the optional zones becomes not only obvious but discriminatory. Negro students living in the Dunbar High School district, but outside the optional zone, and therefore compelled by the neighborhood school logic to attend Dunbar (a predominantly Negro school) are frustrated in their right to equal protection when that logic is withheld from students in the integrated Southwest corner of the Dunbar district to whom it equally applies. If the neighborhood policy anywhere in the District locks Negro students without their consent into predominantly Negro schools, they certainly are entitled to know that in similar circumstances concentrations of whites, and Negroes living near them, are not being accorded undue differential treatment in other parts of the city.

One question is left. The unsupported utterance of a school official respecting the Dunbar zone, but that zone only, was that whites in the zone would sign up at private schools rather than attend the predominantly Negro neighborhood high school, Dunbar. (Tr. 2984–2985.) Even if proved, that fact cannot justify the zone, constitutionally. White students cannot earn for themselves discriminatory preferences by holding over a school board the threat of withdrawal from the public schools. The court need not and does not assume these students all seek escape from Dunbar because of racial prejudice; rather, the court agrees that Negro ghetto schools like Dunbar are inherently unequal educationally, and assumes that many white students want out for this very reason. But, needless to say, that hardly secures their right to discriminatory treatment.

B. TEACHER AND PRINCIPAL SEGREGATION

1. *Teachers.* If the question was ever beclouded by genuine doubt, the Supreme Court dispelled doubts two terms ago in holding that *de jure* teacher segregation is an affront to the constitutional rights of teachers and students alike. Bradley v. School Board, 382 U.S. 103, 86 S.Ct. 224 (1965); Rogers v. Paul, 382 U.S. 198, 86 S.Ct. 358, 15 L.Ed.2d 265 (1965). Teacher assignment in Washington on

a Division I/II basis in the separate-but-equal regime before *Bolling* and *Brown* was, of course, a classic example of this unconstitutional practice. And the Board's policy decision in the aftermath of *Bolling* to let all teachers remain in the schools to which they had been racially assigned before 1954 is a classic illustration of unconstitutional segregation perpetuated.

Clearly, this policy could have been enjoined by an equity court bent on remedying *past* segregation by extirpating all its persevering influences. Moreover, because the policy, detrimental to Negro students in that it shut them in with segregated faculties, capitalized on a factual setting itself the product of unconstitutional action, it was a continuing violation of the students' constitutional rights.

Moreover, the court has found that, despite the decision in *Bolling*, intentional teacher segregation in the District still goes on, not only separating white from Negro teachers but assigning them respectively to schools with predominantly white and Negro student bodies; under these circumstances the strength of the *Rogers* ruling redoubles. The fact that in many schools the equivalent of token integration has been carried out is of no legal moment; the Constitution is not appeased by tokenism. Therefore, this persisting segregation is plainly defective, constitutionally.

This is certainly true to the extent it is attributable to the segregatory teacher assignment practices of assistant superintendents and school principals. In its findings, the court has gone on to question whether a share of the blame should be charged to teachers, the racial preferences of a few of whom the assistant superintendents may have heeded in issuing assignments. Teacher segregation so resulting, it could be argued, does not offend the constitutional rights of the teachers, who were in effect awarded a kind of freedom of choice.

But if any truth is axiomatic, it is that the Negro *students'* equal protection rights to an integrated faculty cannot be undermined or thwarted by the racially induced preferences of the teachers, who after all are minor public officials whose actions must therefore pass constitutional muster. *Rogers* unquestionably extends to every situation in which teacher segregation results from the deliberately segregatory decision of any public officer, or from a pattern of such decisions. Ultimate authority for teacher assignment under the law is vested in the Board of Education. It cannot avoid constitutional responsibility when the public officers, including teachers, to whom it delegates the actual assignment power govern themselves according to illicit racial criteria.

One other question concerning teacher segregation and relevant to the *de facto* issue in this case is the effect teacher segregation has on a neighborhood school policy. The practical consequence of teacher segregation has been accurately described by several Southern courts.

[T]he presence of all Negro teachers in a school attended solely by Negro pupils in the past denotes that school as a 'colored' school just as clearly as if the words were printed across the entrance in six-inch letters.

Correlatively, they rightly say, by appointing all white teachers and principals to other schools, school boards identify those schools as intended for white students.

The context in which Southern courts have confronted this fact of teacher segregation is freedom of choice—the strategy which Southern communities are increasingly turning to as a device for, some say for evasion of, desegregation. If anything, the racial identification resulting from teacher segregation becomes all the stronger in the context of a neighborhood school policy, since under that regime, unlike free choice, Negro students in overwhelming numbers are actually assigned without their consent to, and compelled to attend, these schools defined by Negro faculties. The race of the student body in effect serves as the predicate for an official decision—assignment of a teacher—which in turn confirms and solidifies the school's racial character.

What is very interesting is that the conclusion these courts are drawing in the circumstances of their litigation is that teacher segregation not only is a self-contained legal wrong but also ruins the constitutionality of the free choice plan, since it casts an untoward racial influence on the students' choice of schools. The relation of teacher segregation to the neighborhood school policy has been little touched on; but it is this court's conviction that that teacher segregation, where it is allowed to reinforce pupil segregation, may well be a malignancy in itself destructive of the constitutional health of a neighborhood school system, inasmuch as it effectively invites the entire community, including the Negro children themselves, to regard the school which is predominantly attended by Negro students as an officially Negro school, *compare* Anderson v. Martin, 375 U.S. 399, 84 S.Ct. 454, 11 L.Ed.2d 430 (1964), this being the kind of community attitude which can wreak havoc on the school's spirit. Certainly it is a circumstance driving the *de facto* pupil segregation that much closer to unconstitutionality. *See* pp. 505, 506, *infra*.

2. *Principals*. Principal segregation, the court has found, is a result of the inbreeding of principals within the white schools. That is, when a principal in one of these schools retires, the position is filled by appointing someone already teaching in one of the white schools, or by transferring in a principal from another such school, on the theory that these candidates have had years of experience with the middle class problems which arise in these schools.

Because, however, both before and subsequent to *Bolling* teachers have been assigned to these white schools on a racial basis, the process of principal selection has its foundation in a pattern of teacher assignment marred by illegality. This selection process thereby infects the assignment of principals with the identical unconstitutionality.

V. De Facto Segregation

One of the court's findings of fact is that elements in the school administration, though not necessarily on the Board, are affirmatively satisfied with the segregation which the local neighborhood school policy spawns. (Findings, I–F–5.) But this finding falls somewhat short of showing the kind of actual intent needed if the policy is to be censured under *de jure* principles. Therefore the court approaches the more generalized question of whether the *de facto* or adventitious segregation in Washington is itself unconstitutional. In Washington, as in other Northern cities, this question arises in the context of a neighborhood policy which, superimposed on segregated urban housing, effectively separates white from Negro in the public schools.

It would be wrong to ignore or belittle the real social values which neighborhood schools doubtlessly promote. But due appreciation of these values must not obscure the fact that the price society pays for neighborhood schools, in Washington and other urban centers, is in racially segregated public education. As the court's Findings (I–G) indicate, school segregation, whatever its genesis, typically imposes a twofold disadvantage.

One, the Negro schools provide their Negro students with an education inferior to that which others, white and Negro alike, receive in integrated or predominantly white education settings. This the court finds from the evidence adduced at trial. This finding is confirmed by the Supreme Court in *Brown* I, which, besides noting that "separate" schools are inherently unequal and psychologically harmful to Negro school children, approved the finding entered by the lower court explicitly stating that even unmandated segregation has a "detrimental effect" on Negroes. The court can judicially note that corroborating views can also be found in the conclusions of the federal agency commissioned by Congress to investigate racial questions; in the decisions of federal courts, and of state legislatures and education officers and committees; and in the experienced judgments of American educators and psychologists expert in race relations, who make it clear that the damage segregation causes stems from the sense of confinement it imparts, together with the low esteem which the predominantly Negro school naturally draws from the white as well as the Negro community.

In addition, segregation in the schools precludes the kind of social encounter between Negroes and whites which is an indispensable attribute of education for mature citizenship in an interracial and democratic society. Segregation "perpetuates the barriers between the races; stereotypes, misunderstanding, hatred, and the inability to communicate are all intensified." Education, which everyone agrees should include the opportunity for biracial experiences, carries on, of course, in the home and neighborhood as well at school. In this respect residential segregation, by ruling out meaningful experiences of this type outside of school, intensifies, not eliminates, the need for integration within school.

It is in this light that defendants' appropriation of Horace Mann as the supposed architect of today's neighborhood school policy (Tr. 5032) is singularly unjust. For Mann believed that public schools were at the source of the democratic enterprise; his faith, like that of his fellow reformers, was that the public school, by drawing into the close association of the classroom students from every social, economic and cultural background, would serve as an object lesson in equality and brotherhood and undermine the social class divisions which he and his colleagues felt were inimical to democracy. If there is a characteristically

American philosophy of public school education, this is its apparent substance.

The democratizing relevance of public school education, so intense a concern for the founders of our public schools, has lost none of its urgency in the intervening century, if only because society now is finally beginning to contemplate the assimilation of the Negro, hitherto systematically excluded from participation in our political life and from the abundance of our economy. This relevance was pointedly articulated by a committee of law professors as *amicus* in the law school segregation case, Sweatt v. Painter, 339 U.S. 629, 70 S.Ct. 848, (1950). Their brief read, in part, as follows:

[P]roper teaching of the principle of equality of opportunity requires more than mere inculcation of the democratic ideal. What is essential is the opportunity, at least in the school, to practice it. This requires that the school make possible continuous actual experience of harmonious cooperation between members of various ethnic and religious groups and thus produce attitudes of tolerance and mutual sharing that will continue in later life. In the segregated school, this desirable environment does not exist. The most important instrument for teaching democracy to all people is thus rendered impotent.

We have it, further, on the authority of the Supreme Court, in McLaurin v. Oklahoma State Regents, 339 U.S. 637, 70 S.Ct. 851, 94 L.Ed. 1149 (1950), the companion of Sweatt v. Painter, *supra*, and the last of the cases before *Brown*, that to share experiences with the other race remains an integral aspect of educational opportunity.

In the District, moreover, *de facto* segregation results in even additional harm to Negro students, for here the neighborhood policy enters into alliance with deliberate teacher segregation, with optional zones manifesting the school administration's unwillingness to make white students attend Negro schools, and with the objective inequalities between white and Negro schools recapitulated in Section III *supra*. *Brown* I reported that *de jure* segregation "generates a feeling of inferiority as to their status in the community that may affect [Negro students'] hearts and minds." This court, though unwilling to assume that Negro schoolchildren can readily perceive the sharp difference between *de jure* and *de facto* situations which lawyers note, does not doubt that the personal harm which segregation imparts may, in some circumstances, be somewhat less in the *de facto* situation. What, however, can we expect the Negro children to think and feel when almost all the adult faces they see at their predominantly Negro schools are black, by virtue of a process of deliberate selection which identifies their schools as intended for Negroes, when their own sense of confinement is reinforced by their observation that white students are allowed to desert Negro neighborhood schools for predominantly white schools miles away, when— among other comparative indignities—their own school is jammed with students, though they are aware that schools across the Park have classroom space to spare. These circumstances, the court is convinced, in the context of the local *de facto* segregation conspire to inflict the entire emotional hurt crippling to academic motivation set out in *Brown*.

De facto segregation in the District, in sum, redounds to the academic detriment of Negro students and seriously sets back the working out of racial prejudices. These facts, however, do not conclusively determine its unconstitutionality, for with every inequality-producing classification there remains the question of justification. Indeed, ordinary statutory classifications resulting in inequalities economic in nature are traditionally upheld whenever the reviewing court can imagine a reasonable or rational basis supporting the classification.

But the Supreme Court has been vigilant in erecting a firm justification principle against every legal rule which isolates for differential treatment a disadvantaged minority, whether defined by alienage, Takahashi v. Fish & Game Comm'n, 334 U.S. 410, 68 S.Ct. 1138, 92 L.Ed. 1478 (1948); nationality, Oyama v. State of California, 332 U.S. 633, 68 S.Ct. 269, 92 L.Ed. 249 (1948); or race, Korematsu v. United States, 323 U.S. 214, 65 S.Ct. 193, 89 L.Ed. 194 (1944). While entitled before they succumb to judicial invalidation to a hearing on the justification question, these classifications come freighted with "a heavy burden of justification." McLaughlin v. State of Florida, 379 U.S. 184, 196, 85 S.Ct. 283, 13 L.Ed. 2d 222 (1965). That is, the objectives they further must be unattainable by narrower or less offensive legislative courses; and even if so, those objectives must be of sufficient magnitude to override, in the court's judgment, the evil of the inequality which the legislation engenders. These rules are allowed to relax not even when the right at stake is one which the law itself disfavors. *E. g., McLaughlin, supra* (out-of-wedlock cohabitation).

Next—to shift the focus—regardless of the identity of the injured party, when it is a critical personal right which the classification invades, that law too must be remitted to the gauntlet of a judicial review searching for adequate justification. Skinner v. State of Oklahoma, 316 U.S. 535, 62 S.Ct. 1110, 86 L.Ed. 1655 (1942) (right not to be sterilized); Reynolds v. Sims, 377 U.S. 533, 84 S.Ct. 1362, 12 L.Ed.2d 506 (1964); Carrington v. Rash, 380 U.S. 89, 85 S.Ct. 775, 13 L.Ed.2d 675 (1965) (right to vote). *Cf.* Kotch v. Board of River Port Pilot Comm'rs, 330 U.S. 552, 67 S.Ct. 910, 91 L.Ed. 1093 (1947).

This need for investigating justification is strengthened when the practice, though not explicitly singling out for special treatment any of the groups for which the Constitution has a special solicitude, operates in such a way that one such group is harshly and disproportionately disadvantaged. *See* Griffin v. People of State of Illinois, 351 U.S. 12, 76 S.Ct. 585 (1956), and its progeny, all involving the right to appeal in criminal cases, where practices directed specifically at those who *do* not pay certain fees were held invalid because of the injury they inflicted on those who *can*not pay them. *See also* Harper v. Virginia Bd. of Elections, 383 U.S. 663, 86 S.Ct. 1079, 16 L.Ed.2d 169 (1966) (poverty and the poll tax).

The explanation for this additional scrutiny of practices which, although not directly discriminatory, nevertheless fall harshly on such groups relates to the judicial attitude toward legislative and administrative judgments. Judicial deference to these judgments is predicated in the confidence courts have that they are just resolutions of conflicting interests. This confidence is often misplaced when the vital interests of the poor and of racial minorities are involved. For these groups are not always assured of a full and fair hearing through the ordinary political processes, not so much because of the chance of outright bias, but because of the abiding danger that the power structure—a term which need carry no disparaging or abusive overtones—may incline to pay little heed to even the deserving interests of a politically voiceless and invisible minority. These considerations impel a closer judicial surveillance and review of administrative judgments adversely affecting racial minorities, and the poor, than would otherwise be necessary.

This reasoning, as applied to *de facto* segregation, leads the court to conclude that it must hazard a diligent judicial search for justification. If the situation were one involving racial imbalance but in some facility other than the public schools, or unequal educational opportunity but without any Negro or poverty aspects (*e. g.*, unequal schools all within an economically homogeneous white suburb), it might be pardonable to uphold the practice on a minimal showing of rational basis. But the fusion of these two elements in *de facto* segregation in public schools irresistibly calls for additional justification. What supports this call is our horror at inflicting any further injury on the Negro, the degree to which the poor and the Negro must rely on the public schools in rescuing themselves from their depressed cultural and economic condition, and also our common need for the schools to serve as the public agency for neutralizing and normalizing race relations in this country. With these interests at stake, the court must ask whether the virtues stemming from the Board of Education's pupil assignment policy (here the neighborhood policy) are compelling or adequate justification for the considerable evils of *de facto* segregation which adherence to this policy breeds.

This view of the law is one already endorsed by one federal court. The neighborhood school, stated Chief Judge Zavatt in Blocker v. Board of Educ., E.D. N.Y., 226 F.Supp. 208 (1964), is not "devoid of rationality," a judgment which cannot very successfully be questioned. But mere thin rationality, the court continued, is less than enough: "A closer scrutiny and stronger justification than that are required." *Id.*, at 225, quoting language from Poe v. Ullman, 367 U.S. 497, 554, 81 S.Ct. 1752, 6 L.Ed.2d 989 (1961) (Harlan, J., dissenting). In line with *Blocker* is the stance assumed by the Fifth Circuit, which just recently indicated *en banc*, after reviewing the developing *de facto* law, that "integration is an educational goal to be given a high, high priority among the various considerations involved in the proper administration of a system beset with de facto segregated schools." United States v. Jefferson County, 5 Cir., 372 F.2d 836, 875 (1966), *reaffirmed en banc*, March 29, 1967, 380 F.2d 385.

In their application, these principles require the illumination of concrete expedients or alternatives, the question being whether in view of these alternatives the Board's obeisance to its neighborhood school policy can be justified. One such alternative which cannot fail to arrest the school official eager to explore ways of reducing segregation in the schools would be to transfer and transport volunteering Negro students stuck in overcrowded elementary schools in their neighborhoods into the partly empty white schools west of the Park. From the vantage point of conquering the evils of *de facto* segregation this proposal has much appeal. It is capable of achieving an integrated educational experience for as many as a thousand Negro students—and, it should not be forgotten, for more than two thousand white students. It does so under circumstances which will leave the white students in a clear but not overwhelming majority in the schools, since the typical school in the west has a present enrollment of 200 or 225 against a capacity of 300; many educators feel these are optimal conditions for the success of an integration project.

Arrayed against these social and educational virtues are very few countervailing arguments of any merit. True, the volunteering Negro students would themselves forsake the advantages of the neighborhood schools; but who can doubt that these advantages are susceptible to waiver by Negro parents and students who deem that school integration is of greater value. It may be accurate that the school itself gleans some benefit from its proximity to the homes of its students; even if so, this certainly is a clear case in which the school's slight interest in preserving the status quo is transcended by the student's right to obtain an integrated educational experience. Moreover, this transportation remedy clearly entails no depression of the valid interests of the white students west of the Park. They will remain in the schools in their neighborhoods. These schools will give up only the volume of superfluous space which assuredly they have little real need for presently. And, indeed, the white students will themselves number among those profiting from the access to integrated schooling.

Additional objections to the proposal can be found in Dr. Hansen's reply to the Board arguing against adoption of an equivalent recommendation advanced by the Urban League. These objections, upon review, fail in cogency. Nothing inherent in the transportation provision need halt or impede the construction of school buildings where needed. And the court can assure the school administration that thoughtful, sensible policies for mitigating *de facto* segregation and its attendant iniquities fall under no constitutional ban.

The only respectable demerit to the transportation plan is its cost in the purely budgetary sense. The court notes Dr. Hansen's own argument that public transportation at low fares is available to students, and that the expenses entailed in busing would become "excessive" only if the program is very greatly enlarged; it also is impressed that Baltimore introduced a busing plan of apparently equal ambition when the only end sought was the extenuation of overcrowding. Even if transportation costs do climb to moderate levels, the court cannot conclude that they cancel out the wisdom of a policy so abundant in its integrating potential.

For at least this one alternative, therefore, the resulting social gains far exceed the costs of any and every kind. This confirms that the Board's generally strict adherence to the neighborhood policy is beyond justification in this one instance, which supports the assumption that other proposals can also be framed the net advantages of which in integration terms will also be clear. In light of this great likelihood, the court has decided to in effect remand these proceedings to the Board of Education for its formulation of an integration "plan" which carefully assesses the virtues and costs of the spectrum of integration strategies, as they could be carried out here in the District. The primary focus, of course, should be on junior and senior high schools, which the court's present injunctive order does not affect.

It is not inappropriate to suggest that in the course of its inquiry the Board should reinvestigate the alterations of the Wilson-Coolidge (high schools) and Paul-Deal (junior high) zones recommended by the Urban League. It will plainly be a shame, moreover, if the lines of the new Lincoln Junior High on the edge of Mount Pleasant are not drawn with the goal in mind of opening Lincoln this fall as an integrated school.

Additionally, as Dr. Hansen himself testified at trial, the division of the District from its Maryland and Virginia suburbs is, in terms of education, "artificial." (Tr. 190.) This truth is underlined by the fact that many of the families living in the white suburban "noose" are emigres from the District whose flight may have been prompted in part by their dissatisfaction with the District's school system, for whatever reasons. In many urban areas in the East urban school officials are studying or launching steps which move in the direction of metropolitanizing educational systems. As defendants argue, not more than a minority of Washington's Negroes can be afforded access to integrated education within the present constraints of the District's schools, with their diminished white enrollment. Yet, despite this, there is no evidence that the school administration has devoted more than very minor efforts to contacting the schools in these surrounding suburbs. *See* Tr. 614. The court need not here even remotely consider what the provisions ought to be of any metropolitan school alliance; indeed, the court disavows any power to dictate those terms, or even compel the suburbs to come to the conference table. But none of this alters the fact that the Board of Education seems to have everything to gain (*see* Tr. 5094, 6002) and nothing to lose in seeking to initiate negotiations.

Until it receives and has the chance to study the integration plan it is asking the Board to prepare, the court itself will take no action respecting these and the range of other integration tactics. The exception is the transportation of Negro students into elementary schools west of the Park, which the court here orders should begin this fall. The reason for this exception is that there are two considerations recommending that the court stay its hand until after submission of the plan, and with respect to this remedy neither of these two applies. The first is that if a choice presents itself between more than one integration tactic, ordinarily that choice is committed to the Board. But, for purposes of the immediate future, there seemingly is *no* other practical way of integrating any non-trivial number of elementary school students; and equality, as the civil rights movement rightly reminds us, is now. Of course, if the Board comes into court with a substitute proposal for integrating these elementary schoolchildren, say by construction of an educational park in Rock Creek Park or elsewhere, the court will doubtless accept that substitute and release the Board from the specific transportation policy here endorsed.

The other reason usually favoring judicial delay until after submission of a school board plan is that the courts seek and need school boards' detailed judgments on whether each specific remedial alternative is circumstantially feasible and within the public interest before issuing any order. But Dr. Hansen's elaborated argument in his submission to the Board on the subject of busing for relief of overcrowding and segregation, on the basis of which the Board turned down the Urban League's recommendation, is about as complete and rounded a report as this court can expect on the school administration's attitude on this question. And the equities favoring the transportation remedy seemingly are unimpeachably clear. Any major considerations the court has inadvertently overlooked or greatly underrated can be brought to the court's attention in a motion for amendment of the decree. But it should here be made explicit that, while courts will be enlightened by school boards' judgments as to which considerations are controlling, this enlightenment will not be encouraged to slump into complacent or uncritical acquiescence; to do so would run counter to the principles of judicial review recognized above.

VI. The Track System

Plaintiffs' attack on the track system, Superintendent Hansen's special form of ability grouping, touches yet another phase of the District's administration of the public schools, here the concern being specifically the kind of educational opportunities existing within the classroom. The evidence amassed by both parties with regard to the track system has been reviewed in detail in Part IV of the Findings, where the court has already had occasion to note the critical infirmities of that system. The sum result of those infirmities, when tested by the principles of equal protection and due process, is to deprive the poor and a majority of the Negro students in the District of Columbia of their constitutional right to equal educational opportunities.

At the outset it should be made clear that what is at issue here is not whether defendants are entitled to provide different kinds of students with different kinds of education. Although the equal protection clause is, of course, concerned with classifications which result in disparity of treatment, not all classifications resulting in disparity are unconstitutional. If classification is reasonably related to the purposes of the governmental activity involved and is rationally carried out, the fact that persons are thereby treated differently does not necessarily offend.

Ability grouping is by definition a classification intended to discriminate among students, the basis of that discrimination being a student's capacity to learn. Different kinds of educational opportunities are thus made available to students of differing abilities. Whatever may be said of the concept of ability grouping in general, it has been assumed here that such grouping can be reasonably related to the purposes of public education. Plaintiffs have eschewed taking any position to the contrary. Rather the substance of plaintiffs' complaint is that in practice, if not by design, the track system—as administered in the District of Columbia public schools—has become a system of discrimination founded on socio-economic and racial status rather than ability, resulting in the under-education of many District students.

As the court's findings have shown, the track system is undeniably an extreme form of ability grouping. Students are early in elementary school sorted into homogeneous groups or tracks (and often into subgroups within a track), thereby being physically separated into different classrooms. Not only is there homogeneity, in terms of supposed levels of ability—the intended result—but as a practical matter there is a distinct sameness in terms of socio-economic status as well. More importantly, each track offers a substantially different kind of education, both in pace of learning and in scope of subject matter. At the bottom there is the slow-paced, basic (and eventually almost purely low-skill vocational) Special Academic Track; at the top is the intense and challenging Honors program for the gifted student. For a student locked into one of the lower tracks, physical separation from those in other tracks is of course complete insofar as classroom relationships are concerned; and the limits on his academic progress, and ultimately the kind of life work he can hope to attain after gradua-tion, are set by the orientation of the lower curricula. Thus those in the lower tracks are, for the most part, molded for various levels of vocational assignments; those in the upper tracks, on the other hand, are given the opportunity to prepare for the higher ranking jobs and, most significantly, for college.

In theory, since tracking is supposed to be kept flexible, relatively few students should actually ever be locked into a single track or curriculum. Yet, in violation of one of its principal tenets, the track system is not flexible at all. Not only are assignments permanent for 90% or more of the students but the vast majority do not even take courses outside their own curriculum. Moreover, another significant failure to implement track theory—and in major part responsible for the in-flexibility just noted—is the lack of adequate remedial and compensatory educa-tion programs for the students assigned to or left in the lower tracks because of cultural handicaps. Although one of the express reasons for placing such students in these tracks is to facilitate remediation, little is being done to accomplish the task. Consequently, the lower track student, rather than obtaining an enriched educational experience, gets what is essentially a limited or watered-down cur-riculum.

These are, then, the significant features of the track system: separation of students into rigid curricula, which entails both physical segregation and a disparity of educational opportunity; and, for those consigned to the lower tracks, opportunities decidedly inferior to those available in the higher tracks.

A precipitating cause of the constitutional inquiry in this case is the fact that those who are being consigned to the lower tracks are the poor and the Negroes, whereas the upper tracks are the provinces of the more affluent and the whites. Defendants have not, and indeed could not have, denied that the pattern of grouping correlates remarkably with a student's status, although defendants would have it that the equation is to be stated in terms of income, not race. However, as discussed elsewhere, to focus solely on economics is to over-simplify the matter in the District of Columbia where so many of the poor are in fact the Negroes. And even if race could be ruled out, which it cannot, defendants surely "can no more discriminate on account of poverty than on account of religion, race, or color." Griffin v. People of State of Illinois, 351 U.S. 12, 17, 76 S.Ct. 585, 590, 100 L.Ed. 891 (1951). As noted before, the law has a special concern for minority groups for whom the judicial branch of government is often the only hope for redressing their legitimate grievances; and a court will not treat lightly a showing that educational opportunities are being allocated accord-ing to a pattern that has unmistakable signs of invidious discrimination. Defendants, therefore, have a weighty burden of explaining why the poor and the Negro should be those who populate the lower ranks of the track system.

Since by definition the basis of the track system is to classify students accord-ing to their ability to learn, the only explanation defendants can legitimately give for the pattern of classification found in the District schools is that it does reflect students' abilities. If the discriminations being made are founded on anything other than that, then the whole premise of tracking collapses and with it any justification for relegating certain students to curricula designed for those of limited abilities. While government may classify persons and thereby effect dis-parities in treatment, those included within or excluded from the respective classes should be those for whom the inclusion or exclusion is appropriate; otherwise the classification risks becoming wholly irrational and thus un-constitutionally discriminatory. It is in this regard that the track system is fatally defective, because for many students placement is based on traits other than those on which the classification purports to be based.

The evidence shows that the method by which track assignments are made depends essentially on standardized aptitude tests which, although given on a system-wide basis, are completely inappropriate for use with a large segment of the student body. Because these tests are standardized primarily on and are relevant to a white middle class group of students, they produce inaccurate and misleading test scores when given to lower class and Negro students. As a result, rather than being classified according to ability to learn, these students are in reality being classified according to their socio-economic or racial status, or—more precisely—according to environmental and psychological factors which have nothing to do with innate ability.

Compounding and reinforcing the inaccuracies inherent in test measurements are a host of circumstances which further obscure the true abilities of the poor and the Negro. For example, teachers acting under false assumptions because of low test scores will treat the disadvantaged student in such a way as to make him conform to their low expectations; this acting out process—the self-fulfilling prophecy—makes it appear that the false assumptions were correct, and the student's real talent is wasted. Moreover, almost cynically, many Negro students are either denied or have limited access to the very kinds of programs the track system makes a virtual necessity: kindergartens; Honors programs for the fast-developing Negro student; and remedial and compensatory education programs that will bring the disadvantaged student back into the mainstream of education. Lacking these facilities, the student continues hampered by his cultural handicaps and continues to appear to be of lower ability than he really is. Finally, the track system as an institution cannot escape blame for the error in placements, for it is tracking that places such an emphasis on defining ability, elevating its importance to the point where the whole of a student's education and future are made to turn on his facility in demonstrating his qualifications for the higher levels of opportunity. Aside from the fact that this makes the consequences of misjudgments so much the worse, it also tends to alienate the disadvantaged student who feels unequal to the task of competing in an ethnocentric school system dominated by white middle class values; and alienated students inevitably do not reveal their true abilities—either in school or on tests.

All of these circumstances, and more, destroy the rationality of the class structure that characterizes the track system. Rather than reflecting classifications according to ability, track assignments are for many students placements based on status. Being, therefore, in violation of its own premise, the track system amounts to an unlawful discrimination against those students whose educational opportunities are being limited on the erroneous assumption that they are capable of accepting no more.

REMEDY

The remedy to be provided against the discriminatory policies of the defendants' school administration must center primarily on pupil assignment, teacher assignment and the track system. The overcrowding in the Negro schools results from pupil assignment and the difference in the per pupil expenditure results in the main from the assignment of the more highly paid teachers to the predominantly white schools. Consequently, corrective measures designed to reduce pupil and teacher racial segregation should also reduce overcrowding in the Negro schools as well as the pupil expenditure differential favoring the white children. Pending the implementation of such measures, the court will require that the defendants provide transportation to volunteering children from the overcrowded schools east of the Park to the underpopulated schools west of the Park.

As to the remedy with respect to the track system, the track system simply must be abolished. In practice, if not in concept, it discriminates against the disadvantaged child, particularly the Negro. Designed in 1955 as a means of protecting the school system against the ill effects of integrating with white children the Negro victims of *de jure* separate but unequal education, it has survived to stigmatize the disadvantaged child of whatever race relegated to its lower tracks—from which tracks the possibility of switching upward, because of the absence of compensatory education, is remote.

Even in concept the track system is undemocratic and discriminatory. Its creator admits it is designed to prepare some children for white-collar, and other children for blue-collar, jobs. Considering the tests used to determine which children should receive the blue-collar special, and which the white, the danger of children completing their education wearing the wrong collar is far too great for this democracy to tolerate. Moreover, any system of ability grouping which, through failure to include and implement the concept of compensatory education for the disadvantaged child or otherwise, fails in fact to bring the great majority of children into the mainstream of public education denies the children excluded equal educational opportunity and thus encounters the constitutional bar.

As has been shown, the defendants' pupil placement policies discriminate unconstitutionally against the Negro and the poor child whether tested by the principles of separate-but-equal, *de jure* or *de facto* segregation. The use by the defendants of the neighborhood school policy, intentionally manipulated in some instances to increase segregation, is the primary cause of the pupil assignment discrimination. Because of the 10 to one ratio of Negro to white children in the public schools of Washington and because the neighborhood policy is accepted and is in general use throughout the United States, the court is not barring its use here at this time.

In preparing the plan to alleviate pupil segregation which the court is ordering the defendants to file, however, the court will require that the defendants consider the advisability of establishing educational parks, particularly at the junior and senior high school levels, school pairing, Princeton and other approaches toward maximum effective integration. Where because of the density of residential segregation or for other reasons children in certain areas, particularly the slums, are denied the benefits of an integrated education, the court will require that the plan include compensatory education sufficient at least to overcome the detriment of segregation and thus provide, as nearly as possible, equal educational opportunity to all schoolchildren. Since segregation resulting from pupil assignment is so intimately related to school location, the court will require the defendants to include in their plan provision for the application of the principles herein announced to their $300,000,000 building program.

The plan, too, should anticipate the possibility that integration may be accomplished through cooperation with school districts in the metropolitan suburbs. There is no reason to conclude that all Washingtonians who make their homes in Virginia or Maryland accept the heresy that segregated public education is socially realistic and furthers the attainment of the goals of a democratic society. Certainly if the jurisdictions comprising the Washington metropolitan area can cooperate in the establishment of a metropolitan transit authority (*see* 1 D.C.CODE §§ 1401–1416 (1961)), the possibility of such cooperation in the field of education should not be denied—at least not without first sounding the pertinent moral and social responsibilities of the parties concerned.

The final question is the remedy this court should forge for curing the illegalities in teacher placement. It is clear, first, that an injunction should be directed against every possibility of willful segregation in the teacher assignment process; if the preferences of principals and teachers are to be relied on at all by the assistant superintendents or any other officer making the assignment, measures must be taken to insure that race does not creep into the expression of preference.

Next, assignment of incoming teachers must proceed on a color-conscious basis to insure substantial and rapid teacher integration in every school. And finally, to the extent that these two measures are unable quickly to achieve sufficient faculty integration in the schools, this court, as it indicated by its discussion above concerning the Board's responsibilities in following up on Bolling v. Sharpe, has no doubt that a substantial reassignment of the present teachers, including tenured staff, will be mandatory. A similar call has been sounded by the Office of Education, whose Title VI guidelines establish that "[e]very school system has a positive duty to make staff assignments and re-assignments necessary to eliminate past discriminatory assignment policies." 45 C.F.R. § 181.3(d) (Supp. 1967). *And see* the discussion and decree in United States v. Jefferson County, 5 Cir., 372 F2d 836, 892–894, 900 (1967). In the South, a few courts in their discretion have exacted less inclusive commitments from school boards, relating merely to non-segregatory future assignments and the encouragement of voluntary transfers; but that does not bind the conscience of other chancellors confronted with other factual situations.

The more complex question is the goal or objective toward which the school system should strive through the various means outlined above. Two federal courts have ordered school systems to proportion Negro and white teachers equally in every school, give or take a small margin of error. Dowell v. School Board, W.D.Okla., 244 F.Supp. 971 (1965), *affirmed,* 10 Cir., 375 F.2d 158, *cert. denied,* 387 U.S. 931, 87 S.Ct. 2054, 18 L.Ed.2d 993 (May 29, 1967); Kier v. County School Board, W.D. Va., 249 F.Supp. 239 (1966). It is true, however, that in *Dowell* the court assumed the initiative only after the school board defaulted in the obligation assigned it by the court to draw up a faculty desegregation plan, and *Kier* dealt with a school system with only 25 schools, which may make a difference. Still, there is great appeal in the simplicity and thoroughness of such a decree.

These issues of remedy were ignored at trial by counsel for both sides, each intent instead on establishing or refuting the primary constitutional violation. For this reason, and considering the limitations of time, for the 1967–68 school year the court is content to order "substantial" teacher integration in those schools where complete segregation or token integration of faculty has heretofore existed. The court will remit the question of the longer term goal to the Board for first-instance treatment in the plan which the court in its decree will order the Board to prepare. There will be an abundance of opportunity later for adversary argument on the merits and demerits of the ends (and means) concerning teacher integration which the Board decides to propose.

PARTING WORD

It is regrettable, of course, that in deciding this case this court must act in an area so alien to its expertise. It would be far better indeed for these great social and political problems to be resolved in the political arena by other branches of government. But these are social and political problems which seem at times to defy such resolution. In such situations, under our system, the judiciary must bear a hand and accept its responsibility to assist in the solution where constitutional rights hang in the balance. So it was in Brown v. Board of Education, Bolling v. Sharpe, and Baker v. Carr. So it is in the South where federal courts are making brave attempts to implement the mandate of *Brown*. So it is here.

The decree is attached to, and made part of, this opinion.

DECREE

It is ORDERED, ADJUDGED and DECREED that the defendants, their agents, officers, employees and successors, and all those in active concert and participation with them be, and they are hereby, permanently enjoined from discriminating on the basis of racial or economic status in the operation of the District of Columbia public school system.

It is FURTHER ORDERED, ADJUDGED and DECREED that the defendants be, and they are hereby, permanently enjoined from operating the track system in the District of Columbia public schools. It is FURTHER ORDERED that on October 2, 1967, the defendants file in the record in this case a report of their compliance with this order of the court.

It is FURTHER ORDERED, ADJUDGED and DECREED that on October 2, 1967, the defendants herein file in the record in this case for approval by the court a plan of pupil assignment complying with the principles announced in the court's opinion and the instructions contained in the part styled REMEDY thereof.

It is FURTHER ORDERED, ADJUDGED and DECREED that the defendants, beginning with the school year 1967–68, provide transportation for volunteering children in overcrowded school districts east of Rock Creek Park to underpopulated schools west of the Park. It is FURTHER ORDERED that on October 2, 1967, the defendants file in the record in this case a report of their compliance with this order of the court.

It is FURTHER ORDERED, ADJUDGED and DECREED that, beginning with the school year 1967–68, the following optional zones be abolished: Wilson - Western - Roosevelt; Cardozo - Western; Dunbar - Western; Gordon-MacFarland; Gordon - Banneker; Powell - Hearst. It is FURTHER ORDERED that on October 2, 1967, the defendants file in the record in this case a report of their compliance with this order of the court.

It is FURTHER ORDERED, ADJUDGED and DECREED that the defendants, beginning with the school year 1967–68, provide substantial teacher integration in the faculty of each school. It is FURTHER ORDERED that on October 2, 1967, the defendants file in the record in this case a report of their compliance with this order of the court.

It is FURTHER ORDERED, ADJUDGED and DECREED that on October 2, 1967, the defendants file in the record in this case for approval by the court a plan of teacher assignment which will fully integrate the faculty of each school pursuant to the principles announced in the court's opinion and the instructions contained in the part styled REMEDY thereof.

It is FURTHER ORDERED, ADJUDGED and DECREED that the United States be, and it is hereby, invited to intervene in these proceedings to assist in the implementation of the decree, to suggest amendments to the decree, and to take whatever other steps it deems appropriate in the interest of public education in the District of Columbia. It is FURTHER ORDERED that the United States be served with a copy of this decree in the manner prescribed by Rule 4(d) (4), FEDERAL RULES OF CIVIL PROCEDURE. The parties, of course, may suggest amendments to this decree at any time.

This decree is without costs.

APPENDIX A

Table T-1 Group tests: types and frequency of testing

Grade Given	Name of Test	Aptitude or Achievement	Verbal or Non-verbal
	Mandatory Program		
K	Metro. Readiness (Rev. Form A)	Aptit. (readiness for 1st grade instruction)	*
1	Metro. Readiness (Rev. Form B)	(see *supra*)	*
2†	Metro. Acht. (Prim. II, Form A)	Acht. (reading/ spelling)	V
4	Sequential Tests of Educ. Progress (STEP) (Level 4, Form A)	Acht. (reading/ arith./listening/ writing)	V
	School & College Ability Tests (SCAT) (Level 5, Form A)	Aptit.	V
6 (Genl/Honors)	Stanford Acht. (SAT) (Rev., Partial, Intermed. II, Form W)	Acht.	V
	Otis Quick-Scoring Mental Ability, Beta	Aptit. (IQ)	V
6 (Spec. Ac.)	Metro. Reading & Arith. (Elem. Form A)	Acht.	V
	Tests of General Ability (TOGA), Grades 4–6 (Form A)	Aptit.	Both
9 (Genl/Honors)	STEP (Level 3, Form B)	Acht. (math/ read./listen./ writ.)	V
	SCAT (Level 3, Form B)	Aptit.	V
9 (Spec. Ac.)	SAT (Intermed., Partial, Form W)	Acht.	V
	TOGA, Grades 6–9	Aptit.	Both
11 (Genl/Reg/Honors)	STEP (Level 2, Form A)	Acht. (math *et al.*)	V
	SCAT (Level 2, Form A)	Aptit.	V
11 (Spec. Ac.)	SAT (Advanced, Partial, Form W)	Acht.	V
	Optional Program		
7	TOGA, Grades 6–9	Aptit.	Both
9	Tests of Educ. Ability, Grades 6–9	Aptit.	V
10/12	Flanagan Aptit. Classific. Tests	Aptit.	

* Instructions are oral, test is pictorial; verbal to extent of comprehending instructions as to what question is asking. (Tr. 3233.)
† One principal testified that this test is optional. (Tr. 4070.)

**James Tometz et al., Appellees, v. Board of
Education, Waukegan City School District No. 61
et al., Appellants**
39 Ill.2d 593, 237 N.E. 2d. 498 (1968)
Supreme Court of Illinois

WARD, JUSTICE

On June 13, 1963, the legislature approved an amendment to section 10–21.3
of the Illinois School Code relating to the duties of school boards. (Ill.Rev.Stat.
1967, chap. 122, par. 10–21.3.) This amendment, commonly called the Armstrong Act, provides in part: "As soon as practicable, and from time to time
thereafter, the board shall change or revise existing [attendance] units or create
new units in a manner which will take into consideration the prevention of
segregation and the elimination of separation of children in public schools because
of color, race or nationality."

On August 4, 1965, the plaintiffs, seven children, by their respective parents,
instituted a suit in the circuit court of Lake County claiming that the Waukegan
City School District had violated the Armstrong Act and seeking a mandatory
injunction requiring the district to revise the boundaries of its school attendance
units. The district and the local board of education were named as defendants.

No boundary changes had been made in the school district since the enactment of the Armstrong Act. At the time suit was filed, the percentages of
Caucasian and Negro students in each of the district's attendance units were as
follows:

Name of School	Percentage of Caucasians	Percentage of Negroes
Whittier	15%	85%
Clearview	100%	0%
Glen Flora	98%	2%
Glenwood	100%	0%
Hyde Park	100%	0%

After suit had been filed, Dr. McCall, who was then the superintendent of the
defendant school district, was requested by the board to make a study of the
Whittier and surrounding attendance units. Dr. McCall prepared a comprehensive report, which included four possible revisions of the boundaries for the
school district area, which were designated plans 1, 2, 3, and 4. His observations
concerning each plan's feasibility and desirability were part of the report. On
June 13, 1966, the board considered the report, which, though it described
possible boundary changes, recommended that no changes be made, and voted to
make no revisions of attendance unit boundaries.

Trial was had on the plaintiffs' complaint and at its conclusion on July 20,
1966, the court found *inter alia* that the racial imbalance in the Whittier School
area had not been created by any deliberate conduct on the part of the defendants

and that the defendants had not been guilty of any intentional racial discrimination. Also, the trial court held that the Armstrong Act was constitutional and applicable to "so-called *de facto* segregation in schools, i. e., racial imbalance in schools not created by the deliberate intent of a school board." The trial court judged that the defendants' failure to make any change in the boundaries of the district's attendance units was unreasonable under the circumstances and in violation of the Armstrong Act. The court therefore ordered the defendants to submit a plan making reasonable boundary revisions so as to "in some measure ameliorate the racial imbalance" in the attendance units concerned. August 4, 1966, was set for a hearing to consider the plan to be proposed.

On such date the trial court incorporated in its decree plan 2 of the McCall report with certain modifications. These modifications were proposed by Dr. Van Devander, the new school district superintendent, to improve the original plan 2 by avoiding certain traffic hazards and by more acceptably balancing class loads among the schools. Under the court's decree the distribution of Caucasian and Negro school children in the district was to be:

Name of School	Percentage of Caucasians	Percentage of Negroes
Whittier	57.4%	42.6%
Clearview	100%	0%
Glen Flora	83%	17%
Glenwood	83.6%	16.4%
Hyde Park	79.9%	20.1%

In this direct appeal the defendants challenge the constitutionality of the Armstrong Act, alleging that the Act's requirement that race be considered as a factor in changing or forming school attendance unit boundaries, constitutes a racial classification condemned by the equal protection clause and due process clause of the fourteenth amendment to the United States constitution and the due process clause of the Illinois constitution.

To support this claim, the defendants heavily rely on three Federal cases, each of which held, no State law being involved, that a local school board does not have an affirmative constitutional duty to act to alleviate racial imbalance in the schools that it did not cause. (Deal v. Cincinnati Board of Education (6th Cir. 1966) 369 F.2d 55, cert. denied 389 U.S. 847, 88 S.Ct. 39, 19 L.Ed.2d 114; Downs v. Board of Education of Kansas City (10th Cir. 1964) 336 F.2d 988, cert. denied 380 U.S. 914, 85 S.Ct. 898, 13 L.Ed.2d. 800; Bell v. School City of Gary, Indiana (7th Cir. 1963) 324 F.2d 209, cert. denied 377 U.S. 924, 84 S.Ct. 1223, 12 L.Ed.2d 216.) However, the question as to whether the constitution requires a local school board, or a State, to act to undo *de facto* school segregation is simply not here concerned. The issue here is whether the constitution permits, rather than prohibits, voluntary State action aimed toward reducing and eventually eliminating *de facto* school segregation.

State laws or administrative policies, directed toward the reduction and eventual elimination of *de facto* segregation of children in the schools and racial imbalance, have been approved by every high State court which has considered the issue. . . .

In Springfield School Committee v. Barksdale (1st Cir. 1965) 348 F.2d 261, the school authorities of Springfield, Massachusetts, had passed a resolution to take appropriate action "to eliminate to the fullest extent possible, [*de facto*] racial concentration in the schools within the framework of effective educational procedures." Addressing itself to this resolution, the Court of Appeals for the First Circuit stated at page 266 that: "It has been suggested that classification by race is unlawful regardless of the worthiness of the objective. We do not agree. The defendants' proposed action does not concern race except insofar as race correlates with proven deprivation of educational opportunity. This evil satisfies whatever 'heavier burden of justification' there may be. . . ."

It would seem no more unconstitutional to take into account plaintiffs' special characteristics and circumstances that have been found to be occasioned by their color than it would be to give special attention to physiological, psychological or sociological variances from the norm occasioned by other factors. That these differences happen to be associated with a particular race is no reason for ignoring them. . . .

Here, the legislature has directed school boards "as soon as practicable" to fix or revise the boundaries of school attendance units in a manner that "takes into consideration" the prevention and elimination of segregation. We cannot say that the legislature acted arbitrarily and without a reasonable basis in so directing the school boards of this State.

The legislature is necessarily vested with broad discretion to determine not only what the public interest and welfare require, but what measures are necessary to secure such interests.

We have said: "With the growth and development of the state, the police power necessarily develops, within reasonable bounds, to meet the changing conditions. The power is not circumscribed by precedent arising out of past conditions but is elastic and capable of expansion to keep up with human progress. It extends to the great public needs, that which is sanctioned by usage or held by prevailing morality or strong and preponderant opinion to be greatly and immediately necessary to the public welfare. City of Aurora v. Burns, 319 Ill. 84, 149 N.E. 784."

Too, not to be disregarded is article VIII of the constitution which directs the general assembly to "provide a thorough and efficient system of free schools, whereby all children of this state may receive a good common school education." Ill.Const., art. VIII, sec. 1.

When, in Brown v. Board of Education of Topeka (1954) 347 U.S. 483, 74 S.Ct. 686, 98 L.Ed. 873, the Supreme Court declared unconstitutional *de jure* segregation in public schools, it made clear its position that all segregation of children solely on the basis of race deprives children of the minority group of equal educational opportunities. Though *Brown* directly concerned *de jure* segregation, segregation caused by official governmental action, courts since *Brown* have recognized that *de facto* segregation has a seriously limiting influence on educational opportunity.

The fact that children other than Negro children may be deprived of equal educational opportunities does not form a constitutional impediment to the Act concerned. The legislature is not required to choose between legislating against all evils of the same genus or not legislating at all. It may recognize degrees of harm confining itself to where the need seems most acute.

Too, the Armstrong Act would apply to the offensive segregation of school children of any "color, race or nationality."

We deem that neither the fourteenth amendment nor any provision of the Illinois constitution deprives the legislature of the authority to require school boards "as soon as practicable" to fix or change the boundaries of school attendance units "in a manner which will take into consideration" the prevention and eventual elimination of segregation.

It is apparent from what we have said that our view is that the Armstrong Act was designed to apply to *de facto* school segregation. Illinois has never been classified as a *de jure* segregation State. School authorities in Illinois were forbidden from separating or excluding school children based on race or color as early as 1874. (Chase v. Stephenson, 71 Ill. 383; Hurd. Rev.Stat.1874, chap. 122, par. 100 (now Ill.Rev.Stat.1967, chap. 122, par. 10–22.5); . . .

In 1954, the United States Supreme Court in Brown v. Board of Education of Topeka, 347 U.S. 483, 74 S.Ct. 686, 98 L.Ed. 873, declared *de jure* school segregation by State action unconstitutional. Since then the unconstitutionality of *de jure* segregation has been clear. It would be unreasonable that our legislature, in 1963, in enacting the statute here concerned would be directing its attention superfluously to *de jure* rather than *de facto* school segregation, as defendants maintain. (Accord: Pennsylvania Human Relations Commission v. Chester School District (1967) 427 Pa. 157, 233 A.2d 290, 296.) We concur in the trial court's interpretation that the reference in the Armstrong Act to the "elimination of separation of children in the public schools because of color" is intended to apply to *de facto* segregation.

Too, the appellants question whether the Armstrong Act is so imprecise in defining a school board's duty as to be unconstitutional.

The Act, revised section 10–21.3 of the Illinois School Code (Ill.Rev.Stat. 1967, chap. 122, par. 10–21.3) does not refer to considerations traditionally relevant to the determination of school attendance unit boundaries such as classroom size, distances to school and traffic hazards. However, neither did the prior section 10–21.3 refer to these factors. It simply directed school boards then, as the present section does, to "establish one or more attendance units within the district." (Ill.Rev.Stat.1961, chap. 122, par. 10–21.3, as originally enacted see 1951 Laws of Illinois, pp. 591, 593.) The omission, if it be considered such, does not invalidate the legislation. "When it is necessary, the legislature may commit to others the responsibility for the accomplishment of the details of its expressed purpose. The scope of permissible delegation must be measured in terms of the complexity and diversity of the conditions which will be encountered in the enforcement of the statute." (Department of the Public Works and Buildings v. Lanter, 413 Ill. 581, 589–590, 110 N.E2d 179, 184.) It is known that conditions certainly vary from school district to school district in Illinois and may vary within the same district. As we declared in a context resembling the present one: "It would be both impossible and undesirable for the legislature to draft rigid nondiscretionary standards which would embrace each and every school district boundary change, for conditions surrounding the changes are seldom the same." School Dist. No. 79 v. County Board of School Trustees, 4 Ill.2d 533, 537–538, 123 N.E.2d 475, 477; . . .

We deem that the intention in the enactment was not to eliminate or minimize consideration by boards of factors traditionally weighed in setting school boundaries. Rather, the intent was to direct school boards in forming or changing school units to take into consideration color, race and nationality so that segregation of children on such basis would be prevented and, where appropriate, eliminated.

The Act does not designate when a school is to be considered racially segregated or imbalanced. However, this does not mean the Act lacks adequate specificity to be constitutional. (Accord: Pennsylvania Human Relations Commission v. Chester School District (1967) 427 Pa. 157, 233 A.2d 290, 301.) A statute need not always define each of its terms and detail each of its procedures. "It is only where the legislative act is so indefinite and uncertain that courts are unable to determine what the legislature intended, or when the act is so incomplete or inconsistent that it cannot be executed, that the law will be invalidated by reason of indefiniteness or uncertainty." (People ex rel. Drobnick v. City of Waukegan, 1 Ill.2d 456, 465, 116 N.E.2d 365, 371; . . .)

Here, the Act is capable of being executed. Terms such as "segregation" have a common and recognized meaning.

The Act does not contain any definition of the words "race" or "color". A similar objection was presented to the court in School Committee of Boston v. Board of Education (1967) Mass., 227 N.E.2d 729, where the Supreme Judicial Court of Massachusetts considered the constitutionality of a statute providing for the elimination of racial imbalance in public schools. The court cited its holding in School Committee of New Bedford v. Commissioner of Education (1965) 349 Mass. 410, 208 N.E.2d 814, 818 in dismissing the objection. In that case the court stated: "The city contends that no adequate standards for classifying students as 'white' and 'non-white' are laid down in the request for a racial census. We recognize the difficulties which may arise in particular cases, particularly in communities with a heterogeneous population. These terms, however, seem to us reasonably susceptible of application by school superintendents and teachers for the present general purposes." We do not believe that the criteria of race and color can present substantial difficulty to a board in making a racial census. Here, Dr. McCall and the participating school personnel apparently encountered no problems in determining that the Glen Flora school was 98% Caucasian and the Whittier School 85% Negro. Also, as far as we can ascertain from cases dealing with problems of segregated schools, *de facto* or *de jure*, school authorities are not experiencing any significant difficulties in making color or race determinations of the type required by the Act.

The defendants also argue that the trial court improperly overruled the school board, which had concluded, based on considerations of traffic hazards, walking distances, finances and classroom capacity, that existing attendance unit boundaries should not be revised.

As stated, the Act provides that "as soon as practicable" a school board shall revise attendance unit boundaries "taking into consideration" the prevention and elimination of segregation. Here, a full hearing was conducted by the trial court at which the parties presented detailed evidence. At its conclusion, the trial court ruled *inter alia* that the defendants were in violation of the Armstrong Act and directed the alteration of school boundaries as described.

As the defendants state, the trial judge said that under the Act racial imbalance is a paramount consideration in drawing school attendance unit boundaries. However, it is clear from the opinion of the trial judge that he considered and did not disregard other relevant factors in arriving at his decision. The trial judge stated: "Defendants' evidence concerning traffic, distances of students from school, finances and classroom capacity are not determinative of the issues in the case at bar. In making this statement, the Court does not mean to intimate that in a given case these factors could not be the determining factors and would override any factor of racial consideration. In a certain situation the Court feels this could be true. However, in the instant case, the Court is of the opinion that the evidence on these factors was not conclusive, and did not prove that a serious problem, or even one of very large proportions, existed in any of these categories: namely, traffic, distance, finance or classroom capacity." Later the court observed: ". . . in the case at hand, all of the attendance units involved are contiguous and in a general sense, constitute a neighborhood in the larger sense of the term. This is not an instance where units are separate, nor where any busing or transportation problems are involved."

The trial court found that no serious problems existed with reference to the so-called traditional considerations and that such considerations were outweighed by the factor of racial imbalance in the attendance units concerned.

We are not prepared, following a review of the record, to declare that the holding of the trial court was manifestly against the weight of the evidence or clearly unreasonable.

Accordingly, the judgment of the circuit court of Lake County is affirmed.

Judgment affirmed.

House, Klingbiel and Kluczynski, JJ., dissented.

D. Due Process in the Schools

In Re Gault et al.
Appeal from the Supreme Court of Arizona
387 U.S. 1 (1967)

MR. JUSTICE FORTAS DELIVERED THE OPINION OF THE COURT

This is an appeal under 28 U. S. C. § 1257 (2) from a judgment of the Supreme Court of Arizona affirming the dismissal of a petition for a writ of habeas corpus. 99 Ariz. 181, 407 P. 2d 760 (1965). The petition sought the release of Gerald Francis Gault, appellants' 15-year-old son, who had been committed as a juvenile delinquent to the State Industrial School by the Juvenile Court of Gila County, Arizona. The Supreme Court of Arizona affirmed dismissal of the writ against various arguments which included an attack upon the constitutionality of the Arizona Juvenile Code because of its alleged denial of procedural due process rights to juveniles charged with being "delinquents." The court agreed that the constitutional guarantee of due process of law is applicable in such proceedings. It held that Arizona's Juvenile Code is to be read as "impliedly" implementing the "due process concept." It then proceeded to identify and describe "the particular elements which constitute due process in a juvenile hearing." It concluded that the proceedings ending in commitment of Gerald Gault did not offend those requirements. We do not agree, and we reverse. . . .

[The following abstract of the facts is taken from the headnote provided in the reported opinion.] Appellants' 15-year-old son, Gerald Gault, was taken into custody as the result of a complaint that he had made lewd telephone calls. After hearings before a juvenile court judge, Gerald was ordered committed to the State Industrial School as a juvenile delinquent until he should reach majority. Appellants brought a habeas corpus action in the state courts to challenge the constitutionality of the Arizona Juvenile Code and the procedure actually used in Gerald's case, on the ground of denial of various procedural due process rights. The State Supreme Court affirmed dismissal of the writ. Agreeing that the constitutional guarantee of due process applies to proceedings in which juveniles are charged as delinquents, the court held that the Arizona Juvenile Code impliedly includes the requirements of due process in delinquency proceedings, and that such due process requirements were not offended by the procedure leading to Gerald's commitment.

The Supreme Court [of Arizona] handed down an elaborate and wide-ranging opinion affirming dismissal of the writ and stating the court's conclusions as to the issues raised by appellants and other aspects of the juvenile process.

In their jurisdictional statement and brief in this Court, appellants do not urge upon us all of the points passed upon by the Supreme Court of Arizona. They urge that we hold the Juvenile Code of Arizona invalid on its face or as applied in this case because, contrary to the Due Process Clause of the Fourteenth Amendment, the juvenile is taken from the custody of his parents and committed to a state institution pursuant to proceedings in which the Juvenile Court has virtually unlimited discretion, and in which the following basic rights are denied:

1. Notice of the charges;
2. Right to counsel;
3. Right to confrontation and cross-examination;
4. Privilege against self-incrimination;
5. Right to a transcript of the proceedings; and
6. Right to appellate review.

We shall not consider other issues which were passed upon by the Supreme Court of Arizona. . . .

As to these proceedings, there appears to be little current dissent from the proposition that the Due Process Clause has a role to play.[1] The problem is to ascertain the precise impact of the due process requirement upon such proceedings.

From the inception of the juvenile court system, wide differences have been tolerated—indeed insisted upon—between the procedural rights accorded to adults and those of juveniles. In practically all jurisdictions, there are rights granted to adults which are withheld from juveniles. In addition to the specific problems involved in the present case, for example, it has been held that the juvenile is not entitled to bail, to indictment by grand jury, to a public trial or to trial by jury.[2] It is frequent practice that rules governing the arrest and interrogation of adults by the police are not observed in the case of juveniles.

The history and theory underlying this development are well-known, but a recapitulation is necessary for purposes of this opinion. The Juvenile Court movement began in this country at the end of the last century. From the juvenile court statute adopted in Illinois in 1899, the system has spread to every State in the Union, the District of Columbia, and Puerto Rico.[3] The constitutionality of

1. See Report by the President's Commission on Law Enforcement and Administration of Justice, "The Challenge of Crime in a Free Society" (1967) (hereinafter cited as Nat'l Crime Comm'n Report), pp. 81, 85–86; Standards, p. 71; Gardner, The Kent Case and the Juvenile Court: A Challenge to Lawyers, 52 A. B. A. J. 923 (1966); Paulsen, Fairness to the Juvenile Offender, 41 Minn. L. Rev. 547 (1957); Ketcham, The Legal Renaissance in the Juvenile Court, 60 Nw. U. L. Rev. 585 (1965); Allen, The Borderland of Criminal Justice (1964), pp. 19–23; Harvard Law Review Note, p. 791; Note, Rights and Rehabilitation in the Juvenile Courts, 67 Col. L. Rev. 281 (1967); Comment, Criminal Offenders in the Juvenile Court: More Brickbats and Another Proposal, 114 U. Pa. L. Rev. 1171 (1966).

2. See *Kent* v. *United States*, 383 U. S. 541, 555 and n. 22 (1966).

3. See National Council of Juvenile Court Judges, Directory and Manual (1964), p. 1. The number of Juvenile Judges as of 1964 is listed as 2,987, of whom 213 are full-time Juvenile Court Judges. *Id.*, at 305. The Nat'l Crime Comm'n Report indicates that half of these judges have no undergraduate degree, a fifth have no college education at all, a fifth are not members of the bar, and three-quarters devote less than one-quarter of their time to juvenile matters. See also McCune, Profile of the Nation's Juvenile Court Judges (monograph, George Washington University, Center for the

Juvenile Court laws has been sustained in over 40 jurisdictions against a variety of attacks.[1]

The early reformers were appalled by adult procedures and penalties, and by the fact that children could be given long prison sentences and mixed in jails with hardened criminals. They were profoundly convinced that society's duty to the child could not be confined by the concept of justice alone. They believed that society's role was not to ascertain whether the child was "guilty" or "innocent," but "What is he, how has he become what he is, and what had best be done in his interest and in the interest of the state to save him from a downward career."[2] The child—essentially good, as they saw it—was to be made "to feel that he is the object of [the state's] care and solicitude,"[3] not that he was under arrest or on trial. The rules of criminal procedure were therefore altogether inapplicable. The apparent rigidities, technicalities, and harshness which they observed in both substantive and procedural criminal law were therefore to be discarded. The idea of crime and punishment was to be abandoned. The child was to be "treated" and "rehabilitated" and the procedures, from apprehension through institutionalization, were to be "clinical" rather than punitive.

These results were to be achieved, without coming to conceptual and constitutional grief, by insisting that the proceedings were not adversary, but that the state was proceeding as *parens patriae*.[4] The Latin phrase proved to be a great help to those who sought to rationalize the exclusion of juveniles from the constitutional scheme; but its meaning is murky and its historic credentials are of dubious relevance. The phrase was taken from chancery practice, where, however, it was used to describe the power of the state to act *in loco parentis* for the purpose of protecting the property interests and the person of the child.[5] But there is no trace of the doctrine in the history of criminal jurisprudence. At common law, children under seven were considered incapable of possessing

Behavioral Sciences, 1965), which is a detailed statistical study of Juvenile Court Judges, and indicates additionally that about a quarter of these judges have no law school training at all. About one-third of all judges have no probation and social work staff available to them; between eighty and ninety percent have no available psychologist or psychiatrist. *Ibid.* It has been observed that while "good will, compassion, and similar virtues are . . . admirably prevalent throughout the system . . . expertise, the keystone of the whole venture, is lacking." Harvard Law Review Note, p. 809. In 1965, over 697,000 delinquency cases (excluding traffic) were disposed of in these courts, involving some 601,000 children, or 2% of all children between 10 and 17. Juvenile Court Statistics—1965, Children's Bureau Statistical Series No. 85 (1966), p. 2.

1. See Paulsen, Kent v. United States: The Constitutional Context of Juvenile Cases, 1966 Sup. Ct. Review 167, 174.
2. Julian Mack, The Juvenile Court, 23 Harv. L. Rev. 104, 119–120 (1909).
3. *Id.*, at 120.
4. *Id.*, at 109; Paulsen, *op. cit., supra,* n. 1, at 173–174. There seems to have been little early constitutional object to the special procedures of juvenile courts. But see Waite, How Far Can Court Procedure Be Socialized Without Impairing Individual Rights, 12 J. Crim. L. & Criminology 339, 340 (1922): "The court which must direct its procedure even apparently to do something *to* a child because of what he *has done,* is parted from the court which is avowedly concerned only with doing something *for* a child because of what he *is* and *needs,* by a gulf too wide to be bridged by any humanity which the judge may introduce into his hearings, or by the habitual use of corrective rather than punitive methods after conviction."
5. Paulsen, *op. cit. supra,* n. 1, at 173; Hurley, Origin of the Illinois Juvenile Court Law, in The Child, The Clinic, and the Court (1925), pp. 320, 328.

criminal intent. Beyond that age, they were subjected to arrest, trial, and in theory to punishment like adult offenders.[1] In these old days, the state was not deemed to have authority to accord them fewer procedural rights than adults.

The right of the state, as *parens patriae*, to deny to the child procedural rights available to his elders was elaborated by the assertion that a child, unlike an adult, has a right "not to liberty but to custody." He can be made to attorn to his parents, to go to school, etc. If his parents default in effectively performing their custodial functions—that is, if the child is "delinquent"—the state may intervene. In doing so, it does not deprive the child of any rights, because he has none. It merely provides the "custody" to which the child is entitled.[2] On this basis proceedings involving juveniles were described as "civil" not "criminal" and therefore not subject to the requirements which restrict the state when it seeks to deprive a person of his liberty.[3]

Accordingly, the highest motives and most enlightened impulses led to a peculiar system for juveniles, unknown to our law in any comparable context. The constitutional and theoretical basis for this peculiar system is—to say the least—debatable. And in practice, as we remarked in the *Kent* case, *supra*, the results have not been entirely satisfactory.[4] Juvenile Court history has again demonstrated that unbridled discretion, however benevolently motivated, is frequently a poor substitute for principle and procedure. In 1937, Dean Pound wrote: "The powers of the Star Chamber were a trifle in comparison with those of our juvenile courts . . . ."[5] The absence of substantive standards has not necessarily meant that children receive careful, compassionate, individualized

1. Julian Mack, The Chancery Procedure in the Juvenile Court, in The Child, The Clinic, and the Court (1925), p. 310.
2. See, *e. g.*, Shears, Legal Problems Peculiar to Children's Courts, 48 A. B. A. J. 719, 720 (1962) ("The basic right of a juvenile is not to liberty but to custody. He has the right to have someone take care of him, and if his parents do not afford him this custodial privilege, the law must do so."); *Ex parte Crouse*, 4 Whart. 9, 11 (Sup. Ct. Pa. 1839); *Petition of Ferrier*, 103 Ill. 367, 371–373 (1882).
3. The Appendix to the opinion of Judge Prettyman in *Pee* v. *United States*, 107 U. S. App. D. C. 47, 274 F. 2d 556 (1959), lists authority in 51 jurisdictions to this effect. Even rules required by due process in civil proceedings, however, have not generally been deemed compulsory as to proceedings affecting juveniles. For example, constitutional requirements as to notice of issues, which would commonly apply in civil cases, are commonly disregarded in juvenile proceedings, as this case illustrates.
4. "There is evidence . . . that there may be grounds for concern that the child receives the worst of both worlds: that he gets neither the protections accorded to adults nor the solicitous care and regenerative treatment postulated for children." 383 U. S., at 556, citing Handler, The Juvenile Court and the Adversary System: Problems of Function and Form, 1965 Wis. L. Rev. 7; Harvard Law Review Note; and various congressional materials set forth in 383 U. S., at 546, n. 5.
On the other hand, while this opinion and much recent writing concentrate upon the failures of the Juvenile Court system to live up to the expectations of its founders, the observation of the Nat'l Crime Comm'n Report should be kept in mind:
"Although its shortcomings are many and its results too often disappointing, the juvenile justice system in many cities is operated by people who are better educated and more highly skilled, can call on more and better facilities and services, and has more ancillary agencies to which to refer its clientele than its adult counterpart." *Id.*, at 78.
5. Foreword to Young, Social Treatment in Probation and Delinquency (1937), p. xxvii. The 1965 Report of the United States Commission on Civil Rights, "Law Enforcement—A Report on Equal Protection in the South," pp. 80–83, documents numerous instances in which "local authorities used the broad discretion afforded them by the absence of safeguards [in the juvenile process]" to punish, intimidate, and obstruct youthful participants in civil rights demonstrations. See also Paulsen, Juvenile Courts, Family Courts, and the Poor Man, 54 Calif. L. Rev. 694, 707–709 (1966).

treatment. The absence of procedural rules based upon constitutional principle has not always produced fair, efficient, and effective procedures. Departures from established principles of due process have frequently resulted not in enlightened procedure, but in arbitrariness. The Chairman of the Pennsylvania Council of Juvenile Court Judges has recently observed: "Unfortunately, loose procedures, high-handed methods and crowded court calendars, either singly or in combination, all too often, have resulted in depriving some juveniles of fundamental rights that have resulted in a denial of due process."[1]

Failure to observe the fundamental requirements of due process has resulted in instances, which might have been avoided, of unfairness to individuals and inadequate or inaccurate findings of fact and unfortunate prescriptions of remedy. Due process of law is the primary and indispensable foundation of individual freedom. It is the basic and essential term in the social compact which defines the rights of the individual and delimits the powers which the state may exercise. . . . Due process of law requires notice of the sort we have described—that is, notice which would be deemed constitutionally adequate in a civil or criminal proceeding. It does not allow a hearing to be held in which a youth's freedom and his parents' right to his custody are at stake without giving them timely notice, in advance of the hearing, of the specific issues that they must meet. Nor, in the circumstances of this case, can it reasonably be said that the requirement of notice was waived. . . .

We conclude that the Due Process Clause of the Fourteenth Amendment requires that in respect of proceedings to determine delinquency which may result in commitment to an institution in which the juvenile's freedom is curtailed, the child and his parents must be notified of the child's right to be represented by counsel retained by them, or if they are unable to afford counsel, that counsel will be appointed to represent the child. . . .

We now hold that, absent a valid confession, a determination of delinquency and an order of commitment to a state institution cannot be sustained in the absence of sworn testimony subjected to the opportunity for cross-examination in accordance with our law and constitutional requirements. . . .

1. Lehman, A Juvenile's Right to Counsel in a Delinquency Hearing, 17 Juvenile Court Judges Journal 53, 54 (1966).

Compare the observation of the late Arthur T. Vanderbilt, Chief Justice of the Supreme Court of New Jersey, in a foreword to Virtue, Basic Structure for Children's Services in Michigan (1953), p. x:

"In their zeal to care for children neither juvenile judges nor welfare workers can be permitted to violate the Constitution, especially the constitutional provisions as to due process that are involved in moving a child from its home. The indispensable elements of due process are: first, a tribunal with jurisdiction; second, notice of a hearing to the proper parties; and finally, a fair hearing. All three must be present if we are to treat the child as an individual human being and not to revert, in spite of good intentions, to the more primitive days when he was treated as a chattel."

We are warned that the system must not "degenerate into a star chamber proceeding with the judge imposing his own particular brand of culture and morals on indigent people . . . ." Judge Marion G. Woodward, letter reproduced in 18 Social Service Review 366, 368 (1944). Doctor Bovet, the Swiss psychiatrist, in his monograph for the World Health Organization, Psychiatric Aspects of Juvenile Delinquency (1951), p. 79, stated that: "One of the most definite conclusions of this investigation is that few fields exist in which more serious coercive measures are applied, on such flimsy objective evidence, than in that of juvenile delinquency." We are told that "The judge as amateur psychologist, experimenting upon the unfortunate children who must appear before him, is neither an attractive nor a convincing figure." Harvard Law Review Note, at 808.

For the reasons stated, the judgment of the Supreme Court of Arizona is reversed and the cause remanded for further proceedings not inconsistent with this opinion.

It is so ordered.

Mr. Justice Black, concurring.

Mr. Justice White, concurring.

MR. JUSTICE HARLAN, CONCURRING IN PART AND DISSENTING IN PART

Each of the 50 States has created a system of juvenile or family courts, in which distinctive rules are employed and special consequences imposed. The jurisdiction of these courts commonly extends both to cases which the States have withdrawn from the ordinary processes of criminal justice, and to cases which involve acts that, if performed by an adult, would not be penalized as criminal. Such courts are denominated civil, not criminal, and are characteristically said not to administer criminal penalties. One consequence of these systems, at least as Arizona construes its own, is that certain of the rights guaranteed to criminal defendants by the Constitution are withheld from juveniles. This case brings before this Court for the first time the question of what limitations the Constitution places upon the operation of such tribunals. For reasons which follow, I have concluded that the Court has gone too far in some respects, and fallen short in others, in assessing the procedural requirements demanded by the Fourteenth Amendment. . . .

The foregoing considerations, which I believe to be fair distillations of relevant judicial history, suggest three criteria by which the procedural requirements of due process should be measured here: first, no more restrictions should be imposed than are imperative to assure the proceedings' fundamental fairness; second, the restrictions which are imposed should be those which preserve, so far as possible, the essential elements of the State's purpose; and finally, restrictions should be chosen which will later permit the orderly selection of any additional protections which may ultimately prove necessary. In this way, the Court may guarantee the fundamental fairness of the proceeding, and yet permit the State to continue development of an effective response to the problems of juvenile crime.

Measured by these criteria, only three procedural requirements should, in my opinion, now be deemed required of state juvenile courts by the Due Process Clause of the Fourteenth Amendment: first, timely notice must be provided to parents and children of the nature and terms of any juvenile court proceeding in which a determination affecting their rights or interests may be made; second, unequivocal and timely notice must be given that counsel may appear in any such proceeding in behalf of the child and its parents, and that in cases in which the child may be confined in an institution, counsel may, in circumstances of indigency, be appointed for them; and third, the court must maintain a written record, or its equivalent, adequate to permit effective review on appeal or in collateral proceedings. These requirements would guarantee to juveniles the tools with which their rights could be fully vindicated, and yet permit the States to pursue without unnecessary hindrance the purposes which they believe imperative in this field. Further, their imposition now would later permit more intelligent assessment of the necessity under the Fourteenth Amendment of additional requirements, by creating suitable records from which the character and deficiencies of juvenile proceedings could be accurately judged. . . .

Finally, I turn to assess the validity of this juvenile court proceeding under the criteria discussed in this opinion. Measured by them, the judgment below must, in my opinion, fall. Gerald Gault and his parents were not provided adequate notice of the terms and purposes of the proceedings in which he was adjudged delinquent; they were not advised of their rights to be represented by counsel; and no record in any form was maintained of the proceedings. It follows, for the reasons given in this opinion, that Gerald Gault was deprived of his liberty without due process of law, and I therefore concur in the judgment of the Court.

MR. JUSTICE STEWART, DISSENTING

The Court today uses an obscure Arizona case as a vehicle to impose upon thousands of juvenile courts throughout the Nation restrictions that the Constitution made applicable to adversary criminal trials. I believe the Court's decision is wholly unsound as a matter of constitutional law, and sadly unwise as a matter of judicial policy.

Juvenile proceedings are not criminal trials. They are not civil trials. They are simply not adversary proceedings. Whether treating with a delinquent child, a neglected child, a defective child, or a dependent child, a juvenile proceeding's whole purpose and mission is the very opposite of the mission and purpose of a prosecution in a criminal court. The object of the one is correction of a condition. The object of the other is conviction and punishment for a criminal act. . . .

A State in all its dealings must, of course, accord every person due process of law. And due process may require that some of the same restrictions which the Constitution has placed upon criminal trials must be imposed upon juvenile proceedings. For example, I suppose that all would agree that a brutally coerced confession could not constitutionally be considered in a juvenile court hearing. But it surely does not follow that the testimonial privilege against self-incrimination is applicable in all juvenile proceedings.[1] Similarly, due process clearly

1. Until June 13, 1966, it was clear that the Fourteenth Amendment's ban upon the use of a coerced confession is constitutionally quite a different thing from the Fifth Amendment's testimonal privilege against self-incrimination. See, for example, the Court's unanimous opinion in *Brown* v. *Mississippi*, 297 U. S. 278, at 285–286, written by Chief Justice Hughes and joined by such distinguished members of this Court as Mr. Justice Brandeis, Mr. Justice Stone, and Mr. Justice Cardozo. See also *Tehan* v. *Shott*, 382 U. S. 406, decided January 19, 1966, where the Court emphasized the "contrast" between "the wrongful use of a coerced confession" and "the Fifth Amendment's privilege against self-incrimination." 382 U. S., at 416.

requires timely notice of the purpose and scope of any proceedings affecting the relationship of parent and child. *Armstrong* v. *Manzo*, 380 U. S. 545. But it certainly does not follow that notice of a juvenile hearing must be framed with all the technical niceties of a criminal indictment. See *Russell* v. *United States*, 369 U. S. 749.

In any event, there is no reason to deal with issues such as these in the present case. The Supreme Court of Arizona found that the parents of Gerald Gault "knew of their right to counsel, to subpoena and cross examine witnesses, of the right to confront the witnesses against Gerald and the possible consequences of a finding of delinquency." 99 Ariz. 181, 185, 407 P. 2d 760, 763. It further found that "Mrs. Gault knew the exact nature of the charge against Gerald from the day he was taken to the detention home." 99 Ariz., at 193, 407 P. 2d, at 768. And, as Mr. Justice White correctly points out . . . no issue of compulsory self-incrimination is presented by this case.

I would dismiss the appeal.

Problems and Discussion Questions

1. What specific policies and procedures can school boards adopt to protect students' rights to due process?

2. What policies can school boards adopt to deal effectively with student unrest? How might such policies differ from traditional views on student management? Assume that you are a superintendent of schools in a unit district serving grades K through 12. Draft a policy statement for board review concerning student management and discipline.

3. In the face of alleged discriminatory assessment and evaluation procedures for minority pupils, what alternative testing and grading plans are open to schools? As a school administrator, how would you respond to charges that your school's tests, examinations, placement, promotion, and grading systems are "culturally biased"?

Annotated Bibliography

CUNNINGHAM, Luvern L., "Equality of Opportunity: Is It Possible in Education?", *Administrator's Notebook*, vol. XVI, November, 1967, no. 3, University of Chicago Press.

Cunningham examines the component parts of the concept of "equality of educational opportunity." In amplifying terms such as "equal access," "educative resources," and "essential to needs," he indicates that attaining "equality" demands more than "flat-grant" services and opportunities.

"Discrimination of the Hiring and Assignment of Teachers in Public School Systems," *Michigan Law Review*, 64:692, Fall, 1966.

> The article points out that while the *Brown* decision gave a fairly clear direction toward desegregating schools' student populations, such has not been the case as regards the schools' faculties. In attempts to desegregate, many all-black schools were closed—often leaving a certain percentage of the black faculties with no positions in the newly integrated schools. The article is replete with copious footnotes to substantiate the gist of the text, which, in effect, makes clear the numbers and kinds of obstacles that confront attempts to desegregate school faculties.

GILLMOR, George W. and Alan L. Gosule, "Duty to Integrate Public Schools? Some Judicial Response and a Statute," *Boston University Law Review*, 46:45, Winter, 1966.

> The *Brown* decision (1954) is viewed from two perspectives: (1) the "moral view;" i.e., segregation in fact, and (2) the "sociological" view—meaning the *effect* of segregated schools. The authors hold that the Supreme Court framed its decision in a sociological context but find, through extensive case examination, that "the majority of federal courts" have been hesitant to see "inherent" inequality. These federal courts have shown little concern over de facto segregation and, as a result, demonstrate little feeling of legal duty to provide integrated schools. Massachusetts, however, appears to have overcome this "legal barrier." Gillmor and Gosule provide a thorough examination of the Massachusetts *Act Providing for the Elimination of Racial Imbalance in Public Schools* (enacted 1965).

"Integration: A Tool for the Achievement of the Goal of Quality Education," *Howard Law Journal*, 14:372, Summer, 1968.

> Three approaches to improving public education are discussed here: (1) the "negative" answer—courts which hold or imply there is no duty to achieve racial balance where de jure segregation does not exist; (2) the "affirmative" answer—courts which hold that "there is a constitutional duty to alleviate racial imbalance;" and (3) the "forgotten" approach—that the *first* goal of education is to improve the quality of all schools. The reasoning supporting position (3) is that since proof of the superiority of integrated education over segregated education does not exist, and that "integration on a scale large enough to affect the vast majority of the nations' ghetto population" is not shortly forthcoming, then every effort must be made to provide quality education for all—while, at the same time, striving to remedy racial imbalance.

KURLAND, Philip B., "Equal Educational Opportunity: The Limits of Constitutional Jurisprudence Undefined," *The University of Chicago Law Review*, 35:583, Summer, 1968.

> Professor Kurland (University of Chicago Law School) asserts that "sooner or later the Supreme Court will affirm the proposition that a State is obligated by the equal protection clause to afford equal educational opportunity to all of its public school students." He argues that such a judgment could do more to promote mediocrity in education than to service as an analgesic to the education-race affliction. There are, according to the author, three requirements that the Court must meet in order for its decision to be effective: (1) "that the constitutional standard be a simple one," (2) "that the judiciary have adequate control over the means of effectuating judgment," and (3) "that the public acquiesce . . . in the principle and its application." Kurland speaks to each of these requirements in the context of past cases and future Supreme Court decisions.

"Symposium: De Facto School Segregation," *Western Reserve Law Review*, 16:475–607, May, 1965.

> The symposium appears to cover the full gamut of de facto segregation issues and implications. Included are papers dealing with historical, sociological, educational, legal, and constitutional perspectives—all contributed by experts within their respective domains. The papers and their authors, in order of appearance, are: "Public School Desegregation: Legal Remedies for De Facto Segregation," J. Skelly Wright (Judge of the United States

Court of Appeals for the District of Columbia); "De Facto School Segregation: An Examination of the Legal and Constitutional Questions Presented," Robert L. Carter (General Counsel for the N.A.A.C.P.); "Does the Fourteenth Amendment Forbid De Facto Segregation," Charles J. Bloch (attorney-at-law, and editor of the *Georgia Bar Journal*); "Educational Implications of De Facto School Segregation," William B. Levenson (professor of education, Western Reserve University); "A Historian Looks at School Segregation," Harvey Wish (professor of history, Western Reserve University); "The Social Context of De Facto School Segregation," Sidney M. Peck (associate professor in sociology and anthropology, Western Reserve University), and David K. Cohen (assistant professor in humanities, Case Institute of Technology).

TAYLOR, William L., "Update: Civil Rights," *Kappan*, vol. L, no. 2, October, 1968.

This is a slightly condensed version of an address that the author (staff director of the U.S. Commission on Civil Rights) delivered in 1968 to the Educational Press Association of America. Although it abounds in pessimism—well-founded and explained—it mentions some of the more hopeful school situations (re: equal educational opportunity). The *Kappan* editor states that "Mr. Taylor believes we can reconcile the goals of decentralization and community control with other educational goals, including integration, if strong and imaginative educational leadership can be developed."

TYACK, David, "Catholic Power, Black Power, and the Schools," *The Educational Forum*, vol. XXXII, November, 1967, pp. 27–30.

What begins as a description of a black ghetto uprising in modern times turns out to be a picture of the beginning of Catholic power in the mid-nineteenth century. Tyack, in his brief article, points to some of the similarities between anti-Catholic and anti-Negro treatment and feelings. He also notes the salient differences to be counted as factors in each group's quest for "power."

WALKER, W. W. Jr., "Constitutional Law—Racial Imbalance—Alleviation by Voluntary State Action," *Western Reserve Law Review*, 16:788–792, May, 1965.

Walker explores several recent decisions in the State of New York, and one U.S. Supreme Court decision, regarding the constitutionality of pupil transfer and racial imbalance in public schools. The prevailing sources for all the decisions are the *Brown* decision and the equal protection clause of the Fourteenth Amendment.

4

Pupils, Parents, and School Policies

___

INTRODUCTION

The public schools tend to reflect the unsolved problems of society. As one of the few public institutions common to all communities, schools inherit many dilemmas arising from dysfunctions in the social, moral, and ethical systems in our culture. The problems of racial conflict, religious pluralism, moral relativism, economic imbalance, and a multitude of hard social questions are assigned to the schools for solution. Communities plagued with segregated housing and social structures expect the schools to integrate the pupils, quickly and quietly. We expect the schools to teach moral precepts frequently alien to the community's example. The civics lessons take on a fairytale character when read alongside the newspaper, and our notions about schoolhouse discipline more nearly resemble prisons than places of learning in a free society.

The law regarding pupils in public schools reflects a social order of long ago. The growing unrest in contemporary adult society has spread to the schools, and student militancy challenges the traditional concepts of discipline and control. This chapter deals with the principal legal issues raised by the conflict between state and local board control and the rights of pupils and parents. The implications of school board policies concerning the governance of pupils are raised and discussed in the context of selected cases.

PARENTAL RIGHTS IN EDUCATION

Although the states determine the nature of public school education, parents are free to choose between public and nonpublic schooling for their children. Such nonpublic schooling must be the approximate equivalent to the public schooling and generally does not include home instruction by unqualified teachers. The rule of reason applies in such cases and, although the courts are generally sympathetic to parental alternatives to public school attendance, home study or private schooling of a clearly inferior nature will not be accepted. State compulsory attendance laws provide for exceptions in case of illness, extreme difficulty in transportation, or home circumstances which prevent the child's attendance.

State laws may require that children receive smallpox vaccinations prior to school attendance. When parents have refused to permit such vaccinations on constitutional (religious) grounds, the children have been excluded from public school. Upon prosecution for their failure to comply with mandatory attendance laws, some parents have claimed that the vaccination requirement violated their beliefs, but they have not been sustained by the courts. The state's mandatory attendance law, coupled with reasonable requirements for attendance, has been held superior to the parents' right to refuse vaccination for their children.

The parents' right and duty to send their children to school is subject to reasonable rules of the board. Boards generally have the right to define attendance areas (assign children to schools in a given part of the district). Generally, the parents do not have the right to insist upon their child's attendance at a particular school. Boards may classify and grade pupils according to the child's abilities. Such classification, grading, and assignment procedures will be upheld if they are reasonable and not arbitrary. Boards are empowered by law to make and enforce rules for the management of schools, including rules regulating the conduct of the pupils. Such personal matters as dress, hair styles, and grooming are subject to school board regulation and violations may result in the suspension and expulsion of pupils. In such matters, the balance between board control and parental and pupil rights tips back and forth in the courts. The decided cases present no uniform pattern. The decisions in the matters of personal taste versus board rules, however, show emerging judicial concern for due process (the right to notice and hearing on alleged misconduct) to pupils prior to their suspension or expulsion.

SCHOOL ATTENDANCE

The notion of compulsory school attendance in America dates from the Deluder Satan Act of Massachusetts Colony, enacted in 1642. At a time when education and religion were practically synonymous, the Act aimed toward preparing children for the battle against sin by teaching them to read the Bible. The law required communities of 100 or more householders to organize a school and hire a teacher for the children. The fundamental concepts of universal, compulsory education through a local unit structure find their beginnings in this early legislation. The first state law requiring children to attend schools was enacted by Massachusetts in 1850. The industrial states enacted similar laws within a few years; the predominantly agricultural states followed more slowly. By 1918, compulsory school attendance laws for children were common to all states. These laws stem from the basic belief that education promotes the general welfare of the people and is the proper exercise of the state's police power.

The Illinois law regarding compulsory school attendance (article 26, school code) illustrates the legislation on the subject. Subject to specific exemptions, the parents, guardians, or custodians of any child between the ages of 7 and 16 years are obliged to cause such child's regular attendance at a public school in the district wherein the child resides. Child census, accounting, and reporting procedures are provided to implement the law, and noncompliance by custodians of children carries the threat of a hearing before a court of record and a penalty (fine and imprisonment in the county jail). The Illinois law further imposes a penalty (for a misdemeanor) on any person convicted of inducing a child to truancy or knowingly employing or harboring a truant unlawfully absent from school for three consecutive school days.

Legal controversy developed from parental claims that such compulsory school attendance laws violated their rights of parental control or interfered with the child's rights under the Fourteenth Amendment. Parents' rights in the education of their children have been considered in numerous cases (*Pierce v. Society of Sisters*, 268 U.S. 510 (1925), and *People of the State of Illinois ex rel. McCollum v. Board of Education*, 333 U.S. 203 (1948), are two well-known examples), and the parents' rights have been upheld, subject to reasonable state control. With the legally sanctioned alternatives (private and parochial schools and, in some states, home instruction) open to parents and guardians, the question of whether compulsory attendance laws violate civil rights has not yet been pushed to any ultimate limit. The civil rights movement has raised some troublesome issues for both the schools and the courts: (1) does compulsory attendance at de facto segregated schools violate the pupil's constitutional rights, (2) may parents lawfully boycott schools which allegedly teach social and human values repugnant to the parents and pupils and impose curricula damaging to the child, and (3) do penalties (detention, suspension, expulsion, etc.) imposed for pupil boycotts, peaceful protests, and similar militant activities violate the pupils' civil rights? The balance between state control and civil rights is less clear now than when the vast majority of compulsory attendance laws were enacted and the cases decided. Policies concerning attendance, truancy, discipline, and the like are much more explosive than a school board may realize. The simple ground rules based on statute, regulation, and local custom may not be adequate benchmarks for board action.

State law usually provides that residence in the local district is required for school attendance. The pupil's residence is generally held to be that of his father or, in the absence of a father, the residence of his legal guardian. Districts with a reputation for good school facilities frequently face the problem of determining the residence and legal right of certain pupils to attend their schools. This problem is accentuated in those districts providing high-quality school facilities which attract pupils. Legal residence is a question of intent coupled with an act. Whether a pupil is a legal resident of the school district may turn on the purpose for which he physically resides there. If the child lives with this parents, few problems arise; if, however, he lives with a guardian or foster parent, the question of intent may be crucial. Physical domicile in a district for the primary purpose of attending a certain school may justify the board's charging tuition or denying the child admission. Courts generally take a liberal view of pupil residence and their right to attend the district schools and, unless the residence is clearly for the primary purpose of school attendance, resolve the doubt in favor of the child's attending the district schools. State statutes frequently provide that the receiving school district charge tuition on a formula basis.

Universal state laws concerning attendance, truancy, and parental responsibility to send children to school reflect the importance of school attendance. The public policy of all states favors school attendance, and the law looks with disfavor upon board rules or regulations which limit, restrict, or prohibit school attendance. Although the board generally has the authority to prescribe criteria for pupil admission, promotion, and discharge, the courts will review carefully those rules concerning attendance of married students in public schools. The few cases on the question of whether married students have a right to attend school support the board's prerogative to exclude children for good reason but generally deny the board's authority to impose a separate standard for married pupils. Needless to say, the courts look with favor on marriage and do not consider marriage, per se, to be adequate reason to deny a pupil access to an education. Board decisions to deny admission to married pupils, otherwise qualified to attend school, have generally been reversed by the courts. Such board rules are viewed by the courts as arbitrary and unreasonable and will not be sustained. It is appropriate here to remind the reader that courts hear *particular* cases arising from a *specific* set of facts and, although the court's opinion in a given case may contain statements of broad principles, the decision controls only the specific questions presented. In short, courts decide one case at a time; generalizations drawn may not hold under situations which are even slightly different.

PUPIL CLASSIFICATION AND ASSIGNMENT

Classification and assignment of pupils are the responsibility of the local boards in most states. The procedures adopted by the boards must be reasonable, of course, and not designed or employed to segregate children on racial, religious, or other proscribed bases. State laws generally authorize school boards to establish schools of different grades, adopt regulations for admitting pupils into them, and establish one or more attendance units. The Illinois school code requires the boards to revise the attendance units from time to time to prevent segregation and eliminate pupil separation on the bases of color, race, or nationality. The boards have the responsibility to provide differentiated education but most respect the civil rights of the pupils and their parents. Generally, the pupils or parents cannot insist upon their child's attendance at a particular school. Unless some civil right is violated, boards can exercise judgment in fixing attendance units and assigning pupils to certain schools. Assignment of pupils by attendance units prompts a substantial amount of litigation all over the country. The case of *Tometz v. Board of Education*, Waukegan City School District No. 61, 39 Ill. 2d 593, 237 N.E. 2d (1968), set out earlier in Chapter 3,

illustrates the problem as raised in Illinois. To date, most cases on pupil assignments to attendance units stem from alleged segregation issues and related civil
rights questions.

School boards are free to set criteria for pupil classification. Many states
specifically authorize boards to establish graded schools and assign pupils to
them. The implicit assumption in such authorization is that boards will act
reasonably and without caprice. Problems in pupil classification stem from the
tenuous relation between predicted and actual performance. Few educators will
claim that existing measures or predictors of pupil ability are more than rough
estimations. The validity and reliability of many test instruments do not inspire
confidence in those who decide a child's educational and career future. Likewise,
many teachers experience misgivings about "passing" or "failing" pupils because
performance criteria are vague and open to debate. So far, the courts have skirted
the legal issues in pupil classification so long as the particular scheme passed the
test of reason and was neither demonstrably arbitrary nor discriminatory in
application. There are indications that classification and assignment procedures
will come under closer scrutiny by the courts.

Parents may raise questions under the due-process and equal-protection
clauses of the Fourteenth Amendment in light of the testing, grading, and promotion procedures in many school districts. Do school programs based principally on verbal and quantitative skills give equal protection of the law to those
pupils unable or unwilling to develop such skills? Does the school have any duty
to offer reasonable alternatives to pupils lacking such skills? Do the concepts of
equal educational opportunity, implicit in federal and state laws, extend to
curriculum content, teacher qualifications, and teaching skills? If the state law
requires school attendance, must pupils and parents legally accept the proffered
education, or may they demand something different? May parents legally appeal
the classification and assignment system used on their children in schools and
insist that the burden of proof for curriculum relevance and teaching effectiveness
be on the schools? These are but a few of the issues inherent in the prevailing
systems of classification used in most public schools. The law has chosen not to
treat such questions seriously to date but, as the agenda for civil rights expands,
schools and courts may be pressed to answer.

The case of *Hobson v. Hansen*, 269 F. Supp. 401 (1967), could become the
landmark decision on the question of pupil classification. This case, raised in
the Washington, D.C. school system, presented the basic question of whether the
board of education, in the operation of the public school system, deprived the
black and poor school children of their right to equal educational opportunity
with the district's white and more affluent public school children. In concluding
that the board denied such equal opportunity to the plaintiffs, the Court held
that:

ability grouping as presently practiced in the District of Columbia school system is a
denial of equal educational opportunity to the poor and a majority of the Negroes
attending school in the nation's capital, a denial that contravenes not only the guaran-

tee of the Fifth Amendment but also the fundamental premise of the track system itself.

The various "tracking" and "ability grouping" plans in the schools undoubtedly stem from valid educational motives; the legal fault may lie in their tendency to separate pupils on de facto racial bases. When the courts look behind the educational motives, they may find that the foundations of pupil classification and assignment procedures are so tied to racial separation of pupils as to render the surface motives legally impotent. If the pupil assessment devices, techniques, and instruments are prejudicial, by design or operation, to racial, religious, or ethnic groups, then the loftiest of rationales may not conceal the resultant segregation. Pressure from the civil rights movement may force the development of alternative assessment techniques and a restatement of the pupil classification ground rules.

DISCIPLINE AND PUPIL PERSONNEL POLICIES

School boards have wide discretion in making and enforcing rules in school operations. Many states specifically grant rule-making power to school boards. In the absence of express grants, however, boards have the implied authority to make such rules as are reasonably necessary to manage the schools. Abstract descriptions of the scope of the school's authority over pupils are difficult to frame. Generally, the particular rule or regulation must bear a reasonable relation to the education process and must not be discriminatory in operation or contrary to the pupils' civil rights. The rules must be reasonable and the mode of enforcement must be appropriate to the circumstances, the child, and the educational context. A recent amendment to the Illinois school code (section 24–24) specifically charges teachers and other certificated employees to "maintain discipline in the schools." The scope of the mandate is clear:

In all matters relating to the discipline in and conduct of the schools and the school children, they (the teachers) stand in the relation of parents and guardians to the pupils. This relationship shall extend to all activities connected with the school program and may be exercised at any time for the safety and supervision of the pupils in the absence of their parents or guardians. Nothing in this Section affects the power of the board to establish rules with respect to discipline.

The legislature clearly intends to vest authority for discipline in the boards and the teachers.

The teacher stands *in loco parentis* (in place of the parent) to the child and may administer reasonable corporal punishment. The punishment must be without malice and must not be excessive. Whether or not a particular punishment is excessive or reasonable depends on the circumstances; appropriate corporal punishment of one pupil may be assault and battery of another. The courts appreciate the need for discretion in the teacher and, unless the evidence clearly indicates abuse, malice, or clearly unreasonable punishment, the courts will not interfere with the teacher's reponsibility to discipline pupils. Excessive punishment may result in criminal charges for assault and battery against the teacher and, if the punishment causes injury to the child, civil charges may be brought against the teacher by the child or his parents. The courts recognize a rebuttable presumption that the teacher's conduct in school discipline is reasonable. If, however, evidence rebuts the presumption, the teacher may be held liable criminally, civilly, or both.

The school's authority to regulate pupil conduct extends beyond the school property. Some cases have extended the school's authority to the pupil's conduct at home if such conduct can be shown to adversely affect the school operation. Certainly the pupils' behavior on their way *to* and *from* school can be regulated by the school. Pupil conduct on public carriers, at neighboring schools' athletic and social events, and in the community likewise can be proscribed by the board. Most of the decisions in the cases extending discipline beyond the school day and school boundaries arose a generation ago. *O'Rourke v. Walker*, 102 Connecticut 130 (1925), is an example of the extended discipline cases. Therein the defendant school principal administered moderate corporal punishment to the plaintiffs who were guilty of abusing small children on their way from school. In sustaining the school principal's discipline, the Court held that:

The conduct of pupils outside of school hours and school property may be regulated by rules established by the school authorities if such conduct directly relates to and affects the management of the school and its efficiency.

The inevitable problem in such matters is to determine whether the proscribed conduct "directly relates to and affects" the school operation. Complications may arise when the expected pupil behavior is at substantial variance with the normative public behavior of society at large. Schools might have difficulty, for example, in legally enforcing rules prohibiting smoking by pupils in public places. The same difficulty may attach to enforcement of rules against profanity, participation in civil protests, and similar pupil behavior. As social mores evolve and rules of social behavior become liberalized, the school boards may be forced to liberalize school regulations of pupil conduct. The "outrageous" behavior of yesterday may be so accepted today as to have no adverse effect on school operation. Unless the pupil behavior somehow interferes with the school operation and efficiency, the courts will not be prone to support its proscription by the school authorities. Recent cases involving suspensions and other board disciplinary procedures for student activities in social protest and expression of opinion reinforce the legal requirement that the activity, to be properly prohibited and punished, must interfere with the education process.

The school board's authority to regulate the schools includes the extracurricular aspects of school life. Sororities, fraternities, and secret societies whose membership depends on permission of the group rather than the free choice of the qualified pupils are banned in many states. Some legislative prohibitions of such student organizations are rather pointed. The Illinois statute (section 31–1) defines a public school fraternity, sorority, and secret society as:

any organization composed wholly or in part of public school pupils, which seeks to perpetuate itself by taking in additional members from the pupils . . . on the basis of the decision of its membership rather than upon the free choice of any pupil in the school who is qualified by the rules of the school to fill the special aims of the organization.

The statute further states that any such organization is "inimical to the public good" and authorizes the board to suspend or expel any member or pledge of such an organization. Solicitation of members is unlawful and punishable by fine. The purposes and basic philosophy of such selective organizations are contrary to those of the schools, and the burdens created by such student organizations apparently outweigh any benefits.

Board rules concerning hair, appropriate dress, and grooming have caused a rash of court cases in the last decade. The length of boys' hair and girls' skirts has been a particular object of board rules and teachers' annoyance. The litigated conflicts show no unanimity of legal opinion across the country. In reviewing board suspensions arising from pupils' defiance of dress and grooming rules, the courts have decided cases both ways. The opinions sustaining board penalties for violation rest on the satisfactory proof that such dress interferes with the purposes and operations of the schools. Contrary opinions place greater emphasis on (1) the pupils' right to dress as they please so long as the morals and dignity of the participants are not compromised, and (2) on the school authorities' failure to show any connection between the rule and the education process. Bizarre fashions in hair and clothing are not confined to school children in our society; board efforts to impose unreasonable standards in such matters invite unfortunate conflict and controversy.

SUSPENSION AND EXPULSION

Suspension and expulsion of pupils are two of the most drastic disciplinary measures available to school boards and teachers. State laws generally grant to boards and teachers the power to expel or suspend pupils for serious infractions of school rules. Suspension is the temporary termination of the pupil's right to attend the public school. Expulsion is a more permanent exclusion of the pupil from the schools. The authority to suspend pupils for serious violations of rules or for misconduct may be delegated to local school administrators and teachers by either a statute or by board policy. Teachers and administrators need authority to respond quickly to discipline problems in the schools; the delegated power to suspend pupils meets that need.

Suspensions may be for a fixed number of days or for an indefinite period, the termination of which may depend on some subsequent event (e.g., conference with parents or some evidence of penance by the pupil). Expulsion of a pupil has more serious consequences to the pupil and to society as a whole. To suspend a pupil's attendance for a relatively short period may calm an explosive situation, impress the erring child with the seriousness of his misbehavior, and give the teachers, the pupil, and the parents a cooling-off period. Expelling a child from school sets in motion a complex set of forces (emotional impact, limitations on the child's future, alienation from many positive values of educated society, and the like) which can seriously affect the child's life. The severe consequences of expulsion warrant careful deliberation by the board prior to taking such a drastic step.

The board will be sustained by the courts in suspension and expulsion cases if the violated rule is reasonable and the board does not act in an arbitrary or malicious fashion. The pupil's valuable right to attend school will be protected by the courts. In proper cases, courts may enjoin a school board from carrying out prospective expulsions or may compel a board to readmit a pupil wrongfully expelled. The courts have shown increasing interest in the due-process aspects of suspension and expulsion procedures. The pupil's right to adequate notice of the violation and an appropriate hearing on the charges may come under closer legal scrutiny. This right to a hearing before the board may include the right to counsel and opportunity to hear and examine board evidence—in short, the hallmarks of due process under the Fifth and Fourteenth Amendments. Boards may be required to maintain appropriate records to support expulsion; the days of casual paternalism in pupil personnel matters have ended.

Readings

Crime Investigation in the School: Its Constitutional Dimensions

Lawrence W. Knowles

Associated Professor of Law, University of Louisville School of
Law, Louisville, Kentucky. The research reported here was
supported through the Cooperative Research Program of the Office
of Education, U.S. Department of Health, Education and Welfare.
All policy statements quoted in this article are actual statements of
school officials throughout the country. Regulations of over 350
school districts were collected in a nationwide study of the constitutional implications of school administration. This article is part of
that study.
Journal of Family Law (1964), **4**, 151

The school is not a court of law. The private personal effects of an individual are
regarded as being inviolate. We regard the school as not having the right to search.

School personnel are not policemen. Nevertheless the school is often forced to
play this role. Reports of the presence of dangerous weapons, pornography,
liquor, stolen goods, and dozens of other undesirable, if not very harmful,
objects are familiar to every secondary school teacher and administrator.
Additionally, theft or other illegal acts committed during the school day often
demand immediate and effective action by school authorities. Still again, the
police may ask a school principal to assist them in the questioning, or search of
the person or effects of a student.

Coursing through the foregoing examples is the question of what posture
should the school take toward investigations? Should it assume the same posture
in all cases? Should it act to defend the student against police interrogation in
all instances? Are there times when the school should take the initiative in an
investigation? Furthermore, what rights does a student have? Does he have the
right to refuse a search of his person or his locker? Must he answer all questions?
If a student refuses to cooperate, may the school punish him?

By citing only a few of the basic issues, the total complexity of criminal
investigation in the schools comes to the surface. On one side stands the societal
interest in the detection of crime, and particularly, the interest of the school in
protecting the student body from dangerous persons and weapons. On the

other side stand the rights of young adults, such as the right of privacy and the privilege against self-incrimination.

Between the polestars rest the ambivalent duties of school personnel. School officials are said to be *in loco parentis* to each student.[1] Consequently, they may have a duty to each student to advise him of his rights and protect him against over zealous police investigation. Alternatively school officials are *in loco parentis* to other students in their charge, and must protect them against dangers posed by a particular law breaking student. With the dilemma thus posed, we can now pass to particulars.

I. SEARCHES OF STUDENTS AND LOCKERS

Students are forbidden to bring some things into the school. Search of the person and his effects is a normal procedure in enforcement of these rules. Water pistols, firecrackers, itch-powder and similar items are confiscated.

MERCER COUNTY, WEST VIRGINIA

A. Searching the Person of Students

We do not hesitate to go through their wallets, purses, handbags, notebooks, etc. With the girls, it gets a little tricky when it comes to their clothing. However, with boys, we don't hesitate to check their pockets. CASPER, WYOMING

The Fourth Amendment to the United States Constitution as applied to the States by the Fourteenth Amendment[2] provides:

The right of the people to be secure in their persons, houses, papers, and effects, against unreasonable searches and seizures, shall not be violated . . .

The amendment does not define what is a search, nor does it set out what is an unreasonable search. This was left to the courts to develop. In constructing the definition of a search the courts have interpreted history as modified by the inventions and demands of an advancing society. In the twentieth century a search is an action[3] by a public official[4] compelling[5] the production of non-verbal

---

1. Actually the phrase *in loco parentis* expresses nothing save that the school has certain rights and duties to children in its care. When a court rules that a certain act by a school official is performed *in loco parentis* the court is actually concluding that the act was permissible. When a court rules that an official superseded his powers *in loco parentis*, the court is ruling that the specific act was not legally permissible. Most simply, the phrase *in loco parentis* is no guide to action, but solely a conclusionary label attached to permissible school controls. The phrase is so used here.

2. See Ker v. California, 374 U.S. 23 (1963).

3. On Lee v. U.S., 343 U.S. 747 (1951). A Federal agent, posing as petitioner's friend, engaged in conversation in petitioner's store with a radio transmitter concealed on the agent's person. Incriminating statements made by the petitioner were transmitted outside the store to another Federal agent. Later these were introduced in evidence against the petitioner. The court held that the conduct of these agents did not amount to search. The court compared such an act to the use of bifocals, field glasses, or telescopes. Vision, even with mechanical aids, is not a forbidden search, even if focused without knowledge or consent of the person under scrutiny.

4. Annenberg v. Roberts, 333 Pa. 203, 2 A.2d 612 (1938). A legislative committee demanded certain persons produce incriminating evidence concerning gambling operations. The court held that a witness cannot be compelled, under the guise of a legislative study of conditions bearing upon proposed legislation, to reveal his private and personal affairs, except to the extent to which such disclosure is reasonably required for the general purpose of the inquiry. To compel an individual to

material or information from the possession of another against his will. A crucial point is that a teacher need not forage through the clothes of a student. A search is made if the teacher compels the student to produce or at least expose matter otherwise covered from the plain view of the teacher.[1] Consequently, ordering a student to empty his pockets, remove his coat or shoes, or empty his mouth, is a search regardless whether the student is physically handled in the process.[2]

Another aspect of the law of search and seizure is that a person may cooperate with a search and thereby waive his rights. Cooperate in this sense does not mean to merely accede to a requested search, but to affirmatively volunteer material. For example, if a student responded to an order to empty his pockets, his action would probably not constitute a waiver of his rights to be secure from a search. The age of the student, and his subordinate position vis-a-vis school authorities would appear to give rise to a presumption of non-waiver in such a situation.[3] To rebut this presumption there should be clear and convincing proof that the student willingly acceded to the investigation.

The Fourteenth Amendment does not forbid all searches but only unreasonable searches. The definition of an unreasonable search is, like most definitions, easier to state than to apply. Basically the only time a person may be searched is pursuant to a valid search warrant, or incident to a valid arrest. Only one of these alternatives is open to school officials—the valid arrest opportunity. (The search warrant will probably always be executed by police officers.) Consequently, the main question facing schoolmen, if they act in their capacity

---

produce evidence, under penalties if he refuses, is in effect a search and seizure and unless confined to proper limits, violates his constitutional rights.

5. See Hoppes v. State, 70 Okla. Cr. 179, 105 P.2d 433 (1940), stating: Search implies an invasion and quest, with some sort of force, either actual or constructive. A search, within constitutional immunity from unreasonable search and seizure, implies a quest by an officer of the law acting on the things themselves, which quest may be secret, intrusive, or accomplished by force.

1. Bone v. State, 207 Miss. 868, 43 So. 2d 571 (1949). A law enforcement officer, after being informed that a strange car was parked on a street walked to the car and looked in it without having a search warrant. Inside the car he saw an unusual blanket. Defendant was arrested for a burglary and claimed that his car had never entered the town where the crime was committed. The defendant claimed that the law enforcement officer could not testify that he had seen the car because his acts constituted an unreasonable search. The court held that obtaining information by means of the eye, where no trespass has been committed, does not constitute an unlawful search. "The eye doesn't trespass."

2. School authorities are generally unaware that a search may be conducted without a physical touching. For example, an Illinois school administrator reports: The school district does not have a policy statement relative to searching a person. However, it could be considered common practice for a Principal to request that a child empty his pocket or pocketbook in his presence. This action would be preceded by evidence that the child is carrying prohibited items on his person, such as a pocket knife, matches, lipstick, etc.

An administrator from another State gave a more soul searching, but equally uninformed reply: There might be a question of our legal rights, however, we have asked students to show the contents of their pockets, purses, lockers and even shoes and socks when staff members have been definitely tipped off that certain contraband might be found. To date with 4700 pupils in the district I personally have never had a student refuse to show his effects to me or a staff member when so asked and we have had several cases of stolen articles being recovered with this method.

3. See Haley v. Ohio, 332 U.S. 596 (1948) (Confession of fifteen-year-old boy held to be involuntarily given); Gallegos v. Colorado, 370 U.S. 49 (1962) (Confession of fourteen-year-old boy held to be involuntary).

as private citizens, is when may they arrest a student? A citizen, if he has reasonable grounds to believe a person has or is committing a felony, and a felony has in fact been committed, he may arrest the suspected felon.[1] He may not arrest if the crime committed is a misdemeanor except when the misdemeanor is a breach of the peace, or petit larceny committed in his presence.[2] For example, if a major theft had in fact been committed on school grounds, all students could not be searched by the school authorities. But if one particular student had been seen in the room where the theft occurred, there may be reasonable grounds to arrest that student and then search his person.[3]

The foregoing discussion points up the rights of school personnel acting as private citizens to arrest and search students. Do school officials have added investigative powers because of their special relationship to students? The answer is a very qualified yes. The qualifications break down into considerations of the age of the student searched, the object of the search and the manner of the search.

B. Searches of Young Students

. . . In another case, a student had taken a purse and forged checks from a check book in that purse. The student was asked, "May I see your purse?" The student handed the purse over, the one being sought.   [Name of school district withheld]

A school may search the persons of young school children providing the search is in good faith for a school purpose.[4] Searches of this nature may be justified on several grounds. A principle basis is implied parental consent, positing that parents delegate to the school certain parental rights over the child while the child is in the custody of the school. The dimensions of the delegated rights are greatest at the lower age levels and at these levels would seem to include the right to search. Another reason tending to support searches of

1. The general rule is that an arrest is justified when a felony has in fact been committed by someone, but the person arrested need not be guilty. Suell v. Derricott, 161 Ala. 259, 49 So. 895 (1909). In Imler v. Yeager, 245 S.W. 700 (Mo. 1922) the court stated: When a felony had been committed any private person may, without a warrant, arrest one whom he has reasonable grounds to suspect of having committed it, but such an arrest is illegal if no felony has in fact been committed by anyone, though if a felony has actually been committed, such an arrest is legal, though the party suspected and arrested is innocent.
Several variations of these general rules have been adopted by the different States. The most stringent is that an arrest is justified only if person arrested in fact committed the felony with which charged. Pandjiris v. Hartman, 196 Mo. 539, 94 S.W. 270 (1906).
The liberal view, recognized in a minority of jurisdictions, holds that an arrest is justified if made upon reasonable grounds. Alder v. Commonwealth, 277 Ky. 136, 125 S.W. 2d 986 (1939); Burton v. McNeill, 196 S.C. 250, S.E. 2d 10 (1941).
2. See generally, Alexander, The Law of Arrest In Criminal and Other Proceedings (1949).
3. A good faith requirement is necessary to provide protection against pedophiliacs and similar sexually deviate personnel. If a search or physical intrusion is perpetrated to satisfy abnormal desires then such search may be an invasion of the personal privacy protected by the Fourteenth Amendment. See York v. Story, 324 F.2d 450 (9th Cir. 1963). (Policemen demanded woman to strip and took pictures of her over her objections; held to be violation of the constitutional rights of privacy).
4. Indeed the teacher may have a *duty to search* in situations where the child of tender years is suspected of having articles dangerous to himself and others. See Christofides v. Hellenic East Orthodox Christian Church, 33 Misc. 2d 741, 227 N.Y.S. 2d 946 (1962) (knife with three-inch blade *per se* a dangerous instrumentality in the hands of a child). *Cf.* Lilienthal v. San Leandro Unified School District, 193 Cal. App. 2d 453, 293 P.2d 889 (1956).

elementary school children is that the school owes a duty to all children within its custody, and implicit in this duty is the power to protect children from other children. Consequently, if the purpose of this search is to uncover objects dangerous to children, the search is permissible. A third, and negative, basis supporting the right to search children in the elementary schools is that the children have not reached the age of criminal responsibility, thus placing the search beyond the spirit of the constitutional safeguard against unreasonable searches and seizures.[1]

C. Searches of Older Students

If it is necessary to search students then it should be done—the coach is the logical man for the boys and the dean of women or girls' counselor for the girls. It should be noted clearly what they are searching for and what has happened to make the search necessary. The innocent have to suffer with the guilty until the culprit is found and then he should be punished. Students know each other better than the teachers and they can put their hands on the culprit right off . . . take them to the gym and explain the situation and send them out to find the missing article before they can go home. It won't take long for something to turn up.   HILLROSE, COLORADO

When children reach the age of criminal responsibility, they receive certain constitutional safeguards. They are adults insofar as the criminal law is concerned, and consequently, they are adults insofar as they are entitled to due process of law guaranteed by the Fourteenth Amendment. And implicit in due process of law is the guarantee against unreasonable searches and seizures. What does this mean for school officials? It simply means that they cannot search the persons of older students, unless they arrest a student pursuant to the power of a citizen to arrest persons generally.[2]

Other avenues are open to school officials. If a dangerous weapon is reported or suspected to be in the school, the principal can request suspected students to submit voluntarily to a search. The students who refuse to be searched may be then sent home or otherwise isolated from the student body.[3] The reason for special treatment is not that the non-consenting students are being punished for exercising their rights, but that the school is justified in isolating them because it cannot be certain that they do not possess a dangerous object which the school has reason to believe is on the premises.

At this point the school authorities must decide whether or not they want to search the isolated students. If they do search, they will probably surrender the right to use any evidence so procured as a basis to punish the offending student. Alternatively, the police may be called and a search warrant executed. Evidence procured by this procedure may be used as a basis for punishment, both at school or in the juvenile or criminal courts.

1. Similarly a child's constitutional right of privacy may not develop (save for purposes set out in the previous footnote) until the child is at an age to feel mortification or embarrassment.
2. The safest procedure for the school official is not to arrest the suspected student but to call the police and let them decide whether to arrest the student or not. This procedure will insulate school personnel against a lawsuit for false arrest.
3. It is not unlikely that further interrogation of the isolated students will bring forth the offending party.

One theory may sustain searches of individual students suspected of possessing forbidden articles. It is to analogize the administrative arrests of deportation proceedings to administrative arrests for expulsion from school. In *Abel* v. *U. S.*,[1] the Supreme Court upheld a search of the person and room of an alien taken into custody preliminary to a deportation proceeding. A principal point in the analogy is that the arrest in the *Abel* case occurred as a result of the failure of the alien to register pursuant to Federal law. In the school situation the student must have clearly violated a regulation. This theory will not justify a fishing expedition or general shakedown of students. However, it does support a search of a student incident to taking him into custody for the purposes of suspension or other severe punishment.

D. Consequences of an Unconstitutional Search

Sometimes it is necessary to search students for stolen property. Also for knives or other weapons which are considered dangerous and which are prohibited by law.

RIVERTON, WYOMING

Now to go one step further. What happens if a school official does conduct an illegal search?

TEACHER LIABILITY. As regards a teacher's personal liability, he may be liable for damages under State and Federal laws for a tortious violation of the privacy of the student. In most cases the student will have suffered little or no damages. However, adverse publicity and the expense of a law suit precipitated by an indignant parent are secondary but often costly factors. Moreover the conduct may be cause for dismissal of the teacher.

SUPPRESSION OF THE EVIDENCE. Evidence or contraband produced by an unconstitutional search may not be used in a State or Federal criminal proceeding against the student. Moreover, any evidence or information gained *through the use* of illegally obtained materials is also inadmissible in criminal proceeding. A kind of original sin pervades all subsequent uses of the illegally procured goods. (For example, if the student confessed when confronted by this evidence, his confession would be invalid.) An unconstitutional search in effect may very well prevent a successful criminal prosecution of the person searched.

If the fruits of an illegal search and seizure are inadmissible in a criminal proceeding, are they likewise inadmissible in a proceeding by the school to expel or otherwise punish a student? No court has decided this question but both logic and experience appear to support an exclusionary rule.

For decades the Supreme Court permitted the use of illegally procured evidence in State criminal cases on the theory that a criminal should not go free because the constable bungled. The feeling was that the criminal's wrong should not go unpunished because of the State officer's wrong. The wrong to the criminal could be righted because he could bring a damage suit against the offending

1. 362 U.S. 217 (1960).

official. As dubious as the criminal's relief appears when stated, it was even shallower in practice. Damage suits by convicted criminals against State officers were few and rarely successful. Illegal searches became planned invasions of privacy and not the bungling of constables. In short there was no real protection against unconstitutional searches. In 1961 the Supreme Court of the United States decided that evidence procured from an unreasonable search and seizure must be excluded from State criminal prosecutions.[1] In so holding the Court commented:[2]

Having once recognized that the right to privacy embodied in the Fourth Amendment is enforceable against the States, and that the right to be secure against rude invasions of privacy by state officers is, therefore, constitutional in origin, we can no longer permit that right to remain an empty promise. Because it is enforceable in the same manner and to like effect as other basic rights secured by the Due Process Clause, we can no longer permit it to be revocable at the whim of any police officer who, in the name of law enforcement itself, chooses to suspend its enjoyment. Our decision, founded on reason and truth, gives to the individual no more than that which the Constitution guarantees him, to the police officer no less than that to which honest law enforcement in entitled and, to the courts, that judicial integrity so necessary in the true administration of justice.

The problem for school administrators thus becomes clear. Is a school disciplinary procedure, such as expulsion or suspension, the analogue of a criminal procedure for the purposes of excluding evidence procured by invading a student's privacy? The author believes it is and that the evidence cannot be used against a student.[3]

The only reported case on the issue arose in Tennessee. There a boy broke a school regulation by entering a classroom during recess. When accused he falsely denied so doing. He was punished for lying and breaking the school regulations. A dime was reported missing from the room and the teacher searched the boy (the court's written opinion does not say whether the dime was found). The parents of the child sued the teacher, seeking to recover money damages for an illegal search. The Supreme Court of Tennessee upheld the teacher on the grounds that the teacher's motive in searching the boy was to clear him of any suspicion, and thus the teacher acted for the child's welfare.[4] A previous Tennessee case decided that a teacher who had searched a young girl because the teacher had

1. Mapp v. Ohio, 367 U.S. 643 (1961). The court overruled Wolf v. Colorado, 336 U.S. 25 (1949), a decision decided just twelve years before.
2. *Id.* at 660.
3. In Weeks v. United States the Supreme Court said: The effects of the Fourth Amendment is to put the courts of the United States and Federal officials in the exercise of their power and authority, under limitations and restraints as to the exercise of such power and authority and to forever secure the people, their persons, houses, papers and effects against all unreasonable searches and seizures under the guise of law. *This protection reaches all alike, whether accused of a crime or not, and the duty of giving it force and effect is obligatory upon all entrusted under our Federal System with the enforcement of the laws.* [Emphasis added] 232 U.S. 383, 391 (1914).
    Although this case was a decision concerning Federal officials, the decision in Mapp v. Ohio, 367 U.S. 643 (1961), seems to bring the State exclusionary policies up to the strictness of the Federal policies. *Cf.* Lassoff v. Gray, 207 F. Supp. 843 (W.D. Ky. 1962) (Evidence for tax assessment procured by invasion of taxpayer's privacy excluded from civil action by government tax office). *See also* Rogers v. U.S., 97 F.2d 691 (1st Cir., 1938); Schenck v. Ward 24 F. Supp. 776 (D. C. Mass. 1938).
4. Marlar v. Bill, 181 Tenn. 100, 178 S.W.2d 634 (1944).

lost twenty-one dollars could be held liable in damages to the girl.[1] The court distinguished the earlier case on the basis that the search there was for the teacher's benefit, and not conducted for the child's welfare.[2]

Perhaps some constitutional line drawing should be here. Is it inconsistent to rule that a teacher who searches a student for the welfare of the student or other students cannot be held liable in damages, and also to rule that anything uncovered may not be used as a basis for punishing the student? For example, a report of dangerous weapons in the school may justify a general shakedown of all students. Is it contradictory to hold the school personnel safe from suit, but also forbid any articles found to form a basis for disciplinary action? In balancing a particular student's rights of privacy against the rights of the school to protect him against himself, and other students against him, this may well be the solution.[3] School officials may, under this theory, be said to be acting *in loco parentis*. Conversely if the search may be used to expel or suspend the student, then the search can hardly be denominated *in loco parentis*, or for the child's welfare.

E. Searching School Lockers

[W]e consider this [locker inspection] a general part of the whole disciplinary situation and we would hate to see a situation where the locker was considered "private" and we did not have access.   REHOBETH BEACH, DELAWARE

The search of student lockers within the school poses many problems not presented in the analysis of searches of the person. Basic to the question is whether a locker is an area protected from a search. Another issue is whether the nature of the locker contract with a student, *i.e.*, whether it is a lease or merely a courtesy or privilege granted to a student. The question is further complicated because there are no cases specifically on this issue.

LOCKERS AS A PROTECTED AREA. The Fourth Amendment guarantees the "right of the people to be secure in their persons, houses, papers, and effects." The amendment was drafted and enacted in the eighteenth century, when a person's papers and private possessions were kept almost exclusively in his home. But the agrarian's concept of privacy, the home, has passed.

In the twentieth century personal effects are kept in many places outside the home. Automobiles, safe deposit boxes, desks, business safes, and industrial

1. Phillips v. Johns, 12 Tenn. App. 354.
2. Based on these two Tennessee cases cited in note 4, p. 220, and note 1 *supra*, and the fact that the Kentucky Court of Appeals in numerous cases has held that teachers and officials of public schools stand *in loco parentis* with respect to pupils the Kentucky Office of the Attorney General rendered this opinion on the law of Kentucky: [A] school teacher may search a pupil's pockets or purse and confiscate such articles as cigarette lighters, pocket knives, or key chains with cigarette lighters attached if the teacher acts with reasonable judgment and for good cause, without malice and for the welfare of the child, as well as the school. However, the pupil's parents should be advised of this action and the confiscated articles turned over to said parents. If the pupil is guilty of subsequent offenses of this nature, the teacher might be empowered to retain the articles confiscated until the close of the school year.
3. See Frank v. Maryland, 359 U.S. 360 (1959).

lockers are used to hold important documents and articles. Hotel rooms replace the home for a large number of our citizens. As a result, modern life has demanded and received a new physical dimension of constitutionally protected privacy.

The restrictive characteristics of the Fourth Amendment phrase ". . . secure in their persons, houses, papers, and effects," have been stripped of their proprietary implications. No longer must a citizen own, or rent, a home to be protected from an invasion of his privacy.[1] Consequently, whether a student rents or owns a locker is not crucial to its sanctity. A most significant decision by the Court was handed down in 1964 holding that automobiles were protected areas.[2] This decision extends the homes and persons phrase to mean all closed compartments (even if they are on a public street). The tenure of this decision would support the conclusion that lockers, even though in a public school, may be constitutionally protected compartments. Thus, by using bits and pieces of Supreme Court decisions, a good argument can be made that school lockers are areas of constitutionally protected privacy. Moreover, several decisions in lower Federal courts lend even greater support to this conclusion.

The closest reported court decision to the issue of whether or not a school may search a student's locker is *United States* v. *Blok*,[3] a 1950 District of Columbia case. There a Federal employee was suspected of committing petit larceny. The police asked and received permission from her superiors to search her desk, in which they found incriminating evidence. The Federal Court of Appeals held that even though the government owned the desk and could have gone into it for property needed for official use, the government could not go into the desk seeking evidence of an employee's crime.[4] Other lower court cases, although not as analogous as the *Blok* case, militate to the same end. In *Holzhey* v. *United States*,[5] another government employee was suspected of stealing government property. Federal agents went to the home of the employee's married daughter and secured the daughter's consent to search her garage in which a

1. Hotel rooms are protected despite the duration of a persons stay. Stoner v. California, 376 U.S. 473 (1964).

2. Preston v. United States, 376 U.S. 364 (1964). Actually the point was not even seriously urged by counsel for the government. *Cf.* Carroll v. United States, 267 U.S. 132 (1925); Brinegar v. United States, 338 U.S. 160 (1949).

3. 188 F.2d 1019 (D.C. Cir. 1951).

4. In Freeman v. U. S., 201 A. 2d 22 (D.C. Mun. App. 1964) a government messenger argued that a table from which he was assigned his messages and routes could not be searched by government agents. The court held the employee's interest in the table insufficient stating: Here appellant did not have the exclusive right to use the table at the messenger station on the seventh floor. His assignment there was merely temporary since he could be reassigned to another floor on a daily basis. While he could place personal effects in the table drawer, there was another assigned place in the building for his clothing and lunches. The minimal time spent working at the table and the fact that secretaries and other employees would frequent the room and use paper clips or pencils from the table drawer gave appellant a very limited interest therein. In effect the table was open for common use by other employees of the agency. For these reasons we feel appellant cannot complain that the search by the Veterans Administration investigator violated his right of privacy under the Fourth Amendment and that the seized evidence should have been suppressed. *Id.* at 24.

5. 223 F.2d 823 (5th Cir. 1955). See also Reeves v. Warden, 226 F. Supp. 953 (D.C. Md. 1964). (Mother of suspected rapist could not consent to search of son's room even though she owned the home and had free access to the room).

locked cabinet owned by the employee was stored. The agents searched the cabinet and uncovered incriminating evidence. The Federal Circuit Court of Appeals held that the search was unconstitutional and that even though the daughter owned the garage, she could not authorize a search of the locked personal effects of her mother contained in the garage.

There are several other cases further from the point but sufficiently relevant to merit mention. Foremost of these is the situation where a serviceman's locker is searched. The courts have held that these lockers can be searched, but only where permission is granted by a superior officer.[1] By necessary implication the judicial reasoning is that the lockers are private, but because of the unique character of a serviceman's position, his officers can also consent to a search.[2] The right of privacy was also recognized in a case where police officers hid themselves in a restroom of an amusement park open to the public. The California Supreme Court held that despite the fact that the park owner gave his permission to the officers and that the restrooms were open to the public, eavesdropping in a lavatory violated a fundamental right of privacy.[3]

The only case opposing the mainstream toward greater protection of privacy was decided by the highest court of West Virginia in 1958.[4] There it was decided that a search of a locker in a bus station was constitutional even though the suspected criminal leased the locker, and had a key thereto. The court stated that the locker simply was not a place protected from searches by the Federal Constitution. The only comment which can be made on this case has been made, —that it is an anomaly in current concepts of protected possessions.[5] It would probably not be upheld by the Supreme Court.

CONSENT OF THE STUDENT TO A SEARCH OF THE LOCKER. A student may consent to a search of his locker and thereby legalize what would otherwise be an illegal search.[6] The consent must be freely and knowingly given, however.[7] Because a voluntary and intelligent waiver is necessary to validate the search, there may be

1. Richardson v. Zuppann, 81 F. Supp. 809 (N.D. Pa. 1949) (Locked strongbox found in U.S. government office in Trieste, Italy could be searched when owned by person in the military service).
2. People v. Shepard, 212 Cal. App. 2d 297, Cal. Rptr. 297 (1963).
3. Bulocki v. Superior Court of Los Angeles, 21 Cal. Rptr. 552, 371 P.2d 288 (1962). *But see* U. S. v. Lewis, 227 F. Supp. 433 (S.D.N.Y. 1964); People v. Rodriguez, 4 Cal. Reptr. 456 (1960); McDonald v. U. S., 335 U.S. 451 (1948).
4. State v. Bruner, 143 W. Va. 755, 105 S.E.2d 140 (1958), *cert. denied*, 358 U.S. 937 (1959).
5. The Courts of Appeals of New York decided that a safe deposit box was not protected against a sheriff's inspection for purposes of executing a lien on the contents. Carples v. Cumberland Coal & Iron Co., 240 N.Y. 187, 148 N.E. 185 (1925). Although the purpose of the inspection was not to find evidence of a crime, the court went out of its way to comment on the constitutional aspects of the sheriff's acts, stating: We are unable to see any pertinent analogy between a man's home which is protected by the Constitution and decisions from invasion for the purpose of serving civil process, and a disconnected depository in which he has stored his property, whether a barn, a warehouse, or a safe deposit box. 148 N.E. 185, 187.
6. Johnson v. U. S., 333 U.S. 10 (1948) (the fact that police officers are admitted to an apartment upon request does not constitute consent to a search of the apartment).
7. A West Virginia school administrator reports a unique device for obtaining consent: The principal has a master-key for all locks, and at times has investigated suspicious happenings around the school, but in most cases we ask pupils to see their lock under one pretense or another.

a duty upon the school principal or police officers to tell the student that he has a right to object to a search of his locker.[1] Owing to the age and education of the student, and the possible intimidating presence of police officers, express advisement of his rights would seem necessary to show an exercise of a voluntary choice by the student.[2]

The interests of the school may best be promoted by a preventive procedure adopted at the beginning of the school year, when lockers are originally assigned. The process is not complicated. The school need only to have each student sign a statement to the effect that the school may, at any time and for any purpose, open and inspect the locker of the student.[3] Conceptually this agreement would not be a waiver of a student's right of privacy.[4] However, it would change the character of a school locker from a private compartment to one open to the school and its officers.[5]

Actually many schools retain a master key, or combinations, to lockers. This fact, coupled with a tradition of locker inspection or searches may well be an implicit waiver of exclusive locker control by the students. In fact schools may well have a right to inspect lockers for existing conditions threatening the health of the student body.[6] On the other hand a right to inspect for unhealthy conditions does not extend to the right to inspect for contraband. The former right is a limited one.[7]

1. Johnson v. Zerbst, 304 U.S. 458 (1938) (the right to counsel in Federal courts places a *duty* on Federal judges to advise an accused of his rights).
2. See cases cited note 3, p. 216.
3. In People v. Kelly, 195 Cal. App.2d 669, 16 Cal. Reptr. 177 (1961), it was held that a student who consented to inspection of his room during "emergencies" thereby consented to a search for stolen property. Limiting the stipulated reason for search to "emergencies," "health inspections," or "periodic inspections" may at least cause friction in the event of an investigative search. A preferable stipulation would be "at any time for any purpose deemed to be in the best interests of the school."
4. An Iowa school reports: Whether or not a school retains the right to inspect lockers as a part of a locker-lease agreement is dependent upon the policies, rules and regulations of the respective boards of education. The State of Iowa has no regulations concerning this. The office of the Iowa Attorney General has advised the Department of Public Instruction that there does not seem to be too much doubt that school authorities could go as far as searching a person's locker. There is the possibility that a student may raise a personal right in connection with the searching of a locker. It may be necessary for a student to consent to the search of his locker.
5. This distinction is important. A school system cannot compel a student to surrender his constitutional rights for the privilege of attending school. West Virginia State Board of Education v. Barnette, 319 U. S. 624 (1943). Consequently, if the school exacted a waiver of rights as a condition of attendance it would be violating the Constitution. For this reason, the locker agreement must be construed as changing the character of the locker area, and not as exacting waivers of privacy from students.
6. Frank v. Maryland, 359 U.S. 360 (1959), which did allow a fine of $20 to be imposed on a person who refused a health inspector to his home, may well support searches of lockers made to discover unhealthy or dangerous articles. The decision, however, must be limited to the purpose of the search and the crucial point that the searched individual could only be required to remedy unhealthy conditions uncovered by the search. No punishment was exacted. *Cf.* People *ex rel* Eaton v. Price, 364 U.S. 263 (1960).
7. This limited-right-of-inspection distinction is made clear by the Supreme Court cases involving searches of rented rooms to which landlords had retained a right to enter for cleaning or inspection purposes. The Court held that the landlords' rights of entry did not include the right to enter for purposes of crime investigation, Lustig v. U. S., 338 U.S. 74 (1949); U. S. v. Jeffers, 342 U.S. 48 (1951); Stoner v. State of California, 376 U.S. 473 (1964). *See also* Eng Fung Jem v. U. S., 281 F.2d 803 (9th Cir. 1960); Klee v. U. S., 53 F.2d 58 (9th Cir. 1931).

F. Conclusion

Current locker inspection policies are inadequate to promote the total interests of the schools. Although the schools probably possess the right to inspect lockers for substances endangering the health of the student body, their powers end there. The presence of stolen property, stolen from the school or otherwise, cannot be an object of a locker search. The reason for this is not that the school has made lockers the repositories for all kinds of contraband. The reason is that the schools have failed to clarify their locker policy and in the absence of a published policy clearly reserving the right to inspect the contents of school lockers for any purpose, the lockers would probably be held constitutionally secure against searches for contraband. Consequently, responsible school administration should draft and publicize a clarified locker policy reserving the greatest freedom of action to school authorities. . . .

School Expulsions and Due Process

Terry J. Wuester,
Kansas Law Review (1965), **14,** 108

The expulsion of a student from high school is a serious problem—for both the individual and society. Education through at least the twelfth grade is virtually an economic necessity for the individual;[1] Secretary of Labor Willard Wirtz has said that fourteen years of formal education is necessary for one to compete successfully with machines.[2] Society is equally interested in the problem of school expulsions; the school-aged young person who is not attending school often uses his time for purposes contrary to society's best interests.[3]

Several schools, colleges, and universities have recently experienced serious disciplinary problems in connection with civil rights demonstrations. These situations have produced a few cases that would seem to have due process implications for the more routine school expulsions. In determining the due process rights of students in disciplinary actions, the interests of the individual

1. Based on 1961 figures, the person with an eighth grade education can expect a lifetime income of $168,810, while the person who has completed high school can expect $224,417. Completion of college increases expected lifetime earnings to $360,604. Statistics also indicate that 22.8% of males with one to three years of high school make under $1000 per year. 1963 STATISTICAL ABSTRACT OF THE UNITED STATES 122.

2. Time, Mar. 5, 1965, p. 60.

3. See, *e.g.*, VEDDER, JUVENILE OFFENDERS 60-61 (1963).

[Reprinted with permission of the publisher, *Kansas Law Review*.]

and of society must be weighed against the exigencies of the operation of the school. It would seem obvious that the smooth operation of the school would be seriously hindered if a full hearing were required for every minor disciplinary problem; when contemplated action is expulsion, however, the smooth functioning of the school would not seem so important.

Addressed primarily to the public secondary school level, this comment will focus on the emerging due process rights of the student in such proceedings. A brief summary of existing Kansas statutory law will be included.

EXPULSION POWERS OF SCHOOLS

Under the American scheme, public education is a function of the various states with state legislatures providing the basic statutes under which the schools operate.[1] These statutes delegate a part of the legislative power to the local school districts and boards. Directed by these legislative guidelines, the local boards exercise certain powers, including the power to adopt reasonable rules and regulations which the boards feel necessary for the smooth operation of local schools.[2] Board rules typically provide that upon the proven violation of certain rules, regulations, or customs, students may be suspended or expelled.[3] Suspension is generally within the ambit of the powers of administrative personnel, while board action is customarily necessary before expulsion.[4]

Judicial review of the actions taken by school boards in expulsion cases usually focuses on a finding of whether a board rule was reasonable, and, in a few cases, whether notice and hearing were adequate. Predictably, there is a wide range of difference as to what is reasonable. Boards have been upheld on review for expelling students for violation of rules prohibiting students from attending the movies except on weekends,[5] forbidding the use of cosmetics and the wearing of "transparent hosiery,"[6] against playing football on the school grounds,[7] and prohibiting membership in a high school fraternity.[8] On the other hand, courts have found unreasonable rules compelling students to pay for damages to school property caused by carelessness or by accident,[9] requiring a student to take certain courses against the wishes of parents,[10] and preventing married persons from attending school.[11]

1. HAMILTON & MORT, THE LAW AND PUBLIC EDUCATION 16 (2d ed. 1959).
2. *Id.* at 513.
3. The term *suspension*, as used herein, refers to action resulting in the temporary separation of the student from the school, usually for a period of a few days. *Expulsion* results in a more permanent separation of the student from the school, ordinarily for at least the remainder of the school year. The term *board* or *school board*, will include boards of education, boards of trustees, and school directors who are directly responsible for the operation of local schools. *Administrative personnel* includes those employees of schools who are charged with the administration of the policies of the board.
4. REMMLEIN, SCHOOL LAW 268 (2d ed. 1962).
5. Mangum v. Keith, 147 Ga. 605, 95 S.E. 1 (1918).
6. Pugsley v. Sellmeyer, 158 Ark. 247, 250 S.W. 538 (1923).
7. Kinzer v. Directors of Independent School Dist., 129 Iowa 441, 105 N.W. 686 (1906).
8. Smith v. Board of Educ., 182 Ill. App. 342 (1913).
9. Holman v. School Trustees of Avon, 77 Mich. 605, 43 N.W. 996 (1889).
10. Hardwick v. Board of School Trustees, 54 Cal. App. 696, 205 Pac. 49 (Dist. Ct. App. 1921)

In order to raise the hearing issue specifically, it will be assumed herein that the board rule was reasonable and that the student did violate the rule.

REQUIREMENTS OF DUE PROCESS

A few of the expulsion cases have directly considered the possible right of the student to a hearing prior to expulsion and have suggested that a formal hearing is not required.[1] Various rationales were used, but none gave particular weight to the constitutional due process issue. One of these cases held that since the statutes did not provide for a hearing, a board could expel a student without notice or a formal trial.[2] In another, at the university level, the court held that an expelled medical student was not entitled to a *formal* hearing on charges of cheating, since the university officials had neither power to compel testimony nor to subpoena witnesses.[3] The student was held not to have been deprived of any rights, although she was not told the identity of her accusers nor permitted to give evidence of her innocence. This case brought forth comment from Professor Warren Seavey: "It is shocking that the officials of a state educational institution, which can function properly only if our freedoms are preserved, should not understand the elementary principles of fair play. It is equally shocking to find that a court supports them in denying to a student the protection given to a pickpocket."[4] Professor Seavey argues that schools and courts would do well to adopt the position that the burden is on the schools to prove that the student violated the rules, with an opportunity given the student to meet the charges against him.[5] He concludes: "Although the formalities of a trial in a law court are not necessary, and although the exigencies of school or college life may require the suspension of one reasonably thought to have violated disciplinary rules, it seems fairly clear that a student should not have the burden of proving himself innocent."[6]

The landmark case concerning constitutional due process rights of students in expulsion proceedings is *Dixon v. Alabama State Bd. of Educ.*[7] In this case,

---

(dancing in physical education class); State *ex rel.* Kelley v. Ferguson, 95 Neb. 63, 144 N.W. 1039 (1914) (domestic science); School Bd. Dist. No. 18 v. Thompson, 24 Okla. 1, 103 Pac. 578 (1909) (singing lessons).

11. Nutt v. Board of Educ., 128 Kan. 507, 278 Pac. 1065 (1929); McLeod v. State *ex rel.* Colmer, 154 Miss. 468, 122 So. 737 (1929). See also 9 Kan. L. Rev. 340 (1961).

1. People *ex rel.* Bluett v. Board of Trustees of Univ. of Ill., 10 Ill. App. 2d 207, 134 N.E.2d 635 (1956); State *ex rel.* Ingersoll v. Clapp, 81 Mont. 200, 263 Pac. 433, *cert. denied,* 277 U.S. 591, *error dismissed,* 278 U.S. 661 (1928); Vermillion v. State *ex rel.* Englehardt, 78 Neb. 107, 110 N.W. 736 (1907). See generally Annot., 58 A.L.R.2d 903 (1958).

2. Vermillion v. State *ex rel.* Englehardt, *supra* note 15. Although this case held, and has been widely cited as holding, that a board could expel without a hearing, the court states that "a more satisfactory method of procedure in ordinary cases would probably be to suspend the accused pupil for the present and fix an early day of examining the case, giving all parties interested an opportunity to be heard." *Id.* at 112, 110 N.W. at 737.

3. People *ex rel.* Bluett v. Board of Trustees of Univ. of Ill., 10 Ill. App. 2d 207, 134 N.E.2d 635 (1956).

4 Seavey, *Dismissal of Students: "Due Process,"* 70 Harv. L. Rev. 1406, 1407 (1957).

5. *Id.* at 1409.   6. *Id.* at 1410.

7. 294 F.2d 150 (5th Cir.), *cert. denied,* 368 U.S. 930 (1961).

students of Alabama State College, who were alleged to have caused discord and disorder on the campus by having taken part in a sit-in demonstration, were expelled without a hearing. They were first notified of the school's action in a letter stating they had been expelled. The assertion of their due process rights was made in an action in federal district court to restrain the state board from obstructing their attendance at college. Their assertion was unsuccessful in district court[1] and an appeal was taken. The Fifth Circuit reversed, holding that due process required notice to the students and some opportunity for a hearing before students of public colleges could be expelled for misconduct.[2] The value of an education to the students was indicated, and the court pointed out the probability that these students would be denied admission to other colleges. It was conceded that the college had the governmental power to expel students, but that the school could not arbitrarily exercise the power:

Admittedly, there must be some reasonable and constitutional ground for expulsion or the court would have a duty to require reinstatement. The possibility of arbitrary action is not excluded by the existence of reasonable regulations. There may be arbitrary application of the rule to the facts of a particular case. Indeed, that result is well nigh inevitable when the Board hears only one side of the issue. In the disciplining of college students there are no considerations . . . which should prevent the Board from exercising at least the fundamental principles of fairness by giving the accused students notice of the charges and an opportunity to be heard in their own defense. Indeed, the example set by the Board in failing so to do, if not corrected by the courts, can well break the spirits of the expelled students and of others familiar with the injustice, and do inestimable harm to their education.[3]

The court spelled out in dicta what due process required in the procedure for expulsion from a state college. The student must be given notice containing a statement of the charges which, if proven, would justify expulsion. A hearing is necessary, but the type of hearing required depends upon the nature of the particular charge against the student. The court suggested that a more informal, interview type of hearing would be adequate where the student was being dismissed for failure to meet a scholastic standard. On the other hand, where misconduct is charged and the evidence is so easily colorable, due process requires that each side be given an opportunity to present its arguments in a more formal hearing. Summarizing, the court stated:

This is not to imply that a full-dress judicial hearing, with the right to cross-examine witnesses, is required. Such a hearing, with the attending publicity and disturbance of college activities, might be detrimental to the college's educational atmosphere and impractical to carry out. Nevertheless, the rudiments of an adversary proceeding may be

1. Dixon v. Alabama State Bd. of Educ., 186 F. Supp. 945, 952 (M.D. Ala. 1960).
2. Dixon v. Alabama State Bd. of Educ., 294 F.2d 150, 158 (5th Cir. 1961).
3. *Id.* at 157. The Fifth Circuit pointed out that the cases cited by the district court for the proposition that the school has the right to expel students at any time were situations involving private colleges where relationships between school and students were matters of contract. *Id.* at 157-58.
    For an argument that the same due process requirements are required by both private and public schools because the private schools are affected with "state action," see Comment, *Private Government on the Campus—Judicial Review of University Expulsions*, 72 YALE L.J. 1362, 1409-10 (1963).

preserved without encroaching upon the interests of the college. In the instant case, the student should be given the names of the witnesses against him and an oral or written report on the facts to which each witness testifies. He should also be given the opportunity to present to the Board . . . his own defense against the charges and to produce either oral testimony or written affidavits of witnesses in his behalf. . . . If these rudimentary elements of fair play are followed in a case of misconduct of this particular type, we feel that the requirements of due process of law will have been fulfilled.[1]

It is perhaps fair comment to observe that most subsequent school expulsion cases will cite the *Dixon* case. For example, in the 1963 case of *Due v. Florida A. & M. Univ.*,[2] both the plaintiffs and the defendants referred to *Dixon*. In this case, a number of students were "suspended indefinitely"[3] from a state-supported university by action of the school's disciplinary committee after the students had participated in a civil rights demonstration and had been adjudged guilty of contempt in a local court. The students were called before the committee for a hearing on a charge based on a provision of the student handbook providing for disciplinary action if a student had been convicted of violating any "criminal and/or civil laws."[4] The committee voted to suspend the students indefinitely. Injunctive relief was sought in federal district court where both the adequacy of the notice of hearing and the sufficiency of the hearing itself were challenged. The students asserted that they had been denied right to counsel and the right to confront and cross-examine the witnesses against them, and that there should have been adherence to the rules of evidence and determination by a fair and impartial tribunal. The court, citing *Dixon*, agreed that a substantial fourteenth amendment question was presented, and that the activities of quasi-judicial bodies are subject to judicial review. However, the court upheld the suspensions, deciding that the disciplinary committee was organized by well-defined procedure, that the conviction for contempt in the local courts constituted grounds for suspension according to the handbook, and that the students had been given full opportunity to be heard. This court did not feel that *Dixon* compelled a full scale judicial trial prior to suspension. The court stated:

Procedures are subject to refinement and improvement in the never-ending effort to assure, not only fairness, but every semblance of fairness. More specific routines of notice and advisement may be indicated in this regard, but a foisted system of rigid procedure can become so ritualistic, dogmatic, and impractical as to itself be a denial of due process. The touchstones in this area are fairness and reasonableness.[5]

Due and *Dixon* present different holdings but they can be reconciled on their factual dissimilarity. In *Dixon* the students received neither notice nor hearing prior to expulsion; in *Due* a hearing was provided before the students were indefinitely suspended.

1. 294 F.2d at 159. A dissenting judge indicated that the holding of the court would be a "major blow to our institutions of learning" in that any attempt at discipline by a school could lead to investigation as to whether a federal right had been violated. *Id.* at 165 (Cameron, J., dissenting).
2. 233 F. Supp. 396 (N.D. Fla. 1963).
3. *Id.* at 397. "Suspended indefinitely" as used in this case, means roughly the same as expulsion.
4. *Id.* at 399.
5. *Id.* at 403.

The most recent case involving the due process rights of students to notice and hearing before expulsion arose in a secondary school.[1] In this case students were expelled a few weeks before the close of the school year because of their alleged participation in a civil rights demonstration on a Saturday. They were not allowed to graduate or be promoted. No notice or hearing was provided prior to the action of the school board. A class action was brought in federal district court seeking a temporary restraining order against the enforcement of the board decision. It was alleged that the students had been dismissed in violation of their "right not to be arbitrarily expelled from the public school."[2] The district court denied relief. On appeal, the Fifth Circuit reversed and remanded, ordering the temporary injunction pending final disposition of the case. The court commented:

We are fully aware of the reluctance with which Federal Courts should contemplate the use of the injunctive power to interfere with the conduct of state officers. [Boards of education.] But when there is a deprivation of a constitutionally guaranteed right the duty to exercise the power cannot be avoided. . . . Where there is a clear and imminent threat of an irreparable injury amounting to manifest oppression it is the duty of the court to protect against the loss of the asserted right by a temporary restraining order.[3]

Thus, there would appear general agreement from the recent cases that federal due process requires some kind of notice and hearing before a public school may expel a student. However, only in very general outlines do the opinions set forth the requirements of due process. Future cases will probably bring these requirements into clearer focus.

The expulsion of one student for violation of school rules demands the same due process requirements as in situations involving mass expulsions connected with civil rights demonstrations; mere numerical difference does not justify two due process standards.

EMERGING DUE PROCESS REQUIREMENTS

Since the courts may establish more specifically defined procedures as necessary within the notice and hearing requirements in expulsion cases, some areas of possible development should be noted. Even though the courts do not presently require some of these elements, legislatures and local school boards may desire to incorporate these suggestions into their procedures for expulsions.[4]

1. Woods v. Wright, 334 F.2d 369 (5th Cir. 1964). The court does not distinguish this case from those on the college level.
2. *Id.* at 371.
3. *Id.* at 374-75.
4. A committee of the American Association of University Professors recently published for comment a tentative list of due process requirements.
  IV. Responsibility of Faculty for Procedural Due Process in Cases of Alleged Misconduct
    A. *Notice of Conduct Subject to Discipline.* . . .
    B. *Conduct of Investigation Preliminary to Formal Charges.* . . .
    C. *Notice of Charges.* The student should be informed, in writing, of the reasons for the proposed disciplinary action with sufficient particularity, and in sufficient time, to ensure opportunity for a proper defense.
    D. *Treatment of Student Pending Final Action.* . . .

Due Process Requirement of Notice

Prior to any final proceeding by the board in expulsion, the student must be notified of the action against him and given time to prepare his defense. The Supreme Court, in another context, has indicated that notice is an essential element of due process: "An elementary and fundamental requirement of due process in any proceeding which is accorded finality is notice reasonably calculated, under all the circumstances, to apprise interested parties of the pendency of the action and afford them an opportunity to present their objections."[1] Under the general guidelines of fair play, this notice should go to the parents or guardian as well as to the student himself, so that all parties interested will be fully aware of the importance of the hearing.[2]

Due Process Requirement of Representation by Council

The recent case of *Gideon v. Wainwright*[3] indicates that federal due process requires counsel for the accused in many state criminal trials. Admittedly, there is a vast difference between a criminal trial and the administrative procedure to expel a student; however, the fact remains that in each case the accused is likely to be deprived of some vital interest. The student may have as much or more at stake as many accused criminals. In other areas of administrative law, persons who are called before federal agencies are accorded the right to counsel by the Administrative Procedure Act, Section 5(a).[4] Although this act would not control a hearing for expulsion by a school board, it could be argued that the same kinds of rules ought to be applied in both instances. Counsel would seem necessary in order to protect the student's substantive and procedural rights.

Due Process Requirement of an Impartial Tribunal

Whether due process requires that the function of judging and the functions of

> E. *Hearing.* . . . [Provision for a hearing board to hear the more serious charges.]
>   1. The Hearing Board proceeding should be *de novo*, ... No member of the Hearing Board who is otherwise interested in the particular case should sit in judgment during that proceeding.
>   2. The student appearing before the Hearing Board should have the right to be accompanied and represented by an adviser . . . .
>   3. The burden of proof should rest upon the officials investigating or responsible for establishing the charge.
>   4. The student should be given an opportunity to testify and to present evidence and witnesses relevant to the charge or the penalties involved. Whenever possible, he should be given an opportunity to cross-examine adverse witnesses. . . .
>   5. The decision should be based solely upon matters placed in evidence during the hearing. . . .
>   6. A transcript of the hearing should be made and, subject to the student's waiver, the proceeding before the Hearing Board should be open.
> F. *Further Recourse.* . . .
> *Statement on Faculty Responsibility for the Academic Freedom of Students*, 50 A.A.U.P. 254, 256-57 (1964).

---

1. Mullane v. Central Hanover Bank & Trust Co., 339 U.S. 306, 314 (1950).
2. See, *e.g.*, KAN. STAT. ANN. § 60-304(b) (1964).   3. 372 U.S. 335 (1963).
4. 60 Stat. 240 (1946), 5 U.S.C. § 1005(a) (1958). This statute reads in part: "Any person compelled to appear in person before any agency or representative thereof shall be accorded the right to be accompanied, represented, and advised by counsel . . . ."

complaining and prosecuting be conducted by separate groups has been the subject of much judicial comment. An authoritative treatise indicates the majority opinion is to the effect that due process does not forbid the combination of judging with accusing, investigating, and prosecuting in many areas of administrative law.[1] *Brinkley v. Hassig*[2] is representative of the majority opinion. In this case a doctor's license had been revoked by a state medical board on charges of fraud, immorality, and unprofessional conduct. The accused contended that the members of the board were prejudiced against him and that certain of them had been active in instigating the complaint. The Tenth Circuit concluded:

> The spectacle of an administrative tribunal acting as both prosecutor and judge has been the subject of much comment, and efforts to do away with such practice have been studied for years. . . . But it has never been held that such procedure denies constitutional right. On the contrary, many agencies have functioned for years, with the approval of the courts, which combine these roles.[3]

However, courts frequently condemn such combinations and call for a closer examination of the records:

> Criticisms have often been made of the phenomenon which permits an administrative body to serve in the triple capacity of complainant, prosecutor, and judge. . . . As a result of this combination of roles, its final adjudication often lacks that stamp of impartiality and of disinterested justice which alone can give it weight and authority.
>
> This anomaly in procedure makes it vitally necessary that in reviewing administrative decisions courts zealously examine the record with a view to protecting the fundamental rights of the parties. . . .[4]

Section 4(c) of the Administrative Procedure Act[5] has been interpreted as requiring a separation of the functions of judging and prosecuting in another type of governmental agency.[6] However, in later comparable cases the Supreme Court held that neither due process nor the Administrative Procedure Act compels a complete separation of functions.[7] Two 1962 federal cases indicate that the issue is not yet settled.[8] In view of the foregoing, no definite statement can be made as to whether a court might hold that due process would require the judging in a school expulsion proceeding to be done by those not associated

1. DAVIS, ADMINISTRATIVE LAW TREATISE § 13.02 (1958). See generally 1 AM. JUR. (SECOND) *Administrative Law* §§ 77-78 (1962).
2. 83 F.2d 351 (10th Cir. 1936).
3. *Id.* at 356-57. For a recent case holding that members of the examining board may belong to the same profession and be in competition with the accused, see State *ex rel.* Beddall v. Lonctot, 62 Wash. 2d 845, 384 P.2d 877 (1963). See also Annot., 97 A.L.R.2d 1210, 1220-24 (1964).
4. State *ex rel.* Ging v. Board of Educ., 213 Minn. 550, 565, 7 N.W.2d 544, 553 (1942). Almost the identical wording was used in State *ex rel.* Steele v. Board of Educ., 252 Ala. 254, 261, 40 So. 2d 689, 695 (1949).
5. 60 Stat. 239 (1946), 5 U.S.C. § 1004(c) (1958). This statute reads in part: "No officer, employee, or agent engaged in the performances of investigative or prosecuting functions for any agency in any case shall, in that or a factually related case, participate or advise in the decision, recommended decision, or agency review . . . except as witness or counsel . . . ."
6. Wong Yang Sung v. McGrath, 339 U.S. 33 (1950) (deportation).
7. Marcello v. Bonds, 349 U.S. 302 (1955); Shaughnessy v. United States *ex rel.* Accardi, 349 U.S. 280 (1955). Both of these are deportation cases.
8. Amos Treat & Co. v. SEC, 306 F.2d 260 (D.C. Cir. 1962) (holding a combination of functions to be a denial of due process); Pangburn v. CAB, 311 F.2d 349 (1st Cir. 1962) (holding a combination of functions within an agency does not violate due process).

with the prosecution. It would seem that fundamental fairness would require the functions of adjudication and prosecution to be performed by different parties. If the same person or group performs both functions, there is a greater possibility that the decision will be influenced by factors other than the evidence presented at the hearing.

Due Process Requirement of Cross-examination of Witnesses

None of the recent school expulsion cases indicates that the student has a right to cross-examine his accusers. *Dixon* suggested the student be told the identity of his accusers, but stated that cross-examination and requiring the witnesses to face the accused would be a hardship on the school in that it would be likely to disrupt the college routine.[1] One older case is cited[2] for the proposition that valid expulsion can be decreed only after a formal judicial type hearing using lawful procedures; however, this case seems to stand alone. A 1956 case denying the accused student the right to cross-examine the accusers points out that a school lacks the power to compel attendance and testimony; therefore, any requirement for cross-examination would be futile.[3] An argument could be made that it is violative of fair play for a student to be expelled on the basis of testimony given from ambush, and that it would not be asking too much for the school to disrupt its routine in order that the hearing may proceed fairly, accurately, and promptly to the truth by the use of cross-examination.[4]

Other Possible Due Process Requirements

None of the expulsion cases have indicated that a student has a right not to be expelled because illegally obtained evidence was used. With the states applying the exclusionary rules in criminal proceedings,[5] it is possible to argue that similar rules ought to apply to an expulsion proceeding since in each instance the individual has an interest to lose. This argument will be met with the contention that schools should not have to operate on the same basis as law enforcement agencies, and that to do so would impair efficient discipline.

Another federal due process requirement that has recently been asserted in state criminal cases is the privilege against compulsory self-incrimination.[6] This also may be argued as applicable in an expulsion hearing. However, it appears that both the privileges against self-incrimination and against unlawful search and seizure are limited to the criminal law and would not be readily transferable to the area of expulsion hearings.

1. 294 F.2d at 159.
2. Commonwealth *ex rel.* Hill v. McCauley, 3 Pa. County Ct. 77 (1887).
3. People *ex rel.* Bluett v. Board of Trustees of Univ. of Ill., 10 Ill. App. 2d 207, . . . , 134 N.E.2d 635, 637 (1956).
4. Wigmore states: For two centuries past, the policy of the Anglo-American system of Evidence has been to regard the necessity of testing by cross-examination as a vital feature of the law. The belief that no safeguard for testing the value of human statements is comparable to that furnished by cross-examination, and the conviction that no statement (unless by special exception) should be used as testimony until it has been probed and sublimated by that test, has found increasing strength in lengthening experience. 5 WIGMORE, EVIDENCE § 1367 (3d ed. 1940).
5. Mapp v. Ohio, 367 U.S. 643 (1961).   6. Malloy v. Hogan, 378 U.S. 1 (1964).

The courts may later adopt several of these suggested requirements; in any case, however, an argument can be made that legislatures or local school boards should provide for certain of these procedures either by statute or board policy. Clearly a state may provide for procedures which go beyond the requirements of the due process clause of the fourteenth amendment.

KANSAS PUBLIC SCHOOLS AND THE KANSAS EXPULSION STATUTE

Even without a statute expressly authorizing a board to expel students, it could be held that in the exercise of its general powers to make rules reasonably necessary to operate a school, the board could make a rule authorizing expulsions.[1] However, if there is a statute covering expulsions, board regulations must not contradict it.

The older Kansas statute on expulsions was repealed in 1959 and a new statute enacted.[2] Expulsion under the new provision may come from direct board action or from the superintendent or principal if the board has properly delegated the authority. In either situation, the student must be guilty of "gross misconduct or persistent disobedience"[3] and the expulsion must be in "the best interests of the other students or the school."[4] If expulsion is by direct board action, there would seem to be no express provisions for either notice or hearing. On the other hand, if expulsion is by the superintendent or principal, then upon application by the student within thirty days, the board has a statutory duty to review the action. It would seem that the demands of the statute might not be sufficient in that neither notice nor hearing prior to expulsion is expressly required.

To avoid possible litigation it would be wise for boards to provide for both notice and hearing,[5] although the statute does not expressly so require.[6] Where

1. Hamilton & Mort, THE LAW AND PUBLIC EDUCATION 513 (2d ed. 1959).
2. The new Kansas statute reads: The governing body of any school district may suspend or expel or by regulation authorize the superintendent or principal having charge of a school, to suspend or expel any pupil guilty of gross misconduct or persistent disobedience, when such suspension or expulsion is to the best interests of the other students or the school: *Provided, however,* That in all cases where such suspension or expulsion is exercised by the superintendent or principal, such action shall be subject to review before said governing body upon application therefor filed with said governing body by said pupil or a person acting in his behalf, within 30 days after such suspension or expulsion. No suspension shall extend beyond the current school semester; and no expulsion shall extend beyond the current school year. . . . KAN. STAT. ANN. § 72-1029b (1964).
3. The statute does not say that a *rule* has to be broken. It seems broad enough to say that if the behavior is detrimental to the other students, expulsion may be used, even though no particular school rule is violated.
4. Logically, it seems easy to justify this on the idea that the interests of all students are more important than those of the one. However, the "or the school" phrase could be taken to mean for the convenience of the school, and if so taken, would seemingly make the convenience of the school too important. Schools exist to educate students, not to perpetuate school convenience.
5. If the student were an immediate threat to the wellbeing of the other students, he could be temporarily suspended, pending notice and a hearing before final determination is taken on his expulsion.
6. The question arises as to whether the terms of the statute must provide procedures sufficient to meet due process requirements as suggested by Wuchter v. Pizzutti, 276 U.S. 13, 18-19 (1928); or, whether the courts will find due process satisfied so long as the procedure actually used meets the

the expulsion has come from the superintendent or principal, a provision for review by the board is available at the option of the student. This seems to place upon the student the obligation of raising the issue; whereas it seems due process would require the school to provide both hearing and notice. Again, it may be wise for the board, on its own initiative, to give notice and provide for a hearing before final action on the expulsion is taken.

CONCLUSION

It is submitted that the individual's opportunity for an education is a valuable right, and that this interest ought not be denied unless due process requirements have been met. Further, the inconvenience to the school resulting from giving adequate notice and a fair hearing seems nominal when compared with the prospect of litigation in either a state or federal suit. Perhaps in the vast majority of expulsion proceedings the outcome would be the same, but the procedures suggested would have protected the student's rights. Schools may voluntarily adopt such practices, or perhaps be compelled to do so—after prolonged and expensive litigation. The risk seems too great when the prevention is so easy. A well-worn cliche seems apropos: an ounce of prevention is worth a pound of cure.

---

requirements. The latter position was implied by National Equip. Rental, Ltd. v. Szukhent, 375 U.S. 311, 315 (1964).

Cases

A. Board Authority to
Expel Pupils

School Board Dist. No 18, Garvin County, et al. v.
Thompson et al.
24 Okla. 1, 103 P. 578 (1909)

KANE, C. J.

This was an action in mandamus, commenced in the district court of Garvin county by the defendants in error to compel the school authorities of the city of Pauls Valley, in said county, to reinstate their children in the public schools, from which they were expelled for the reason that under direction of their parents they refused to take singing lessons, which it seems were a part of the prescribed course of study in said schools. The school board, and teachers of the schools, were informed by the appellees that they did not wish their children to take singing lessons, that they would not supply them with the necessary singing books to do so, and requested them to excuse their children from this branch of the regular course. The school authorities refused to grant the request of appellees, and the appellees refused to furnish the singing books, and the children refusing to participate in the singing exercises, were expelled. It is agreed by both sides that, when boiled down, the only question really involved in this case is whether a patron of the public schools may make a reasonable selection from a course of study prescribed by the proper school authorities for his child to pursue, in opposition to a rule prescribed by such authorities requiring the child to take all the studies in such course. The trial court decided this question in favor of the appellees, and the appellants, not being satisfied with the judgment, bring the case to this court by petition in error.

There is some conflict as to the power to suspend or expel pupils for failure to participate in certain required studies or exercises if the parents of the pupil request that the child be excused; but it seems to us that the weight of authority and the better reasoning sustain the judgment of the trial court. At common law the principal duties of parents to their legitimate children consisted in their maintenance, their protection, and their education. These duties were imposed upon principles of natural law and affection laid on them not only by Nature herself, but by their own proper act of bringing them into the world. It is true the municipal law took care to enforce these duties, though Providence has done it more effectually than any law by implanting in the breast of every parent that natural insuperable degree of affection which not even the deformity of person or mind, not even the wickedness, ingratitude, and rebellion of children, can totally suppress, or extinguish. 1 Lewis' Blackstone, § 447. The statutes of Oklahoma defining the relation between parent and child are in the main declaratory of the common law. Section 3763, Wilson's Rev. & Ann. St. 1903, provides that the parent entitled to the custody of a child must give him support and education suitable to his circumstances. Section 3769, Wilson's Rev. & Ann. St. 1903, provides that:

The authority of a parent ceases, first, upon the appointment by a court of a guardian of the person of the child; second, upon the marriage of the child; third, upon its attaining majority.

Section 3768, Wilson's Rev. & Ann. St. 1903, provides that:

The abuse of parental authority is the subject of judicial cognizance in a civil action in the district court brought by the child, or by its relatives within the third degree, or by the officers of the poor where the child resides; and when the abuse is established, the child may be freed from the dominion of the parent, and the duty of support and education enforced. . . .

At common law the parent, and especially the father, was vested with supreme control over the child, including its education, and, except where modified by statute, that authority still exists in the parent.

It is true that with the organization of the common school system throughout the state statutes have been passed modifying more or less the authority of the parent over the child in school matters. Before statehood the general control and management of the schools of this jurisdiction was under the general supervision and management of the superintendent of public instruction, and the district schools were under the immediate control of the district school boards. The district school boards, in so far as the branches of study to be followed in such schools after they had complied with the law requiring the studying of certain branches, might substitute any other studies that might be determined upon by them. The board was authorized under the statute to suspend from school pupils who were guilty of immoral conduct and continued violation of the rules of the school.

It is admitted that these laws in so far as they are not repugnant to the Constitution of the state nor locally inapplicable, are still in force; but counsel for plaintiff in error contends that, no matter what the rule may have been under the old territorial laws, there can now be no doubt that under sections 308, 311, 312, 313, and 314, Bunn's Ann. Const., the management of the public schools is absolutely turned over to the Legislature of the state, and that the compulsory education clause of the Constitution absolutely destroys the old common-law doctrine that the parent had the entire control over the education of his child, and that the uniform text-book law of the state absolutely places the course of study that is to be used in all the public schools in this state in the hands of a text-book commission. The sections of the Constitution referred to by counsel provide: (1) That the Legislature shall establish and maintain a system of free public schools wherein all the children of the state may be educated; (2) that it shall provide for the compulsory attendance at some public or other school, unless other means of education are provided, of all the children in the state who are sound in mind and body, between the ages of 8 and 16 years, for at least three months in each year; (3) that the supervision of instruction in the public schools shall be vested in a board of education, whose powers and duties shall be prescribed by law; and (4) that the Legislature shall provide a uniform system of text-books for the common schools of the state. To our mind the right of the board of education to prescribe the course of study and designate the textbooks to be used does not carry with it the absolute power to require the pupils to study all of the branches prescribed in the course in opposition to the parents' reasonable wishes in relation to some of them. . . .

Our laws pertaining to the school system of the state are so framed that the parent may exercise the fullest authority over the child without in any wise impairing the efficiency of the system. The only decided departure from the common-law rule is the section of our Constitution providing for the compulsory attendance at some public or other school, unless other means of education are provided, of all the children of the state who are sound in mind and body, between the ages of 8 and 16 years, for at least three months in each year. Blackstone says that the greatest duty of parents to their children is that of giving them an education suitable to their station in life; a duty pointed out by reason, and of far the greatest importance of any. But this duty at common law was not compulsory; the common law presuming that the natural love and affection of the parents for their children would impel them to faithfully perform this duty, and deeming it punishment enough to leave the parent, who neglects the instruction of his family, to labor under those griefs and inconveniences which his family, so uninstructed, will be sure to bring upon him. Lewis' Blackstone, book 1, § 451. Our Constitution provides for compulsory education; but it leaves the parents free to a great extent to select the course of study. They may send their children to public schools and require them to take such of the studies prescribed by the rules as will not interfere with the efficiency or discipline of the schools, or they may withdraw them entirely from the public schools and send them to private schools, or provide for them other means of education. . . .

We have made careful examination of the authorities directly in point on the question presented by the record here and have found that the courts of last resort of four states have passed squarely upon it. Three of the states, Illinois, Nebraska, and Wisconsin, sustain our views. A case from Indiana (*State v. Webber et al.*, 108 Ind. 31, S N. E. 708, 58 Am. Rep. 30), seems to take the contrary view. Mr. Chief Justice Howk, who delivered the opinion of the court in *State v. Webber, supra*, based his opinion upon the fact that the parent did not assign any cause or reason why his son should not participate in the musical studies and exercises of the high school, and that therefore it may be fairly assumed that he had none. We believe the presumption ought to be the other way. There are certain virtues that may safely be attributed to the generality of mankind, among which are love of country and love of offspring. The perpetuation of the public school system of the state is probably as dear to the defendants in error as it is to the plaintiffs in error, and their interest in its efficiency, discipline, and course of study, as deep. They undoubtedly approve of the entire curriculum, except the singing lessons. We think it would be a reversal of the natural order of things to presume that a parent would arbitrarily and without cause or reason insist on dictating the course of study of his child in opposition to the course established by the school authorities. A better rule, we think, would be to presume, in the absence of proof to the contrary, that the request of the parent was reasonable and just, to the best interest of the child, and not detrimental to the discipline and efficiency of the school. The school authorities of the state have the power to classify and grade the scholars in their respective districts and cause them to be taught in such departments as they may deem expedient. They may also prescribe the courses of study and text-books for the use of the schools, and such reasonable rules and regulations as they may think needful. They may also require prompt attendance, respectful deportment, and diligence in study. The parent, however, has a right to make a reasonable selection from the prescribed course of study for his child to pursue, and this selection must be respected by the school authorities, as the right of the parent in that regard is superior to that of the school officers and the teachers.

We believe the court below reached the right conclusion, and its judgment is therefore affirmed.

All the Justices concur.

Robert Richards, Jr., a minor, by his father and next friend, Mr. Robert Richards v. Roger Thurston, as Principal of Marlboro High School
United States District Court D. Massachusetts
Sept. 23, 1969

Supplementary Opinion Sept. 23, 1969

Second Supplementary Opinion Oct. 3, 1969

Third Supplementary Opinion Oct. 6, 1969

304 F. Supp. 449 (1969)

OPINION

WYZANSKI: CHIEF JUDGE

Plaintiff, 17 years old, by his next friend, his father, has filed in the United States District Court, against the principal of the Marlboro High School, a comprehensive general high school, a complaint seeking restoration to his status as a member of the senior class there. He alleges that the defendant principal suspended him on the sole ground that he refused to have his hair, which he wears in a style reminiscent of the English singers called "The Beatles", and in a tidy style that Albert Einstein as scholar or master rarely displayed, cut to an extent approved by the principal. Plaintiff contends that he has a cause of action under the Civil Rights Act, 42 U.S.C. Sec. 1983, and under the Fourteenth Amendment to the United States Constitution. He claims that the Court has jurisdiction under 28 U.S.C. Sec. 1343(3).

There is no evidence that a formal written regulation of any school authority sets the maximum length or other aspects of a student's hairdress. Nor has any party shown any reason for the principal's official act except possibly the principal's personal prejudice, the community conventions of the first half of the Twentieth Century, and the views of some contemporaries, who may or may not be a majority of Marlboro's population, or of its parents, or of its students.

No factual foundation has been offered to show that plaintiff's hair style involves a health or sanitary risk to him or to others, or will interfere with plaintiff's or with others' performance of their school work, or will create disciplinary problems of a kind reasonably thought to be a concern of public officials.

This Court takes judicial notice that hairstyles have altered from time to time throughout the ages. Samson's locks symbolically signified his virility. Many of the Founding Fathers of this country wore wigs. President Lincoln grew a beard at the suggestion of a juvenile female admirer. Chief Justice Hughes' beard furnished the model for the frieze over the portico of the Supreme Court of the United States proclaiming "equal justice under law." Today many of both the younger and the older generations have avoided the increased cost of barbering by allowing their locks or burnsides to grow to greater lengths than when a haircut cost a quarter of a dollar.

Whether hair styles be regarded as evidence of conformity or of individuality, they are one of the most visible examples of personality. This is what every woman has always known. And so have many men, without the aid of an anthropologist, behavioral scientist, psychiatrist, or practitioner of any of the fine arts or black arts.

The Commonwealth of Massachusetts, at least since the desuetude of the Puritans' blue laws, has not attempted to regulate hair styles.

Massachusetts G.L. c. 76, which governs school attendance, and cognate provisions of Massachusetts law do not include any clauses regarding hirsute adornment.

But it may be argued that the principals of public schools are free to set their own standards for their own pupils, especially because the laws of the Commonwealth do not purport to require attendance at *public* schools but, on the contrary, merely create an opportunity, and leave every minor child, such as plaintiff, (or, more accurately, his parents, as his natural guardians,) free to choose a private school more to his taste.

The contention, in effect, is that inasmuch as plaintiff chose, without being required to do so, to attend the particular institution called the Marlboro High School he voluntarily became subject to the prejudices of its governing authorities and has no right to set his own terms and no standing to complain of an official direction that he can avoid by going to some other school. Such an argument might seek support in McAuliffe v. City of New Bedford, 155 Mass. 216, p. 220, 29 N.E. 517, a case where local authorities dismissed a policeman because of his political activities and Justice Oliver Wendell Holmes, Jr., wrote for the state court an opinion denying the policeman's claim for a reinstatement on the ground that "The petitioner may have a constitutional right to talk politics, but he has no constitutional right to be a policeman."

However, recent decisions about public school teachers (see the cases beginning with Garner v. Board of Public Works of City of Los Angeles, 341 U.S. 716, 71 S.Ct. 909, 95 L.Ed. 1317 and culminating in Keyishian v. Board of Regents, 385 U.S. 589, 87 S.Ct. 675, 17 L.Ed.2d 629) and about civil servants generally (see United Public Workers v. Mitchell, 330 U.S. 75, 67 S.Ct. 556, 91 L.Ed 754) indicate that Holmes, J.'s epigram somewhat simplified the problem.

The current view is that a state has not upon an arbitrary basis an absolutely unlimited right to refuse, opportunities such as education in the public schools, or employment in the public service. Often this, in somewhat circular terms, is referred to as the principle that there is a distinction between constitutional and unconstitutional conditions. At other times, this is said to present the problem of weighing the state's claims or interests against the individual's claims or interests.

Order can be defined properly only in terms of the liberties for which it exists, as liberty can be defined properly only in terms of the ordered society in which it thrives. As Albert Camus implied in *The Rebel*, order and liberty must find their limits in each other.

Whatever be the formulation of the governing principles under our Constitution, the duty of a court is to give scope to the state's claims of order, organization, and public purposes, yet not to allow such claims to prevail over individual liberty in the absence of a demonstrated rationality in the state's claims. Merely arbitrary choices of states or their official representatives cannot be enforced against any individual's serious claims of liberty. This is as true of minors as it is of adults. Tinker v. Des Moines School Dist., 393 U.S. 503, 89 S.Ct. 733, 21 L.Ed.2d 731; Griffin v. Tatum, (M.D.Ala.) 300 F.Supp. 60, 64. And when the personal liberty claimed by a minor or an adult has a high order of importance the state must make a strong showing of the need of its curtailment. United States v. O'Brien, 391 U.S. 367, 377, 88 S.Ct. 1673, 20 L.Ed.2d 672.

Clear illustration of this approach is given by the decision in West Virginia State Board of Education v. Barnette, 319 U.S. 624, 63 S.Ct. 1178, 87 L.Ed. 1628. There a public school authority sought to make attendance contingent upon a pupil saluting the American flag. A student whose religious faith precluded a flag salute was held to have a right to have the school authorities enjoined from enforcing its demand upon him.

It is the flag salute case rather than the City of New Bedford case which supplies the precedent which today has the greater relevance to this case. To be sure, plaintiff's claimed liberty to appear as he wills is not so significant as a Jehovah's Witness' claimed liberty to worship as he wills. But a principal's personal prejudice against the long hair of his pupils is not so significant as a state's claim to indoctrinate students by such patriotic symbolism as may inhere in saluting the American flag.

In summary, the state in the case now at bar has no such rational ground for dictating hair style to a pupil in a general high school as to support an official order interfering with his liberty to express in his own way his preference as to whatever hair style comports with his personality and his search for his own identity.

Plaintiff's claim to liberty as to his appearance is entitled to protection from action by the state or its agents both under the broad terms of the "due process" clause of the Fourteenth Amendment (see Griswold v. Connecticut, 381 U.S. 479, 85 S.Ct. 1678, 14 L.Ed.2d 510) and under the specific provisions of the Civil Rights Act which treat that claim to liberty as a civil right, 42 U.S.C. Sec. 1983, and give to the United States District Courts jurisdiction to enforce that right against an interfering agent seeking to exercise state authority. 28 U.S.C. Sec. 1343(3).

Nothing herein refers to the problems which might arise not in a general high school but in a school or other educational institution having a military or like disciplinary character. Arguably, uniformity may have some substantive merit in such specialized training establishments where individual liberty may need to be weighed against other rational, legitimate objects of a peculiar applicability. See Breen v. Kahl, W.D. Wis., 296 F.Supp. 702, 708.

But in schools of general comprehensiveness the constitutional premise is that "from different tones comes the best tune." Heraclitus frag. 8; Jaeger Paideia (1939) I, 18. They illustrate our national motto E PLURIBUS UNUM.

This Court's opinion is consistent with opinions of three other United States District Courts. Those are by Johnson, C. J. of the Middle District of Alabama in Griffin v. Tatum, 300 F.Supp. 60 (which at p. 62 states that "the Constitution protects the freedoms to determine one's own hair style and otherwise to govern one's personal appearance."), by James E. Doyle, D. J. of the Western District of Wisconsin in Breen v. Kahl, 296 F.Supp. 702 (which at pp. 705–706 declares that with respect to adults, "freedom to wear one's hair at a certain length or to wear a beard is constitutionally protected, even though it expresses nothing but individual taste", and that "the freedom of an adult male or female to present himself or herself physically to the world in the manner of his or her choice is a highly protected freedom" and that a like freedom exists for minor students unless the school authorities bear, as it said at p. 709, "a substantial burden of justification"), and by Lynne, C. J. in the Northern District of Alabama in Zachry v. Brown, 299 F.Supp. 1360 (which, referring to the equal protection clause of the Fourteenth Amendment, holds that the classification of male students "by their hair style is unreasonable and fails to pass constitutional muster.")

Some federal courts, which look in a contrary direction are cited in Breen v. Kahl, 296 F.Supp. 702, 708. The only court of appeals decision, Ferrell v. Dallas Independent School District, 392 F.2d 697 (5th Cir.) concludes that hair style is not a civil right protected by the First or the Fourteenth Amendment. However, that judgment in Ferrell loses much weight because of the dissent of Tuttle, C. J.

Leonard v. School Committee of Attleboro, 349 Mass. 704, 212 N.E.2d 468, 14 A.L.R.3d 1192, while an opinion of the full court by Spalding, J., is merely an interpretation of Massachusetts statutory and common law and does not reach questions presented by the United States Constitution or federal statutes.

Plaintiff is entitled to a decree (1) that he be reinstated forthwith as a student in good standing in the Marlboro High School with the same rights, privileges, and immunities as those he had before his suspension, (2) that there be expunged from that school's records any notation of the suspension against which he complained and of the absences due thereto, (3) that defendant be enjoined from suspending or disciplining him on account of his hair style, and (4) that plaintiff recover his costs.

SUPPLEMENTARY OPINION

I have received so many approving and disapproving comments which misunderstood the thrust of my opinion filed September 23 in this case that I deem it appropriate to file this supplemental opinion.

1. The object of the opinion was to shoot like a rifle at the parties' target and not like a cannon at a public issue.
2. With that object in mind, the opinion carefully noted that in this case there was no applicable Massachusetts statute and there was no formal school regulation with respect to hair styles.
3. The opinion emphasized that no factual foundation had been laid to show that there was in issue any point with respect to health, sanitation, or discipline.
4. The opinion made it clear that the situation arose in a general or comprehensive public high school. It did not involve a private school, secular or religious in nature. It did not involve a grammar school or other institution below secondary school level.
5. What the case clearly pointed out was that the principal had issued an *ad hominem* order based solely on what the lawyers would call his *ipse dixit*. In short, he acted autocratically without any regulation to support him, and without offering in court any rational basis for his conduct.
6. This Court not only left unsettled what disposition would be correct if there were a showing that health or cleanliness was involved, but indicated that there might be a showing of reasonable disciplinary demands which

would be determinative. Of course, rational discipline has a value, and there are circumstances in which the young must be taught the worth of conformity as well as the worth of individuality. But an attempt to impose conformity for the sake of conformity, or merely to accord with a principal's prejudices is not entitled to prevail over the personal liberty of a student to choose his hair style.

7. Aesthetic considerations having a rational objective foundation may also properly be taken into account by a representative of a state in determining policy. In Village of Euclid, Ohio v. Ambler Realty Co., 272 U.S. 365, 47 S.Ct. 114, 71 L.Ed. 303 the Supreme Court sustained the right of a state or a subdivision thereof to regulate on aesthetic grounds a man's development of his own property. Mr. Justice Sutherland observed the impropriety of "a pig in the parlor." (p. 388, 47 S.Ct. p. 118). That test might have application to some students in some classrooms. But plaintiff Robert Richards appeared more like Little Lord Fauntleroy, the hero of Frances Hodgson Burnett's celebrated book, than a character out of *Johnny Crow's Garden*.

SECOND SUPPLEMENTARY OPINION

My attention has been called to Crews v. Cloncs, (S.D.Ind.) 303 F.Supp. 1370, as reported in 38 U.S. Law Week 2187. There a student sought to have a principal enjoined from suspending him for having violated a regulation against wearing long hair. Chiefly on the ground that "The school authorities unequivocally state that long hair disrupts classroom atmosphere, impedes classroom decorum, disturbs other students, creates class disruption, and involves health and safety standards in physical education classes", the court denied relief. It seems that the court concluded that plaintiff was barred principally because his long hair caused others to be disorderly. This Court takes the position that that is not a valid ground for denying plaintiff's liberty to wear his hair as he pleases. A man may not be restrained "from doing a lawful act merely because he knows that his doing it may cause another to do an unlawful act." Beatty v. Gillbanks, 9 Q.B.D. 308, 314 (1882) (where it was held that the Salvation Army could not be forbidden to parade merely because hostile groups choose to start a disturbance.) As Professor Zecheriah Chafee, Jr. observed in Free Speech In The United States (1941) pp. 151–152, 160–161, it is absurd to punish a person "because his neighbors have no self-control and cannot refrain from violence." And as an illustration of such absurdity Professor Chafee referred to the imprisonment of Joseph Palmer because he persisted in wearing such a long beard that people kept mobbing him.

B. Marriage as a Ground for Pupil Expulsion

**Board of Education of Harrodsburg, Kentucky, et al.,
Appellants, v. Joy Burgin Bentley, Appellee**
Court of Appeals of Kentucky 383 S.W. 2d 677 (1964)

DAVIS, COMMISSIONER

This appeal tests the validity of a school board regulation requiring that any student who shall marry shall withdraw from the school, subject to being re-admitted after one year. The trial court adjudged that the regulation is invalid and granted a permanent injunction against enforcement of the regulation as applied to appellee.

The Board of Education of Harodsburg Independent School District (hereinafter designated as the Board) duly adopted the questioned resolution in 1957; the text of the resolution is:

Any student, either boy or girl, who marries, automatically must withdraw immediately from school and cannot re-enter school for one full year, and then only as a special student with permission of the principal. A special student cannot attend home room or study halls or enter into any class activities, social events or athletics. If, upon re-entering school after the year has elapsed, the student becomes pregnant, she will automatically withdraw until after the birth of the child.

The record reflects that the Board's policy, as enunciated by the resolution, was widely publicized, and was known to the appellee prior to the time of her marriage. Although the text of the resolution remained unchanged, it is admitted that the Board had uniformly followed the policy of permitting a student to complete the six-week term in progress at the time of the marriage.

Appellee was a regularly enrolled student at Harrodsburg High School and a member of the junior class when she married April 10, 1964. The six-week term then current lacked one and a half weeks of completion. Appellee was permitted to remain as a student until the close of that six-week period; she was required to withdraw from school and dropped from its rolls April 24, 1964.

Appellee then enrolled in Mercer County High School, but remained there only a day and a half. Her mother withdrew her from that school, and sought to have her reinstated in Harrodsburg High School. The Board, at a specially called session, heard the request of appellee and her parents, but expressed the view that it could not make an exception as to appellee since it had uniformly invoked the rule theretofore. This suit resulted.

Certain fundamental precepts were recognized by the trial court, and are acknowledged by the litigants: The Board is vested with the duty and power to control and manage the Harrodsburg High School. The Board is authorized to enforce reasonable regulations, including disciplinary rules. KRS 160.160; 160.290; 160.370.

The Board is empowered to suspend or expel pupils for violations of lawful regulations of the school. Other grounds for suspension or expulsion are prescribed. KRS 158.150.

The government and conduct of public schools, in general, is committed to the discretion of the school board. Courts will not interfere with the board's exercise of such discretion unless it appears the board has acted arbitrarily or maliciously. Casey County Bd. of Ed. v. Luster, Ky., 282 S.W.2d 333, and authorities therein discussed.

It is also recognized by all that KRS 158.100 mandatorily directs that each board of education shall provide public educational facilities for residents of its district who are under twenty-one years of age. There is no specific statutory provision dealing with the matter of married pupils under age twenty-one.

With these accepted principles in mind, we turn to the specific controversy at bar. The appellee was sixteen years old at the time of her marriage. The marriage ceremony was publicly performed in a Harrodsburg church. The marriage must have been approved by appellee's parents, pursuant to the provisions of KRS 402.210, although the record is silent as to that.

There is no suggestion that any sensationalism or scandal preceded or followed the wedding. It is admitted that appellee is now, and has been throughout her lifetime, a moral and respectable person. There has been no complaint of misbehavior or misconduct on her part. She has maintained a creditable, above average scholastic record.

For the Board, it was shown that the 1957 regulation had been adopted, upon public demand of parents and patrons, by reason of an "epidemic" of marriages of high school students. Moreover, the Board predicated its policy upon its belief, from experience and counsel of its superintendent, that such marriages during school term cause discussion and excitement, thereby disrupting school work and leading to dropping out of school. The Board expressed its view that student marriage is detrimental to the best interests and welfare of a good and successful school system.

It is recalled that the regulation in question provides for readmission of a married student after "one full year, and then only as a special student with permission of the principal." However, the record reflects that it has been the uniform policy in enforcement of the rule that the married student be permitted to complete the current six-week term. It was explained that the disruptive impact of student marriage is by reason of widespread student body discussion and excitement just prior to and just following the marriage. Apparently, the regulation as originally promulgated sought to alleviate the disruption generally said to be attendant at the time just before and just following the marriage. As noted, however, quite the opposite practice has been consistently followed. The pupil (including the present appellee) is allowed to remain actively in full school routine during the immediate time following the marriage—but no longer than the end of the then current six-week term.

It is accepted, of course, that marriage is favored by public policy. 35 Am. Jur., Marriage, § 3. The General Assembly has imposed various requirements looking toward preservation of the institution of marriage. KRS Chapter 402. Specifically, Kentucky's legislature has placed its sanction upon marriage of a female who has attained age sixteen. KRS 402.020(5). The safeguard of written consent from one in *loco parentis* is demanded for marriage participants under age twenty-one. KRS 402.210.

On the other hand, no question arises as to the sincerity of purpose of the Board here. It has acted upon the counsel of its superintendent and its own experience in administration of the affairs of the school under its jurisdiction. We have neither the right nor the inclination to substitute our view for the Board's view as to the exercise of its sound discretion as it relates to matters within the province of the Board's responsibilities. It does become our function to examine the regulation and determine whether it is unreasonable or arbitrary, and therefore illegal. (There is no suggestion that the Board has acted maliciously.) In 47 Am.Jur., Schools, § 155, it is said:

However, a pupil may not be excluded from school because married, where no immorality or misconduct of the pupil is shown, nor that the welfare and discipline of the pupils of the school is injuriously affected by the presence of the married pupil.

. . . For the appellee it is pointed out that all persons meeting the residence, moral and mental qualifications are entitled to an opportunity for publicly furnished education until attaining age twenty-one. In today's economy we judicially note the increasing demand for education as a prerequisite for employment. Certainly, there is no reason to suppose that the marriage of a student will diminish the need of that student for an education—indeed, just the contrary would appear the case.)

It is our conclusion that the decision of the trial court is correct; the instant regulation is arbitrary and unreasonable, and therefore void. The fatal vice of the regulation lies in its sweeping advance determination that every married student, regardless of the circumstances, must lose at least a year's schooling. Moreover, the manner of enforcement of the regulation accentuates the fact that the regulation is not realistically related to its purported purpose. It is asserted for the Board that the most intense disruptive impact of a student marriage occurs during the time just preceding and just following the marriage. Yet, under the uniformly followed pattern of administration of this regulation, the married student is permitted to remain in school during all of the time preceding the marriage, and may remain for a maximum of six weeks thereafter. Such procedure, even though premised on the Board's commendable desire to permit the student to complete the current term, effectively frustrates the prime purpose of the regulation. Additionally, after it may be reasoned that the disturbing influence of the event has subsided, the situation is returned to the "spotlight' of student attention by compelling withdrawal of the married student; after a year, assuming the principal is willing, the student is to be reinstated, thus injecting another occasion for student body agitation.

The regulation has a further inherent weakness in that it merely provides that a married student *may* be permitted to resume school if, but only if, the principal permits it. Of course, we will not assume that the principal would arbitrarily deny permission—but there is a complete absence of any standard or guideline for the principal; neither has the ousted student any gauge by which to estimate whether the principal's consent will be forthcoming after a year.

Implicit in this record is the desire of the Board to permit this appellee to "work something out" so that her education would not be interrupted. A review of the Board's minutes warrants the conclusion that the Board felt that its hands were tied—principally because it never had made any previous exception in such cases. The unreasonable and arbitrary effect of the regulation is thus demonstrated, since it imposes the identical result in every case, without regard to the circumstances of any case. The Board's discretion is foreclosed in advance, no matter what the facts. Such prejudgment is unreasonable and arbitrary.

We are not to be understood here as deciding that some reasonable and appropriate regulation in this area may not be adopted; we do hold the instant regulation invalid.

Without undertaking to restate the arguments which may be advanced in support of either side of the question, we state that we are persuaded that the view quoted (47 Am.Jur., Schools, Sec. 155) is sound. Consequently, it is our holding that the regulation here is an arbitrary and unreasonable one.

The judgment is affirmed.

C. Membership in Fraternities and Sororities

Holroyd et al., Appellants, v. Eibling, Supt., et al., Appellees
Court of Appeals of Ohio, 188 N.E. 2d 797 (1962)

COLLIER, PRESIDING JUDGE

This action was brought by H. James Holroyd and Helen M. Holroyd, husband and wife, and Patricia A. Holroyd, their minor child, by her father and next friend, H. James Holroyd, and Dwight Ely and Dorothy S. Ely, husband and wife, and their minor child, Marilyn Sue Ely, by her father and next friend, Dwight Ely, on behalf of themselves and other parents and children similarly situated, in the Common Pleas Court of Franklin County, Ohio, seeking to enjoin the defendants Harold H. Eibling, Superintendent of Schools of the City of Columbus, Ohio, and Edgar W. House, Principal of North High School Columbus, Ohio, from enforcing Regulation, Section 10.22, enacted by the Board of Education of the City of Columbus, Ohio.

After a hearing in the Common Pleas Court, the injunctive relief sought was denied and final judgment was entered against the plaintiffs. The plaintiffs have perfected their appeal to this court on questions of law and fact, and by stipulation of the parties the case has been submitted to this court on the record of the testimony taken in the trial court, the oral arguments and briefs of counsel.

Plaintiffs, in their petition, allege that the two minor plaintiffs are enrolled as pupils in North High School, which is a part of the public school system of the city of Columbus and the state of Ohio; that they have joined a youth organization which is identified with an adult service organization; that this organization, with other similar organizations, requires a high standard of grades and morals; that it does not meet on school property, but in the homes of the parents of the members; that the meetings are not secret but are attended by parents or group supervisors; that these organizations are not fraternities or sororities and have no secret initiation or secret ritual; and that they (the organizations) encourage participation in school and community activities and recognition of the responsibility of the citizen. Plaintiffs claim further that if Regulation 10.22 is enforced, the defendants will take complete control of a pupil's activities so far as associations are concerned at all times throughout the year, both summer and winter, thereby denying the parents their responsibility in selecting associates for their children outside school hours and away from school property; and that the pupils will be denied the rights and privileges to participate in regular school work and activities. The prayer of the petition is for a permanent injunction, enjoining the defendants from enforcing such regulation or any part thereof in the public schools of the city of Columbus.

The defendants, in their answer, after admitting the identity of the parties, that the minor plaintiffs and others represented are pupils in North High School and members of the alleged youth organizations, and the enactment of such regulation by the Board of Education of the City of Columbus, deny generally all other allegations of the petition.

The record shows that on March 15, 1960, the Board of Education of the City of Columbus enacted its Regulation, Section 10.22, which reads as follows:

Section 10.22. Prohibition Upon Public Affiliation with Certain Organizations.

(a) It shall be unlawful for any pupil enrolled in the Columbus Public Schools, in any manner, to organize, join, or belong to any school fraternity, sorority, society, or organization, as defined in sub-section (b), or to solicit members for such organizations, or to attend meetings of such organizations, or to engage in activities sponsored by such organizations, or to wear or display rings, pins, or any type of emblem, symbol or attire, which signifies or designates membership in any such organizations. Any such fraternity, sorority, society or organization as defined and referred to in this section, is declared an obstruction to education, inimical to the best interests of the Columbus Public Schools and to the public welfare, and illegal.

(b) For purposes of this section, a school fraternity, sorority, society or organization, referred to in sub-section (a) is hereby defined and determined to be any organization whose active membership is composed wholly or in part of pupils enrolled in the Columbus Public Schools, and which perpetuates itself by admitting additional members from the pupils enrolled in the Columbus Public Schools on the basis of the decision of its membership rather than upon the right and free choice of any pupil who is qualified by the rules of his school to be a member of and take part in any class or group exercises designated and qualified according to sex, subjects required by the course of study, or program of school activities fostered and promoted by his school, except for organizations officially approved by the Superintendent of Schools as having sufficient education merit to justify their existence.

(c) Any pupil enrolled in the Columbus Public Schools, who is in violation of this section, shall be barred from, declared ineligible for and shall forfeit his right and opportunity to participate in any athletic, literary, military, musical, dramatic, service, scientific, scholastic, and other similar activities and organizations of his school, including honor societies or honor organizations. It is the purpose and intent of such bar to cause the forfeiture of participation in those activities and organizations incidental to regular school work.

Such pupils shall also be barred from, declared ineligible for, and shall forfeit his right and opportunity to hold any school or class office, to participate in any class election, to receive any honor whatsoever based upon scholastic or other achievement, or to represent the school in any activity or organization.

(d) It shall be the duty of the principal of each school of the Columbus public school system to enforce the provisions of this section, subject, however, to the right of the Superintendent of the Columbus public school system, at his discretion, to review the actions of the school principal in the performance of the duties enjoined upon him by this section.

(e) The provisions of this section shall be in force and shall apply to all students enrolled in the Columbus public school system, who are scheduled for graduation during or after June, 1962.

The evidence consists of the testimony of the minor plaintiffs and several other pupils in North High School, all members of youth organizations, one parent of a pupil, and the defendants, the Superintendent of the Columbus City Schools, and the Principal of North High School. The testimony of these witnesses shows the history and operation of these youth organizations, which are not called fraternities or sororities but are referred to as social clubs. There are six clubs, three for boys and three for girls. The names of the boys' clubs are: Link, Okays and York. The names of the girls' clubs are: Waikiki, Siotes and Arro. Each club has a membership of approximately 30 pupils, a total membership of less than 200. All clubs have been in existence for a number of years. The total enrollment of North High School is approximately 1,900. These clubs have many, if not all, of the characteristics of a fraternity or sorority. In describing the operations and functions of these groups, the witnesses used such familiar terms as, "rushing," "pledges," "initiation", etc. Each club has a pin, a ring, and a club song and poem which is supposed to be known only by the members. Such testimony discloses that the membership is based entirely upon invitation and approval by the club members; that the members of the clubs are all students in North High School, except one or two members in each club; that each club has a court for the discipline of its members; that the club meetings are held in the homes of the parents; and that the club members hold positions in the various school programs and activities, in numbers out of proportion to their comparative number with the school enrollment. The testimony of the defendants is that they have not attempted to enforce Regulation 10.22 and will not do so until the present litigation is determined; and that they have not classified any of these six clubs as falling within the purview of Regulation 10.22 and, therefore, to be banned. They say, however, that these clubs have a divisive influence in the school and present difficult problems for the school authorities. The only reasonable assumption is that the primary purpose of the board of education in adopting this regulation was to abolish these six clubs and all other similar organizations in the Columbus City Schools.

The above summary of facts as shown by the transcript of the testimony taken in the Common Pleas Court, consisting of 566 pages, as we view the situation, presents one question to be determined. That is, does the Board of Education of the City of Columbus have authority to adopt Regulation 10.22, prohibiting pupils in the public schools from affiliating with social clubs, such as the six clubs herein described, under penalty of rendering such pupils ineligible to participate in certain extra-curricular activities? . . .

Section 3313.20, Revised Code, provides as follows:

The board of education shall make such *rules and regulations* as are necessary for its government and the government of its employees and the pupils of the schools. . . . (Emphasis added.)

It appears that in the many cases from other jurisdictions cited and examined the case of Wright v. Board of Education, 295 Mo. 466, 246 S.W. 43, 27 A.L.R. 1061, stands almost alone in holding such a regulation is invalid. The rationale of these decisions is that a board of education is vested with broad discretionary powers in adopting a policy prohibiting affiliation with such organizations in the government, management and discipline of the schools; that such regulations do not deprive the pupils or parents of any *natural* or constitutional rights or privileges; that, when, in the opinion of the school authorities, such organizations have a deleterious influence and are found to be inimical to the best interests of the school, a school board is authorized, even in the absence of a specific statute granting such power, to adopt regulations prohibiting them; and that such power is inherent in a board of education. . . .

Our conclusions are that the Board of Education of the City of Columbus acted within the scope of its authority in adopting Regulation 10.22; that such authority is granted to the board by Section 3313.20, Revised Code, and is also inherent in the board; that the provisions of this regulation are not unreasonable or arbitrary; that the enforcement of this regulation in a reasonable manner, which must be assumed, will not deprive the plaintiffs of any constitutional rights or natural privileges as citizens or pupils of the public schools; that this court has no authority to interfere with the exercise of the discretion vested in the Board of Education of the City of Columbus in this matter; and that the plaintiffs are not entitled to the relief sought. Therefore, the prayer of plaintiffs' petition is denied and plaintiffs' petition is dismissed, at the cost of plaintiffs, the appellants herein.

Plaintiff's petition is hereby dismissed and judgment rendered for the defendants.

Judgment accordingly.

Donahue and Brown, JJ., concur.

D. Board Control of Pupil Activism

Burnside v. Byars
363 F. 2d 744 (1966)

GEWIN, CIRCUIT JUDGE

Plaintiffs brought a civil rights action under 42 U.S.C. § 1983 for a preliminary injunction pursuant to 28 U.S.C. § 1343 against officials of the Booker T. Washington High School of Philadelphia, Mississippi. It was alleged that plaintiffs' children's rights under the First and Fourteenth Amendments of the United States Constitution were breached by school officials in that they denied to the children the right to wear "freedom buttons" while attending school. Plaintiffs appeal from the order of the United States District Court for the Southern District of Mississippi denying a preliminary injunction.

Several days prior to September 21, 1964, Mr. Montgomery Moore, Principal of the Booker T. Washington High School of Philadelphia, Mississippi, learned that a number of his students were wearing "freedom buttons" obtained from the headquarters of the COFO organization which had been established in Philadelphia, Mississippi. The buttons were circular, approximately $1\frac{1}{2}$ inches in diameter, containing the wording "One Man One Vote" around the perimeter with "SNCC" inscribed in the center. Thereupon he announced to the entire student body that they were not permitted to wear such buttons in the school house or in their various classes. Mr. Moore testified that this disciplinary regulation was promulgated because the buttons "didn't have any bearing on their education," "would cause commotion," and would be disturbing [to] the school program by taking up time trying to get order, passing them around and discussing them in the classroom and explaining to the next child why they are wearing them." Despite Mr. Moore's announcement, on September 21, 1964, three or four children appeared at school wearing the buttons. All were given an opportunity to remove the buttons and remain in school but three of the children elected to keep them and return home. The following day all the children returned to school without their buttons. On the morning of September 24, 1964, Mr. Moore was summoned to the school by one of the teachers who reported that 30 or 40 children were displaying the buttons and that it was causing a commotion. Mr. Moore then assembled the children in his office, reminded them of his previous announcement, and gave them the choice of removing their buttons or being sent home. The great majority elected to return home and Mr. Moore thereupon suspended them for a period of one week. Mr. Moore then delivered a letter to each parent concerning the suspension, and all parents agreed to cooperate in the matter except Mrs. Burnside, Mrs. English and Mrs. Morris, whereupon injunctive proceeds were instituted against the school officials to enjoin them from enforcing the regulation.

Appellants contend that the school regulation forbidding "freedom buttons" on school property is an unreasonable rule which abridges their children's First and Fourteenth Amendment freedom of speech. It is the contention of the appellees that the regulation imposed by the principal is reasonable in maintaining proper discipline in the school and the District Court did not abuse its discretion in declining to issue a preliminary injunction.

The Negro school children who attended an all Negro high school wore the "freedom buttons" as a means of silently communicating an idea and to encourage the members of their community to exercise their civil rights. The right to communicate a matter of vital public concern is embraced in the First Amendment right to freedom of speech and therefore is clearly protected against infringement by state officials. Thornhill v. State of Alabama, 310 U.S. 88, 101, 60 S.Ct. 736, 84 L.Ed. 1093, 1102. Particularly, the Fourteenth Amendment protects the First Amendment rights of school children against unreasonable rules and regulations imposed by school authorities.

The Fourteenth Amendment, as now applied to the States, protects the citizen against the State itself and all of its creatures—Boards of Education not excepted.

West Virginia State Board of Education v. Barnette, 319 U.S. 624, 637, 63 S.Ct. 1178, 1185, 87 L.Ed. 1628, 1637.

But the liberty of expression guaranteed by the First Amendment can be abridged by state officials if their protection of legitimate state interests necessitates an invasion of free speech. Dennis v. United States, 341 U.S. 494, 510, 71 S.Ct. 857, 95 L.Ed. 1137, 1153; Whitney v. People of State of California, 274 U.S. 357, 376, 47 S.Ct. 641, 71 L.Ed. 1095, 1106. The interest of the state in maintaining an educational system is a compelling one, giving rise to a balancing of First Amendment rights with the duty of the state to further and protect the public school system. The establishment of an educational program requires the formulation of rules and regulations necessary for the maintenance of an orderly program of classroom learning. In formulating regulations, including those pertaining to the discipline of school children, school officials have a wide latitude of discretion. But the school is always bound by the requirement that the rules and regulations must be reasonable. It is not for us to consider whether such rules are wise or expedient but merely whether they are a reasonable exercise of the power and discretion of the school authorities.

Regulations which are essential in maintaining order and discipline on school property are reasonable. Thus school rules which assign students to a particular class, forbid unnecessary discussion in the classroom and prohibit the exchange of conversation between students are reasonable even though these regulations infringe on such basic rights as freedom of speech and association, because they are necessary for the orderly presentation of classroom activities. Therefore, a reasonable regulation is one which measurably contributes to the maintenance of order and decorum within the educational system.

The regulation which is before us now prohibits the wearing of "freedom buttons" on school property. The record indicates only a showing of mild curiosity on the part of the other school children over the presence of some 30 or 40 children wearing such insignia. Even the principal testified that the children were expelled not for causing a commotion or disrupting classes but for violating the school regulation. Thus it appears that the presence of "freedom buttons" did not hamper the school in carrying on its regular schedule of activities; nor would it seem likely that the simple wearing of buttons unaccompanied by improper conduct would ever do so. Wearing buttons on collars or shirt fronts is certainly not in the class of those activities which inherently distract students and break down the regimentation of the classroom such as carrying banners, scattering leaflets, and speechmaking, all of which are protected methods of expressions, but all of which have no place in an orderly classroom. If the decorum had been so disturbed by the presence of the "freedom buttons," the principal would have been acting within his authority and the regulation forbidding the presence of buttons on school grounds would have been reasonable. But the affidavits and testimony before the District Court reveal no interference with educational activity and do *not* support a conclusion that there was a commotion or that the buttons tended to distract the minds of the students away from their teachers. Nor do we think that the mere presence of "freedom buttons" is calculated to cause a disturbance sufficient to warrant their exclusion from school premises unless there is some student misconduct involved. Therefore, we conclude after carefully examining all the evidence presented that the regulation forbidding the wearing of "freedom buttons" on school grounds is arbitrary and unreasonable, and an unnecessary infringement on the students' protected right of free expression in the circumstances revealed by the record. . . .

We wish to make it quite clear that we do not applaud any attempt to undermine the authority of the school. We support all efforts made by the school to fashion reasonable regulations for the conduct of their students and enforcement of the punishment incurred when such regulations are violated. Obedience to duly constituted authority is a valuable tool, and respect for those in authority must be instilled in our young people.

But, with all of this in mind, we must also emphasize that school officials cannot ignore expressions of feelings with which they do not wish to contend. They cannot infringe on their students' right to free and unrestricted expression as guaranteed to them under the First Amendment to the Constitution, where the exercise of such rights in the school buildings and schoolrooms do not materially and substantially interfere with the requirements of appropriate discipline in the operation of the school.

The order entered by the District Court denying the preliminary injunction sought is hereby vacated, the judgment is reversed and the cause is remanded with directions to the District Court to grant a preliminary injunction enjoining the officials of the Booker T. Washington High School from the enforcement of the disciplinary regulation forbidding their students from wearing "freedom buttons" on the school premises. Although there was a full evidentiary hearing in which the facts were rather fully developed, such judgment and order by the District Court shall be without prejudice to the making of a further order and judgment if additional, different or more complete facts are developed upon final hearing which would authorize the entry of such additional judgment.

Reversed and remanded with directions.

Tinker v. Des Moines Independent Community School District no. 21
89 S.Ct. 733, (1969)
United States Supreme Court

MR. JUSTICE FORTAS DELIVERED THE OPINION OF THE COURT

Petitioner John F. Tinker, 15 years old, and petitioner Christopher Eckhardt, 16 years old, attended high schools in Des Moines. Petitioner Mary Beth Tinker, John's sister, was a 13-year-old student in junior high school.

In December 1965, a group of adults and students in Des Moines, Iowa, held a meeting at the Eckhardt home. The group determined to publicize their objections to the hostilities in Vietnam and their support for a truce by wearing black armbands during the holiday season and by fasting on December 16 and New Year's Eve. Petitioners and their parents had previously engaged in similar activities, and they decided to participate in the program.

The principals of the Des Moines schools became aware of the plan to wear armbands. On December 14, 1965, they met and adopted a policy that any student wearing an armband to school would be asked to remove it, and if he refused he would be suspended until he returned without the armband. Petitioners were aware of the regulation that the school authorities adopted.

On December 16, Mary Beth and Christopher wore black armbands to their schools. John Tinker wore his armband the next day. They were all sent home and suspended from school until they would come back without their armbands. They did not return to school until after the planned period for wearing armbands had expired—that is, until after New Year's Day.

This complaint was filed in the United States District Court by petitioners, through their fathers, under § 1983 of Title 42 of the United States Code. It prayed for an injunction restraining the defendant school officials and the defendant members of the board of directors of the school district from disciplining the petitioners, and it sought nominal damages. After an evidentiary hearing the District Court dismissed the complaint. It upheld the constitutionality of the school authorities' action on the ground that it was reasonable in order to prevent disturbance of school discipline. 258 F. Supp. 971 (1966). The court referred to but expressly declined to follow the Fifth Circuit's holding in a similar case that prohibition of the wearing of symbols like the armbands cannot be sustained unless it "materially and substantially interfere[s] with the requirements of appropriate discipline in the operation of the school." *Burnside* v. *Byars*, 363 F. 2d 744, 749 (1966).

On appeal, the Court of Appeals for the Eighth Circuit considered the case *en banc*. The court was equally divided, and the District Court's decision was accordingly affirmed, without opinion. 383 F. 2d 988 (1967). We granted certiorari. 390 U. S. 942 (1968).

I

The District Court recognized that the wearing of an armband for the purpose of expressing certain views is the type of symbolic act that is within the Free Speech Clause of the First Amendment. See *West Virginia* v. *Barnette*, 319 U. S. 624 (1943); *Stromberg* v. *California*, 283 U. S. 359 (1931). Cf. *Thornhill* v. *Alabama*, 310 U. S. 88 (1940); *Edwards* v. *South Carolina*, 372 U. S. 229 (1963); *Brown* v. *Louisiana*, 383 U. S. 131 (1966). As we shall discuss, the wearing of armbands in the circumstances of this case was entirely divorced from actually or potentially disruptive conduct by those participating in it. It was closely akin to "pure speech" which, we have repeatedly held, is entitled to comprehensive protection under the First Amendment. Compare *Cox* v. *Louisiana*, 379 U. S. 536, 555 (1965); *Adderley* v. *Florida*, 385 U. S. 39 (1966).

First Amendment rights, applied in light of the special characteristics of the school environment, are available to teachers and students. It can hardly be argued that either students or teachers shed their constitutional rights to freedom of speech or expression at the schoolhouse gate. This has been the unmistakable holding of this Court for almost 50 years. In *Meyer* v. *Nebraska*, 262 U. S. 390 (1923), and *Bartels* v. *Iowa*, 262 U. S. 404 (1923), this Court, in opinions by Mr. Justice McReynolds, held that the Due Process Clause of the Fourteenth Amendment prevents States from forbidding the teaching of a foreign language to young students. Statutes to this effect, the Court held, unconstitutionally inter fere with the liberty of teacher, student, and parent. See also *Pierce* v. *Society of Sisters*, 268 U. S. 510 (1925); *West Virginia* v. *Barnette*, 319 U. S. 624 (1943); *McCollum* v. *Board of Education*, 333 U. S. 203 (1948); *Wieman* v. *Updegraff*, 344 U. S. 183, 195 (1952) (concurring opinion); *Sweezy* v. *New Hampshire*, 354 U. S. 234 (1957); *Shelton* v. *Tucker*, 364 U. S. 479, 487 (1960); *Engel* v. *Vitale*, 370 U. S. 421 (1962); *Keyishian* v. *Board of Regents*, 385 U. S. 589, 603 (1967); *Epperson* v. *Arkansas*, 393 U. S. 97 (1968).

In *West Virginia* v. *Barnette, supra*, this Court held that under the First Amendment, the student in public school may not be compelled to salute the flag. Speaking through Mr. Justice Jackson, the Court said:

The Fourteenth Amendment, as now applied to the States, protects the citizen against the State itself and all of its creatures—Boards of Education not excepted. These have, of course, important, delicate, and highly discretionary functions, but none that they may not perform within the limits of the Bill of Rights. That they are educating the young for citizenship is reason for scrupulous protection of Constitutional freedoms of the individual, if we are not to strangle the free mind at its source and teach youth to discount important principles of our government as mere platitudes. *319 U. S., at 637.*

On the other hand, the Court has repeatedly emphasized the need for affirming the comprehensive authority of the States and of school authorities, consistent with fundamental constitutional safeguards, to prescribe and control conduct in the schools. See *Epperson* v. *Arkansas, supra*, at 104; *Meyer* v. *Nebraska, supra*, at 402. Our problem lies in the area where students in the exercise of First Amendment rights collide with the rules of the school authorities.

II

The problem presented by the present case does not relate to regulation of the length of skirts or the type of clothing, to hair style or deportment. Compare *Ferrell* v. *Dallas Independent School District*, 392 F. 2d 697 (1968); *Pugsley* v. *Sellmeyer*, 158 Ark. 247, 250 S. W. 538 (1923). It does not concern aggressive, disruptive action or even group demonstrations. Our problem involves direct, primary First Amendment rights akin to "pure speech."

The school officials banned and sought to punish petitioners for a silent, passive, expression of opinion, unaccompanied by any disorder or disturbance on the part of petitioners. There is here no evidence whatever of petitioners' interference, actual or nascent, with the school's work or of collision with the rights of other students to be secure and to be let alone. Accordingly, this case does not concern speech or action that intrudes upon the work of the school or the rights of other students.

Only a few of the 18,000 students in the school system wore the black armbands. Only five students were suspended for wearing them. There is no indication that the work of the school or any class was disrupted. Outside the classrooms, a few students made hostile remarks to the children wearing armbands, but there were no threats or acts of violence on school premises.

The District Court concluded that the action of the school authorities was reasonable because it was based upon their fear of a disturbance from the wearing of the armbands. But, in our system, undifferentiated fear or apprehension of disturbance is not enough to overcome the right to freedom of expression. Any departure from absolute regimentation may cause trouble. Any variation from the majority's opinion may inspire fear. Any word spoken, in class, in the lunchroom or on the campus, that deviates from the views of another person, may start an argument or cause a disturbance. But our Constitution says we must take this risk, *Terminiello* v. *Chicago*, 337 U. S. 1. (1959); and our history says that it is this sort of hazardous freedom—this kind of openness—that is the basis of our national strength and of the independence and vigor of Americans who grow up and live in this relatively permissive, often disputatious society.

In order for the State in the person of school officials to justify prohibition of a particular expression of opinion, it must be able to show that its action was caused by something more than a mere desire to avoid the discomfort and unpleasantness that always accompany an unpopular viewpoint. Certainly where there is no finding and no showing that the exercise of the forbidden right would "materially and substantially interfere with the requirements of appropriate discipline in the operation of the school," the prohibition cannot be sustained. *Burnside* v. *Byars, supra,* at 749.

In the present case, the District Court made no such finding, and our independent examination of the record fails to yield evidence that the school authorities had reason to anticipate that the wearing of the armbands would substantially interfere with the work of the school or impinge upon the rights of other students. Even an official memorandum prepared after the suspension that listed the reasons for the ban on wearing the armbands made no reference to the anticipation of such disruption.

On the contrary, the action of the school authorities appears to have been based upon an urgent wish to avoid the controversy which might result from the expression, even by the silent symbol of armbands, of opposition to this Nation's part in the conflagration in Vietnam. It is revealing, in this respect, that the meeting at which the school principals decided to issue the contested regulation was called in response to a student's statement to the journalism teacher in one of the schools that he wanted to write an article on Vietnam and have it published in the school paper. (The student was dissuaded.) . . .

The principal use to which the schools are dedicated is to accommodate students during prescribed hours for the purpose of certain types of activities. Among those activities is personal intercommunication among the students. This is not only an inevitable part of the process of attending school. It is also an important part of the educational process. A student's rights therefore, do not embrace merely the classroom hours. When he is in the cafeteria, or on the playing field, or on the campus during the authorized hours, he may express his opinions, even on controversial subjects like the conflict in Vietnam, if he does so "without materially and substantially interfering with appropriate discipline in the operation of the school" and without colliding with the rights of others. *Burnside* v. *Byars, supra,* at 749. But conduct by the student, in class or out of it, which for any reason—whether it stems from time, place, or type of behavior—materially disrupts classwork or involves substantial disorder or invasion of the rights of others is, of course, not immunized by the constitutional guaranty of freedom of speech. Cf. *Blackwell* v. *Issaquena City Bd. of Educ.,* 363 F. 2d 749 (C. A. 5th Cir., 1966).

Under our Constitution, free speech is not a right that is given only to be so circumscribed that it exists in principle but not in fact. Freedom of expression would not truly exist if the right could be exercised only in an area that a benevolent government has provided as a safe haven for crackpots. The Constitution says that Congress (and the States) may not abridge the right to free speech. This provision means what it says. We properly read it to permit reasonable regulation of speech-connected activities in carefully restricted circumstances. But we do not confine the permissible exercise of First Amendment rights to a telephone booth or the four corners of a pamphlet, or to supervised and ordained discussion in a school classroom.

If a regulation were adopted by school officials forbidding discussion of the Vietnam conflict, or the expression by any student of opposition to it anywhere on school property except as part of a prescribed classroom exercise, it would be obvious that the regulation would violate the constitutional rights of students, at least if it could not be justified by a showing that the students' activities would materially and substantially disrupt the work and discipline of the school. . . .

In the circumstances of the present case, the prohibition of the silent, passive "witness of the armbands," as one of the children called it, is no less offensive to the Constitution's guaranties.

As we have discussed, the record does not demonstrate any facts which might reasonably have led school authorities to forecast substantial disruption of or material interference with school activities, and no disturbances or disorders on the school premises in fact occurred. These petitioners merely went about their ordained rounds in school. Their deviation consisted only in wearing on their sleeve a band of black cloth, not more than two inches wide. They wore it to exhibit their disapproval of the Vietnam hostilities and their advocacy of a truce, to make their views known, and by their example, to influence others to adopt them. They neither interrupted school activities nor sought to intrude in the school affairs or the lives of others. They caused discussion outside of the classrooms, but no interference with work and no disorder. In the circumstances, our Constitution does not permit officials of the State to deny their form of expression.

We express no opinion as to the form of relief which should be granted, this being a matter for the lower courts to determine. We reverse and remand for further proceedings consistent with this opinion.

Reversed and remanded.

Mr. Justice White, concurring. . . .

Mr. Justice Stewart, concurring. . . .

Mr. Justice Harlan, dissenting. . . .

MR. JUSTICE BLACK, DISSENTING

The Court's holding in this case ushers in what I deem to be an entirely new era in which the power to control pupils by the elected "officials of state supported public schools . . ." in the United States is in ultimate effect transferred to the Supreme Court. . . .

Assuming that the Court is correct in holding that the conduct of wearing armbands for the purpose of conveying political ideas is protected by the First Amendment compare, *e. g.*, *Giboney* v. *Empire Storage & Ice Co.*, 336 U. S. 490 (1949), the crucial remaining questions are whether students and teachers may use the schools at their whim as a platform for the exercise of free speech—"symbolic" or "pure"—and whether the Courts will allocate to themselves the function of deciding how the pupils school day will be spent. While I have always believed that under the First and Fourteenth Amendments neither the State nor Federal Government has any authority to regulate or censor the content of speech. I have never believed that any person has a right to give speeches or engage in demonstrations where he pleases and when he pleases. This Court has already rejected such a notion. In *Cox* v. *Louisiana*, 379 U. S. 536 (1964), for example, the Court clearly stated that the rights of free speech and assembly "do not mean that anyone with opinions or beliefs to express may address a group at any public place and at any time." 379 U. S. 536, 554 (1964). . . .

I deny, therefore, that it has been the "unmistakable holding of this Court for almost 50 years" that "students" and "teachers" take with them into the "schoolhouse gate" constitutional rights to "freedom of speech or expression." Even *Meyer* did not hold that. It makes no reference to "symbolic speech" at all; what it did was to strike down as "unreasonable" and therefore unconstitutional a Nebraska law barring the teaching of the German language before the children reached their eighth grade. One can well agree with Justice Holmes and Mr. Justice Sutherland, as I do, that such a law was no more unreasonable than it would be to bar the teaching of Latin and Greek to pupils who have not reached the eighth grade. In fact, I think the majority's reason for invalidating the Nebraska law was that they did not like or in legal jargon that it "shocked

the Court's conscience," "offended its sense of justice" was "contrary to fundamental concepts of the English-speaking world," as the Court has sometimes
said. See, *e. g., Rochin* v. *California*, 342 U. S. 165, and *Irvine* v. *California*,
347 U. S. 128. The truth is that a teacher of kindergarten, grammar school, or
high school pupils no more carries into a school with him a complete right to
freedom of speech and expression than an anti-Catholic or anti-Semitic carries
with him a complete freedom of speech and religion into a Catholic church or
Jewish synagogue. Nor does a person carry with him into the United States
Senate or House, or to the Supreme Court, or any other court, a complete
constitutional right to go into those places contrary to their rules and speak his
mind on any subject he pleases. It is a myth to say that any person has a constitutional right to say what he pleases, where he pleases, and when he pleases. Our
Court has decided precisely the opposite. See, *e. g., Cox* v. *Louisiana*, 379 U. S.
536, 555; *Adderley* v. *Florida*, 385 U. S. 39.

In my view, teachers in state-controlled public schools are hired to teach
there. Although Mr. Justice McReynolds may have intimated to the contrary in
Meyers v. *Nebraska, supra*, certainly a teacher is not paid to go into school and
teach subjects the State does not hire him to teach as a part of its selected curriculum. Nor are public school students sent to the schools at public expense to broadcast political or any other views to educate and inform the public. The original
idea of schools, which I do not believe is yet abandoned as worthless or out of
date, was that children had not yet reached the point of experience and wisdom
which enabled them to teach all of their elders. It may be that the Nation has
outworn the old-fashioned slogan that "children are to be seen not heard,"
but one may, I hope, be permitted to harbor the thought that taxpayers
send children to school on the premise that at their age they need to learn, not
teach. . . .

Change has been said to be truly the law of life but sometimes the old and
the tried and true are worth holding. The schools of this Nation have undoubtedly contributed to giving us tranquility and to making us a more law-
abiding people. Uncontrolled and uncontrollable liberty is an enemy to domestic
peace. We cannot close our eyes to the fact that some of the country's greatest
problems are crimes committed by the youth, too many of school age. School
discipline, like parental discipline, is an integral and important part of training
our children to be good citizens—to be better citizens. Here a very small number
of students have crisply and summarily refused to obey a school order designed
to give pupils who want to learn the opportunity to do so. One does not need to
be a prophet or the son of a prophet to know that after the Court's holding today
that some students in Iowa schools and indeed in all schools will be ready, able,
and willing to defy their teachers on practically all orders. This is the more unfortunate for the schools since groups of students all over the land are already
running loose, conducting break-ins, sit-ins, lie-ins, and smash-ins. Many of these
student groups, as is all too familiar to all who read the newspapers and watch
the television news programs, have already engaged in rioting, property seizures

and destruction. They have picketed schools to force students not to cross their picket lines and have too often violently attacked earnest but frightened students who wanted an education that the picketers did not want them to get. Students engaged in such activities are apparently confident that they know far more about how to operate public school systems than do their parents, teachers, and elected school officials. It is no answer to say that the particular students here have not yet reached such high points in their demands to attend classes in order to exercise their political pressures. Turned loose with law suits for damages and injunctions against their teachers like they are here, it is nothing but wishful thinking to imagine that young, immature students will not soon believe it is their right to control the schools rather than the right of the States that collect the taxes to hire the teachers for the benefit of the pupils. This case, therefore, wholly without constitutional reasons in my judgment, subjects all the public schools in the country to the whims and caprices of their loudest-mouthed, but maybe not their brightest, students. I, for one, am not fully persuaded that school pupils are wise enough, even with this Court's expert help from Washington, to run the 23,390 public school systems in our 50 States. I wish, therefore, wholly to disclaim any purpose on my part, to hold that the Federal Constitution compels the teachers, parents, and elected school officials to surrender control of the American public school system to public school students. I dissent.

Scoville v. Board of Education of Joliet
TP. H.S. Dist. 204, 286 F. Supp. 998 (1968)
United States District Court

NAPOLI DISTRICT JUDGE

On January 15, 1968, minor plaintiffs Raymond Scoville and Arthur Breen, 17 year old students at Joliet Central High School, distributed 60 copies of a 14 page mimeographed "literary journal", entitled "Grass High", to other students and faculty members at Joliet Central High School. A copy of "Grass High" attached as an exhibit to the complaint shows that it contained various editorials, poetry, motion picture and record album reviews, and miscellaneous anecdotes. One prominent editorial, entitled "My Reply, ' read in part:

. . . The pamphlet started with a message from the principal, David Ross. This is logical because the entire pamphlet is supposed to be "The Principal's Report to Parents." In this article Ross states why the pamphlet was put out and the purpose it is supposed to accomplish namely, the improvement of communication between parents and administration. He has got to be kidding. Surely, he realizes that a great majority of these pamphlets are thrown away by the students, and in this case that is how it should have been. I urge all students in the future to either refuse to accept or destroy upon acceptance all propaganda that Central's administration publishes . . .

The editorial went on to criticize school attendance regulations as "utterly idiotic and asinine", and concluded that "Our whole system of education with all its arbitrary rules and schedules seems dedicated to nothing but wasting time." Elsewhere, the editorial accused the senior dean of the school of having a "sick mind." It is alleged in the complaint, and must be assumed true in passing on the pending motion to dismiss, that the distribution of "Grass High" created no disturbance which did, or could have caused, any commotion or disruption of classes at Joliet Central High School.

On January 18, 1968, minor plaintiffs were instructed not to report for their final examinations for the Fall semester, 1967/1968. On January 20, 1968, minor plaintiffs were told they could no longer participate in debate team activity. On January 22, 1968, minor plaintiffs were told that they were to be suspended for the first five days of the spring 1968 semester at Joliet Central High School. On January 31, 1968, minor plaintiff Scoville was removed as editor of the school newspaper. Thereafter, recommendations were sent to the Joliet School Board that minor plaintiffs be expelled from Joliet Central for the remainder of the term ending in June, 1968. Parents of the minor plaintiffs, including plaintiffs Merrill Scoville and Jerry Breen, were notified that expulsion of the boys would be recommended at a school board meeting on February 23, 1968; and that as parents of the boys they were invited to attend. The parents of the boys did not attend, but instead sent letters to the school board asking for clemency. At the Board meeting on February 23, a resolution was adopted, expelling minor plaintiffs from the day school at the high school for the Spring 1968 terms. The Board found that the publication of "Grass High" constituted a public use of inappropriate and indecent language; a violation of established rules of the school district; a disregard of and contempt for the authorities charged with the administration of Joliet Central campus and the school district; an encouragement to disregard and disobey orders promulgated by the duly constituted authorities of the school and the school district; and an involvement of other students as parties to the preparation and distribution of "Grass High" who were in fact not parties thereto.

Thereafter, a plan was worked out whereby the boys attended night school at Joliet Central, where they were able to make up some, but not all, of the subjects they were formerly taking. They were also permitted to take their physics course, on a "probationary basis," at the day school. They were obliged to pay tuition for the night school classes.

On April 17, 1968, plaintiffs filed this action against the Joliet school authorities, seeking a declaratory judgment that the action of the school board was in violation of plaintiffs' constitutional rights; and seeking a permanent injunction against enforcement of the expulsion order. Plaintiffs contend that the expulsion order constituted a denial of the rights of the minor plaintiffs of free speech and free press; and that the expulsion order constituted an exercise of authority in excess of the power delegated to the school board by the State of Illinois. . . .

The sole authority cited by defendants for their actions here is Illinois Revised Statutes, Chapter 122, § 10–22, which provides,

§ 10–22. Powers of the Board.

The school board shall have the powers enumerated in sections 10–22.1 through 10–22.34 . . .

§ 10–22.6 Suspension or expulsion of pupils

(a) to expel pupils guilty of gross disobedience or misconduct, and no action shall lie against them for such expulsion. Expulsion shall take place only after the parents have been requested to appear at a meeting of the board to discuss their child's behavior. Such request shall be made by registered or certified mail and shall state the time, place and purpose of the meeting. The board at such meeting shall state the reasons for dismissal and the date on which the expulsion is to become effective.

(b) To suspend or by regulation to authorize the superintendent of the district or the principal of any school to suspend pupils guilty of gross disobedience or misconduct for a period not to exceed 7 days or until the next regular meeting of the board, whichever first occurs, and no action shall lie against them for such suspension. . . .

I. JURISDICTION OVER THE SUBJECT MATTER

Plaintiffs allege that defendants have applied a statute of the State of Illinois, Ill.Rev.Stat., Chapter 122, Section 10–22.6, in such a manner that plaintiffs were deprived of their First Amendment rights under the Constitution of the United States. The allegations of a federally guaranteed constitutional right, and the alleged deprivation of that right by defendants acting under color of state law, are sufficient to give the Court jurisdiction over the subject matter. Accordingly, judgment must be on the merits, not via dismissal for want of jurisdiction. cf. Bell v. Hood, 327 U.S. 678, 66 S.Ct. 773, 90 L.Ed. 939 (1946).

II. CIVIL RIGHTS ACT CLAIM

Public schools boards, as well as the states from which they draw their authority, are not immune from First Amendment limitations. Thus it has been held that compulsory flag salute laws for school children, West Virginia State Board of Education v. Barnette, 319 U.S. 624, 63 S.Ct. 1178, 87 L.Ed. 1628, and short voluntary nondenomination school prayers, Engel v. Vitale, 370 U.S. 421, 82 S.Ct. 1261, 8 L.Ed.2d 601 (1962), are violative of the First Amendment prohibition against establishment of religion. Even in a special purpose public building such as a high school, speech may not be suppressed where it presents absolutely no threat to the state's legitimate interest in providing an orderly, efficient classroom atmosphere. Burnside v. Byars, 5 Cir., 363 F.2d 744 (1966). (regulation forbidding high school students from wearing "freedom buttons" held unconstitutional where there is absolutely no showing that educational activity had been interfered with.) Compare Blackwell v. Issaquena County Board of Education, 5 Cir., 363 F.2d 749 (1966) (wearing of "freedom buttons" in high school may be punished, where there is evidence of commotion, boisterousness, and undermining of authority as a result of the wearing of buttons.)

State supported public high schools are special purpose public buildings.

As such, there is no constitutional objection to limiting speech therein which interferes with the purpose to which they are dedicated. Even granting that freedom of speech occupies a preferred position in the hierarchy of constitutional values, it does not follow that it may be exercised at any time, in any manner, on any state-owned property without regard to the primary use to which the property has been dedicated. cf. Adderly v. State of Florida, 385 U.S. 39, 87 S.Ct. 242, 17 L.Ed.2d 149 (1966). Despite the First Amendment, speech may be regulated where there is a "clear and present danger" that substantive evil will result. Schenck v. United States, 249 U.S. 47, 52, 39 S.Ct. 247, 63 L.Ed. 470 (1919). "In each case (courts) must ask whether the gravity of the 'evil', discounted by its improbability, justifies such invasion of free speech as is necessary to avoid the danger." Dennis v. United States, 341 U.S. 494, 510, 71 S.Ct. 857, 868, 95 L.Ed. 1137 (1951) (quoting Judge Hand in the lower court, United States v. Dennis, 2 Cir., 183 F.2d 201, 212.)

It is apparent from the face of the complaint here that the minor plaintiffs had engaged in speech on school grounds which amounted to an immediate advocacy of, and incitement to, disregard of school administrative procedures. Particularly in elementary and secondary schools, the state has a compelling interest in maintaining an atmosphere conducive to an orderly program of classroom learning, and to respect for legitimate and necessary administrative rules. "The interest of the state in maintaining an educational system is a compelling one, giving rise to a balancing of First Amendment rights with the duty of the state to further and protect the public school system." Burnside v. Byars, 5 Cir., 363 F.2d 744, 748 (1966). The speech here, unlike the speech in Burnside v. Byars, supra, and Tinker v. Des Moines Independent Community School District, supra, itself constitutes a direct and substantial threat to the successful operation of the school. Even if it were not directed to an immature audience, its suppression might be justified under the rule of Dennis v. United States, supra. Furthermore, although we are in a period when the rights of the minor vis-a-vis the state are being closely reexamined, cf. In re Gault, 387 U.S. 1, 87 S.Ct. 1428, 18 L.Ed.2d 527 (1967), the Supreme Court has recently affirmed the right of the state to protect its younger citizens from certain forms of speech which would, if the audience were adult, be protected by the First Amendment. Ginsberg v. New York, 390 U.S. 629, 88 S.Ct. 1274, 20 L.Ed.2d 195 (April 22, 1968).

Under most circumstances, responsible criticism of school administrative officials is no less protected by the First Amendment than responsible criticism of other state officials. See Pickering v. Board of Education, 391 U.S. 563, 88 S.Ct. 1731, 20 L.Ed.2d 811 (1968). However, where speech takes the form of immediate incitement to disregard of legitimate administrative regulations necessary to orderly maintenance of a public high school system; and where the speech occurs, not on a street or on a public park, where the rights of free speech are virtually absolute, but rather on the very property dedicated to a special public use, the education of younger citizens; and where the speech is directed to an audience which, because of its immaturity, is more likely than an adult audience to react to the detriment of the school system, then it is the opinion of this Court that the interest of the state in maintaining the school system outweighs the protection afforded the speaker by the First Amendment. Since the circumstances surrounding the dissemination of "Grass High" are set forth in the complaint itself, defendants are entitled to judgment on the pleadings as to the Civil Rights Act claim made by plaintiffs here. . . .

I hold that the dissemination of "Grass High" under the circumstances alleged, was reasonably found by the Board to constitute "gross misconduct.", and that Illinois Revised Statutes, Chapter 122, § 10–22.6 has sufficiently delegated the authority to defendants to make such a finding.

Because the Court finds that the language quoted from the editorial entitled "My Reply" is unprotected by the First Amendment, under the circumstances alleged in the complaint, and that the minor plaintiffs may reasonably be punished for their conduct in disseminating it to students on school grounds, under the applicable Illinois statute, it will be unnecessary to consider whether certain other language in "Grass High", found to be "inappropriate and indecent" by the School Board, would, if standing alone, be entitled to First Amendment protection under the circumstances; or whether dissemination of a newspaper on high school grounds to high school students, containing only that language, would constitute "gross misconduct." It will also be unnecessary to pass upon the question of whether a state statute such as Ill.Rev.Stat., Ch. 122, § 10–22.6, can grant immunity from a federally created cause of action.

For the reasons given, defendants' motion to dismiss must be, and is hereby, allowed.

E. Pupil's Right to Legal Counsel

Victor Madera, Ramiro Madera and Manuela Madera, Plaintiffs-Appellees, v. Board of Education of the City of New York, Bernard E. Donovan, as Superintendent of Schools of the City of New York, Theresa S. Rakow, as District Superintendent for District One in the City of New York, Defendants-Appellants
386 F. Supp. 778 (1967)

BEFORE MOORE, FRIENDLY AND ANDERSON, CIRCUIT JUDGES

MOORE, CIRCUIT JUDGE

On February 2, 1967, plaintiff Victor Madera, was a 14-year-old student in the seventh grade in Junior High School No. 22, District No. 1 of the New York City public school system. On that date, after a period of more than a year of behavioral difficulties, Victor was suspended from school by the principal. Victor's principal notified the District Superintendent of District No. 1, Miss Theresa Rakow, of the suspension. Miss Rakow notified Victor's parents, requesting their presence at a Guidance Conference to be held in her office on February 17, 1967, with regard to Victor's suspension.

After Victor's parents received the notice, they sought the aid of legal counsel who wrote to Miss Rakow asking to appear on behalf of Mr. and Mrs. Madera and their son at the conference. Miss Rakow's office advised the attorney that he could not attend the conference. General Circular No. 16 (1965–1966), promulgated by the Board of Education of the City of New York and the Superintendent of Schools, provides:

Inasmuch as this is a guidance conference for the purpose of providing an opportunity for parents, teachers, counselors, supervisors, et al., to plan educationally for the benefit of the child, attorneys seeking to represent the parent or child may not participate. (page 5)

On February 16, 1967, the Maderas sought and obtained a temporary restraining order from the district court, restraining appellants:

From holding any proceeding at which the plaintiffs may be affected and, particularly, from conducting the 'Assistant Superintendent's Hearing' scheduled for February 17, 1967, without permitting plaintiffs' legal counsel to be present and to perform his tasks as an attorney.

After a trial, the district court issued a permanent injunction and held that "the right to a hearing is a due process requirement of such constitutional significance as to void application of defendants' 'no attorneys provision' to the District Superintendent's Guidance Conferences." 267 F.Supp. at 373. Defendants, the Board of Education, have appealed the issuance of that injunction. Pending the decision of the appeal, this Court on May 1, 1967, granted a stay.

At the very outset it should be made clear what this case does *not* involve. First, the Guidance Conference is not a criminal proceeding; thus, the counsel provision of the Sixth Amendment and the cases thereunder are inapplicable. Second, there is no showing that any attempt is ever made to use any statement at the Conference in any subsequent criminal proceeding. The record is to the contrary (186–87), and the district court so found, 267 F.Supp. at 372. Therefore, there is no need for counsel to protect the child in his Fifth Amendment privilege against self-incrimination.

The issue is one of procedural "due process" in its general sense, free from the "specifics" of the Fifth and Sixth Amendments. What constitutes due process under any given set of circumstances must depend upon the nature of the proceeding involved and the rights that may possibly be affected by that proceeding. Cafeteria and Restaurant Workers Union v. McElroy, 367 U.S. 886, 895, 81 S.Ct. 1743, 6 L.Ed.2d 1230 (1961). Thus, it will be necessary to describe the nature and purpose of the District Superintendent's Guidance Conference in some detail.

Article XI, Section 1 of the New York Constitution states that "the legislature shall provide for the maintenance and support of a system of free common schools, wherein all the children of this state may be educated." In New York, a person over five and under twenty-one is "entitled" to attend the free public schools in the school district or city in which he resides. § 3202(1), New York Education Law, McKinney's Consol. Laws, c. 16. Attendance at school is a statutory requirement for minors between the ages of seven and sixteen. § 3205(1), Education Law.

The suspension of a pupil who is insubordinate or disorderly or who endangers the safety or morals of himself or other minors, is authorized by section 3214(6) of the Education Law. There are two kinds of suspensions, the "principal suspense" (meaning by the "principal" of a school) and the "administrative suspense." Under the principal suspense the school principal has the authority to suspend the child from classes for a period of no more than five days. Generally, the principal tries to meet with the parents of the child to try to solve the problem before the suspension, but sometimes the situation requires an immediate suspension with a later conference before the child is returned to school. Normally, a principal suspense does not require any consideration by the District Superintendent. (168–170).

If the principal feels that a simple suspension will not solve the problem, he may suspend the child and refer the suspension to the District Superintendent. This is what is referred to as an "administrative suspense," a suspense which remains in effect pending an administrative decision. Section 3214(6)(b) vests the responsibility for dealing with the suspended child with the District Superintendent. There is no statutory requirement that a parent be granted a hearing prior to invoking this power. Cosme v. Board of Education, 50 Misc.2d 344, 270 N.Y.S.2d 231 (1966), affirmed without opinion, 27 App.Div.2d 905, 281 N.Y.S.2d 970 (1st Dept. 1967). Section 3214, subd. 5(a) requires only that a hearing be held prior to sending a child to a special day school or to confinement. However, pursuant to procedure promulgated by the Board of Education of the City of New York and the Superintendent of Schools and distributed in General Circular No. 16, hearings, or "Guidance Conferences," relating to the suspension are held in all cases. The principal, after suspending the student, notifies the parents that a conference will be held and the District Superintendent's office notifies them of the date of the conference.

In attendance at the Guidance Conference are the child and his parents, the principal, the guidance counselor of the suspended child's school, the District Superintendent, her assistant, the guidance counselor assigned to her office, and the school-court coordinator assigned to the district. If the parents do not speak English, they may bring an interpreter with them or one will be provided. In addition to his parents, the suspended child may have a representative from any social agency to whom the family may be known, attend the Guidance Conference. Students and their parents have never been represented at any of these Conferences by counsel. (184–85).

The function of the school-court coordinator is to provide a liaison between the Family Court and the schools. He interprets to the court "the program and facilities" of the school and he "interprets to the school the decisions of the court and the recommendations of the courts." (171). In some cases the Family Court may make use of the District Superintendent's decision at the Guidance Conference, and when requested to do so by the court, it is the school-court coordinator who takes this information to the court. In such a case, the court would receive only the school record of the child containing the fact that the child had been suspended and some notation as to where he had been transferred or where he had been placed after the suspense. (355–56). Apparently as a matter of convenience, the school-court coordinator will also take notes at the Guidance Conference. (180). However, it is clear that no statements made during such a preliminary conference could be admitted into evidence at any adjudicatory hearing before the Family Court. Section 334 of the Family Court Act provides that "No statement made during a preliminary conference may be admitted into evidence at an adjudicatory hearing under this act or in a criminal court at any time prior to conviction."

The District Superintendent's guidance counselor coordinates the activities of the District Superintendent's office with the Bureau of Child Guidance. The guidance counselor takes notes and keeps records of the Guidance Conference. When the child returns from suspension, the guidance counselor helps to place him in the proper school situation. (172).

At the Guidance Conference it is made clear to the parents and the child that it is not intended to be punitive, but it is, rather, an effort to solve his school problems. Each one present, including the child if he is old enough, is asked what he thinks should be done and contributes to the discussion. Sometimes either the parents or the child will be asked to step outside for a moment so that one might discuss problems that would be difficult to discuss in front of the other. (173–74).

The sole purpose of the conference is to study the facts and circumstances surrounding the temporary suspension of this student by his school principal, and to place the child in a more productive educational situation. At these conferences the assistant superintendent interviews the child, his parents and school personnel to learn the cause of the child's behavior. The conference is conducted in an atmosphere of understanding and cooperation, in a joint effort involving the parent, the school, guidance personnel and community and religious agencies. There is never any element of the punitive, but rather an emphasis on finding a solution to the problem.

After full and careful study and discussion a plan is formulated to deal more adequately with the problems presented by the child. Every effort is bent towards the maintenance of a guidance approach. The emphasis is on returning the child as rapidly as possible to an educational setting calculated to be most useful to him.

At the very beginning of the conference, the District Superintendent's staff may gather to go over the school records and background of the case before the parents and child arrive, but the parents are asked what they think should be done with the child and "no decision is made until the parent and child have participated" (303).

It is important to note that there are only three things that can happen to a student as a direct result of the District Superintendent's conference:

1. The suspended child might be reinstated in the same school, in the same or a different class, or
2. The suspended child might be transferred to another school of the same level, or
3. The suspended child—but only with the parents' consent—might be transferred to a special school for socially maladjusted children. (Gen. Circular No. 16).

Schools for socially maladjusted pupils (formerly known as "600" schools) were established about eighteen years ago. They are schools which are provided with special services for rehabilitation of children who are socially maladjusted or are problem children. These schools have smaller classes, specially trained teachers and special programs. More money is allocated to them so that they are able to provide more equipment and field trips for the children. (100–101). There is evidence that these schools are presently inadequate to meet the needs of the New York public school system, but no practical alternative has been offered for educating the disruptive child. (445–51). It is undoubtedly true that a certain social stigma attaches to being placed in a school for socially maladjusted children. But this is true of many decisions of educational placement, such as, deciding not to promote a child or to remove him from a rapid advancement class or even the decision to give him a low or failing mark. Furthermore, the only schools for socially maladjusted children to which the District Superintendent could refer a child after a Guidance Conference are those which provide for attendance during regular school hours as in any other school. (236). In deciding as to which school to refer the child, an effort is made to reduce any stigma by sending him to a school out of the neighborhood if possible. (246).

Thus, aside from a decision that the child should be returned to the school he has been attending, the District Superintendent is only authorized finally to decide that the child be transferred to another school. The most that is involved is a change of school assignment. However, after the Guidance Conference, the District Superintendent may also:

4. Refer the student's case to the Bureau of Child Guidance or other social agency for study and recommendation, or
5. Refer the case to the Bureau of Attendance for court action. (Gen. Circular No. 16).

If the compulsory school attendance law, § 3205, Education Law, is being violated, it is the responsibility of the Bureau of Attendance to take the matter to the Family Court. If, after the guidance conference, the District Superintendent determines that the child should be enrolled in a special school for socially maladjusted children, his parents are told to report to that school with the child. The written consent of the parent or person in parental relation to the child, is necessary before he may be required to attend a school for socially maladjusted children. § 3214, subd. 5(a), Education Law. However, if the parents refuse to give such consent they may be prosecuted for violation of the compulsory education laws. §§ 3214, subd. 5(c)(1), 3212, subd. 2(b). If the child does not report for admission, the Bureau of Attendance is notified and appropriate action is commenced in the Family Court.

The Bureau of Child Guidance (BCG) is the "clinical arm of the Board of Education. Its employees are social workers, psychologists, and psychiatrists." (175). When the District Superintendent refers a child to the BCG, it makes a study of the child "as seems indicated to help" the District Superintendent or to advise her "of what may be [the] best educational placement." (176). The BCG has no authority to order a particular placement for a child, but can only recommend various alternatives to the District Superintendent. (307–08). What these alternatives are would depend on the individual child but, in general, they are the following:

1. The child is able to attend school but should be sent to a school with a particular kind of program.
2. The child should be sent to a special day school for socially maladjusted pupils or a residential institution where the Board of Education operates such a school.
3. The child should be instructed at home.
4. The child should be temporarily exempted from school while his parents seek institutional help.

5. The child should receive a medical suspension or exemption.
6. The child should be exempt from school. (176).

I

The Fourteenth Amendment prohibits a state from depriving "any person of life, liberty, or property, without due process of law." Thus it has long been clear that where a government affects the private interest of an individual, it may not proceed arbitrarily, but must observe due process of law. Wynehamer v. People, 13 N.Y. 378 (1856).

... The 'liberty' mentioned in that amendment means, not only the right of the citizen to be free from the mere physical restraint of his person, as by incarceration, but the term is deemed to embrace the right of the citizen to be free in the enjoyment of all his faculties; to be free to use them in all lawful ways; to live and work where he will; to earn his livelihood by any lawful calling; to pursue any livelihood or avocation and for that purpose to enter into all contracts which may be proper, necessary, and essential to his carrying out to a successful conclusion the purposes above mentioned. Allgeyer v. State of Louisiana, 165 U.S. 578, 589, 17 S.Ct. 427, 431, 41 L.Ed. 832 (1897).

It has been held that any action that would effectively deny an education must meet with the minimal standards of due process.

... It requires no argument to demonstrate that education is vital and, indeed, basic to civilized society. Without sufficient education the plaintiffs would not be able to earn an adequate livelihood, to enjoy life to the fullest, or to fulfill as completely as possible the duties and responsibilities of good citizens. Dixon v. Alabama State Board of Education, 294 F.2d 150, 157 (5th Cir.), cert. denied, 368 U.S. 930, 83 S.Ct. 368, 7 L.Ed.2d 193 (1961). ...

As noted above, it is the school principal that initially issues the administrative suspense. After this preliminary suspension, aside from a decision that the child should return to the school he has been attending, the District Superintendent's Guidance Conference is only authorized finally to decide whether or not he should be transferred to another school. At most what is involved would be a change of school assignment.

The court below found that "a 'Guidance Conference' can *ultimately* result in loss of personal liberty to a child or in a suspension which is the functional equivalent of his expulsion from the public schools or in a withdrawal of his right to attend the public schools." 267 F.Supp. at 369 (emphasis supplied). The difficulty with this holding is, of course, the word "ultimately." The trial court by a series of hypothetical assumptions, in effect, turned a mere Guidance Conference relating to Victor's future educational welfare into a quasi-criminal adversary proceeding. The possibilities of Youth House, the Psychiatrist Division of Kings County Hospital or Bellevue Hospital, institutionalization, or attendance enforcement proceedings were mentioned. 267 F.Supp. at 371–372. When, as and if, in the future, Victor or his parents find themselves faced with charges in the Family Court, there would seem to be adequate safeguards in the law for preservation of their constitutional rights, including the right to counsel. Family Court Act § 741. At the most, the Guidance Conference is a very preliminary investigation, if it can be considered an investigation at all. After the conference, aside from a school reassignment, if any, a whole series of further investigations, hearings and decisions must occur before the child is subjected to any of the "serious consequences" which the district court suggested "flow for the juvenile involved in a District Superintendent's Guidance Conference." 267 F. Supp. at 370. The real question is at what point along this chain is the full panoply of due process safeguards to apply. . . .

While it is arguable that in view of the limited character of the action that may be taken, a Guidance Conference cannot result in a deprivation of "liberty" within the meaning of the Fourteenth Amendment, the contrary will be assumed for present purposes and the question whether the due process clause requires the presence of counsel at such a conference will be considered forthwith.

II

If due process is applicable to such a conference, it would not follow that the school must permit the presence of counsel. The "differing rules of fair play" encompassed by the concept of the due process "[vary] according to specific factual contexts . . . and differing types of proceedings." Hannah v. Larche, 363 U.S. 420, 442, 80 S.Ct. 1502, 1514, 4 L.Ed. 2d 1307 (1960). . . .

The right to representation by counsel is not an essential ingredient to a fair hearing in all types of proceedings.

. . . The utmost devotion to one's profession and the fullest recognition of the great role of lawyers in the evolution of a free society cannot lead one to erect as a constitutional principle that no administrative inquiry can be had *in camera* unless a lawyer be allowed to attend." In re Groban, 352 U.S. 330, 336, 77 S.Ct. 510, 515, 1 L.Ed. 2d 376 (Frankfurter, J., concurring). . . .

Recent Supreme Court decisions concerning procedures of the juvenile courts are not to the contrary. Kent v. United States, 383 U.S. 541, 86 S.Ct. 1045, 16 L.Ed.2d 84 (1966), involved the referral of a youthful offender from the juvenile court to the adult criminal court. The Court there stressed the "tremendous consequences" of such a decision and held that before it was made, the juvenile was entitled to a hearing and to the assistance of counsel. But the "tremendous consequences" to which the Court was referring in that case were "that the child will be taken from the Receiving Home for Children and transferred to jail along with adults, and that he will be exposed to the possibility of a death sentence instead of treatment for a maximum, . . . until he is 21." 383 U.S. at 553–554, 86 S.Ct. at 1053.

In In re Gault, 387 U.S. 1, 87 S.Ct. 1428, 18 L.Ed.2d 527 (1967), the Supreme Court held that due process required that in a proceeding to determine delinquency which may result in commitment to an institution in which the juvenile's freedom is curtailed, the child and his parents must be notified of the child's right to be represented by retained counsel, or if they are unable to afford counsel, that counsel will be appointed to represent the child. However, in writing for the majority, Justice Fortas clearly implied that the right to counsel does not exist at early stages of procedures involving juveniles:

The Nat'l Crime Comm'n Report recommends that 'Juvenile courts should make fullest feasible use of preliminary conferences to dispose of cases short of adjudication.' . . . Since this 'consent decree' procedure would involve neither adjudication of delinquency nor institutionalization, nothing we say in this opinion should be construed as expressing any views with respect to such procedure. The problems of pre-adjudication treatment of juveniles, and of post-adjudication disposition, are unique to the juvenile process; hence what we hold in this opinion with regard to the procedural requirements at the adjudicatory stage has no necessary applicability to other steps of the juvenile process." At 31, 87 S.Ct. at 1445, note 48 (citations omitted). . . .

What due process may require before a child is expelled from public school or is remanded to a custodial school or other institution which restricts his freedom to come and go as he pleases is not before us. . . .

Appellees also argue that the presence of counsel is necessary because the decision of the Guidance Conference depends to a certain degree on the school's statement of the child's misbehavior and that this statement may be incorrect. In the present case there were eleven incidents of misbehavior reported by seven different teachers. The mere attendance of counsel at the conference would do little to aid this problem without also granting the other rights accorded in adversary proceedings—calling of witnesses, cross-examinations, etc. To do so would be destructive of the original purpose of the Guidance Conference—to provide for the future education of the child. The conference is not a judicial or even a quasi-judicial hearing. Neither the child nor his parents are being accused. In saying that the provision against the presence of an attorney for the pupil in a District Superintendent's Guidance Conference "results in depriving plaintiffs of their constitutionally protected right to a hearing" (267 F.Supp. at 373), the trial court misconceives the function of the conference and the role which the participants therein play with respect to the education and the welfare of the child. Law and order in the classroom should be the responsibility of our respective educational systems. The courts should not usurp this function and turn disciplinary problems, involving suspension, into criminal adversary proceedings —which they definitely are not. The rules, regulations, procedures and practices disclosed on this record evince a high regard for the best interest and welfare of the child. The courts would do well to recognize this.

III

While it is most doubtful that there is any basis in law or fact for considering Victor Madera and his parents to be representatives of, and champions for, a class, a ruling on this point becomes unnecessary in view of the decision that the complaint must be dismissed for failure to state a claim on which relief can be granted.

Judgment reversed; injunction vacated and complaint dismissed.

Problems and
Discussion Questions

1. What role should pupils play in school policymaking and implementation? How may this role be structured?

2. To what extent should pupils and their parents be participants in school policy-making? How can school governance machinery take account of the interests of teachers, pupils, and parents?

3. Design alternatives to pupil suspension and expulsion procedures. Show educational advantages of such alternative procedures.

4. Draft a student Bill of Rights to accommodate school objectives, due process for pupils and teachers, and the interests of the adult community and the state.

5. Suspension and expulsion of pupils from school does little to solve educational problems. Given the reality of disruptive pupil behavior, what alternative procedures are open to schools for such pupils?

Annotated Bibliography

HALLECK, S. L., M.D. "Hypotheses of Student Unrest," *Kappan*, vol. L, no. 1, September, 1968.

> The author, a professor of psychiatry at the University of Wisconsin, Madison, presented this paper before the Twenty-Third National Conference on Higher Education. In it he catalogs and explains fifteen different hypotheses of student unrest. Included among them are "The Civil-Rights Hypothesis," "The War-in-Vietnam Hypothesis," and "The Media Hypotheses" ("diplomats have always lied to one another, but what is new about this world is that children can now watch them lie in living color").

"Constitutional Law—Right to Counsel," *New York University Law Review*, 42:961, November, 1967.

> In essence, this article is a concise statement of theory, principle, fact, and constitutional philosophy of the students' right to counsel—even in an administrative investigation or a guidance conference. Several analogies are drawn from juvenile and criminal court cases with special references to ostensibly nonadjudicative school hearings. The article raises problems arising from the students' right to have legal counsel in school proceedings.

"Legal Aspects of Student-Institutional Relationships: A Conference," *Denver Law Journal*, 45:497, Special 1968.

> This special issue is the result of a three-day conference held in May, 1968, under the auspices of the American Council on Education, the University of Denver College of Law, and assisted by the Danforth Foundation. Although the papers and comments are attuned solely to the area of higher education, they are well worth reading in light of the fact that the student involvement, unrest, and demands which began at the college level moved into public schools. Three papers in particular provide some insight into the student/public

school relationship. "The Student as Private Citizen," by Robert B. Mackay (comments by Stephen Wright, Robert Lutz, and Paul H. Cashman) discusses the surrogate parenthood of universities, and tests the principles of protests and demonstrations, William W. VanAlstyne's "The Student as University Resident" (comments by C. Peter Magrath, Rachel Scott, and Roy Lucas) thoroughly investigates the plenary and proprietary powers of colleges and universities, as well as their procedural due process. "The Student as a Student," by Phillip Moneypenny (comments by Neal R. Stamp, Robert S. Powell, Jr., and Earle W. Clifford), has special application to the obligations that colleges and universities in general have to their students.

MORGAN, Warren G., "A Look at the Law of Pupil Management," *Pennsylvania Bar Association Quarterly*, 39:101, October, 1967.

Although the article refers to public education in Pennsylvania, there is no reason to believe that the judicial opinions reviewed here are not indicative of others that might be delivered at the same level in other states. Morgan, through examination of a number of cases, points out that in the matter of pupil management (i.e., discipline) the courts tend to give the school board full discretionary power. Indeed, the weight of proof seems to bear solely on the plaintiff, and the allegations of board error, if they are to be received favorably by the court, must be other than lack of wisdom or mistaken judgment.

PLASCO, Marvin R. "School Student Dress and Appearance Regulations," *Cleveland-Marshall Law Review*, 18:143, January, 1969.

Plasco reviews the extensive case history in his commentary regarding the students' attempts for freedom of dress, appearance, etc. He points out strongly the apparent inconsistency that exists not only between states, but within single states, and—on at least one occasion—within a single school district. The author's view is that, while school boards, administrators, etc., are saying that certain student dress and behavior *could* be disruptive, the students are asking for judgment based on proof of disruption *in fact*.

RAY, Montfort S. "Constitutional Law—A Student's Right to Govern His Personal Appearance," *Journal of Public Law*, 17:151, 1968.

Ray indicates that courts, in recent decades, have adopted a laissez-faire attitude regarding student-school appearance conflicts. Examination of a number of cases shows that courts tend to apply the "test of reasonableness:" i.e., if the school regulation in question appears reasonable, then it is allowed to stand with little attention paid by the court to the constitutional issues at hand. The article also points out that the student's right to control his personal appearance is protected by the First Amendment and by a constitutional right of privacy. Ray makes judicious use of cases, opinions, and interpretations throughout.

SALZ, Arthur E., "Local Control vs. Professionalism," *Phi Delta Kappan*, vol. L, no. 6, February, 1969.

Salz, an education professor at Queens College, City University of New York, notes that growing teacher autonomy plus increased community interest in education creates a formula for inevitable conflict. Although his article relates specifically to the New York City educational conflict, the author feels that the general events and implications are nationwide. The suggestion is made that the teaching profession's lack of control over entry into the profession is detrimental to the teachers' drive towards being a viable power in education policymaking.

TURNER, Larry S., "Schools—Rules and Regulations Affecting Married Students—Reasonableness and Validity," *Western Reserve Law Review*, 16:792–799, May, 1965.

Ostensibly, this writing is based on an Ohio court case. Turner, however, takes advantage of the occasion to review decisions handed down in Mississippi, Louisiana, Kentucky, Tennessee, Texas, Utah, Michigan, Iowa, and Nebraska as well. In a concluding statement, the author opines that neither school boards nor courts are making progress in helping to cure "a very grave social problem" by punishing married students, and suggests that corrective steps are more in order than punitive measures.

5

Teacher–Board Relations

INTRODUCTION

Teacher–board employment relations is a rapidly developing area in school law. With nearly two million teachers employed in nearly 23,000 public school districts, one should expect a broad range of employment problems. Traditional legal issues arising from contracts, salary disputes, tenure, and dismissal procedures have been overshadowed recently by those stemming from collective bargaining and negotiations. In this context, employment relations include contracts of employment, loyalty oaths, teacher tenure laws, dismissal procedures, teacher-organization movements, teacher-board bargaining, and teacher strikes, sanctions, and other work stoppages.

State laws generally control eligibility for employment as a teacher through certification requirements and procedures. Some states legislate minimum salary schedules, tenure provisions, retirement regulations, and general conditions of employment. Through permissive legislation, boards are authorized to make such other terms of employment as they choose, subject to the usual bounds of reason and constitutional limitations. Within the framework of state regulations, local boards are free to develop the teacher employment relations which best serve their district.

CONTRACTS OF EMPLOYMENT

Subject to state and federal laws dealing with discrimination in hiring, school boards are free to employ whomever they wish so long as the employee meets the minimum qualifications prescribed by the law. Boards are generally free to add additional requirements for employment. They may require additional education, experience, or any other criteria which do not violate the applicants' constitutional rights. Teacher qualifications are set forth by the states through licensing or certification laws. States regulate employment of teachers on the premise that teaching is a specialized responsibility and requires specialized preparation. Another reason for state regulation is the protection of its citizens from the ill effects of teaching by unqualified employees. The protection argument is analogous to the regulation of other professions, such as law, dentistry, and medicine, where clientele must trust their well-being to people whose skills are not readily ascertained. Most parents cannot go to the marketplace for the education of their children; they must take the local public schools or none at all.

Certification laws typically include general and specific requirements. The general requirements usually include such factors as age, character, and citizenship. Specific requirements differentiate the training for various teaching levels (elementary or secondary) and teaching fields (art, music, special education, etc.). The complexity of teacher-certification provisions is illustrated by the state of Illinois, which grants eleven different teaching certificates.

The employment of a teacher is based on a contract between the school board and the teacher. The contract, usually written, includes all the elements required by common law: (a) mutual assent (the board makes an offer which is accepted by the teacher), (b) competent parties (the board and the teacher are legally capable of making the agreement), (c) consideration (the board agrees to pay the teacher for his services), (d) legal bargain (the agreement is not prohibited by law), and (e) agreement made in the form required by law. The elements of mutual assent, legal bargain, and required form create few legal problems; most contract litigation stems from consideration and the teacher's professional credentials.

Simply stated, consideration in this context is the teacher's promise to render professional service in return for the board's promise to pay a certain sum of money. Problems arise when boards assign teachers to duties allegedly not promised. Extracurricular assignments frequently trigger disputes between the teacher and the board. For example, does a contract to teach English include services as dramatic coach, cafeteria supervisor, and similar nonteaching roles? The general rule seems to be that a contract to teach includes the obligation to perform such other services as are reasonably related to the teacher's professional preparation and the welfare of the school. Thus, it may be proper to expect English teachers to sponsor dramatic activities and supervise children in non-classroom settings, but improper to assign them to coach athletic teams.

The courts generally agree that board rules constitute a part of the teaching contract. Thus the teacher's contractual obligation stems from both the written contract and the rules adopted by the board. Some states extend this obligation to include board rules enacted *after* the contract was made. This rule seems to rest on the notion that progress in school operation depends on the board's authority to alter, add to, or change work rules at any time.

Teaching contracts, like other contracts of employment, may be breached. The teacher may fail to perform, or the board may unlawfully discharge the teacher or fail to pay the teacher's salary. The law provides two basic remedies for breaches of contract: (1) money damages and (2) specific performance. Recovery of money damages is appropriate when money is equivalent to the damage caused by the breach. Specific performance compels a defaulting party to perform under the contract. The general rule bars specific performance of personal-services contracts. This rule is based on the court's inability to assure proper performance of a decree ordering personal service. Pragmatically, most school boards realize that enforced teaching may be more harmful than helpful to the pupils.

Teachers may be sued in damages for their breach of contract but will not be forced to perform. Boards, however, may be forced to perform by permitting the teacher to carry out the agreed duties. The reason for the contradictory result rests on the fragile nature of professional reputations. If a teacher is discharged unjustly, however, the news may precede his application for other teaching posts. The recovery of money damages will not necessarily repair the damage to his reputation as a teacher. Prospective employers may have neither the opportunity nor the time to investigate the legality of the discharge. In short, money damages to the teacher would be inadequate and reinstatement to the teaching position is required.

Within the past decade, collective contracts between the board and representatives of some or all of the teachers have modified the traditional concept of individual teacher contracts in many school districts. Under the collective contracts, boards enter into agreements with teachers' organizations on such matters as salary, duties, hours of employment, rights, and obligations of teachers and board, and many other details subsumed under "professional working conditions." Although the negotiated agreement may not be personally acceptable to every teacher, if the teacher organization is the sole bargaining agent, the board must conform the individual teacher contracts with the master or collective agreement. As noted above, the board rules are normally incorporated by reference or by law into the individual teacher contract. Although the individual contracts rarely limited the board's policymaking prerogatives, the collective contracts frequently include specific agreements on policy matters.

TEACHER LOYALTY OATHS

It is well settled that states and local school districts have a legitimate interest in who teaches in the public schools. All states prescribe requirements for certification of teachers and, with a few exceptions, require teachers' certification as a condition of their employment in the public schools. The purpose of such laws is to exercise reasonable controls over the preparation and presumed competence of teachers. So far as such requirements are reasonable and not administered so as to violate the teachers' rights under the state or federal constitutions, the courts generally uphold them.

Since World War II, a substantial body of legislation has been enacted to eliminate subversive activities by public school employees. This legislation generally takes the form of loyalty oaths or disclaimers of membership in specific subversive groups and requires school employees to answer certain questions about their activities and associations. The loyalty oaths and related board rules, with some exceptions, have been upheld by the courts. Loyalty-oath laws generally are attacked on two bases: (a) the claim that the oath and related questions violate the Fifth Amendment (which protects citizens against self-incrimination) and (b) the oath and the consequences of refusal to make it violate the due-process clause of the Fourteenth Amendment. A further line of argument, more popularly phrased, points out that requiring a loyalty oath presumes guilt, contrary to the common-law tradition that a man is innocent until proven guilty. Commentators have noted that the loyalty oaths rest more on emotion than logic. Teachers devoted to subversive activity or to the violent overthrow of the government would be inclined, in all likelihood, to sign anything, including loyalty oaths, to "cover" their intentions. The loyalty oaths have been upheld in numerous decisions on the theory that the public interest in education and qualifications of teachers justifies reasonable efforts to deny employment to and remove from public employment those who are committed to the overthrow of the federal or state government. The courts view the commitment to overthrow the government, inferred from certain organizational membership and associations, as a disqualification for employment in public schools. A distinction is made, obviously, between the right to unorthodox religious views and the right to subversive political views regarding qualifications for public employment. In general, states may require loyalty oaths of public school personnel so long as the content and penalties prescribed do not violate due process under the state and federal constitutions.

DISMISSAL PROCEDURES

The board's power to appoint teachers carries the implied power to dismiss, subject to the restrictions provided by law. Although the school board has the power to dismiss teachers for cause during the school year, most dismissals come at the end of the contract period. There are circumstances when immediate discharge is appropriate, particularly when the welfare of the pupils and the school demands prompt action. The board may suspend a teacher from teaching duties to protect the pupils or the school even though the teacher's contract breach has not been proven. In this event, the board may choose to assign the teacher to other appropriate duties and continue the payment of salary, or it may suspend the teacher from employment subject to review, possible reinstatement, and the payment of accrued salary. Guidelines for board action depend on the applicable state law, and advice of counsel is appropriate in such sensitive matters. The law generally provides for suspension and revocation for cause of the teaching certificate or license by the granting authority and, in some states, by the chief state school executive officer. The Illinois school code, for example, empowers the state superintendent of public instruction to suspend teachers' certificates for immorality or "other unprofessional conduct" (sec. 2–3.9). Section 21–23 of the code expands the concept of suspension and revocation:

Any certificate issued pursuant to this Article may be suspended for a period not to exceed one calendar year by either the county superintendent of schools or Superintendent of Public Instruction upon evidence of immorality, a condition of health detrimental to the welfare of pupils, incompetency, unprofessional conduct, the neglect of any professional duty, or other just cause. Unprofessional conduct shall include refusal to attend or participate in institutes, teachers' meetings, professional readings, or to meet other reasonable requirements of the county superintendent of schools or Superintendent of Public Instruction. It shall also include neglect or unnecessary delay in making of statistical and other reports required by school officers. . . . Any certificate may be revoked for the same reasons or for suspension by the Superintendent of Public Instruction. . . .

The code provides that the teacher may appeal a suspension or revocation of teaching certificate to the state teacher certification board and may take the matter into the court system to review the administrative decisions of the state superintendent, the county school superintendent, and the state teacher certification board. Suspension and revocation of the teaching certificate are serious matters to the teacher and merit protection.

TEACHER TENURE

Teachers are employed under three types of contracts: (1) term contracts (normally for the school year), (2) continuing contractual service (contract renewed unless either party elects nonrenewal), or (3) tenure contracts. The term contracts create few legal issues inasmuch as both parties retain the right to renegotiate succeeding contracts as they choose. The other two types raise the bulk of the litigation about continued teaching service. The two types frequently are used interchangeably despite their substantial differences. Continuing contracts are those teaching contracts which, if not terminated by either party by certain procedures (usually notice by a given date), continue on a year-to-year basis. Under continuing contracts, no reason for termination is required, and the board's compliance with the requisite notice provisions leaves the teacher with no recourse. Tenure contracts, on the other hand, provide for continued contractual service unless the board terminates the service for specified cause.

Tenure legislation for teachers is of recent origin. The peripatetic teacher is a familiar figure in American folk history, and teacher mobility was considered to be part of the occupation. The rise of professionalism paralleled the development of the notion that stability of teaching staff might benefit the schools and the communities. By attracting and retaining able teachers who served long enough to become familiar with the pupils and the community, schools derived increased professional benefit. From the teachers' point of view, service solely at the pleasure of the board placed jobs in annual jeopardy. The discharge of teachers under annual contracts could be as capricious as the board chose, and the constant threat of arbitrary discharge encouraged teachers to curry favor with the board on personal bases rather than on professional teaching performance. To remedy this condition, many states enacted teacher tenure legislation.

Tenure laws produce litigation for a number of reasons. Once such laws are enacted, the limits and applicability must be "tested" through disputes presented to the courts. School boards and administrators frequently resist the grant of new power to teachers and quite naturally seek to retain their power to "hire and fire" at will. The basic structure of tenure laws is remarkably simple; after a period of probationary service, during which time the board can assess the teacher's performance, the board may choose to release the teacher without cause or retain the teacher. If the board elects to retain the teacher after the probationary period, the teacher is entitled to continued contracts unless the board raises and sustains cause for discharge. The state laws vary somewhat, but the causes for discharge of tenured teachers are identical with those for teachers generally, as noted above. The procedures for discharging tenured teachers, however, are quite different from those applicable to non-tenured teachers.

Four procedural characteristics are common to most tenure laws:

1. Notice to the teacher of professional shortcomings which, if not remedied, may lead to dismissal.
2. Written statement of specific charges served by the board upon the teacher a specified time *prior* to the effective date of the dismissal or removal. The period of notice and specificity of charges are intended to give the teacher adequate opportunity to prepare his response to the charges.
3. Hearing on the charges with the right to counsel, witnesses, recorded testimony, and other record-making requirements and
4. Right of judicial review of the administrative proceedings.

State laws generally permit the board to discharge teachers upon the bona-fide elimination of teaching positions, but they may require that seniority principles be followed in determining which teachers are released. Tenured teachers may terminate their services to the employing board. The laws generally prohibit the teacher's termination of services while the school is in session or during a stated period prior to the beginning of the school term except by agreement with the board. Violation of the termination provision may result in the suspension of the teacher's certificate for unprofessional conduct. The Illinois school code (sec. 24–14) exemplifies this kind of legislation:

> No teacher who has entered upon contractual continued service may terminate such service during the part of the school year when school is in session nor for a period of 60 days just previous to the beginning of the school term except by agreement of the board and the teacher. . . . Any teacher terminating said service not in accordance with this section is guilty of unprofessional conduct and liable to suspension of certificate. . . .

"Contract-jumping" by teachers is treated seriously by many state tenure laws.

The purpose of tenure laws is not to staff schools with untouchable incompetents; on the contrary, the tenure laws, when intelligently implemented, should result in vastly upgraded, capable staffs and eliminate the professional incompetents. Popular criticism of tenure laws tends to exaggerate the "protection" of teachers and the alleged inability of school boards to discharge incompetent but tenured teachers. Such criticism usually ignores the board's opportunity and responsibilities to select, screen, supervise, and evaluate the teachers *prior* to and *during* tenured employment. If the school board and its administrative agents choose to neglect their responsibility to supervise and evaluate the teachers' performance, their subsequent difficulty in supporting charges against teachers cannot be blamed on the tenure legislation.

The school board's authority to dismiss teachers should be distinguished from its authority to refuse to renew a teacher's contract. In the absence of tenure or continuing-contract laws, boards have no legal duty to renew a teacher's contract. The laws in most states differentiate the dismissal of tenured and non-tenured teachers. The difference usually lies in the procedural requirements. Until the teacher qualifies for "continuing contractual service" or "tenure," the board is free to renew or terminate the contract. State laws usually define the board's power to dismiss teachers for (1) incompetency, (2) cruelty, (3) negligence, (4) immorality, and (5) whenever, in the board's opinion, the teacher is not qualified to teach or the interests of the schools require dismissal. The board may choose not to remove teachers for the enumerated causes, and such discretion will generally be upheld by the courts. In other words, board authority to remove teachers for cause is permissive, not legally mandatory.

The causes for dismissal of teachers are not easy to prove. Supervisors and administrators rarely maintain records adequate to legally support allegations of cause, and the burden to prove the cause rests on the board. Teaching competency, for example, has not been defined clearly. Reasonable men may disagree as to alleged incompetency by a teacher in a given instance. The presumption of competency for a licensed teacher must be overcome by evidence presented by the board. The same difficulty applies to the other enumerated causes for dismissal. Boards, then, have the authority to dismiss teachers for cause, but such dismissal frequently requires evidence of a nature not readily available to the school board.

Tenure laws formalize responsible, professional teacher-board relations and inject order into the sometimes casual employment procedures in education. The laws seek to eliminate arbitrary and capricious board decisions in teacher employment. Few critics of tenure will raise objection to the purposes of the tenure system; the objections generally are to its faulty operation. As urbanization continues and school districts grow in size and complexity, teacher employment relations become less personal and more formal in operation. The evidence suggests the probability of more, not less, bureaucracy and concomitant organizational problems. Tenure laws for teachers are well established in the profession; it does not appear likely that they will fade away. The laws serve a useful purpose to teachers, boards, and the schools. The probability seems greater for improved, refined, and better-implemented tenure provisions than for their demise.

TEACHER ORGANIZATIONS AND THE LAW

Teacher organizations challenge the traditional distribution of power in the public schools. Through collective action, teachers demand (and seem to get) more control of curriculum, class size, allocation of school funds, salaries, and many other facets of school operation. The teachers' drive toward organizational power has transformed teacher-board relations from a basic master-servant model into a three-way struggle for supremacy among teachers, administrators, and school boards. Teacher organizations threaten administrative prerogatives and board power in the public schools; they raise basic legal questions about school organization and operation.

As noted in Chapter 1, the legal structures of public education vest the governing authority of schools in elected or appointed school boards. The board's power, subject to statutory limitations, is plenary in the local district. Boards employ administrators to execute board policies and hire teachers to provide instruction under administrative supervision. Both teachers and administrators are responsible to the school board, which is traditionally vested with the authority and responsibility to make all final decisions about school matters. By granting complete management powers to the school boards, the legislatures in most states reinforced this denial of teacher participation in the decision-making process.

The courts have not been sympathetic to either the teachers' organizational efforts or to their demands for a share in the governance of the schools. Early organizational efforts by teachers met with hostility from the courts. An Illinois decision (*People ex rel Fursman v. Chicago*, 278 Ill. 318, 116 N.E. 158 [1917]) validated a rule enacted by the Chicago board of education which prohibited teacher membership in unions or union-affiliated organizations. In a later decision, the Supreme Court of Washington (*Seattle High School American Federation of Teachers et al. v. Sharples et al.*, 159 Wash. 424, 293 P. 994 [1930]) upheld a board resolution which conditioned initial or continued employment in the district on the teachers' disavowal of membership in the American Federation of Teachers or any local thereof. These two cases illustrate the courts' resistance to teacher organizational efforts.

Both the National Education Association (NEA) and the American Federation of Teachers (AFT) have lobbied at the state and national levels for legislation sympathetic to teacher organizations. Their efforts, competitive in spirit, seem to have produced the desired results in many states. As early as 1935, the AFT adopted collective bargaining as the basic technique in teacher-board relations. Some twelve years later the NEA accepted the bargaining procedure, and since 1947 both groups have pushed further toward overt teacher power in school decisions. Teachers have won the legal right to organize in most states; the right to collectively negotiate or bargain with the school board seems to be the next organizational goal. To date, seventeen states have enacted laws either permitting or requiring collective bargaining between teachers and school boards. Teacher organizations and collective action will continue to influence the law of teacher-board relations through "test cases" and sponsored legislation.

TEACHER–BOARD BARGAINING

The law concerning collective bargaining between teachers and school boards is in transition. Since 1959, when Wisconsin enacted the first legislation for teacher-board bargaining, seventeen states[1] have enacted legislation permitting or mandating some type of teacher–school board bargaining procedure. The statutes, though varying widely in scope and detail, can be classified in two ways: (1) permissive or mandatory and (2) conference or bargaining. Permissive legislation grants teachers and boards the right to confer or bargain at the option of one or the other; mandatory legislation requires such dialog. The conference-type legislation gives official sanctions to teacher-board dialog in employment relations but imposes few obligations on either party. Bargaining laws introduce new concepts and impose new obligations into teacher-board relations. Representative elections, good-faith participation, the give-and-take strategies of bargaining, and written agreements with more or less elaborate grievance and appeal machinery are new responsibilities for both sides in the teacher-board bargaining process.

In addition to mandating or permitting teacher-board bargaining or the "right to meet and confer," the legislation may define such basic elements as the scope of negotiations (what issues are subject to negotiation), unit representation (which employees constitute the bargaining unit—teachers, administrators, service personnel, noncertificated employees, etc.), procedural matters (how, when, and by whom issues are placed on the agenda), appellate procedures (steps to avoid or resolve impasses), and other issues related to the settlement of disputes.

An overview of selected negotiation statutes may be helpful in understanding the varied legislative responses to the teacher-board relations problems. The legislation in Connecticut, Michigan, and California set forth below exemplifies three approaches to the content, structure, and expected operation of sanctioned teacher-board relations.

Public Law 298 of Connecticut recognizes two bargaining units in a local or regional school district: (a) employees in positions requiring a teaching or special-service certificate, and (b) those in positions requiring an administrative or supervisory certificate. The representatives elected by each unit are the exclusive agent for all employees in the unit for negotiations with the board. Employees, however, retain the right to individually or collectively petition the board on any grievance. The statute imposes on the board and the teachers' representative the duty "to negotiate with respect to salaries and other conditions of employment, and such duty shall include the obligation of such board of education to meet at reasonable times, . . . and confer in good faith" with respect to salaries, conditions of employment, a negotiated agreement, or any question arising under such negotiations. The statute expressly provides that the obligation to bargain does not compel either party to make a concession. Section 4 of the law expressly prohibits strikes:

No certificated professional employee shall, in an effort to effect a settlement of any

---

1. Alaska, California, Connecticut, Florida, Maryland, Massachusetts, Michigan, Minnesota, Nebraska, New Hampshire, New Jersey, New York, Oregon, Rhode Island, Texas, Washington, and Wisconsin.

salary disagreement with his employer-board of education, engage in any strike or concerted refusal to render services.

Mediation by the secretary of the state board of education is provided and, if said officer cannot resolve the disagreement, three-party advisory arbitration may be compelled.

Michigan enacted comprehensive legislation to place disputes in public employment (sections 423.201, 423.203, 423.206, and 423.207 of the Compiled Laws of 1948, as amended). The title of the statute clearly indicates the legislative intent (and aspirations):

An act to prohibit strikes by certain public employees; to provide review from disciplinary action with respect thereto; to provide for the mediation of grievances and the holding of elections; to declare and protect the rights and privileges of public employees; and to prescribe means of enforcement and penalties of the provisions of this act.

The "no-strike" provision expressly preserves the employees' right to express a grievance, complaint, or opinion on any matter related to public employment so long as the exercise of such right does not interfere with the duties of employment. Public employees may organize, join, or assist labor organizations in lawful concerted activities for the purpose of collective negotiation or bargaining "in respect to rates of pay, wages, hours of employment, or other conditions of employment" (sec. 11). The parties are obligated to meet at reasonable times and confer in good faith but need not agree to a proposal or make concessions. The labor mediation board hears, determines, and penalizes unfair labor practices. Enforcement of and appeal from board orders may be petitioned from the courts. The law specifically mandates the board to administer separately the labor-relations and mediation functions of the act.

The California statute (Education Code, Part 2, Division 10, Chapter 1, article 5, sec. 13080 through 13088) exemplifies the mandatory "meet and confer" type with a unique negotiating council provision. This legislation, covering all public school employees, opens "all matters relating to employment conditions and employer-employee relations" to discussion. The negotiating council consists of five to nine members (the number on the council is determined by the employer) appointed by employee organizations represented among the certificated employees. As nearly as practicable, a constituent-teacher organization shall appoint council members in the same ratio its membership bears to the total number of certificated employees holding membership in employee organizations. For example, given a school district employing six hundred certificated employees with a negotiating council of nine members and given the following employee organization membership—one hundred nonmembers, two hundred members of organization A, three hundred members of organization B—the council would consist of four members from A and five members from B. The one hundred nonmembers are not represented on the council but, under the statute, have the right to individual discussion with the employer. The statute specifically protects the employees' rights of nonmembership teacher organizations (sec. 13082) and prohibits the employers' interference,

intimidation, restraint, coercion, or discrimination against employees because
of their exercise of organizational rights (sec. 13086).

As noted above, seventeen states have enacted legislation concerning teacher-
board relations. Of the seventeen, only six states (Connecticut, Massachusetts,
Michigan, New York, Rhode Island, and Wisconsin) mandate collective negotiations between teachers and school boards; the other eleven states permit or
require less. In the remaining thirty-three, where states are legislatively silent on
the question, boards may adopt one of two basic positions: (a) absent permissive
or mandatory legislation, the school board may not bargain with teachers, or
(b) absent permissive or mandatory legislation, each board is free to meet,
confer, or bargain with teachers. In the absence of legislation on the questions
surrounding teacher-board bargaining, the teachers and school boards must look
to other sources for guidance. In some states, although the legislature has not
spoken on the questions, there are court decisions and opinions of the attorney
general to which the parties can refer.

Three principal objections to teacher-board bargaining are raised by opponents: (1) the sovereignty theory, (2) the delegation-of-power theory, and (3) the
essential nature of teachers' services. The sovereignty theory holds that no
government can be called to account without its consent. The notion that the
"king can do no wrong" persisted in our systems of law by virtue of state
adoption of common law. The government's immunity to suit by individuals is
one manifestation of the theory; the resistance to bargaining between the government employer and its employees is another. The argument against teacher-
board bargaining based on sovereign immunity seems to be less appealing in a
democracy than elsewhere.

The second principal argument rests on the constitutional principle that
legislative power once delegated (from the legislature to the school board)
cannot be redelegated (to teachers). State legislatures vest legislative power in
the school board and, so the argument goes, the board cannot relinquish its
responsibility by conferring the delegated power on the teachers. Collective
bargaining does not mean an abdication of power by the board; it does mean a
responsible role for teachers in school decision making. The bargaining dialog
should focus additional expertise (from the teachers) on school problems and
facilitate more intelligent, effective decisions than unilateral action by the board.

Opponents of collective bargaining in the public sector raise a third argument
that government service, including teaching, is so vital that interference by
bargaining and employee demands cannot be tolerated. In the face of bargaining
and strikes permitted by law in such private-sector employment as transportation, communications, and medical services, the argument takes on a specious
ring against teachers.

Two cases included in this chapter illustrate the courts' rationale for treating
teacher-board bargaining issues when the legislature has not acted on the matter.
Norwalk Teachers' Association v. Board of Education, 138 Connecticut 269, 83
A.2d 482 (1951), was decided fourteen years prior to the enactment of the

Connecticut Public Law 298. The second case, *Chicago Division Illinois Education Association v. Board of Education*, 76 Illinois Appellate 2d 456 (1966), upheld the Chicago board's agreement to bargain with the Chicago Teachers Union despite the absence of enabling legislation. Future trends and developments in collective action by teachers are not clear at this time. The traditional objections to teacher-board bargaining are giving way to the equities and persuasion in the teachers' drive for more participation in school decisions. Conflicts in teacher-board relations are inherent in the employment relationship and must be resolved in an orderly, efficient manner. The legality of bargaining and negotiations between teachers and boards may become a moot issue; if militant action produces positive results for schools and teachers, enabling legislation may legitimize extorted power but is not vital to its acquisition by teachers.

STRIKES, SANCTIONS, AND CONFLICT RESOLUTION

Militant collective action by teachers states a new proposition in teacher-board relations; teacher demands for increased power in school affairs are supported by their concerted action in the form of strikes and sanctions. The paternalistic employer-employee model of the past no longer satisfies a substantial number of teachers. Their demands for a greater voice in policymaking and greater control over school operations conflict with traditional powers and prerogatives held by school boards and school administrators. In addition to salaries and working conditions, the conflicts arise as to class size, extracurricular assignments, discipline procedures, textbook selection, and many other specifics historically within the sole province of school boards and their agents. Teacher requests take on the nature of demands backed by explicit or implicit threats of militant action to enforce them. Organized teachers' action repertoire has expanded from persuasion and petition to strikes and sanctions. A strike is defined as the cessation of work by a group of workmen for the purpose of coercing an employer to accede to some demand which they have made upon him and which he has refused. In the context of teacher-board relations, sanctions are procedures taken by organized teachers against school districts or other political subdivisions to coerce the target agency to satisfy teachers' demands.

State legislatures, court decisions, and opinions of the attorneys general uniformly prohibit teacher strikes. Many decisions by appellate courts and courts of last resort support the prohibition, among which is the decision in the case of *Norwalk Teachers' Association v. Board of Education*, 138 Conn. 269, 83 A. 2d 482 (1951), which stated:

Few cases involving the right of unions of government employees to strike to enforce their demands have reached courts of last resort. That right has usually been tested by an application for an injunction forbidding the strike. The right of the governmental body to this relief has been uniformly upheld. It has been put on various grounds: public policy; interference with governmental function; illegal discrimination against the right of any citizen to apply for governmental employment (where the union sought a closed shop). The following cases do not necessarily turn on the specific right to strike, but the reasoning indicates that, if faced with that question, the court would be compelled to deny that right to public employees . . . *Miami Water Works Local No. 654 v. Miami*, 157 Florida 445, 26 So. 2d 194: *Ry. Mail Association v. Murphy*, 180 Misc. 868, 44 New York State 2d 601; . . . *People ex rel Fursman v. Chicago*, 278 Illinois 318, 116 N.E. 158. . . .

There seems to be no doubt that the law prohibits strikes by teachers. The uniform prohibition, however, does not prevent teacher strikes. A recent (December, 1968) press release by the NEA reported 114 teacher strikes during the 1967–8 school year involving 163,000 teachers in 21 states and the District of Columbia. The release noted that 295 teacher strikes occurred in the past 8 years. Legal prohibitions do not prevent strikes by teachers.

The NEA developed sanctions as its "professional" alternative to teacher strikes. Sanctions consist of a sequence of escalated pressures by the organized teaching profession against school districts, intermediate educational agencies, and even entire states (the state of Florida was recently placed under sanctions by the NEA). The several levels of professional sanctions, imposed after extensive investigation, are:

1. An advisory issued by the NEA to member teachers informing them of the unsatisfactory working conditions.
2. A request to all member teachers that they do not seek employment in the "offending" district or educational unit.
3. A request to members employed in the district or unit to seek employment elsewhere upon completion of their contracts.
4. A request to members to refrain from employment in the district or unit coupled with the threat of expulsion of any members of the NEA or its affiliates who accept such employment.

The NEA considered the sanction procedures to be more "professional" than teacher strikes. The distinctions between strikes and sanctions were explained by an NEA official (T.M. Stinnett in the *N.A.S.S.P. Bulletin*, 48:93–105, April, 1964) as follows:

Sanctions do not violate a contract. Services to children are not interrupted. There are no picket lines. School districts are given several months notice and told that existing conditions make possible only inferior programs for children; that professional people cannot under the existing conditions provide first-rate services.

In light of recent NEA policy shifts toward the strikes as the ultimate weapon in the NEA arsenal, the professional-sanctions approach to power tactics may be obsolete. Each major advance in organizational weaponry tends to render its predecessor obsolete; the same principle may apply to teacher-board relations.

Readings

Are Teacher Loyalty Oaths Valid?

Hendrick C. De Bruin

Hendrick De Bruin is assistant professor, College of Education,
Butler University, Indianapolis, Indiana.

American School Board Journal (February, 1967), **155**, 49–50

Within the last few years the attitude of the courts regarding the allegiance of
teachers has been undergoing a change.[1] It is generally recognized that a school
teacher, as a citizen of the United States, possesses the same privileges and guarantees enjoyed by all Americans. He has a guarantee against self-incrimination
and violation of life, liberty, and property. He has the right to join any organization, either professional or nonprofessional. But as a "public" school teacher,
he must exercise his right with due consideration to the effect it will have on
others, namely the school children.

Teaching is a privilege extended to properly certified individuals by a
governmental agency, and not a constitutional right. State and local governmental units have the right to determine who will teach their children and may
invoke at their discretion, various restrictions and requirements deemed necessary, so long as they fall within the legal framework delegated to the states.

One of the requirements for securing a teaching certificate has been the
taking of a "loyalty" oath. Currently 40 states have some form of loyalty oath
provisions. Most often the provisions are attached to the application for a
teacher's certificate. The Indiana application for a teacher's certificate is typical
of this form of legislation.[2]

Generally speaking, both educational and legislative authorities have felt
that oath taking was a just part of the requirement for teacher qualification.
When disagreements have occurred, the legality and constitutional validity of
the oath will be determined by the specific statute under consideration.

When considering the constitutional validity of loyalty oaths and the
grounds upon which they are attacked, the courts will consider all relevant facts

1. This is a summary of a presentation made at the Workshop in School Law, June 20–24, 1966,
School of Education, Indiana University, Bloomington, Ind.
2. State of Indiana, Department of Public Instruction, Division of Teacher Licensing, *Application for Teachers Certificate*, *Burns Indiana Statutes Annotated*, 28–5112.

surrounding the specific oath. These are carefully examined and include such
things as:

1. The general purpose of the oath.
2. Who must subscribe to the oath.
3. What effect the oath has on the rights and privileges of the individual.
4. What relationship the oath has regarding one's past and present allegiance.
5. Are there conflicts between statutory and constitutional provisions?
6. Who is objecting to the oath taking?

The most recent decision regarding the validity of loyalty oaths was handed
down by the federal supreme court on April 18, 1966, in the case of Elfbrandt v.
Russell.[1]

Mr. and Mrs. Vernon Elfbrandt, who are teachers in the Tucson, Arizona,
school system, and Quakers, challenged the loyalty oath of the State of Arizona,
not on religious grounds, but on the grounds that the law under question provided no hearing procedure by which they could explain their stand. The case
had been before the courts for five years. It was held by the supreme court
that:

Since the statute did not require a showing that an employee was an active member
with the specific intent of assisting in achieving the unlawful ends of an organization
which had as one of its purposes the violent overthrow of the government, the statute
infringed unnecessarily on the freedom of association protected by the First Amendment to the Federal Constitution, made applicable to the states through the 14th
Amendment, and was unconstitutionally broad.[2]

The court said:

Those who join an organization but do not share its unlawful purposes and who do not
participate in its unlawful activities surely pose no threat, either as citizens or as public
employees.[3]

Still quoting this decision, we find the following statement:

A law which applies to membership without specific intent to further the illegal aims
of the organization infringes unnecessarily on protected freedoms. It rests on the doctrine of "guilt by association," which has no place here.[4]

PURPOSES OF STATE STATUTES

A state statute then must be narrowly drawn to define and punish specific conduct. And this conduct must constitute a clear and present danger to an interest
of the state, namely the public school system. Laws cannot be passed that will
stifle and handicap fundamental liberties. We can say from this decision that
a loyalty oath cannot subject a person to criminal penalties and discharge from
employment unless one can prove that he is an active participant in the organization under question.

1. Elfbrandt v. Russell, U. S., 16 L.Ed. 2nd 231, 86 S.Ct. 1238, (1966).
2. *Ibid.*
3. *Ibid.*
4. *Ibid.*

On June 1, 1964, the U. S. Supreme Court ruled in Baggett v. Bullitt[1] that the loyalty oath required by employees of the State of Washington offended the due process clause because the language used was unduly vague, uncertain, and broad.

A class action was started in a federal district court by 64 members of the faculty and student body of the University of Washington, a state institution, challenging the constitutionality of two loyalty oaths. Contested for the first time was the oath of allegiance that had been in existence since 1931, which required all Washington teachers to swear or affirm they would support the Constitution and the laws of the state and the federal government, and by precept and example promote respect for the flag.

Also under attack in this case was a 1955 loyalty oath which had been in litigation since 1957. The oath required every state employee to swear or affirm that he was not a subversive person, a member of the Communist party, or knowingly a member of any other subversive organization. Both oaths provided the subject penalties for perjury.

The plaintiffs in the case contended that the statutes invaded the constitutional guarantees of freedom of speech, association, belief, and religion under the first Amendment; that the statutes were destructive of academic freedom, and that the vagueness of the statutory language violated due process.

VIOLATION OF DUE PROCESS

The court applied the rule that "a law forbidding or requiring conduct in terms so vague that men of common intelligence must necessarily guess at its meaning and differ as to its application, violates due process of law."[2]

The court stated further:

Those with a conscientious regard for what they solemnly swear or affirm, sensitive to the perils posed by the oath's indefinite language, avoid the risk of loss of employment, and perhaps profession, only by restricting their conduct to that which is unquestionably safe. Free speech may not be so inhibited . . .[3]

The court reaffirmed its position taken in Cramp v. Board of Public Instruction,[4] when ruling on the loyalty oath of the state of Florida. Here again the oath was challenged on the due process clause of the 14th Amendment by saying that employees must take the oath or risk perjury or immediate dismissal. The language that was held to be too vague read: ". . . That I have not (lent) or will lend my aid, support,[5] advice, counsel or influence to the Communist party . . ."

Consequently, out of the entire oath, only this section was eliminated. It ruled that when this section was deleted, it left a valid, coherent, workable

1. Baggett v. Bullitt, 84 S.Ct. 1316 (1964).
2. *Ibid.*
3. *Ibid.*
4. Cramp v. Board of Public Instruction, 363 U. S. 278 (1961).
5. *Ibid.*

statute. The remainder of the oath continues in force, and teachers are bound by statute to execute the oath.

With regard to membership in various questionable organizations, the Supreme Court in 1962 ruled that a statute in Arkansas was unconstitutional when it required teachers to file a yearly statement listing organizations in which they hold membership.[1]

CONCLUSIONS AND IMPLICATIONS

For the practicing school administrator and the school board member, these decisions regarding loyalty oath taking have certain implications. Those states planning to recodify their school statutes should examine the loyalty oath provisions carefully to see that the statute is not unconstitutionally broad. The language used must be specific and clear in meaning.

Laws cannot be passed that will stifle fundamental liberties by subjecting a person to prosecution for perjury or discharge from office because of his refusal to take the oath unless there is proof of his guilt. Guilt by association has no place in loyalty oath provisions.

Loyalty oaths cannot be used as grounds for dismissal unless it can be shown that the individual is an active participant in a questionable organization. In fact, even an individual who belongs to a questionable group, but does not share or participate in its views, seems to pose no threat to our society.

Generally speaking, legislatures and professional educators still may question a person's loyalty, and oaths can be a total part of the requirement for teacher certification. They may invoke restrictions and requirements they deem necessary so long as they fall within the legal framework delegated to the states.

Connecticut Statute
Public Law 298

An Act Concerning the Right of Teachers' Representatives to Negotiate with Boards of Education

SECTION I. (*a*) Any organization or organizations of certificated professional employees of a local or regional board of education may be selected for the purpose of representation in negotiations concerning salaries and all other

1. Shelton v. Tucker, 31 S.Ct. 247 (1962).

conditions of employment. Representatives may be designated or selected for the purpose of negotiating by the majority of the employees in the entire group of employees of said board of education or school district below the rank of superintendent or by the majority of the employees in separate units as described in subsection (*b*). (*b*) All certificated professional personnel below the rank of superintendent, other than temporary substitutes, employed and engaged either (i) in positions requiring a teaching of special services certificate or (ii) in positions requiring an administrative or supervisory certificate, may select a separate representative by a secret ballot decision of a majority of the personnel voting in each of the two said categories. If twenty per cent or more of the certificated professional employees of a local or regional board of education below the rank of superintendent in either the entire group or in the separate units described in (i) or (ii) above file with the secretary of the state board of education a petition requesting that a teacher representation referendum be held to select an organization for the purpose of representation, said secretary shall file notice of such petition with the local or regional board of education. The signatures on such petition shall remain confidential with the secretary of said board. Any organization having an interest in representing teachers in any of the units authorized by this section may intervene within fifteen days by filing with the secretary of the state board of education a petition supported by ten per cent of the employees of such unit. The local or regional board and the petitioning organization and any intervening teacher's organization may agree on an impartial person or agency to conduct such a referendum consistent with the other provisions of this section, provided not more than one such referendum shall be held in any one school year. In the event of a disagreement on the agency to conduct the referendum, the method shall be determined by the board of arbitration selected in accordance with section 2 of this act. An election shall be held to determine the representatives of the appropriate unit or units, as the case may be, within forty-five days after the filing of the petition with the secretary of the state board of education. (*c*) The representatives designated or selected as provided in subsection (*a*) of this section shall be the exclusive representatives of all the employees in such unit for the purposes of negotiating with respect to salary schedules and personnel policies relative to employment of certificated professional employees, provided any certificated professional employee or group of employees shall have the right at any time to present any grievance to such persons as the local or regional board of education shall designate for that purpose.

SECTION 2. Any dispute as to the eligibility of personnel to vote in an election, or the agency to conduct the election required by section 1 hereof, shall be submitted to a board of arbitration as provided by section 5 (*b*) of this act except that, where there are two or more organizations seeking to represent employees, each shall be permitted to name an arbitrator and such arbitrators, together with an equal number designated by the board of education, shall select an additional impartial member thereof. The agency selected to conduct the election shall decide on matters relating thereto.

SECTION 3. The local or regional board of education and the organization designated as exclusive representatives for the appropriate unit, through designated officials or their representatives, shall have the duty to negotiate with respect to salaries and other conditions of employment, and such duty shall include the obligation of such board of education to meet at reasonable times, including meetings appropriately related to the budget-making process, and confer in good faith with respect to salaries and other conditions of employment, or the negotiation of an agreement, or any question arising thereunder and the execution of a written contract incorporating any agreement reached if requested by either party, but such obligation shall not compel either party to agree to a proposal or require the making of a concession. The local or regional board of education, and its representatives, agents and superintendents shall not interfere, restrain or coerce employees in the rights guaranteed by this act, and in the absence of any certification as the exclusive representative as provided by section 1, all organizations seeking to represent members of the teaching profession shall be accorded equal treatment with respect to access to teachers, principals, members of the board of education, records and participation in discussions with respect to salaries and other conditions of employment.

SECTION 4. No certificated professional employee shall, in an effort to effect a settlement of any salary disagreement with his employing board of education, engage in any strike or concerted refusal to render services.

SECTION 5. (a) In the event of any disagreement as to the terms and conditions of employment between the board of education of any town or regional school district and the organization or organizations of certificated professional employees of said board, selected for the purpose of representation, the disagreement shall be submitted to the secretary of the state board of education for mediation. The parties shall meet with him or his agents and provide such information as he may require. The secretary may recommend a basis for settlement but such recommendations shall not be binding upon the parties. (b) In the event mediation by the secretary of the state board of education provided by subsection (a) of this section fails to resolve the disagreement, either party may submit the unresolved issue or issues to an impartial board of three arbitrators. Each party to the dispute shall designate one member of the board and the arbitrators so selected shall select the third. The decision of such board, after hearing all the issues, shall be advisory and shall not be binding upon the parties to the dispute. If the parties are unable to agree upon a third arbitrator, either party may petition the superior court or, if the court is not is session, a judge thereof, to designate the third arbitrator in the manner provided by section 52–411 of the general statutes or, if either party refuses to arbitrate, an action to compel arbitration may be instituted in the manner provided by section 52–410 of the general statutes.

SECTION 6. This act shall take effect from its passage.

Michigan Statute

An act to amend the title and sections 1, 3, 6 and 7 of Act No. 336 of the Public Acts of 1947, entitled "An act to prohibit strikes by certain public employees; to provide certain disciplinary action with respect thereto; to provide for the mediation of grievances; and to prescribe penalties for the violation of the provisions of this act," being sections 423.201, 423.203, 423.206 and 423.207 of the Compiled Laws of 1948; and to add 8 new sections to stand as sections 9 to 16; and to repeal certain acts and parts of acts.

The people of the State of Michigan enact:

SECTION 1. The title and sections 1, 3, 6 and 7 of Act No. 336 of the Public Acts of 1947, being sections 423.201, 423.203, 423.206 and 423.207 of the Compiled Laws of 1948, are hereby amended and 8 new sections are added to stand as sections 9 to 16, the amended title and amended and added sections to read as follows:

TITLE

An act to prohibit strikes by certain public employees; to provide review from disciplinary action with respect thereto; to provide for the mediation of grievances and the holding of elections; to declare and protect the rights and privileges of public employees; and to prescribe means of enforcement and penalties for the violation of the provisions of this act.

SECTION 1. As used in this act the word "strike" shall mean the concerted failure to report for duty, the wilful absence from one's position, the stoppage of work, or the abstinence in whole or in part from the full, faithful and proper performance of the duties of employment, for the purpose of inducing, influencing or coercing a change in the conditions, or compensation, or the rights, privileges or obligations of employment. Nothing contained in this act shall be construed to limit, impair or affect the right of any public employee to the expression or communication of a view, grievance, complaint or opinion on any matter related to the conditions or compensation of public employment or their betterment, so long as the same is not designed to and does not interfere with the full, faithful and proper performance of the duties of employment.

SECTION 3. No person exercising any authority, supervision or direction over any public employee shall have the power to authorize, approve or consent to a strike by public employees, and such person shall not authorize, approve or consent to such strike, nor shall any such person discharge or cause any public employee to be discharged or separated from his or her employment because of participation in the submission of a grievance in accordance with the provisions of section 7.

SECTION 6. Notwithstanding the provisions of any other law, any person holding such a position who, by concerted action with others, and without the lawful approval of his superior, wilfully absents himself from his position, or abstains in whole or in part from the full, faithful and proper performance of his duties for the purpose of inducing, influencing or coercing a change in the conditions or compensation, or the rights, privileges or obligations of employment shall be deemed to be on strike but the person, upon request, shall be entitled to a determination as to whether he did violate the provisions of this act. The request shall be filed in writing, with the officer or body having power to remove or discipline such employee, within 10 days after regular compensation of such employee has ceased or other discipline has been imposed. In the event of such request the officer or body shall within 10 days commence a proceeding for the determination of whether the provisions of this act have been violated by the public employee, in accordance with the law and regulations appropriate to a proceeding to remove the public employee. The proceedings shall be undertaken without unnecessary delay. The decision of the proceeding shall be made within 10 days. If the employee involved is held to have violated this law and his employment terminated or other discipline imposed he shall have the right of review to the circuit court having jurisdiction of the parties, within 30 days from such decision, for determination whether such decision is supported by competent, material and substantial evidence on the whole record.

SECTION 7. Upon the request of the collective bargaining representative defined in section 11, or if no representative has been designated or selected, upon the request of a majority of any given group of public employees evidenced by a petition signed by said majority and delivered to the labor mediation board, or upon request of any public employer of such employees, it shall be the duty of the labor mediation board to forthwith mediate the grievances set forth in said petition or notice, and for the purposes of mediating such grievances, the labor mediation board shall exercise the powers and authority conferred upon said board by sections 10 and 11 of Act No. 176 of the Public Acts of 1939.

SECTION 9. It shall be lawful for public employees to organize together or to form, join or assist in labor organizations, to engage in lawful concerted activities for the purpose of collective negotiation or bargaining or other mutual aid and protection, or to negotiate or bargain collectively with their public employers through representatives of their own free choice.

SECTION 10. It shall be unlawful for a public employer or an officer or agent of a public employer (a) to interfere with, restrain or coerce public employees in the exercise of their rights guaranteed in section 9; (b) to initiate, create, dominate, contribute to or interfere with the formation or administration of any labor organization: Provided, That a public employer shall not be prohibited from permitting employees to confer with it during working hours without loss of time or pay; (c) to discriminate in regard to hire, terms or other conditions of employment in order to encourage or discourage membership in a labor organization; (d) to discriminate against a public employee because he has given testimony or instituted proceedings under this act; or (e) to refuse to bargain collectively with the representatives of its public employees, subject to the provisions of section 11.

SECTION 11. Representatives designated or selected for purposes of collective bargaining by the majority of the public employees in a unit appropriate for such purposes, shall be the exclusive representatives of all the public employees in such unit for the purposes of collective bargaining in respect to rates of pay, wages, hours of employment or other conditions of employment, and shall be so recognized by the public employer: Provided, That any individual employee at any time may present grievances to his employer and have the grievances adjusted, without intervention of the bargaining representative, if the adjustment is not inconsistent with the terms of a collective bargaining contract or agreement then in effect, provided that the bargaining representative has been given opportunity to be present at such adjustment.

SECTION 12. Whenever a petition shall have been filed, in accordance with such regulations as may be prescribed by the board:

(a) By a public employee or group of public employees, or an individual or labor organization acting in their behalf, alleging that 30% or more of the public employers within a unit claimed to be appropriate for such purpose wish to be represented for collective bargaining and that, their public employer declines to recognize their representative as the representative defined in section 11, or assert that the individual or labor organization, which has been certified or is being currently recognized by their public employer as the bargaining representative, is no longer a representative as defined in section 11; or

(b) By a public employer or his representative alleging that 1 or more individuals or labor organizations have presented to him a claim to be recognized as the representative defined in section 11; the board shall investigate the petition and, if it has reasonable cause to believe that a question of repesentation exists, shall provide an appropriate hearing after due notice. If the board finds upon the record of the hearing that such a question of representation exists, it shall direct an election by secret ballot and shall certify the results thereof. Nothing in this section shall be construed to prohibit the waiving of hearings by stipulation for the purpose of a consent election in conformity with the rules and regulations of the board.

SECTION 13. The board shall decide in each case, in order to insure public employees the full benefit of their right to self-organization, to collective bargaining and otherwise to effectuate the policies of this act, the unit appropriate for the purposes of collective bargaining as provided in section 9e of Act No. 176 of the Public Acts of 1939: Provided, That in any fire department, or any department in whole or part engaged in, or having the responsibility of, fire fighting no person subordinate to a fire commission, fire commissioner, safety director, or other similar administrative agency or administrator, shall be deemed to be a supervisor.

SECTION 14. An election shall not be directed in any bargaining unit or any subdivision within which, in the preceeding 12-month period, a valid election has been held. The board shall determine who is eligible to vote in the election and shall establish rules governing the election. In an election involving more than 2 choices, where none of the choices on the ballot receives a majority vote, a runoff election shall be conducted between the 2 choices receiving the 2 largest numbers of valid votes cast in the election. No election shall be directed in any bargaining unit or subdivision thereof where there is in force and effect a valid collective bargaining agreement which was not prematurely extended and which is of fixed duration: Provided, however, No collective bargaining agreement shall bar an election upon the petition of persons not parties thereto where more than 3 years have elapsed since the agreement's execution or last timely renewal, whichever was later.

SECTION 15. A public employer shall bargain collectively with the representatives of its employees as defined in section 11 and is authorized to make and enter into collective bargaining agreements with such representatives. For the purposes of this section, to bargain collectively is the performance of the mutual obligation of the employer and the representative of the employees to meet at reasonable times and confer in good faith with respect to wages, hours, and other terms and conditions of employment, or the negotiation of an agreement, or any question arising thereunder, and the execution of a written contract, ordinance or resolution incorporating any agreement reached if requested by either party, but such obligation does not compel either party to agree to a proposal or require the making of a concession.

SECTION 16. Violations of the provisions of section 10 shall be deemed to be unfair labor practices remediable by the labor mediation board in the following manner:

(*a*) Whenever it is charged that any person has engaged in or is engaging in any such unfair labor practice, the board, or any agent designated by the board for such purposes, may issue and cause to be served upon the person a complaint stating the charges in that respect, and containing a notice of hearing before the board or a member thereof, or before a designated agent, at a place therein fixed, not less than 5 days after the serving of the complaint. No complaint shall issue based upon any unfair labor practice occurring more than 6 months prior to the filing of the charge with the board and the service of a copy thereof upon the person against whom the charge is made, unless the person aggrieved thereby was prevented from filing the charge by reason of service in the armed forces, in which event the 6 month period shall be computed from the day of his discharge. Any complaint may be amended by the member or agent conducting the hearing or the board, at any time prior to the issuance of an order based thereon. The person upon whom the complaint is served may file an answer to the original or amended complaint and to appear in person or otherwise and give testimony at the place and time fixed in the complaint. In the discretion of the member or agent conducting the hearing or the board, any other person may be allowed to intervene in the proceeding and to present testimony. Any proceeding shall be conducted in accordance with the provisions of section 5 of Act No. 197 of the Public Acts of 1952, as amended, being section 24.105 of the Compiled Laws of 1948.

(*b*) The testimony taken by the member, agent or the board shall be reduced to writing and filed with the board. Thereafter the board upon notice may take further testimony or hear argument. If upon the preponderance of the testimony taken the board is of the opinion that any person named in the complaint has engaged in or is engaging in the unfair labor practice, then it shall state its findings of fact and shall issue and cause to be served on the person an order requiring him to cease and desist from the unfair labor practice, and to take such affirmative action including reinstatement of employees with or without back pay, as will effectuate the policies of this act. The order may further require the person to make reports from time to time showing the extent to which he has complied with the order. If upon the preponderance of the testimony taken the board is not of the opinion that the person named in the complaint has engaged in or is engaging in the unfair labor practice, then the board shall state its findings of fact and shall issue an order dismissing the complaint. No order of the board shall require the reinstatement of any individual as an employee who has been suspended or discharged, or the payment to him of any back pay, if the individual was suspended or discharged for cause. If the evidence is presented before a member of the board, or before examiners thereof, the member, or examiners shall issue and cause to be served on the parties to the proceeding a proposed report, together with a recommended order, which shall be filed with the board, and if no exceptions are filed within 20 days after service thereof upon the parties, or within such further period as the board may authorize the recommended order shall become the order of the board and become effective as prescribed in the order.

(c) Until the record in a case has been filed in a court, the board at any time, upon reasonable notice and in such manner as it deems proper, may modify or set aside, in whole or in part, any finding or order made or issued by it.

(d) The board may petition for the enforcement of the order and for appropriate temporary relief or restraining order, and shall file in the court the record in the proceedings. Upon the filing of the petition, the court shall cause notice thereof to be served upon the person, and thereupon shall have jurisdiction of the proceeding and shall grant such temporary or permanent relief or restraining order as it deems just and proper, enforcing, modifying, enforcing as so modified, or setting aside in whole or in part the order of the board. No objection that has not been urged before the board, its member or agent, shall be considered by the court, unless the failure or neglect to urge the objection is excused because of extraordinary circumstances. The findings of the board with respect to questions of fact if supported by competent, material and substantial evidence on the record considered as a whole shall be conclusive. If either party applies to the court for leave to present additional evidence, and shows to the satisfaction of the court that the additional evidence is material and that there were reasonable grounds for the failure to present it in the hearing before the board, its member or agent, the court may order the additional evidence to be taken before the board, its member or agent, and to be made a part of the record. The board may modify its findings as to the facts, or make new findings, by reason of additional evidence so taken and filed, and it shall file the modifying or new findings, which findings with respect to questions of fact if supported by competent, material and substantial evidence on the record considered as a whole shall be conclusive, and shall file its recommendations, if any, for the modification or setting aside of its original order. Upon the filing of the record with it the jurisdiction of the court shall be exclusive and its judgment and decree shall be final, except that the same shall be subject to review by the supreme court in accordance with the general court rules.

(e) Any person aggrieved by a final order of the board granting or denying in whole or in part the relief sought may obtain a review of such order in the court of appeals by filing in the court a complaint praying that the order of the board be modified or set aside, with copy of the complaint filed on the board, and thereupon the aggrieved party shall file in the court the record in the proceeding, certified by the board. Upon the filing of the complaint, the court shall proceed in the same manner as in the case of an application by the board under subsection (e), and shall grant to the board such temporary relief or restraining order as it deems just and proper, enforcing, modifying, enforcing as so modified, or setting aside in whole or in part the order of the board. The findings of the board with respect to questions of fact if supported by competent material and substantial evidence on the record considered as a whole shall be conclusive.

(*f*) The commencement of proceedings under subsections (*e*) or (*f*) shall not, unless specifically ordered by the court, operate as a stay of the board's order.

(*g*) Complaints filed under this act shall be heard expeditiously by the court to which presented, and for good cause shown shall take precedence over all other civil matters except earlier matters of the same character.

(*h*) The board shall have power, upon issuance of a complaint as provided in subsection (*b*) charging that any person has engaged in or is engaging in an unfair labor practice, to petition any circuit court within any circuit where the unfair labor practice in question is alleged to have occurred or where such person resides or exercises or may exercise its governmental authority, for appropriate temporary relief or restraining order, in accordance with the general court rules, and the court shall have jurisdiction to grant to the board such temporary relief or restraining order as it deems just and proper.

(*i*) For the purpose of all hearings and investigations, which, in the opinion of the board, are necessary and proper for the exercise of the powers vested in it under this section, the provisions of section 11 shall be applicable, except that subpoenas may issue as provided in section 11 without regard to whether mediation shall have been undertaken.

(*j*) The labor relations and mediation functions of this act shall be separately administered by the board.

Section 2. Sections 4, 5 and 8 of Act No. 336 of the Public Acts of 1947, being sections 423.204, 423.205 and 423.208 of the Compiled Laws of 1948, are repealed.

This act is ordered to take immediate effect.

California Statute

An act to amend Section 3501 of the Government Code and to add Article 5 (commencing with Section 13080) to Chapter 1 of Division 10 of Part 2 of the Education Code, relating to public school employee organizations.

The people of the State of California do enact as follows:

SECTION 1. Section 3501 of the Government Code is amended to read:

3501. As used in this chapter:

(*a*) "Employee organization" means any organization which includes employees of a public agency and which has as one of its primary purposes representing such employees in their relations with that public agency.

(*b*) Except as otherwise provided in this subdivision, "public agency" means the State of California, every governmental subdivision, every district, every public and quasi-public corporation, every public agency and public service corporation and every town, city, county, city and county and municipal corporation, whether incorporated or not and whether chartered or not. As used in this chapter, "public agency" does not mean a school district or a county board of education or a county superintendent of schools or a personnel commission in a school district having a merit system as provided in Chapter 3 (commencing with Section 13580) of Division 10 of the Education Code.

(*c*) "Public employee" means any person employed by any public agency excepting those persons elected by popular vote or appointed to office by the Governor of this state.

SECTION 2. Article 5 (commencing with Section 13080) is added to Chapter 1 of Division 10 of Part 2 of the Education Code, to read:

ARTICLE 5. EMPLOYEE ORGANIZATIONS

13080. It is the purpose of this article to promote the improvement of personnel management and employer-employee relations within the public school systems in the State of California by providing a uniform basis for recognizing the right of public school employees to join organizations of their own choice and be represented by such organizations in their professional and employment relationships with public school employers and to afford certificated employees a voice in the formulation of educational policy. Nothing contained herein shall be deemed to supersede other provisions of this code and the rules and regulations of public school employers which establish and regulate tenure or a merit or civil service system or which provide for other methods of administering employer-employee relations. This article is intended, instead, to strengthen tenure, merit, civil service and other methods of administering employer-employee relations through the establishment of uniform and orderly methods of communication between employees and the public school employers by which they are employed.

13081. As used in this article:

(*a*) "Employee organization" means any organization which includes employees of a public school employer and which has as one of its primary purposes representing such employees in their relations with that public school employer.

(*b*) "Public school employer" means a school district, a county board of education, a county superintendent of schools, or a personnel commission of a school district which has a merit system as provided in Chapter 3 of this division.

(*c*) "Public school employee" means any person employed by any public school employer excepting those persons elected by popular vote or appointed by the Governor of this state.

13082. Except as otherwise provided by the Legislature, public school employees shall have the right to form, join and participate in the activities of employee organizations of their own choosing for the purpose of representation on all matters of employer-employee relations. Public school employees shall also have the right to refuse to join or participate in the activities of employee organizations and shall have the right to represent themselves individually in their employment relations with the public school employer.

13083. Employee organizations shall have the right to represent their members in their employment relations with public school employers. Employee organizations may establish reasonable restrictions regarding who may join and may make reasonable provisions for the dismissal of individuals from membership. Nothing in this section shall prohibit any employee from appearing in his own behalf in his employment relations with the public school employer.

13084. The scope of representation shall include all matters relating to employment conditions and employer-employee relations, including, but not limited to wages, hours and other terms and conditions of employment.

13085. A public school employer or the government board thereof, or such administrative officer as it may designate, shall meet and confer with representatives of employee organizations upon request with regard to all matters relating to employment conditions and employer-employee relations, and in addition, shall meet and confer with representatives of employee organizations representing certificated employees upon request with regard to all matters relating to the definition of educational objectives, the determination of the content of courses and curricula, the selection of textbooks, and other aspects of the instructional program to the extent such matters are within the discretion of the public school employer or governing board under the law. The designation of an administrative officer as provided herein shall not preclude an employee organization from meeting with, appearing before, or making proposals to the public school employer at a public meeting if the employee organization requests such a public meeting.

Notwithstanding the provisions of Sections 13082 and 13083, in the event there is more than one employee organization representing certificated employees, the public school employer or governing board thereof shall meet and confer with the representatives of such employee organizations through a negotiating council with regard to the matters specified in this section, provided that nothing herein shall prohibit any employee from appearing in his own behalf in his employment relations with the public school employer. The negotiating council shall have not more than nine nor less than five members and shall be composed of representatives of those employee organizations who are entitled to representation on the negotiating council. An employee organization representing certificated employees shall be entitled to appoint such number of members of the negotiating council as bears as nearly as practicable the same ratio to the total number of members of the negotiating council as the number of members of the employee organization bears to the total number of certificated employees of the public employer who are members of employee organizations representing certificated employees. Each employee organization shall adopt procedures for selecting its proportionate share of members of the negotiating council, provided that such members shall be selected no later than October of each school year. Within 10 days after October 31, the members of the negotiating council shall meet and select a chairman, and thereafter such negotiating council shall be legally constituted to meet and confer as provided for by the provisions of this article. Employee organizations shall exercise the rights given by Section 13083 through the negotiating council provided for in this section.

13086. Public school employers and employee organizations shall not interfere with, intimidate, restrain, coerce or discriminate against public school employees because of their exercise of their rights under Section 13082.

13087. A public school employer shall adopt reasonable rules and regulations for the administration of employer-employee relations under this article.

Such rules and regulations shall include provision for verifying the number of certificated employees of the public school employer who are members in good standing of an employee organization on the date of such verification, and where a negotiating council is required by Section 13085, for the size of the negotiating council. The public school employer may require an employee organization to submit any supplementary information or data considered by the public school employer to be necessary to the verification of the number of members in an employee organization and such information or data shall be submitted by the organization within 10 days after request, provided that membership lists, if requested, shall not be used as a means of violating section 13086. In addition such rulings include provisions for (a) verifying the official status of employee organization officers and representatives, (b) access of employee organization officers and representatives to work locations, (c) use of official bulletin boards and other means of communication by employee organizations, (d) furnishing complete and accurate nonconfidential information pertaining to employment relations to employee organizations and (e) such other matters as are necessary to carry out the purposes of this article.

13088. The enactment of this article shall not be construed as making the provisions of Section 923 of the Labor Code applicable to public school employees.

Developments— Academic Freedom 1

Harvard Law Review (1968), **82**, 1084–1105

STATUTORY AND CONTRACTUAL RIGHTS

At the nonconstitutional level, academic freedom often gains some protection through statutory or contractual teacher tenure arrangements. Such systems are essentially employment security devices under which the teacher attains a permanent status guaranteeing him against either dismissal or the application of other specified sanctions except for stated cause. Certain procedural safeguards are also provided. Tenure systems of this sort are an attempt to minimize the undesirable aspects of the employment relationship under which teachers act. The untenured teacher is subject to many types of sanctions which may tend to reduce his freedom of action inside and outside the classroom. He may be dismissed, suspended, forced to take a compulsory leave of absence, refused promotion to a position consonant with his experience and ability, given a cut in salary, or transferred to unpleasant or insignificant tasks, all for reasons which may or may not relate to the welfare of the school. Tenure systems can control the application of at least some of these sanctions. But they are not an unmixed blessing. Secure employment may attract the duller, less adventurous teacher, who desires a steady job rather than an opportunity for intellectual inquiry, while teachers who have once gained tenure, knowing that they can maintain a minimal output and still retain their jobs, may grow stale. The publicity and expense attendant upon a full tenure dismissal proceeding may lead the school administration to retain such inferior teachers. For the more competent teachers, tenure may also represent an unwanted substitution of bureaucratic security for the chance of rapid advancement, higher wages, and other attractive fringe benefits. Finally, where, due to competitive pressures, the probationary period is relatively short, both the teacher and the institution may suffer by a forced decision to grant or deny tenure before the teacher's capabilities have been demonstrated. On the other hand, added security for the teacher can help create an atmosphere conducive to the development of academic freedom since the tenured teacher, freed from worry over renewal of his contract, can concentrate on teaching and research and can exercise intellectual leadership both inside and outside the classroom despite the unpopularity of his individual views. The protection which can thus be afforded academic freedom makes tenure a desirable safeguard, in spite of its potential drawbacks.[1]

1. For discussions of the comparative disadvantages and advantages of the tenure system, see Byse, *Tenure and Academic Freedom*, in CHALLENGE AND CHANGE IN AMERICAN EDUCATION 313, 313–27 (S. Harris ed. 1965); Machlup, *In Defense of Academic Tenure*, in ACADEMIC FREEDOM AND TENURE 306, 312–26 (L. Joughin ed. 1967).

1. STATUTORY TENURE SYSTEMS

Statutory tenure schemes vary considerably, both in the degree of protection afforded and in the number of teachers covered. Private institutions are never included under tenure statutes,[1] and public universities, although treated in separate provisions in a few states,[2] are also generally not bound.[3] A small minority of the states have no tenure systems at all; an equally small minority have "spring notification" legislation, which provides for a continuing contract between the teacher and the board of education, subject to nonrenewal by either party upon stated advance notice. The majority of the states, however, have some form of true tenure legislation, under which a teacher's continuing contract is subject to termination only for cause after compliance with stated procedural safeguards.[4] As of December 1967, thirty-six states had enacted such tenure laws for all or most of their primary and secondary public schools, while six others had laws applicable to selected school districts.[5]

(A) PROCEDURAL GUARANTEES UNDER STATUTORY TENURE SYSTEMS. Tenure laws generally specify the procedural safeguards to be applied in dismissal or demotion proceedings involving tenured teachers.[6] The typical statute requires the serving of written notice of intention to dismiss or demote and a statement of charges; a copy of the tenure law itself is frequently attached. The teacher may

---

1. Private institutions may, however, create their own tenure systems by contracts.

2. E.g., WIS. STAT. ANN § 37.31 (1966). Even where such tenure laws exist they need not cover all state colleges and universities. Compare, e.g., id. (Wisconsin state colleges) with, e.g., WIS. STAT. § 36.06(2) (1963) (University of Wisconsin). The tenure laws for public universities are often less detailed about cause and/or procedure than those for primary and secondary schools, thereby vesting somewhat more discretion in the governing bodies of the former than the latter. Compare, e.g., WIS. STAT. ANN. § 37.31 (1966) (state colleges), with, e.g., WIS. STAT. ANN. § 118.23 (School Law Rev. Supp. 1967) (populous counties). See also CAL. EDUC. CODE §§ 24201, 24305–09 (West Supp. 1967) (no tenure by statute in state colleges, but board of trustees must enact tenure regulations consonant with rather detailed statutory minima).

3. Public universities not included in tenure laws often, however, adopt tenure systems by by-law or rule.

4. Although both the local and state boards of education are powerless to alter statutory tenure arrangements to the detriment of the teacher, the extent to which the teacher is protected from legislative interference depends on the wording of the statute. In three cases decided during the late 1930's, the United States Supreme Court distinguished between two types of tenure laws. Under the more common type, the tenured teacher has only a legislatively created status, which may be altered or eliminated by subsequent acts of the legislature. Phelps v. Board of Educ., 300 U.S. 319 (1937); Dodge v. Board of Educ., 302 U.S. 74 (1937). However, the law may be so worded as to regulate and become part of the continuing contract between teacher and school board; in such a case U.S. CONST. art. 1, § 10 (obligation of contracts) is applicable, and only valid exercises of the police power for other than purely political motives will justify the legislature in impairing the stated contractual rights. Indiana ex rel. Anderson v. Brand, 303 U.S. 95 (1938). In order to avoid so binding themselves, some legislatures have inserted specific provisions in the tenure laws disclaiming any contractual obligations. E.g., ARIZ. REV. STAT. ANN. § 15–260 (1956).

5. See National Educ. Ass'n of the United States, Research Div., Tenure and Contracts, Dec. 1967 (to be published in 1968). The NEA lists 33 states (including the District of Columbia) with statewide tenure laws, three states with statewide laws with certain school districts excepted, and six states with tenure laws applying to certain cities, counties, or school districts only. Nine states are listed as without any tenure law whatsoever; five of these states have "spring notification" provisions. In addition, spring notification provisions apply to the nontenure areas in five other states.

6. See also ALA. CODE tit. 52, §§ 356–57 (1958) (procedural guarantees upon transfer).

then request an open or closed hearing before the board of education, at which he is entitled to be represented by counsel, to present and subpoena evidence and witnesses, and to confront and cross-examine opposing witnesses, who are to be examined under oath. A stenographic record of the proceedings is usually kept. Although the statute may require the decision of the board to be in writing, the decision generally need not include findings of fact or conclusions of law.[1] Individual tenure laws do, however, vary considerably from this pattern; they may be more or less detailed,[2] and they may require different parties to take the initiative at various stages of the proceedings.[3]

Some form of review of an adverse decision of the board is always available to the teacher, but appellate procedures vary widely. Appeal may be provided to the state board or commissioner of education,[4] to a state tenure commission,[5] or alternatively or exclusively to the courts.[6] The review may be on the administrative record or on the basis of a new hearing.[7] Some form of review will ultimately be available in the courts, but the reviewing court may be satisfied if it finds that the decision below was based on "substantial evidence"[8] or even that it was something more than "arbitrary and capricious."[9] Where an administrative appeal is provided, this remedy may have to be exhausted before the courts will grant a hearing.[10] A decision in favor of the teacher at any level will result in reinstatement or a remand for further proceedings.[11]

In order to prevent procedural laxity from eroding substantive guarantees,

---

1. *But see* N.M. STAT. ANN. 77–8–16(E) (Supp. 1967).

2. *Compare* HAWAII REV. LAWS § 38–5.3 (Supp. 1965) *with* N.Y. EDUC. LAW § 3012 (McKinney Supp. 1967) *and* ME. REV. STAT. ANN. tit. 20, § 161.5 (1964). *See also* M. L. Leahy, A New Tenure Act, Nov. 1966 (American Federation of Teachers model tenure act).

3. For example, a statement of charges may be automatically provided with the notice of intention to dismiss, or it may be available only at the request of the teacher. *Compare* CAL. EDUC. CODE § 13405 (West 1960) (charges to be included) *with* MASS. GEN. LAWS ch. 71, § 42 (Supp. 1966) (request necessary).

4. N.M. STAT. ANN. § 77–8–17 (Supp. 1967) (state board); N.Y. EDUC. LAW § 3012.3 (McKinney Supp. 1967) (commissioner).

5. ALA. CODE tit. 52, § 360 (1958).

6. N.Y. EDUC. LAW § 3012.3 (McKinney Supp. 1967) (alternative remedy); OHIO REV. CODE ANN. § 3319.16 (Page 1960) (exclusive remedy).

7. *Compare* Pearson v. Board of Educ., 12 Ill. App. 2d 44, 138 N.E.2d 326 (1956), *with* Rehberg v. Board of Educ., 345 Mich. 731, 740, 77 N.W.2d 131, 135 (1956).

8. *See* Hauswald v. Board of Educ., 20 Ill. App. 2d 49, 155 N.E.2d 319 (1958); Swisher v. Darden, 59 N.M. 511, 287 P.2d 73 (1955).

9. *See* Board of Educ. v. Allen, 6 N.Y.2d 127, 160 N.E.2d 60, 188 N.Y.S.2d 515 (1959) (arbitrary and capricious standard of review under statute prohibiting review "in any place or court whatever").

10. *E.g.*, Moore v. Starkey, 185 Kan. 26, 340 P.2d 905 (1959). *But. cf.* State v. Yoakum, 201 Tenn. 180, 193–94, 297 S.W.2d 635, 641 (1956). Where initial appeals are provided alternatively to the courts or an administrative body, the problem is more complex. The New York courts have drawn a distinction between cases in which there is a violation of a clear legal right—for example when a statutory duty has been violated—and cases within administrative discretion and school policy. In the latter case they will apparently defer to the discretion of the educational authorities and refuse to hear the initial appeal. *Cf.* Lombardo v. Board of Higher Educ., 18 App. Div. 2d 444, 447–48, 240 N.Y.S. 2d 119, 123–24 (dictum), *aff'd mem.*, 13 N.Y.2d 1097, 196 N.E.2d 266, 246 N.Y.S.2d 631 (1963). *Compare* Frankle v. Board of Educ., 173 Misc. 1050, 19 N.Y.S.2d 588 (Sup. Ct. 1940), *modified*, 259 App. Div. 1006, 21 N.Y.S.2d 511, *aff'd per curiam*, 285 N.Y. 541, 32 N.E.2d 830 (1941) (violation of statute), *with In re* Lamberti, 26 Misc. 2d 56, 211 N.Y.S.2d 894 (Sup. Ct. 1960) (alternative holding) (discretionary action).

11. *See* State *ex rel.* Ball v. McPhee, 6 Wis. 2d 190, 94 N.W.2d 711 (1959).

tenure statutes should be quite explicit in describing procedural rights and obligations.[1] In particular, teachers, should be granted the right to be present. to introduce evidence, to subpoena witnesses, to have counsel present, and to receive a full transcript of the hearing.[2] In addition, where fellow teachers are called as witnesses, their testimony should be considered privileged in order to prevent reprisals. However, legislative prescription of these fundamentals of a fair hearing need not result in a formal judicial trial before the board; a just and effective hearing might be had if additional procedures less rigid than those used in courts were followed.[3] The board might, for instance, be allowed to consider "expert" evidence not fully developed at the hearing, such as evaluations prepared for the purpose of the case by the teacher's superiors. The sources of such evidence would be identified in order to allow the teacher to challenge the information, present rebuttal evidence, and confront and cross-examine the individuals involved if he wishes. In effect, this procedure would have evidence stipulated unless challenged and would shift only the burden of inertia to the teacher. Similarly, the common law rules of evidence could be waived.[4] The members of the hearing board should not be expected to be experts in the law of evidence; and because they have some familiarity with the parties and issues involved, they would be justified in receiving a wider range of evidence than would be admissible in court. Of course, routine school records should be admissible, although open to challenge.[5] A requirement of relevance, a limitation of the evidence to the charges,[6] and possibly a statute of limitations on admissible evidence[7] should be sufficient safeguards. Such a procedure would be less cumbersome than the rigid procedural requirements of a court-like "trial," but would not endanger any of the teacher's substantive rights.

Because the most important part of any procedural system is the impartiality of the decision-making body, the wisdom of having the board of education hear the charges against the teacher may be questioned. Although the board may not in actuality be an "adversary" of the teacher[8] and may attempt to consider the case with an open mind, in some instances the board will be acting both as prosecutor and judge.[9] Even where a subordinate official initiates or presents the charges, the board, in its role as administrator of the school system, may regard a seemingly minor inconvenience to the teacher, or the welfare of "only

1. A court may not require procedures not explicitly granted in the statute. *See* Knox County Bd. of Educ. v. Willis, 405 S.W.2d 952 (Ky. Ct. App. 1966) (board not required to adopt formal procedural rules for hearings).
2. Because of the great expense involved in preparing transcripts, use of a tape recording, which need only be transcribed if an appeal is taken and an agreed statement of facts cannot be arrived at, would be a satisfactory alternative.
3. *See* N.M. Stat. Ann. § 77–8–16 (Supp. 1967).
4. *Cf.* Cal. Educ. Code § 13426 (West 1960); N.M. Stat. Ann. § 77–8–16(C) (Supp. 1967).
5. *See* Cal. Educ. Code § 13434 (West 1960).
6. *E.g.*, Hawaii Rev. Laws § 38–5.3 (Supp. 1965).
7. *See* N.Y. Educ. Law § 3012.4 (McKinney Supp. 1967).
8. In New York, for example, charges against the teacher are to be made to the board by the superintendent of schools or filed with the clerk of the board (presumably by an outside party). N.Y. Educ. Law § 3012.3 (McKinney Supp. 1967).
9. *See, e.g.*, McFarlane v. East Detroit Bd. of Educ., 364 Mich. 103, 110 N.W.2d 808 (1961).

one" teacher, as outweighed by what it sees as the short or long term interests of the whole system. In addition, the board may feel that it has an interest in maintaining the reputation of, and amicable relations with, the superintendent or other administrator whom it has appointed and who has brought charges against the teacher. In a close case, it may thus hear the evidence with an open mind. In addition, the board is ordinarily elected for a short term, and thus is both subject to popular pressure and reflective of popular prejudice. While such a highly representative body is desirable for administering a democratic system of education, a more insulated tribunal would be preferable in the quasi-judicial role of hearing tenure proceedings.

One way to avoid this problem is to transfer the tenure hearing to the courts. Under California law, for example, if the teacher requests a hearing and the board persists in its intention to dismiss him, it must file a complaint in the superior court, which is empowered to determine the truth of the charges and their sufficiency under the code, and to render a decision on the merits.[1] The formalities and publicity of court litigation are not, however, the only alternative. One sensible compromise provided under a former Oregon law deserves consideration.[2] The initial hearing was to be held before the board of education, but alternative appeals were provided to the courts or a state teacher tenure commission composed of disinterested citizens. Review by the commission was normally on the record, but if the board had been closely divided the teacher might request a hearing de novo. If an adequate record along with full findings of fact and conclusions of law are presented by the board, the establishment of a nonprofessional tenure commission with the power to review exercises of board discretion should adequately protect the teacher's rights.

A better solution would be for the initial hearing to be held before a faculty or mixed faculty-administration tenure committee.[3] A pure faculty committee would give teachers an independent voice on the delicate and complex questions relating to competency and academic freedom often raised in tenure proceedings.[4] And it would utilize the independence enjoyed by the tenured faculty member to assure a fair hearing. However, a claim of faculty expertise will be valid only in certain cases: although realistic in some cases where unprofessional conduct

---

1. CAL. EDUC. CODE §§ 13412–13 (West, 1960).

2. Act of Feb. 28, 1935, ch. 125, §§ 15–18, [1935] Ore. Laws 193–95 (repealed 1965).

3. Both procedures are found in higher education. C. BYSE & L. JOUGHIN, TENURE IN AMERICAN HIGHER EDUCATION 58–60 (1959). Despite the obvious differences in institutional structure and discipline between higher and lower educational institutions, such tenure committees should be adaptable to the elementary and high schools covered by tenure statutes.

Colorado provides a somewhat analogous arrangement under its tenure law. The hearing is before a panel composed of one member selected by the teacher, one by the board, and one by the other two. Teacher Employment, Dismissal, and Tenure Act of 1967, ch. 435, § 1, [1967] Colo. Sess. Laws 981–83 (to be codified in COLO. REV. STAT. ANN. § 123–18–17). Absent board review of the panel's findings (which is also provided), this would be an acceptable alternative to the tenure committee, although there is a slight danger that the panel members may view themselves in a partisan role. *See* C. BYSE & L. JOUGHIN, *supra*, at 59–60.

4. *See* Joughin, *Academic Due Process*, 28 LAW & CONTEMP. PROB. 573, 584–86 (1963). The discussion of the tenure committee is directed to the university, but the reasons are not inapplicable to elementary and secondary schools, except for those limitations discussed in the text.

or incompetence is charged,[1] where the teacher is accused of immorality, expertise will be irrelevant. And despite the advantages gained by faculty independence, the faculty, like a body of administrators, may have a potential bias based on its vested interests. At least at the lower levels of public education, where most tenure statutes are applicable, the need for faculty self-government may not be sufficient to justify a pure faculty tenure committee. Administrative interests are greater at the primary and secondary levels than they are in colleges and universities, where all-faculty tenure committees are more common; the greater impressionability of younger students and the need for tighter controls over curriculum justify greater restrictions on faculty autonomy. The conflicting interests involved would probably best be resolved by providing for a mixed tenure committee.

Although it would be desirable for tenure proceedings to be conducted by a tenure committee, regulation of school policy and the setting of standards of competence should remain within the province of the board of education, for although at present the discretion exercised in dismissal proceedings is often excessive, the need for properly channelled discretion in the hands of a public body remains. Both the public interest in allowing the board to set policy and the need for an impartial adjudicator could be met by allowing the board to retain a rule-making power to set standards which would be binding on the tenure committee and by giving the board a more limited policy-making role during the adjudicatory process. The board would exercise this latter function by retaining an initial power of decision; it could make ex parte investigations and decide whether to bring charges. At the hearing the board could present to the committee the standards under which it believes the teacher should be judged. To the extent that such standards are reasonable—and the committee would be obliged to accord them a presumption of reasonableness even though they had not previously been enunciated in formal regulations[2]—the tenure committee would be bound by them. The role of the committee in such a case would be threefold. It would decide whether the facts support the charges, whether the charges constitute a sufficiently grave violation of the board's standards to justify dismissal,[3] and whether the adjudicatory standards advanced are reasonable within the framework of the statutory scheme. When the board's standards had been advanced as formal rules before the conduct complained of took place, the committee would be free to exercise its discretion on the first two issues, but

---

1. *Cf.* CAL. EDUC. CODE § 13417 (West Supp. 1967) (expert witnesses on professional matters).

2. There might be some danger under this scheme that the board, by failing to promulgate formal regulations, would improperly delegate part of its policy-making responsibility to the committee by default. In order to guard against this, it might be necessary to require the board by statute to issue formal rules.

3. This would help to alleviate the problem faced recently by a Massachusetts court, under a statute which it interpreted as providing for a trial de novo of the facts but not a new determination of the appropriateness of the board's action. The court concluded that a teacher with an excellent record of 23 years service was subject to dismissal for conduct unbecoming a teacher when, at a school committee meeting, she had muttered under her breath that the superintendent of schools was a "son of a bitch." MacKenzie v. School Comm., 342 Mass. 612, 174 N.E.2d 657 (1961) (dictum).

not on the third. It would in any case be responsible for imposing a reasonable sanction. Either administrative or judicial review could then be provided from the tenure committee's decision under a substantial evidence test.

(B) LIMITED SANCTIONS   (I) DENIAL OF PERMANENT STATUS. Because of the relative immunity from dismissal afforded the tenured teacher, most tenure systems provide for a probationary period, generally of two to five years, before tenure is granted.[1] The probationary teacher is ordinarily given only short-term contracts, which the board may decline to renew at will without giving any statement of charges,[2] although there may be constitutional limitations on arbitrary action by the board[3] and, under state law, timely notice of intention not to renew may be required.[4] However, the probationary teacher does at least enjoy the security of his employment contract; he cannot be dismissed during the school year for cause,[5] and he will ordinarily be entitled to a hearing on the charges against him in such a case.[6]

The granting of tenure following probation is ordinarily a discretionary action on the part of the governing board, dependent upon a finding of prior satisfactory performance, and under ordinary circumstances, not reviewable in the courts.[7] Although an affirmative grant of tenure is usually mentioned in the statute, reemployment at the end of the probationary period even without such a formal action automatically confers permanent status.[8] An attempted denial of tenure is ineffective if coupled with hiring for an additional year after probation;[9] the teacher may be said to gain tenure by estoppel.[10] Since notice of the withholding of tenure at the end of the probationary period is usually required by statute,[11] even failure to give such notice will probably create a tenure by estoppel.[12] The board therefore is left with little power to circumvent the probationary system.[13]

1. *E.g.*, N.Y. EDUC. LAW § 3012.1 (McKinney 1953) (three years probation). *But see* WASH. REV. CODE § 28.67.070 (Cum. Supp. 1959) (no probationary period).
2. Parker v. Board of Educ., 237 F. Supp. 222 (D. Md.), *aff'd per curiam*, 348 F.2d 464 (4th Cir. 1965), *cert. denied*, 382 U.S. 1030 (1966). *See also* Cochran v. Vernon Parish School Bd., 125 So. 2d 259 (La. Ct. App. 1960) (complete discretion in initial hiring).
3. *See* note 3, p. 318.
4. *E.g.*, School Dist. No. 6 v. Barber, 85 Ariz. 95, 332 P.2d 496 (1958); Mo. ANN. STAT. § 168.221 (1) (Supp. Nov. 1967).
5. *See, e.g.*, Johnson v. Board of Educ., 101 Ariz. 268, 419 P.2d 52 (1966); Act of April 13, 1967, ch. 382, § 1, [1967] Kan. Laws 717. *But see* N.Y. EDUC. LAW § 3012.1 (McKinney 1953).
6. Kuehn v. School Dist. No. 70, 221 Minn. 443, 22 N.W.2d 220 (1946); Town of North Kingstown v. Robinson, 207 A.2d 389 (R.I. 1965). *But see* Act of July 1, 1967, ch. 890, § 1, [1967] Minn. Laws 1886 (written statement of statutory cause required but no right to hearing or appeal).
7. *Cf.* Lombardo v. Board of Higher Educ., 18 App. Div. 2d 444, 240 N.Y.S.2d 119, *aff'd mem.*, 13 N.Y.2d 1097, 196 N.E.2d 266, 246 N.Y.S.2d 631 (1963). *But cf.* PA. STAT. ANN. tit. 24, § 11–1108 (1962).
8. *E.g.*, N.Y. EDUC. LAW § 3012.2 (McKinney 1953).
9. *E.g.*, La Shells v. Hench, 98 Cal. App. 6, 276 P. 377 (1929).
10. Eulalie M. Sanders, 72 N.Y. Dep't R. 39 (Educ. Dep't 1951).
11. *See, e.g.*, N.Y. EDUC. LAW § 3012.2 (McKinney 1953) (60 days notice); ILL. REV. STAT. ch. 122, § 24–11 (1967) (written notice containing specific reason required).
12. *See* Donahoo v. Board of Educ., 413 Ill. 422, 109 N.E.2d 787 (1952). *Compare* School Dist. No. 6 v. Barber, 85 Ariz. 95, 332 P.2d 496 (1958), *with* Alexander R. Geruso, 71 N.Y. Dep't R. 158 (Educ. Dep't 1950). *But cf.* Fallon v. Board of Higher Educ., 14 Misc. 2d 9, 178 N.Y.S.2d 459 (Sup.

Although the typical probationary system follows this pattern, wide variations are common. In New York, for example, the tenure law abrogates all
contract rights for the probationary teacher and provides for dismissal at any
time by a majority of the board of education upon recommendation of the
superintendent of schools. No hearing or statement of charges is required.[1]
At the opposite end of the spectrum is Washington, in which there is no probationary period at all.[2] In California a probationary teacher dismissed during
the term is entitled to the same protection, both substantive and procedural, as
the tenured teacher;[3] if he is not rehired at the end of the year he still has the
right to a hearing before the board of education and a statement of reasons,
which must be based on a cause related to the welfare of the schools and their
pupils, but the board's determination of such cause is deemed conclusive.[4]

There are valid reasons for treating the probationary teacher differently from
the permanent teacher. The period of probation allows the board to evaluate the
new teacher on the basis of actual performance rather than past records or
educational experience alone. It also enables the board gradually to increase the
quality of its teaching staff by developing higher standards of competence for
new teachers without jeopardizing the job security of teachers hired at earlier
times. A probationary period also enables the board to attempt to assemble
a compatible faculty even though differences in personality are impermissible
reasons for dismissal once tenure is achieved. Finally, placing all teachers on
immediate tenure and then weeding out the unsatisfactory ones through complicated tenure procedures would place a large administrative burden on the schools.

Despite the advantages of probation, there is little reason to give the board of
education completely unbridled discretion. The younger teacher may have fresh
ideas and an aggressive outlook which can be frustrated by a hostile board
absent some protection for the teacher. Even if the ideas are wrong and the
aggressiveness objectionable, the interest of the probationary teacher and the
community in academic freedom[5] requires that some safeguards against arbitrary
board action be provided.[6] One solution would be for the probationary teacher
to have guarantees similar to those granted the tenured teacher, but with different

Ct. 1958), *aff'd per curiam*, 9 App. Div. 2d 766, 192 N.Y.S.2d 239 (1959) (failure of one administrator
to give notice is not equivalent of requisite affirmative action by separate board).

13. *See* Wilson v. Flint Bd. of Educ., 361 Mich. 691, 106 N.W.2d 136 (1960) (school board, under
statute providing for two year probationary period with discretionary third year, may not establish
mandatory three year period). *Contra*, Independent School Dist. v. Samuelson, 222 Iowa 1063, 270
N.W. 434 (1936) (contractual waiver of statutory tenure rights upheld).

1. N.Y. Educ. Law § 3012.1 (McKinney 1953); *see* Pinto v. Wynstra, 22 App. Div. 2d 914,
255 N.Y.S.2d 536 (1964).
2. Wash. Rev. Code § 28.67.070 (Cum. Supp. 1959).
3. Cal. Educ. Code § 13442 (West 1960).
4. Raney v. Board of Trustees, 239 Cal. App. 2d 256, 48 Cal. Rptr. 555 (1966); Cal. Educ.
Code § 13443 (West Supp. 1967).
5. *See* American Ass'n of Univ. Professors & Ass'n of American Colleges, *1940 Statement of
Principles on Academic Freedom and Tenure*, in Academic Freedom and Tenure 33, 38 (L. Joughlin
ed. 1967).
6. *Cf.* Henkel, *The Right of Teachers Employed in the Colorado Public School System to Notice and
Hearing Before Dismissal*, 31 Dicta 341, 341–42 (1954).

although definable standards governing dismissal. A board wishing to maintain or create standards of excellence could then set its level of required competency as high as it wished during the probationary period.[1] In the alternative, the burden of proof of competence could be shifted to the new teacher for the period of probation, should the board wish to dismiss him. In either case, all the other protections of the tenure system should be given the probationary teacher. Although the new teacher would still be more vulnerable than his tenured associate and the board's ability to mold a desirable homogeneity would be curtailed, the danger of arbitrary action by the board would be substantially reduced. Any added administrative burden which would be incurred is justified by community interests in encouraging independence and originality among young teachers.

(II) TRANSFERS. Under many statutory tenure systems teachers are insulated from sanctions less direct than dismissal or failure to grant tenure. There are, for example, certain limitations on transfers. A teacher often acquires tenure status within a more or less broadly defined category, usually that of elementary or secondary school teacher,[2] or even, in some jurisdictions, high school teacher in a particular subject.[3] The teacher will be immune from transfer from one such tenure "area" to another without his consent,[4] but if he voluntarily assumes a position in a different tenure area he must go through a new period of probation.[5] Within any tenure area, the board has discretion to transfer teachers, even from one school to another within its jurisdiction, so long as this is not done in bad faith.[6] Although there may be a statutory right to a hearing whenever a teacher objects to a transfer,[7] such a provision is rare. The teacher may not, however, be assigned to unreasonable or dangerous positions, or to inaccessible schools,[8] and then be dismissed for insubordination upon refusal to comply with such an order. Nor, it would appear, can a teacher be transferred to some nonteaching position in an effort to induce a resignation.[9] Thus, even where the board has the authority to rotate teachers at its discretion, unreasonable transfers are subject to limited judicial review.[10]

1. *Cf.* State *ex rel.* Schroeder v. Board of School Directors, 225 Wis. 444, 448–49, 274 N.W. 301, 303 (1937).

2. *See* Frederick E. Trani, 1 N.Y. Educ. Dep't R. 184 (1958). *But see In re* Santee, 397 Pa. 601, 156 A.2d 830 (1959).

3. State *ex rel.* Ging v. Board of Educ., 213 Minn. 550, 7 N.W.2d 544 (1942).

4. *See* Opinion No. 41, Counsel Educ. Dep't, 1 N.Y. Educ Dep't R. 740 (1951). *But cf.* Teacher Employment, Dismissal, and Tenure Act of 1967, ch. 435, § 1, [1967] Colo. Sess. Laws 980 (to be codified in COLO. REV. STAT. ANN. § 123–18–14(1)).

5. *See* Opinion No. 41, Counsel Educ. Dep't, 1 N.Y. Educ. Dep't R. 740 (1951).

6. *See* Selma Lefkowitch, 1 N.Y. Educ. Dep't R. 546 (1960), *aff'd*, 29 Misc. 2d 14, 220 N.Y.S. 2d 917 (Sup. Ct. 1961); ALA. CODE tit. 52, § 355 (1958).

7. *See* ALA. CODE tit. 52, §§ 356–57 (1958).

8. Dutart v. Woodward, 99 Cal. App. 736, 279 P. 493 (1929); State v. Yoakum, 201 Tenn. 180, 297 S.W.2d 635 (1956).

9. *See* Dutart v. Woodward, 99 Cal. App. 736, 740, 279 P. 493, 494–95 (1929) (dictum). *But cf.* Van Heusen v. Board of Educ., 26 App. Div. 2d 721, 271 N.Y.S.2d 898 (1966) (assignment to full-time study-hall duty sustained).

10. *See* Dutart v. Woodward, 99 Cal. App. 736, 279 P. 493 (1929).

(III) SALARY. Although the board has great discretion in setting salaries, there are some statutory restraints. Minimum schedules are often prescribed.[1] Some jurisdictions prohibit demotions or reductions in salary unless a hearing is granted;[2] in others reductions may be made only if salaries generally, or those of a specified percentage of teachers, are reduced.[3] An alternate approach is to allow the board discretion in fixing the salaries of tenured teachers so long as salary schedules are adopted prior to the start of the school year, differentials based on years of training and experience are uniform and subject to reasonable classification, and the schedule is not arbitrary, unreasonable, or discriminatory.[4] Thus reductions may ordinarily be made, but cannot be used as a means of reprisal against any one teacher. However, the board can condition salary increases on such factors as satisfactory performance[5] or continued professional training.[6]

(IV) FAILURE TO PROMOTE. Just as in the granting of tenure, the board is vested with discretion in giving promotions. Since promotions are based on many factors, such as increased professional stature and capacity, which the courts may not be qualified to evaluate and which in any case will be difficult of proof, judicial review of this phase of board discretion seems practically foreclosed, even where improper motives are alleged.[7]

(C) DISMISSAL FOR CAUSE. The heart of the tenure system is the requirement of specified cause for dismissal. There are two general categories of reasons justifying dismissal. The first, and less important, includes reasons unrelated to the teacher. When enrollment declines or a specific teaching post is abolished and the number of teachers must be reduced, tenured teachers may be dismissed, often without the benefit of a hearing. However, provision is usually made for dismissal on the basis of seniority, and preferred reemployment is guaranteed for a stated period of time.[8] It would be preferable to leave the board with as little discretion as possible in this area, since if the board wishes to consider factors personal to the teacher, it ought to be remitted to the stricter procedures ordinarily used where dismissal is for other than administrative reasons.[9] If the

1. *E.g.*, N.Y. EDUC. LAW §§ 3103, 3105 (McKinney 1953), *as amended*, (McKinney Supp. 1967).
2. *E.g.*, PA. STAT. ANN. tit. 24, § 11–1151 (Supp. 1966).
3. *E.g.*, Teacher Employment, Dismissal, and Tenure Act of 1967, ch. 435, § 1, [1967] Colo. Sess. Laws 978 (to be codified in COLO. REV. STAT. ANN. § 123–18–5(4)).
4. Rible v. Hughes, 24 Cal. 2d 437, 150 P.2d 455 (1944).
5. Heinlein v. Anaheim Union High School Dist., 96 Cal. App. 2d 19, 214 P.2d 536 (1950).
6. Rible v. Hughes, 24 Cal. 2d 437, 150 P.2d 455 (1944).
7. *Cf.* Lombardo v. Board of Higher Educ., 18 App. Div. 2d 444, 240 N.Y.S.2d 119, *aff'd mem.*, 13 N.Y.2d 1097, 196 N.E.2d 266, 246 N.Y.S.2d 631 (1963).
8. *E.g.*, CAL. EDUC. CODE §§ 13447–48 (West 1960). *But see* State *ex rel.* Ging v. Board of Educ., 213 Minn. 550, 7 N.W.2d 544 (1942) (board has discretion on the order of dismissal within tenure group).
9. *Cf.* N.J. REV. STAT. § 18:13–19 (Supp. 1964). In a situation in which some teachers must be dismissed, it would be reasonable that the board could retain only the most competent members of its teaching staff, even where those dismissed are not incompetent in the statutory sense. *See* PA. STAT. ANN. tit. 24, § 11–1125 (1962), *as amended*, (Supp. 1966). Although such a system would entail some decrease in the teacher's tenure security, with proper safeguards to protect academic freedom the

grounds for dismissal are strictly circumscribed by statute, there will ordinarily be no need for an initial hearing; the only question is whether the statutory grounds for reduction of the staff have been met and the statutory standards of preference have been applied.[1]

The more significant category of reasons for dismissal of tenured teachers relates to the teacher's personal conduct or ability. A tenured teacher serves "during good behavior and efficient and competent service,"[2] until some specified age is reached, at which time he may be retired or continued without tenure.[3] The tenure statute commonly lists those causes which justify dismissal. The most common are incompetency, immorality, insubordination, physical or mental unfitness, and neglect of duty.[4] Other reasons may be cruelty,[5] drunkenness,[6] conduct unbecoming a teacher,[7] conviction of a felony or a crime involving moral turpitude,[8] or failure to give evidence of professional growth.[9] In addition many states have laws banning teachers who are members of the Communist Party, advocate Communism, or refuse to sign loyalty oaths.[10] Finally, there is usually some broad discretionary ground, such as "other sufficient cause," or "whenever . . . the interests of the schools require it."[11] The state law may also distinguish between cause necessary for dismissal during the term and at the end of the year.[12]

Standing alone, the specification of causes provides some protection from arbitrary dismissal by defining a legal standard which is subject to review by the courts. An additional safeguard is provided in some states, in the form of a

---

benefit to the schools would outweigh such a disadvantage. Nevertheless, since under such a system every teacher would have to be rated competitively, *id.* § 11–1123, administrative difficulties make it too unwieldy to be of great practical importance.

1. An exceptional situation has been presented by consolidation of schools in the process of integration in the South, the result of which has been the dismissal of and the failure to reemploy Negro teachers. A system of dismissals strictly according to seniority would eliminate the discrimination but would not be entirely satisfactory because the disparity in quality between the white and Negro schools has frequently resulted in the setting of lower qualifications for teachers in the Negro schools than for those in the white schools. A strictly mechanical system would result in the retention of many poorly qualified teachers. In such a special type of situation some form of comparative evaluation with satisfactory safeguards becomes essential. *Cf.* Franklin v. County School Bd., 242 F. Supp. 371 (W.D. Va. 1965), *rev'd on other grounds*, 360 F.2d 325 (4th Cir. 1966).
2. N.Y. EDUC. LAW § 3012.2 (McKinney 1953).
3. *E.g.*, CAL. EDUC. CODE § 13325 (West 1960). The marriage of a female teacher may also be a cause for dismissal. Greco v. Roper, 145 Ohio St. 243, 61 N.E.2d 307 (1945); *accord*, Act of April 20, 1967, ch. 388, § 1, [1967] Kan. Laws 728. *Contra*. State *ex rel.* Schmidtkunz v. Webb, 230 Wis. 390, 284 N.W. 6 (1939). Since the rationale for such action seems to be the disruption caused by pregnancy, a less drastic remedy, such as mandatory leave of absence during and immediately following such pregnancy, would be a more satisfactory solution. *Cf.* State *ex rel.* Sepulvado v. Rapides Parish School Bd., 236 La. 482, 108 So. 2d 96 (1959). *But cf.* Arlington Indep. School Dist. v. Weekley, 313 S.W.2d 929 (Tex. Civ. App. 1958) (mandatory resignation for pregnancy).
4. *See, e.g.*, CAL. EDUC. CODE § 13403 (West 1960).
5. ILL. REV. STAT. ch. 122, § 10–22.4 (1965).
6. FLA. STAT. ANN. § 231.36(3) (Supp. 1966).
7. N.Y. EDUC. LAW § 3012.2 (McKinney 1953).
8. CAL. EDUC. CODE § 13403(h) (West 1960).
9. NEB. REV. STAT. § 79–1260(6) (1966).
10. *E.g.*, CAL. EDUC. CODE §§ 13403(i)–(k) (West 1960).
11. ILL. REV. STAT. ch. 122, § 10–22.4 (1965).
12. *E.g.*, FLA. STAT. ANN. §§ 231.36(1), (3) (Supp. 1966).

provision requiring notice of and an opportunity to correct remediable faults.[1] Such a procedure—along with some form of mandatory informal conference before the formal preferring of charges, which could help to reconcile imagined differences before the two sides polarize[2]—is certainly desirable. Unfortunately, despite the limitations placed on the board by the tenure laws, the statutes often are broadly construed,[3] and school boards are thus allowed to exercise rather extensive and often unnecessary control over teachers' activities both within and without the classroom.[4]

(i) ACTIVITIES OUTSIDE THE CLASSROOM. Several considerations justify the exercise of some administrative control over teachers' extra-curricular activities. Because the teacher is expected to be a model to his pupils and may have a great influence on their character development,[5] some "immoral" activities should perhaps be forbidden. In addition, certain of the teacher's outside activities may reduce his teaching effectiveness by reducing his available time or tending to involve the schools in outside controversies. On the other hand, the teacher has a valid interest in the assertion of his individuality; the tenure laws should not be used to enforce conformity with community standards of conduct absent some compelling justification related to teaching efficiency or the welfare of the students. Thus, although the teacher's extracurricular conduct may lessen the confidence of the general community in his ability and character, limitations on such conduct are justifiable only when there is likely to be some impact on students; the parents clearly have a valid interest in the proper education of their children, but the very purpose of tenure is to protect the teacher from the pressures of popular prejudice.[6] The resulting independence granted teachers is calculated both to increase the quality of education and to promote participation by an intellectually trained group in community affairs.

At the present time, several quite different types of outside conduct may place the teacher's career in jeopardy. The ubiquitous restrictions on political activities and beliefs and on the right of free speech raise constitutional problems, which are discussed elsewhere. Another difficult area is that of dismissals for "immorality" or unprofessional conduct. Circumstances which have been held to justify dismissal have included arrest for being drunk and disorderly;[7]

1. *E.g.*, CAL. EDUC. CODE § 13407 (West Supp. 1967); *see* Hauswald v. Board of Educ., 20 Ill. App. 2d 49, 155 N.E.2d 319 (1958).
2. *See* Joughin (note 4, p. 310), at 578–80.
3. *See, e.g.*, Beilan v. Board of Pub. Educ., 357 U.S. 399 (1958), *aff'g* 386 Pa. 82, 125 A.2d 327 (1956).
4. *But cf.* N.Y. EDUC. LAW § 6206.10(d) (McKinney Supp. 1967) (grounds for dismissal shall not be interpreted to restrict academic freedom).
5. *Cf., e.g.*, CAL. EDUC. CODE § 7851 (West Supp. 1967) (teacher responsible for impressing on pupils morality, truth, justice, patriotism, citizenship, kindness to domestic pets, manners and morals of free government, and avoidance of idleness, profanity, and falsehood).
6. Unfortunately, where a teacher's personal conduct is sufficiently "scandalous," the disapproval of the parents might possibly be transmitted to the child and teaching effectiveness could thereby be indirectly impaired. No institutional safeguard will protect the teacher against this form of community pressure.
7. Williams v. School Dist. No. 40, 4 Ariz. App. 5, 417 P.2d 376 (1966).

continual drunkenness in public, resulting in a public scandal;[1] acting as a waitress and occasional bartender in a beer garden owned by the teacher's husband and helping to operate a pinball machine on the premises;[2] drinking within the boundary of the schoolhouse;[3] a male teacher's entering a school building with some young woman under rather suspicious circumstances;[4] and indictment for adultery, even though the charges were later dropped.[5]

Because of the great influence which the schools may have on the child, the board of education does bear a responsibility for the development of character in its pupils. The role of the teacher as exemplar makes the question of his morality quite relevant. Unfortunately, where "immorality" is a cause for dismissal, the school boards often apply the concept too broadly: teachers may be dismissed for holding or practicing unpopular views without any finding of actual or probable impairment of education, and dismissal may result from conduct which is not generally condemned in practice by the culture and which, in terms of the teacher's effect on his pupils, is relatively harmless. The teacher's right and community interests could be better protected by regulating conduct more directly related to the students. Thus actual or probable misuse of the academic position to foster "immoral" views or to "corrupt" the child may well justify dismissal, but simply holding the same views privately, no matter how unpopular they may be, should not. In all cases the probable detrimental effects on the pupil should be determinative.

Where the charge against the teacher is the commission of a crime rather than the vague accusation of "immoral conduct," the teacher's liberty is in theory no longer being restrained, for the law already forbids what the teacher claims freedom to do. And the board's power to define permissible conduct is suitably limited, since a social judgment from a valid source—the legislature—has already been obtained. But a per se rule of dismissal is still inappropriate; it should be necessary to decide whether the antisocial conduct with which the teacher is charged is of sufficient gravity to indicate a personality unfit to associate with students. The commission of a crime involving little or no moral turpitude may not indicate a serious or dangerous flaw in the character of the teacher. Some acts of civil disobedience, for example, may not have a significant impact upon teaching efficiency or the standing of the teacher as an example of good citzenship; in many instances the teacher may be engaging in the very conduct which academic freedom is designed to foster. On the other hand, young pupils may not be sufficiently sophisticated to comprehend the difference between social protest and criminal conduct. The nature of the offense as well as the age level of the pupils must be taken into account in each case. In addition,

1. Scott v. Board of Educ., 20 Ill. App. 2d 292, 156 N.E.2d 1 (1959).
2. Horosko v. Mount Pleasant Twp. School Dist., 335 Pa. 369, 6 A.2d 866, *cert. denied*, 308 U.S. 553 (1939) (the "cause" here was alternatively incompetence or immorality). *But see* Colorado School of Mines v. Neighbors, 119 Colo. 399, 203 P.2d 904 (1949).
3. Tracy v. School Dist. No. 22, 70 Wyo. 1, 243 P.2d 932 (1952).
4. Gover v. Stovall, 237 Ky. 172, 35 S.W.2d 24 (1931).
5. Freeman v. Inhabitants of Bourne, 170 Mass. 289, 49 N.E. 435 (1898) (superintendent).

some teachers, because of the type of contact they have with the students, will not have a significant enough influence on their pupils to require judging their conduct harshly. And at some point, perhaps at the high school or university level, the private activities of the teacher should become almost wholly irrelevant, as long as they do not impinge on classroom behavior or directly affect the students.[1] Dismissal under tenure laws should be essentially for unfitness rather than as a punishment in addition to that imposed by the criminal law.[2]

(II) CLASSROOM ACTIVITIES. The clearest justification for dismissal of any teacher is incompetence. Problems arise, however, when judgments of teaching ability are mixed in with conflicts over what should be taught and how the material should effectively be conveyed. It is the function of the schools to help create educated citizens capable of independent and penetrating thought. But it must also be recognized that, at least up to a certain stage, the student is not yet fit to cope with the "free marketplace of ideas." The striking of a satisfactory balance between curriculum control and faculty autonomy and, at times, between the academic freedom of the teacher and the needs of the student, is in the first instance the task of the school board.

In this area the differences between higher and lower education become the most striking. Where the university teacher is effective and successful in covering the desired curriculum, no further inquiry should be permitted. Even control over what minimum curriculum is to be covered may be limited, especially where the course offered is one quite personal to the teacher. A decision about what is to be taught is usually made simultaneously with that of who is to teach it. At the lower levels more control can be justified. If a state has a right to require compulsory education, it has a corresponding right and duty to set minimum standards to be attained by students. The superintendent and the board should prescribe basic course outlines and set the minimum standards in order to achieve both completeness and coherence in an educational process which of necessity exposes students to a succession of different teachers. But since society's interests will only be harmed by additional instruction to the extent that it is in some sense "pernicious," less control is justifiable over maximum than over minimum curriculum content.

A related problem arises when the control over curriculum is exercised indirectly through supervision of teaching methods. A requirement that lesson plans be filed in advance evidences board concern in this area.[3] A directive

1. *See generally* Emerson & Haber, *Academic Freedom of the Faculty Member as a Citizen*, 28 LAW & CONTEMP. PROB. 525, 569–72 (1963).
2. Where the teacher has been indicted for a crime sufficiently heinous to justify dismissal under the tenure laws, problems of proof arise. Even acquittal in the prior criminal action has been held not to bar dismissal after a hearing by the board. Jenkyns v. Board of Educ., 294 F.2d 260 (D.C. Cir. 1961) (per curiam). This is a satisfactory result, since guilt must be proved beyond a reasonable doubt in a criminal proceeding but only by a preponderance of the evidence in civil and, presumably, tenure actions. There is no problem of moral fiat where the charge is based upon a defined crime, and proper procedure precludes abuse of board discretion.
3. *Cf.* James R. Worley, 1 N.Y. Educ. Dep't R. 475 (1960), *aff'd*, 12 App. Div. 2d 411, 212 N.Y.S.2d 236 (1961).

requiring the plans to be prepared is easily justified by the need for continuity when substitute teachers are called upon to take over classes. But a requirement that a teacher submit his plans in advance to the principal can serve as a check upon teaching content and method and facilitate administrative interference with the teacher's classroom autonomy. The board may also wish to control the teacher's grading policy or approach to his students.[1] Perhaps the most direct conflict arises when the teacher departs from the required or approved syllabus, contending that the teaching materials with which he is presented are inappropriate and unsuccessful in arousing any interest in his pupils.[2] The quality of education is the concern both of the classroom teacher and of the administration. While the establishing of standards is properly the function of the school board, teaching method, if effective, seems peculiarly within the personal province of the teacher. On the other hand, the distinction between teaching substance and method will at times be illusory and the choice of a "method" of teaching will often be a question of educational policy.[3] The teacher's conduct here, if it must be overruled by the board, should not in any but the most extreme cases be a ground for dismissal. Less extreme sanctions would be more appropriate. This is also the type of situation in which procedural channels should be open for reconciliation rather than polarization and discipline.[4]

Faced with a conflict of this nature, it should be open to the teacher to exonerate himself by demonstrating the effectiveness of his teaching methods. Such a showing could be made in a number of ways. Direct testimony of students and fellow faculty members might be introduced. In some cases, however, the pupils may not be competent to give satisfactory testimony about the ability of the teacher; even occasional faculty visits to the classroom may present a distorted picture. But it is sometimes possible to compare the achievement of pupils under one teacher with those under others—and thereby to evaluate the comparative effectiveness of the teacher and his teaching methods—on the basis of both objective tests during or at the close of the year and later performance in higher grades or higher level courses.[5] It may require some time to accumulate such objective data, but in the absence of a demonstrated inability to handle students it does not seem unfair to students or administration to give the teacher an opportunity to prove his ability.

1. *Cf.* Raney v. Board of Trustees, 239 Cal. App. 2d 256, 48 Cal. Rptr. 555 (1966).

2. Such a confrontation was dramatically presented recently in Boston, when Jonathan Kozol was dismissed after teaching an anti-establishment poem by Langston Hughes to fourth-grade pupils in a ghetto school. *See* J. KOZOL, DEATH AT AN EARLY AGE chs. 18, 19 (1967). *See also* Parker v. Board of Educ., 348 F.2d 464 (4th Cir. 1965), *cert. denied*, 382 (U.S. 1030 (1966) (nontenured teacher dismissed for teaching from proscribed book); State *ex rel.* Wasilewski v. Board of School Directors, 14 Wis. 2d 243, 111 N.W.2d 198 (1961), *appeal dismissed*, 370 U.S. 720 (1962) (dismissal of tenured teacher for flagrant discussion of sexual matters in 12th grade speech class).

3. Although they may be viewed as choices of teaching method, such decisions as whether to teach the "new" math or the "old," whether or not the student will learn by rote, and what textbooks will be employed are in fact matters of policy properly within the discretion of the board.

4. *See* Joughin (note 4, p. 310), at 578–80.

5. *See* Isabel M.S. Whittier, 64 N.Y. Dep't R. 264 (Educ. Dep't 1942).

2. OTHER TENURE SYSTEMS

Not all states have statutory tenure systems, nor do the statutes that exist ordinarily cover state colleges and universities; private institutions are never included under the tenure laws. Nevertheless, the benefits of tenure systems are sometimes provided by private contract. In addition, in some areas contractual modifications of the tenure laws have been attempted, although the asserted inability of the parties to limit the statutory discretion of the board sometimes causes difficulties.

(A) CONTRACTUAL RIGHTS. Absent any tenure system, the teacher's employment rights are limited to those embodied in his contract with the institution. The teacher has no right to renewal at the end of the contract period. The discretion vested in the board of education or trustees is thus practically unlimited. However, during the term of the contract the teacher may be dismissed only for sufficient justification, analogous to statutory cause,[1] unless the contract provides for termination upon stated notice.[2] Because of the traditional equity rule against specific performance of employment contracts,[3] the aggrieved teacher can obtain legal relief only through an action for damages, even if his contract is with a public institution.[4] A damage action, however, has some severe disadvantages for the teacher. He remains out of his job even if he prevails in the action. In addition, if he is in need of work and procures another position, he may receive only nominal damages because of application of the mitigation principle.[5] Thus, the untenured teacher is left with little recourse, even if he feels explicit contract terms have been violated.

(B) TENURE IN THE ABSENCE OF A STATUTE. Where there is no tenure statute applicable, the governing board might agree to adopt a tenure system by regulation or by-law, and such regulations may be incorporated into the contract of employment.[6] Contractual tenure systems are in force in a wide variety of public, private, and sectarian institutions, at the elementary, secondary, and college levels. Under all such contractual schemes, a primary object is the promotion of academic freedom through employment security; however, somewhat different considerations will apply in educational institutions at different academic levels.

Most elementary and secondary public schools are included under tenure laws;[7] in those which remain, contractual tenure arrangements do not appear to

1. *See* Millar v. Joint School Dist., 2 Wis. 2d 303, 86 N.W.2d 455 (1957).
2. *Cf.* Independent School Dist. v. Samuelson, 222 Iowa 1063, 270 N.W. 434 (1936).
3. *See, e.g.,* Greene v. Howard Univ., 271 F. Supp. 609, 615 (D.D.C. 1967) (dictum).
4. *Cf.* Independent Dist. No. 68 v. Deibert, 60 S.D. 424, 244 N.W. 656 (1932).
5. *Cf.* Coble v. School Dist., 178 Pa. Super. 301, 116 A.2d 113 (1955). In the absence of a statute enabling the school board to be sued, the teacher may also find his action for damages barred by the principle of sovereign immunity. *Cf.* Note, *The Sovereign Immunity of the States: The Doctrine and Some of Its Recent Developments,* 40 MINN. L. REV. 234, 257–59 (1956).
6. *See* State *ex rel.* Keeney v. Ayers, 108 Mont. 547, 92 P.2d 306 (1939).
7. *See* note 5, p. 307.

be common. Where tenure regulations are promulgated, however, judicial enforcement may be denied on the theory that the rules unlawfully limit the statutory power of the board to dismiss arbitrarily and without cause.[1] There is, on the other hand, persuasive authority for enforcing the tenure rules and reinstating the teacher through the use of the prerogative writs,[2] despite the similarity of such a remedy to specific enforcement of a contract of employment. This would seem to be the preferable view. Teacher tenure laws have been recognized as benefiting the whole school system, not just the individual teacher,[3] and contractual tenure should be viewed in a similar light; the enactment of a tenure system by regulation would seem to be a valid exercise of the board's discretion to provide a high quality of education for the student by attracting the most qualified personnel available. With such judicial enforcement possible, there should be no functional difference between statutory and contractual tenure systems in lower public schools.[4]

The most important category of nonstatutory tenure systems is found in institutions of higher education. The considerations shaping the structure of the systems do not differ materially between public and private institutions, for the major difference in this context between the two—the greater availability of judicial review in public institutions—has little practical effect on the operation of tenure systems.[5]

Because of the special needs of the university, both public and private, great discretion must be given it in decisions about the renewal of contracts during the probationary period. In deciding whether to rehire or grant tenure, the considerations involved go well beyond a judgment about general teaching competence. College professors are ordinarily specialists teaching particular courses. In seeking to mold a balanced department, the institution must take into account the particular contributions which each potential teacher will make to the department as a whole; for this purpose personal factors, such as the political or economic biases of the professor, may well be legitimate considerations. An attempt must also be made to evaluate the potential academic contributions of the new teacher, as well as his teaching ability. In addition, in many institutions the practice is to hire several probationary teachers in contemplation of filling one tenured position. A decision not to rehire thus does not involve

1. State *ex rel.* Hunsicker v. Board of Regents, 209 Wis. 83, 244 N.W. 618 (1932); *cf.* Posin v. State Bd. of Higher Educ., 86 N.W.2d 31 (N.D. 1957) (alternative holding) (state college); Worzella v. Board of Regents of Educ., 77 S.D. 447, 93 N.W.2d 411 (1958) (state college), *strongly criticized in* Byse, *Academic Freedom, Tenure, and the Law: A Comment on Worzella v. Board of Regents,* 73 HARV. L. REV. 304 (1959).
2. *See* State *ex rel.* Keeney v. Ayers, 108 Mont. 547, 92 P.2d 306 (1939) (mandamus; state university); State *ex rel.* Richardson v. Board of Regents, 70 Nev. 144, 261 P.2d 515 (1953) (certiorari on theory that board's action was quasi-judicial in character; state university). *But see* Davis, *Enforcing Academic Tenure: Reflections and Suggestions,* [1961] WIS. L. REV. 200, 216–18.
3. *See* McSherry v. City of St. Paul, 202 Minn. 102, 106–08, 277 N.W. 541, 543–44 (1938).
4. There is a paucity of case law relating to tenure systems at private schools below the college level, but such systems undoubtedly exist. Most considerations applicable to lower public schools would be applicable here, with the difference that private interests are involved and a decree of specific performance unavailable.
5. *See* note 8, p. 323.

issues of "proof" of the teacher's unsuitability; it involves rather a complex comparative and evaluative process. Although dismissal during the term of the contract must entitle the probationary teacher to a full hearing,[1] to grant such a hearing to all probationary teachers who are not rehired would be both administratively too burdensome and practically useless, for the issues involved may not be suitable for adjudicatory resolution. It would be desirable, however, for the teacher to be given some statement of the reasons for failure to rehire him.[2] In order to provide at least minimal protection for the probationary teacher, he should also be entitled to a hearing when he feels his nonretention was for a reason violative of academic freedom; in such a case he would have to sustain the burden of proving such a violation.[3] Even if the tenure committee itself proves biased, such a procedure would expose to public view unacceptable reasons for failure to rehire. Non-legal sanctions, possibly including AAUP censure, could then be brought to bear on the institution.

Once a professor has tenure, his rights should be well protected. In order to achieve this goal, the tenure procedures at the university must reflect the limitations on judicial remedy, the tradition of faculty self-government, and special interests peculiar to individual institutions. They must therefore not be devised in a way which relies on forces outside the university to guarantee faculty autonomy. A tenure system creates what is in substance private grievance machinery operating under privately developed standards. Failure to comply with the procedural requirements will subject the institution to an action for damages. However, if the formal procedures are followed, a court may decline to consider even an indefensible result in a contract action,[4] unless some explicit contract term has been violated.[5] Such a restrictive attitude is not inevitable; by analogy with another type of private grievance adjustment—labor arbitration— the courts could exercise at least limited control over a contractual tenure system. But in any case, increased judicial supervision is of limited value. The academic community is generally quite autonomous; the teacher rarely seems to desire a judicial remedy in academic matters, preferring to seek aid from professional organizations or just to find other employment.[6] The tenure system should

1. American Ass'n of Univ. Professors & Ass'n of American Colleges, *1958 Statement on Procedural Standards in Faculty Dismissal Proceedings* ¶ 1, in ACADEMIC FREEDOM AND TENURE 40, 42 (L. Joughin ed. 1967) [hereinafter cited as *1958 Statement on Procedural Standards*].

2. *But see* American Ass'n of Univ. Professors, *Letter No. 13: Stating Reasons for Nonreappointment*, in ACADEMIC FREEDOM AND TENURE 136 (L. Joughin ed. 1967).

3. The AAUP recommends a similar procedure. *See* American Ass'n of Univ. Professors, *Academic Freedom and Tenure in the Quest for National Security* ¶ 11, in ACADEMIC FREEDOM AND TENURE 47, 56 (L. Joughin ed. 1967).

4. *See* Koch v. Board of Trustees, 39 Ill. App. 2d 51, 187 N.E.2d 340 (1962), *cert. denied*, 375 U.S. 989 (1964).

5. The court might also find the enactment of the tenure system to be illegal as an ultra vires action of the board of trustees under the charter. Such an argument was advanced in Cobb v. Howard Univ., 106 F.2d 860 (D.C. Cir.), *cert. denied*, 308 U.S. 611 (1939), although the court did not find it necessary to rule on it.

6. Because of this disinclination to engage in litigation, it is necessary to discount the possibility in some jurisdictions of judicial reinstatement to a post in a public university which has tenure regulations. *See* State *ex rel.* Keeney v. Ayers, 108 Mont. 547, 92 P.2d 306 (1939); State *ex rel.* Richardson

therefore be structured in a way which obviates as much as possible the need for intervention by the courts.

One possible tenure arrangement is that recommended by the American Association of University Professors.[1] Under the AAUP system dismissal proceedings would be heard by an all-faculty tenure committee. The governing board would review the committee's decision, and if it disagreed with the faculty group it would be required to remand the case to the committee, specifying its objections. Only after considering the tenure committee's second decision could the board finally overrule it.

The AAUP contemplates that in most instances the decision of the tenure committee will be final, and this assumption is probably correct. However, in those cases which involve a fundamental disagreement between the board and the faculty committee—and such cases are likely to involve difficult questions of academic freedom—the ultimate power of decision which remains in the board, coupled with the general lack of judicial control, could nullify the protections offered by the tenure system.[2]

One solution to this problem would be to adopt a procedure similar to that discussed in the context of statutory tenure systems. The hearing would be held before a mixed faculty-administration tenure committee, which in reaching its decision would be bound by any regulations previously issued by the governing board or other appropriate body. For the purposes of any particular case the board could also advance "adjudicatory" standards; such standards would be accorded a presumption of validity, and to the extent that they are not unreasonable or inconsistent with previously issued regulations or contract provisions, the committee would be bound by them. The tenure committee would thus have the function of determining the applicability of both prior regulations and the adjudicatory standards to the particular case and of evaluating the reasonableness of the relevant adjudicatory standards put forward by the board.

It would be necessary under this system to have a mixed rather than a pure faculty committee. A pure faculty committee, immune from outside pressures because of the tenure enjoyed by its members, would be unlikely to act in a manner consciously detrimental to the best interests of the school; but it might represent only faculty attitudes and fail to give due weight to relevant administrative and institutional considerations. If the board is to relinquish its final veto power, individuals who may reflect the board's viewpoint should be represented on the committee in order to prevent an overbalancing in favor of faculty interests. Such substantial, although not controlling, administrative represen-

---

v. Board of Regents, 70 Nev. 347, 269 P.2d 265 (1954) (reinstatement). *But see* Posin v. State Bd. of Higher Educ., 86 N.W.2d 31 (N.D. 1957); Worzella v. Board of Regents of Educ., 77 S.D. 447, 93 N.W. 2d 411 (1958) (no reinstatement).

    1. *1958 Statement on Procedural Standards.*
    2. *Cf.* Koch v. Board of Trustees, 39 Ill. App. 2d 51, 187 N.E.2d 340 (1962), *cert. denied*, 375 U.S. 989 (1964). *But cf.* Joughin (note 4, p. 310), at 597–98.

tation on the tenure committee, combined with the board's policy-making power through the issuance of binding regulations and adjudicatory standards, as well as the great discretion exercised during the probationary period, should sufficiently safeguard the interests of the board.

A tenure system of this nature would be capable of accommodating the special interests of public as well as private institutions. Such interests may be significant. The private sectarian institution, for example, has some legitimate interest in regulating the religious beliefs of its faculty, or at least of those faculty members engaged in religious instruction, in order to nourish a satisfactory religious atmosphere for its students. Considerations of academic freedom applicable to most institutions must therefore at least be modified in sectarian schools. Other private institutions may have strong ideas or values which they wish to promote or especially high standards they wish to maintain. Such interests could all be protected within the structural tenure framework suggested for public and private colleges, through the board's use of binding regulations and presumptively valid adjudicatory standards.

(c) ADDITIONAL LIMITATIONS UNDER STATUTORY SYSTEMS. Even where tenure systems are in effect, the parties may wish to make modifications by contract. Although it has been held that a contractual modification under which the teacher lost all the protection of the tenure law was valid,[1] such frustration of statutory guarantees should not be permitted.[2] Perhaps some distinction could be drawn between tenure laws viewed as contractual and those thought to establish a public policy; but where the legislature has seen fit to establish a tenure system, no matter how the law is characterized, patent evasions should not be permitted.[3]

At the opposite extreme is the situation in which the board attempts to give up some of its statutory discretion, binding itself to a more restrictive system by regulation or a collective bargaining agreement. It has been held that the board has no statutory power to do this.[4] Such a holding is more easily justified where there are tenure laws than in nontenure states since the legislature has created a framework in which the system is to operate by carefully defining permissible grounds for dismissal and circumscribing the extent of the board's discretion. The statute could be seen as striking a balance between the need for employment security and the danger of creating a dull, "civil service" mentality among teachers. However, it would be more satisfactory to view the tenure laws as minimal guarantees for the teacher, which may be increased by private agreement, subject to certain limitations in the public interest. Under this theory, the validity of nonstatutory limitations under the tenure laws would be judged by evaluating the need to maintain the board discretion which they seek to restrict.

1. *See* Independent School Dist. v. Samuelson, 222 Iowa 1063, 270 N.W. 434 (1936).
2. *See generally* Machlup, *In Defense of Academic Tenure*, in ACADEMIC FREEDOM AND TENURE 306, 326–27 (L. Joughin ed. 1967).
3. *Accord*, La Shells v. Hench, 98 Cal. App. 6, P. 377 (1929).
4. *See, e.g.*, Norwalk Teachers' Ass'n v. Board of Educ., 138 Conn. 269, 83 A.2d 482 (1951).

A regulation which establishes notice procedures and requires conferences with the teacher before he is transferred would be enforced because the limitation it imposes is only on arbitrary or summary action by the board.[1] Collective bargaining agreements, which have frequently been struck down in the absence of enabling legislation,[2] would be invalid if they prevented the board from dismissing for incompetency or if they restricted the board's power to hire by establishing a union shop.[3] But where the collective bargaining agreement establishes formal procedural safeguards in addition to those provided by statute or regulates working conditions while providing for the submission of disputed matters to arbitration, it should be upheld. On matters such as these, the board's full discretion in its role as an employer is not necessary for the proper exercise of its educational functions.

Developments— Academic Freedom 2

Harvard Law Review, (1968) **82**, 1121–1128

COLLECTIVE BARGAINING

Collective bargaining in education, although not new, is just beginning to come of age. Through the first decades of the century, teachers contracted with school boards individually.[4] This system gradually gave way to uniform schedules for salaries, under which all teachers in the system were rated on the basis of professional preparation and years of experience. Grouping teachers for salary decisions suggested that teachers face the school board at contract time as an organized unit, at least to facilitate discussion. Concurrently, local affiliates of the NEA multiplied, so that administrators and the school boards became accustomed to the idea of local teachers organizations. Collective bargaining was the logical next step, but in the absence of statutory authorization formidable legal barriers were thought to prevent collective negotiations in public employment.[5] At least thirteen states now have passed laws giving teachers the

1. *Accord,* AFT v. Oakland Unified School Dist., 59 Cal. Rptr. 85 (Dist. Ct. App. 1967).
2. *See, e.g.,* Norwalk Teachers' Ass'n v. Board of Educ., 138 Conn. 269, 83 A.2d 482 (1951).
3. *Cf.* Benson v. School Dist. No. 1, 136 Mont. 77, 344 P.2d 117 (1959).
4. *See* R. DOHERTY & W. OBERER, TEACHERS, SCHOOL BOARDS, and COLLECTIVE BARGAINING 8 (1967).
5. *See generally* Comment, *Public Employee Collective Bargaining Contract: The Chicago Teachers,* 33 U. CHI. L. REV. 852 (1966); Note, *Labor Relations in the Public Service,* 75 HARV. L. REV. 391 (1961).

right to bargain with school boards;[1] in view of the strong support given to collective bargaining by both the AFT and, more recently, the NEA,[2] it is likely that more states soon will follow. Among secondary school teachers, a broad movement toward accepting collective bargaining may be discerned.[3] At present more than 600,000 teachers[4] are covered by some sort of negotiated agreement;[5] about half of them have contracts sophisticated enough to contain impasse resolution procedures.[6]

Thus far little attention has been paid specifically to academic freedom in teaching contracts, probably because this area is of less concern to most teachers than the achievement of improved working conditions and higher salaries.[7] Newly established unions concentrate on these more salient issues since they still must prove their power to school boards and teachers alike. Potentially, collective bargaining agreements could expand the protection afforded to the academic freedom of teachers, and to their interest in autonomy generally, in three directions: limiting the substantive grounds on which a school board may discipline or discharge a teacher; strengthening the procedural safeguards afforded to a teacher threatened with adverse action; and establishing a grievance procedure, terminating in binding arbitration, as a means through which a teacher may seek reversal of official action taken against him. However, in each of these three areas a state statute may limit the school board's legal ability to relinquish or delegate its existing discretionary power.

1. PERMISSIBLE SCOPE OF THE CONTRACT

Most public employee bargaining statutes authorize the parties to bargain over all "conditions of employment."[8] Notwithstanding this, it is clear that more specific education statutes, such as tenure laws, may limit the ability of the parties to agree on contract provisions which depart from statutory require-

---

1. *E.g.*, CONN. GEN. STAT. ANN. §§ 10–53b to –53f (1967).
2. For an account of the NEA's gradual shift from opposition to support of collective bargaining see R. DOHERTY & W. OBERER (note 4, p. 326), at 33–38.
3. The reasons for this sudden growth include the increased competition between the NEA and the AFT, the growth and bureaucratization of school systems, rendering the relationship between teacher and administrator impersonal, and improvements in salaries and conditions which in turn have generated higher expectations. *See* Doherty, *The Impact of Teacher Organizations upon Setting School Policies*, 40 THE CLEARING HOUSE 515, 520–21 (1966).
4. *See Five Types of Negotiation Agreements*, NEGOTIATION RESEARCH DIGEST, Nov. 1967, at B–1, B–2.
5. Collective bargaining at the college level is the subject of a broad campaign now being undertaken by the AFT. *See* AMERICAN TEACHER, June, 1967, at 3, col. 2. Faced with this intrusion into its preserve, the AAUP is torn between two positions. Some members feel that collective bargaining would demean the dignity of the profession; others hold that, despite the value of maintaining an informal relationship between faculty and administration, collective bargaining is certain to come and that it should not be left to the AFT. *Compare Representation of Economic Interests*, 52 A.A.U.P. BULL. 229 (1966), *with* Bierstedt & Malchup, *Dissenting Statement to Representation of Economic Interests*, 52 A.A.U.P. BULL. 232 (1966).
6. *See Five Types of Negotiation Agreements, supra* note 6.
7. When polled for their preferences on items for negotiations, San Francisco classroom teachers gave priority to class size, discipline, salary, and clerical help. R. DOHERTY & W. OBERER, *supra* note 1, at 20.
8. *E.g.*, CONN. GEN. STAT. ANN § 10–153d (1967).

ments. For example, a contract vesting the right to hire and fire teachers in a professional association would be an illegal delegation of the school board's statutory power to make these decisions.[1] But often it may be possible for the parties to supplement the provisions of a statute; a law requiring that the board give notice before transfering a teacher need not prevent the parties from agreeing in the contract that the board also hold a conference with the teacher.[2] The basic inquiry to be made is whether a given statute reflects a legislative balancing of the interest of teachers in greater security against the interest of the public in retaining discretionary power in the school board. If a balance has been struck, the parties are not free to alter it. If the statute can be read as only establishing certain minimum rights for teachers, however, the parties should be free to provide for additional contractual obligations so long as they do not impair the functioning of the educational system. Because of the relative novelty of collective bargaining in education, these questions have been litigated infrequently.[3]

(A) SUBSTANTIVE GROUNDS FOR BOARD ACTION. The school board almost certainly cannot abnegate by contract its power to discipline or discharge a teacher for a cause specified in a statute. If the tenure laws say that teachers may be discharged for immorality, this must be read as a binding legislative judgment that the board retain discretion to remove an immoral teacher. However, the parties may be able to provide in the contract a clarifying definition of a vague statutory phrase; thus, immorality might be defined as conduct sufficiently notorious to bring the individual into public disrepute and so impair his service as a teacher.[4] Such a definition would serve as a guide to administrators in disciplinary proceedings and would alleviate the potentially inhibiting effect upon teachers of an undefined statutory term. The definition should not be voided as an impermissible limitation on the board's discretion if it is a reasonable explication of the statutory provision's underlying rationale.[5]

A clause intended to protect the academic freedom of teachers[6] presents a more complex version of this same question since it can be viewed as limiting the board's discretion to act under several statutory grounds, such as incompetency or insubordination. But a court should give effect to the clause until it comes into direct conflict with one of these statutory provisions; the possibility of conflict does not justify the prospective invalidation of the entire clause in the absence of a legislative determination that such provisions are undesirable.[7]

1. *Cf.* Benson v. School Dist. No. 1, 136 Mont. 77, 344 P.2d 117 (1959).
2. *Cf.* AFT v. Oakland Unified School Dist., 59 Cal. Rptr. 85 (Dist. Ct. App. 1967).
3. For a discussion of contractual tenure rights at the university level see pp. 322–326.
4. Florida Educ. Ass'n, Rules of the Florida Professional Teaching Practices Commission § 287–4.09(2) (Dec. 1966).
5. *Cf.* Cotter v. City of Chelsea, 329 Mass. 314, 108 N.E.2d 47 (1952).
6. Although this sort of provision is not common, an occasional example can be found: "The private and personal life of any teacher is not within the appropriate concern or attention of the board except when it impairs the teacher's effectiveness in the classroom or position." Agreement Between Hancock, Mich. Public Schools and Hancock Educ. Ass'n, in *Unusual Provisions of Agreements*, NEGOTIATION RESEARCH DIGEST, May 1967, at A–4.
7. *Cf.* Ill. Governor's Advisory Comm'n on Labor-Management Policy for Public Employees, *Final Report*, in *id.* at E–1, E–8.

Finally, the contract might create substantive limitations in an area where the board, absent any specific statutory authority or limitation, proceeds under its general grant of power to establish and maintain the schools. Normally, for example, there are no statutory limits on the board's power to dismiss untenured teachers. This legislative silence should not be read automatically as a requirement that the board's discretion be unlimited.[1] Rather, the limits created by the contract should be examined to see whether they impair the board's ability to operate its educational program efficiently. Thus, in the context of untenured teachers, the board's interest in retaining broad discretion to dismiss would appear to be greatest with regard to decisions based on incompetency, but less compelling in the area of extramural political activities.

(b) PROCEDURAL SAFEGUARDS. The parties generally should be able to provide in the contract that the board observe certain procedural safeguards, such as giving notice and holding a hearing, beyond those required by statute.[2] These provisions do not limit the board's ultimate decisionmaking power, but rather help to insure that the board will not act in an arbitrary or capricious manner. An exception must be made, however, where the legislature has enacted a comprehensive procedural system. This indicates that the legislature has mediated between the desire of teachers for job security and the public interest in not burdening the school board with procedural requirements which frustrate its ability to exercise its substantive powers.[3] At the other extreme is a statute which establishes a substantive right for teachers but provides no procedure for its enforcement.[4] Here the legislature has singled out a particular area of teacher activity as worthy of protection, an intent which presumably is fostered if specific procedures are included in the collectively bargained contract.

The inclusion in the contract of a grievance procedure which does not terminate in binding arbitration seems to present no special ground for objection. These procedures represent only an elaboration of the basic notice and hearing requirements, providing the board with an opportunity to reconsider the decision of a possibly overzealous administrator. The slightly increased administrative burden is justified by the added security and fairness afforded to teachers and by the benefits accruing to the entire system in having decisions rationally reached and publically reasoned.

(c) BINDING ARBITRATION. Most teachers presumably would prefer to process their grievances to binding arbitration rather than have the school board's final decision reviewable only in the courts. Arbitration would provide a quicker and less expensive method of review,[5] and, in view of the hospitable attitude which

1. *See generally* H. HART & A. SACKS, THE LEGAL PROCESS 1394–97 (tent. ed. 1957).
2. *Cf.* AFT v. Oakland Unified School Dist., 59 Cal. Rptr 85 (Dist. Ct. App. 1967).
3. *Cf.* City of Springfield v. Clouse, 356 Mo. 1239, 206 S.W.2d 539 (1947) (contract may not alter obligations arising from statutory civil service system).
4. *Cf.* MASS. GEN. LAWS ANN. ch. 71, § 44 (1966).
5. *Cf.* H. HART & A. SACKS (*supra* note 1), at 340–47.

the courts generally have manifested toward school board actions, the teacher's prospects for success might be greater before an arbitrator. However, relatively few teaching contracts to date have included arbitration provisions,[1] a fact which may reflect doubt concerning their legality.

The extent to which an arbitration clause is vulnerable to attack as a delegation of the board's decisionmaking power will depend on the scope of the arbitrator's jurisdiction and on the standard of review he applies. Arbitration should be permissible at least so long as it is limited to contract provisions[2] which do not repeat or define statutory language. Here arbitration is a direct substitute for a judicial process of contract construction, and, of course, the validity of the contract provisions remains for the court to decide. But the union may wish to include in the contract verbatim state laws which limit the board's power,[3] thus in effect giving the arbitrator jurisdiction over violations of the board's statutory obligations. The novelty of this scheme in public education argues against its validity, but the question may turn on the standard of review the arbitrator applies. If he proceeds under the normal arbitration standard of reasonableness or just cause,[4] the result would be a materially more extensive inquiry into the board's actions than would occur under the arbitrary or capricious standard customarily used by the courts. This reduction in the board's discretion should be objectionable only when a dispute involves a difficult question of educational policy. Here the preservation of a wide area of discretion for the board is essential if it is to fulfill effectively its statutory responsibilities, and thus an attempt to give an arbitrator this expanded power of review should fail.[5] This question should be answered on a case by case basis, however, for the area over which the board actually needs the power to act unreasonably should be held within narrow confines.

2. RIGHTS OF THE INDIVIDUAL IN GRIEVANCE ARBITRATION

When academic freedom disputes are subject to arbitration under a collectively bargained agreement, the question arises of the extent to which the individual teacher should be given control over his grievance. Most teaching contracts

1. T. STINNETT, J. KLEINMANN & M. WARE, PROFESSIONAL NEGOTIATION IN PUBLIC EDUCATION 171 (1966).
2. Local 953, State, County & Municipal Employees v. School Dist., 66 L.R.R.M. 2419 (Mich. Cir. Ct. Oct. 12, 1967); cf. Local 1226, Rhinelander City Employees v. City of Rhinelander, 35 Wis. 2d 209, 151 N.W.2d 30 (1967). Contra, Norwalk Teachers' Ass'n v. Board of Educ., 138 Conn. 269, 84 A.2d 482 (1951).
3. Teaching contracts frequently incorporate state bans on racial and religious discrimination. See also Agreement Between the School Committee of Cambridge, Mass. and the Cambridge Teachers Ass'n, Oct. 1, 1967 ("Teachers will be entitled to full right of citizenship, and no religious or political activities of any teacher, or the lack thereof, will be grounds for any discipline or discrimination with respect to the professional employment of such teacher").
4. See generally Cox, Reflections upon Labor Arbitration, 72 HARV. L. REV. 1482, 1501–02 (1959).
5. See Norwalk Teachers' Ass'n v. Board of Educ., 138 Conn. 269, 279–80, 83, A.2d 482, 487 (1951).

having arbitration clauses adopt the prevailing industrial practice[1] that the individual grievant needs the union's authorization to take a grievance to arbitration; usually he is accorded the right to process grievances up to arbitration on his own. Union control of arbitration may involve only the power to determine that the complaint will not be taken to arbitration, leaving the individual recourse against the employer in the courts. However, the Supreme Court in *Vaca v. Sipes*[2] has extended greatly the consequences of union control under federal labor law. The Court held that whenever a union given exclusive control over the grievance machinery refuses to take a grievance to arbitration, the individual grievant may not maintain a court action against the employer unless he can prove that the union's refusal constituted "arbitrary or bad-faith conduct" in violation of its duty of fair representation.[3]

The *Vaca* requirement that either subjective bad faith or gross malfeasance be proved represents a very strict standard, and strong arguments can be made that the decision unnecessarily sacrifices the individuals's interest in controlling his grievance.[4] State courts nonetheless may proceed by analogy to *Vaca* in construing education contracts, and consequently it is necessary to consider whether the reasoning of *Vaca* is persuasive when applied to grievances stemming from academic freedom controversies. The Court justified its rule by the danger that if the individual were given complete control of the grievance, or the union forced to prosecute all claims, the resulting flow of frivolous claims would undermine the union's stature as bargaining representative, and in addition make arbitration so costly that both sides would be likely to abandon it.[5] The Court saw little danger to the individual in allowing the union to balance the interests of its membership in determining in good faith which claims were meritorious enough to prosecute.

Academic freedom disputes should be treated under a less restrictive rule than *Vaca*. Since these disputes are relatively infrequent there is little danger of a flood of frivolous claims. But it is in the few cases which do arise that the danger to the individual's interest from exclusive union control is most acute. The union's membership may reflect the same ideological consensus as that which led the community, through the school board, to take repressive action against an outspoken teacher. Thus the union may refuse to press the grievance to arbitration or may process it perfunctorily. In either case under the *Vaca* standard it would be difficult to prove bad faith, and indeed the union officials may have acted in good faith if their consensus viewpoint leads them to conclude that the grievance is without substance.

Academic freedom, with its close ties to crucial first amendment rights, demands greater protection. The right to assert this highly personal interest in

---

1. *See generally*, Cox, *Rights Under a Labor Agreement*, 69 HARV. L. REV. 601, 606–13 (1956).
2. 386 U.S. 171 (1967).
3. *Id.* at 193.
4. *See* Note, *Individual Control over Personal Grievances Under Vaca v. Sipes*, 77 YALE L.J. 559 (1968).
5. Vaca v. Sipes, 386 U.S. 171, 191–92 (1967).

intellectual freedom should not be vested exclusively in a union with virtually unlimited discretion. There is little reason to allow the union to balance the interests of its membership here, because it is difficult to see what legitimate opposing interests other teachers could have in not pressing the grievance to arbitration. If the infrequent academic freedom dispute threatens to overbear the limited resources of a small union in what seems to it a frivolous cause, the teacher could be required to pay the cost of arbitration if he insists on arbitration and later loses.[1] The danger that the arbitration of tenuous academic freedom claims would lead to restrictive decisions applicable to all teachers can be overcome by allowing the union to designate some arbitrations as having no precedential value.

In order to afford academic freedom grievances special treatment, such as by giving the grievant greater control over these claims, it is necessary that a court or arbitrator be able to determine which disputes fall within this excepted category. This is most easily accomplished if the contract contains a specific academic freedom clause which resolves the problem of definition[2] and grants individuals the right to prosecute grievances falling within its terms. Even here there will be preliminary problems of proof, however. The teacher may advance frivolous grievances under an allegation that the school's true motivation was one comprehended within the academic freedom clause; or, conversely, the school may hide an issue of academic freedom under a vague charge such as insubordination. In either case the arbitrator, if given the power to do so in the contract, must determine whether the facts bring the dispute within the clause before allowing the individual grievant to invoke his jurisdiction. If the arbitrator decides this jurisdictional question in favor of the teacher, he would proceed to rule on the merits of the claim; if he decides that academic freedom is not involved, the claim would remain in the status of a grievance subject to the exclusive control of the union and be dismissed.

In the absence of a special contract provision, a court wishing to take academic freedom claims out of the union's exclusive control would have to construct its own definition. This definition should encompass those areas in which the union's ideological bias might frequently impair its ability to process grievances on their merits. It thus should cover, basically, actions by the board of education stemming from a teacher's political activities outside the classroom, or from his manner of presenting a controversial issue within.[3]

If a court can segregate out academic freedom claims from other grievances where the *Vaca* approach is less objectionable, it might proceed in either of two ways to provide special treatment for these claims. First, the court could rule, as a matter of public policy, that a contract could not prevent a teacher from taking an academic freedom grievance to arbitration if his union refused to do so.[4] This approach might have the consequence of leading the union never to

---

1. *See* note 4, p. 331, at 567.   2. *See, e.g.,* note 6, p. 328; and note 3, p. 330.
3. *See* note 3, p. 330.
4. *Cf* Donnelly v. United Fruit Co., 40 N.J. 61, 190 A.2d 825 (1963).

prosecute an academic freedom grievance since it no longer would possess any real decisionmaking power in this area. This is undesirable since without union participation, and in particular its willingness to accept some arbitrations as binding precedents, the development of a useful general body of arbitrational case law on academic freedom is impeded.

The preferable approach would be to adopt a broader definition of the union's duty of fair representation where academic freedom grievances are involved—that the union must prosecute all academic freedom disputes where it reasonably concludes that the claim is frivolous. This objective test in effect would create a presumption that the union must carry the grievance to arbitration, but recognize the virtue of retaining union participation in the basic grievance machinery. To save time and expense it seems desirable as a general practice for a court, whenever it decides that a union has breached its duty, then to go on and decide the grievance on its merits, rather than merely remanding and requiring the union to arbitrate. There still is a danger that the union would process some grievances in a perfunctory manner, feeling compelled to do so by the scope given to its fair representation duty, but disagreeing with the grievant's contentions. To insure that the teacher's grievance is presented effectively he should be allowed to intervene in the arbitration and be represented, at his expense, by his own lawyer.[1]

Rights of School Teachers to Engage in Labor Organizational Activities

Reynolds C. Seitz

Dean and Professor of Labor Law, Marquette University Law School. Formerly assistant to the superintendent of public schools in Omaha and in St. Louis; senior attorney, National Labor Relations Board, Washington, D.C.; Montgomery Ward and Co., Chicago; executive, Chicago Daily News; associate professor labor law, communications law and school law at Northwestern University. Experienced labor arbitrator. President National Organization on Legal Problems of Education during 1958 and 1959. (Discussion delivered at annual meeting of the National School Boards Association, Chicago, Illinois, April 25, 1960.)
Marquette Law Review, **44**, 36–44

There would likely be no purpose to this discussion if the objective were to present the extent to which a public school teacher and employee organization

1. *See generally* Shapiro, *Some Thoughts on Intervention Before Courts, Agencies, and Arbitrators*, 81 HARV. L. REV. 721, 770–72 (1968).

or union, could compel a School Board to recognize it and respond to its efforts at concerted activities by making agreements of the type common in the field of commercial industrial relations.

Unless there is enabling statutory legislation (and generally throughout the country there is not such legislation) there are no established procedures by which unions or organizations of teachers and school personnel can compel School Boards to recognize them and bargain collectively. This differs from the situation in private industry where state and federal laws require that the employer must bargain with the union chosen as the bargaining agent by a majority of employees in an appropriate unit.

Not only is there generally an absence of statutes compelling School Board participation in collective bargaining, there is also no solid body of court-fashioned law which would so require. Indeed, in some early cases[1] courts have refused to promote the philosophy of the right to organize and engage in collective bargaining by finding no constitutional impairment of the right to assemble in the little legislation which had gone so far as to deny to teachers who joined unions the opportunity of employment.

Why, then, go on with the discussion? The full justification can be found in the fact that many School Boards may be so prompted by sentiments of fair dealing or a public relations sense which sees valuable dividends in the form of good will and strengthened morale.

Then, too, the discussion should serve to predict the extent of the requirement to negotiate if legislation in particular states or local communities should decree a duty to bargain. The analysis has additional use as suggesting a yardstick which courts will undoubtedly use, if there should be any disposition to find a common law right for school personnel to assemble and bargain collectively.

Granting, therefore, that there is good reason for the discussion, the task presently becomes primarily that of determining to what extent School Boards may voluntarily engage in collective bargaining and bind themselves contractually through agreements with public school employee organizations and unions.

The greatest obstacle[2] to acceptance of the right of School Boards to voluntarily engage in collective bargaining, culminating in contract agreements, is the position of many public officials that the public employer is under a sovereign disability to emulate the practice in the private employment relationship. The outlook of the public bodies which follow such philosophy is based upon the doctrine that the determination of employment conditions in the public service is an inherent legislative function and that neither the executive nor legislature may delegate to any outside group, such as a labor organization, the functions entrusted to it under the basic scheme of government. As a corollary, it is contended that exclusive recognition and bargaining are plainly at odds with the

1. People ex. rel Fursman v. City of Chicago, 278 Ill. 318, 116 N.E. 158 (1917), and Seattle High School Chapter No. 200 v. Sharples, 159 Wash. 424, 293 Pac. 994 (1930).

2. Report of the Committee on Law of Government Employee Relations, 1959 Proceedings of Section of Labor Relations Law, American Bar Association, page 87.

principles which characterize the legislative civil service and merit system provisions.[1]

In spite of such prevailing attitudes and similar expressions by some courts,[2] many governmental units have gone a long way to fashion their labor relations policy along lines similar to that controlling in the commercial and industrial area. Four current case histories are analyzed in the *1959 Proceedings of the Section on Labor Law of the American Bar Association*.[3] Not all the case histories involved a record of the activity of teachers or school personnel, but the principles enunciated are controlling in the area of workers in education.

It becomes pertinent now to turn directly to an analysis of the support which courts have given to those governmental units that wish voluntarily to respond favorably to some of the efforts of public employees to engage in the concerted activities common for labor organizations. The same study will furnish a foundation for judgment as to the extent to which legislative provisions may support the endeavors of public employees to participate in concerted activities familiar in the area of industrial relations.

The springboard case which leads into this discussion is the 1951 Connecticut Supreme Court decision of *Norwalk Teachers' Ass'n. v. Board of Education of the City of Norwalk*.[4] The Court bluntly stated that in the absence of a prohibitory statute, or regulation, no good reason appears as to why public employees should not organize as labor unions.

This seems utterly sound. Indeed, it would not be surprising if future litigation was able to establish that statutes prohibiting the joining of unions were offensive to the United States Constitution First Amendment protection to freedom to assemble. Some state court holdings to the contrary do not seem persuasive. The state decisions asserting no first amendment rights, proclaim that employees overlook the fact that no one has a right to demand that he be employed in governmental service[5] and that employees ignore the principle that by voluntarily accepting employment with a governmental unit, they assume the obligations incident to such employment and implicitly agree to come under the conditions as they existed.[6] In the face of the clear first amendment right of freedom to assemble, such arguments appear no more plausible than would the contention that first amendment freedom of religion rights would give way to a pronouncement that governmental employees were not to become members of a certain recognized church.

1. The restrictive principles mitigating against development of a labor relations policy comparable to that found in private industry are spelled out in detail in Report of the Committee on State Labor Legislation, 1958 Proceedings of the Section on Labor Relation Law, American Bar Association, page 147. See also Labor Relations in Public Service, 10 Syracuse L. Rev. 183 (1959).

2. Mugford v. Mayor and City Council of Baltimore, 185 Md. 206, 44 A. 2d 745 (1945); City of Cleveland v. Division 268, Amalgamated Assoc. of Street, Electric and Motor Coach Employees of Amer., 30 Ohio Opin. 395 (1945), Nutter v. Santa Monica, 74 Cal. App. 2d 292, 168 P. 2d 741 (1946); Springfield v. Clouse, 356 Mo. 1239, 205 S.W. 2d 539 (1947); Miami Water Works, Local No. 654 v. Miami, 157 Fla. 445, 26 S. 2d 194 (1946); Wagner v. Milwaukee, 177 Wis. 410, 188 N.W. 487 (1922), and C.I.O. v. City of Dallas, 198 S.W. 2d 143 (Tex. 1946).

3. Pp. 87–113. See also Klaus, Labor Relations in Public Service, 10 Syracuse L. Rev. (1959); Labor Relations for Employees of the City of New York, 12 Ind. & Lab. Rel. Rev. 618 (1959).

4. 138 Conn. 269, 83 A. 2d 482 (1951).

5. Fursman v. City of Chicago (note 1, p. 334).   6. C.I.O. v. City of Dallas, *supra*, note 2.

The only logical justification for prohibiting public employees from joining a labor union, would seem to require a finding that labor unions generally seek to force their employee members to do something which is inconsistent with the position of the employee as a governmental worker. For instance, if it could be established that all unions advocated that government employees use the strike weapon, it might be reasonable for the legislature to forbid governmental employees to join a union. All unions do not, however, agitate for use of improper methods or attainment of unlawful goals. There appears, therefore, no valid ground on which prohibition of union membership can be based.

Of course, merely granting employees of government the privilege of joining a union will not put them on a plane of equality with industrial workers. To approach such equality the employees must have the right to be represented in collective bargaining by an organization or union. And the unit of government must have the power to bind itself through certain contractual terms which are the product of collective bargaining.

The *Norwalk Teachers* case is perhaps the best example which points the way to approval, within reasonable limits, of permitting a union, representing public employees, and a governmental unit to bargain collectively for certain meaningful goals. In *Norwalk* the fundamental limitation placed on the teacher association therein involved, was that it could only bargain for the teachers it actually represented. This is different than the attitude in the business-industrial field, where the rule is that the union selected as the representative of the majority in an appropriate unit bargains, for all employees that fall within the unit, including those who are not members of the union.

The authorities[1] seem to agree that in the absence of a specific statute, authorizing a union representing a majority of public employees in an appropriate unit to represent all in the unit, the union may only negotiate for its members. In other words, the School Board may recognize a union of public employees, but as the representative of its members only. This is made clear by the language in *Norwalk:*

It would seem to make no difference theoretically whether the negotiations are with a committee of the whole association or with individuals or small related groups, so long as any agreement made with the committee is confined to members of the Association.[2]

Other reasonable limitations placed upon collective bargaining can best be viewed from the positive approach of noting what kind of collectively bargained contract terms have been approved, and the reasons stated for the approval. In the reasoning, distinctions are made which spell out limitations. The logic of the decisions in this area strike most directly at the philosophy shared by some, that bargaining and agreement constitute a usurpation of the legislative function and, therefore, cannot be sanctioned.

In *Norwalk*, dealing specifically, with collective bargaining with a teachers'

1. Ryne, Labor Unions and Municipal Employee Law, pp. 134–35 (1946), and Union Activity in Public Employment, 55 Colum. L. Rev. 343 (1955).
2. *See* note 4, p. 335, at 486.

association,[1] the Court makes clear that there can be negotiations over salaries. The judges qualify by pronouncing that the parties are restrained as to the outer limits by any statutes which might place ultimate budget control in some other official governmental body. Obviously an effective check would be created by any legislation putting a brake on total revenue which could be collected for school purposes.

The *Norwalk* decision further approved negotiating on such matters of concern to teachers as employment, working conditions and grievance procedures. But again the admonition is clear that a School Board may not sign a contract which contains a provision contrary to law. As a matter of fact, this is not a principle unique to labor relations law as it applies to governmental employees. Even in the commercial field, collective bargaining does not carry with it the implication that existing statutes may be nullified or abridged.

The Arizona Supreme Court makes this philosophy quite clear in its statement:

If a civil service scheme provides for the regulation of matters normally contained in a collective bargaining agreement the conflicting terms of both could not exist concurrently. The inconsistency would be resolved in favor of the statute.[2]

A matter which would surely be of interest to any union bargaining for its constituents, would be provisions concerning tenure. If statutory law were silent on tenure, a School Board might very well permit bargaining for contractual tenure. If a tenure law existed it would probably foreclose negotiations. The usual tenure legislation contains provisions for a probationary period, prohibition against discharge after permanent status attaches, except for stated cause and a procedure for dismissing a teacher—including notice of charges, investigation, trial and decision by the School Board. The usual specific tenure legislation is such that it would appear certain to leave little room for collective bargaining.

Frequently laws on retirement and pension legislation are rather detailed. Most often the field has undoubtedly been preempted as against collective bargaining.

Since legislation is not too common in all areas of working conditions, a Board of Education might very well agree to bargain over certain matters which it might eventually permit to be incorporated into a contract. For example, the parties could agree on responsibilities for supervision at extra curricular events, such as student dances and athletic events. A great many other matters bearing upon working conditions could become the subject of discussion and solutions might eventually appear in contract form.

In the commercial field of labor relations, negotiating parties have often

1. Some efforts have been made to forbid bargaining with a union affiliated with a national or international labor organization and permit it with an unaffiliated teacher organization. The justification for such a distinction is said to lie in the belief that a national and international union is more apt to induce work stoppage. For reasons noted hereafter this does not seem to be too sound a theory.
2. Local 266, International Brotherhood of Electrical Workers, AFL v. Salt River Project Agricultural Improvement and Power District, 78 Ariz. 30, 275 P. 2d 393, 397 (1954).

manifested an awareness of the fact that provisions for the arbitration of controversies arising under contracts, are the most peaceful and efficient way of settling disputes which have arisen under contracts. Certainly such provisions provide a less cumbersome way of settlement than a lawsuit. The standard contract providing for arbitration, contains clauses spelling out the grievance procedure which is to be followed prior to going to arbitration. The courts have given considerable attention to the question of whether public employees can include an arbitration clause in any contract which results from collective bargaining.

The tone of court thinking is strictly along the lines of reasoning that has been previously outlined. Some courts think the provision would be a complete abdication of authority delegated to the School Board by legislative act. The Ohio court expressed this attitude when it said:

Under the civil service laws of the state and city, it would seem a vain and futile thing for the Transit Board to refer the issues to an arbitrator who with the best intentions, but in ignorance of civil service law, might make an award which it would be legally impossible for the Transit Board to accept.[1]

The *Norwalk* case takes a more moderate view. As was true in connection with the issue of bargaining for certain contract advantages, the court recognized that there is no reason to deny altogether the power of a School Board to enter voluntarily into a contract to arbitrate a specific matter. On the other hand, the Court shows an awareness that an agreement to submit all disputes to arbitration would be in a different category and improper. This, indicated the Court, might put the School Board in a position where it likely would find itself committed to surrender the discretion and responsibility imposed on it by law. As an illustration, the Court stated the School Board could not commit to arbitration the question of whether a teacher was discharged "for cause." Since legislation gives the School Boards authority to make investigations, hold hearings and make a determination as to whether there is "cause" for dismissal, the Court concluded a School Board could not delegate its duties to an arbitrator or board of arbitrators.

The ultimate answer is, therefore, likely to depend upon the degree of specificity by which the legislature has imposed a responsibility upon the School Board. As was true in connection with the part of this discussion which had to do with bargaining on salaries, there will be certain limits which an arbitrator may receive a delegation to function. The keeping of an arbitrator confined within limits, insures that the School Board will not have to surrender the essence of its power.

No discussion concerning the ability of public school teachers and employees to engage in concerted activities common for labor organizations can be complete without facing up to the right to strike and picket in support of strikes. The judicial attitude in this regard is uniform. All courts and authorities[2] agree

1. City of Cleveland (note 2, p. 335).
2. For a summary of authorities see Seasongood and Barrow, Unionization of Public Employees, 21 U. of Cinc. L. Rev. 327 (1952). Also see Ryne (note 1, p. 336), at 44. The *Norwalk* case is in accord..

that the right does not exist. The philosophy which supports this conclusion has been variously expressed. The Attorney General of the State of Minnesota told the Board of Regents of the University of Minnesota that "should we accept the doctrine permitting strikes we would in effect transfer to such employees all legislative, executive and judicial powers now vested in the duly elected or appointed public officers." Calvin Coolidge, in dealing with the question of strikes by public employees, took the position that there is "no right to strike against public safety by anybody anywhere at any time." Woodrow Wilson called strikes by public employees "an intolerable crime against civilization."[1] The *Norwalk* case quotes Franklin D. Roosevelt, whom it identifies as certainly no enemy of labor, as saying "a strike of public employees manifests nothing less than an intent on their part to prevent or obstruct the operation of government and such action is unthinkable and intolerable."

It appears particularly logical to conclude that a state can halt the strike and picketing in support of strike activities. Continued operation of schools is certainly vital to general welfare. State police power can surely insure that such operation is not interrupted by picketing and strikes. Furthermore, school personnel, most particularly teachers, work in a sensitive area. Picket lines would be especially disruptive of pupil morale. Teachers on strike might likely lose the respect of enough pupils so as to destroy their usefulness as instructors. The reason also suggests that no real distinction can be made between teacher picketing in aid of a strike and that in support of recognition or organizational efforts.

Some may feel that there is not the same danger in connection with organizational and recognition picketing by school personnel other than teachers. A valid distinction based on such facts seems doubtful. If picketing produces any repercussions which would hinder normal functioning of a school, it obviously could be halted. Furthermore, it seems totally inappropriate to allow pickets to parade around a school. The immature, impressionable minds of youth, who have no real concept of what a picket line may validly stand for, may be subtly influenced to have less respect for school authority. The danger that this could happen is one that School Boards do not have to risk.

The mere conclusion that picketing and striking on the part of school personnel is not sanctioned, does not fully explain the right of the School Board in combating such tactics. The injunction can be used to halt the activity. School personnel can be discharged and disciplined. Contract rights may be pursued. There is, however, no way by which individuals can be forced to return to work.

Since it is so generally agreed that public employees, particularly teachers, do not have the right to picket and strike, the argument is made that all privilege to join unions, bargain collectively and enter into negotiated agreements should be denied. This is on the premise that permitting the joining of unions, bargaining collectively and entering into negotiated agreements is entrenching an

1. These attitudes are quoted by Vogel in What About the Right of the Public Employee, 1 Lab. L. J. 604 (1950).

organization which by tradition is impelled to use the economic weapon of the picket line and strike. This argument does not persuade. As long as courts stand firm against use of picketing and strikes by public employees, unions and associations of public employees are not likely to use the pressure of such weapons. Furthermore, unions and organizations of public employees should realize that if such pressures are applied the governmental employer is not apt, under existing circumstances, to voluntarily agree to bargain and adhere to contract terms. In this connection it is appropriate to recall again that unless a statute provides to the contrary (and few do) the School Board is not required to recognize a union or association of school personnel. Even if statutes should be passed encouraging recognition and bargaining they will undoubtedly provide severe penalties if strikes or picketing pressure is used.

By way of moving to conclusion, it is appropriate to think about the policy question as to whether School Boards should voluntarily agree to recognize and bargain collectively with associations or unions of school personnel. The philosophy of good employee and public relations would appear to dictate an affirmative answer. Good faith bargaining is one of the best ways of keeping the school personnel public realistically informed about vital problems of school administration. The teacher segment of the school personnel group ought to be especially responsive to this kind of approach. Another benefit of good faith collective bargaining can be the creating of a climate which will enlighten the general public as to problems of the school and enlist assistance for their solution.

One further point needs to be made clear. The very meaning of collective bargaining affords protection to School Boards. Collective bargaining does not require that there must ultimately be capitulation. Even in the industrial arena parties are required only to bargain in good faith.

The facts involved in each bargaining situation dictate the elements of good faith. The present does not permit exhaustive analysis. One of the frequent requirements is an exchange of factual information to support certain positions which a party may assume. Often a party must reasonably explain why a certain concession will not be granted. An employer does not bargain in good faith if he takes an arbitrary position that he need make no response or do anything unless he receives a suggestion which seems reasonable. Some counter proposals must be submitted.

The application to School Boards of the "good faith" collective bargaining mandate is, of course, legally affected by the fact that in the vast majority of communities (unless legislation intervenes) the law does not compel School Boards to bargain collectively. Hence if a School Board voluntarily agrees to bargain, the law would not impose a legal duty to follow the rules of good faith negotiations. But if School Boards are motivated to bargain collectively by a desire to maintain good relations with employees and the public, it would defeat the purpose if the Boards did not bargain in good faith.

In conclusion it seems realistic to predict that the future position of School

Boards in labor relations, may be regulated by statutory enactments to a greater extent than at present. Legislation may decree collective bargaining. Reasons spelled out in this article suggest that there are no complete barriers to such development. Previous discussion has indicated that any legislative evolution will have to be within the framework of other relevant statutes. The task of determining if any existing legislation places limitations on subjects which can be topics for collective bargaining and contractual agreement will continue to exist.

The Superintendent's Role in Negotiation

NEA Research Bulletin (October), 1967, pp. 84–86.

Four superintendents in 10 in school systems with written teacher-school board negotiation procedures report that they are advisors to the negotiators for both the school board and the teachers. This finding was made by the NEA Research Division in its 1966–67 survey of written negotiation procedures in education. This survey was conducted in response to the increasing interest in teacher-school board negotiation; it provides comprehensive and reliable data on negotiation.

Questionnaires were sent to the 7,157 school systems with enrollments of 1,000 or more. Replies were received from 6,115, of which 1,531 reported having negotiation procedures and included copies of them along with the completed questionnaires. Sixteen of the questionnaires did not contain responses on the superintendent's role in negotiation. The remaining 1,515 responses were divided on the role of the superintendent as follows:

Negotiator with full authority	324
Negotiator with limited authority	239
Advisor to negotiators for school board only	201
Advisor to negotiators for school board and teachers	614
Neutral resource person	101
Nonparticipant	16
Other	20
	1,515

While the 1,531 school systems considered to have written negotiation procedures in 1966–67 represented only one in four of the responding school systems, they employed over 41 percent of the 1,560,000 instructional staff members in the replying school systems.

MORE ADVISORS THAN NEGOTIATORS

Just over half the superintendents consider themselves advisors to the negotiators: 40.5 percent for both the school board and the teachers, and 13.3 percent for the school board only. Just over a third consider themselves negotiators: 21.4 percent with full authority and 15.8 percent with limited authority.

As used here, the term *negotiator* means a person representing either the school board or the teachers in a face-to-face session designed to come to an agreement on salaries, working conditions, personnel policies and practices, the instructional program and/or other items of common concern.

STATE DIFFERENCES

About two-thirds of the 324 responses which indicated that the superintendent was negotiator with full authority (for the school board) came from California and Michigan. Both of these states have mandatory negotiation statutes. Responses from the other states with mandatory negotiation statutes (Connecticut, Massachusetts, Oregon, Rhode Island, Washington and Wisconsin) and from those without statutes indicated that the superintendent's role was *advisory* to the negotiators for the teachers and/or the school board. The New Jersey, New York, and Ohio responses indicate this role as well, none of the latter three states having negotiation statutes at the time of the survey.

Although the superintendent's role is determined by legislation, it appears to be influenced by the size of the school system: as school system enrollment decreases, the superintendent's role shifts from that of negotiator with full authority to that of advisor to the negotiators for both the school board and teachers.

The amounts and types of state negotiation legislation that will be enacted in the next few years should help to define more clearly the superintendent's role in teacher-school board negotiation.

1   Role of Superintendent in negotiation sessions

State*	Total number of responses	NEGOTIATOR WITH		ADVISOR TO NEGOTIATORS				
		Full authority	Limited authority	School board only	Board and teachers	Neutral resource person	Non-participant	Other
Alaska	3	2	0	0	0	1	0	0
Arizona	10	2	0	0	8	0	0	0
California	297	115	88	10	59	13	5	7
Colorado	17	3	5	0	8	1	0	0
Connecticut	55	5	4	14	27	5	0	0
Delaware	7	0	1	0	4	1	0	1
Florida	5	2	0	1	2	0	0	0
Idaho	14	3	2	0	7	2	0	0
Illinois	62	9	7	10	30	6	0	0
Indiana	29	0	6	4	19	0	0	0
Iowa	8	0	1	1	6	0	0	0
Kansas	25	5	4	1	15	0	0	0
Kentucky	1	0	0	0	1	0	0	0
Maine	5	0	1	1	3	0	0	0
Maryland	5	2	1	0	2	0	0	0
Massachusetts	64	1	0	21	32	7	3	0
Michigan	238	98	47	58	22	6	4	3
Minnesota	18	0	1	5	12	0	0	0
Mississippi	1	1	0	0	0	0	0	0
Missouri	20	6	2	0	12	0	0	0
Montana	5	0	0	0	5	0	0	0
Nebraska	2	0	0	1	0	1	0	0
Nevada	1	0	0	0	1	0	0	0
New Hampshire	5	0	0	0	5	0	0	0
New Jersey	145	5	7	13	96	20	0	4
New Mexico	5	0	2	1	2	0	0	0
New York	76	14	11	8	39	4	0	0
North Carolina	1	0	0	0	1	0	0	0
North Dakota	1	0	0	0	1	0	0	0
Ohio	116	29	24	9	42	10	1	1
Oklahoma	3	2	0	0	1	0	0	0
Oregon	54	0	1	10	31	11	1	0
Pennsylvania	41	6	3	1	27	3	1	0
Rhode Island	9	1	0	3	3	2	0	0
South Carolina	1	1	0	0	0	0	0	0
South Dakota	4	0	0	1	3	0	0	0
Tennessee	1	0	0	1	0	0	0	0
Texas	3	1	1	0	1	0	0	0
Utah	5	1	0	1	3	0	0	0
Vermont	6	0	0	0	5	1	0	0
Virginia	2	0	0	0	0	1	1	0
Washington	74	9	16	3	44	0	0	2
West Virginia	1	0	0	0	1	0	0	0
Wisconsin	67	1	4	23	31	6	0	2
Wyoming	3	0	0	0	3	0	0	0
Total	1,515	324	239	201	614	101	16	20

* At the time of the survey no negotiation agreements were reported from Alabama, Arkansas, District of Columbia, Georgia, Hawaii, and Louisiana.

Cases

A. Teacher Dismissal

Beilan v. Board of Public Education, School District of Philadelphia
357 U.S. 399 (1958)
Certiorari to the Supreme Court of Pennsylvania, Eastern District

MR. JUSTICE BURTON DELIVERED THE OPINION OF THE COURT

The question before us is whether the Board of Public Education for the School District of Philadelphia, Pennsylvania, violated the Due Process Clause of the Fourteenth Amendment to the Constitution of the United States when the Board, purporting to act under the Pennsylvania Public School Code, discharged a public school teacher on the ground of "incompetency", evidenced by the teacher's refusal of his Superintendent's request to confirm or refute information as to the teacher's loyalty and his activities in certain allegedly subversive organizations. For the reasons hereafter stated, we hold that it did not.

On June 24, 1952, Herman A. Beilan, the petitioner, who had been a teacher for about 22 years in the Philadelphia Public School System, presented himself at his Superintendent's office in response to the latter's request. The Superintendent said he had information which reflected adversely on petitioner's loyalty and he wanted to determine its truth or falsity. In response to petitioner's suggestion that the Superintendent do the questioning, the latter said he would ask one question and petitioner could then determine whether he would answer it and others of that type. The Superintendent, accordingly, asked petitioner whether or not he had been the Press Director of the Professional Section of the Communist Political Association in 1944. Petitioner asked permission to consult counsel before answering and the Superintendent granted his request.

On October 14, 1952, in response to a similar request, petitioner again presented himself at the Superintendent's office. Petitioner stated that he had consulted counsel and that he declined to answer the question as to his activities in 1944. He announced he would also decline to answer any other "questions similar to it," "questions of this type," or "questions about political and religious beliefs . . . ." The Superintendent warned petitioner that this "was a very serious and a very important matter and that failure to answer the questions might lead to his dismissal." The Superintendent made it clear that he was investigating "a real question of fitness for [petitioner] to be a teacher or to continue in the teaching work." These interviews were given no publicity and were attended only by petitioner, his Superintendent and the Assistant Solicitor of the Board.

On November 25, 1953, the Board instituted dismissal proceedings against petitioner under § 1127 of the Pennsylvania Public School Code of 1949. The only specification which we need consider charged that petitioner's refusal to answer his Superintendent's questions constituted "incompetency" under § 1122 of that Code. The Board conducted a formal hearing on the charge. Petitioner was present with counsel but did not testify. Counsel for each side agreed that petitioner's loyalty was not in issue and that evidence as to his disloyalty would be irrelevant. On January 7, 1954, the Board found that the charge of incompetency had been sustained and, by a vote of fourteen to one, discharged petitioner from his employment as a teacher.

On an administrative appeal, the Superintendent of Public Instruction of Pennsylvania sustained the local Board. However, on petitioner's appeal to the County Court of Common Pleas, that court set aside petitioner's discharge and held that the Board should have followed the procedure specified by the Pennsylvania Loyalty Act, rather than the Public School Code. Finally, on the Board's appeal, the Supreme Court of Pennsylvania, with two justices dissenting, reversed the Court of Common Pleas and reinstated petitioner's discharge. 386 Pa. 82, 98, 110, 125 A. 2d 327, 334, 340. We granted certiorari. 353 U. S. 964.

In addition to the Public School Code, Pennsylvania has a comprehensive Loyalty Act which provides for the discharge of public employees on grounds of disloyalty or subversive conduct. Purdon's Pa. Stat. Ann., 1941 (Cum. Ann. Pocket Pt., 1957), Tit. 65, §§ 211–225. Petitioner stresses the fact that the question asked of him by his Superintendent related to his loyalty. He contends that he was discharged for suspected disloyalty and that his discharge is invalid because of failure to follow the Loyalty Act procedure. However, the Pennsylvania Supreme Court held that the Board was not limited to proceeding under the Loyalty Act, even though the questions asked of petitioner related to his loyalty. We are bound by the interpretation thus given to the Pennsylvania statutes by the Supreme Court of Pennsylvania.

The only question before us is whether the Federal Constitution prohibits petitioner's discharge for statutory "incompetency" based on his refusal to answer the Superintendent's questions.

By engaging in teaching in the public schools, petitioner did not give up his right to freedom of belief, speech or association. He did, however, undertake obligations of frankness, candor and cooperation in answering inquiries made of him by his employing Board examining into his fitness to serve it as a public school teacher.

A teacher works in a sensitive area in a schoolroom. There he shapes the attitude of young minds towards the society in which they live. In this, the state has a vital concern. It must preserve the integrity of the schools. That the school authorities have the right and the duty to screen the officials, teachers, and employees as to their fitness to maintain the integrity of the schools as a part of ordered society, cannot be doubted. *Adler* v. *Board of Education*, 342 U. S. 485, 493.

As this Court stated in *Garner* v. *Board of Public Works*, 341 U. S. 716, 720, "We think that a municipal employer is not disabled because it is an agency of the State from inquiring of its employees as to matters that may prove relevant to their fitness and suitability for the public service."

The question asked of petitioner by his Superintendent was relevant to the issue of petitioner's fitness and suitability to serve as a teacher. Petitioner is not in a position to challenge his dismissal merely because of the remoteness in time of the 1944 activities. It was apparent from the circumstances of the two interviews that the Superintendent had other questions to ask. Petitioner's refusal to answer was not based on the remoteness of his 1944 activities. He made it clear that he would not answer any question of the same type as the one asked. Petitioner blocked from the beginning any inquiry into his Communist activities, however relevant to his present loyalty. The Board based its dismissal upon petitioner's refusal to answer any inquiry about his relevant activities—not upon these activities themselves. It took care to charge petitioner with incompetency, and not with disloyalty. It found him insubordinate and lacking in frankness and candor—it made no finding as to his loyalty.

We find no requirement in the Federal Constitution that a teacher's classroom conduct be the sole basis for determining his fitness. Fitness for teaching depends on a broad range of factors. The Pennsylvania tenure provision specifies several disqualifying grounds, including immorality, intemperance, cruelty, mental derangement and persistent and willful violation of the school laws, as well as "incompetency." However, the Pennsylvania statute, unlike those of many other States, contains no catch-all phrase, such as "conduct unbecoming a teacher," to cover disqualifying conduct not included within the more specific provisions. Consequently, the Pennsylvania courts have given "incompetency" a broad interpretation. This was made clear in *Horosko* v. *Mt. Pleasant School District*, 335 Pa. 369, 371, 374–375, 6 A. 2d 866, 868, 869–870:

If the fact be that she 'now commands neither the respect nor the good will of the community' and if the record shows that effect to be the result of her conduct within the clause quoted, it will be conclusive evidence of incompetency. It has always been the recognized duty of the teacher to conduct himself in such way as to command the respect and good will of the community, though one result of the choice of a teacher's vocation may be to deprive him of the same freedom of action enjoyed by persons in other vocations. Educators have always regarded the example set by the teacher as of great importance. . . .

The term "incompetency" has a 'common and approved usage'. The context does not limit the meaning of the word to lack of substantive knowledge of the subjects to be taught. Common and approved usage give a much wider meaning. For example, in 31 C. J., with reference to a number of supporting decisions, it is defined: "A relative term without technical meaning. It may be employed as meaning disqualification; inability; incapacity; lack of ability, legal qualifications, or fitness to discharge the required duty." In Black's Law Dictionary (3rd edition) page 945, and in Bouvier's Law Dictionary, (3rd revision) p. 1528, it is defined as "Lack of ability or fitness to discharge the required duty." Cases construing the word to the same effect are found in Words and Phrases, 1st series, page 3510, and 2nd series, page 1013. Webster's New International Dictionary defines it as "want of physical, intellectual, or moral ability; insufficiency; inadequacy; specif., want of legal qualifications or fitness." Funk & Wagnalls Standard Dictionary defines it as "General lack of capacity of fitness, or lack of the special qualities required for a particular purpose."

In the *Horosko* case, a teacher was discharged for "incompetency" because of her afterhours activity in her husband's beer garden, serving as a bartender and waitress, occasionally drinking beer, shaking dice with the customers for drinks and playing the pinball machine. Cf. *Schwer's Appeal*, 36 Pa. D. & C. 531, 536.

In the instant case, the Pennsylvania Supreme Court has held that "incompetency" includes petitioner's "deliberate and insubordinate refusal to answer the questions of his administrative superior in a vitally important matter pertaining to his fitness." 386 Pa., at 91, 125 A. 2d, at 331. This interpretation is not inconsistent with the Federal Constitution.

Petitioner complains that he was denied due process because he was not sufficiently warned of the consequences of his refusal to answer his Superintendent. The record, however, shows that the Superintendent, in his second interview, specifically warned petitioner that his refusal to answer "was a very serious and a very important matter and that failure to answer the questions might lead to his dismissal." That was sufficient warning to petitioner that his refusal to answer might jeopardize his employment. Furthermore, at petitioner's request, his Superintendent gave him ample opportunity to consult counsel. There was no element of surprise.

Our recent decisions in *Slochower* v. *Board of Education*, 350 U. S. 551, and *Konigsberg* v. *State Bar of California*, 353 U. S. 252, are distinguishable. In each we envisioned and distinguished the situation now before us. In the *Slochower* case, at 558, the Court said:

It is one thing for the city authorities themselves to inquire into Slochower's fitness, but quite another for his discharge to be based entirely on events occurring before a federal committee whose inquiry was announced as not directed at "the property, affairs, or government of the city, or . . . official conduct of city employees." In this respect the present case differs materially from *Garner* [341 U. S. 716], where the city was attempting to elicit information necessary to determine the qualifications of its employees. Here, the Board had possessed the pertinent information for 12 years, and the questions which Professor Slochower refused to answer were admittedly asked for a purpose wholly unrelated to his college functions. On such a record the Board cannot claim that its action was part of a bona fide attempt to gain needed and relevant information.

In the *Konigsberg* case, *supra*, at 259–261, this Court stressed the fact that the action of the State was not based on the mere refusal to answer relevant questions—rather, it was based on inferences impermissibly drawn from the refusal. In the instant case, no inferences at all were drawn from petitioner's refusal to answer. The Pennsylvania Supreme Court merely equated refusal to answer the employing Board's relevant questions with statutory "incompetency."

Inasmuch as petitioner's dismissal did not violate the Federal Constitution, the judgment of the Supreme Court of Pennsylvania is affirmed.

In the Matter of Dorothy H. Schwartz, Appellant, v. Isidore Bogen et al., constituting the Board of Examiners, Board of Education of the City of New York, Respondents
28 A.D. 2d 692, 281 N.Y.S. 2d 279 (1967)
New York Supreme Court

Before Christ, Acting P. J., and Rabin, Benjamin, Munder and Nolan, JJ.

MEMORANDUM BY THE COURT

Judgment of the Supreme Court, Kings County, dated January 10, 1966, reversed on the law, without costs; respondents' determination dismissing petitioner's appeal is annulled; and respondents are directed (1) to furnish petitioner with the standard answers and rating directions applicable to the essay-type parts of her examination and (2) to afford petitioner a reasonable time to prepare and file an appeal, if she be so advised, from such parts of the examination. No questions of fact have been considered.

In our opinion, the refusal of respondents to permit petitioner to examine the standard against which her performance was measured was unreasonable and substantially impaired her right of appeal. The results of the examination should be so stated that the applicant can "check up the conclusions by some objective comparison" (Matter of Andresen v. Rice, 277 N.Y. 271, 282, 14 N.E.2d 65, 70). In Matter of Gassner v. Board of Examiners of City of N.Y. (27 A.D.2d 662, 277 N.Y.S.2d 822 revg. 51 Misc.2d 467, 273 N.Y.S.2d 264), this court held that the petitioner had a right to inspect the rating schedule upon which her training and experience were evaluated, in order to obtain an adequate review of her case. Furnishing a prospective appellant with photocopies of his examination papers and a rating sheet does not, in our opinion, provide him with a sufficient explanation for his failing grade. It compels him to challenge a standard he has never seen or forego his right of review. We think that is an unreasonable choice to impose.

Respondents argue that the procedure of not furnishing standard answers has been followed for many years and that thousands of applicants have been able to prepare and file appeals; that of the hundreds of such appeals filed each year approximately 15% of the appellants are successful; and that, if standard answers were furnished to prospective appellants, these answers would be improperly applied and endless litigation would result. We do not find these arguments persuasive. If a procedure is unreasonable, it does not become less arbitrary with age. The fact that some appellants have managed successfully to overcome a handicap that should not have been imposed is no argument for continuity of that handicap. Nor does it necessarily follow that furnishing the standard answers will result in substantially increased litigation. Faced with the excellence of the standard against which his performance was measured, a prospective appellant can see the deficiencies of his answers and weigh intelligently the probability of success on an appeal. Under the present procedure, he is confronted with an unknown standard answer which must be challenged in "scatter-gun" fashion because he must argue against every conceivable answer save his own. The maintenance of secret standards does not inspire confidence in the objectivity and fairness of these examinations. If increased appeals and litigation should be the result of furnishing these answers, the Board and the courts must be prepared to accept those burdens.

> ## Pickering v. Board of Education of Township High School District 205, Will County
> 391 U.S. 563 (1968)
> Appeal from the Supreme Court of Illinois

MR. JUSTICE MARSHALL DELIVERED THE OPINION OF THE COURT

Appellant Marvin L. Pickering, a teacher in Township High School District 205, Will County, Illinois, was dismissed from his position by the appellee Board of Education for sending a letter to a local newspaper in connection with a recently proposed tax increase that was critical of the way in which the Board and the district superintendent of schools had handled past proposals to raise new revenue for the schools. Appellant's dismissal resulted from a determination by the Board, after a full hearing, that the publication of the letter was "detrimental to the efficient operation and administration of the schools of the district" and hence, under the relevant Illinois statute, Ill. Rev. Stat., c. 122, § 10–22.4 (1963), that "interests of the school require[d] [his dismissal]."

Appellant's claim that his writing of the letter was protected by the First and Fourteenth Amendments was rejected. Appellant then sought review of the Board's action in the Circuit Court of Will County, which affirmed his dismissal on the ground that the determination that appellant's letter was detrimental to the interests of the school system was supported by substantial evidence and that the interests of the schools overrode appellant's First Amendment rights. On appeal, the Supreme Court of Illinois, two Justices dissenting, affirmed the judgment of the Circuit Court. 36 Ill. 2d 568, 225 N. E. 2d 1 (1967). We noted probable jurisdiction of appellant's claim that the Illinois statute permitting his dismissal on the facts of this case was unconstitutional as applied under the First and Fourteenth Amendments. 389 U. S. 925 (1967). For the reasons detailed below we agree that appellant's rights to freedom of speech were violated and we reverse.

I

In February of 1961 the appellee Board of Education asked the voters of the school district to approve a bond issue to raise $4,875,000 to erect two new schools. The proposal was defeated. Then, in December of 1961, the Board submitted another bond proposal to the voters which called for the raising of $5,500,000 to build two new schools. This second proposal passed and the schools were built with the money raised by the bond sales. In May of 1964 a proposed increase in the tax rate to be used for educational purposes was submitted to the voters by the Board and was defeated. Finally, on September 19, 1964, a second proposal to increase the tax rate was submitted by the Board and was likewise defeated. It was in connection with this last proposal of the School Board that appellant wrote the letter to the editor (which we reproduce in an Appendix to this opinion) that resulted in his dismissal.

Prior to the vote on the second tax increase proposal a variety of articles attributed to the District 205 Teachers' Organization appeared in the local paper. These articles urged passage of the tax increase and stated that failure to pass the increase would result in a decline in the quality of education afforded children in the district's schools. A letter from the superintendent of schools making the same point was published in the paper two days before the election and submitted to the voters in mimeographed form the following day. It was in response to the foregoing material, together with the failure of the tax increase to pass, that appellant submitted the letter in question to the editor of the local paper.

The letter constituted, basically, an attack on the School Board's handling of the 1961 bond issue proposals and its subsequent allocation of financial resources between the schools' educational and athletic programs. It also charged the superintendent of schools with attempting to prevent teachers in the district from opposing or criticizing the proposed bond issue.

The Board dismissed Pickering for writing and publishing the letter. Pursuant to Illinois law, the Board was then required to hold a hearing on the dismissal. At the hearing the Board charged that numerous statements in the letter were false and that the publication of the statements unjustifiably impugned the "motives, honesty, integrity, truthfulness, responsibility and competence" of both the Board and the school administration. The Board also charged that the false statements damaged the professional reputations of its members and of the school administrators, would be disruptive of faculty discipline, and would tend to foment "controversy, conflict and dissension" among teachers, administrators, the Board of Education, and the residents of the district. Testimony was introduced from a variety of witnesses on the truth or falsity of the particular statements in the letter with which the Board took issue. The Board found the statements to be false as charged. No evidence was introduced at any point in the proceedings as to the effect of the publication of the letter on the community as a whole or on the administration of the school system in particular, and no specific findings along these lines were made.

The Illinois courts reviewed the proceedings solely to determine whether the Board's findings were supported by substantial evidence and whether, on the facts as found, the Board could reasonably conclude that appellant's publication of the letter was "detrimental to the best interests of the schools." Pickering's claim that his letter was protected by the First Amendment was rejected on the ground that his acceptance of a teaching position in the public schools obliged him to refrain from making statements about the operation of the schools "which in the absence of such position he would have an undoubted right to engage in." It is not altogether clear whether the Illinois Supreme Court held that the First Amendment had no applicability to appellant's dismissal for writing the letter in question or whether it determined that the particular statements made in the letter were not entitled to First Amendment protection. In any event, it clearly rejected Pickering's claim that, on the facts of this case, he could not constitutionally be dismissed from his teaching position.

II

To the extent that the Illinois Supreme Court's opinion may be read to suggest that teachers may constitutionally be compelled to relinquish the First Amendment rights they would otherwise enjoy as citizens to comment on matters of public interest in connection with the operation of the public schools in which they work, it proceeds on a premise that has been unequivocally rejected in numerous prior decisions of this Court.

The problem in any case is to arrive at a balance between the interests of the teacher, as a citizen, in commenting upon matters of public concern and the interest of the State, as an employer, in promoting the efficiency of the public services it performs through its employees.

III

The Board contends that "the teacher by virtue of his public employment has a duty of loyalty to support his superiors in attaining the generally accepted goals of education and that, if he must speak out publicly, he should do so factually and accurately, commensurate with his education and experience." Appellant, on the other hand, argues that the test applicable to defamatory statements directed against public officials by persons having no occupational relationship with them, namely, that statements to be legally actionable must be made "with knowledge that [they were] . . . false or with reckless disregard of whether [they were] . . . false or not," *New York Times Co.* v. *Sullivan*, 376 U. S. 254, 280 (1964), should also be applied to public statements made by teachers. Because of the enormous variety of fact situations in which critical statements by teachers and other public employees may be thought by their superiors, against whom the statements are directed, to furnish grounds for dismissal, we do not deem it either appropriate or feasible to attempt to lay down a general standard against which all such statements may be judged. However, in the course of evaluating the conflicting claims of First Amendment protection and the need for orderly school administration in the context of this case, we shall indicate some of the general lines along which an analysis of the controlling interests should run.

An examination of the statements in appellant's letter objected to by the Board reveals that they, like the letter as a whole, consist essentially of criticism of the Board's allocation of school funds between educational and athletic programs, and of both the Board's and the superintendent's methods of informing, or preventing the informing of, the district's taxpayers of the real reasons why additional tax revenues were being sought for the schools. The statements are in no way directed towards any person with whom appellant would normally be in contact in the course of his daily work as a teacher. Thus no question of maintaining either discipline by immediate superiors or harmony among coworkers is presented here. Appellant's employment relationships with the Board and, to a somewhat lesser extent, with the superintendent are not the kind of close working relationships for which it can persuasively be claimed that personal loyalty and confidence are necessary to their proper functioning. Accordingly, to the extent that the Board's position here can be taken to suggest that even comments on matters of public concern that are substantially correct, such as statements (1)–(4) of appellant's letter, see Appendix, *infra*, may furnish grounds for dismissal if they are sufficiently critical in tone, we unequivocally reject it.

We next consider the statements in appellant's letter which we agree to be false. The Board's original charges included allegations that the publication of the letter damaged the professional reputations of the Board and the superintendent and would foment controversy and conflict among the Board, teachers, administrators, and the residents of the district. However, no evidence to support these allegations was introduced at the hearing. So far as the record reveals, Pickering's letter was greeted by everyone but its main target, the Board, with massive apathy and total disbelief. The Board must, therefore, have decided, perhaps by analogy with the law of libel, that the statements were *per se* harmful to the operation of the schools.

However, the only way in which the Board could conclude, absent any evidence of the actual effect of the letter, that the statements contained therein were *per se* detrimental to the interest of the schools was to equate the Board members' own interests with that of the schools. Certainly an accusation that too much money is being spent on athletics by the administrators of the school system (which is precisely the import of that portion of appellant's letter containing the statements that we have found to be false, see Appendix, *infra*) cannot reasonably be regarded as *per se* detrimental to the district's schools. Such an accusation reflects rather a difference of opinion between Pickering and the Board as to the preferable manner of operating the school system, a difference of opinion that clearly concerns an issue of general public interest.

In addition, the fact that particular illustrations of the Board's claimed undesirable emphasis on athletic programs are false would not normally have any necessary impact on the actual operation of the schools, beyond its tendency to anger the Board. For example, Pickering's letter was written after the defeat at the polls of the second proposed tax increase. It could, therefore, have had no effect on the ability of the school district to raise necessary revenue, since there was no showing that there was any proposal to increase taxes pending when the letter was written.

More importantly, the question whether a school system requires additional funds is a matter of legitimate public concern on which the judgment of the school administration, including the School Board, cannot, in a society that leaves such questions to popular vote, be taken as conclusive. On such a question free and open debate is vital to informed decision-making by the electorate. Teachers are, as a class, the members of a community most likely to have informed and definite opinions as to how funds allotted to the operation of the schools should be spent. Accordingly, it is essential that they be able to speak out freely on such questions without fear of retaliatory dismissal.

In addition, the amounts expended on athletics which Pickering reported erroneously were matters of public record on which his position as a teacher in the district did not qualify him to speak with any greater authority than any other taxpayer. The Board could easily have rebutted appellant's errors by publishing the accurate figures itself, either via a letter to the same newspaper or otherwise. We are thus not presented with a situation in which a teacher has carelessly made false statements about matters so closely related to the day-to-day operations of the schools that any harmful impact on the public would be difficult to counter because of the teacher's presumed greater access to the real facts. Accordingly, we have no occasion to consider at this time whether under such circumstances a school board could reasonably require that a teacher make substantial efforts to verify the accuracy of his charges before publishing them.

What we do have before us is a case in which a teacher has made erroneous public statements upon issues then currently the subject of public attention, which are critical of his ultimate employer but which are neither shown nor can be presumed to have in any way either impeded the teacher's proper performance of his daily duties in the classroom or to have interfered with the regular operation of the schools generally. In these circumstances we conclude that the interest of the school administration in limiting teachers' opportunities to contribute to public debate is not significantly greater than its interest in limiting a similar contribution by any member of the general public.

IV

The public interest in having free and unhindered debate on matters of public importance—the core value of the Free Speech Clause of the First Amendment—is so great that it has been held that a State cannot authorize the recovery of damages by a public official for defamatory statements directed at him except when such statements are shown to have been made either with knowledge of their falsity or with reckless disregard for their truth or falsity.

In sum, we hold that, in a case such as this, absent proof of false statements knowingly or recklessly made by him, a teacher's exercise of his right to speak on issues of public importance may not furnish the basis for his dismissal from public employment. Since no such showing has been made in this case regarding appellant's letter, see Appendix, *infra*, his dismissal for writing it cannot be upheld and the judgment of the Illinois Supreme Court must, accordingly, be reversed and the case remanded for further proceedings not inconsistent with this opinion.

It is so ordered.

Mr. Justice Douglas, with whom Mr. Justice Black joins, concurs in the judgment of the Court for the reasons set out in his concurring opinions in *Time, Inc.* v. *Hill*, 385 U. S. 374, 401, *Rosenblatt* v. *Baer*, 383 U. S. 75, 88, and *Garrison* v. *Louisiana*, 379 U. S. 64, 80, and in the concurring opinions of Mr. Justice Black in *Curtis Publishing Co.* v. *Butts*, 388 U. S. 130, 170, and *New York Times Co.* v. *Sullivan*, 376 U. S. 254, 293.

APPENDIX TO OPINION OF THE COURT

A. Appellant's letter

LETTERS TO THE EDITOR
**** Graphic Newspapers, Inc.
Thursday, September 24, 1964, Page 4

Dear Editor:

I enjoyed reading the back issues of your paper which you loaned to me. Perhaps others would enjoy reading them in order to see just how far the two new high schools have deviated from the original promises by the Board of Education. First, let me state that I am referring to the February thru November, 1961 issues of your paper, so that it can be checked.

One statement in your paper declared that swimming pools, athletic fields, and auditoriums had been left out of the program. They may have been left out but they got put back in very quickly because Lockport West has both an auditorium and athletic field. In fact, Lockport West has a better athletic field than Lockport Central. It has a track that isn't quite regulation distance even though the board spent a few thousand dollars on it. Whose fault is that? Oh, I forgot, it wasn't supposed to be there in the first place. It must have fallen out of the sky. Such responsibility has been touched on in other letters but it seems one just can't help noticing it. I am not saying the school shouldn't have these facilities, because I think they should, but promises are promises, or are they?

Since there seems to be a problem getting all the facts to the voter on the twice defeated bond issue, many letters have been written to this paper and probably more will follow, I feel I must say something about the letters and their writers. Many of these letters did not give the whole story. Letters by your Board and Administration have stated that teachers' salaries total $1,297,746 for one year. Now that must have been the total payroll, otherwise the teachers would be getting $10,000 a year. I teach at the high school and I know this just isn't the case. However, this shows their "stop at nothing" attitude. To illustrate further, do you know that the superintendent told the teachers, and I quote, "Any teacher that opposes the referendum should be prepared for the consequences." I think this gets at the reason we have problems passing bond issues. Threats take something away; these are insults to voters in a free society. We should try to sell a program on its merits, if it has any.

Remember those letters entitled "District 205 Teachers Speak," I think the voters should know that those letters have been written and agreed to by only five or six teachers, not 98% of the teachers in the high school. In fact, many teachers didn't even know who was writing them. Did you know that those letters had to have the approval of the superintendent before they could be put in the paper? That's the kind of totalitarianism teachers live in at the high school, and your children go to school in.

In last week's paper, the letter written by a few uninformed teachers threatened to close the school cafeteria and fire its personnel. This is ridiculous and insults the intelligence of the voter because properly managed school cafeterias do not cost the school district any money. If the cafeteria is losing money, then the board should not be packing free lunches for athletes on days of athletic contests. Whatever the case, the taxpayer's child should only have to pay about 30¢ for his lunch instead of 35¢ to pay for free lunches for the athletes.

In a reply to this letter your Board of Administration will probably state that these lunches are paid for from receipts from the games. But $20,000 in receipts doesn't pay for the $200,000 a year they have been spending on varsity sports while neglecting the wants of teachers.

You see we don't need an increase in the transportation tax unless the voters want to keep paying $50,000 or more a year to transport athletes home after practice and to away games, etc. Rest of the $200,000 is made up in coaches' salaries, athletic directors' salaries, baseball pitching machines, sodded football fields, and thousands of dollars for other sports equipment.

These things are all right, provided we have enough money for them. To sod football fields on borrowed money and then not be able to pay teachers' salaries is getting the cart before the horse.

If these things aren't enough for you, look at East High. No doors on many of the classrooms, a plant room without any sunlight, no water in a first aid treatment room, are just a few of many things. The taxpayers were really taken to the cleaners. A part of the sidewalk in front of the building has already collapsed. Maybe Mr. Hess would be interested to know that we need blinds on the windows in that building also.

Once again, the board must have forgotten they were going to spend $3,200,000 on the West building and $2,300,000 on the East building.

As I see it, the bond issue is a fight between the Board of Education that is trying to push tax-supported athletics down our throats with education, and a public that has mixed emotions about both of these items because they feel they are already paying enough taxes, and simply don't know whom to trust with any more tax money.

I must sign this letter as a citizen, taxpayer and voter, not as a teacher, since that freedom has been taken from the teachers by the administration. Do you really know what goes on behind those stone walls at the high school?

Respectfully,

Marvin L. Pickering.

B. Analysis

The foregoing letter contains eight principal statements which the Board found to be false. Our independent review of the record convinces us that Justice Schaefer was correct in his dissenting opinion in this case when he concluded that many of appellant's statements which were found by the Board to be false were in fact substantially correct. We shall deal with each of the statements found to be false in turn. (1) Appellant asserted in his letter that the two new high schools when constructed deviated substantially from the original promises made by the Board during the campaign on the bond issue about the facilities they would contain. The Board based its conclusion that this statement was false on its determination that the promises referred to were those made in the campaign to pass the second bond issue in December of 1961. In the campaign on the first bond issue the Board stated that the plans for the two schools did not include such items as swimming pools, auditoriums, and athletic fields. The publicity put out by the Board on the second bond issue mentioned nothing about the addition of an auditorium to the plans and also mentioned nothing specific about athletic fields, although a general reference to "state required physical education" facilities was included that was similar to a reference made in the material issued by the Board during the first campaign.

In sum, the Board first stated that certain facilities were not to be included in the new high schools as an economy measure, changed its mind after the defeat of the first bond issue and decided to include some of the facilities previously omitted, and never specifically or even generally indicated to the taxpayers the change. Appellant's claim that the original plans, as disclosed to the public, deviated from the buildings actually constructed is thus substantially correct and his characterization of the Board's prior statement as a "promise" is fair as a matter of opinion. The Board's conclusion to the contrary based on its

determination that appellant's statement referred only to the literature distributed during the second bond issue campaign is unreasonable in that it ignores the
word "original" that modifies "promises" in appellant's letter.

(2) Appellant stated that the Board incorrectly informed the public that
"teachers' salaries" total $1,297,746 per year. The Board found that statement
false. However, the superintendent of schools admitted that the only way the
Board's figure could be regarded as accurate was to change the word "teachers"
to "instructional" whereby the salaries of deans, principals, librarians, counselors, and four secretaries at each of the district's three high schools would be
included in the total. Appellant's characterization of the Board's figure as incorrect is thus clearly accurate.

(3) Pickering claimed that the superintendent had said that any teacher who
did not support the 1961 bond issue referendum should be prepared for the
consequences. The Board found this claim false. However, the statement was
corroborated by the testimony of two other teachers, although the superintendent
denied making the remark attributed to him. The Illinois Supreme Court appears
to have agreed that something along the lines stated by appellant was said, since
it relied, in upholding the Board's finding that appellant's version of the remark
was false, on testimony by one of the two teachers that he interpreted the remark
to be a prediction about the adverse consequences for the schools should the
referendum not pass rather than a threat against noncooperation by teachers.
However, the other teacher testified that he didn't know how to interpret the
remark. Accordingly, while appellant may have misinterpreted the meaning of
the remark, he did not misreport it.

(4) Appellant's letter stated that letters from teachers to newspapers had to
have the approval of the superintendent before they could be submitted for
publication. The Board relied in finding this statement false on the testimony by
the superintendent that no approval was required by him. However, the Handbook for Teachers of the district specifically stated at that time that material
submitted to local papers should be checked with the building principal and submitted in triplicate to the publicity coordinator. In particular, the teachers'
letters to which appellant was specifically referring in his own letter had in fact
been submitted to the superintendent prior to their publication. Thus this statement is substantially correct.

The other four statements challenged by the Board, are factually incorrect in
varying degrees. (5) Appellant's letter implied that providing athletes in the
schools with free lunches meant that other students must pay 35¢ instead of 30¢
for their lunches. This statement is erroneous in that while discontinuing free
lunches for athletes would have permitted some small decrease in the 35¢ charge
for lunch to other students, the decrease would not have brought the price down
to 30¢. (6) Appellant claimed that the Board had been spending $200,000 a year
on athletics while neglecting the wants of teachers. This claim is incorrect in that
the $200,000 per year figure included over $130,000 of nonrecurring capital
expenditures. (7) Appellant also claimed that the Board had been spending

$50,000 a year on transportation for athletes. This claim is completely false in that the expenditures on travel for athletes per year were about $10,000. (8) Finally, appellant stated that football fields had been sodded on borrowed money, while the Board had been unable to pay teachers' salaries. This statement is substantially correct as to the football fields being sodded with borrowed money because the money spent was the proceeds of part of the bond issue, which can fairly be characterized as borrowed. It is incorrect insofar as it suggests that the district's teachers had actually not been paid upon occasion, but correct if taken to mean that the Board had at times some difficulty in obtaining the funds with which to pay teachers. The manner in which the last four statements are false is perfectly consistent with good-faith error, and there is no evidence in the record to show that anything other than carelessness or insufficient information was responsible for their being made.

Mr. Justice White, concurring in part and dissenting in part. . . .

B. Teacher–Board Bargaining

Norwalk Teachers' Association v. Board of Education of the City of Norwalk
138 Conn. 269 (1951)

JENNINGS, J.

This is a suit between the Norwalk Teachers' Association as plaintiff and the Norwalk board of education as defendant for a declaratory judgment, reserved on the admitted allegations of the complaint for the advice of this court.

The complaint may be summarized as follows: The plaintiff is a voluntary association and an independent labor union to which all but two of the teaching personnel of approximately 300 in the Norwalk school system belong. In April, 1946, there was a dispute between the parties over salary rates. The board of estimate and taxation was also involved. After long negotiations, 230 members of the association rejected the individual contracts of employment tendered them and refused to return to their teaching duties. After further negotiations, in which the governor and the state board of education took part, a contract was entered into between the plaintiff and the defendant, and the teachers returned to their duties. The contract, subject to conditions precedent therein set forth, recognized the plaintiff as the bargaining agent for all of its members, defined working conditions and set up a grievance procedure and salary schedule. Similar contracts were entered into for the succeeding school years, including 1950-1951.

From September, 1946, to the present, and particularly with reference to the contract for 1950-1951, much doubt and uncertainty have arisen concerning the rights and duties of the respective parties, the interpretation of the contract and the construction of the state statutes relating to schools, education and boards of education. "In addition," the complaint states, "there has been the possibility of strikes, work stoppage or collective refusals to return to work by the teachers through their organization and the possibility of discharges or suspensions by the defendant by reason of difficult personnel relations, all of which tends to disharmony in the operation of the school system and to the ever present possibility that either, or both, the parties may be unwittingly violating statutes by reason of mistaken or erroneous interpretation thereon." The parties agreed that the contract for the school year 1949-1950 would govern their relations for the school year 1950-1951, that they would join in this action, and "that whatever contractual obligations exist will be forthwith modified so soon as they shall have received from the Court judgments and orders declaring their respective rights, privileges, duties and immunities." The specific points of dispute are stated in the questions reserved, printed in the footnote.[1]

This court is not required to advise on abstract principles of law.

In the case at bar, the admitted facts show that Norwalk has suffered from one disrupting teachers' strike. While the complaint is couched in diplomatic language, it is obvious that the city is likely to be faced with another in the fall. Section 249 of the Practice Book authorizes the Superior Court to render declaratory judgments "as to the existence or nonexistence . . . of any right, power, privilege or immunity." It is obvious that a determination of the right of the teachers to strike comes within this definition.

Question (e) will be considered first.

Under our system, the government is established by and run for all of the people, not for the benefit of any person or group. The profit motive, inherent in

1. The plaintiff claimed a declaratory judgment answering and adjudicating the following questions:

"(a) Is it permitted to the plaintiff under our laws to organize itself as a labor union for the purpose of demanding and receiving recognition and collective bargaining?

"(b) Is it permitted to the plaintiff organized as a labor union to demand recognition as such and collective bargaining?

"(c) Is it permissible under Connecticut law for the defendant to recognize the plaintiff for the purpose of collective bargaining?

"(d) Is collective bargaining to establish salaries and working conditions permissible between the plaintiff and the defendant?

"(e) May the plaintiff engage in concerted action such as strike, work stoppage, or collective refusal to enter upon duties?

"(f) Is arbitration a permissible method under Connecticut law to settle or adjust disputes between the plaintiff and the defendant?

"(g) Is mediation a permissible method under Connecticut law to settle or adjust disputes between the plaintiff and the defendant?

"(h) If the answer to the previous questions is yes, are the State's established administrative facilities, such as the State Board of Mediation and Arbitration and the State Labor Relations Board, available, as they are available in industrial disputes, to the plaintiff and the defendant?

"(i) Does the continuing contract law, so-called, create a status of employment within which the plaintiff may claim employment subject to the right to bargain salaries and working conditions?

"(j) Has the plaintiff the right to establish rules, working conditions and grievance resolution procedures by collective bargaining?"

the principle of free enterprise, is absent. It should be the aim of every employee of the government to do his or her part to make it function as efficiently and economically as possible. The drastic remedy of the organized strike to enforce the demands of unions of government employees is in direct contravention of this principle. It has been so regarded by the heads of the executive departments of the states and the nation. Most of the text writers refer to one or more of the following statements by three of our recent presidents. They are quoted, for example, in 1 Labor Law Journal 612 (May, 1950): "There is no right to strike against public safety by anybody anywhere at any time" (Calvin Coolidge on the Boston police strike). This same strike was characterized by President Wilson as "an intolerable crime against civilization." President Franklin D. Roosevelt said in a letter to the president of the National Federation of Federal Employees on August 16, 1937: "Particularly, I want to emphasize my conviction that militant tactics have no place in the functions of any organization of Government employees. . . . [A] strike of public employees manifests nothing less than an intent on their part to prevent or obstruct the operations of Government until their demands are satisfied. Such action, looking toward the paralysis of Government by those who have sworn to support it, is unthinkable and intolerable." As the author of the article cited says, "The above statement by President Roosevelt, who certainly was no enemy of labor unions, epitomizes the answer to the problem. It seems to be axiomatic."

The commentators, generally, subscribe to this proposition. National Institute of Municipal Law Officers Reports No. 76, 116, 129; 1 Teller, Labor Disputes & Collective Bargaining (1947 Sup.) § 171; 18 N. Y. U. L. Q. Rev. 247; 94 U. of Pa. L. Rev. 427. Notwithstanding this fact, Ziskind was able to publish a well-documented book entitled "One Thousand Strikes of Government Employees," which contains an elaborate bibliography. See also Spero, "Government as Employer." This would indicate that the law on the subject is still in the process of development.

Few cases involving the right of unions of government employees to strike to enforce their demands have reached courts of last resort. That right has usually been tested by an application for an injunction forbidding the strike. The right of the governmental body to this relief has been uniformly upheld. It has been put on various gounds: public policy; interference with governmental function; illegal discrimination against the right of any citizen to apply for government employment (where the union sought a closed shop). The following cases do not necessarily turn on the specific right to strike, but the reasoning indicates that, if faced with that question, the court would be compelled to deny that right to public employees. For example, *Perez* v. *Board of Police Commissioners*, 78 Cal. App. 2d 638, 178 P. 2d 537, held that the board could, by rule, prevent police officers from joining a labor union. If it could do this, it would certainly be upheld in an attempt to enjoin a strike called by the union.

In the American system, sovereignty is inherent in the people. They can delegate it to a government which they create and operate by law. They can give to that government the power and authority to perform certain duties and furnish certain services. The government so created and empowered must employ people to carry on its task. Those people are agents of the government. They exercise some part of the sovereignty entrusted to it. They occupy a status entirely different from those who carry on a private enterprise. They serve the public welfare and not a private purpose. To say that they can strike is the equivalent of saying that they can deny the authority of government and contravene the public welfare. The answer to question (e) is "No."

Questions (a) and (b) relate to the right of the plaintiff to organize itself as a labor union and to demand recognition and collective bargaining. The right to organize is sometimes accorded by statute or ordinance.

The right to organize has also been forbidden by statute or regulation.

In Connecticut the statutes are silent on the subject. Union organization in industry is now the rule rather than the exception. In the absence of prohibitory statute or regulation, no good reason appears why public employees should not organize as a labor union. *Springfield* v. *Clouse*, 356 Mo. 1239, 1246, 206 S. W. 2d 539. It is the second part of question (a) that causes difficulty. The question reads: "Is it permitted to the plaintiff under our laws to organize itself as a labor union for the purpose of demanding and receiving recognition and collective bargaining?" The question is phrased in a very peremptory form. The common method of enforcing recognition and collective bargaining is the strike. It appears that this method has already been used by the plaintiff and that the threat of its use again is one of the reasons for the present suit. As has been said, the strike is not a permissible method of enforcing the plaintiff's demands. The answer to questions (a) and (b) is a qualified "Yes." There is no objection to the organization of the plaintiff as a labor union, but if its organization is for the purpose of "demanding" recognition and collective bargaining the demands must be kept within legal bounds. What we have said does not mean that the plaintiff has the right to organize for all of the purposes for which employees in private enterprise may unite, as those are defined in § 7391 of the General Statutes. Nor does it mean that, having organized, it is necessarily protected against unfair labor practices as specified in § 7392 or that it shall be the exclusive bargaining agent for all employees of the unit, as provided in § 7393. It means nothing more than that the plaintiff may organize and bargain collectively for the pay and working conditions which it may be in the power of the board of education to grant.

Questions (c) and (d) in effect ask whether collective bargaining between the plaintiff and the defendant is permissible. The statutes and private acts give broad powers to the defendant with reference to educational matters and school management in Norwalk. If it chooses to negotiate with the plaintiff with regard to the employment, salaries, grievance procedure and working conditions of its members, there is no statute, public or private, which forbids such negotiations. It is a matter of common knowledge that this is the method pursued in most school systems large enough to support a teachers' association in some form. It would seem to make no difference theoretically whether the negotiations are with a committee of the whole association or with individuals or small related groups, so long as any agreement made with the committee is confined to members of the association. If the strike threat is absent and the defendant prefers to handle the matter through negotiation with the plaintiff, no reason exists why it should not do so. The claim of the defendant that this would be an illegal delegation of authority is without merit. The authority is and remains in the board. This statement is not to be construed as approval of the existing contracts attached to the complaint. Their validity is not in issue.

As in the case of questions (a) and (b), (c) and (d) are in too general a form to permit a categorical answer. The qualified "Yes" which we give to them should not be construed as authority to negotiate a contract which involves the surrender of the board's legal discretion, is contrary to law or is otherwise ultra vires. For example, an agreement by the board to hire only union members would clearly be an illegal discrimination. *Mugford* v. *Baltimore*, 185 Md. 266, 270, 44 A. 2d 745; Rhyne, Labor Unions & Municipal Employe Law, pp. 34, 137, 157. Any salary schedule must be subject to the powers of the board of estimate and taxation. "The salaries of all persons appointed by the board of education . . . shall be as fixed by said board, but the aggregate amount of such salaries . . . shall not exceed the amount determined by the board of estimate and taxation. . . . " 21 Spec. Laws 285, No. 315, § 3; *Board of Education of Stamford* v. *Board of Finance*, 127 Conn. 345, 349, 16 A. 2d 601. One of the allegations of the complaint is that the solution of the parties' difficulties by the posing of specific issues is not satisfactory. Whether or not this is so, that course will be necessary if this discussion of general principles is an insufficient guide.

Question (f) reads, "Is arbitration a permissible method under Connecticut law to settle or adjust disputes between the plaintiff and the defendant?" The power of a town to enter into an agreement of arbitration was originally denied on the ground that it was an unlawful delegation of authority. *Griswold* v. *North Stonington*, 5 Conn. 367, 371. It was later held that not only the amount of damages but liability could be submitted to arbitration. *Hine* v. *Stephens*, 33 Conn. 497, 504; *Mallory* v. *Huntington*, 64 Conn. 88, 96, 29 A. 245. The principle applies to the parties to the case at bar. If it is borne in mind that arbitration is the result of mutual agreement, there is no reason to deny the power of the defendant to enter voluntarily into a contract to arbitrate a specific dispute. On a proposal for a submission, the defendant would have the opportunity of deciding whether it would arbitrate as to any question within its power. Its power to submit to arbitration would not extend to questions of policy but might extend to questions of liability. Arbitration as a method of settling disputes is growing in importance and, in a proper case, "deserves the enthusiastic support of the courts."

Agreements to submit all disputes to arbitration, commonly found in ordinary union contracts, are in a different category. If the defendant entered into a general agreement of that kind, it might find itself committed to surrender the broad discretion and responsibility reposed in it by law. For example, it could not commit to an arbitrator the decision of a proceeding to discharge a teacher for cause. So, the matter of certification of teachers is committed to the state board of education. General Statutes §§ 1432, 1433, 1435. The best answer we can give to question (f) is, "Yes, arbitration may be a permissible method as to certain specific, arbitrable disputes."

From what has been said, it is obvious that, within the same limitations, mediation to settle or adjust disputes is not only permissible but desirable. The answer to question (g) is "Yes." The state board of mediation and arbitration and the state labor relations board, however, are set up to handle disputes in private industry and are not available to the plaintiff and defendant for reasons given in the opinion of the attorney general dated July 6, 1948. 25 Conn. Atty. Gen. Rep. 270. This was confirmed as to Norwalk teachers by an opinion dated June 12, 1950, not yet published.

The answer to question (h) is "No."

General Statutes, Sup. 1949, § 160a, provides in part: "The contract of employment of a teacher shall be renewed for the following school year unless such teacher has been notified in writing prior to March first of that year that such contract will not be renewed." Question (i) asks whether this law creates "a status of employment within which the plaintiff may claim employment subject to the right to bargain salaries and working conditions?" The meaning of this is not clear and the briefs do not clarify it. It is the type of question that should be related to a specific state of facts. It cannot be answered in vacuo.

As to question (j), the plaintiff has no right to establish rules. As stated above, the right is and remains in the board.

Question (g) is answered, "Yes, but not under chapter 369 of the General Statutes as amended." Questions (e), (h) and (j) are answered "No." Question (i) is not answered. No purpose would be served by answering the other questions categorically. Questions (a) and (b) are answered, "Yes, with relation to the plaintiff's own members, provided its demands are kept within legal bounds." Questions (c) and (d) are answered, "Yes, with relation to the plaintiff's own members, provided that this answer shall not be construed as approval of any specific contract which has been or may be entered into between the parties." Question (f) is answered, "Yes, arbitration may be a permissible method as to certain specific, arbitrable disputes." In answering some of these questions we have gone beyond the requirements of the specific questions asked in order to render such assistance as we properly may in helping to solve the difficulties of the parties.

No costs will be taxed in this court to either party.

In this opinion the other judges concurred.

Chicago Div. Ill. Ed. Ass'n v. Board of Ed.
76 Ill. App. 2d 456 (1966)

MR. JUSTICE MURPHY DELIVERED THE OPINION OF THE COURT

Plaintiff and intervenor-plaintiff appeal from an "Opinion and Decree," which dismissed their separate complaints, after making findings and declarations of law, the effect of which was to approve collective bargaining by the Board of Education of the City of Chicago with a sole collective bargaining agency to be selected by its teachers.

The plaintiff (Chicago Division), an Illinois not-for-profit corporation, is an association of school teachers and other educational personnel organized for the purpose of representing its members and other teachers and educational personnel who desire it to present grievances to, and negotiate with, the defendant Board of Education of the City of Chicago (Board), regarding working conditions, welfare and professional responsibilities. The intervenor-plaintiff is James D. Broman, a citizen and taxpayer of the City of Chicago.

The intervenor-defendant, the Chicago Teachers Union (CTU), is an unincorporated association in the nature of a labor union or labor organization. Its members, also, are teachers and educational personnel employed by the defendant Board of Education. It is alleged that CTU has "about 12,000 members who are active classroom teachers in the schools of Chicago."

Since 1964, the Board has recognized the Chicago Division, the CTU and the Chicago Principals Club as collective bargaining agents for their teacher members and other educational personnel who desired one of these organizations to speak for them. With the Board's approval, a "Memorandum of Understanding," which prescribed procedures for the resolution of professional problems and grievances, was entered into with each organization by the General Superintendent of Schools.

In a verified two-count complaint filed October 5, 1965, plaintiff sought (1) both a declaratory judgment to have its "Memorandum of Understanding" (contract) with the defendant Board, dated March 11, 1964, and effective November 12, 1964, determined to be a valid and subsisting contract, in force and effect at least until November 12, 1966, and to restrain the Board "from proceeding with the preparation for and the conducting of the election among its employees, school teachers and educational personnel to determine what organization they wish to have represent them as their sole bargaining agent until a hearing and determination of this cause be had by this Court"; and (2) relief against the "Board's adoption of Resolutions 73408 and 73409 in September, 1965," which resolutions plaintiff claimed breached its contract; and relief against the Board's discrimination reflected by the Board's activities leading up to the adoption of the resolutions and its continued demonstrated prejudicial action thereafter against plaintiff and in favor of Chicago Teachers Union.

The intervenor-plaintiff, James D. Broman, filed a complaint in which he alleged that "as a result of threats and intimidation by the intervenor-defendant, the Chicago Teachers Union, unlawfully to disrupt the operation of the school system by causing an illegal strike of its members, and in unlawful agreement with the Chicago Teachers Union, the Board of Education has engaged in and embarked upon a course of conduct which has required and will require that the Board perform acts not authorized by The School Code or by any other statute of the State of Illinois, and which acts are and will be contrary to the laws and public policy of the State of Illinois and which constitute an abdication and illegal sharing and delegation of their duties as public officials . . . ." Injunctive relief was sought, temporary and permanent, restraining the Board from recognizing CTU, or any organization, as the sole bargaining agent or as a collective bargaining agent for its employees "upon any question upon which power of decision has been entrusted to the said Board of Education by the Illinois State Legislature." Other relief sought included restraint of the Board from "authorizing or holding a referendum or any other kind of election for the purpose of selecting a sole bargaining agent."

Defendant Board and intervenor-defendant CTU filed motions to strike and dismiss the complaints of the Chicago Division and of Broman.

On February 23, 1966, the trial court, after considering the pleadings, affidavits and exhibits, and the briefs filed by all parties, and having heard the arguments of counsel, entered an "Opinion and Decree," which included findings and declarations of law, allowed the motions to strike and dismiss both complaints, and dismissed the cause subject to expressed "limitations."

The findings included:

2. The Memorandum of Understanding entered into between Chicago Division of the Illinois Education Association and the General Superintendent of Schools and adopted by the Board of Education of the City of Chicago November 12, 1964 is a valid agreement, subsisting until terminated by either of the parties thereto, or by the Board of Education of the City of Chicago, after notice given the other party prior to October 1 of any year that it will be modified or terminated November 12 of that year. . . .

4. Board Resolution No. 73409 of September 23, 1965 authorizes the teachers employed by the Board of Education of the City of Chicago to hold a referendum election at which they may select a sole collective bargaining agent concerning wages, working conditions, fringe benefits, and other professional problems; and provides that regardless of the outcome of the election any teacher may join any employee organization of his own choosing and that persons not members of the organization selected at the election have the right to present grievances and submit suggestions to the Board as individuals.

The order included:

". . . that the Board of Education agrees to incorporate in the collective bargaining agreement a provision that on any and all matters which are proper subjects of collective bargaining, which are brought to the attention of the Board of Education or school administration by any individual or organization, the Union shall be informed, and any action or decision on the matter shall be made only after negotiation with the Union," is without force or effect.

3. Board Resolution No. 73409 is lawful and is not a delegation, dilution, or sharing of powers delegated to the Board of Education of the City of Chicago by the General Assembly; however, that Resolution may not be effectuated until notice of intent to terminate the existing Memoranda of Understanding has been given by the Board of Education to the other parties thereto.

4. Any collective bargaining agreement which the Board of Education of the City of Chicago may enter into with an agency representing its teachers or other educational personnel, whether or not with a sole collective bargaining agency selected by its teachers, shall contain specific provisions whereby the employee organization shall agree not to strike, not to picket in any manner which would tend to disrupt the operation of any public school in the City of Chicago or of the administrative offices of the Board of Education of the City of Chicago, that the benefit of any and all decisions and conclusions the Board of Education may reach after having negotiated with the employee organization selected shall apply equally to all teachers and other educational personnel employed by the Board of Education; and that, should negotiations fail to resolve differences, the decision of the Board of Education shall be final.

5. Subject to the limitations hereinabove expressed, the motions to strike the complaint as amended of Chicago Division of the Illinois Education Association and the complaint of James D. Broman are allowed, and the complaint as amended of Chicago Division of the Illinois Education Association and the complaint of James D. Broman are hereby stricken and the cause dismissed.

The plaintiff and intervenor-plaintiff Broman both appealed from the decree and filed separate briefs asserting different grounds to show that the lower court was in error in entering the decree and in not issuing restraining orders.

The record of proceedings in this court shows that subsequent to the entry of the decree and on March 25, 1966, the Board gave written notice of intent to terminate the "Memoranda of Understanding" of both plaintiff and the Chicago Teachers Union and authorized a referendum election to be held on May 27, 1966. Thereafter, this court denied plaintiff's motion for a temporary restraining order enjoining the holding of the election.

Initially, we consider whether the trial court was correct in striking Broman's complaint. This raises the basic question of whether the Board may bargain collectively with an exclusive employee representative. Broman contends:

1. "The central question raised in this Court is whether the Board of Education of the City of Chicago has authority to engage in collective bargaining, and to enter into a collective bargaining agreement, with an exclusive representative of its employees. It is not disputed that the power to do so has not been expressly conferred on the Board by the legislature. Both defendants have argued, rather, that the authority to engage in such bargaining, and to conclude a contract, may be implied from general legislation empowering the Board to contract and to do all things 'necessary or proper' for the operation of the schools. Neither defendant has argued that the authority to bargain collectively is *necessary* to the operation of the schools. Instead, both have argued that collective bargaining is a *proper* function of the Board, and may be engaged in by the Board at its discretion."

2. "The courts of this state—like those in a majority of other jurisdictions—

should leave to the legislature the many policy questions presented by the question of whether, and under what restrictions and conditions, the institution of collective bargaining should be imported into the public sector."

The authorities cited by Broman include International Brotherhood v. Grand River Dam Authority (Okla), 292 P2d 1018 (1956) which, Broman asserts, stands for the proposition "that public employees have no common law right of collective bargaining, and that even a statute giving a public agency authority to contract does not, inferentially, create in public employees the *right* to bargain collectively." City of Jackson v. McLeod, 199 Miss 161, 24 So2d 319 (1946), which was a suit by a policeman who had been discharged because of his membership in a labor union. There the court upheld the Civil Service Commission in its finding that union membership was incompatible with a policeman's duty to the community. Levasseur v. Wheeldon, 79 SD 442, 112 NW 2d 894 (1962), cited for the rule that "absent statute public employees have no right to engage in collective bargaining." Philadelphia Teachers' Ass'n v. Labrum, 415 Pa 212, 203 A2d 34 (1964) cited to suggest that "Pennsylvania law does not uphold collective bargaining between public employees and public employers." Mugford v. Mayor and City Council of Baltimore, 185 Md 266, 44 A2d 745 (1946), where "the precise question of a municipality's authority to bargain collectively with its employees was decided negatively by the trial court and not appealed." International Union of Operating Engineers, Local Union No. 321 v. Water Works Board of City of Birmingham, 276 Ala 462, 163 So2d 619 (1964), which followed "the strongest current of opinion from the highest courts of states where the question has been presented . . . that a public agency has no authority to bargain or contract with a labor union in the absence of express statutory authority." International Longshoreman's Ass'n, AFL–CIO v. Georgia Ports Authority, 217 Ga. 712, 124 SE2d 733 (1962), which holds that picketing by public employees for bargaining rights is enjoinable because it contravenes the public policy denying public employers the authority to bargain. Wichita Public Schools Employees Union, Local 513 v. Smith, 194 Kan 2, 397 P2d 357 (1964), "where the court held that the state's general legislation conferring collective bargaining rights did not extend to governmental employees." Delaware River & Bay Authority v. International Organization, 45 NJ 138, 211 A2d 789 (1965), where, "in appealing an order enjoining it from picketing or striking, a union of Bay Authority employees argued that the constituent compacts' *general* conferral of power to contract empowered the Authority to enter into *collective bargaining contracts*. The court rejected that argument on grounds that the power to enter collective bargaining contracts would be contrary to established state policy. The court ruled . . . that a change in that policy required action by the legislature."

From these authorities, Broman argues that since 1958 the courts of nine states have reiterated the basic principle contended for by taxpayer Broman— that public employees have no right to bargain collectively unless and until the legislature has conferred that right and defined the manner of its exercise. As evidence of an Illinois policy against collective bargaining by public employees, Broman points out that "the legislature has ten times refused *general* authorization for public collective bargaining but has, during the same period, authorized collective bargaining for two specified public agencies." Broman argues that the Illinois Supreme Court in Board of Education of Community Unit School Dist. No. 2 v. Redding, 32 Ill2d 567, 207 NE2d 427 (1965), recognized and explicitly relied upon the fundamental distinction between public and private employment in ruling that public employees could not engage in concerted refusals to work or disruptive picketing. He asserts that neither the Illinois Labor Peace Act, Ill Rev Stats, c 10, §§ 20–30, nor the Illinois Anti-Injunction Act, Ill Rev Stats, c 48, § 2a, are applicable to public employment. These manifestations of public policy, he concludes, evidence both legislative and judicial intent not to authorize or permit collective bargaining in public employment.

The Board contends that specific legislation is unnecessary, and that existing general legislation is more than sufficient to authorize exclusive collective bargaining by the Board, and that the collective bargaining agreement authorized by the decree preserves the Board's statutory authority and that its provisions are mandatory. It argues that Broman's authorities are not relevant, and that "few of these foreign authorities considered any specific collective bargaining agreement, not to say one containing provisions similar to those required to be included in any collective bargaining agreement the Board may enter."

The Board asserts that "a review of the activity of state and the federal legislatures can be argued to demonstrate that legislation is needed to prevent collective bargaining by governmental agencies, not to authorize it," and that existing Illinois legislation authorizes collective bargaining by the Board. Ill Rev Stats 1965, c 102, § 35.2, and c 48, § 852. The Board claims that the power of the Board here questioned "exists independently of *specific* statutory provisions and is legislatively recognized by the cited Acts." It agrees that Article 34 of the School Code, which governs school boards, does not specifically authorize the Board to engage in collective bargaining, but neither does it "provide otherwise."

As to the general rule set forth in 31 ALR2d 1142, 1170:

Public employers cannot abdicate or bargain away their continuing legislative discretion and are therefore not authorized to enter into collective bargaining agreements with public employee labor unions,

the Board states that "the decree at bar prohibits the Board from entering into any collective bargaining agreement under which it would 'abdicate or bargain away its continuing legislative discretion'. Such a collective bargaining agreement cuts the ground from under the general rule as stated in American Law Reports. The *reason* for the rule being absent, there is *no* reason for it here."

The Board further agrees that it cannot delegate authority conferred on it by the legislature, nor delegate its discretionary powers in any collective bargaining agreement (Stroh v. Casner, 201 Ill App 281 (1916)), but claims that Broman's assertion that "collective bargaining *necessarily* grants to the collective bargaining agent a role in the decision-making process of the Board which was neither created nor approved by the legislature," ignores the provisions of the instant decree. The Board points out that under the decree it must maintain "sole responsibility for effecting the statutory duties delegated to it," and that the decree "prohibits the Board's entry into *any* collective bargaining agreement which could result in any delegation of its statutory powers or duties."

The Board contends that the decree is in accord with the Illinois Supreme Court opinion in Board of Education of Community Unit School Dist. No. 2 v. Redding, 32 Ill2d 567, 207 NE2d 427 (1965) and that Redding does not speak of the legality of collective bargaining by public school employees. Rather, it holds only that such employees cannot strike or otherwise engage in conduct deleterious to the efficient operation of the schools. In the Redding case, where the court enjoined both the strike and picketing of schools, it is said (p 571):

And while there is some effort to divert us to a determination of whether public school employees may lawfully organize into unions at all, (see: People ex rel. Fursman v. City of Chicago, 278 Ill 318,) that issue was not raised or passed upon below. Rather, the scope of our review is limited to a consideration of whether such employees may strike against their school board employer, and whether they may picket to support their strike.

Although this is a case of first impression in a reviewing court of this jurisdiction, it is, so far as we can ascertain, the universal view that there is no inherent right in municipal employees to strike against their governmental employer, whether Federal, State, or a political subdivision thereof, and that a strike of municipal employees for any purpose is illegal.

And at p 572:

Our own constitution impresses the General Assembly with the duty to 'provide a thorough and efficient system of free schools,' (const of 1870, art VIII, sec 1), and we believe it logically follows that those who, under the implementing statutes, become the agents to fulfill the will of the people in such respect are themselves charged with a duty to refrain from conduct which will render our schools less efficient and thorough. The drastic remedy of organized strikes against employing school boards is in direct contravention of such duty.

The Board, in support of the decree and its provisions, asserts that it "accords with the pronouncements of all relevant precedent in or out of this State," and that "the collective bargaining agreement held lawful by the chancellor cannot conceivably serve as a vehicle for delegating legislative power." The Board argues that the "propriety and mandatory nature of the entire Decree is established by judicial pronouncement . . . :

'The rules of courts of chancery in granting relief are flexible, such court not being bound by formulas or restrained by any limitation which tends to trammel the free exercise of discretion. When all the parties are before the court, the whole case may be considered, all interests protected, and a complete decree made which will be binding on all parties who have a substantial beneficial interest in the litigation.' 7 ILP 582; DuPage County v. Henderson, 402 Ill 179; McMechan v. Yenter, 301 Ill 508,

and that a decree of a court of equity must be reasonably construed, and must be interpreted as an entirety. Neidhardt v. Frank, 325 Ill 596, 156 NE 769 (1927).

On the issue of collective bargaining in public employment, the intervenor-defendant, CTU, contends that "employees, including those employed by government, have a right to organize for the purpose of collective bargaining under the First and Fourteenth Amendments to the United States Constitution," and that the right of employees to organize has been treated in several U. S. Supreme Court cases as protected by the Constitution. Lincoln Union v. Northwestern Co., 335 US 525 (1949); Communications Ass'n v. Douds, 339 US 382 (1950).

Other authorities relied on include City of Springfield v. Clouse, 356 Mo 1239, 206 SW2d 539, 542 (1947), where it is said:

All citizens have the right preserved by the First Amendment to the United States Constitution . . . to peaceably assemble and organize for any proper purpose. . . .

International Union, United Automobile Workers v. Wisconsin Employment Relations Board, 336 US 245 (1949), where it is said (p 259):

The right to strike, because of its more serious impact upon the public interest, is more vulnerable to regulation than the right to organize and select representatives for lawful purposes of collective bargaining which this Court has characterized as a "fundamental right". . . .

Labor Board v. Jones & Laughlin, 301 US 1 (1937), where the Supreme Court upheld the validity of the National Labor Relations Act and pointed out that the Act was designed to "protect" the right to organize and the right to organize included the right to organize for the purpose of collective bargaining, which right existed separate from the Act.

The CTU, in asserting that the right of employees to organize for collective bargaining is a right also enjoyed by public employees, states, "employment by government does present the occasion for limitation of rights, but until government actually attempts to limit rights they remain unfettered," Wieman v. Updegraff, 344 US 183 (1952); United Public Workers v. Mitchell, 330 US 75 (1947), and "while Taxpayer Broman seemingly assumes that by entering public service employees thereby cede all their rights and have only those which the government gives, the exact opposite is true. Thus public employees in Illinois maintain their right to organize for the purpose of collective bargaining, at least until that right is legitimately limited," and "the proper question then is whether the instant Board of Education is under some legal inhibition."

In contending that Illinois belongs among those states which approve collective bargaining in public employment, the CTU admits there is a genuine split on this issue existing in this country, and that the list of fourteen states submitted by Broman appears to be formidable, but argues, "it loses much of its impressiveness when subjected to analysis," and that the "jurisdictions he can reliably cite are only Alabama, Colorado, Georgia, Kansas, Missouri, New Jersey and Tennessee."

As additional authority, the CTU states that "New York City and 86 unions representing the various employees of the city established a Memorandum of Understanding dated March 31, 1966, which includes the following provisions:

"Collective bargaining is the most effective means in our society for matching employer requirements with employee needs. A healthy bargaining relationship provides the maximum promise that labor-management disputes will be resolved by peaceful measures, to the great advantage of the disputants and, in the case of public employment, to the even more important advantage of the public . . . .

"It is the policy of the City of New York to engage in collective bargaining and enter into written agreements with employee organizations . . . ."

But the City of New York is not alone. The Board of Education in that city has an exclusive bargaining agreement with the United Federation of Teachers which represents some 44,000 teachers. . . . New York, Pennsylvania and Connecticut are but three among many jurisdictions where local governmental bodies have adopted policies favoring collective bargaining.

The CTU notes that "The American Federation of Teachers, of which the Chicago Teachers Union is a local, represents teachers in Philadelphia, New York, Detroit, Cleveland and numerous smaller cities and communities. Illinois locals currently have written exclusive collective bargaining agreements in Cicero, Maywood, and Proviso school districts. Proviso and East St. Louis were among the very first school boards in the United States authorizing collective bargaining elections. Within the last several months, school boards in Kankakee, Calumet City and Stickney Township have adopted pro collective bargaining policies. . . . Alaska, California, Connecticut, Delaware, Massachusetts, Michigan, Minnesota, New Hampshire, Oregon, Rhode Island, Washington and Wisconsin have by legislative pronouncement demonstrated that collective bargaining is within sound good public policy."

As to whether the Board of Education of the City of Chicago may in its discretion engage in collective bargaining, the CTU observes, "There appears to be no disagreement over the fact defendant Board of Education has the power to employ 20,000 teachers. The central issue of this case lies in disagreement over the means used to determine the contract terms of those 20,000 employees. It is submitted that the board is the best judge of the most efficient method of arriving at those terms; this court is without authority to deny the board's exercise of discretion in choosing the method unless the choice is manifestly unreasonable.". . .

The CTU argues that the Illinois courts have approved broad discretion in school board contractual relationships which have genuine bargaining as their basis, and cites Wilson v. Board of Education of Chicago, 233 Ill 464, 84 NE 697 (1908), where it is said (p 475):

It is for the board of education, within the reasonable exercise of its power and discretion, to say what is best for the successful management and conduct of the schools, and not for the courts.

The CTU also cites a number of authorities to show that collective bargaining does not involve a delegation of power. NLRB v. American National Ins. Co., 343 US 395 (1952); Norwalk Teachers Ass'n v. Board of Education, 138

Conn 269, 83 A2d 482 (1951); Local 266 v. Salt River Project, 78 Ariz 30, 275 P2d 393 (1954); and Fellows v. LaTronica, 151 Colo 300, 377 P2d 547 (1962), where it is said in a concurring opinion (p 551):

The fact that the municipality engages in collective bargaining does not necessarily mean that it has surrendered its decision making authority with respect to public employment. The final decision as to what terms and conditions of employment the municipality will agree to, or whether it will agree at all, still rests solely with its legislative body.

On the "central question," the right of collective bargaining in public employment in the absence of legislative authority, the briefs show exhaustive research, which has been of great assistance to this court, and the contentions of all parties are well stated. We conclude that the Board of Education of the City of Chicago does not require legislative authority to enter into a collective bargaining agreement with a sole collective bargaining agency selected by its teachers, and we hold that such an agreement is not against public policy. Therefore, the order of the trial court, which struck and dismissed the Broman complaint, was proper and within the court's power.

In considering the "Opinion and Decree" and this record, we believe the trial court was presented with questions of substantial public interest, in a highly sensitive area, for which there were no precise limits or guidelines in this state. The court was required to act summarily if its action was to be effective. For the reasons given, the "Opinion and Decree" is affirmed.

Affirmed.

Kluczynski, P. J. and Burman, J., concur.

Pinellas County Classroom Teachers' Association, Inc. v. Board of Public Instruction of Pinellas County, Florida
214 So. 2d 34 (1968) Supreme Court of Florida

THORNAL, J.

We take jurisdiction of a direct appeal from a final decree of a circuit court which construes controlling provisions of the Florida and United States Constitutions.

Our ultimate decision is concluded by the power of a chancellor to enjoin a strike by public school teachers.

On January 11, 1967, the appellant, Pinellas County Classroom Teachers' Association, Inc., entered into a Professional Affairs Agreement with the appellee, Board of Public Instruction of Pinellas County. In this opinion we shall refer to the Agreement by that designation. The appellant association shall be called C. T. A., and the Board shall be so called. By the Agreement the Board recognized C. T. A. as the organization with which it would negotiate concerning salaries and working conditions of teachers. Both parties accepted "their individual obligations to assure the uninterrupted operation of the School System." By its terms it remained effective until January 15, 1968. Numerous Conferences were held pursuant to the agreement. In April, 1967, new contracts were sent to all teachers employed on an annual contract basis and to those moving into a continuing contract or tenure status. Testimony was that not a single contract was returned to the Board with any statement of reservations. As a result, before the beginning of the 1967-68 school term, the Board had received executed contracts from every teacher who was returning to the system either under tenure or on an annual contract basis. In the former category there were 2,699, and in the latter, 1,073. Copies of the two types of contracts were attached to the complaint and a list of the names of all teachers who signed them was placed in evidence. Additionally, there were 252 teachers under so-called binder agreements. These were new teachers whose certification from the State had not yet been received. In this status they were not members of C. T. A. when suit was filed. However, each of these had previously *received* and *accepted* a formal "notification of appointment" which the chancellor correctly held constituted an enforceable agreement.

Each *annual contract* recited a base salary and then expressly provided that the Board agrees to employ the teacher "at a salary not less than that shown above, and in accordance with the officially adopted salary schedule." Each *continuing contract* provided that the teacher was employed on a continuing basis "at an annual salary schedule heretofore or hereafter adopted by the County Board." The so-called *binder agreement* stated that "*The signatures on this offer will indicate that this agreement is binding* on the part of the County Board and you." The binder provided also that "The salary scale for the coming school year recognizing certification, rank, and acceptable experience, will be observed." This was accepted by the 252 new teachers.

Normally, under state regulations the budget of the Board should have been submitted to the State Superintendent of Public Instruction by August 3, 1967. However, due to legislative delays occasioned by teacher salary problems at the time, the Board could not adopt its 1967-68 salary schedule until August 10, 1967. The Chancellor held that the delay was excusable and we agree.

At the August 10, 1967, Board Meeting the vice-president of C. T. A. read a prepared statement to the effect that the salary schedule was unacceptable despite increases in all categories. On August 15, 1967, the president of C. T. A. delivered to the County Superintendent a written communication to the effect that the teachers could not begin the performance of services until "such things as salaries and general working conditions could be agreed and incorporated in their respective contracts."

With schools scheduled for opening on August 16, 1967, and the announced intention of the teachers to stay away from the classrooms, the Board sought and obtained a temporary injunction to prohibit the strike. The temporary injunction was granted on August 15, 1967, and was made permanent on August 31, 1967, after two days of extensive hearings.

By the injunctive decree the Chancellor announced: "That the Pinellas

County Classroom Teachers Association, Inc., and each of its members who hold an appointment with the Board of Public Instruction of Pinellas County, Florida, be and they are hereby permanently enjoined from striking, failing to report to work, stopping work, or failing to perform all or part of their duties of employment for the purpose of inducing, influencing or coercing a change in compensation or conditions of employment."

The Chancellor supplemented the formal decree with an explanatory opinion which was expressly incorporated into the decree. It is this decree which we now review on appeal.

Although appellants claim that the teachers were only negotiating and had never finalized contracts this record is abundantly clear that all three classes of teachers had binding contracts with the Board. While the stipulated salaries were stated to be the minimums or those stated in the schedule to be adopted by the Board, the fact remains that all elements of a contract were present and agreed upon in writing. The Chancellor correctly held that all parties bound by his decree had valid and enforceable contracts to teach in the Pinellas County schools for the year 1967-68, beginning August 16, 1967.

Appellants raise various objections to the pleadings. The complaint was properly brought against the appellant Association in order to bind its members by the decree. The Association represented the teachers who had acted in concert through C. T. A. as their bargaining agency. The members of C. T. A. were the only ones bound by the decree. Non-member teachers had not threatened to strike. Relief against them was neither sought, nor obtained.

The complaint adequately alleged bases for declaratory relief. Under Fla. R. Civ. P. 1.130(a), it was sufficient to attach copies of each of the several contracts and allege that they were signed respectively by the three categories of teachers.

Appellants have come directly here, claiming that the trial judge passed directly on the validity of Fla. Stat. § 839.221 (1967). This statute, in effect, prohibits governmental officers and employees from participating in strikes against the government. It states that "no person shall accept or hold any . . . employment in the service of the state, of any county or of any municipality . . ." who participates in any strike against the governmental employer. The statute guarantees the right to bargain as a member of a union or labor organization but precludes the right to strike against government.

The Chancellor did not really pass on the validity of the statute. He recognized the statute and then announced that even if it were inapplicable, "a person holding a government position has no right to strike without clear and direct legislative authority to do so." He based his ultimate judgment on the general powers of equity to prevent the breakdown of an essential aspect of government because of an unauthorized work stoppage by its employees. In following this course the Chancellor relied upon sound concepts and precedents. *Miami Water Works Local No. 654 v. City of Miami 26 So. 2d* 194 (Fla. 1946); *Dade County v. Amalgamated Association of Street Electric Railway & Motor Coach Employees of America*, [48 LC ¶ 50,964] 157 So. 2d 176 (3d Dist. Ct.

App. Fla. 1963); *Norwalk Teachers' Ass'n v. Board of Education of City of Norwalk*, [20 LC ¶ 66,543] 83 A. 2d 482 (Conn. 1951). In referring to strikes by public employees the decision last cited credits the late President Franklin D. Roosevelt with the statement that "Such action, looking toward the paralysis of Government by those who have sworn to support it, is unthinkable and intolerable." We share this view so clearly announced by one whom history records as a political patron saint of the modern labor movement. The Chancellor wisely made clear that his injunction could not preclude an unconditional termination of employment, nor could it be employed to impinge on freedom of speech, assembly or association short of the advocacy of a strike against the government.

The Chancellor did, however, construe the so-called "involuntary servitude" provisions of the state and federal Constitutions. Fla. Dec. of Rights § 19, provides in part: "Neither slavery nor involuntary servitude . . . shall ever be allowed in this state." Substantially identical proscriptions are announced by U. S. Const. amend. XIII.

Appellants insist that the injunction requires involuntary servitude as proscribed by the foregoing provisions. The Chancellor specifically held that it does not. He clearly stated that involuntary servitude is not involved simply because all he was doing was prohibiting a strike by a group of teachers who had been duly appointed and who had not terminated their employment. The Chancellor did not force the teachers to work. He merely offered them alternatives, which were: (1) to work and thereby comply with their contracts; (2) resign in accordance with the terms of their contracts; or, (3) resign in violation of their contracts and subject themselves to the provisions of Fla. Stat. § 231.36 (1965), which would make them ineligible for employment in the school system for a period of one year from the date of such violation.

We are not here confronted by an arbitrary mandate to compel performance of personal service against the will of the employee. These people were simply told that they had contracted with the government and that they could, if they wished, terminate the contract legally or illegally, and suffer the results thereof. They could not, however, strike against the government and retain the benefits of their contract positions.

Appellants place great reliance on *Henderson v. Coleman*, 150 Fla. 185, 7 So. 2d 117 (1942). This decision does not control the instant case. *Henderson* merely held that one man cannot be forced to serve another against his will. It then held that where "there was no contractual relation" between a union and a truck operator, the union members could not be required to work for the operator. In the case before us there was the "Professional Affairs Agreement" between the Board and C. T. A. Even more importantly, perhaps, the appellants were told that they could resign or breach their contracts, but they could not strike and bargain for a return to work while retaining their teacher status under contract terms. This is a significant aspect of the instant matter which should be carefully noted in employing this opinion in any future situation.

A "strike is ordinarily thought of as the physical act of employees leaving their workbenches or office desks and departing from their place of employment, but not including in such departure a severance of the employer-employee relationship." Forkosch, A Treatise on Labor Law (1965). The teachers here were not quitting their jobs or severing the employer-employee relationship. They were free to do that before and after the injunction. What they were really attempting to do here was to exert pressure on the School Board by refusing to go to work, but at the same time laying claim to their positions and asserting the right to go back to work on terms more acceptable to them. This, indeed, was a typical strike . . . .

The conclusion is almost inescapable that the action announced by members of appellant C. T. A. was a strike by any standard. It was a strike against the government which all authorities agree cannot be tolerated in the absence of expressed consent by the government. . . .

We affirm the holding of the Chancellor to the effect that in the absence of specific statutory authority an employee of government has no right to strike, as herein defined, in order to coerce a change in compensation or conditions of employment. To this end, we agree with the Chancellor when he stated:

To allow such action would permit the breakdown of governmental functions, would sanction the control of a governmental function for private gain; and further, to allow such action is the same as saying that governmental employees may deny the authority of government through its duly elected representatives. To permit this is to take the first step toward anarchy.

The decree is affirmed.

Caldwell, C. J., Thomas, Roberts, Drew and Adams (Retired), JJ., concur.

Problems and Discussion Questions

1. As teacher–board relations formalize through negotiations, grievance procedures, and collective-employment contracts, what changes follow for the role of the school's principal? How is the superintendent's role affected?

2. Short of strikes, sanctions, or other forms of concerted withholding of services what power mechanisms are available to teacher organizations? How can the public interest be recognized in teacher–board conflict?

3. Does collective action by teachers complement or contradict the concepts of professionalism? Why?

4. How might the organized teaching profession (teachers, administrators, and school boards) participate in political decisions as they concern schools?

5. Draft model grievance procedures which take into account the interests of teachers, pupils, administrators, and the community. Include machinery to resolve impasses.

6. What problems do teacher loyalty oaths seek to solve? What alternatives to loyalty oaths might protect the states' interest in education?

Annotated Bibliography

CARLTON, Patrick W., and Harold I. Goodwin (eds.), *The Collective Dilemma: Negotiations in Education*, Worthington, Ohio: Charles A. Jones Publishing Company, 1969.

This collection of thirty readings explores negotiations from both the operational and analytical levels. The readings are arranged under three major headings: the organized teacher, the practitioners, and the academicians. The pieces range in scope from the operational and specific (what is negotiable and the resolution of impasse) to the theoretical and general (analysis of power bases and the anatomy of militant professionalism). The selected readings deal with the significant and timely issues of role, process, and outcomes of negotiations in education. This collection provides an invaluable resource of analysis and informed opinion for the professional educator and interested layman alike.

DOHERTY, Robert E., and Walter E. Oberer, *Teachers, School Boards, and Collective Bargaining: A Changing of the Guard*, Ithaca, New York: New York State School of Industrial and Labor Relations, Cornell University, 1967.

In a lively, readable style, the authors in this modest book responded to four questions posed by them in this fashion: What has prompted this movement toward bilateral determination of employment conditions in the schools? What is the character of the teacher organizations behind this movement? What are the legal questions raised by collective action among teachers and what legislation has been and should be enacted? What implications does teacher bargaining have for the quality of the educational enterprise?

Although some data in the book are dated (much has developed in this area of education since 1966), the fundamental issues and strategies of teacher bargaining are much the same now as then. The questions and answers about bargaining legislation set out in Chapter III are particularly useful to teachers, administrators, and laymen interested in schools.

ELAM, Stanley M., Myron Lieberman, and Michael H. Moskow (eds.), *Readings on Collective Negotiations in Public Education*, Chicago: Rand McNally & Co., 1967.

The editors have organized this book into seven sections, with four to seven readings per section. The section titles are: I. The Background of Collective Negotiations in Public Education; II. The Legal and Political Framework for Collective Negotiations; III. Organizational Approaches to Collective Negotiations; IV. Organizational Issues in Collective Negotiations; V. Collective Negotiations and School Administration; VI. Strategy and Tactics in Collective Negotiations; VII. Special Issues in Collective Negotiations.

This collection of readings, as every good collection should, appears to studiously avoid an, editorial bias. This neutrality is most obviously attained by including readings of conflicting viewpoints within each section by authors noted for their expertise in their particular domain. Some of the more prominent authors are W. Willard Wirtz (Section I), Wesley A. Wildman (II); Alan M. West and Charles Cogen (III); Elam, Lieberman, and Moskow (IV); Bernard E. Donovan and Luvern L. Cunningham (V); David Selden (VI); Charles S. Benson (VII).

EPSTEIN, Benjamin, "*What is Negotiable?*" *Professional Negotiations Pamphlet Number One*, Washington, D.C.: The National Association of Secondary School Principals.

In speaking of the teacher, Epstein says that "he resents and feels in conflict with any individual, group, or set of factors which may, for any reason, limit, control, or curtail his freedom or which impose patterns of instructional methods or content other than the ones he feels most suitable." (p. 7) Substantiating this, Allan West (NEA) is quoted as saying: "We take the position that everything that affects the quality of education is negotiable." (p. 8) Also, Charles Cogen (AFT): "There's no limit to how far we'll go." (p. 8)

The author itemizes specific points currently being negotiated in various agreements between teachers and school boards—including headings such as "personal rights of teachers," "grievance machinery," and "educational practice and policy." The pamphlet closes with a discussion of seven criteria for negotiation proposed by the NASSP.

LIEBERMAN, Myron, and Michael H. Moskow, *Collective Negotiations for Teachers: An Approach to School Administration*, Chicago: Rand McNally & Co., 1966.

The authors present comprehensive sources for material on collective negotiations in education. The extensive bibliography (346 items) and the ten extremely important appendices (e.g., state statutes, judicial decisions, attorney general rulings, federal regulations, collective agreements, arbitration cases) attest to their search for relevant and useful information.

The framework within which the thirteen chapters are organized may be seen as a six-unit structure: introductory (Chap. I), history (II, III), constraints and procedures (IV, V, VI, VII), negotiations per se (VIII, IX, X, XI), impact on school administration (XII), the future of collective negotiations (XIII). Perhaps the whole of the work, however, points to Chapter IX—"The Process of Negotiations."

In this chapter, Lieberman and Moskow explore, in a rather concise fashion, the various dimensions of the negotiations process: the who, where, when, and how; influential factors confronting the parties; establishment and modification of goals; the attainment and ratification of agreements.

ROSENTHAL, Alan, *Pedagogues and Power*, New York: Syracuse University Press, 1969.

The major portion of this book (the first five chapters out of eight) is devoted to a rather intensive study of the similarities and differences between the National Education Association and the American Federation of Teachers. Dealing first at the national level, Rosenthal soon concentrates on New York City, Boston, San Francisco, and Chicago as the arenas for the study of leader motivation, dimensions of militancy, and patterns of organizational behavior—always contrasting or comparing the NEA-affiliated organizations to those of the AFT (as well as discussing some attempts made by a few independent organizations).

In Chapter VI ("The Government of Education") the author analyzes the distribution of "educational power" in the cities mentioned above, as well as the city of Atlanta. The next chapter ("Organizational Influence") enumerates both the efforts and effects of the previously discussed teachers' organizations as regards educational policymaking (e.g., in matters of economic welfare, curriculum, working conditions, etc.).

In a summary chapter, the author concludes that "organizational imperatives now impel teachers to behave militantly. Contests between unions and associations, the conduct of professional organizers assigned to local affiliates, intra-group competition, and the achievements of the union in New York City all encourage action." (p. 185)

."*School Boards in an Era of Conflict*," Stanford University: Cubberly Conference Highlights, July 26–28, 1966 (*Education U.S.A.* Special Report).

The conference brought together an impressive group of teacher-scholars, including H. Thomas James, Wesley A. Wildman, John Guy Fowlkes, David W. Minar, Max J. Rubin, Jerry Fine, Alan K. Campbell, Roald F. Campbell.

In addition to presenting a synopsis of each participant's contributions, the editors of this report have included a bibliography of the items used as reference by each of them. In essence, the conference emphasized that the role of the school board is not well understood—by anyone —and that there is an urgent need for clarification of this role so that teacher-administrator-board-community relationships can improve, and thus provide a unified support for improving elementary and secondary public education.

TISDEL, Richard P., "Academic Freedom—Its Constitutional Context," *University of Colorado Law Review*, 40:600, Summer, 1968.

Following a brief narrative of the history of the "academic freedom" concept, Tisdel turns to a thorough discussion of several judicial opinions handed down in cases in which the concept has been the issue. The author notes that "the courts have not formulated a workable definition of academic freedom." Although the Supreme Court has recently approached the view of holding academic freedom as an independent right, with independent constitutional status, Tisdel presents a strong argument that such a view is both unnecessary and impractical.

Tisdel's point is that academic freedom should be constitutionally interpreted and treated as "an interest of society rather than as a personal right of a small sector of the society."

When Boards Negotiate or Bargain, Springfield, Ill.: Illinois Association of School Boards, December, 1967.

This pamphlet is third in a four-step program "designed to assist boards, administrators and other school officers when they face this (collective negotiations) problem." (p. ii)

Step One was the preparation of the *Statement of Principles on Board-Staff Relationships*, Step Two, an IASB Leadership Seminar; Step Four—December 1967 and January 1968—a series of workshops for board members, administrators and other school officers.

The pamphlet offers suggestions and states principles regarding preparations for negotiations, who shall bargain, and what to do in case of an impasse. After explaining grievance machinery—what it is and why it is an item at nearly every bargaining table—Wesley Wildman outlines model grievance procedures.

6

School Funds, School Property, and the Law

INTRODUCTION

Public education is a state responsibility supported by local, state, and federal resources. State and local taxes provide 92 cents of every school dollar; the remaining 8 cents come from federal sources. The local school districts use their tax funds to pay salaries of teachers, administrators, and support personnel; maintain and operate school plants; purchase goods and services necessary for school operation; and pay interest on school debts. Capital improvement and new construction expenses normally come from the sale of bonds issued by the school board with approval of the district voters. This chapter outlines some basic legal problems in school finance, the tax-support structures, the use of school funds and school property, and some implications of federal support to public elementary and secondary schools. School-support laws vary widely among the states; an exhaustive treatment of school finance is beyond the scope of this chapter.

STATE AND LOCAL TAX SUPPORT

State laws generally provide for school support through public taxation. State school funds come from a wide range of tax sources: personal income taxes, sales taxes, use and occupation taxes, franchise and license fees, inheritance and gift taxes, and other taxes on specific objects, events, or activities. Some states designate certain taxes for education; others draw upon the general tax funds to meet their obligations to local districts. The states vary considerably in the machinery used to channel state tax funds to local districts. Two common devices are the flat grant and the equalization grant. The mechanisms for state support of schools focus on incentives for local district efforts and aim for equality of educational opportunity for all children in the state.

The state may encourage local taxation for education by setting minimum tax rates to qualify the district for state support. These qualifying tax rates are expressed either in mills (tenth of a cent) per dollar or cents per $100 dollars of assessed valuation. State law or state constitutions may set upper limits on local school taxes; below that limit, the voters in the district may authorize a tax rate on all taxable property in the district. Many local districts are near their upper limits of taxation for schools and face severe economic problems in school finance. The state flat grants generally go to districts on the basis of average daily attendance during the previous school year. Some states provide for adjustments of attendance bases during the current year to account for rapid increases in school enrollments. The grants, computed on district reports, are paid to the local school units periodically during the fiscal year.

Equalization support from state sources aims to bring some degree of equality to district school funds. State funds are apportioned to local districts by statutory formulas involving district property valuation, local tax rate for education, and number of pupils. Under such plans, state funds are allocated on the basis of local need. Achievement of equality of educational opportunity in a given state depends on the effectiveness of the tax-allocation system among the school districts. As urbanization continues, the polarization of school income into rich and poor districts is likely to continue. Unless some equalization machinery intervenes, the rich districts will continue to offer their children substantially more educational resources than the poor districts. Wide disparities in per-pupil expenditure for education exist within and among the states. In 1966–1967, Alabama spent $380 per pupil and New York spent $1,140. Even allowing for variations in the schools' cost of living, the inequities are apparent. The constitutional provisions for school finance vary widely, but the need for revised plans for school support is evident.

Local taxation provides the bulk of school funds in over half the states; state funds provide the major support in the rest of the states. Local taxes are imposed under taxing power granted to the district by the legislature. The power to tax cannot be implied from the boards' power to operate and maintain schools; the power is not "necessary" and alternative support schemes can be provided. Whenever the state laws grant local school districts the power to tax, the statute will be construed strictly and must be followed on procedural matters. Generally, the districts' tax objects are real and personal property, although some states extend local school taxes to other objects and sources. Computation of local school taxes is a simple formula: school tax rate (expressed in mills or cents) times the assessed valuation of taxable property equals the school tax. Assessed valuation may not be the market value of property but rather some fraction of its market value. In some states, assessed valuation may be less than one-half the market value; in other states it may be nearer the market value.

Subject to constitutional or statutory limitations, the local school board determines its budget in advance of the fiscal year, estimates the assessed valuation of taxable property in the district, and computes the rate necessary to raise the needed amount of revenue. The board may be fiscally dependent or independent; if dependent, the board must seek budget approval from some other public body, such as the city, county, or intermediate governing body. Fiscally independent boards determine their own budgets and tax rates. The law generally provides opportunity for public inspection and objection to the school budget. Public hearings may be held to give the public an opportunity to discuss proposed expenditures with the school board or its agents. The school tax may be coupled with other governmental units and a single tax bill prepared for the owners of property. In some states, tax-assessment and tax-collection functions are performed by different public officials. Regardless of the scheme, the local school districts ultimately receive local tax funds for school use. The payments may come to the district in periodic installments. Upon their receipt, the local board may have the power to invest excess operating funds in certain types of securities until the funds are needed. State laws generally restrict the board's power to invest school funds. These limitations safeguard the public against the board's speculation and diminution or loss of tax monies. The management of school-tax funds is a technical matter and reference to specific state laws is necessary for an accurate understanding of the procedures and limitations.

Most states provide for public participation in decisions about school taxes. The upper limits of school taxation may be provided by statute; periodic referenda to qualified electors in the district are common forms of public participation. The referendum, conducted under statutory authority and specified procedures, presents the issue of tax increases to the voters. If the referendum fails, the board must adjust projected expenditures downward to stay within its school income. Borrowing against future tax income is permitted in many states. Whenever the board cannot meet its fiscal needs from current tax income, the evidence of future tax receipts (commonly known as tax-anticipation warrants) may be "sold" to lending institutions and the receipts used for current school expenses. By trimming future expenses or by receiving increased tax income by virtue of increased future assessments or an increased tax rate, the school board repays "borrowed" funds in subsequent fiscal years. It should be noted that the board cannot depend on the receipt of all taxes due. In a given fiscal year, a portion of anticipated taxes are not paid and the school must await the collection of these delinquent taxes. The board's failure to anticipate delinquent taxes in its accounting can cause financial embarrassment to the district. Tax funds generally must be used for current operating expenses (expenses incurred during a given fiscal year, such as salaries, supplies, materials, utilities, and maintenance costs). Accumulation of excess operating funds is generally limited by statute. The purpose of this limitation is to hold school-tax income to a level near to school needs and minimize "overtaxation" for school purposes. To permit systematic overtaxation would impose unnecessary burdens on taxable property.

Funds for capital expenditures for major school plant improvement and new construction generally come from the sale of bonds. The board's authority to issue bonds must be granted by the state law; such authority will not be implied. Bonds are certificates evidencing a debt by the school district and generally must be approved by the voters in a special election called for that purpose. Upon approval by the voters, the school district sells the bonds and uses the proceeds for the purposes specified in the bond referendum. Some states permit the board to use certain tax funds in conjunction with proceeds from bond issues on capital improvement projects.

The legal issues in school-tax and school-bond matters usually arise from (1) alleged violation of statutory procedural requirements for school budgets, referenda, notice, and other technical requirements surrounding the imposition of the tax or the issuance and sale of the bonds, and (2) alleged use of school funds for unauthorized purposes. The school board's power to tax and issue bonds is not inherent but must come from specific statutory authority. The statutory requirements as to procedural details generally must be met by the school board. When procedural irregularities occur, the court must determine whether the statutory provisions are mandatory or directory. In determining the validity of tax procedures, the basic problem for the court is to preserve the substantial rights of the public without unduly hampering the school-funding process. Whether an irregularity deprives the public of substantial rights turns on whether the public right to participate in the tax decision was impaired.

State legislatures usually surround the district's authority to tax and to issue bonds with procedures designed to protect the district and the public from misuse and mismanagement of public funds. The courts are sensitive to alleged irregularities in the board's exercise of district taxing or bonding authority. Support of the public schools rest on the voters' confidence in the judgment and integrity of board members executing their public trust as a board. The substantial influence and power entrusted to the board and their employees over the lives and resources of the community explain in part the narrow limits and broad oversight of fiscal matters imposed by the legislature and the courts.

USE OF SCHOOL FUNDS

The purposes for which school boards may lawfully authorize the expenditure of school funds generally are specified in the state laws concerning schools or derived by implication from the purposes of the school district. Spending authority may be granted to the board by the legislature in broad, general language. The grant of authority seldom includes the myriad of specific objects of services for which boards may spend tax funds. For example, the legislature may authorize the board to employ teachers but refrain from specifying salary levels, increments, schedules, or differential salaries for various levels of experience or role responsibility. The authority to make such specific role and salary decisions and the express authority to employ teachers, however, probably would not support any implied power to pay salary bonuses to teachers from tax funds.

A fundamental proposition of school finance is that public tax funds can be spent only for public purposes and only those public purposes authorized to the board by express or implied legislative delegation. School boards have no legal authority to expend public funds for private purposes. Prospective expenditures of public funds may be enjoined by the court in an appropriate legal action; partial or complete execution of *ultra vires* contracts raises more difficult problems. In the latter case, there is a split of authority; some states permit recovery by the injured party on an implied contract for the value of goods or services supplied, and other states leave the parties where they are found and refuse to inject the power of the court into illegal situations. School districts are quasi-corporate bodies with limited power; the duty to ascertain the limits of such power rests on those who deal with the board. This view, coupled with the urgent need to protect public funds, may account for the weight of authority holding that no recovery can be had on *ultra vires* contracts.

Expenditures authorized by the legislature but circumscribed by statutory procedures present a different issue. In such cases, the court must determine whether the procedural requirements were directory rather than mandatory. As noted earlier, the general rationale in such matters is to protect substantial public rights. If the board's noncompliance with statutory procedures denied the public's substantial rights, the general rule holds such action void. If no substantial rights have been injured by procedural irregularities, the procedure may be considered directory only or the board may subsequently correct the error or ratify the contracts, and the expenditure and surrounding contracts are upheld. These questions raised by the board's unauthorized expenditure of tax funds are difficult and no completely satisfactory solutions have been found.

USE OF SCHOOL PROPERTY

The board's authority to use school property for purposes other than strictly educational (classroom and extracurricular activities for children) programs frequently comes under attack. The board's authority to lease or rent school land, buildings, or facilities; to operate bookstores and cafeterias; to sponsor athletic, cultural, and entertainment events open to the paying public and similar ventures of a commercial nature has been legally challenged. Further complications may develop from the board's inconsistency in permitting nonschool groups to use school facilities. The problem frequently arises from the board's refusal of use to religious and political groups. Generally, the board is free to refuse the use of school property to all nonschool groups. If the board chooses to allow nonschool use and the statutes permit, the board must not discriminate unfairly against any group. Criteria for nonschool use must be developed and followed by the board in considering applications for use. If the board has authority to grant permission, the courts are reluctant to set aside the board's decision unless it is clearly arbitrary and capricious. Whenever the state statutes specify use of school premises by outside groups, few problems seem to arise. The few problems stem from conflicts of interpretation of the statute as to permitted uses and groups. The problems seem to come from states with either cryptic legislation or legislative silence on the question of use.

Among the states with no explicit statutory guidelines concerning the use of school property, the cases reveal considerable conflict. One line of decisions restricts the use of school property to strictly school purposes on the ground that money raised by taxation for one purpose may not be used for another. Another line of cases, reflecting a more liberal view, permits the board to use school property for other than school purposes, provided the permitted use does not interfere with the primary purpose of the schools, particularly when district school funds are augmented by the permitted use. In these cases, the court looks at the wording and import of the statute, if any, and at the public policy regarding use as expressed through the prior cases. The use of school premises for community social and cultural events seems to be gaining broad legal acceptance.

The determination of whether specific uses are school-related is not without difficulty. Some legal opinions reflect a cautious view of board authority; in such views, boards may use school property only for those purposes expressly granted by statute or necessarily implied from the powers granted. Contrary opinions speak of changing times, social needs, legislative intent; these opinions support those uses not prohibited by statute and not contrary to the fundamental objects of education. As our understanding of the educational needs matures and expands to include social, emotional, physical, and intellectual experiences, so should the laws move beyond the narrow, parochial interpretations of school uses. If judicial construction of statutory purpose cannot reach the needs, the legislatures must recast the statutes to accommodate rather than frustrate these needs.

One can fairly predict continued litigation on the use of school funds and school property. The general dissatisfaction with public schools and their programs will surely promote public demands for drastic revision in the present system. The traditional views about board power over school resources will be challenged by the social activism movement in general and the student militancy in particular. It seems unlikely that the law can remain encased in nineteenth-century views.

FEDERAL SUPPORT TO EDUCATION

Federal aid to education is channeled through numerous agencies. The Office of Education, the Office of Economic Opportunity, and the National Science Foundation have pumped billions of dollars into public education over the past two decades. These funds come to schools both directly from the federal agencies and indirectly through state agencies. The schools use the federal funds for equipment, special services, training facilities, development of curriculum materials, experimentation with different methods of teaching, and for new organizational patterns of teachers, pupils, and school facilities for learning. Federal funding seeks to improve the quality of public schooling through the creation and application of new knowledge, better practices, and by encouraging increased local and state effort. Matching and "seed-money" grants to states and school districts encourage additional financial effort on these levels. The major piece of federal legislation for public schools, the Elementary and Secondary Education Act, was enacted in 1965. This act, set out in the reading section of chapter 1, provides financial assistance for special programs for educationally deprived children by local school districts; for improving instructional materials for local district schools; for special services, research, and grants to strengthen state departments of education.

Federal grants are categorical; the funds must be used for the specific purposes set forth in the statutes. The spirit behind these federal bills is to encourage schools and universities to rethink persistent problems and design imaginative alternatives to traditional programs. Enterprising school districts have benefited considerably from these opportunities; the vast majority of districts have not. Funding guidelines generally require specific proposals and detailed plans of attack from the applicant schools and agencies. Proposal writing is a high-risk enterprise in competitive funding situations. Many districts have neither the writing skill nor the inclination to make the risk investment necessary to obtain federal funds. The very schools which so desperately need help do not get it through the federal programs. This unfortunate state of affairs may be a partial result of the local control pattern in our schools. The federal government cannot force any program onto local schools; it can only offer assistance, encourage participation in the programs. For a variety of reasons, local school authorities may choose to ignore the opportunity. Unless alternative funding sources are available, the educational benefit is denied to children in those districts. Local pride, political views, fear of federal "control," and local power-structure conflicts may promote local decisions against participation in federal programs. Regardless of the educational impact such decisions may have on children in the local schools, the federal agencies are powerless to intervene.

Some legal issues have been raised by federal aid. Districts receiving federal funds must comply, of course, with the regulations and guidelines in the particular legislation. Alleged violations of civil rights among pupils in participating districts have prompted federal inquiry and review of policies and practices in the schools. Federal funds have been blocked in a few instances while charges of civil-rights violations were investigated. Busing plans, sponsored by federal funds, have created dissension and civil disturbances in some school districts.

The legality of federal aid to private schools has not been settled in any sense. Federal funds are available to private schools through a variety of funding agencies. The legal fiction employed in Title II of ESEA, for example, is to vest title to the school materials in a public school although the materials themselves may be housed and used in private schools (Secs. 203 and 205 of Title II). The fiction is necessary to circumvent the obvious legal difficulty in using public funds for private purposes and, in the case of aid to parochial schools, the prohibitions of the First Amendment. To date, the United States Supreme Court has not spoken on the issue of federal aid to private schools. There are ample precedents and fictions (the "child benefit" theory, for example, as enunciated in

Board of Education v. Allen, 392 U.S. 236 [1968]) to suggest that federal aid to private schools could be permitted under the constitution.

(Congress has no legal obligation to act on educational matters but does so voluntarily.) Despite periodic crises in the national budget, there is little reason to expect the federal government to withdraw from public school support. Many school problems, such as functional illiteracy, high dropout rates among the poor and minority groups, and inadequate local and state resources, transcend state and regional lines. The states have demonstrated neither the ability nor intent to solve such problems on state or regional bases. National goals are closely interlocked with education and, to paraphrase, "everyone's business is no one's responsibility"; to leave all educational matters to state or local decisions is to play roulette with too many children. National self-interest, if nothing else, will require continued federal support to education.

Cases

A. School Taxes

Dean v. Coddington
131 N.W. 2d 700 (1964) (South Dakota)

RENTTO, JUDGE

By the enactment of Ch. 67, Laws of 1959, now SDC 1960 Supp. 15.2246, this state initiated a foundation program of state support to school districts. This act was in effect re-enacted with amendments and additional provisions by Ch. 76, Laws of 1961 and Ch. 77, Laws of 1963. Ch. 365, Laws of 1963 appropriated $4,500,000.00 for the fiscal year ending June 30, 1964 and a similar amount for the year ending June 30, 1965, from the State Treasury to be distributed to the eligible schools in the manner provided in said Ch. 77.

In this proceeding plaintiff is asking that Ch. 77, Laws of 1963, be declared invalid and that the defendants be enjoined from making distribution of the 1963 appropriation. He asserts that said Ch. 77 violates that part of Sec. 17, Art. VI of our Constitution which provides that all taxation shall be equal and uniform. He makes the further claim that it denies him equal protection of the law in violation of the 14th Article of Amendment to the Constitution of the United States. The defendants' motion to dismiss the complaint for failure to state a claim upon which relief could be granted was sustained. This appeal is from the order of dismissal.

In Ch. 77 the legislative purpose of the program is declared to be as follows:

It is hereby declared to be the policy of this state that education is a state and local function and whereas some relief should be provided from local property tax as a source of school revenue where such tax is excessive, and that other sources of revenue should contribute to the total funds needed for public education; that in order to provide reasonable equality in school tax rates among the various school districts in the state and to provide reasonable equality of educational opportunity for all the children in the state, the state shall assist in giving a basic educational opportunity to each student, but that the state should be obligated to contribute to the support of the basic educational program only if the district provides a program which meets the requirements and standards hereinafter set forth.

The act establishes a foundation program fund to include all funds appropriated to, or designated to it by law, gift or grant including any money appropriated by the Federal Congress for purposes of equalizing school opportunity. It prescribes rules for determining the eligibility of school districts to receive funds and sophisticated formulas concerning the amount thereof. The eligibility requirements and payment formulas are designed to encourage improvement of education at the local level.

The stipulation by which the pertinent facts involved were presented to the court reveals that plaintiff is a resident and taxpayer of Lakeview Common School District No. 3 in Hutchinson County, South Dakota. Such district did not maintain a secondary or an elementary school during the school year 1962–63, and did not plan to maintain any during the 1963–64 school year. The students living in the district attended school in the Independent School District of Scotland, Bon Homme County, South Dakota. The tuition for the high school students was paid to the Scotland district from the County High School Tuition Fund. This fund is raised by a tax levied on all common school districts in the county. The tuition for those in the elementary grades was paid by the Lakeview district out of money raised by taxing the property of that district.

The Lakeview district, under the Foundation Program, was not eligible to receive any of the funds appropriated to the foundation by Ch. 365, Laws of 1963 for the fiscal year ending June 30, 1964 because it had not operated a school during the previous school fiscal year. Further, the Lakeview children attending the Scotland school were by the formula counted in its enrollment thus enhancing the payment from the foundation to the Scotland district. These results are complained of by the plaintiff and made the basis of his claim of unconstitutionality. He asserts that the effect of the law is to lower taxes in the Scotland district while leaving them constant in the Lakeview district.

Art. VI, § 17 of our Constitution, so far as here material provides: "all taxation shall be equal and uniform". The test of uniformity under this section is substantially the same as under the 14th Amendment to the United States Constitution. State ex rel. Botkin v. Welsh, 61 S.D. 593, 251 N.W. 189. Plaintiff admits that the taxes levied upon the taxpayers of the state to raise the $9,000,000.00 appropriated by Ch. 365, Laws of 1963 were probably uniformly raised, but he contends that the uniformity provision of our constitution is not satisfied unless they are uniformly distributed. As observed by the trial judge the effect of plaintiff's contention would apply this section of our constitution as though it read—and all *expenditures* shall be equal and uniform.

The general rule applicable in this situation is stated in 84 C.J.S. Taxation § 34 to be:

It is generally held that the constitutional provisions requiring equality and uniformity relate to the levy of taxes, and not to the distribution or application of the revenue derived therefrom; and hence statutes relative to the distribution or application of such money cannot be held invalid on this ground.

After observing that it was not unusual for states after collecting taxes on a statewide basis to make distribution of revenues to municipal corporations, particularly school districts, the court in Hess v. Mullaney, 213 F.2d 635, 15 Alaska 40, Cert. denied Hess v. Dewey, 348 U.S. 836, 75 S.Ct. 50, 99 L.Ed. 659, goes on to say: "No requirements of uniformity or of equal protection of the law limit the power of a legislature in respect to allocation and distribution of public funds. . . .

The act in question does not levy a tax, nor is it an appropriation measure. It is concerned only with the distribution of money accruing to the foundation fund. The only assets that the fund has had for distribution are those that have been appropriated to it by the legislature. None of such money was raised by an ad valorem tax on the property of the plaintiff or anyone else in the state. As above indicated no claim is made that the levies by which the state raises revenue for its general fund are not uniform. . . .

The guiding principles which we think govern in this field are well stated in 79 C.J.S. Schools and School Districts § 411, wherein it is written:

In the absence of constitutional regulation the method of apportioning and distributing a school fund, accruing from taxes or other revenue, rests in the wise discretion of the state legislature, which method, in the absence of abuse of discretion or violation of some constitutional provision, cannot be interfered with by the courts. Apportionment statutes are designed to promote equality of facilities, and if the purpose of public welfare is kept in view in making the distribution, the fact that the fund is distributed unequally among the different districts or political subdivisions does not render it invalid.

Accordingly the trial court did not err in dismissing plaintiff's complaint. . . .

Affirmed.

All the Judges concur.

Herschel C. Latham et al., Appellants, vs. The Board of Education of the City of Chicago et al., Appellees
31 Ill. 2d 178 (1964)

Appeal from the Circuit Court of Cook County; the Hon. Walker Butler, Judge, presiding.

MR. JUSTICE UNDERWOOD DELIVERED THE OPINION OF THE COURT

Plaintiffs appeal from an order of the circuit court of Cook County sustaining a motion to strike their complaint for declaratory judgment and for injunction, denying them leave to file an amended and supplemental complaint and dismissing the suit. The presence of constitutional questions warrants this direct appeal.

This is a representative suit filed by plaintiffs as citizens, taxpayers, voters, and residents of the city of Chicago wherein they seek a judgment declaring the statutes providing for the creation and corporate existence of the Board of Education of the City of Chicago to be unconstitutional, and also seek to enjoin the levy, collection and expenditure of any and all taxes for the support of the School District of the City of Chicago.

Plaintiffs' original complaint consists of five counts, the first of which alleges the status of plaintiffs to maintain the action and states, in substance, that the procedures required by article 34 of the School Code (Ill. Rev. Stat. 1963, chap. 122, art. 34,) which applies only to cities having a population over 500,000, result in the Board of Education of the City of Chicago levying taxes for the city's educational system, and that such levy by the Board, whose members are appointed rather than elected, constitutes an unlawful exercise of the power to tax in violation of section 9 of article IX of the constitution of the State of Illinois. The procedures referred to involve a detailed report of estimated financial needs and receipts by the general superintendent to the Board, Board preparation of a budget, hearings thereon prior to submission thereof to the city council, and, it is alleged, determination by the Board of the rate of tax to be extended in order to produce the revenue desired. Plaintiffs contend these acts constitute the actual tax levy and that the subsequent passage of a levy ordinance by the city council is a perfunctory act.

To support their argument that, in fact, the Board rather than the city council levies the taxes needed to support the Chicago school system, plaintiffs points to language found in sections 34—53, 34—54, 34—57 and 35—58 of the School Code. Of the four provisions the principal one is section 34—53, and the pertinent language therein is as follows: "For the purpose of establishing and supporting free schools . . . the board of education *and the authorities of such district or city* . . . may levy annually . . . a tax . . . provided that the taxes so levied . . . shall not exceed the estimated amounts of taxes to be levied for such year . . . and set forth in the annual school budget of the Board. . . . (Italics ours). It is significant that in this section and in sections 34—54 and 34—57 the statutory language authorizing the levy is always framed in the conjunctive, joining the Board *and* the municipal authorities. Only section 34—58 of the provisions cited by plaintiffs does not contain such conjunctive language but states that: . . . the board may levy or cause to be levied annually for the purpose of carrying out the provisions thereof a tax. . . . Such language considered alone might be thought to indicate that the Board itself may levy a tax. However, in section 34—55 the legislature expressly negates such an implication by the following language: "This Article does not authorize the board to levy or collect any tax, but the city council shall, upon the demand and under the direction of the board, annually levy all school taxes." Ill. Rev. Stat. 1963, chap. 122, par. 34—55. . . .

The substance of count II charges that the provisions of article 34 which provide for the appointment of members to the board of education in cities exceeding 500,000 population, whereas board members are elected elsewhere in the State, is special legislation violative of section 22 of article IV of the constitution of Illinois, and that the classification thus established on the basis of population bears no reasonable relationship to the objectives sought to be accomplished. . . .

The controlling rule is well established that: "Classification on the basis of population is not objectionable where there is a reasonable basis therefor in view of the object and purposes to be accomplished by the legislation and such an act is not local or special merely because it operates in only one place, if that is where the conditions necessary to its operation exist." . . .

When drafting article 34 the legislature determined that it should apply only to cities having a population exceeding 500,000 and that each such city should constitute one school district. The legislature further provided that in each such district, the Board members should be appointed by the mayor with the approval of the city council. In the briefs of both parties herein may be found statistics suggesting the magnitude of the Chicago school system. The fact that, in 1964, the Chicago Board of Education will spend in excess of $300,000,000, or that in the Chicago School District there are more than 1,700,000 voters are but examples. Moreover, this court takes judicial notice that the problems inherent in the supervision and management of a school system in a metropolitan area of 500,000 or more, and particularly, in the city of Chicago, are far more complex and may well require different modes of operation than a system in an average-size district. The intricacies of a metropolitan school district of this magnitude require an especially high degree of competence in the members of the Board. The legislature has determined that such personnel can best be obtained as Board members in large cities having a population of over 500,000 by the appointive process rather than by a general city election, and has so provided in sections 34—1 to 34—4. Whether or not the General Assembly has chosen the best method to accomplish an objective is a legislative and not a judicial question.

Hence, the classification found in article 34, restricting its operation to cities having a population exceeding 500,000, being based upon exigencies found in such metropolitan areas, does not create local or special legislation and is therefore constitutionally valid. The trial court properly dismissed count II.

In count III plaintiffs allege that article 34 denies them equal protection of the laws because it establishes an arbitrary classification and because it deprives them of the right to vote for members of the Board of Education which franchise is given residents of smaller districts. In *People ex rel. Heydenreich* v. *Lyons*, 374 Ill. 557, this court said at 564: "The constitutional guaranty of equal protection of the laws is interposed against discriminations that are purely arbitrary. The fourteenth amendment does not purport to prevent a State from adjusting its legislation to differences in situation and to that end to make a justifiable classification. It merely requires that the classification shall be based on a real and substantial difference having a rational relation to the subject of the particular legislation. . . . The classification need not, however, be accurate, scientific, logical or harmonious, so long as it is not arbitrary and will accomplish the legislative design."

Our discussion of count II established the propriety of the legislative classification found in sections 34—1 through 34—4 of article 34. Where a classification is reasonable and the statute is uniform in its operation on all members of the class to which it applies, there is no violation of the constitutional guaranty of equal protection of law. . . .

Plaintiffs' contention that article 34 denies them their inherent right to directly elect members of the Board of Education in their school district is adequately answered in *People* v. *Deatherage*, 401 Ill. 25, where we said at page 35: "The legislature possessing all power to legislate in reference to public school matters, limited only by the stated limitations found in section 1 of article VIII of the constitution, no resident of a school district has an inherent right of franchise insofar as school elections are concerned. His right to vote therein is purely a permissive one bestowed by legislative grace in furtherance of the policy of the legislature."

Count IV alleges article 34 of the School Code is violative of due process in that it is an arbitrary delegation of police power and governmental functions to a board not responsible to the electorate, reposes unregulated discretion in an appointive board, is an unlawful delegation of legislative power and that the power to tax so delegated deprives plaintiffs of their property without due process. The legislature is mandated by the constitution of Illinois to establish a system of free schools for all the children of the State and in furtherance of such legitimate legislative responsibilities the General Assembly may delegate to such agencies as it sees fit the power to do those things which it might properly but cannot understandingly or advantageously do itself. This court has said: "The power of the legislature to create public corporations is practically unlimited. It may create any conceivable kind of a corporation it sees fit for the more efficient administration of public affairs and endow such corporation with such powers and functions as it deems necessary and proper for the administration of such corporate powers and affairs. (*People ex rel. Wies* v. *Bowman*, 247 Ill. 276)."

Moreover, since the Board's functions and powers are expressly defined in article 34, as are the maximum rates at which taxes may be levied, it is apparent that the powers of the Board are not absolute, unregulated or undefined as argued by plaintiffs. In addition to the above we regard what we have said with reference to Counts I, II and III as dispositive of the argument made with reference to count IV, and no error resulted from its dismissal.

Count V of the complaint alleges that although section 34—3 confers upon the mayor of the city of Chicago responsibility for appointment of members of the Board of Education, subject to the approval of the city council, the mayor's practice of making such appointments from a list of nominees submitted to him by an "Advisory Commission on School Board Nominations" constitutes an "unconstitutional delegation of legislative authority and powers to private individuals". The commission is stated to be composed of the heads of universities, civic, business, labor and professional organizations who serve at the mayor's request, meeting to consider recommendations to be made to the mayor whenever appointments to the Board of Education are required. It is further alleged that the commission has, on occasion, adopted criteria for consideration of nominees in addition to the statutory qualifications for appointment set forth in section 34—4. The amended complaint added the allegation that the mayor had "bound himself" to make appointments only from the list of nominees submitted by the commission. While the method by which the mayor "bound himself" is not specified in the pleadings, it is stated in the briefs that he did so by statements made during his election campaigns.

That serious consideration of count V is unmerited is apparent. No action by the mayor could bind the members of the city council, whose approval is required by section 34—3. The mayor has not, by seeking the advice and suggestions of the advisory commission, legally restricted his appointees to those individuals thus recommended. If such pre-election statements of intention were made, they would not prevent his subsequent action to the contrary if his judgment so dictates. As the trial court aptly stated in referring to the relationship between the mayor and the commission, "consultation is not abdication". . . .

The judgment of the circuit court of Cook County is therefore affirmed.

Use of School Property

Herald v. Board of Education
65 W. Va. 765 (1909)

Appeal from Circuit Court, Harrison County.

Bill by John Herald and others against the Board of Education and others. Decree for defendants, and plaintiffs appeal.

Reversed.

BRANNON, JUDGE

By deed dated 29th August, 1892, Isaac N. Harbert and others conveyed to The Board of Education of Sardis District and their successors in office, sixty-five poles of land, in Harrison county, "for the purpose of building a school house on the same for the benefit of free schools." The parcel of land is in use for free school purposes. It is used as a site for a school house, which is in actual use as a school house. The board of education passed a resolution, 27th May, 1907, authorizing a lease to W. J. Rowland and F. L. Grove of the lot for the purpose of the production of oil and gas, and under that resolution the president of the board made a lease of the lot to Rowland and Grove for the purpose of the production of oil and gas for one year and as long thereafter as oil or gas either should be produced from the lot. In July, 1907, John Herald and several others suing for themselves and other residents, citizens and tax payers of said district, brought a chancery suit against the board of education and Rowland and Grove stating that the plaintiffs were residents within School District No. 20 in the District of Sardis, and were tax payers within that district, and that they were patrons of the free school within that district, and that the said lot was situate within sub-district No. 20, and that children of the plaintiff's attended school on the said lot, and alleging that the said lease was unauthorized and beyond the power of the board to make and seeking to have it annulled as illegal and void. They prayed that said lessees be enjoined from using the said lot for the development of oil and gas. A provisional injunction was granted; but later a decree was pronounced declaring that the board of education had authority of law to execute the said lease, and that the lessees under it had authority to bore for oil and gas on the said lot, and to produce oil and gas therefrom, provided that in so doing their operations should not interfere with, disturb or prevent the orderly conduct of the public school in session at any time during such oil productions, and that such school was not then in actual session, and would not be until later in the year. Thereupon it was decreed that the injunction be so modified and dissolved to such an extent as to admit Rowland and Grove to proceed with operation until the school in the district should begin, and that thereafter such operation should be conducted only before and after school hours and not while the school was in session or while such school house and lot were in actual use during school hours for school purposes. The plaintiffs appeal to this Court.

This is a very important case. It involves the power of a government corporation performing the most important function to divert public property to uses other than those contemplated by law.

The defense contests the right to the plaintiffs to interfere in the action of a public board. They say that the board has title, and the plaintiffs have no interest. But these people are the very persons most deeply and clearly interested in the use of the lot for school purposes for their children. It is said no individual can enjoin a public nuisance, unless he has a special interest affected. *Talbott* v. *King*, 32 W. Va. 6. But these plaintiffs have a direct, immediate, practical interest as parents. Are they to wait for the county superintendent or attorney-general to act? Who will surely vindicate their rights which they surely have? I quote the following from Spelling on Extra. Relief, see, 684: "The letting of property belonging to a municipal corporation for any unauthorized uses will be enjoined at the suit of resident tax payers; and the use of a school house for religious worship, when not expressly authorized, is held to warrant the granting of an injunction to restrain the officers of the school district from permitting such use at the suit of a tax payer, without his showing special damage, since he is within means of redress at law. School officers may be enjoined from leasing a public school house for the purpose of keeping a private school, and the use of a public school house for private purposes, such as the holding of religious or political meetings, social gatherings and the like, is unauthorized by law and may be restrained at the instance of any party injured thereby; and this, though a majority of the electors and tax payers of the District assent to such use and an adequate rental is paid therefor; and it is immaterial in such case that the majority of the citizens and the Directors of the District have consented to the illegal use." "A tax payer or property owner has also the undoubted right to prevent by injunction public authorities from wasting or disposing of public property, or to restrain the diversion or misappropriation of public property which a public corporation holds, acquired either by private gift or through the use of public money, as a trust for special uses and purposes. This right in some states is definitely given by statute. In accord with this same principle, it has been held in many, many cases that private persons may oppose and prevent the making of illegal contracts which involve the use of public monies or property, or the granting of licenses or privileges by public legislative bodies, which, although without their discretionary powers, yet in effect result in a waste, misappropriation or misuse of public funds or property." 3 Abbot Munic. Corp. sec. 1158. These parents and tax payers are, before all others, most seriously affected in this case. In *Bull* v. *Read*, 13 Grat. 47, inhabitants suing for themselves and other inhabitants were allowed to sue to test an act to establish free schools against the school commissioners appointed under it. The authorities there collected will warrant the right to sue in this case. In *Shinn* v. *Board*, 39 W. Va. 497, citizens and tax payers were allowed to sue to enjoin payment of drafts issued by a board of education. In *Osburn* v. *Stealey*, 5 W. Va. 85, tax payers and residents enjoined the removal of public records from Shepherdstown to Charlestown. A resident and a tax payer is allowed to sue to prevent diversion to private use of land dedicated for town site. *Davenport* v. *Buffington*, 97 Fed. (C. C. A.) 234.

Is that lease valid? That depends upon the power of the board of education to make it. A board of education is a public corporation having its birth and existence by statute. Code, chapter 45, section 7. The board of education is not a corporation vested with general powers of a business corporation. The books call it rather a *quasi* corporation. 27 Am. St. R. 412. It is a public corporation, in that it is a part of the governmental structure and performs an important function in the body politic in the administration of government, a government agency. "School districts are organized under the general laws of the State and fall within the class of corporations known as *quasi* corporations. . . .

This designation distinguishes them on the one hand from private corporations aggregate, and on the other from municipal corporations proper, such as cities or towns acting under charters, or incorporating statutes, and which are invested with more powers and endowed with special functions relating to the particular or local interests of the municipality, and to this end are granted a larger measure of corporate life." 1 Dillon Munic. Corp., secs. 24, 25. Their functions are assigned by our statues. They have no other than those so assigned, and those necessarily implied—I say necessarily implied—because essential to carry out the functions assigned—mere creatures of the statute for the performance of functions specified by the statute. . . .

Counties, school districts, road districts, library or educational boards, park commissions, municipal corporations proper and others, are each created with the idea that they shall carry out effectually some act included within the governmental power. Each one of these corporations may acquire, under grant of express power or the existence of the implied one above suggested, property which is to be used only for the purpose germane to the object for which the particular governmental subdivision was organized. The restricted and limited power of public corporations as governmental agencies cannot be too strictly maintained and strongly urged." . . .

I do not deny the power of the board to even dispose of the lot, so it be in furtherance of education and appropriate to the execution of the duties of the board in the work of education. . . .

There is a limitation upon the power of disposition. The sale must be for money, and the money go into the building fund. That does not contemplate a lease for oil. Here the board has made a partial sale, but not such as the statute contemplates. How utterly foreign to the purposes of education is the leasing of this lot for oil. The lot is very small. It is true the decree provides that work shall not go on to the disturbance of the school; but there might be an explosion of gas while the children were in the school, thus endangering their lives, though no actual operations were going on. The lessees might violate these restrictions. The lease gives the lessees power to mine, lay pipe lines, build tanks, station or other structures on the lot to take care of oil and gas. Thus this little lot might be filled with greasy, unsightly oil tanks and other structures occupying the ground rendering it unsightly and useless for the children as a play ground, and exposing them to strangers and destroying privacy—in other words, practically destroying its usefulness, as we can readily see, for free school purposes. Did the Legislature ever intend to vest any such power in a school board? If such boards may wield such powers, where is the limit, and how far may it not frustrate the whole purpose of the ownership of the board? We are told that the board has the legal title in fee simple. So it has, but it is not a private owner, because it holds such title in trust for these plaintiffs and their children, and for those that may come after them. I can scarcely imagine a use to which this lot could be put more foreign to the purpose for which the law has invested the board with title.

Until ch. 70, Acts of 1905, Code ch. 45, 333, provided that if the board should decide to sell a lot, the former owner should have right to buy it back, or to a reconveyance, if he had given it. Does not this tend to show that a school lot was not designed to be generally transferable? The fact that the act of 1905 omits this right of reclamation would not change the right of the original owner or the character of title in the board.

We therefore reverse the decree, annul the lease and perpetuate the injunction.

Reversed.

**American Civil Liberties Union of Southern
California et al., Petitioners, v. Board of Education
of the City of Los Angeles, Respondent**
Supreme Court of California,
28 Cal. Reptr. 700, 379 P. 2d 4 (1963)

PETERS, JUSTICE

Petitioners, a nonprofit corporation and its Executive Director, seek mandate to compel the respondent Board of Education to grant its application for a permit to use John Burroughs Junior High School Auditorium for a series of public bi-monthly meetings on the subject of "The Bill of Rights." Respondent denied that application upon the sole ground that petitioners refused to file a statement of information as required by respondent's rule 1316. The sole question presented by this proceeding is whether respondent has the legal right to make compliance with that rule a prerequisite to an otherwise lawful use of the school premises.

The use for which the school premises is requested is admittedly a proper use, within the Civic Center Act (ch. 4, div. 12, Ed. Code), which makes school property available for any public use which does not interfere with the school program. Petitioners' request does not entail any such interference. Petitioners' refusal to comply with respondent's rule 1316 was based solely on principle, in that they believe the requirements thereof are unconstitutional. The parties hereto are the same as the parties in American Civil Liberties Union v. Board of Education, 55 Cal.2d 167, 10 Cal.Rptr. 647, 359 P.2d 45, filed January 24, 1961, in which this court reiterated the principle (previously stated in Danskin v. San Diego Unified Sch. Dist., 28 Cal.2d 536, 545–546, 171 P.2d 885) that while "[t]he state is under no duty to make school buildings available for public meetings . . . [i]f it elects to do so . . . it cannot arbitrarily prevent any member of the public from holding such meetings . . . [n]or . . . make the privilege of holding them dependent on conditions that would deprive any members of the public of their constitutional rights." In that decision we also held that sections 16564 and 16565 of the Education Code (a portion of the Civic Center Act) were unconstitutional insofar as they required an applicant for use of school property to file a statement that the property would not be used "to further any program or movement the purpose of which is to accomplish the overthrow of the Government of the United States by force, violence or other unlawful means," and that the organization applying does not advocate such and is not a communist-action or communist-front organization. The tenor of the opinion was that the statutory requirement was aimed not at the use to which the school property would be put, but was intended to bar certain organizations from use because of their political beliefs; in other words, that the statute ignored the fact that such an organization might desire to use the school property for perfectly legitimate purposes.

When that decision became final, the respondent board investigated the

necessity and propriety of filling (by local rule) the gap left by this court's holding that section 16565 was unconstitutional. . . .

Thus the basic question is whether respondent's rule 1316 is in conflict with
any provision of the state or federal Constitutions. . . .

Respondent's rule 1316 does not establish an unconstitutional abridge-
ment of the rights of free speech and assembly:

Since petitioners in this portion of their argument rely principally upon our
previous decision in American Civil Liberties Union v. Board of Education,
supra, 55 Cal.2d 167, 10 Cal.Rptr. 647, 359 P.2d 45, the basic distinction between
the statute there involved and rule 1316 should be noted. Section 16565 of the
Education Code provided that an applicant could be denied the use of school
property solely because of that applicant's political beliefs, and not because of
the use to which it intended to put the premises. Respondent's rule 1316, on the
other hand, requires no information regarding the applicant itself, but is restricted to a negative statement of the purpose for which it intends to use the building
—that is, a statement that the property will not knowingly be used for the commission of any illegal act. The Education Code section was directed exclusively
to communist activities, or activities ordinarily associated with communist
organizations, whereas respondent's rule refers in general to "any act which is
prohibited by law." These distinctions not only provide the basis for determining
that the latter does not abridge the rights of free speech and assembly, but are also
germane to the other legal issues here presented. Thus, the claim that the rule
subverts our former opinion is unsound. . . .

Thus, where the subject matter of the intended speech or assembly is such
that it may properly be prohibited by law, and where there is an intention to
assemble or speak under such circumstances as requires prior governmental
license, the conditioning of such license upon a restraint against violating the
law is not such prior restraint as is repugnant to the constitutional guarantees.

There is a great difference between the exercise of those fundamental rights
which do not require prior permit and those which, while they may not be
denied arbitrarily, require permit or licensing by a public authority. It undoubtedly would be improper to refuse a permit to hold a parade in the public
streets merely because the permitting authority is not in sympathy with the cause
which applicant espouses. But it would be entirely reasonable to demand that
such applicant agree, *in advance*, to comply with existing municipal ordinances,
including (but not confined to) use of the streets during hours of heavy traffic,
blockage of intersections beyond a specified time limit, inciting of riot, bearing
loaded weapons, setting off of fireworks, etc. The licensing authority has both
the right and the duty to place such reasonable restrictions on the freedom of
assembly. Such restrictions or limitations would create no less a prior restraint
than is to be found in respondent's rule 1316; and it would be neither more nor
less of a restraint by reason of grouping all such limitations into one demand
that the licensee obey all civic ordinances. . . .

To require an applicant to state that it does not knowingly intend to use the property in any illegal manner is a logical method of fulfilling that mandate. It follows that the prior restraint, if any, inherent in respondent's rule 1316 is not (in light of the Times Film Corp. decision) repugnant to any constitutional guarantee, and is not inimical to what we said in our opinion rendered in the previous action between these parties. . . .

Respondent's rule does not violate due process of law by reason of being too broad, vague, arbitrary or unreasonable:

Petitioners contend that insofar as rule 1316 requires an applicant to state that the school property "will not be used for the commission of any act that is prohibited by law," it fails to meet the standards of legislative clarity. They also argue that since the applicant is required to state that he will not use the premises for the commission of any crime, it follows that "acts prohibited by law" must refer to something other than crime. While the enactment may be redundant, it is not vague. Acts prohibited by law and acts which constitute the commission of a crime may be one and the same thing, but the meaning of each phrase is clear. Each of the two phrases simply requires an applicant to assure the governing board that the school property will not knowingly be used for *any* purpose which is prohibited by law. . . .

"Reasonable certainty is all that is required. A statute will not be held void for uncertainty if any reasonable and practical construction can be given to its language." (45 Cal. Jur.2d, Statutes, § 37, p. 561, and cases cited in fn. 20.) . . .

The requirement of the rule here involved is similar to that of many statutes requiring an applicant to give information in advance of receiving a particular privilege or benefit allowed by law to persons who qualify according to a factual standard set forth in the statute. In such situations the applicant is required to file a statement (usually under oath) setting forth those facts which bring him within the statute. Frequently such information is required to be given in the same general form as required herein. Such requirements are not unconstitutional because the statute or rule containing the requirement is not penal in nature. Its purpose is simply to limit the granting of the benefits to those persons qualified under the respective statutes. The requirement that an applicant for the use of school property state that it will not knowingly use the premises for any illegal act is subject to the same interpretation. . . .

Respondent was not barred from further legislation in the field by reason of state preemption:

Petitioners argue that the fact that the provisions of Education Code section 16565 have been held unconstitutional does not remove the state's occupation of the field. The full implication of such argument is that when the state completely occupies a certain field of legislation, and subsequently a portion thereof is stricken by judicial action, the latter action does not reinstate local power to legislate, since the state has expressed its intent to occupy the entire field . . . the

Civic Center Act did not preempt the field. A further indication that the state did not intend to preempt the field is to be found in the very sections (16564 and 16565) held by us to be unconstitutional in our prior opinion. . . .

Rule 1316 of the respondent board is not invalid for any of the reasons suggested by petitioners. The alternative writ of mandate heretofore issued should be discharged and a peremptory writ denied. It is so ordered.

Gibson, C. J., and Traynor, Schauer, McComb, Tobriner and Peek, JJ., concur.

Problems and Discussion Questions

1. In many communities, the school facilities constitute the major facilities for adult education, community recreation, and cultural enrichment. What guidelines would you propose to direct school board policy in community use of school facilities?

2. Most public school districts receive funds from local, state, and federal sources. Among these several sources, what control arrangements may effectively accommodate their separate and common interests? How do such arrangements differ from current arrangements in your state school system?

3. Develop a rationale to support or oppose federal support for public education. What is the "federal interest" in education; what historical foundations express this interest; what are the principal constitutional bases for the federal role?

4. Analyze the school finance structure in your state. What relative position (among the fifty states) does your state occupy as to (a) per capita income, (b) total state revenue, (c) percent of state revenue allocated to public schools, (d) measures of economic production, and (e) average annual education expenditure per pupil? How might the equities among local, state, and federal support be improved?

Annotated Bibliography

American Association of School Administrators, *The Federal Government and Public Schools*, Washington, D.C.: AASA, 1965.

The first four chapters of this seventy page booklet give concise descriptions of the historical rationale of federal involvement in public education, the establishment and growth of several "broadening" federal acts (e.g., Smith-Hughes, George-Barden, School Lunch, Economic Opportunity), the sense of federal responsibility for educating various groups of individuals (e.g., American Indians, war veterans, Cuban refugees), and the history and rationale behind the National Science Foundation and the National Defense Education Act. Chapter Five concentrates on the ways in which the federal government attempts to compensate for state-local taxing deficiencies—largely under the various titles of Public Law 874 and Public Law 815. In the sixth and final chapter, the discussion centers on the emergence of a "new" federal-state-local public school "partnership"—stressing that the traditional federal role has been "basically noncoercive and supplementary." An appendix illustrates the federal funds for elementary and secondary education for the years 1955, 1960, 1964, and 1965.

BURKHEAD, Jesse, *Public School Finance: Economics and Politics*, New York: Syracuse University Press, 1964 (with chapters by Bertram M. Gross and Charles S. Benson).

Based on the findings of the Project for Research in Educational Finance, the bulk of this volume (eleven of the fifteen chapters) consists of the author's summaries of individual monographs. Burkhead has divided his work into three sections: general economic and political concerns (Chapters I–IV); the economics and politics of state and local finance (Chapters V–IX); federal aid to education (Chapters X–XIV).

In his final chapter (XV. "Patterns for Resource Mobilization") Burkhead collates, in a prescriptive manner, the ideas that were pursued through research study reports in the first fourteen chapters. As examples:

The necessary resources for improving education are available, but a new means of mobilization is necessary.

The internal organization of education is in need of change.

Innovative steps must be taken to update the sources and techniques of finance at the levels of state and local support.

The administration of the property tax (most viable means of local support) is in dire need of renovation.

"Research in educational methods must somehow be made more honorific" (p. 362); i.e., school boards must be convinced of the value of such research so that they will support it with monies.

There should be a high degree of citizen involvement in fiscal analysis at the individual district level.

The U.S.O.E. must be strengthened—enhancing existing programs and taking on new responsibilities in categorical aid.

BURKHEAD, Jesse, *State and Local Taxes for Public Education*, New York: Syracuse University Press, 1963.

This monograph explores the three general sources of state and local support for public education; namely, the property tax, state aid from general state revenue, and local non-property taxes. Written by an economist and expressed largely in the terminology of economics, this work does not attempt to provide definitive answers as to what will and what will not be an effective source of revenue; instead, "an effort has been made to explore the framework in which local tax and expenditure decisions are made and to examine the behavior of economic, political, and administrative variables that determine the responsiveness of state and local sources of tax support." (p. 103)

Burkhead considers the property tax as having, on the whole, a high degree of elasticity, as a continuing viable means of support for public education, and as the object of many legitimate criticisms (which he enumerates and explains). Further, in a discussion on how property taxes are administered, the author offers suggestions as to why the forces for reform have been relatively ineffective to date.

CLARK, Harold F., *Cost and Quality in Public Education*, New York: Syracuse University Press, 1963.

Although both an educator and an economist, Clark, in writing this monograph, has purposely avoided the use of esoteric jargon. In layman's terms he explores educational and economic inputs and outputs of American elementary and secondary (public) schools.

The cost-quality problem is, of course, the question of whether increased expenditures on education would bring about commensurate gains in the quality of the output. Clark speaks to this point when he indicates that although a correlation does indeed exist between cost and quality, it is far from 1.0; and, further, the most significant variable affecting this correlation (or lack of it) is, in all probability, inefficiency. In support of this position, the author reviews a number of conflicting studies and offers considerable insight into the variety of possible interpretations.

Financial Status of the Public Schools—1969, Committee on Educational Finance, National Education Association, Washington, D.C.: NEA, 1969.

In this sixth annual report by the committee, Chairman William D. Firman notes that "schools were better financed in 1968–69 than in previous years, and the outlook for next year is good, under pending state legislation on taxes and school funding, although partly clouded by inflation." (p. 4)

Organized into four major sections, this 74-page report offers considerable data regarding the past, present, and future of public school finance in America. The sections are: 1—"Dimensions of Formal Education;" 2—"Employment in the Schools;" 3—"Expenditures;" 4—"Revenue."

7

Tort Liability of Teachers and Schools

INTRODUCTION

The notion that every person should be responsible for his wrongful conduct is fundamental in our society. Except for those persons under some legal disability, such as children below the age of reason, the law imposes penalties upon those whose wrongful acts cause damage or injury to persons and property. An offense against the state is a crime and constitutes a positive or negative breach of some duty which an individual owes to the community. A tort is a legal wrong which proximately causes injury to person or property. The same act may be a crime and a tort. For example, the physical assault of one by another may be the crime of assault and battery (a wrong against the state), a penalty for which may be imposed through a criminal prosecution, and a tort (a civil or private wrong against the victim), damages for which may be assessed through civil proceedings. Tort liability is independent of a contract relation between parties. For example, the school board's violation of the teacher's contract is not tortuitous although injury may result for which the board could be held liable.

Negligence is the most common tort. Negligence is the failure to exercise that degree of care expected of a reasonable, prudent man in the same or similar circumstances. The concept of negligence presumes a duty of care owed by one person to others, the breach of that duty, and resultant damage or injury to the other person or his property. The question of negligence frequently arises in schools from the teacher's alleged breach of some duty of care owed to the pupil or his parents. A similar question of liability may arise when a person or property is injured or damaged by some act or omission of the school boards. The doctrine of *respondeat superior* arises frequently in alleged wrongful acts of the board. This doctrine, based on the principles of agency and derived from the ancient master-servant laws, means that a master is liable in certain cases for the wrongful acts of his servant. The doctrine means that the school district may be charged with liability for the wrongful acts of its teachers, administrators, and other employees. This chapter discusses tort liability of teachers, the diverse legal positions on the matter of school board liability, the bases for the board's

405

immunity from liability, and some implications of tort law for teachers and school boards.

TORT LIABILITY OF TEACHERS

Like everyone else, teachers are responsible for the consequences of their conduct. This legal accountability is not different from that imposed upon other members of the community, but the specific duties of care imposed on the teacher may be different from that of the ordinary person. As discussed earlier, the teacher stands *in loco parentis* to the pupils. This special relationship carries special privileges and special responsibilities. To the extent that disciplinary action is reasonable, most courts refrain from imposing liability on the teacher for punishment administered to the child. The same conduct toward children may be proper for a teacher but legally improper for others. For example, teachers may direct and control pupils in and out of school, but ordinary citizens may not. The special relationship between teachers and pupils permits teachers to impose punishment on pupils and be legally immune from the consequences. Ordinary citizens do not have this kind of privilege or immunity. The special relationship carries with it special responsibilities and duties which may impose liability on teachers beyond that imposed on others.

Teachers are obliged to exercise that degree of care toward pupils which a reasonably prudent person would exercise under the circumstances. In legal contemplation, the duty of care owed by a teacher to a pupil is of no higher degree than the care owed by others; the circumstances, however, dictate the dimensions of the teacher's duties. What might constitute reasonable care by the general public may not be reasonable for the teacher. Teachers, for example, may be obliged to intervene in school playground fights and might be charged with negligence for failure to act if a child were injured thereby. The ordinary citizen would have no legal duty to intervene. Children are under the care and supervision of the teachers during their class work and extracurricular activities of the school; the teachers must exercise reasonable care towards the children according to the circumstances. The specific duty of care depends on the situation. Thus, the teacher's duty to "supervise" children may require totally different teacher behaviors in an English class and in a chemistry laboratory. The cases do not speak of prospective "duties"; rather, they deal with alleged past "breaches of duty." The specific duties of care owed to another can only be inferred from the court's determination of alleged breaches of duty. Although teachers must exercise reasonable care, they do not ensure the safety and well-being of pupils in their charge; their duty requires only reasonable care.

The teacher's duty of reasonable care includes warning children of any known dangers or risks in school activities. In some classes and extracurricular activities, pupils may use tools, machines, or equipment which require training prior to use. Certain sports activity may require physical conditioning and preparation; the teacher's failure to plan and supervise such physical conditioning may result in liability for negligence. Failures to do this may expose the teacher to liability for injuries to pupils arising in the school program.

Teachers may be negligent for their failure to properly supervise pupils. Whether the teacher supervises in a proper fashion is a question of fact; each circumstance will determine the specific duty on the teacher. School boards frequently impose their own rules on teacher conduct in an effort to minimize the possibility of teacher negligence. A common board rule requires teachers to be in their classrooms at all times when pupils are present. The board is well within its power to make the rules; but the teacher's presence does not necessarily mean "no negligence" nor does his absence mean negligence. Circumstances may arise when a teacher must leave a classroom or place where pupils are engaged in school matters; the question of negligence or breach of duty does not depend on the teacher's absence but on the question of the reasonableness of the teacher's actions. If, under the circumstances, the teacher acted as a reasonably prudent person, the courts will not impose tort liability; if the teacher failed to so act, liability may be so imposed. Teachers and pupils are exposed to many situations wherein "careless" or "willful" negligence can occur. Children are prone to take risks, act carelessly, and ignore the simple cautions of temperance in their school activity. In matters of pupil supervision and safety, teachers cannot be too careful. There is no known case of a teacher being liable for careful behavior; there are many cases holding teachers liable for careless behavior. Until some better guidelines than the present ex post facto legal determination of negligence comes along, teachers are well advised to act carefully, reasonably, and cautiously in their dealings with pupils.

✓Teachers are particularly vulnerable to charges of negligence toward pupils. Some states, in recognition of this vulnerability and the serious burden of lawsuits on teachers, authorize school boards to purchase liability insurance for all board employees. These laws typically authorize school boards to indemnify and protect board members and employees (some include student teachers) against claims for death, bodily injury, and property damage caused by alleged negligent or wrongful acts alleged to have been committed in the scope of employment. The phrase "scope of employment" is sometimes difficult to define but it generally means those activities within the reasonable and customary teaching duties. Teachers engaged in classroom instruction, supervision of pupils in or out of the school premises (such as the supervision of school-sponsored social, cultural, and educational events), and similar responsibilities sanctioned by the school board are generally acting within the "scope of employment." In the absence of legislative immunity to liability for torts, teachers should consider purchasing liability insurance.

TORT LIABILITY OF SCHOOLS

Public schools, as instruments or agents of the state, may be immune to tort liability. This immunity protects the public school from action for negligence by its officers, agents, and employees. Some states have chosen to remove the immunity in whole or part, but the great majority of states still cloak the school district with governmental immunity to tort liability.

School districts exist only in legal contemplation, not as tangible entities. School districts, as noted in Chapter 1, are quasi-municipal corporations, created and endowed with such powers and duties as the state legislatures choose and subject to the limitations imposed by the state and federal constitutions. A school district does not act in and of itself. Any alleged wrongs by the district must be imputed from the acts of its officers, employees, or agents. The doctrine of *respondeat superior* is the only way to hold the district liable for the wrongful acts of its employees and agents.

The school districts' immunity to tort liability (frequently referred to as "governmental immunity") is based on the rejection of the doctrine of *respondeat superior* and three major arguments. Most courts reject the doctrine as inapplicable to governmental bodies, including the schools. The reasons for this rejection vary but the substance of the rationale is the peculiar character of the state and the need to preserve its machinery from interruption and interference from another of its parts. The three co-equal branches of the state could suffer irreparable harm if the legislature (or the school district as its agent) were subject to the power of the judicial branch through suit by a private citizen. Further, the courts have been reluctant to impose the same liability on nonprofit schools as on profit-making ventures. The rationale for this reluctance is not clear; both enterprises produce more or less measurable products.

The most frequent and perhaps the least defensible argument against school liability for tort is the notion of governmental sovereignty. This notion, based on the monarchial tradition that "the king can do no wrong," denies the right of the individual's redress for wrongs inflicted by the state or its instruments. In fact, the argument denies that a wrong occurred at all. The sovereignty argument apparently entered our laws by way of the common law, adopted by the states following the American Revolution. As a part of the common law, the notion of sovereign immunity remains imbedded in the state laws (except in Louisiana, which adopted the Napoleonic Code), except as superseded by statute.

The sovereignty argument seems particularly offensive to our fundamental belief in government by the consent of the governed. The public schools are invested with broad responsibilities and power over children and their parents. Neither the children nor their parents have any direct control of the persons, places, or things employed in the educational process. Teachers may or may not be able to pay damages incurred as a result of their tortious acts; school facilities, equipment, and materials may or may not be safe; and the school may not be a reasonably safe environment. The school district, through its officers and employees, creates the school setting and, in large measure, controls the risks to the pupils and their parents. The district selects the teachers, the equipment, the materials; it determines the physical and human environment for the pupils. If bodily injury or property damages result from teacher negligence or material failure, in most states the victim is barred from recovery against the district and, generally, its officers. Recovery, if any, is confined to the teacher who is far less able to respond in damages than the district. The sovereignty argument still prevails in many states but has come under serious attack in recent years.

A second argument against tort liability of school districts is based on the "trust-fund" concept. This argument starts with the premise that school funds are impressed with a public purpose; namely, to pay the costs of education in the district. The school district holds the funds in trust for the educational benefit of the pupils and, using them in any other way (such as paying damages under a court judgment) would violate that trust. A further wrinkle to this argument adds the notion that to use public funds to pay for private injuries would unlawfully divert public funds to a private purpose. Some states take the position that, because the school funds are thus impressed with a trust for their use and since the districts have no other funds with which to satisfy judgments, suits against the districts are futile and pointless, and consequently would not be entertained by the courts. The injured party is limited to recovery against the individual wrong-doer (teacher or board member) and, in practical effect, left without a legal remedy. The effect of the trust-fund argument is as harsh to the victim as the sovereignty argument: no recovery for damages in tort against the school district.

The third argument in favor of tort immunity for school is ingenious in its rationale: the district acts only through its officers to carry out the bona fide purposes of the school and not to act negligently. Therefore, any negligence by such officers is clearly *ultra vires* and void so far as the district is concerned. This argument permits the district to take the benefits of board action but avoid any burden arising from board folly. The courts are reluctant to charge individual members of the board with liability for wrongs committed by the board. Unless the victim can prove malice, recovery against individual board members is unlikely and, under the fiction of district immunity for unauthorized acts of the board, the injured party is left without remedy. The district's immunity to tort liability is fictional and the rationale of arguments for it are arbitrary and indefensible.

The court's reluctance to hold individual board members liable in tort for the consequences of board decisions can be understood. School boards make policies which necessarily must be implemented by employees and agents. Despite the school board's best motives and best efforts to protect the public against employee negligence, the board cannot supervise and directly control the risks to pupils and the public. To hold individual board members responsible would have two adverse effects: (1) encourage responsible citizens to refuse to serve on school boards, and (2) encourage school boards to avoid any decisions which conceivably might result in liability.

EXCEPTIONS TO SCHOOL DISTRICT IMMUNITY

Some states make exceptions to school district immunity by legislation and court decisions. The trust-fund theory protects school districts from liability only to the extent that school funds are exempt from judgments for damages; if nonschool funds are available, damages can be recovered. Those districts which have liability insurance can have damages assessed without violating the trust impressed on school tax funds. Some states distinguish the dual capacities of school boards; governmental (quasi-legislative decision making) and ministerial or proprietary (implementing the decisions). Districts may be immune to liability for torts caused by governmental acts but liable for torts arising from the board's ministerial acts. The criteria for the two kinds of board action are vague; and any distinctions serve little useful purpose, since the courts rarely explain their decisions other than to categorize the specific act as governmental and grant immunity, or label it as ministerial and impose liability.

Most states impose tort liability on school districts for nuisances maintained by the district. Nuisance may be defined as anything which is injurious to health or interferes with another's free use of his property. School district liability for nuisance seems to rest on the notion that ownership of a property carries the duty to refrain from using it to the harm of others. Thus, the district's tort liability arises from its ownership (and wrongful use) of property. The courts apparently regard property rights and their protection of such importance as to impose liability on school districts.

Some states impose liability on school districts by express statute or by judicial interpretation. New York holds district officers liable under certain circumstances but restricts the accountability to the torts by the officers. A few states impose liability on school districts by express statute. California and Illinois are two states in this position. Some states have modified the immunity by providing administrative machinery to hear claims in tort against districts, and exclude such claims from regular judicial channels. Alabama, Mississippi, and North Carolina are examples of such state efforts to breach the general immunity rule as to school districts. A few states permit or require school districts to indemnify teachers against judgments and legal expenses arising from the teachers' negligent acts. Such "save harmless" provisions indirectly subject districts to extensive tort liability.

The dissatisfaction with the rule of nonliability for districts may be seen in those states which adhere to it but permit school districts to purchase liability insurance. Despite the general rule of tort immunity some states permit districts to use school funds for liability insurance premiums. Even prior to the *Molitor* decision, the Illinois legislature permitted school districts to purchase liability insurance, although the district was immune from liability. A case arose wherein the insured school district was sued for the alleged negligence of one of its teachers. The school board raised the usual defense of immunity arising from its performance of a governmental function. The Illinois appellate court noted the district's liability insurance and held that the immunity rule did not apply so far as the district was covered by insurance. The court observed that the only reason for tort immunity was the public policy to protect the district's funds from diversion to pay damages. Since the district funds were preserved, the reason for the rule of immunity failed and the district was held liable (*Thomas v. Broadlands Community Consolidated School District*, 348 Ill. App. 567, 109 N.E. 2d 636 [1952]). The evolution of Illinois law regarding tort liability of school districts is set forth in the *Molitor* decision below.

TORT LIABILITY OF BOARD MEMBERS

School district immunity to tort liability does not extend to the members of the school district. Although the decisions indicate the courts' reluctance to hold board members to the usual standard of conduct, they can be individually liable in tort. As noted above, there are sound reasons for the courts' reluctance to impose tort liability on board members. Most board members serve the district as volunteers and the public reaps substantial benefit from their service. To charge board members with tort liability growing out of their decisions would not only discourage their volunteer service but would seriously restrict their discretion in board matters. Certainly if board members act in a corrupt, malicious, or negligent manner, they should be held accountable. The law clearly protects the board members in their governmental or discretionary acts but may impose liability for torts arising from their ministerial or proprietary capacity. As stated earlier in the chapter, the distinction between the two types of acts is not always clear in specific situations. The Supreme Court of Indiana attempted to distinguish the two acts in a case brought against a school district for injuries sustained by a spectator at a board-sponsored "field day exhibition." In *Adams v. Schneider* 71 Ind. App. 249, 124 N.E. 718 (1919), the court stated:

. . . we hold that the . . . members of the school board, in determining that there should be field day exercises . . . were acting within their jurisdiction, and that such act, together with their action in determining the manner in which such exercises should be conducted was discretionary, and that for injuries resulting therefrom they were not liable, but that the duties performed in making preparation for such field day exercises and the general management thereof were ministerial acts, for the negligent performance of which, if so performed whether, performed by themselves, by their agent, or by an independent contractor, they were liable for damages for injuries suffered by reason thereof.

The courts' reluctance to impose tort liability on members of the school board falls short of immunity. Cases involving violations of express statutory duties, illegal expenditures of school funds, and illegal suspension of expulsion of pupils demonstrate the circumstances under which tort liability may be imposed on board members.

Future developments in tort law as it concerns schools, school boards, and teachers are not at all clear. One can reasonably expect some change, either through restrictive legislation or widespread insurance protection for teachers and board employees. The interaction between pupils and teachers undoubtedly will continue to get public attention and our sharpened sense of individual rights may prompt more litigation. The law is not static; it moves and adjusts to human forces just as surely as does society itself. The transition of school board tort liability in some states from complete immunity based on indefensible premises to liability illustrates the evolutionary process. Public servants presently seek the rights and privileges of private employees in labor relations and employment practices. The achievement of this role equality may bring with it the parallel responsibilities under the law. We should expect the government privileges and immunities derived from irrelevant traditions to come under serious examination; how much of the schools' tort liability immunity survives is yet to be determined.

Readings

Legal Responsibility under Tort Law of School Personnel and School Districts as Regards Negligent Conduct toward Pupils

Reynolds C. Seitz

The thrust of this article is the discussion of the law as it touches public school personnel and school districts. The material, however, which deals with the duties that rest on individual teachers has equal application to teachers in the private school. Of course, in the religious school the individual teacher who is a religious has no money and is, therefore, judgment proof. The recourse, however, may be against the corporation that operates the private school unless the jurisdiction holds to the immunity doctrine of non-profit, eleemosynary, charitable institutions. The article will reveal that more school districts are losing governmental immunity against tort action. The tide of judicial thinking is also beginning to run in the direction of abrogating immunity of private schools, even one operated by a church. The many cases involving liability of private hospitals are of significance in this respect. See for a more direct example the 1963 Wisconsin case, Widell v. Holy Trinity Catholic Church, 19 Wis. 2d 648, 121 N.W.2d 249, 254 (1963), which, although involving a church corporation, gives indication that the rule of immunity of a private school against actions based on a claim of negligence is very likely abolished. The language of the court is significant:

> There can be no quarrel with the argument [that] the public benefits generally from the work of religious institutions. . . . [T]he question is whether the benefit to the many should be at the expense of the innocent sufferer of injuries caused by the negligence of an agent of the religious institution. . . . Certainly institutions teaching divine justice, the dignity of man and his obligations to his fellowmen . . . would not claim . . . they ought to be exempt from repairing the injury done by themselves or their agents to another. . . .
>
> We do not believe the result of abolishing immunity . . . casts any insuperable financial burden upon them. . . . [They can minimize the burden by insurance.]

Hastings Law Journal, (May, 1964), **45**, 495

The title selected for this article is likely to startle the discerning reader. It is rather apparent that adequate treatment of the suggested subject matter would more readily lend itself to a full length volume rather than a law review article. Realistically, therefore, the approach has been to select for discussion those

[Reprinted with permission of *The Hastings Law Journal*.]

areas of exposure which may likely present the greatest possibility of risk of liability.

A further technique has suggested itself. An article of this nature will have maximum usefulness if in addition to being a helpful guide to school board attorneys, it has meaning to teachers, administrators and school board members. Since many of the individuals in the latter categories do not have a professional foundation in legal education, the approach will at times present basic material which may not be customary in articles which are designed to be read almost exclusively by trained legal scholars and lawyers.

There is full justification for giving enough slant to an article of this type so that teachers, administrators and school board members can find meaning in it. The primary reason, although the danger does exist, is not to alert school personnel and school boards to the threat of recovery of money damages. The basic justification is that school personnel have as much reason to safeguard children against injury resulting from harm induced by breach of duty as they have to protect young people from the result of an improper psychological approach to teaching.

THE POSITION OF THE INDIVIDUAL TEACHER AND SCHOOL ADMINISTRATOR

In society generally an individual must take reasonable care to avoid acts or omissions which he can reasonably foresee would be likely to injure his neighbor. If he does not, he subjects himself to the probability that he will be required by a court to pay money damages to an injured party. Under tort law a neighbor is one who is so closely and directly affected by an act that an individual ought reasonably to have had him in contemplation as being affected when he was directing his mind to acts or omissions. A negative statement serves to emphasize the principle. There are some people to whom an individual owes no duty to be concerned about his conduct. The concept of whether a duty is owed is a question of law for a court to determine. Courts have generally recognized that pupils fall within the category of neighbors so as to cause teachers and administrators to have them in contemplation when they act or omit to act.

Under familiar principles of tort law the concrete duty imposed by this attitude is that teachers and administrators must act toward pupils as would the reasonable, prudent person or parent under the circumstances. This standard does not make teachers the insurers of the safety of children. If school personnel have acted as the reasonable, prudent parent under the circumstances and nevertheless a child is injured, the teacher or administrator cannot be held responsible. The teacher and administrator are not liable for pure accidents.

It is obvious that the determination of negligence measured by the yardstick of whether teachers and administrators acted toward pupils as the reasonable, prudent parent would do under the extremely complex circumstances found in varied school situations is not simple. It is far more difficult than the application of the same yardstick to the conduct of the driver of an automobile.

Since a great majority of fact situations alleging negligence on the part of teachers are going to present an issue which will not warrant a court directed verdict either in favor of the plaintiff or the defendant, a jury is most frequently going to be directed to work with the yardstick of determining whether a teacher or administrator did such acts or omitted "to take such a precaution that under the circumstances present he, as an ordinarily prudent person, ought reasonably to [have foreseen] that he will thereby expose the interest of another to an unreasonable risk of harm."[1]

In facing up to the difficult question of whether in a particular situation liability should attach because of the conduct of a school teacher or administrator there are some principles of tort law that may have significant application.

In discussing probability of harm resulting from a certain type of conduct authorities in tort law have pointed out that as the gravity of the possible harm increases, the apparent likelihood of its occurrence need be correspondingly less.[2] This explains why, although the odds may be 1,000 to 1 in favor of an automobile driver going 90 miles an hour not meeting a train at a railroad crossing, the risk of death is sufficiently serious to impose upon him more caution. Does this principle suggest, however, that often a teacher or administrator, as a defense to an allegation that his action was negligent and produced harm to a pupil, could assert that since the gravity of possible harm is not great, it is proper to think in terms of statistical odds on harm?

Another concept in tort law expresses the attitude that against the probability and gravity of risk must be balanced the utility of the type of conduct in question.[3] The recognized problem here is whether the game is worth the candle and the realism of appreciating that sometimes risk may reasonably be run with the full approval of the community.

The disclosure of the yardstick which will be put into the hands of jurors and the particular principles to which attention has just been drawn suggests the difficulty of predicting the jury reaction to a particular school fact situation in which negligence of school personnel is alleged. Even appellate courts may differ on the matter as to whether a jury verdict should be let stand.

This uncertainty as to outcome points to the reasonableness of giving advice to school personnel which leans toward the conservative, with the qualification that the advice should not be so cautious as to put the educator in the kind of a legal strait jacket which would have an undesirable effect upon the ability of children to learn and develop responsibility.

In the light of what has been stated, and to the extent that space will permit, it now seems desirable to discuss some of the kinds of fact situations which arise in the school field.

1. Part of the instruction in Osborne v. Montgomery, 203 Wis. 223, 242, 234 N.W. 372, 379 (1931).
2. PROSSER, TORTS 121-22 (2d ed. 1955).
3. *Id.* at 122.

Duty to Supervise in General

It is obvious that many questions concerning liability can arise out of situations where it is alleged that the pupil was injured during a period when a teacher failed to supervise.

Fortunately the operation of schools has not produced anything like the amount of litigation found in the area of the use of the automobile. It is, therefore, often necessary to speculate as to outcome of cases alleging failure to properly supervise. This is done through the application of basic principles and by analogy suggested by certain decided cases. As previously indicated, the approach here adopted is a reasonably conservative one. In spite of the liberality of certain courts, as portrayed in immediately following paragraphs, prudence dictates offering advice to school personnel which will be calculated to keep them out of the hands of juries. Unless there is a meaningful educational goal to be attained, it does not seem wise to encourage teachers or administrators to probe to see if juries and courts will follow the pattern of some liberally decided cases.

The New York case, *Ohman v. Board of Educ.*,[1] will serve as an introduction to a discussion of the responsibilities of teachers and administrators in respect to supervision. In *Ohman* the trial court had found a teacher negligent on evidence that she had been out of the room to which she was assigned for the purpose of sorting papers and storing materials for perhaps an hour and fifteen minutes. During the time she was gone a thirteen year old boy was struck in the eye by a pencil hurled by a pupil at a particular classmate who ducked to avoid the object. The appeal court felt the absence of the teacher was not the proximate cause of the injury and, therefore, concluded that the length of absence was immaterial. The court talked about the act of the third party as one which could hardly have been anticipated in the reasonable exercise of the teacher's duty toward the plaintiff. This, the court felt, was because there was no proof of similar accidents. Also, the court asserted that it could not be contended that a pencil in the hands of a school pupil is a dangerous instrumentality. The event, stressed the court, could have occurred equally as well in the presence of a teacher as during her absence. Two dissenters in the *Ohman* case argued most persuasively that the jury could properly conclude that if a teacher left a room full of children unsupervised, there could be horseplay which could result in injury to a pupil.

The position of the dissenters and the jury seemed utterly sound. Certainly the reasonable, prudent teacher can foresee that when she leaves a normal sized room containing thirteen year olds, especially for an extended period of time, the psychology of group behavior will induce some horseplay which would result in injury. It seems utterly immaterial that the pencil was thrown at one pupil and hit another. While it is true a similar event could have happened while the teacher was in the room, carefully supervising, and there would have been no

1. 300 N.Y. 306, 90 N.E.2d 474 (1949).

liability, the chances of the episode taking place were greatly heightened by the absence of the teacher from the room. There is no requirement that the teacher foresee the exact injury that would take place in her absence. True, there must be a relationship between the absence from the classroom and the injury. The happening in *Ohman* is in no way similar to that where a boy might be injured because he bumped his head in a basketball game while the teacher was out of the gymnasium. It could realistically be said in such case that the absence of the teacher from the gymnasium had nothing to do with the injury.

If there is any rational explanation for the majority viewpoint in the *Ohman* case, it would seem to rest on the presumption that in terms of statistical odds the likelihood of possible harm was not great. It seems, however, that this principle, standing alone, should not be a valid defense to excuse lack of supervision. Some reasonable showing of the utility of the conduct would appear to be required.

All courts, however, are not requiring it. In Ohio[1] the court held that a teacher who was out of the room was not negligent when one pupil threw a milk bottle which struck another pupil in the head, causing him eventually to lose the sight of one eye and impairing the vision of the other. On the other hand all courts do not accept the philosophy of the Ohio and New York courts. In the state of Washington,[2] where the ability to foresee the exact injury was more difficult than in the case just discussed, the court found no problem in finding a physical education teacher liable who left the gymnasium unsupervised when during his absence a boy dragged a girl into an adjacent room and perpetrated an immoral act.

SUPERVISION OF NORMAL SIZE CLASSROOMS. In spite of many assertions of teachers that necessity prompts frequent leaving of classrooms unsupervised, a thoughtful analysis of most concrete situations points to the fact that there are actually few occasions when it can be said that worthwhile educational purposes support leaving the room for any appreciable period of time. It would be probable, although by no means certain, that courts would find more occasion to conclude that there was no negligence if the teacher was out of the room for a short period of time for a purpose connected with an educational matter.

SUPERVISION OF CERTAIN SPECIAL GROUPS. The "under the circumstances" phrase in the basic test for negligence would often dictate that the make-up of certain groups was such that no prudent teacher would leave the group alone for even a brief time. On the other hand the utility of the endeavor might suggest that if the approach was that of the reasonable, prudent man, such things as unsupervised study halls might be set up. If they were, it would seem that prudence would dictate that only those pupils would be routed into such rooms that teachers had vouched for as reliable. It would also appear wise to support the unsupervised

1. Guyten v. Rhodes, 65 Ohio App. 163, 29 N.E.2d 444 (1940).
2. McLeod v. Grant County Dist. No. 128, 42 Wash. 2d 316, 255 P.2d 360 (1953).

study hall by enlisting the aid of a student council willing to accept the responsibility of reporting infractions of study hall regulations.

Certainly small study groups of five to six could be left unsupervised provided there was not in the group a known and consistent trouble maker. This is because the reasonable prudent parent would not hesitate to leave certain small groups unsupervised in his home. As to the question concerning when a small group becomes too large, this presents the typical problem of the line of demarcation with which the law is often confronted and as to which the answer could vary from jury to jury and court to court.

SUPERVISION DURING RECESS. The responsibility to supervise elementary school pupils during recess periods rests upon the individual teacher. Surely if a teacher must supervise her group within a classroom, she would have to do the same on a recess playground. Negligence has been found when a teacher fails to enforce adequate play rules, which the court felt was the cause of the injury.[1]

SUPERVISION OF SHOPS, LABORATORIES, GYMNASIUMS, SWIMMING POOLS, PLAYGROUNDS. A particular responsibility rests upon teachers who instruct in areas where students work with equipment, materials and machines which are inherently dangerous if care is not used. Specifically, shop, physical education, science and home economics teachers work in such areas. The teacher not only has the duty to supervise carefully. He also has the duty to instruct in the proper use of equipment.[2] There is often a tendency on the part of shop, science and home economics teachers to concentrate on the work of a few conducting a particular experiment in a laboratory or shop. In view of the potential danger that exists, conservative advice suggests that such concentration should not be too obvious for an unreasonable time. On the other hand a New York court made clear that there is no requirement that the teacher have under constant and unremitting scrutiny the precise spots wherein every phase of activity is being pursued. Nor is there any compulsion that the general supervision be continuous and direct.[3] This philosophy is simply a frank recognition of the practicalities of the situation.

SUPERVISING AT DISMISSAL AND DURING MOVEMENT BETWEEN CLASSES. Particular supervisory duties exist at times of dismissal and movement between classes. Under certain circumstances the duty rests solely on the individual teacher. Since, for instance, it can reasonably be foreseen that very young children in the

---

1. Germond v. Board of Educ., 10 App. Div. 2d 139, 197 N.Y.S.2d 548 (1960); Forgnone v. Salvadore Union Elementary School Dist., 41 Cal. App. 2d 423, 106 P.2d 932 (1940), involving a situation where during recess one pupil twisted another pupil's arm; Miller v. Board of Educ., 291 N.Y. 25, 50 N.E.2d 529 (1943), presented a pupil injured when playing on a fire escape at recess. Improper supervision was found in the latter two cases.
2. Mastrangelo v. West Side Union High School Dist., 2 Cal. 2d 540, 42 P.2d 634 (1935).
3. See Nestor v. City of New York, 28 N.Y. Misc. 2d 70, 211 N.Y.S.2d 975 (1961), involving supervision on a playground, but the philosophy would be equally applicable to supervision of shops and science laboratories.

primary grades jostle and push by nature, a teacher in control of such group would be prudent to accompany her children down stairs and along corridors at dismissal time. As the child becomes more mature, the factors previously discussed, of the probability of harm and the utility of the type of conduct, should often excuse a teacher from accompanying her group out of the building at dismissal time and at the time of movement between classes.[1] But as indicated hereafter in connection with the discussion of the responsibility of administrators, some strategic supervision seems necessary. The planning for this rests primarily upon the administrator.

SUPERVISION DURING LUNCH PERIODS—BEFORE AND AFTER SCHOOL. In addition to the problem of supervising children at dismissal time and during movement between classes there exists the question of responsibility for supervision of lunch room and playground during lunch periods. It is obvious that because of lack of manpower, foolproof supervision cannot be furnished during the time allotted for lunch. Teachers must have time to eat and relax. Prudence, however, dictates the need for some strategic supervision. The duty to plan for such supervision rests primarily on the administrator.[2] It appears probable that if the administrator sits down with his staff and faces up to the problem of the strategic use of manpower that is available, a court will not find any personal liability on the part of the administrator on the ground that the plan devised was the best possible under the circumstances. Unless the plan devised is utterly arbitrary, it is obvious that teachers must perform the duties assigned to them or face the risk of liability if a child is injured while the teacher is not supervising.

Later in this article discussion will deal with the matter of school district liability. If the state of the law in a particular jurisdiction permits the imposition of such liability, the way is open to act to establish that the district did not make enough personnel available for supervision of lunch room and playgrounds. It has been held, for instance, that one teacher cannot supervise a large playground where 150 pupils of various ages play.[3]

There appears to be no need to supervise just because groups gather before school and remain after school.[4] The school will fulfill its responsibility in respect to pupils who so gather by making reasonable endeavors to acquaint the student body and parents as to when supervision will begin and end. This will place upon those who come early and remain late the assumption of the risk.

SUPERVISION BY UNCERTIFIED SCHOOL PERSONNEL. Questions have arisen as to liability of school teachers or administrators if a child is injured while some individual other than a certified teacher is supervising in the room or on the playground. Such individuals may be a parent, an older child, a custodian or a guest lecturer. Although there may occasionally arise fact situations which might

1. Leibowitz v. Board of Educ. 112 N.Y.S.2d 698 (Sup. Ct., Trial Term, 1952).
2. Thompson v. Board of Educ., 255 App. Div. 786, 6 N.Y.S.2d 921 (1938).
3. Charonnat v. San Francisco Unified School Dist., 56 Cal. App. 2d 840, 133 P.2d 643 (1943).
4. Lutzker v. Board of Educ., 287 N.Y. 822, 41 N.E.2d 97 (1942).

seem to give hope of using the justification of little probability of harm and utility of the use of such supervision, it would appear that teachers and school administrators should generally recognize the hazard in such decision. Surely it can be foreseen that individuals without particular training in child psychology and the handling of young people in groups will generally not have the skill to control the group. If, therefore, horseplay results in injury, it seems likely that the teacher or administrator would be vulnerable to liability. Illustrative is the New York decision holding a school custodian not qualified to supervise a play area.[1]

Indeed, the legal adviser of the San Francisco Board of Education sounds a note of caution concerning the use of practice teachers unless there is protection granted by statute.[2] It is submitted that this would be too conservative a viewpoint to be accepted by many courts. It would seem that most courts could be convinced that it is necessary to give practice teachers experience in controlling the room on their own and that such courts would only find negligence if those who are charged with observing the work of the practice teacher allowed her to be on her own before it was prudent to do so.

SUPERVISION ON FIELD TRIPS. Certainly if it is necessary to supervise within classrooms, it is even more so on field trips. It is likely that the reasonable prudent parent yardstick will often suggest that a teacher cannot supervise the same size group on a field trip that she can in a classroom. The utility of such trips, when weighed against the likelihood of harm, should influence courts to permit teachers to enlist the aid of other adults who will go along as assistants. The responsibility of the teacher would then be realistic orientation of the duties expected from helpers and acceptance of the responsibility to see that the assistants selected actually do live up to their commitment to help supervise. A standard of due care will often require that a teacher avoid taking children on certain trips if it can be foreseen that the reasonable prudent parent would not present his child with the dangers involved. Of course, in any decision of such sort the age of the child will be an important factor. Field trips impose upon school personnel the most careful planning. To avoid harassment from parents who may claim that they would not have consented to the child going on the trip, parents should be asked to sign permission slips. These slips should give parents complete details as to the method of transportation, approximate time of departure and return and the destination. There is no way in which verbiage can be put on a permission slip which will absolve teachers from the duty to carefully supervise on field trips. A parent cannot consent to a teacher being negligent toward his child. For the same reason a parent cannot consent to allow a teacher to take his child on a trip or to a destination which would not be approved by the reasonable prudent parent.

1. Garber v. Central High School Dist. No. 1, 251 App. Div. 214, 295 N.Y. Supp. 850 (1937).
2. Breyer, *The Power to Use Student Teachers and Special Non-Professional Lecturers*, in LAW AND THE SCHOOL PRINCIPAL 169-89 (Seitz ed. 1961).

CONTRIBUTORY NEGLIGENCE AS DEFENSE TO FAILURE TO SUPERVISE. A teacher charged with negligence, especially that based upon an allegation of failure to properly supervise, may allege contributory negligence or in those jurisdictions which follow the doctrine try to reduce damages through a comparative negligence formula. Under some sets of facts the teacher can succeed. If, for example, strong evidence indicated that an older pupil had been thoroughly instructed in the danger of using certain chemicals and was warned not to use them but nevertheless did so while the teacher was out of the room and was seriously injured, the court would undoubtedly find contributory negligence. The problem with contributory negligence as a defense is that the court is going to face up to the fact that the yardstick it must use is that degree of care which the great mass of children of like age, intelligence and experience would ordinarily exercise under the circumstances. The prudent teacher would not want to take too many chances that a jury or court would be liberal in the application of such a standard. The problem is that the court may often conclude that although pupils recognize that a warning of danger has been given, they do not fully comprehend the extent of the danger. The court is likely to see in the failure to properly supervise the creating of an improper atmosphere of temptation to experiment. The duty of one charged with supervising to warn of danger often exists even though a pupil could recognize some danger. In a California situation the teacher failed to warn that the guard on a power saw was broken. Although the pupil could observe the fact and knew of the danger, the court held that although the pupil did know there was some danger, he did not know the amount of it.[1]

Responsibilities Other than for Supervising

There are a number of occasions other than in the area of supervision which frequently present the issue of due care toward pupils.

FIRST AID AND MEDICAL TREATMENT. The mere plea of good Samaritan will not excuse the school man who gives medical attention when he should recognize that the injury is a serious one and appreciate that he does not know how to administer proper treatment.[2]

Due care in such circumstances would be to take reasonably prudent steps to summon as quickly as possible the emergency attention that is necessary. Depending upon the circumstances this might range from calling a nurse, doctor, or first aid expert in the school building, contacting a physician or a police emergency squad. Parents or guardians should also be notified promptly.

If school personnel improperly treat an injury which does not present an emergency, it is even more apparent that due care has not been used.[3]

REQUESTING PUPIL AID. Teachers and administrators subject themselves to liability

1. Ridge v. Boulder Creek Union Jr.-Sr. High School Dist., 60 Cal. App 2d 453. 140 P.2d 990 (1943).
2. Conner v. Winton, 8 Ind. 315 (1856); Commonwealth v. Pierce, 138 Mass. 165 (1884).
3. Guerrieri v. Tyson, 147 Pa. Super. 239, 24 A.2d 468 (1942).

for injury when they request aid which they should recognize is beyond the experience and physical capacity of the child. An obvious example would be asking pupils to move a heavy piano in a situation which requires lifting. Even though the pupils asked to help may be physically strong, it can be foreseen that since they do not have experience as movers of heavy equipment, they may injure themselves in the effort. Also it would not be prudent to ask students unused to climbing high ladders to decorate the high ceiling of a gymnasium for a school dance or other affair.

SENDING PUPILS HOME DURING SCHOOL DAY. Several possibilities for incurring liability suggest themselves in connection with sending pupils home during the school day. If the parent is not contacted ahead of time and permission received a teacher who sent a child home for disciplinary reasons would likely be held capable of foreseeing that the individual might not go home and might go to places which would subject him to danger of harm. The parent would also need to be contacted before an ill child was sent home. If the child could not get into the home and his illness became more acute, the teacher would likely be vulnerable. Furthermore, in the instance of the ill child prudence would often dictate that he should not be allowed to leave the school without assistance.

If a teacher or administrator contemplates sending a young child home during school hours, she should, as a reasonable prudent person, reflect upon whether she is exposing the child to dangers to which it would not be exposed if it were dismissed at the normal hour. For instance, if the child would be exposed to a very dangerous crossing when no patrol help was on duty and it was injured, it would place the teacher in a precarious position as respects liability.

KEEPING PUPILS AFTER SCHOOL. The principle just previously enunciated should be kept in mind when a teacher or administrator is thinking of keeping a pupil after school. If by doing so the child is exposed to dangers to which he should not be subjected because of his age, the practice is hazardous. A danger in addition to exposing young children to an unpatrolled dangerous crossing is that which could exist in some neighborhoods if girls are kept after dark. Obvious hazards could arise if pupils traveling long distances miss bus connections. Of course if the teacher arranges for a child to be picked up by a parent or a reputable party whom the parent delegates, the problem is solved.

SENDING STUDENTS ON ERRANDS. A liability problem can arise for the teacher in connection with sending pupils on errands. This would happen, however, only if the child is injured while on the assignment.

Caution would suggest not sending a student off the school grounds on any errand that was for anything other than an educational purpose. If the errand is for a good educational purpose it would seem the hazard of injury is small if the pupil selected is not put in a position which confronts him with dangers any more serious than is usual at his present age and experience. Naturally it would be unwise to select any student who had demonstrated irresponsibility. Teachers can incur liability for sending pupils on errands within a school building if the facts establish that the teacher could have foreseen that the child would encounter danger of harm. For instance, if an art teacher sent a child to the storeroom to secure some paint and knew that to get to the paint the child would have to move some stage equipment, the teacher would surely be found negligent if the child would move the equipment and it fell on and injured her.

There is another aspect to sending a pupil on an errand off the school grounds. If he is sent for a sound educational purpose it can be argued that he is made an agent of the school, and if he is negligent and injures someone the school district may be liable under a doctrine that will be discussed hereafter.

TRANSPORTING PUPILS. School bus drivers are liable for injuries their negligence causes pupils. In addition to being required to use the care which is imposed upon the driver of any automobile, the bus driver should be prudent at times of loading and unloading. Opening the bus door before bringing the bus to a stop was held to be negligence.[1] So too is the stopping of a bus away from the curb and not at the regular bus stop.[2] Drivers must be alert for the presence of children on school grounds and drive with great caution. One court, pointing out that often the age of the child should be considered, indicated that a bus driver could be found to have a duty to warn pupils about approaching vehicles at the time of unloading.[3] Failure to discharge pupils in a safe place is dangerous. A driver who stopped his bus without drawing to the right side of the road was held to be negligent and responsible when a pupil was injured by a speeding car, even though the driver failed to stop for the school bus as required by statute.[4] A North Carolina court found a duty resting on a bus driver to see that children who must cross the road after leaving the bus are in a place of safety before he starts his vehicle.[5]

A driver was found negligent when he started his bus suddenly while a child was standing in the aisle.[6] Similarly negligence was found when a driver pulled to a halt without warning after traveling at a high rate of speed and a pupil was thrown out of the bus.[7]

Drivers have some responsibility for supervising as well as operating the vehicle. If rowdyism is such that a reasonable man would become aware of it the driver has a duty to stop the bus and quell the disturbance.[8]

School administrators have the responsibility for setting up a plan for the orderly loading and unloading of buses.

1. Taylor v. Cobble, 28 Tenn. App. 167, 187 S.W.2d 648 (1945).
2. Webb v. City of Seattle, 22 Wash. 2d 596, 157 P.2d 312 (1945).
3. Cartwright v. Graves, 182 Tenn. 114, 184 S.W.2d 373 (1944).
4. Davidson v. Horne, 86 Ga. App. 220, 71 S.E.2d 464 (1952).
5. Greene v. Mitchell County Bd. of Educ., 237 N.C. 336, 75 S.E.2d 129 (1953).
6. Van Clare v. Illinois Coach Co., 344 Ill. App. 127, 100 N.E.2d 398 (1951).
7. Roberts v. Baker, 57 Ga. App. 733, 196 S.E. 104 (1938).
8. Maley v. Children's Bus Service, Inc., 203 Misc. 559, 117 N.Y.S.2d 888 (1952), *aff'd*, 282 App. Div. 920, 125 N.Y.S.2d 643 (1953).

As will be indicated hereafter, negligent bus drivers may impose liability upon school districts. Of course, if the transportation system is operated by a private contractor, liability would rest on the private contractor. The district might likely be held for direct negligence if it did not require the private contractor to carry adequate insurance.

USE OF A SCHOOL PATROL[1]. There are a number of states which by statute sanction operating pupil patrols at crossings near schools. If the legislature does not sanction setting up a patrol, some responsible school board attorneys take the view that students should not be used on a patrol because it can be foreseen that in an emergency a young patrolman might, in the course of carrying out his duties, put himself in the path of danger. In practice many school administrators establish student patrols, even though they are not authorized to do so by a specific statute. This may be justified on the basis of utility and the greater good versus likelihood of harm. There is enough logic, however, in the position of those who argue for caution in setting up a student patrol to induce the advice that if a permissive statute does not exist, the school administrator should not set up a patrol unless efforts to get responsible adult help have failed. If funds are not available to secure adult assistance, if responsible volunteer adult help is not available, and if police assistance cannot be secured, it would seem that the courts would uphold as reasonable the decision to set up a patrol on the balance of utility versus probability of harm. In areas where a district has lost governmental immunity, it could be that courts would be induced to hold that the district had the responsibility to furnish adult assistance.

All authorities agree that a student should never be asked to stand in the street to direct traffic.

Responsibilities in Connection with Buildings, Grounds and Equipment

As respect liability of the individual teacher or administrator for defects in buildings, grounds and equipment which are the cause of injury to a pupil, the decision will be based upon whether under the circumstances the schoolman, as a reasonable prudent person, should have checked for the defect or have noted it. The shop teacher should be careful to frequently check the condition of his equipment for defects that could be discerned by ordinary inspection The ordinary teacher would not be charged with the same duty of vigilance to check buildings and grounds. The administrator, in some school systems may have more responsibility in such respect, although in large school systems the primary responsibility for periodic checks would undoubtedly rest on a building or grounds department. However, teachers and administrators who become aware of dangerous defects have a duty to report them to the proper authorities. Often, to the extent it is physically possible, teachers and administrators would

---

1. For a more detailed discussion of the legality of the school patrol see Hetzel, *State and Local Salary Legislation Applicable to Principals*, in LAW AND THE SCHOOL PRINCIPAL 105-19 (Seitz ed. 1961).

have a duty to block off the dangerous area or stop the use of the defective piece of equipment. It would also be their duty to warn pupils of known hazards.

Defects in buildings, grounds and equipment which induce injury to pupils seem particularly to stimulate legal action against the school district. If, as will be discussed hereafter, the law of the jurisdiction permits recovery against the district, it is vulnerable if it or its employees knew or should have known of the condition and failed to take corrective steps to remedy or protect against it within a reasonable time after actual notice. If the hazardous condition exists for an undue length of time, it may become difficult for the school district to rebut the presumption that it should have known of the situation.

It will be useful to present some fact situations which have produced liability as a result of injury to pupils who allege defects in buildings, grounds and equipment. New York imposed liability after a pupil fell on an unlighted stairway when there was also a gap in the handrailing.[1] In California recovery was permitted when a loosened locker attached to a gymnasium wall fell on a pupil.[2] Washington awarded damages when a top-heavy piano on casters was left in a playroom in such a position that children had to move it and when it was being moved it overturned and injured a pupil. In another Washington case the court found negligence in permitting an elevated step at an exit.[3] A pupil recovered in New York when he was injured when his sweater caught in a shop machine. No aprons were furnished to protect against such happening.[4] A pupil studying carpentry who fell from a scaffolding without a handrail was permitted to recover.[5] However, when a boy was pulled down by another boy and injured because he fell on a clinker on a school playground, the New York court did not find the unsafe surface of the playground the proximate cause of the injury. Rather, the court said the cause was the intervention of another pupil.[6] This New York case represents a court obviously bending over backwards. If the clinker was known to be on the playground, it is likely many courts would conclude that an event of the very type which happened could be foreseen. . . .

CONCLUSION

Since there has been so much discussion of liability in this article it seems necessary to stress again that neither the teacher nor the school district is the insurer of the safety of children against pure accidents. Teachers and administrators need not be apprehensive about the imposition of liability. The record reveals that courts recognize that the teacher and administrator work in a complex

1. Hovey v. State of New York, 287 N.Y. 663, 39 N.E.2d 287 (1941).
2. Freud v. Oakland Bd. of Educ., 28 Cal. App. 2d 246, 82 P.2d 197 (1938).
3. Kidwell v. School District No. 300, Whitman County, 54 Wash. 2d 672, 335 P.2d 805 (1959); Ekerson v. Ford's Prairie School District No. 11 of Lewis County, 3 Wash. 2d 475, 101 P.2d 345 (1940).
4. Edkins v. Board of Educ., 287 N.Y. 505, 41 N.E.2d 75 (1942).
5. Weber v. State, 267 App. Div. 325, 45 N.Y.S.2d 834 (1944), *aff'd*, 53 N.Y.S.2d 598 (Ct. Cl. 1945).
6. May v. Board of Educ., 295 N.Y. 948, 68 N.E.2d 44 (1946).

situation and have given every indication that they will reasonably apply the yardstick which tests for negligence when the allegation is that a schoolman has fallen down in his duty of care and a pupil has been injured. Teachers, however, would be ill-advised to rely upon the most liberal theory that can be presented. It is again suggested that the conservative approach of this article is best calculated to keep the schoolman out of the hands of juries. It is submitted that this approach will not put the educator in a legal strait jacket which will interfere with his ability to best develop the pupils under his charge.

The existence of "save harmless" statutes and liability insurance should not be looked upon by the truly professional schoolman as protection which will cause him to think less of his legal responsibilities to avoid negligence which may affect pupils. He will fully appreciate a professional need to do otherwise. He will understand that money damages do not fully compensate an injured pupil. From the utterly materialistic viewpoint he will realize that he may impair his standing with his employer if his negligence too wantonly and too often imposes a liability upon the employer and too often affects relations with parents and school patrons.

Cases

A. School Liability for Employees' Negligence

Norma Molitor et al. vs. Kaneland Community Unit
District No. 302, Appellee (Thomas Molitor, Appellant)
18 Ill. 2d 11 (1959)

MR. JUSTICE KLINGBIEL DELIVERED THE OPINION OF THE COURT

Plaintiff Thomas Molitor, a minor, by Peter his father and next friend, brought this action against Kaneland Community Unit School District for personal injuries sustained by plaintiff when the school bus in which he was riding left the road, allegedly as a result of the driver's negligence, hit a culvert, exploded and burned.

The complaint alleged, in substance, the negligence of the School District, through its agent and servant, the driver of the school bus; that plaintiff was in the exercise of such ordinary care for his own safety as could be reasonably expected of a boy of his age, intelligence, mental capacity and experience; that plaintiff sustained permanent and severe burns and injuries as a proximate result of defendant's negligence, and prayed for judgment in the amount of $56,000. . . .

Thus we are squarely faced with the highly important question —in the light of modern developments, should a school district be immune from liability for tortiously inflicted personal injury to a pupil thereof arising out of the operation of a school bus owned and operated by said district?

It appears that, while adhering to the old immunity rule, this court has not reconsidered and re-evaluated the doctrine of immunity of school districts for over fifty years. During these years, however, this subject has received exhaustive consideration by legal writers and scholars in articles and texts, almost unanimously condemned the immunity doctrine. . . .

Historically we find that the doctrine of the sovereign immunity of the state, the theory that "the King can do no wrong," was first extended to a subdivision of the state in 1788 in *Russell* v. *Men of Devon*, 2 Term Rep. 671, 100 Eng. Rep. 359. As pointed out by Dean Prosser (Prosser on Torts, p. 1066), the idea of the municipal corporate entity was still in a nebulous state at that time. The action was brought against the entire population of the county and the decision that the county was immune was based chiefly on the fact that there were no corporate funds in Devonshire out of which satisfaction could be obtained, plus a fear of multiplicity of suits and resulting inconvenience to the public.

It should be noted that the *Russell case* was later overruled by the English courts, and that in 1890 it was definitely established that in England a school board or school district is subject to suit in tort for personal injuries on the same basis as a private individual or corporation. (*Crisp* v. *Thomas*, 63 L. T. N. S. 756 (1890).) Non-immunity has continued to be the law of England to the present day.

The immunity doctrine of *Russell* v. *Men of Devon* was adopted in Illinois with reference to towns and counties in 1870 in *Town of Waltham* v. *Kemper*, 55 Ill. 346. Then, in 1898, eight years after the English courts had refused to apply the *Russell* doctrine to schools, the Illinois court extended the immunity rule to school districts in the leading case of *Kinnare* v. *City of Chicago*, 171 Ill. 332, where it was held that the Chicago Board of Education was immune from liability for the death of a laborer resulting from a fall from the roof of a school building, allegedly due to the negligence of the Board in failing to provide scaffolding and safeguards. That opinion reasoned that since the State is not subject to suit nor liable for the torts or negligence of its agents, likewise a school district, as a governmental agency of the State, is also "exempted from the obligation to respond in damages, as master, for negligent acts of its servants to the same extent as is the State itself." Later decisions following the *Kinnare* doctrine have sought to advance additional explanations such as the protection of public funds and public property, and to prevent the diversion of tax moneys to the payment of damage claims. *Leviton* v. *Board of Education*, 374 Ill. 594; *Thomas* v. *Broadlands Community Consolidated School Dist.* 348 Ill. App. 567.

Surveying the whole picture of governmental tort law as it stands in Illinois today, the following broad outlines may be observed. The General Assembly has frequently indicated its dissatisfaction with the doctrine of sovereign immunity upon which the *Kinnare case* was based. Governmental units, including school districts, are now subject to liability under the Workmen's Compensation and Occupational Disease Acts. . . .

The State itself is liable, under the 1945 Court of Claims Act, for damages in tort up to $7,500 for the negligence of its officers, agents or employees. (Ill. Rev. Stat. 1957, chap. 37, pars. 439 1-439.24.) Cities and villages have been made directly liable for injuries caused by the negligent operation of fire department vehicles, and for actionable wrong in the removal or destruction of unsafe or unsanitary buildings. (Ill. Rev. Stat. 1957, chap. 24, pars. 1—13, 1—16.) Cities and villages, and the Chicago Park District, have also been made responsible, by way of indemnification, for the nonwilful misconduct of policemen. (Ill. Rev. Stat. 1957, chap. 24, par. 1—15.1; chap. 105, par. 333.23K.) In addition to the tort liability thus legislatively imposed upon governmental units, the courts have classified local units of government as "quasi-municipal corporations" and "municipal corporations." And the activities of the latter class have been categorized as "governmental" and "proprietary," with full liability in tort imposed if the function is classified as "proprietary." . . .

Of all the anomalies that have resulted from legislative and judicial efforts to alleviate the injustice of the results that have flowed from the doctrine of sovereign immunity, the one most immediately pertinent to this case is the following provision of the Illinois School Code: "Any school district, including any non-high school district, which provides transportation for pupils may insure against any loss or liability of such district, its agents or employees, resulting from or incident to the ownership, maintenance or use of any school bus. Such insurance shall be carried only in companies duly licensed and authorized to write such coverage in this state. Every policy for such insurance coverage issued to a school district shall provide, or be endorsed to provide, that the company issuing such policy waives any right to refuse payment or to deny liability thereunder within the limits of said policy, by reason of the non-liability of the insured school district for the wrongful or negligent acts of its agents and employees, and, its immunity from suit, as an agency of the state performing governmental functions."

Thus, under this statute, a person injured by an insured school district bus may recover to the extent of such insurance, whereas, under the *Kinnare* doctrine, a person injured by an uninsured school district bus can recover nothing at all.

Defendant contends that the quoted provision of the School Code constitutes a legislative determination that the public policy of this State requires that school districts be immune from tort liability. We can read no such legislative intent into the statute. Rather, we interpret that section as expressing dissatisfaction with the court-created doctrine of governmental immunity and an attempt to cut down that immunity where insurance is involved. The difficulty with this legislative effort to curtail the judicial doctrine is that it allows each school district to determine for itself whether, and to what extent, it will be financially responsible for the wrongs inflicted by it.

Coming down to the precise issue at hand, it is clear that if the above rules and precedents are strictly applied to the instant case, plaintiff's complaint, containing no allegation as to the existence of insurance, was properly dismissed. On the other hand, the complaint may be held to state a good cause of action on either one of two theories, (1) application of the doctrine of *Moore* v. *Moyle*, 405 Ill. 555, or (2) abolition of the rule that a school district is immune from tort liability.

As to the doctrine of *Moore* v. *Moyle*, that case involved an action for personal injuries against Bradley University, a charitable educational institution. Traditionally, charitable and educational institutions have enjoyed the same immunity from tort liability as have governmental agencies in Illinois. (*Parks* v. *Northwestern University*, 218 Ill. 381.) The trial court dismissed the complaint on the ground that Bradley was immune to tort liability. The Supreme Court reversed, holding that the complaint should not have been dismissed since it alleged that Bradley was fully insured. Unfortunately, we must admit that the opinion in that case does not make the basis of the result entirely clear. . . .

However, the court there said, p. 564: ". . . the question of insurance in no way affects the liability of the institution, but would only go to the question of the manner of collecting any judgment which might be obtained, without interfering with, or subjecting the trust funds or trust-held property to, the judgment. The question as to whether or not the institution is insured in no way affects its liability any more than whether a charitable institution holding private nontrust property or funds would affect its liability. These questions would only be of importance at the proper time, when the question arose as to the collection of any judgment out of nontrust property or assets. . . . Judgments may be obtained, but the question of collection of the judgment is a different matter." If we were to literally apply this reasoning to the present school district case, we would conclude that it was unnecessary that the complaint contain an allegation of the existence of insurance or other nonpublic funds. Plaintiff's complaint was sufficient as it stood without any reference to insurance, and plaintiff would be entitled to prosecute his action to judgment. Only at that time, in case of a judgment for plaintiff, would the question of insurance arise, the possession of nonpublic funds being an execution rather than a liability question. It cannot be overlooked, however, that some doubt is cast on this approach by the last paragraph of the *Moore* opinion, where the court said: "It appears that the trust funds of Bradley will not be impaired or depleted by the prosecution of the complaint, and therefore it was error to dismiss it." These words imply that if from the complaint it did not appear that the trust funds would not be impaired, the complaint should have been dismissed. If that is the true holding in the case, then liability itself, not merely the collectibility of the judgment, depends on the presence of nontrust assets, as was pointed out by Justice Crampton in his dissenting opinion. The doctrine of *Moore* v. *Moyle* does not, in our opinion, offer a satisfactory solution. Like the provision of the School Code above quoted, it would allow the wrongdoer to determine its own liability.

It is a basic concept underlying the whole law of torts today that liability follows negligence, and that individuals and corporations are responsible for the negligence of their agents and employees acting in the course of their employment. The doctrine of governmental immunity runs directly counter to that basic concept. What reasons, then, are so impelling as to allow a school district, as a quasimunicipal corporation, to commit wrongdoing without any responsibility to its victims, while any individual or private corporation would be called to task in court for such tortious conduct?

The original basis of the immunity rule has been called a "survival of the medieval idea that the sovereign can do no wrong," or that "the King can do no wrong." . . .

In *Kinnare* v. *City of Chicago*, 171 Ill. 332, the first Illinois case announcing the tort immunity of school districts, the court said: "The State acts in its sovereign capacity, and does not submit its action to the judgment of courts and is not liable for the torts or negligence of its agents, and a corporation created by the State as a mere agency for the more efficient exercise of governmental functions is likewise exempted from the obligation to respond in damages, as master, for negligent acts of its servants to the same extent as is the State itself, unless such liability is expressly provided by the statute creating such agency." This was nothing more nor less than an extension of the theory of sovereign immunity. Professor Borchard has said that how immunity ever came to be applied in the United States of America is one of the mysteries of legal evolution. (Borchard, Governmental Liability in Tort, 34 Yale L. J, 1, 6.) And how it was then infiltrated into the law controlling the liability of local governmental units has been described as one of the amazing chapters of American common-law jurisprudence. (Green, Freedom of Litigation, 38 Ill. L. Rev. 355, 356.) "It seems, however, a prostitution of the concept of sovereign immunity to extend its scope in this way, for no one could seriously contend that local governmental units possess sovereign powers themselves." 54 Harv. L. Rev. 438, 439.

We are of the opinion that school district immunity cannot be justified on this theory. As was stated by one court, "The whole doctrine of governmental immunity from liability for tort rests upon a rotten foundation. It is almost incredible that in this modern age of comparative sociological enlightenment, and in a republic, the medieval absolutism supposed to be implicit in the maxim, 'the King can do no wrong,' should exempt the various branches of the government from liability for their torts, and that the entire burden of damage resulting from the wrongful acts of the government should be imposed upon the single individual who suffers the injury, rather than distributed among the entire community constituting the government, where it could be borne without hardship upon any individual, and where it justly belongs." . . .

Likewise, we agree with the Supreme Court of Florida that in preserving the sovereign immunity theory, courts have overlooked the fact that the Revolutionary War was fought to abolish that "divine right of kings" on which the theory is based.

The other chief reason advanced in support of the immunity rule in the more recent cases is the protection of public funds and public property. This corresponds to the "no fund" or "trust fund" theory upon which charitable immunity is based. This rationale was relied on in *Thomas* v. *Broadlands Community Consolidated School Dist.* 348 Ill. App. 567, where the court stated that the reason for the immunity rule is "that it is the public policy to protect public funds and public property, to prevent the diversion of tax moneys, in this case school funds, to the payment of damage claims." This reasoning seems to follow the line that it is better for the individual to suffer than for the public to be inconvenienced. From it proceeds defendant's argument that school districts would be bankrupted and education impeded if said districts were called upon to compensate children tortiously injured by the negligence of those districts' agents and employees.

We do not believe that in this present day and age, when public education constitutes one of the biggest businesses in the county, that school immunity can be justified on the protection-of-public-funds theory.

In the first place, analysis of the theory shows that it is based on the idea that payment of damage claims is a diversion of educational funds to an improper purpose. As many writers have pointed out, the fallacy in this argument is that it assumes the very point which is sought to be proved, *i.e.*, that payment of damage claims is not a proper purpose. "Logically, the 'No-fund' or 'trust fund' theory is without merit because it is of value only after a determination of what is a proper school expenditure. To predicate immunity upon the theory of a trust fund is merely to argue in a circle, since it assumes an answer to the very question at issue, to wit, what is an educational purpose? Many disagree with the 'no-fund' doctrine to the extent of ruling that the payment of funds for judgments resulting from accidents or injuries in schools is an educational purpose. Nor can it be properly argued that as a result of the abandonment of the common-law rule the district would be completely bankrupt. California, Tennessee, New York, Washington and other states have not been compelled to shut down their schools." (Rosenfield, Governmental Immunity from Liability for Tort in School Accidents, 5 Legal Notes on Local Government, 376–377.) Moreover, this argument is even more fallacious when viewed in the light of the Illinois School Code, which authorizes appropriations for "transportation purposes" (Ill. Rev. Stat. 1957, chap. 122, par. 17—6.1), authorizes issuance of bonds for the "payment of claims" (Ill. Rev. Stat. 1957, chap. 122, par. 19—10), and authorizes expenditures of school tax funds for liability insurance covering school bus operations. (Ill. Rev. Stat. 1957, chap. 122, par. 29—11a). It seems to us that the payment of damage claims incurred as an adjunct to transportation is as much a "transportation purpose" and therefore a proper authorized purpose as are payments of other expenses involved in operating school buses. If tax funds can properly be spent to pay premiums on liability insurance, there seems to be no good reason why they cannot be spent to pay the liability itself in the absence of insurance.

Neither are we impressed with defendant's plea that the abolition of immunity would create grave and unpredictable problems of school finance and administration. We are in accord with Dean Green when he disposed of this problem as follows: "There is considerable talk in the opinions about the tremendous financial burdens tort liability would cast upon the taxpayer. In some opinions it is stated that this factor is sufficient to warrant the courts in protecting the taxpayer through the immunity which they have thrown around municipal corporations. While this factor may have had compulsion on some of the earlier courts, I seriously doubt that it has any great weight with the courts in recent years. In the first place, taxation is not the subject matter of judicial concern where justice to the individual citizen is involved. It is the business of other departments of government to provide the funds required to pay the damages assessed against them by the courts. Moreover, the same policy that would protect governmental corporations from the payment of damages for the injuries they bring upon others would be equally pertinent to a like immunity to protect private corporations, for conceivably many essential private concerns could also be put out of business by the damages they could incur under tort liability. But as a matter of fact, this argument has no practical basis. Private concerns have rarely been greatly embarrassed, and in no instance, even where immunity is not recognized, has a municipality been seriously handicapped by tort liability. This argument is like so many of the horribles paraded in the early tort cases when courts were fashioning the boundaries of tort law. It has been thrown in simply because there was nothing better at hand. The public's willingness to stand up and pay the cost of its enterprises carried out through municipal corporations is no less than its insistence that individuals and groups pay the cost of their enterprises. Tort liability is in fact a very small item in the budget of any well organized enterprise." Green, Freedom of Litigation, 38 Ill. L. Rev. 355, 378.

We are of the opinion that none of the reasons advanced in support of school district immunity have any true validity today. Further we believe that abolition of such immunity may tend to decrease the frequency of school bus accidents by coupling the power to transport pupils with the responsibility of exercising care in the selection and supervision of the drivers. As Dean Harno said: "A municipal corporation today is an active and virile creature capable of inflicting much harm. Its civil responsibility should be co-extensive. The municipal corporation looms up definitely and emphatically in our law, and what is more, it can and does commit wrongs. This being so, it must assume the responsibilities of the position it occupies in society." (Harno, Tort Immunity of Municipal Corporations, 4 Ill. L. Q. 28, 42.) School districts will be encouraged to exercise greater care in the matter of transporting pupils and also to carry adequate insurance covering that transportation, thus spreading the risk of accident, just as the other costs of education are spread over the entire district. At least some school authorities themselves have recognized the need for the vital change which we are making. See Editorial, 100 American School Board Journal 55, Issue No. 6, June, 1940.

"The nation's largest business is operating on a blueprint prepared a hundred, if not a thousand, years ago. The public school system in the United States, which constitutes the largest single business in the country, is still under the domination of a legal principle which in great measure continued unchanged since the Middle Ages, to the effect that a person has no financial recourse for injuries sustained as a result of the performance of the State's functions. . . . That such a gigantic system, involving so large an appropriation of public funds and so tremendous a proportion of the people of the United States, should operate under the principles of a rule of law so old and so outmoded would seem impossible were it not actually true." Rosenfield, Governmental Immunity from Liability for Tort in School Accidents, 9 Law and Contemporary Problems 358, 359.

We conclude that the rule of school district tort immunity is unjust, unsupported by any valid reason, and has no rightful place in modern day society.

Defendant strongly urges that if said immunity is to be abolished, it should be done by the legislature, not by this court. With this contention we must disagree. The doctrine of school district immunity was created by this court alone. Having found that doctrine to be unsound and unjust under present conditions, we consider that we have not only the power, but the duty, to abolish that immunity. . . .

The judgment of the Appellate Court sustaining the dismissal of plaintiff's complaint is reversed and the cause is remanded to the circuit court of Kane County with instructions to set aside the order dismissing the complaint, and to proceed in conformity with the views expressed in this opinion.

Reversed and remanded, with directions.

B. The School's Duty of Care

Nuvia A. Lawes, an Infant, by Her Guardian ad Litem, Leon Lawes, et al., Respondents, v. Board of Education of the City of New York, Appellant, et al., Defendant
Court of Appeals of New York
16 N.Y. 2d 302, 266 N.Y.S. 2d 364 (1965)

BERGAN, JUDGE

Plaintiff Nuvia Alicia Lawes, a pupil at Public School No. 144 in Brooklyn, was struck by a snowball thrown by a fellow pupil while she was on her way from her home to her classroom after lunch on February 17, 1960. Plaintiff, then 11 years old, suffered a serious eye injury. A judgment for $45,000 has been rendered against the Board of Education and affirmed by a divided Appellate Division.

The snowball was thrown on school property in a yard between the street and school entrance, but this was not during a recreation period. Children were then on the property on their way into the school after having been home to lunch. The school had made a rule against snowball throwing and plaintiff's teacher had warned her pupils not to throw snowballs.

If a school is to become liable to one pupil for a snowball thrown at him by a fellow pupil, the rule governing such responsibility should be laid down clearly and be precise enough to be generally understood in the schools.

No one grows up in this climate without throwing snowballs and being hit by them. If snow is on the ground as children come to school, it would require intensive policing, almost child by child, to take all snowball throwing out of play. It is unreasonable to demand or expect such perfection in supervision from ordinary teachers or ordinary school management; and a fair test of reasonable care does not demand it.

The classic New York statement of the measure of school care for children is laid out in Judge Loughran's noted opinion in Hoose v. Drumm, 281 N.Y. 54, 57–58, 22 N.E.2d 233, 234: "Teachers have watched over the play of their pupils time out of mind. At recess periods, not less than in the class room, a teacher owes it to his charges to exercise such care of them as a parent of ordinary prudence would observe in comparable circumstances."

A parent of ordinary prudence would not invariably stop his children from making and throwing snowballs. Indeed, he might encourage it. He would stop dangerous throwing, if he learned hard frozen snow or ice had come into play, or the pelting of one child by several others, but ordinary snowball throwing would not necessarily be stopped.

A reasonable measure of a school's responsibility for snowball throwing is to control or prevent it during recreation periods according to its best judgment of conditions, and to take energetic steps to intervene at other times if dangerous play comes to its notice while children are within its area of responsibility.

The facts in the present case do not spell out any notice of special danger. There is no proof whatever in the record that teachers had notice of any other snowball throwing on the day plaintiff was hit. Proof that a snowball was thrown on the previous day is very thin and, even if fully credited, would not give fair notice of the kind of continued danger which should have been prevented by the active intervention of teachers.

A fellow pupil and friend of plaintiff testified that she was struck by a snowball on February 16 and that she reported this to a teacher. She did not testify that she reported that she was injured. She said: "I told her I got hit. Somebody hit me with a snowball."

The teacher denied having been told this and the Education Department records marked for identification, which the trial court refused to receive, show that this pupil reported in writing that she had been struck by a snowball, not before, but some five weeks after, plaintiff's injury.

No requirement on this kind of a record is imposed on teachers to enforce the rule against snowballs by standing outside in the cold to watch to see that children do not violate the rule as they come into the school. And it is an undue burden on the school to impose a liability because teachers did not stand outside for active intervention in the circumstances shown by this record.

A school is not liable for every thoughtless or careless act by which one pupil may injure another (Hoose v. Drumm, 281 N.Y. 54, 22 N.E.2d 233, supra; Ohman v. Board of Educ. of City of New York, 300 N.Y. 306, 90 N.E.2d 474; Wilber v. City of Binghamton, 296 N.Y. 950, 73 N.E.2d 263; Clark v. City of Buffalo, 288 N.Y. 62, 41 N.E.2d 459). Nor is liability invariably to fall on it because a school rule has been violated and an injury has been caused by another pupil (Maurer v. Board of Educ. of City of New York, 294 N.Y. 672, 60 N.E.2d 759).

It is not easy to find a decided case either in New York or other jurisdictions where a school has been cast in liability for a snowball thrown by one pupil at another and no authority sustaining such a liability is cited by respondents. . . .

In its result the judgment in this case imposes a greatly enlarged risk of liability on a school without showing notice of a particular danger at a particular time. A long line of decisions should cause us to proceed warily toward such an enlarged area of liability. (See, e. g., Ohman v. Board of Educ. of City of New York, supra, a thown lead pencil; Wilber v. City of Binghamton, supra, a batted stone; May v. Board of Educ. Union Free School Dist. No. 1, 295 N.Y. 948, 68 N.E.2d 44, cinders in the schoolyard pavement; Mayer v. Board of Educ. of City of New York, supra, inadequately supervised swimming, and Clark v. City of Buffalo, supra, a thown piece of glass.)

The order should be reversed and the complaint dismissed, without costs.

BURKE, JUDGE (DISSENTING)

The majority opinion has correctly outlined the duty of care imposed by law upon a school for the protection of its students in a case such as this, i. e., "A reasonable measure of a school's responsibility for snowball throwing is to control or prevent it during recreation periods according to its best judgment of conditions, and to take energetic steps to intervene at other times if dangerous play comes to its notice while children are within its area of responsibility." However, I disagree with the majority's determination that as a matter of law the Board of Education did not breach this duty, notwithstanding contrary findings of fact affirmed in the Appellate Division.

Although the plaintiff was passing through the schoolyard on her way into the school, the other children were not merely passing through. They had returned from their lunch and were playing in the schoolyard awaiting the commencement of their afternoon classes. That the remainder of a luncheon recess, after school children have returned from lunch and are playing in the schoolyard, is a "recreation period" as used by the majority in defining the board's duty is hardly controvertible. Furthermore, a duty of supervision over such playground activity is clearly imposed upon the Board of Education by subdivision 16 of section 1709 of the Education Law, Consol.Laws, c. 16. (Decker v. Dundee Cent. School Dist., 4 N.Y.2d 462, 464, 176 N.Y.S.2d 307, 309, 151 N.E. 2d 866, 867 [1958].) In recognition of this duty, the school authorities promulgated a regulation forbidding the thowing of snowballs on the school premises. Once this particular standard of care was adopted, whether or not it was reasonably complied with was a question of fact to be submitted to the jury. The Appellate Division unanimously agreed that plaintiff had established a prima facie case; the principal cause for the dissent was the admissibility of certain evidence, *not* a disagreement as to the duty imposed upon the Board of

Education. That the snowball throwing was a dangerous activity, that the school authorities had notice thereof, and that they failed to act reasonably under the circumstances, proximately causing plaintiff's damages, are affirmed findings of fact which cannot be disputed here. For these reasons I would affirm in all respects.

Dye, Fuld, Van Voorhis and Scileppi, JJ., concur with Bergan, J.

Burke, J., dissents in an opinion in which Desmond, C. J., concurs. . . .

Cioffi v. Board of Education of City of New York
278 N.Y.S. 2d 249 (1967)

Before Botein, P. J., and Stevens, Steuer and Rabin, JJ.

PER CURIAM

Judgment appealed from affirmed, with $50 costs and disbursements to respondent. From the evidence in the record the jury could properly find inadequate supervision. This is not the case of ordinary snowballing or of an isolated incident where a snowball is thrown and injury results (cf. Lawes, v. Board of Education of City of New York, 16 N.Y.2d 302, 266 N.Y.S.2d 364, 213 N.E.2d 667). Hard frozen snow or ice lay upon the ground in the area in the upper yard of the school. The school authorities knew or should have known of this condition. From the testimony some twenty or thirty boys were engaged in iceball throwing with the infant plaintiff as their immediate target. Statements to that effect were obtained by the school authorities from certain students directly after the accident. There was common knowledge of the propensity of children to engage in snowball throwing and at least one teacher testified she had many times witnessed snowballing by the students. The upper yard where the accident occurred was considered a school yard, and though there was evidently a fairly large group of children playing in that area, no teacher was present to supervise their activities. The circumstances here present measure up to that dangerous condition of which the Court of Appeals spoke, where "hard frozen snow or ice had come into play", and a single child was being pelted by several others (see, Lawes v. Board of Education of City of New York, supra, p. 305, 266 N.Y.S.2d p. 366, 213 N.E.2d p. 668). The case was submitted to the jury on an unexceptionable charge and the judgment should be affirmed.

All concur except Steuer, J., who dissents in the following memorandum:

STEUER, JUSTICE (DISSENTING)

I dissent on the ground that no breach of any duty to plaintiff was established. Plaintiff, an 11 year old schoolboy, was returning to the school building after the noon recess. He elected to enter the building through a yard contiguous to it and part of the school premises, which was quite usual and permitted. The yard was used for recreational purposes, and when so used was supervised. On the day in question, February 21, 1962, there was a large accumulation of snow in in the yard, due to snowfalls two and three days before. It was plaintiff's proof that a substantial portion of this snow had turned to ice. On plaintiff's entry into the yard, a group of boys then in the yard started throwing snowballs at him. These were naturally from the snow which had fallen there, and one, at least, which struck plaintiff consisted of ice and caused his injuries. From the weather reports, it could fairly be concluded that the school authorities might have learned that at least some of the snow had turned to ice and that the authorities were aware that pupils on their way to and from school did throw snowballs at each other. From this it is a reasonable deduction that some of these snowballs might be composed partly or wholly of ice.

The courts of this state now recognize that throwing snowballs and being hit by them is among the commonest seasonal incidents of childhood in this climate. And it is not an undesirable experience. True, on occasion injury results, as it does from any play activity of children. In Lawes v. Board of Education of City of New York, 16 N.Y.2d 302, 305, 266 N.Y.S.2d 364, 366, 213 N.E.2d 667, 668, the extent of liability for the consequences of snowball throwing is stated to be to supervise (but not prevent) it during recreational periods. At other times it is to take "energetic steps to intervene . . . if dangerous play comes to its notice while children are within its area of responsibility."

It is a fair assumption that the contiguous area is the area of responsibility as it is not reasonably to be expected that snowballs will be thrown in the building itself. And it is further incontrovertible that throwing frozen snow or ice, and the practice of several boys ganging up on one, are dangerous practices. But these are only actionable against the school if its personnel failed to prevent the practice after notice.

The fact that fallen snow has partly turned to ice is not notice that ice is going to be thrown. Nor is the fact that on prior occasions there were instances of snowball throwing by pupils (see Lawes v. Board of Education of City of New York, supra, p. 305, 266 N.Y.S.2d p. 366, 213 N.E.2d p. 668). Nor is there any claim that there was notice that the boys coming into school from the yard would suddenly pick on the plaintiff.

It should be emphasized that the normal reaction of children to snow is not a dangerous practice in and of itself and prevention of it is not enjoined. It is the unusual that should be stopped, and because of its rarity the authorities are under no obligation unless on notice. Notice of the unusual is not to be deduced from existence of the usual, and that is all that this record discloses.

The judgment should be reversed and the complaint dismissed on the law.

Lois M. Kerwin, Individually, and Richard Courtney, a minor, by his Guardian ad litem, Lois M. Kerwin, Plaintiffs and Appellants, v. County of San Mateo, etc., et al., Defendants, Jefferson Elementary School District, Defendant and Respondent
1 Cal. Reptr. 437 (1959)

BRAY, PRESIDING JUSTICE

Plaintiffs appeal from a judgment in favor of Jefferson Elementary School District (hereinafter referred to as defendant) entered after order sustaining demurrer to first amended complaint without leave to amend.

Question Presented

Did defendant owe any duty to plaintiff minor to protect him on his way home from his brother's school?

Record

The complaint alleged:

Plaintiff, 11-year-old Richard Courtney, and his brother, 6-year-old Thomas, were pupils of defendant school district. Thomas attended Garden Village School and Richard attended Benjamin Franklin School. On May 14, 1956, Thomas became ill while in attendance at the Garden Village School. The school authorities called Thomas' home and directed Richard, who was at home alone and absent from school because of illness, to come to the Garden Village School and take Thomas home. Richard then proceeded to the school on a bicycle built for one rider. The complaint then alleged: "When said plaintiff complied with defendants' directions and instructions, as aforesaid, he became, was and continued under their control, care, management and supervision. At said time and place, defendants negligently and carelessly supervised, controlled, managed and cared for said plaintiff and his said brother Thomas and negligently and carelessly undertook to provide transportation for said plaintiff and his said brother to their home, in that defendants, well knowing that said plaintiff and his said brother both were students and pupils of defendant school district and subject to the control, care, management, rules, instructions and supervision of defendants, failed and neglected to investigate, inspect and ascertain the mode and means of transportation to be used by said minors, and the safety and adequacy thereof, and negligently and carelessly failed and omitted to arrange for and provide a safe and adequate mode and means of transportation for said minors, and negligently and carelessly ordered, directed and instructed said plaintiff then and there to transport his said brother and himself from said school toward their said home on means of transportation to be selected by said plaintiff, and negligently and carelessly permitted both of said minors to ride from said school toward their said home on a bicycle built for one rider. Pursuant to the directions and instructions of defendants, as aforesaid, said plaintiff did endeavor to so transport his said brother and himself upon said bicycle and from said school. Said bicycle was an inadequate unsafe and dangerous mode and means of transporting both of said minors and defendants knew or should have known it was so inadequate, unsafe and dangerous." As a direct and proximate cause of defendants' negligence and the unsafe character of the bicycle, on the way home the bicycle tipped over, resulting in injuries to Richard.

Was There a Duty?

Plaintiffs' first contention is that defendant owed a duty to exercise reasonable care for the protection of plaintiff minor on his way home, (a) because of the school district-pupil relationship and (b) by affirmatively placing plaintiff minor in a position of danger.

(A) THE RELATIONSHIP. Plaintiff, the boy who was hurt, did not go to the school as a pupil. He went there at defendant's request to take his brother home. Both boys were ill[1] but the illness of neither caused the accident, nor did it make it dangerous for them to go home without an adult. Nor were they unable to walk home. It is not alleged that defendant knew that the boys were riding on one bicycle. In fact, it is alleged that defendant directed plaintiff to transport his brother "on means of transportation to be selected by said plaintiff." A school district is under no duty to supervise, or provide for the protection of its pupils, on their way home, unless it has undertaken to provide transportation for them, which defendant did not do.

So, even if plaintiff had been a pupil at this particular school, defendant violated no duty as to him.

Hanson v. Reedley Joint Union High School Dist., 1941, 43 Cal.App.2d 643, 111 P2d 415, is not in point. There the teacher arranged with another student whom she knew to have a defective car and a tendency to drive recklessly, to take home certain students in the latter's automobile, agreeing to give him gasoline for the purpose. Due in large part to the condition of the car and the faulty driving of the driver, an accident occurred in which one student was killed and another injured. In holding the district liable the court pointed out that the teacher undertook to provide transportation for the students and failed to provide reasonably safe transportation—a much different situation from that here. The district here did not undertake to provide transportation for plaintiff or his brother, and while there is a catch-all allegation that the district "knew or should have known it [the bicycle] was . . . [an] inadequate, unsafe and dangerous" mode of transportation, there is no allegation that the district knew that plaintiff was going to take his brother home on a bicycle. Moreover, a reading of the entire complaint and plaintiffs' brief demonstrates that the complaint is based not upon any knowledge by the district of the fact that plaintiff was going to

1. It does not appear whether the defendant district knew that plaintiff was ill.

use a bicycle, but upon the theory that the district had a duty to either provide transportation for plaintiff and the younger boy or to determine the manner in which plaintiff was going to transport him. No such duty existed. (It must be remembered that we are dealing with an injury to the 11-year-old boy, and not one to the 6-year-old.) As there was no duty to provide transportation, as the district did not undertake to provide transportation, and as there is no claim that the boys were unable to walk home, defendant was under no duty to ascertain the manner in which the boys were going home.

Nor is Satariano v. Sleight, 1942, 54 Cal. App.2d 278, 129 P.2d 35, applicable here. There in passing from the gymnasium to the athletic field a student was injured while crossing a public street. In setting aside a nonsuit the court held that it was a question of fact whether ordinary care for the student's protection did not require the school authorities who had knowledge of the dangerous practice of the students in crossing the street outside of a crosswalk, to do something more than to give sporadic warnings to individuals and groups. In our case the accident did not occur on or near the school grounds, nor is there any claim of dangerous knowledge by defendant.

Plaintiff cites two New Mexico decisions. McMullen v. Ursuline Order of Sisters, 1952, 56 N.M. 570, 246 P.2d 1052, held that where the plaintiff student was injured while digging shale at a mine as a part of a school activity, a jury could reasonably infer that the school was negligent in not supervising the activity. In Thompson v. Anderman, 1955, 59 N.M. 400, 285 P.2d 507, judgment for the minor plaintiff was affirmed where the defendant bus driver was found negligent in allowing the plaintiff to get off a school bus at other than a regular stopping place. Obviously there is no similarity between those cases and ours.

(B) DID DEFENDANT PLACE THE MINOR PLAINTIFF IN A POSITION OF DANGER? Plaintiff cites no authorities which would warrant such a finding under the allegations of the complaint. Defendant merely directed plaintiff to take his sick brother home. As pointed out before, there was nothing in the situation which would impose a duty to supervise, transport, or protect plaintiff on his way home. Nothing is alleged to indicate that there is any lack of ordinary care in a school sending a 6-year-old boy home with an 11-year-old one.

No reason is alleged why an 11-year-old boy could not safely return home. Thousands of 11-year-old schoolboys, as well as those of much younger years, travel to and from school daily without school supervision. Defendant had the right to assume unless something occurred to put it on notice to the contrary, that the two boys would walk home. Nothing is alleged to cause defendant to believe otherwise, or that an 11-year-old boy would not substantially appreciate the dangers to be encountered on the streets.

Section 13229, Education Code, provides: "Every teacher in the public schools shall hold pupils to a strict account for their conduct *on the way to and from school*, on the playgrounds, or during recess." (Emphasis added.) Plaintiff seems to confuse the italicized portion, which is the pupils' duty, with the duty of a teacher. Obviously this section does not impose a duty on the teacher or the district to supervise the pupils on their way home. The section refers to the behavior of school children and not to the safe conduct to and from school.

No condition is made that pertinent additional facts could be alleged. The court properly sustained the demurrer without leave to amend.

The judgment is affirmed.

Tobriner and Duniway, JJ., concur.

Charles B. Elgin, Sr., Individually and as Next Friend of John Elgin, a Minor, Appellant, v. District of Columbia, Appellee
337 F. 2d 152, 119 U.S. App. D.C. (1964)

McGOWAN, CIRCUIT JUDGE

In this litigation, liability in tort is claimed to have accrued by reason of an accident which occurred while John Elgin, a minor and a full-time student at a public school owned and operated by the District of Columbia, was engaged in a required recreation program on the school playground. He fell into a depressed areaway immediately adjacent to the playground, which areaway itself surrounded the basement of the school building. The complaint, in one count, alleged that the fall was the result of the District's negligence in failing either to provide, or to maintain properly, an adequate railing or other safeguard around the depressed areaway or to warn of the resultingly dangerous condition, or in exposing Elgin to this dangerous condition through mandatory participation in activities likely to result in injury because of it. A second count in the complaint, relying upon the same factual allegations, sets forth a claim of nuisance. The District Court, upon motion prior to trial, dismissed the complaint, presumably upon the ground that the doctrine of municipal immunity precluded recovery. This appeal seeks, through reversal of that action, an opportunity to prove the allegations of the complaint at a trial.

Three points are urged upon us as warranting such reversal. One is a plea that we join the growing number of courts which have put an end to the shelter from tort liability afforded to municipal governments by the immunity doctrine. For the reasons set forth in the margin, we do not deal with the merits of this proposal. A second is an argument that, whatever the vulnerability of the negligence count in the complaint, the second count, stated in terms of nuisance, is good under the long-standing exception to municipal immunity for this kind of wrong. Although a superficial examination of this contention suggests that the facts alleged appear to fall short of the common law concept of nuisance, we do not deal with the matter definitely in view of the disposition we make of the third issue raised on this appeal.

This third contention, which was the one principally pressed upon us as upon the court below, derives from the familiar learning with respect to the differentiation in functions performed by a municipality. Almost from the very moment of creation by the courts of an immunity initially resting upon the ancient dogma that the king can do no wrong, the judges have been alert to insist that the king be acting as such at the time injury occurs. With kings replaced by city councils as the embodiments of the grace by which men permit themselves to be governed, this alertness was verbalized in somewhat different terms, but the core of the judicial insight remained the same. It is, we believe, essentially this: If a king, or a city countil, is to do the job of governing well, then there is something to be said for withholding the threat of answerability in damages for at least some of the actions and decisions which governing necessarily entails. He who rules must make choices among competing courses of action and in the face of conflicting considerations of policy. The capacity and the incentive to govern effectively are arguably not enhanced by the prospect of being sued by those citizens who may be adversely affected by the choice eventually made. Thus it has been thought wise to sweep this restrictive cloud from the horizon and to let those responsible for the conduct of public affairs calculate their courses of action free of this intimidating influence. By the same token, in those areas of governmental action where the reason for the rule does not apply, the rule itself is disregarded.

This is, in our view, the origin and the present significance of the exception to municipal tort immunity rooted in the contrasting of "governmental" functions, as to which immunity is assumed to obtain, with those said to be a "proprietary" nature, where it does not. It is not a useful exercise to catalogue the many cases in this and other jurisdictions where the distinction has purported to be drawn. They frequently defy logical classification, and they reflect varying, and often inconsistent, rationalizations, as might be expected in an area where there is a growing conviction that a strict rule of immunity from liability has outlived its time. We do think it significant that, in the traditional formularization of the opposed concepts as "governmental" and "proprietary," there has been an increasing tendency to substitute "ministerial" for "proprietary." This sounds upon our ears as the knell of the old rationale, which was stated in terms of activities customarily associated with government as compared with those ordinarily carried on by the private sector of society. This was, at best, a tangential articulation of the most sensible support to be found for the immunity grant; and the use of the word "ministerial" both eliminates any continuing utility it might have and focuses attention upon a sharper and more satisfying analysis.

That analysis is more concerned with trying to distinguish between the functions performed within an area of readily recognizable governmental responsibility, than with undertaking to define precisely where the boundaries of that area lie. And, with such functions so identified and differentiated, it next inquires whether an injury inflicted as a consequence of one of such functions can be subjected to judicial redress without thereby jeopardizing the quality and efficiency of government itself. "Ministerial" connotes the execution of policy as distinct from its formulation. This in turn suggests differences in the degree of discretion and judgment involved in the particular governmental act. Where those elements are important, it is desirable that they operate freely and without the inhibiting influence of potential legal liability asserted with the advantage of hindsight. To the extent that the rule of municipal tort immunity continues to serve any useful purpose, this would appear to be that purpose; and its illumination in any given set of facts has been, and is, sought through the function-discriminating exception. . . .

In the case before us, the facts alleged in substance are that a guardrail erected by the school authorities to separate a school playground from a depressed areaway adjoining it had its protective purpose and capacity impaired because a section of it became missing; and that, although a dangerous condition was thus created, nothing was done to remedy it, nor were the required recreational activities on the playground suspended until repairs were effected. These are, we repeat, the allegations. They may or may not be established to the satisfaction of a court or jury after trial. The question before us now is not whether they are true, but whether the opportunity should have been given to prove them to be true.

We think it should have been. In so concluding, we accept the proposition that it is the appropriate business, and indeed the urgent responsibility, of the District of Columbia to provide and operate schools and their accompanying playgrounds. We apprehend also that the discharge of that responsibility will frequently involve the performance of functions calling for the highest degrees of discretion and judgment; and it will be time enough, when and if such claims are before us, for this court to deal with the question of the District's liability in tort for harms allegedly flowing from such functions. We think that *Urow* and its forebears presently provide a considerable degree of guidance in this area to the trial courts, wholly apart from the resolution one way or the other of the abstract issue of municipal tort immunity.

We are not persuaded, however, that the function of repairing broken guardrails imposes upon the District determinations of such delicacy and difficulty that its ability to furnish public education will be ponderably impaired by liability for neglect in failing to make such repairs. If "ministerial" is to be given anything like its accepted usage, it surely has patent applicability to these circumstances. If we accept, as this court has, the right of a pedestrian on a public sidewalk to get to the jury on his claim of the District's liability in negligence for permitting a depressed area alongside such sidewalk to exist unguarded (Elliott v. District of Columbia, 82 U.S. App.D.C. 64, 160 F.2d 386 (1947)), we do not see how we can deny the same right on the facts alleged here. From the standpoint of the school child here involved, the school playground was not only a public area which he was privileged to traverse but one in which he was affirmatively required to be at the time of his injury. In the posture which this case has before us, a remand for the purpose of permitting the complaint to be pursued in appropriate proceedings impresses us as well within the scope which this court has already given for the assertion of claims against the District of Columbia sounding in tort.

It is so ordered.

Bazelon, Chief Judge, concurring. . . .

Louis Husser, Jr., a Minor by his Parent and Natural Guardian Louis Husser, and Louis Husser In his own right, Appellants, v. The School District of Pittsburgh
Supreme Court of Pennsylvania
425 Pa. 249, 228 A. 2d 910 (1967)

OPINION

Per Curiam

The minor plaintiff attended a public high school in the city of Pittsburgh. While leaving the school through the boys' exit at the end of the day's classes on February 11, 1965, he was accosted, assaulted and seriously beaten by a group of rowdy youths when he refused their demands for money. This action for damages against the school district was later instituted. The lower court sustained preliminary objections to the complaint in the nature of a demurrer and dismissed the action. The plaintiffs appeal.

The complaint alleges that similar criminal acts occurred with great frequency in and about the same school during the months immediately prior to the attack involved; that the school district and its agents knew of the existence of these occurrences and the danger present to those attending the school; and neglected and refused to take any precautionary measures to protect the safety of the minor plaintiff or the other pupils attending the school.

Appellants' counsel earnestly argues that the Pennsylvania rule, which protects a school district while engaged in the exercise of its governmental functions from vicarious liability for the tortious infliction of injury by its agents and employees, should be abolished. The rule was recently reiterated in Dillon v. York City School District, 422 Pa. 103, 220 A.2d 896 (1966). We again affirm our ruling in this respect.

Appellants also contend, that the conduct of the defendant was tantamount to the maintenace of a nuisance on the school property to which the immunity rule does not apply. The acts complained of may constitute negligence on the part of the school district, but do not constitute a nuisance in law. . . .

Judgment affirmed.

Jones, J., concurs in the result.

Roberts, J., filed a concurring and dissenting opinion.

Musmanno, J., filed a dissenting opinion.

DISSENTING OPINION

Musmanno, Justice

If the defendant school district had permitted a Bengal tiger to roam the school yard of the Schenley High School, and the minor plaintiff, Louis Husser, Jr., had been mangled by that savage beast, I cannot believe that the Majority of this Court would say that the defendant would not be guilty of neglect in allowing such a peril to life and limb to exist. The responsibility of holding in leash a raging mob of juvenile delinquents intent on ruinous mischief cannot be less.

The school authorities knew of the criminal tidal wave which from time to time inundated the school property. The newspapers, as well as radio and television news programs, frequently referred to this disgraceful victimization of the small and the weak by the big and the brutal, but the authorities initiated no measures to offer protection to the school children. In consequence, Louis Husser suffered a broken jaw, facial paralysis, disfigurement and serious anatomical breakage.

He comes into court through his father and seeks redress, but this Court summarily disposes of the litigation by saying that never in the past did a school district have to respond in damages for injuries done to children, no matter how negligent the district might be. Not only that, the Majority says, why, just recently in the case of Dillon v. York City School District, 422 Pa. 103, 220 A.2d 896, we reiterated our rule that if a child breaks its leg or in any other way is injured because of the averred negligence of a school district, the courts will not listen to any such complaint. The Majority advances this self-stultifying proposition with an aplomb that says in effect that the recency of an aggression justifies its continuing repetition.

The Majority advances no rationalization for denying the injured plaintiff in this case a forum. It merely says we never allowed a school child any right to sue a school district, and we do not propose to open the court doors now to such cases.

This injustice cannot endure forever. I am satisfied that the day will arrive, and it cannot be far off, when people will laugh at solemn decisions of the courts of law which declare that everybody is responsible for his civil wrongs at law,— everybody but the government. What is government, but an institution set up by the people to protect the people? To say that anyone injured by the government cannot sue the government is like saying that a ship built by certain individuals may transport anyone but the builders. . . .

Roberts, J., concurring and dissenting opinion.

C. Teachers' Rights to Discipline Pupils

Suits v. Glover
260 Ala. 449 (1954)

SIMPSON, JUSTICE

Tort action by appellant, a schoolboy suing by his father as next friend, against appellee, a former schoolteacher, claiming damages in three counts of the complaint for assault and battery. A jury trial was had resulting in a verdict in favor of appellee. The appellant's motion for new trial, the grounds of which were that the verdict was contrary to the law and was not sustained by the preponderance of the evidence, was overruled and he now appeals to this court. . . .

There was no conflict but that certain punishment was administered to the appellant, a school pupil, by the appellee, a schoolmaster. The evidence was however, conflicting as to the type of instrument used to administer the punishment; the appellant's evidence tending to show that he was whipped with a slat from an apple crate and the appellee's evidence tending to show that the instrument used was a ping-pong paddle, commonly used by the school for administering such punishment. There was evidence that the appellee was responsible for maintaining order and discipline and to administer corporal punishment as was deemed necessary as punishment for infractions of the school rules. Further, there was evidence of an infraction of the school rules by the appellant, the nature of which was insubordination and scuffling in the school hall. The appellant's medical expert testified that in his opinion there was no permanent injury and the evidence showed that the appellant remained in school the remainder of the school day the incident occurred (February 22nd) and did not miss any time from school, at least until March 9th, except the day following the incident (February 23rd). The evidence further showed that the appellant was eight and a half years old, well developed, fat and in good health; and there was evidence warranting the inference that the appellee was in no wise angry or aggravated with the appellant when he administered the spanking. The evidence was also conflicting on the issue of the severity of the punishment, the appellee's evidence tending to show that the appellant was paddled on his buttocks only, the skin was not broken, and approximately only five licks were administered.

A schoolmaster is regarded as standing in *loco parentis* and has the authority to administer moderate correction to pupils under his care. To be guilty of an assault and battery, the teacher must not only inflict on the child immoderate chastisement, but he must do so with legal malice or wicked motives or he must inflict some permanent injury. In determining the reasonableness of the punishment or the extent of malice, proper matters for consideration are the instrument used and the nature of the offense committed by the child, the age and physical condition of the child, and the other attendant circumstances. . . .

It appears from the foregoing there was evidence which, if believed by the jury, justified the verdict and we conclude that the trial court committed no error in overruling the motion for new trial. Smith v. Smith, 254 Ala. 404, 48 So.2d 546.

Affirmed.

Lawson, Stakely and Merrill, JJ., concur.

Problems and Discussion Questions

1. Tort liability and the doctrine of *in loco parentis* seem to be frequently misunderstood by teachers, administrators, and parents. To document this misconception, design and administer a survey instrument to sample populations of teachers or graduate students to determine their understanding on the matters. Cases decided in your state court of last resort could provide definitive case-study examples and leading questions could be drawn thereform. This study could involve a team of student researchers.

2. What explicit or implicit safety procedures for schools and pupils are found in your state school code? How are these statutory provisions related to the concepts of tort liability?

3. After reviewing the legislation and case-law in your state concerning tort liability of schools and teachers, draft model legislation to promote and protect preservice internships in teacher education programs.

4. In light of the legal position of your state concerning school tort liability, what policies should school boards adopt concerning: (a) supervision of pupils, (b) discipline of pupils, and (c) teacher reports of school accidents and pupil discipline?

Annotated Bibliography

DeBonis, Joseph A., "Teacher's Liability for Pupil's Injuries—Duty of Supervision," *Maine Law Review*, 19:111, 1967.

The author, through examination of a Vermont liability case, suggests that a more viable and consistent means of placing the responsibility of liability be brought into effect. One such suggestion, in cases where teachers are the defendants, is to implement or impose vicarious liability, i.e., the teacher's alleged misfeasance or nonfeasance could be imputed to the school district.

DUGAN, Thomas A., "Teachers' Tort Liability," *Cleveland-Marshall Law Review*, 11:512, 1962.

Dugan attempts to write an article on tort liability directed to teachers as much, or more, as to attorneys. Although he writes within the context of Ohio statutes, his cases and discussions are on a nationwide basis. The primary reference points of his article are negligent torts and intentional torts—offers definitions, cases, interpretations, and suggestions.

LINN, John Phillip, "Tort Liability and the Schools," *North Dakota Law Review*, 43:765, Summer, 1967.

An interesting but brief history of schools' tort immunity prefaces a discussion of various cases that have led to a breakthrough in the historically impregnable wall of immunity that surrounds a school district. Linn notes, through these cases, that not all states have accepted a non-immunity role in their courts, but that the courts—notably in Iowa and Colorado—appear to be waiting for the legislature to make the change. In states where schools are liable (often to the extent of insurance coverage only) they must answer to claims such as "creating a nuisance," trespass, and school-bus accidents.

NELSON, Lawrence J., "Right of a Teacher to Administer Corporal Punishment to a Student," *Washburn Law Journal*, 5:75, Winter, 1965.

Some attention is given in this article to the reasonableness of the punishment meted out by the teacher—pointing out factors which juries may consider in deciding reasonableness. Nelson also gives a brief description and discussion of various state statutes that relate to teacher-administered corporal punishment. It is pointed out that, at common law, most states grant teachers conditional immunity from liability for corporal punishment.

PROEHL, Paul O., "Tort Liability of Teachers," *Vanderbilt Law Review*, 12:273, 1958-1959.

The teacher's social function, the relative ignorance of the laity of the professional's subject matter, and the lack of a clearly established norm of teacher's responsibilities (vis-a-vis liability), offers the teacher a "partial immunity" to tort liability. The author, with extensive documentation, discusses the teacher's source, nature, and domain of authority. Specific areas of liability included are corporal punishment (assault and battery) and the far-reaching areas of negligence (e.g., classroom supervision, playground supervision, physical education classes, and others).

Appendix

Constitution of the United States

We the People of the United States, in Order to form a more perfect Union, establish Justice, insure domestic Tranquility, provide for the common defense, promote the general Welfare, and secure the Blessings of Liberty to ourselves and our Posterity, do ordain and establish this Constitution for the United States of America.

ARTICLE I

SECTION 1. All legislative Powers herein granted shall be vested in a Congress of the United States, which shall consist of a Senate and House of Representatives.

SECTION 2. The House of Representatives shall be composed of Members chosen every second Year by the People of the several States, and the Electors in each State shall have the Qualifications requisite for Electors of the most numerous Branch of the State Legislature.

No Person shall be a Representative who shall not have attained to the age of twenty-five Years, and been seven Years a Citizen of the United States, and who shall not, when elected, be an Inhabitant of that State in which he shall be chosen.

[Representatives and direct Taxes shall be apportioned among the several States which may be included within this Union, according to their respective Numbers, which shall be determined by adding to the whole Number of free Persons, including those bound to Service for a Term of Years, and excluding Indians not taxed, three fifths of all other Persons.] The actual Enumeration shall be made within three Years after the first Meeting of the Congress of the United States, and within every subsequent Term of ten Years, in such Manner as they shall by Law direct. The Number of Representatives shall not exceed one for every thirty Thousand, but each State shall have at Least One Representative; and until such enumeration shall be made, the State of New Hampshire shall be entitled to chuse three, Massachusetts eight, Rhode-Island and Providence Plantations one, Connecticut five, New York six, New Jersey four, Pennsylvania eight, Delaware one, Maryland six, Virginia ten, North Carolina five, South Carolina five, and Georgia three.

When vacancies happen in the Representation from any State, the Executive Authority thereof shall issue Writs of Election to fill such Vacancies.

The House of Representatives shall chuse their Speaker and other Officers; and shall have the sole Power of Impeachment.

SECTION 3. [The Senate of the United States shall be composed of two Senators from each State, chosen by the Legislature thereof, for six Years; and each Senator shall have one Vote.]

Immediately after they shall be assembled in Consequence of the first Election, they shall be divided as equally as may be into three Classes. The Seats of the Senators of the first Class shall be vacated at the Expiration of the second Year, of the second Class at the Expiration of the fourth Year, and of the third Class at the Expiration of the sixth Year, so that one third may be chosen every second Year; [and if Vacancies happen by Resignation, or otherwise, during the Recess of the Legislature of any State, the Executive thereof may make temporary Appointments until the next Meeting of the Legislature, which shall then fill such Vacancies.]

No person shall be a Senator who shall not have attained to the Age of thirty Years, and been nine Years a Citizen of the United States, and who shall not, when elected, be an Inhabitant of that State for which he shall be chosen.

The Vice President of the United States shall be President of the Senate, but shall have no Vote, unless they be equally divided.

The Senate shall chuse their other Officers, and also a President pro tempore, in the Absence of the Vice President, or when he shall exercise the Office of President of the United States.

The Senate shall have the sole Power to try all Impeachments. When sitting for that Purpose, they shall be on Oath or Affirmation. When the President of the United States is tried, the Chief Justice shall preside: And no Person shall be convicted without the Concurrence of two thirds of the Members present.

Judgment in Cases of Impeachment shall not extend further than to removal from Office, and disqualification to hold and enjoy any Office of honor, Trust or Profit under the United States: but the Party convicted shall nevertheless be liable and subject to Indictment, Trial, Judgment and Punishment, according to Law.

SECTION 4. The Times, Places and Manner of holding Elections for Senators and Representatives, shall be prescribed in each State by The Legislature thereof; but the Congress may at any time by Law make or alter such Regulations, except as to the Places of chusing Senators.

The Congress shall assemble at least once in every Year, and such Meeting shall be on the first Monday in December, unless they shall by Law appoint a different Day.]

SECTION 5. Each House shall be the Judge of the Elections, Returns and Qualifications of its own Members, and a Majority of each shall constitute a Quorum to do Business; but a smaller Number may adjourn from day to day, and may be authorized to compel the Attendance of absent Members, in such Manner, and under such Penalties as each House may provide.

Each House may determine the Rules of its Proceedings, punish its Members for disorderly Behaviour, and, with the Concurrence of two thirds, expel a Member.

Each House shall keep a Journal of its Proceedings, and from time to time publish the same, excepting such Parts as may in their Judgment require Secrecy; and the Yeas and Nays of the Members of either House on any question shall, at the Desire of one fifth of those Present, be entered on the Journal.

Neither House, during the Session of Congress, shall, without the Consent of the other, adjourn for more than three days, nor to any other Place than that in which the two Houses shall be sitting.

SECTION 6. The Senators and Representatives shall receive a Compensation for their Services, to be ascertained by Law, and paid out of the Treasury of the United States. They shall in all Cases, except Treason, Felony and Breach of the Peace, be privileged from Arrest during their Attendance at the Session of their respective Houses, and in going to and returning from the same; and for any Speech or Debate in either House, they shall not be questioned in any other Place.

No Senator or Representative shall, during the Time for which he was elected, be appointed to any civil Office under the Authority of the United States, which shall have been created, or the Emoluments whereof shall have been encreased during such time; and no Person holding any Office under the United States, shall be a Member of either House during his Continuance in Office.

SECTION 7. All Bills for raising Revenue shall originate in the House of Representatives; but the Senate may propose or concur with Amendments as on other Bills.

Every Bill which shall have passed the House of Representatives and the Senate, shall, before it become a Law, be presented to the President of the United States; If he approve he shall sign it, but if not he shall return it, with his Objections to that House in which it shall have originated, who shall enter the Objections at large on their Journal, and proceed to reconsider it. If after such Reconsideration two thirds of that House shall agree to pass the Bill, it shall be sent, together with the Objections, to the other House, by which it shall likewise be reconsidered, and if approved by two thirds of that House, it shall become a Law. But in all such Cases the Votes of both Houses shall be determined by yeas and Nays, and the Names of the Persons voting for and against the Bill shall be entered on the Journal of each House respectively. If any Bill shall not be returned by the President within ten Days (Sundays excepted) after it shall have been presented to him, the Same shall be a Law, in like Manner as if he had signed it, unless the Congress by their Adjournment prevent its Return, in which Case it shall not be a Law.

Every Order, Resolution, or Vote to which the Concurrence of the Senate and House of Representatives may be necessary (except on a question of Adjournment) shall be presented to the President of the United States; and before the Same shall take Effect, shall be approved by him, or being disapproved by him, shall be repassed by two thirds of the Senate and House of Representatives, according to the Rules and Limitations prescribed in the Case of a Bill.

SECTION 8. The Congress shall have Power To lay and collect Taxes, Duties, Imposts and Excises, to pay the Debts and provide for the common Defence and general Welfare of the United States; but all Duties, Imposts and Excises shall be uniform throughout the United States;

To borrow Money on the credit of the United States;

To regulate Commerce with foreign Nations, and among the several States and with the Indian Tribes;

To establish an uniform Rule of Naturalization, and uniform Laws on the subject of Bankruptcies throughout the United States;

To coin Money, regulate the Value thereof, and of foreign Coin, and fix the Standard of Weights and Measures;

To provide for the Punishment of counterfeiting the Securities and current Coin of the United States;

To establish Post Offices and post Roads;

To promote the Progress of Science and useful Arts, by securing for limited Times to Authors and Inventors the exclusive Right to their respective Writings and Discoveries;

To constitute Tribunals inferior to the supreme Court;

To define and punish Piracies and Felonies committed on the high Seas, and Offences against the Law of Nations;

To declare War, grant Letters of Marque and Reprisal, and make Rules concerning Captures on Land and Water;

To raise and support Armies, but no Appropriation of Money to that Use shall be for a longer Term than two Years;

To provide and maintain a Navy;

To make Rules for the Government and Regulation of the land and naval Forces;

To provide for calling forth the Militia to execute the Laws of the Union, suppress Insurrections and repel Invasions;

To provide for organizing, arming, and disciplining, the Militia, and for governing such Part of them as may be employed in the Service of the United States, reserving to the States respectively, the Appointment of the Officers, and the Authority of training the Militia according to the discipline prescribed by Congress;

To exercise exclusive Legislation in all Cases whatsoever, over such District (not exceeding ten Miles square) as may, by Cession of particular States, and the Acceptance of Congress, become the Seat of the Government of the United States, and to exercise like Authority over all Places purchased by the Consent of the Legislature of the State in which the Same shall be, for the Erection of Forts, Magazines, Arsenals, dock-Yards, and other needful Buildings;—And

To make all Laws which shall be necessary and proper for carrying into Execution the foregoing Powers, and all other Powers vested by this Constitution in the Government of the United States, or in any Department or Officer thereof.

SECTION 9. The Migration or Importation of such Persons as any of the States now existing shall think proper to admit, shall not be prohibited by the Congress prior to the Year one thousand eight hundred and eight, but a Tax or duty may be imposed on such Importation, not exceeding ten dollars for each Person.

The Privilege of the Writ of Habeas Corpus shall not be suspended, unless when in Cases of Rebellion or Invasion the public Safety may require it.

No Bill of Attainder or ex post facto Law shall be passed.

No Capitation, or other direct, Tax shall be laid, unless in Proportion to the Census or Enumeration herein before directed to be taken.

No Tax or Duty shall be laid on Articles exported from any State.

No Preference shall be given by any Regulation of Commerce or Revenue to the Ports of one State over those of another: nor shall Vessels bound to, or from, one State, be obliged to enter, clear or pay Duties in another.

No Money shall be drawn from the Treasury, but in Consequence of Appropriations made by Law; and a regular Statement and Account of the Receipts and Expenditures of all public Money shall be published from time to time.

No Title of Nobility shall be granted by the United States: And no Person holding any Office of Profit or Trust under them, shall, without the Consent of the Congress, accept of any present, Emolument, Office, or Title, of any kind whatever, from any King, Prince, or foreign State.

SECTION 10. No State shall enter into any Treaty, Alliance, or Confederation; grant Letters of Marque and Reprisal; coin Money; emit Bills of Credit; make any Thing but gold and silver Coin a Tender in Payment of Debts; pass any Bill of Attainder, ex post facto Law, or Law impairing the Obligation of Contracts, or grant any Title of Nobility.

No State shall, without the Consent of the Congress, lay any Imposts or Duties on Imports or Exports, except what may be absolutely necessary for executing it's inspection Laws: and the net Produce of all Duties and Imposts, laid by any State on Imports or Exports, shall be for the Use of the Treasury of the United States; and all such Laws shall be subject to the Revision and Controul of the Congress.

No State shall, without the Consent of Congress, lay any Duty of Tonnage, keep Troops, or Ships of War in time of Peace, enter into any Agreement or

Compact with another State, or with a foreign Power, or engage in War, unless actually invaded, or in such imminent Danger as will not admit of delay.

ARTICLE II

SECTION 1. The executive Power shall be vested in a President of the United States of America. He shall hold his Office during the Term of four Years, and, together with the Vice President, chosen for the same Term, be elected, as follows

Each State shall appoint, in such Manner as the Legislature thereof may direct, a Number of Electors, equal to the whole Number of Senators and Representatives to which the State may be entitled in the Congress: but no Senator or Representative, or Person holding an Office of Trust or Profit under the United States, shall be appointed an Elector.

[The Electors shall meet in their respective States, and vote by Ballot for two Persons, of whom one at least shall not be an Inhabitant of the same State with themselves. And they shall make a List of all the Persons voted for, and of the Number of Votes for each; which List they shall sign and certify, and transmit sealed to the Seat of the Government of the United States, directed to the President of the Senate. The President of the Senate shall, in the Presence of the Senate and House of Representatives, open all the Certificates, and the Votes shall then be counted. The Person having the greatest Number of Votes shall be the President, if such Number be a Majority of the whole Number of Electors appointed; and if there be more than one who have such Majority, and have an equal Number of Votes, then the House of Representatives shall immediately chuse by Ballot one of them for President; and if no Person have a Majority, then from the five highest on the List the said House shall in like Manner chuse the President. But in chusing the President, the Votes shall be taken by States, the Representation from each State having one Vote; A quorum for this Purpose shall consist of a Member or Members from two thirds of the States, and a Majority of all the States shall be necessary to a Choice. In every Case, after the Choice of the President, the Person having the greatest Number of Votes of the Electors shall be the Vice President. But if there should remain two or more who have equal Votes, the Senate shall chuse from them by Ballot the Vice President.]

The Congress may determine the Time of chusing the Electors, and the Day on which they shall give their Votes; which Day shall be the same throughout the United States.

No person except a natural born Citizen, or a Citizen of the United States, at the time of the Adoption of this Constitution, shall be eligible to the Office of President; neither shall any Person be eligible to that Office who shall not have attained to the Age of thirty five Years, and been fourteen Years a Resident within the United States.

In Case of the Removal of the President from Office, or of his Death,

Resignation, or Inability to discharge the Powers and Duties of the said Office, the Same shall devolve on the Vice President, and the Congress may by Law provide for the Case of Removal, Death, Resignation or Inability, both of the President and Vice President, declaring what Officer shall then act as President, and such Officer shall act accordingly, until the Disability be removed, or a President shall be elected.

The President shall, at stated Times, receive for his Services, a Compensation, which shall neither be encreased nor diminished during the Period for which he shall have been elected, and he shall not receive within that Period any other Emolument from the United States, or any of them.

Before he enter on the Execution of his Office, he shall take the following Oath or Affirmation:—"I do solemnly swear (or affirm) that I will faithfully execute the Office of President of the United States, and will to the best of my Ability, preserve, protect and defend the Constitution of the United States."

SECTION 2. The President shall be Commander in Chief of the Army and Navy of the United States, and of the Militia of the several States, when called into the actual Service of the United States; he may require the Opinion, in writing, of the principal Officer in each of the executive Departments, upon any Subject relating to the Duties of their respective Offices, and he shall have Power to grant Reprieves and Pardons for Offences against the United States, except in Cases of Impeachment.

He shall have Power, by and with the Advice and Consent of the Senate, to make Treaties, provided two thirds of the Senators present concur; and he shall nominate, and by and with the Advice and Consent of the Senate, shall appoint Ambassadors, other public Ministers and Consuls, Judges of the supreme Court, and all other Officers of the United States, whose Appointments are not herein otherwise provided for, and which shall be established by Law: but the Congress may by Law vest the Appointment of such inferior Officers, as they think proper, in the President alone, in the Courts of Law, or in the Heads of Departments.

The President shall have Power to fill up all Vacancies that may happen during the Recess of the Senate, by granting Commissions which shall expire at the End of their next Session.

SECTION 3. He shall from time to time give to the Congress Information of the State of the Union, and recommend to their Consideration such Measures as he shall judge necessary and expedient; he may, on extraordinary Occasions, convene both Houses, or either of them, and in Case of Disagreement between them, with Respect to the Time of Adjournment, he may adjourn them to such Time as he shall think proper; he shall receive Ambassadors and other public Ministers; he shall take Care that the Laws be faithfully executed, and shall Commission all the Officers of the United States.

SECTION 4. The President, Vice President and all civil Officers of the United

States, shall be removed from Office on Impeachment for, and Conviction of, Treason, Bribery, or other high Crimes and misdemeanors.

ARTICLE III

SECTION 1. The judicial Power of the United States, shall be vested in one supreme Court, and in such inferior Courts as the Congress may from time to time ordain and establish. The Judges, both of the supreme and inferior Courts, shall hold their Offices during good Behaviour, and shall, at stated Times, receive for their Services, a Compensation, which shall not be diminished during their Continuance in Office.

SECTION 2. The judicial Power shall extend to all Cases, in Law and Equity, arising under this Constitution, the Laws of the United States, and Treaties made, or which shall be made, under their Authority;—to all Cases affecting Ambassadors, other public Ministers and Consuls;—to all Cases of admiralty and maritime Jurisdiction;—to Controversies to which the United States shall be a Party;—to Controversies between two or more States;—between a State and Citizens of another State;—between citizens of different States;—between Citizens of the same State claiming Lands under Grants of different States, and between a State, or the Citizens thereof, and foreign States, Citizens or Subjects.

In all Cases affecting Ambassadors, other public Ministers and Consuls, and those in which a State shall be Party, the supreme Court shall have original Jurisdiction. In all the other Cases before mentioned, the supreme Court shall have appellate Jurisdiction, both as to Law and Fact, with such Exceptions, and under such Regulations as the Congress shall make.

The Trial of all Crimes, except in Cases of Impeachment, shall be by Jury; and such Trial shall be held in the State where the said Crimes shall have been committed; but when not committed within any State, the Trial shall be at such Place or Places as the Congress may by Law have directed.

SECTION 3. Treason against the United States, shall consist only in levying War against them, or in adhering to their Enemies, giving them Aid and Comfort. No Person shall be convicted of Treason unless on the Testimony of two Witnesses to the same overt Act, or on Confession in open Court.

The Congress shall have Power to declare the Punishment of Treason, but no Attainder of Treason shall work Corruption of Blood, or Forfeiture except during the Life of the Person attainted.

ARTICLE IV

SECTION 1. Full Faith and Credit shall be given in each State to the public Acts, Records, and judicial Proceedings of every other State. And the Congress may

by general Laws prescribe the Manner in which such Acts, Records and Proceedings shall be proved, and the Effect thereof.

SECTION 2. The Citizens of each State shall be entitled to all Privileges and Immunities of Citizens in the several States.

A Person charged in any State with Treason, Felony, or other Crime, who shall flee from Justice, and be found in another State, shall on Demand of the executive Authority of the State from which he fled, be delivered up, to be removed to the State having Jurisdiction of the Crime.

No Person held to Service or Labour in one State, under the Laws thereof, escaping into another, shall, in Consequence of any Law or Regulation therein, be discharged from such Service or Labour, but shall be delivered up on Claim of the Party to whom such Service or Labour may be due.

SECTION 3. New States may be admitted by the Congress into this Union; but no new State shall be formed or erected within the Jurisdiction of any other State; nor any State be formed by the Junction of two or more States, or Parts of States, without the Consent of the Legislatures of the States concerned as well as of the Congress.

The Congress shall have Power to dispose of and make all needful Rules and Regulations respecting the Territory or other Property belonging to the United States; and nothing in this Constitution shall be so construed as to Prejudice any Claims of the United States, or of any particular State.

SECTION 4. The United States shall guarantee to every State in this Union a Republican Form of Government, and shall protect each of them against Invasion; and on Application of the Legislature, or of the Executive (when the Legislature cannot be convened) against domestic Violence.

ARTICLE V

The Congress, whenever two thirds of both Houses shall deem it necessary, shall propose Amendments to this Constitution, or, on the Application of the Legislatures of two thirds of the several States, shall call a Convention for proposing Amendments, which, in either Case, shall be valid to all Intents and Purposes, as Part of this Constitution, when ratified by the Legislatures of three fourths of the several States, or by Conventions in three fourths thereof, as the one or the other Mode of Ratification may be proposed by the Congress; Provided that no Amendment which may be made prior to the Year One thousand eight hundred and eight shall in any Manner affect the first and fourth clauses in the Ninth Section of the first Article; and that no State, without its Consent, shall be deprived of it's equal Suffrage in the Senate.

ARTICLE VI

All Debts contracted and Engagements entered into, before the Adoption of this Constitution, shall be as valid against the United States under this Constitution, as under the Confederation.

This Constitution, and the Laws of the United States which shall be made in Pursuance thereof; and all Treaties made, or which shall be made, under the Authority of the United States, shall be the supreme Law of the Land; and the Judges in every State shall be bound thereby, any Thing in the Constitution or Laws of any State to the Contrary notwithstanding.

The Senators and Representatives before mentioned, and the Members of the several State Legislatures, and all executive and judicial Officers, both of the United States and of the several States, shall be bound by Oath or Affirmation, to support this Constitution; but no religious Test shall ever be required as a Qualification to any Office or public Trust under the United States.

ARTICLE VII

The Ratification of the Conventions of nine States, shall be sufficient for the Establishment of this Constitution between the States so ratifying the Same.

done in Convention by the Unanimous Consent of the States present the Seventeenth Day of September in the Year of our Lord one thousand seven hundred and Eighty seven and of the Independance of the United States of America the Twelfth. In witness whereof We have hereunto subscribed our Names,

GO: WASHINGTON,—Presidt.
and deputy from Virginia

New Hampshire	{ JOHN LANGDON NICHOLAS GILMAN
Massachusetts	{ NATHANIEL GORHAM RUFUS KING
Connecticut	{ WM: SAML. JOHNSON ROGER SHERMAN
New York . .	ALEXANDER HAMILTON
New Jersey	{ WIL: LIVINGSTON DAVID BREARLEY WM. PATERSON. JONA: DAYTON

Pennsylvania
- B FRANKLIN
- THOMAS MIFFLIN
- ROBT MORRIS
- GEO. CLYMER
- THOS. FITZSIMONS
- JARED INGERSOLL
- JAMES WILSON
- GOUV MORRIS

Delaware
- GEO: READ
- GUNNING BEDFORD jun
- JOHN DICKINSON
- RICHARD BASSETT
- JACO: BROOM

Maryland
- JAMES MCHENRY
- DAN OF ST THOS. JENIFER
- DANL CARROLL

Virginia
- JOHN BLAIR—
- JAMES MADISON, Jr.

North Carolina
- WM. BLOUNT
- RICHD. DOBBS SPAIGHT
- HU WILLIAMSON

South Carolina
- J. RUTLEDGE
- CHARLES COTESWORTH PINCKNEY
- CHARLES PINCKNEY
- PIERCE BUTLER

Georgia
- WILLIAM FEW
- ABR BALDWIN

In Convention Monday, September 17th 1787.

Present

The States of

New Hampshire, Massachusetts, Connecticut, Mr. Hamilton from New York, New Jersey, Pennsylvania, Delaware, Maryland, Virginia, North Carolina, South Carolina and Georgia.

Resolved,

That the preceding Constitution be laid before the United States in Congress assembled, and that it is the Opinion of this Convention, that it should afterwards be submitted to a Convention of Delegates, chosen in each State by the People thereof, under the Recommendation of its Legislature, for their Assent and Ratification; and that each Convention assenting to, and ratifying the

Same, should give Notice thereof to the United States in Congress assembled. Resolved, That it is the Opinion of this Convention, that as soon as the Conventions of nine States shall have ratified this Constitution, the United States in Congress assembled should fix a Day on which Electors should be appointed by the States which shall have ratified the same, and a Day on which the Electors should assemble to vote for the President, and the Time and Place for commencing Proceedings under this Constitution. That after such Publication the Electors should be appointed, and the Senators and Representatives elected: That the Electors should meet on the Day fixed for the Election of the President, and should transmit their Votes certified, signed, sealed and directed, as the Constitution requires, to the Secretary of the United States in Congress assembled, that the Senators and Representatives should convene at the Time and Place assigned; that the Senators should appoint a President of the Senate, for the sole Purpose of receiving opening and counting the Votes for President; and, after that he shall be chosen, the Congress, together with the President, should, without Delay, proceed to execute this Constitution.

By the Unanimous Order of the Convention

Go: WASHINGTON Presidt.

W. JACKSON Secretary

ARTICLES IN ADDITION TO, AND AMENDMENT OF, THE CONSTITUTION OF THE UNITED STATES OF AMERICA, PROPOSED BY CONGRESS, AND RATIFIED BY THE SEVERAL STATES, PURSUANT TO THE FIFTH ARTICLE OF THE ORIGINAL CONSTITUTION

Amendment [I]

Congress shall make no law respecting an establishment of religion, or prohibiting the free exercise thereof; or abridging the freedom of speech, or of the press; or the right of the people peaceably to assemble, and to petition the Government for a redress of grievances.

Amendment [II]

A well regulated Militia, being necessary to the security of a free State, the right of the people to keep and bear Arms, shall not be infringed.

Amendment [III]

No Soldier shall, in time of peace be quartered in any house, without the consent of the Owner, nor in time of war, but in a manner to be prescribed by law.

Amendment [IV]

The right of the people to be secure in their persons, houses, papers, and effects, against unreasonable searches and seizures, shall not be violated, and no

Warrants shall issue, but upon probable cause, supported by Oath or affirmation, and particularly describing the place to be searched, and the persons or
things to be seized.

Amendment [V]

No person shall be held to answer for a capital, or otherwise infamous crime,
unless on a presentment or indictment of a Grand Jury, except in cases arising in
the land or naval forces, or in the Militia, when in actual service in time of War
or public danger; nor shall any person be subject for the same offence to be
twice put in jeopardy of life or limb; nor shall be compelled in any criminal case
to be a witness against himself, nor be deprived of life, liberty, or property,
without due process of law; nor shall private property be taken for public use,
without just compensation.

Amendment [VI]

In all criminal prosecutions, the accused shall enjoy the right to a speedy and
public trial, by an impartial jury of the State and district wherein the crime shall
have been committed, which district shall have been previously ascertained by
law, and to be informed of the nature and cause of the accusation; to be confronted with the witnesses against him; to have compulsory process for obtaining witnesses in his favor, and to have the Assistance of Counsel for his defence

Amendment [VII]

In Suits at common law, where the value in controversy shall exceed twenty
dollars, the right of trial by jury shall be preserved, and no fact tried by jury,
shall be otherwise re-examined in any Court of the United States, than according
to the rules of the common law.

Amendment [VIII]

Excessive bail shall not be required, nor excessive fines imposed, nor cruel and
unusual punishments inflicted.

Amendment [IX]

The enumeration in the Constitution, of certain rights, shall not be construed
to deny or disparage others retained by the people.

Amendment [X]

The powers not delegated to the United States by the Constitution, nor prohibited by it to the States, are reserved to the States respectively, or to the people.

Amendment [XI]

The Judicial power of the United States shall not be construed to extend to any
suit in law or equity, commenced or prosecuted against one of the United States
by Citizens of another State, or by Citizens or Subjects of any Foreign State.

Amendment [XII]

The Electors shall meet in their respective states and vote by ballot for President and Vice-President, one of whom, at least, shall not be an inhabitant of the same state with themselves; they shall name in their ballots the person voted for as President, and in distinct ballots the person voted for as Vice-President, and they shall make distinct lists of all persons voted for as President, and of all persons voted for as Vice-President, and of the number of votes for each, which lists they shall sign and certify, and transmit sealed to the seat of the government of the United States, directed to the President of the Senate;—The President of the Senate shall, in the presence of the Senate and House of Representatives, open all the certificates and the votes shall then be counted;—The person having the greatest number of votes for President, shall be the President, if such number be a majority of the whole number of Electors appointed; and if no person have such majority, then from the persons having the highest numbers not exceeding three on the list of those voted for as President, the House of Representatives shall choose immediately, by ballot, the President. But in choosing the President, the votes shall be taken by states, the representation from each state having one vote; a quorum for this purpose shall consist of a member or members from two-thirds of the states, and a majority of all the states shall be necessary to a choice. And if the House of Representatives shall not choose a President whenever the right of choice shall devolve upon them, before the fourth day of March next following, then the Vice-President, shall act as president, as in the case of the death or other constitutional disability of the President.—The person having the greatest number of votes as Vice-President, shall be the Vice-President, if such number be a majority of the whole number of Electors appointed, and if no person have a majority, then from the two highest numbers on the list, the Senate shall choose the Vice-President; a quorum for the purpose shall consist of two-thirds of the whole numbers of Senators, and a majority of the whole number shall be necessary to a choice. But no person constitutionally ineligible to the office of President shall be eligible to that of Vice-President of the United States.

Amendment XIII

SECTION 1. Neither slavery nor involuntary servitude, except as a punishment for crime whereof the party shall have been duly convicted, shall exist within the United States, or any place subject to their jurisdiction.

SECTION 2. Congress shall have power to enforce this article by appropriate legislation.

Amendment XIV

SECTION 1. All persons born or naturalized in the United States, and subject to the jurisdiction thereof, are citizens of the United States and of the State wherein they reside. No State shall make or enforce any law which shall abridge the privileges or immunities of citizens of the United States; nor shall any

State deprive any person of life, liberty, or property, without due process of law; nor deny to any person within its jurisdiction the equal protection of the laws.

SECTION 2. Representatives shall be apportioned among the several States according to their respective numbers, counting the whole number of persons in each State, excluding Indians not taxed. But when the right to vote at any election for the choice of electors for President and Vice President of the United States, Representatives in Congress, the Executive and Judicial officers of a State, or the members of the Legislature thereof, is denied to any of the male inhabitants of such State, being twenty-one years of age, and citizens of the United States, or in any way abridged except for participation in rebellion, or other crime, the basis of representation therein shall be reduced in the proportion which the number of such male citizens shall bear to the whole number of male citizens twenty-one years of age in such State.

SECTION 3. No person shall be a Senator or Representative in Congress, or elector of President and Vice President, or hold any office, civil or military, under the United States, or under any State, who, having previously taken an oath, as a member of Congress, or as an officer of the United States, or as a member of any State legislature, or as an executive or judicial officer of any State, to support the Constitution of the United States, shall have engaged in insurrection or rebellion against the same, or given aid or comfort to the enemies thereof. But Congress may by a vote of two-thirds of each House, remove such disability.

SECTION 4. The validity of the public debt of the United States, authorized by law, including debts incurred for payment of pensions and bounties for services in suppressing insurrection or rebellion, shall not be questioned. But neither the United States nor any State shall assume or pay any debt or obligation incurred in aid of insurrection or rebellion against the United States, or any claim for the loss or emancipation of any slave; but all such debts, obligations and claims shall be held illegal and void.

SECTION 5. The Congress shall have power to enforce, by appropriate legislation, the provisions of this article.

Amendment XV

SECTION 1. The right of citizens of the United States to vote shall not be denied or abridged by the United States or by any State on account of race, color, or previous condition of servitude.

SECTION 2. The Congress shall have power to enforce this article by appropriate legislation.

Amendment XVI

The Congress shall have power to lay and collect taxes on incomes, from whatever source derived, without apportionment among the several States, and without regard to any census or enumeration.

Amendment [XVII]

The Senate of the United States shall be composed of two Senators from each State, elected by the people thereof, for six years; and each Senator shall have one vote. The electors in each State shall have the qualifications requisite for electors of the most numerous branch of the State legislatures.

When vacancies happen in the representation of any State in the Senate, the executive authority of such State shall issue writs of election to fill such vacancies: *Provided*, That the legislature of any State may empower the executive thereof to make temporary appointments until the people fill the vacancies by election as the legislature may direct.

This amendment shall not be so construed as to affect the election or term of any Senator chosen before it becomes valid as part of the Constitution.

Amendment [XVIII]

Repealed. See Amendment XXI, post.

Amendment [XIX]

The right of citizens of the United States to vote shall not be denied or abridged by the United States or by any State on account of sex.

Congress shall have power to enforce this article by appropriate legislation.

Amendment [XX]

SECTION 1. The terms of the President and Vice President shall end at noon on the 20th day of January, and the terms of Senators and Representatives at noon on the 3d day of January, of the years in which such terms would have ended if this article had not been ratified; and the terms of their successors shall then begin.

SECTION 2. The Congress shall assemble at least once in every year, and such meeting shall begin at noon on the 3d day of January, unless they shall by law appoint a different day.

SECTION 3. If, at the time fixed for the beginning of the term of the President, the President elect shall have died, the Vice President elect shall become President. If a President shall not have been chosen before the time fixed for the beginning of his term, or if the President elect shall have failed to qualify, then the Vice President elect shall act as President until a President shall have qualified; and the Congress may by law provide for the case wherein neither a President elect nor a Vice President elect shall have qualified, declaring who shall then act as President, or the manner in which one who is to act shall be selected, and such person shall act accordingly until a President or Vice President shall have qualified.

SECTION 4. The Congress may by law provide for the case of the death of any of the persons from whom the House of Representatives may choose a President whenever the right of choice shall have devolved upon them, and for the case of the death of any of the persons from whom the Senate may choose a Vice President whenever the right of choice shall have devolved upon them.

SECTION 5. Sections 1 and 2 shall take effect on the 15th days of October following the ratification of this article.

SECTION 6. This article shall be inoperative unless it shall have been ratified as an amendment to the Constitution by the legislatures of three-fourths of the several States within seven years from the date of its submission.

Amendment [XXI]

SECTION 1. The eighteenth article of amendment to the Constitution of the United States is hereby repealed.

SECTION 2. The transportation or importation into any State, Territory, or possession of the United States for delivery or use therein of intoxicating liquors, in violation of the laws thereof, is hereby prohibited.

SECTION 3. This article shall be inoperative unless it shall have been ratified as an amendment to the Constitution by conventions in the several States, as provided in the Constitution, within seven years from the date of the submission hereof to the States by the Congress.

Amendment [XXII]

SECTION 1. No person shall be elected to the office of the President more than twice, and no person who has held the office of President, or acted as President, for more than two years of a term to which some other person was elected President shall be elected to the office of President more than once. But this Article shall not apply to any person holding the office of President when this Article was proposed by the Congress, and shall not prevent any person who may be holding the office of President, or acting as President, during the term within which this Article becomes operative from holding the office of President or acting as President during the remainder of such term.

SECTION 2. This article shall be inoperative unless it shall have been ratified as an amendment to the Constitution by the legislatures of three-fourths of the several States, within seven years from the date of its submission to the States by the Congress.

Amendment [XXIII]

SECTION 1. The District constituting the seat of Government of the United States shall appoint in such manner as the Congress may direct:

A number of electors of President and Vice President equal to the whole number of Senators and Representatives in Congress to which the District would be entitled if it were a State, but in no event more than the least populous State; they shall be in addition to those appointed by the States, but they shall be considered, for the purposes of the election of President and Vice President, to be electors appointed by a State; and they shall meet in the District and perform such duties as provided by the twelfth article of amendment.

SECTION 2. The Congress shall have power to enforce this article by appropriate legislation.

Amendment [XXIV]

SECTION 1. The right of citizens of the United States to vote in any primary or other election for President or Vice President, for electors for President or Vice President, or for Senator or Representative in Congress, shall not be denied or abridged by the United States or any State by reason of failure to pay any poll tax or other tax.

SECTION 2. The Congress shall have power to enforce this article by appropriate legislation.

Glossary

AMICUS CURIAE. An individual, usually a lawyer, who interposes himself in a lawsuit, and, for the court's assistance, voluntarily provides information regarding a matter of law about which the court is doubtful or mistaken. Ordinarily this interposition is undertaken on behalf of a person who is interested in the outcome of a case but is not actually a party to it.

ANSWER. A defendant's response in writing made to the charges stipulated against him in a plaintiff's complaint.

BILL OF ATTAINDER. A legislative act that pronounces a particular person guilty of an alleged crime (usually treason) and punishes him accordingly. This legislative determination is arrived at without the benefit of trial or the recognized rules of criminal procedure being afforded the accused. Such act is prohibited by the United States Constitution.

CAVEAT. A formal caution or warning given to a ministerial or judicial officer by an interested party. Ordinarily this warning advises against the officer's undertaking of a particular act within his power until the warning party is heard in opposition to the initiation of the act at issue.

CERTIORARI. A review or reexamination, by a superior tribunal, of an inferior tribunal's decision or proceedings.

CHATTEL. Personal property; any type of property except freeholds and fees in realty.

CLASS ACTION. An action brought by one or more individuals on behalf of other individuals similarly interested in a particular proceeding or suit.

COLLATERAL ATTACK. An attempt to avoid or defeat the results of one judicial proceeding by resort to another judicial proceeding which is outside of the ordinary appellate procedure provided for by law.

COMMON LAW. As distinguished from legislatively created law, the common law consists of those traditionally held legal principles, usually enunciated in court decisions, which derive their force and effect from the historic acceptance and recognition given those principles by a society and its judiciary. Ordinarily, the term refers to the unwritten law of England.

COMPLAINT. A plaintiff's first formal pleading in a civil suit. This document, filed with the court and delivered to the defendant, is intended to inform the defendant of the factual grounds upon which the plaintiff is relying in his lawsuit.

DE FACTO. In reality, in fact. This term is used to describe an entity or event which is not constituted in a regular and legal fashion but which nonetheless must be accepted for all practical purposes. The phrase is used to characterize the illegal but real existence of a public official, a state of affairs, a past action, a government, etc. Distinguished from de jure.

DE JURE. By a lawful title, of right. The contrary of de facto.

DE MINIMIS. A term used to describe matters brought before a court which are so trifling or of such insignificance that the law will not take notice of them.

DECLARATORY JUDGMENT. That form of judgment rendered by a court in which only a declaration of the rights of the parties or an opinion on a question of law is given. Unlike most judgments in civil actions, a declaratory judgment does not require or order anything to be done pursuant to the judgment rendered.

DEFENDANT. The party against whom a lawsuit is brought.

DEMURRER. The formal means by which one party to a lawsuit argues against the legal sufficiency of the other party's claim. A demurrer basically contends that, even if all the facts which the other party alleges are true, nonetheless, these facts do not give rise to a legal cause of action.

DICTUM. An opinion or observation expressed by a judge, in pronouncing his decision upon a cause, which is addressed to a point not necessarily arising or involved in the case in question or necessary for determining the rights of the involved parties. The doctrine of *stare decises* is inapplicable to those rulings rendered in an opinion which are deemed to be dictum.

ELEEMOSYNARY CORPORATION. A private corporation created for charitable purposes.

ET AL. And others. When the words "et al" are used in an opinion, the court is thereby indicating that there are unnamed parties, either plaintiffs or defendants, also before the court in the case.

EX POST FACTO LAW. A law which retrospectively changes the legal consequences of an act which has already been performed. Article 1, section 10 of the United States Constitution forbids the passage of ex post facto laws.

EX REL. (Ex relatione) An informational phrase, used in those legal proceedings which are initiated and conducted by the state, designating the private individual at whose instance the state is acting.

INJUNCTION. A judicial order requiring the person or persons to whom it is addressed to do or not to do a particular act or acts. This remedy is ordinarily granted only when the remedy at law for the offense committed is inadequate.

IN LOCO PARENTIS. Replacing a parent; in the place of a parent.

INTER ALIA. Among other things. The term is used in pleading when a portion of a text (usually a statute) is quoted, but quoted only in part.

IPSO FACTO. By the fact itself.

LACHES. Neglect to do something at the proper time; an undue delay to do a thing that should be done or failure to enforce a right at the time required.

MANDAMUS. A writ, issued from a superior court to an inferior court, corporation, or officer, which commands the performance of a legally required public act.

MITIGATION. The reduction in a fine, penalty, sentence, or damages initially assessed or decreed against a defendant.

NIHIL OBSTAT. Nothing obstructs. The certification, by the Catholic Church, that a particular publication has been studied and found to be free from serious errors of faith or morals.

ORDINANCE. The term applied to a municipal corporation's legislative enactments. An ordinance should be distinguished from a statute.

PARENS PATRIAE. The term applied to the authority of the government, as sovereign, over its citizens; in particular, the government's power of guardianship over minors, insane and incompetent people, and the like.

PER CURIAM. By the court. The phrase distinguishing an opinion concurred in by all the justices of the court from an opinion of any one or several justices.

PETITIONER. One who initiates a proceeding and requests some relief be granted on his behalf. A plaintiff. When the terminology "petitioner" is used, the one against whom the petitioner is complaining is referred to as the respondent.

PLAINTIFF. One who initiates a lawsuit; the party bringing suit.

PLEADINGS. The formal statements of claims and defenses submitted to the court by the parties to a lawsuit.

PRIMA FACIE CASE. At first view, before investigation; sufficient until contradicted. Absent opposing counsel's arguments, a lawyer has established a prima facie case when he has alleged sufficient facts which, if true, will justify the granting of a verdict in his favor.

QUO WARRANTO. A proceeding whereby the right of a person or office to exercise a certain power is challenged. This proceeding is designed to prevent the illegal exercise of governmental or governmentally conferred powers.

REMAND. To send back; the return of a case by a superior court to the inferior court from which the case was appealed; ordinarily this return is accompanied with instructions by the superior court as to what further proceedings should be undertaken by the inferior court.

RESPONDENT. One who makes an answer in a legal proceeding. This term is frequently used in appellate and divorce cases, rather than the more customary term, defendant.

SOVEREIGN IMMUNITY. The freedom of a governmental body from suit without its permission. Sometimes referred to as "governmental immunity."

SPECIAL VERDICT. The finding, by a jury, of particular issues of fact which the court desires answered before it applies the law to those facts found by the jury.

STATUTE OF LIMITATIONS. A statute which sets forth the time period within which litigation may be commenced in a particular cause of action.

TORT. A private or civil wrong (other than a breach of trust or contract) for which the law requires compensation. Ordinarily, the compensation granted is for injury, either willful or negligent, caused to one's person, property, or reputation.

TROVER. The common-law remedy for any wrongful interference with or conversion of another's personal property.

TRUST. A right in property, of a fiduciary nature, whereby the title to property, either real or personal, is held by one person (the trustee) for the benefit of another person (the beneficiary).

ULTRA VIRES. Beyond the power. A term commonly used to describe that act of a corporation which goes beyond the permissible authority granted that corporation by its articles of incorporation or charter.

VESTED. The right to or enjoyment of absolute ownership in all or any part of real or personal property.

WAIVER. An intentional or uncoerced release of a known right.

WRIT OF ERROR. A writ of review by a court of superior jurisdiction of alleged errors committed by a court of inferior jurisdiction. This writ, issued by the superior court, requires that the inferior court present to it the record of the case at issue so that a final determination of the alleged errors may be made and the lower court's judgment be reversed, corrected, or affirmed as is necessary.

Index

Index of Cases